Astrology through History

Astrology through History

Interpreting the Stars from Ancient Mesopotamia to the Present

WILLIAM E. BURNS, EDITOR

ABC-CLIO™

An Imprint of ABC-CLIO, LLC
Santa Barbara, California • Denver, Colorado

Library of Congress Cataloging-in-Publication Data

Names: Burns, William E., 1959- editor.
Title: Astrology through history : interpreting the stars from ancient Mesopotamia to the present / William E. Burns, editor.
Description: Santa Barbara : ABC-CLIO, 2018. | Includes bibliographical references and index. |
Identifiers: LCCN 2018025825 (print) | LCCN 2018026668 (ebook) | ISBN 9781440851438 (eBook) | ISBN 9781440851421 (hardcopy : alk. paper)
Subjects: LCSH: Astrology—History—Encyclopedias.
Classification: LCC BF1655 (ebook) | LCC BF1655 .A88 2018 (print) | DDC 133.509–dc23
LC record available at https://lccn.loc.gov/2018025825

ISBN: 978-1-4408-5142-1 (print)
978-1-4408-5143-8 (ebook)

22 21 20 19 18 1 2 3 4 5

This book is also available as an eBook.

ABC-CLIO
An Imprint of ABC-CLIO, LLC

ABC-CLIO, LLC
130 Cremona Drive, P.O. Box 1911
Santa Barbara, California 93116-1911
www.abc-clio.com

This book is printed on acid-free paper ∞

Manufactured in the United States of America

Dedicated to the Memories of Lucretia Sargent
and Chris Sargent

Contents

Alphabetical List of Entries

Topical List of Entries

Biographical

American

Adams, Evangeline (1868–1932)
Goodman, Linda (1925–1995)
Omarr, Sydney (1926–2003)
Quigley, Joan (1927–2014)
Righter, Carroll (1900–1988)
Rudhyar, Dane (1895–1985)

Arabic

Abū Ma'shar Al-Balkhī (787–886)
Al-Qabīṣī (d. 967)
Mashāllāh Ibn Athari (740–815)

British and Irish

Ashenden, John
Ashmole, Elias (1617–1692)
Chaucer, Geoffrey (ca. 1340–1400)
Dee, John (1527–1609)
Forman, Simon (1552–1611)
Gadbury, John (1627–1704)
Leo, Alan (1860–1917)
Lilly, William (1602–1675)
Partridge, John (1644–1715)
Pont, Robert (1524–1606)
Sibly, Ebenezer (ca. 1750–1799)
Yeats, William Butler (1865–1939)

Chinese

Sima Qian (ca. 145–87 BCE)

Roman

Firmicus Maternus, Julius (Fourth Century CE)
Manilius, Marcus

The Astrological Skies

Asteroids
Comets
Decans
Fixed Stars
House Systems
Zodiacs

Astrology in Times and Places

Chinese Astrology
Enlightenment
Hellenistic Astrology
Indian Astrology
Islamic Astrology
Medieval European Astrology
Mesoamerican Astrology
Mesopotamian Astrology
Nazism and the Third Reich
Renaissance and Reformation Astrology
Roman Astrology
Thai Astrology

Astrology and Society

Age of Aquarius
Agriculture
American Stars Debate
Antiastrological Thought
Apocalypticism
Art
Astral Magic
Astrological Associations

Astrological Terms and Tools

Texts and Media

Preface

"What's your sign?" Whether or not you believe in astrology, you almost undoubtedly know your sun sign. Astrology, the practice of divining human meaning in the motions of the stars and planets, permeates our society. Its validity remains fiercely debated, but despite the efforts of those who oppose it as unscientific or even blasphemous it remains widely believed among all social levels and throughout much of the world.

Astrology has a long history. Ancient Mesopotamia, sometimes called the "cradle of civilization," was also the cradle of astrology. It was further developed in Greece, Egypt, and India and transmitted to Rome, the Islamic World, and medieval Europe. Other astrological traditions were found in China and Mesoamerica. Astrology flourished in the European Renaissance, to be largely but not entirely abandoned in the Enlightenment, then revived in the 19th century. In the 20th century it rapidly expanded, reaching mass audiences through newspapers and then the Internet while facing a variety of new challenges.

Astrology is not practiced in a separate realm apart from the rest of what people do. Over the millennia it has influenced politics, religion, science, and art as well as many other areas of human endeavor. Great scientists, historians, philosophers, and poets have practiced it, and it has profoundly influenced their work. But for a long time astrology was seen as a subject unworthy of serious study, merely a superstition identified with people living in the past and their "irrational" beliefs. The fact that astrology was associated with socially marginal groups in 20th-century society—the lower classes, the uneducated, and women—didn't help. Fortunately, in the past few decades this has changed. Astrologers have become more aware of the historical roots of their discipline and have reprinted and translated many of the classic works of Western astrology (the Internet has been a big help here). Historians, sociologists, and anthropologists, following the "cultural turn," have taken astrology, along with other "disreputable" subjects, more seriously. A flood of good books and articles on astrology in its social and historical context has poured from university and other academic presses. Many of the scholars who have contributed to this revival of interest are also contributors to this volume.

There are already numerous reference books on astrology, some of them excellent, but their purpose is very different from this book. Their subject is astrology, and they concentrate on astrological terms, techniques, and concepts. This book's subject is the history of astrology. The most common question I was asked when I told people I was editing a reference book on the history of astrology was whether I believed in it. My response is that it doesn't matter. The influence of astrology in human history is undeniable whether one "believes" in it or not, and that is the subject of this book. Contributors to this volume include practicing astrologers and nonbelievers in astrology, and the articles are designed to be informative to everyone, regardless of their position on astrology's credibility. The book is divided into an introduction, giving an overview of the history of astrology concentrating on the Western tradition; a timeline of the history of astrology; a glossary giving brief definitions of key terms; and a selected bibliography for those interested in learning more about the history of astrology. The heart of the work is a collection of more than a hundred articles on astrology and its history, arranged in an A–Z format.

My first thanks go to the contributors, who have turned in excellent articles. The Gelman Library of George Washington University has been a fine resource, as have the Washington Research Library Consortium and the Folger Shakespeare Library. George Butler and Barbara Patterson at ABC-CLIO have been a great help.

Introduction

Astrology, the effort to relate occurrences on Earth and in our lives to the movements of the sky and celestial bodies, is one of humanity's oldest known intellectual quests. The earliest evidence of astrology comes from Mesopotamia in the late third millennium BCE, and the Mesopotamian tradition is at the origin of Western and probably of Indian astrology. Mesopotamian astrologers traced the correlation of celestial phenomena like solar and lunar eclipses with public events including natural disasters and changes in the royal houses that ruled the land. Late in its history, Mesopotamian astrology made the crucial step of inquiring after the fates of private individuals as well as kings and kingdoms. The first surviving "natal" horoscope, recounting the condition of the skies at the time of birth, comes from the Mesopotamian tradition and dates from the late fifth century BCE. The Babylonians or "Chaldeans" of Mesopotamia were particularly identified with astrological knowledge among peoples as distinct as the Greeks, Jews, and Romans.

Astrology in the Greco-Roman World

The fourth-century BCE conquests of Alexander the Great in the Middle East exposed Greek thinkers to Mesopotamian and Middle Eastern culture, including astrology, and ushered in the Hellenistic period. In adapting Mesopotamian astrology to their own culture, the Greeks took a more cosmological approach, emphasizing how the planets moved through the sky rather than just their positions at particular moments. The Hellenistic city of Alexandria in Egypt, home of the famous library, became the new center of astrology where Mesopotamian, Greek, and Egyptian traditions were synthesized. The new Hellenistic astrology was also introduced into India, where it helped establish the rich tradition of Indian astrology. However, Indian astrology, which flourishes to this day, developed in a fundamentally different way, with a sidereal zodiac based on the stars rather than a tropical one based on the sun's rising and with far more emphasis given to the rising and descending lunar nodes.

Astrology arrived in Rome along with other aspects of Greek culture. The Roman ruling elite condemned it at first, associating it with popular superstition and forms of divination unauthorized by the state. Following the first-century BCE Roman conquest of the Hellenistic eastern Mediterranean, elite Romans became more interested in astrology. The earliest known Roman astrologers are found in this period. Astrology became particularly prominent in the Roman Empire, as the first Emperor Augustus Caesar (r. 27 BCE–14 CE) employed it in his propaganda.

Subsequent emperors, including Augustus's successor Tiberius, employed court astrologers, and rebels and aspirants to the imperial throne consulted astrologers to estimate their chances for success—a practice that led to legal repression of political astrology.

Although Romans such as Manilius and Firmicus Maternus wrote astrological works in Latin, the most important astrological writer in the history of the Roman Empire was the second-century CE Greek astronomer Ptolemy, author of the most influential ancient astrological book, *Tetrabiblios*. Ptolemy synthesized a great deal of ancient knowledge and presented astronomy as a scientific and mathematical discipline rather than a mystical or magical one. His work has continued to shape astrology to the present day.

The early Christians attacked astrology, associating it with determinism and the worship of the pagan gods and goddesses after whom the planets were named. Many of the most influential fathers of the church, such as St. Augustine in the Latin west, and St. John Chrysostom in the Greek-speaking east, denounced the science of the stars. The Christian Roman Empire included astrology in its strong antidivination laws, which like the laws of its pagan predecessor were, however, only sporadically enforced.

Medieval Astrology

Knowledge of astrology, like many ancient disciplines, declined in the Latin west after the fall of the Roman Empire. Few Westerners were able to draw an astrological chart or read the classic astrological works, which with a few exceptions were in Greek.

The most important theoreticians and practitioners in the early middle ages were Arabic-speakers in the Islamic world. Arabic and Persian-language astrologers, whether Muslim, Christian, or Jewish, translated classical Greek astrological works into Arabic and developed important astrological ideas, such as the correlation of patterns in human history with the conjunctions of Jupiter and Saturn, the so-called great conjunctions. The most prominent Arabic astrologer, Abū Ma'shar, became an authority in both the Muslim and Christian worlds rivaled only by Ptolemy.

Greek and Arabic works of astrological theory were translated into Latin only in the 12th and 13th centuries and helped bring about an intellectual revolution in the Latin west. Medieval intellectuals like Albertus Magnus and his disciple Thomas Aquinas endorsed astrology but in order to do so had to reconcile what was commonly viewed as the determinism of astrology with the Christian doctrine of the freedom of the individual will. They resolved this issue by claiming that the stars exerted a physical influence that affected only the body, and not the soul. Aquinas conceded that the stars influenced human passions, pointing out that astrological predictions were often correct because most people were ruled by their passions. The wise man, however, could resist his passions, and thus the stars could not determine his actions. The medieval emphasis on the power of the stars over the body helped astrology become closely allied with medicine.

Not all late medieval intellectuals accepted the new astrology as put forth by Scholastic philosophers like Albertus and Aquinas. Six propositions of Bishop Etienne Tempier's famous list of prohibited ideas in 1277 condemned astrology, mostly because of its lingering associations with determinism. The Scholastic philosopher Nicolas Oresme also vigorously opposed astrology. He reiterated the Christian attack on astrological determinism and added new arguments based on the scientific unknowability of the velocities of the heavenly bodies. The attack on astrology as unscientific would have a long future to the present day.

Astrology in the Age of Renaissance, Reformation, and Scientific Revolution

The 15th and 16th centuries saw fundamental transformations in the role of astrology linked with the cultural transformations of their time. Renaissance humanists, admirers of the ancient Greek tradition in the sciences, claimed to be recovering the astronomy of Ptolemy and other ancients from its subsequent corruption by Arab and medieval Latin writers, although the medieval astrologers continued to be studied. Renaissance philosophers, particularly those influenced by the revival of Neoplatonic mysticism and ancient astral magic, also incorporated the influences of the stars into their picture of the universe as a cosmic harmony. Although the great Protestant reformers Martin Luther and John Calvin both condemned astrology, many of their followers were believers and even practitioners. Given Protestantism's emphasis on the Bible, Protestant astrologers were particularly interested in reconciling astrology with the sacred text. They spent much intellectual effort reconciling the cycles of the stars with the apocalyptic timetables of the Bible, hoping to predict the time of the world's ending. The printing press, introduced to Europe in the mid-15th century, was also leading to an explosion of astrological tracts and almanacs.

Astrology continued to be an important support for professional astronomers in the late middle ages and Renaissance. Many patrons of astronomy were interested in it mainly for its astrological applications. The leaders of the "scientific revolution" of the 16th and 17th centuries differed in their opinions of astrology. Some, like the astronomers Tycho Brahe and Johannes Kepler, drew horoscopes for the monarchs they served in the traditional role of court astrologer. Changes in science in the mid-17th century made it less friendly to astrology. The new heliocentric Copernican astronomy that was winning growing acceptance did not "disprove" astrology, but astrologers did picture the universe as geocentric and the shift to a sun-centered cosmos did cast doubt on traditional astrological representations of the heaven. The fashionable "mechanical philosophers" of the 17th century, believing only in matter and motion, denied the doctrine of the influence of the stars on the Earth that astrology was based on, as it had no mechanical explanation.

Astrology lost its central intellectual role in the late 17th century. With the need for accurate star charts for long-distance voyages astronomers increasingly justified their science as useful in navigation and cartography rather than astrology. The major European astronomical observatories founded in the late 17th century, the

Paris and Greenwich Observatories, were founded for these utilitarian purposes, which, rather than astrology, appealed to the rulers who founded them. Astrology was losing its presence at European courts and court astrologers had largely disappeared. The late 17th century saw a major movement of astrological reform involving Placidus in Italy, J. B. Morin in France, and John Gadbury and John Partridge in England. Reformers took different paths, either hoping to refound astrology on an empirical basis like Gadbury or to purify it by returning to Ptolemy like Placidus and Partridge, but in any case their efforts turned out to be in vain as the gap between astrology and science widened.

Enlightenment Decline

As Europe entered the 18th century, the idea of an age of reason in which vulgar and archaic superstition would be rejected in favor of a more "scientific" worldview took hold, and astrology like other branches of magic suffered as a result. Although many ordinary people continued to believe in astrology, most scientists, intellectuals, and members of the social and political elite had ceased to take it seriously. Elements of astrology, such as the belief that the stars could influence the weather, persisted in the Enlightenment period, but astrology itself was in its decline, and there is no significant astrologer in Europe between the death of John Partridge and the rise of Ebenezer Sibly. The belief that astrology was superstition, unworthy of the educated, established in the Enlightenment would have a long history to the present.

19th- and 20th-Century Revival

The 19th century saw a major revival of Western astrology, beginning in England. The work of Ebenezer Sibly was followed by the establishment of almanacs by "Raphael" and "Zadkiel" that brought astrology back into the public eye.

But what really transformed astrology was the occult revival of the mid-19th century and particularly the founding of the Theosophical Society, an occult group founded in 1875 that attracted numerous astrologers. Their astrology was now integrated into an occult system focused on personal spiritual development. Theosophy not only revived Western astrology but contributed to the revival of Indian astrology. A Theosophically influenced English astrologer, Alan Leo, transformed astrology by providing cheap character analyses based on the sun sign. In the 20th century, sun sign astrology, in the form of the newspaper horoscope column, would become by far the most widely circulated form of astrology. The revival of astrology in the 20th century also affected politics, from the inner circles of the Third Reich, to newly independent nations raising their flags at an astrologically chosen moment, to the astrological advisers of President Ronald Reagan.

The 20th century was also marked by an increased participation of women in astrology, which up until that point had been a heavily male profession. The increasing prominence of women astrologers such as Evangeline Adams in America and Elisabeth Ebertin in Germany accompanied the rise of women as a target market for astrology. Hollywood women were a crucial constituency in the rise of such popular American male astrologers as Carroll Righter and Sydney Omarr.

Linda Goodman became one of America's most popular astrologers through her appeal to women. Late 20th century astrologers such as Geraldine Hatch Hanon created new syntheses of feminism and astrology, often associated with growing astrological interest in asteroids and other recently discovered celestial objects.

Astrology also benefited from the rise of the New Age movement. Drawing on Theosophy among other movements, the New Age has legitimized various forms of occult practice, astrology prominent among them.

The astrological revival did not go unchallenged, as opposition to astrology has never been more active. Although opposition on the part of religious fundamentalists continues, the validity of astrology is now less seen as a religious issue, and more in the context of the "superstition vs. science" dichotomy that is so much a part of the modern world.

Astrology in the 21st Century

Like everything else, astrology in the past few decades has been revolutionized by computers and the Internet. Astrological software has made the endless tedious calculations practiced by astrologers for millennia virtually disappear. The Internet has provided a new way for astrologers to disseminate their ideas and analyses over the world. It contributes to global astrology-based movements, such as the excitement around the year 2012, caused by a misreading of ancient Maya astronomical and astrological texts.

Despite its many opponents, astrology in the contemporary world continues to flourish. The newspaper astrology column has declined along with the newspaper but lives on in a variety of print and online environments. Astrological books, ranging from pop astrology aimed at a mass market to scholarly reprints and translations of astrological classics, pour from the presses, both ink-and-paper and electronic. The Indian astrological tradition maintains a vigorous presence in India and other countries influenced by India, such as Sri Lanka and Thailand. Astrology promises to play a role in society and culture for a long time to come.

Timeline

ca. 720 BCE	Composition of the *Enūma Anu Enlil*, the earliest surviving compendium of Mesopotamian astrology.
410 BCE	Date of the earliest extant birth chart.
169 BCE	First expulsion of astrologers from Rome.
11 CE	Roman emperor Augustus issues decree against diviners, including astrologers.
ca. 160 CE	Composition of Ptolemy's *Tetrabiblos*.
762	Baghdad, capital of the Abbasid Caliphate, is founded, at a moment selected four years earlier as astrologically favorable.
785–805	Work of the Hellenistic astrologer Dorotheus of Sidon is translated into Chinese by Persian astronomers at the Chinese court.
806	The Buddhist monk Kukai introduces Chinese astrology to Japan.
1277	Bishop Etienne Tempier of Paris condemns many astrological propositions.
1327	Cecco d'Ascoli is executed by the Inquisition for casting the nativity of Christ.
1371	French king Charles V endows a college of astrology and medicine at the University of Paris.
1441	Two astrologers are tried, condemned, and executed for casting a horoscope predicting the death of King Henry VI of England.
1555	First appearance of Nostradamus's prophecies.
1580	The Istanbul Observatory is shutdown following a failed astrological prediction.
1586	Pope Sixtus V issues *Coeli et terrae creator deus*, forbidding judicial astrology.
1630	Orazio Morandi is tried and condemned for predicting the death of Pope Urban VIII.
1631	Pope Urban VIII issues *Inscrutabilis iudiciorum Dei*, reaffirming the prohibition on judicial astrology, particularly the casting of horoscopes for Popes, royalty, and their relations.
1647	William Lilly's *Christian Astrology* is published.
1650	Placidus's *Physiomathematica sive coelestis philosophia* is published.

1652	"Black Monday" eclipse embarrasses English astrologers.
1681	Jean-Baptiste Morin's *Astrologia Gallica* is published posthumously.
1685	King James II of Great Britain bans astrological predictions from almanacs.
1687	Placidus's *Physiomathematica sive coelestis philosophia* is put on the Index of Forbidden Books, a list of books that Catholics are forbidden to own or read.
1695	Western Jesuit Juan Antonio Arnedo is appointed court astrologer in Vietnam.
1708	"Bickerstaff hoax" occurs, as British satirist Jonathan Swift mockingly predicts death of astrologer John Partridge.
1781	Uranus is discovered.
1782	Bangkok is founded as the capital city of Siam, later Thailand, with the drawing of a horoscope for the founding of the city that becomes a national horoscope.
1801	Ceres is discovered, the first asteroid to be identified.
1831	First appearance of *Zadkiel's Almanac*.
1846	Neptune is discovered.
1875	The Theosophical Society is founded.
1890	Alan Leo and F. W. Lacey found *The Astrological Magazine* in England.
1895	*Astrological Magazine*, the first Indian astrological periodical, is founded by Bangalore Suryanarain Rao.
1896	The Astrological Society is founded by English astrologer Alan Leo.
1915	Astrological Lodge of London is founded as a Theosophical organization by Alan Leo and others.
1917	Alan Leo is convicted of fortune-telling.
1925	The "Hamburg School" of astrology is founded.
	Marc Edmund Jones and Elsie Wheeler create the Sabian symbols.
1930	The first newspaper astrology column appears in the *London Sunday Express*.
	Pluto is discovered.
	B. V. Raman takes over editorship of the Indian *Astrological Magazine*, which he will hold until his death in 1998.
1938	American Federation of Astrologers is founded.
1941	Following Rudolf Hess's flight to Britain, Nazi Germany launches broad crackdown on occultists, including astrologers.
1951	Carroll Righter's sun sign newspaper column begins; it will continue until his death in 1988.

1952	The National Association of Radio and Television Broadcasters bans astrological programming from American television.
1953	Marc Edmund Jones's *The Sabian Symbols in Astrology* is published.
1954	Michel Gauquelin's *The Influence of the Stars* is published
1958	Astrological Association of Great Britain is founded.
1968	*Linda Goodman's Sun Signs*, the first astrology book to make the *New York Times* best seller list, is published.
1969	"Age of Aquarius/Let the Sun Shine In" by the Fifth Dimension tops the American pop charts for six weeks.
1972	The Republic of Sri Lanka is proclaimed on a date and time chosen by astrologers as auspicious.
1975	"Objections to Astrology: A Statement by 186 Leading Scientists" is published in *The Humanist*.
1977	Chiron, the first "centaur," a celestial object between the orbits of Saturn and Uranus, is discovered. It quickly becomes popular with astrologers.
1984	B. V. Raman founds the Indian Council of Astrological Sciences.
1985	California Supreme Court decision *Spiritual Psychic Science Church v. City of Azusa* wipes out local prohibitions on taking money for astrology or other divinatory practices as violations of the state constitution.
1987	Following the assassination of Prime Minister Indira Gandhi three years earlier, India outlaws astrological or other divination predicting the death of a high-ranking public official.
	Harmonic Convergence as "grand trine" alignment of planets arouses apocalyptic expectations.
1988	Former White House chief of staff Don Regan reveals that U.S. president Ronald Reagan has been consulting an astrologer, setting off a scandal. The astrologer is later identified as Joan Quigley.
1993	American Council of Vedic Astrology is founded, later the Council of Vedic Astrology, to promote Indian astrology.
2008	British Consumer Protection Act establishes new requirements for consulting astrologers.
2012	Expectations of an apocalypse based on Western interpretations of Mayan astrology are disappointed.
2013	First Queer Astrology conference is held in San Francisco, California, United States.

A

ABŪ MA'SHAR AL-BALKHĪ (787–886)

Abū Ma'shar Ja'far b. Muḥammad al-Balkhī was one of the most influential astrologers in the Islamic and Christian worlds. He was born in the ancient city of Balkh in what is now Afghanistan, and it is possible that he died in Wāsiṭ (Iraq). The dates of his birth and death, respectively August 10, 787, and March 9, 886, are indefinite, as we know the former from an anonymous horoscope found in his *Kitāb Taḥāwīl sinī al-mawālīd (Book of the Revolutions of the Years of Nativities)* and the latter from the famous catalog of books and anecdotes *al-Fihrist*, composed by the bookseller al-Nadīm (d. 990). In his *al-Āthār al-bāqiya*, the astrologer al-Bīrūnī (973–1048) writes that Abū Ma'shar lived till 893. He lived in Baghdad and was a prominent astrologer in the 'Abbasid court. One of the most sensational accounts about him is the story about how he came to be an astrologer. Al-Nadīm tells us that he was at first a scholar of ḥadīth, the traditions of Muḥammad and his companions, and philosophy, and in particular the philosopher al-Kindī (801–873). Through a careful stratagem al-Kindī got Abū Ma'shar interested in arithmetic, geometry, and astrology. Abū Ma'shar was not so proficient in the first two. As for astrology, which he began to study at the age of 47, his mastery was undisputed. Because none of his works display any knowledge of ḥadīth, al-Nadīm may have confused our astrologer with Abū Ma'shar al-Sindī, jurist and historian.

In *Nishwār al-muḥāḍara wa ahbār al-mudhākara*, we are told by Abū 'Alī al-Muḥassin b. 'Alī al-Tanūkhī (891–959) that Abū Ma'shar and his companion al-Buḥthurī were suffering from financial difficulties. To improve their situation they decided to gain favor with al-Mu 'tazz (r. 866–869) who was at that time incarcerated. Abū Ma'shar predicted that al-Mu 'tazz would become a caliph. When his prediction was realized, the new caliph lavished him with financial rewards and made him chief of astrologers at court. Ibn Ṭawūs (1193–1266) in *Faraj al-mahmūm* relates this incident and refers to Abū Ma'shar as the "foremost Muslim authority in astrology, [he] was exemplary in this science." We find in this work 13 tales about Abū Ma'shar, including one that shows the astrologer predicting the appearance of a calf's fetus in the presence of al-Muwaffaq's army and another that tells of an incident that took place in the presence of the same caliph who had asked Abū Ma'shar and his companion to guess the thing he was hiding. Having cast a horoscope, the companion answered that it was a fruit; Abū Ma'shar declared it an animal. When revealed, it was an apple. A perplexed Abū Ma'shar reexamined the horoscope for an hour and then rushed toward the apple. He broke it and exclaimed, "God is great!" The apple was full of worms! Al-Muwaffaq was very impressed and granted the astrologer a reward. Abū Ma'shar's pupil Abū Sa 'īd Shādhān relates in his *Mudhākarāt* how his master exposed a fake-prophet through astrology at the court of the Caliph al-Maʾmūn. Shādhān's text is particularly interesting as it shows a glimpse of Abū Ma'shar's personality, teachings, and worldview.

Abū Ma'shar's most influential works are *Kitāb al-milal wa al-duwal* (*Religions and Dynasties*) also known as *Kitab al-qirānāt* (*On Conjunctions*), which deals with the effects of celestial conjunctions on nations, dynasties, and rulerships; *Kitab tahāwīl sinī al-mawālīd* (*The Revolutions of the Years of Nativities*), which describes casting horoscopes for the birthdays of clients and how to derive information for the following year by comparing these horoscopes with the clients' birth charts; and *Kitāb al-madkhal al-kabīr ilā 'ilm aḥkām al-nujūm* (*The Book of the Great Introduction to Astrology*) in which he provides a comprehensive philosophical model.

Arguably, Abū Ma'shar's most significant contribution is the systematic justification of astrology found in his *Great Introduction*. It is founded upon Aristotelian physical principles of causality and motion. According to Abū Ma'shar, the stars indicate terrestrial events because they are the efficient causes of the generation and corruption of all animals, plants, and minerals. Their variation of species and genera is attributed to the diverse astrological configurations that were active at the time of their generation. Furthermore, the motion of the celestial bodies causes the transformation of elements in the natural world, thus having an impact on the circumstances surrounding human beings and the physical well-being of their bodies, because these are also composed of the elements. By astrological (fore) knowledge, one is able to anticipate and prepare for the changes of circumstances; this fact attests to the benefit of astrology.

Abū Ma'shar dedicates large sections in the first book of the *Great Introduction* and elsewhere to argue for astrology's benefits. In fact, he explains that what impelled him to write this work was that "many people thought that astrology is something stumbled upon by intuition and guesswork without having a sound origin to work with or from which syllogisms [*qiyas*] can be made [. . .] and so we composed our present book to establish the judgements [of astrology] with convincing arguments and demonstration [*burhan*]" [II, 3]. In addition to embedding astrology in natural philosophy, Abū Ma'shar addresses and responds to 10 groups of skeptics that include: those who reject that the celestial bodies indicate anything in the sublunary world; those who believe they indicate general things like species and the transformation of the elements but never individuals; those who reject that they can indicate contingent events but only the impossible and the necessary; those who only consider the effect of the stars on the seasons; and those who contest that astrology cannot be verified by repetitive experience.

At the heart of his arguments against these groups is demonstrating rationally the superiority of this astrology on the bases of natural philosophy and medicine: if one wants to address and fix a problem in the sublunary world, one needs to consider the causes, as Aristotle, Galen, and Hippocrates have shown.

The works of Abū Ma'shar circulated widely in the Latin West during the Middle Ages and the Renaissance. His *Great Introduction* was translated twice in the 12th century: by John of Seville in 1133 and by Hermann of Carinthia in 1140. The reception of Abū Ma'shar's works during the 12th century contributed to the sense of the universe's intelligibility, which came to be one of the features of this century of rebirth fostered, for example, in the School of Chartres, its associates, and those possessed by this spirit such as Thierry of Chartres, Bernard Silvestris, William of Conches, and Adelard of Bath. In the 15th century, Pico della Mirandola's *Disputations against Astrology* uses Abū Ma'shar's argument *for* astrology to argue that true astrology is a science that acknowledges astral causality but is not used as a divinatory art. During the 16th century, we see the influence of Abū Ma'shar's astrological theory on *The Defence of Judiciall Astrology* by Sir Christopher Heydon (1561–1623). The fame of Abū Ma'shar extended to literature: a 1615 play by Thomas Tomkis (ca. 1580–1634) was entitled *Albumazar*:

> Pandolofo: My marriage *Cricca!* hee foresee's my marriage:
> O most Celestiall *Albumazar!* (Act I, scene 5, 1–9)

Liana Saif

See also: Albertus Magnus; D'Ailly, Pierre; Islamic Astrology; Mundane Astrology

Further Reading

Abū al-Faraj Muḥammad Ibn Isḥāq al-Nadīm. 1998. *The Fihrist*, ed. and trans. Bayard Dodge. Chicago: Great Books of the Islamic World.

Abū Ma'shar al-Balkhī. 1994. *The Abbreviation of the Introduction to Astrology*, eds. and trans. Charles Burnett, Keiji Yamamoto, and Michio Yano. Leiden: Brill.

Abū Ma'shar al-Balkhī. 2000. *On Historical Astrology: The Book of Religions and Dynasties (on the Great Conjunctions)*, ed. and trans. Keiji Yamamoto and Charles Burnett, 2 vols. Leiden: Brill.

Adamson, Peter. 2002. "Abū Ma'shar, al-Kindī and the Philosophical Defence of Astrology." *Recherches de philosophie et théologie médiévales* 69: 245–270.

Burnett, Charles. 2002. "The Certitude of Astrology: The Scientific Methodology of al-Qabīsī and Abū Ma'shar." *Early Science and Medicine* 7: 198–213.

Saif, Liana. 2015. *The Arabic Influences on Early Modern Occult Philosophy*. Basingstoke, UK: Palgrave Macmillan.

Saif, Liana. 2015. "Astrology: Homocentric Science in Heliocentric Universe." In *Astrology in Time and Place: Cross-Cultural Questions in the History of Astrology*, ed. Nicholas Campion and Dorian Gieseler Greenbaum, 159–172. Newcastle upon Tyne, UK: Cambridge Scholars Publishing.

Thorndike, Lynn. 1954. "Albumasar in Sadan." *Isis* 45, no. 1: 22–32.

ADAMS, EVANGELINE (1868–1932)

Evangeline Smith Adams was a successful American consulting astrologer. She achieved widespread fame for her successful legal defense of her astrological practice and wrote several popular books on astrology. Adams's most lasting legacy was perhaps her effort to legitimize astrology through her writing and her popular radio show. Adams popularized astrology, making it accessible to everyone, while her writing ranged from celebrity gossip to serious attempts to understand the connections between the universe and human endeavors.

In the early 20th century, no American astrologer was better known than Adams but her practice of what she considered her natural born talent was difficult. She was arrested at least twice for giving readings. Adams had to convince clients and courts that her astrology was not fortune-telling and that it had scientific merits; both were interconnected. To accomplish this, Adams structured her astrological practices using norms she articulated as scientific and then fashioned herself as an astrologer after the model of the expert professional.

Although Adams wrote an autobiography, *The Bowl of Heaven* (1926), it did little to clarify much of her early life as she focused on her astrological abilities and career rather than her personal life. She claimed to be a descendant of former presidents John Adams and John Quincy Adams, yet one of her few telling moments in the book is her admission that her father died when she was only 15 months old. She claimed that through no fault of his own he lost almost all of his money. Adams does not elaborate on the causes of his death or financial losses. Her family moved to Boston shortly afterward.

Adams moved to New York on her 31st birthday. She lodged at the Windsor Hotel and immediately told the owner that the hotel was in imminent danger. The next day, the Windsor Hotel caught fire and Adams's prophecy made headlines.

This photograph of Evangeline Adams in her study in the 1920s combines a businesslike setting with the statue of a cat (at top), linking her to an old tradition of magical wise women. (Bettmann/Getty Images)

The resulting publicity brought Adams immediate national fame. Adams's services were much in demand by the wealthy and famous, such as actress Mary Pickford and financier J. P. Morgan.

Adams was arrested for fortune-telling in 1914, in what appeared to be a case of entrapment, under the anti-fortune-telling clause of the 1824 Vagrancy Act. Rather than pay the fine, she insisted on going to court. She went to trial armed with reference books and proceeded to explain the principles of astrology. At the conclusion of her testimony, she read a chart of an unknown individual. The anonymous horoscope was that of the trial judge's son. The judge, John H. Freschi, was impressed with the accuracy of Adams's reading, and, although the charges were dismissed, she gained great publicity from the case. This was an important case in the professionalization of astrology, which, according to Freschi, raised it to "the dignity of an exact science." This classification of her discipline outside of the realm of fortune-telling was bound up with its classification as a science, which, in turn, required Adams to command a certain level of intellectual, professional, and scientific authority.

Adams continued to practice and to promote the science of the stars to the general public. She wrote *Monthly Forecasts*, a publication featuring her predictions about political and economic events, plus several books on astrology including simple introductory texts: *Astrology: Your Place in the Sun* (1927), *Astrology: Your Place among the Stars* (1930), and *Astrology for Everyone* (1931). Adams's final book, published posthumously, was *The Evangeline Adams Guide for 1933*, in which the political and economic events for the year were predicted. It was a move away from the celebrity gossip with which Adams began her career and a bid for her science to be granted even greater respect. Many credit Adams with predicting the stock market crash of 1929 and World War II, as well as the deaths of her astrological clients, tenor Enrico Caruso (1873–1921) and actor Rudolph Valentino (1895–1926).

From her office in New York City's Carnegie Hall, Adams gave astrological readings to tens of thousands and reached over a million more through mail-order horoscopes, newspaper columns, books, and a radio show that she started in April 1930; she began to broadcast on the radio three times a week. As a result, she further increased requests for astrological charts over the next months, and, a year later, requests and letters were still being sent to her, often at the rate of 4,000 a day.

Adams's astrology complicates the picture that philosophers, sociologists, and historians of science have drawn about the demarcation between science and nonscience. Her story is an example of boundary work, with the new paths she opened in her transformation from a fortune-teller, whose practice was illegal, into a professional astrologer, who could freely read the stars from her office in Carnegie Hall.

Martin J. Manning

See also: Legal Regulation of Astrology; Medical Astrology; Politics; Righter, Carroll

Further Reading

Adams, Evangeline. 1926. *The Bowl of Heaven.* New York: Dodd, Mead.

Christino, Karen. 2002. *Foreseeing the Future: Evangeline Adams and Astrology in America.* Amherst, MA: One Reed Publications.

Crowley, Aleister, with Evangeline Adams. 2002. *The General Principles of Astrology: Liber DXXXVI*, ed. Hymenaeus Beta. Boston: Weiser Books.

Levine, Nick. 2014. *The Dignity of an Exact Science: Evangeline Adams, Astrology, and the Professions of the Probable, 1890–1940.* Senior thesis. New Haven, CT: Yale University.

Video footage on YouTube of Evangeline Adams, with early newsreel coverage of her trial from the TV series *Secrets in the Stars* (1999), narrated by Leonard Nimoy. https://www.youtube.com/watch?v=m7FN6MnufgM

AGE OF AQUARIUS

The Age of Aquarius is the supposed historical period that the Earth has recently entered, is now entering, or will enter in the future. Its astronomical basis is the progressive slippage of the stars against the 12 tropical zodiac signs in use in standard Western astrology. The tropical zodiac is fixed in relation to the seasons and begins at the so-called first point of Aries, or vernal point, the sun's location at the spring equinox, usually March 21. The movement of the stars in relation to the tropical zodiac is known as "precession of the equinoxes" and takes approximately 25,920 years for a complete cycle, or 2,156 years per tropical zodiac sign.

The tropical zodiac was adopted as the standard model in the Hellenistic world by the first century CE, as a result of which it was later used in medieval and Renaissance Europe, as well as in modern Western astrology. (Indian astrologers use a version of 12 zodiac signs—the so-called sidereal zodiac—which moves with the stars.) Claims that precession was regarded as astrologically significant in the classical world are circumstantial and lack any textual support. However, in 1791 the French radical François Delaunaye, influenced by Isaac Newton, suggested that world history could be divided into phases defined by the passage of the stars over the vernal point.

The scheme assumes that the period of around 2,000 years when the stars of a particular constellation are passing over the vernal point is an astrological age. The period when Aquarius is passing over the vernal point is then known as the Age of Aquarius. The whole system runs in reverse order so that the preceding age was the Age of Pisces, the one before that the Age of Aries. Aries is preceded by the Ages of Taurus, Gemini, and Cancer, and so on. However, there is no standard measuring system and so no agreement about when the ages begin. Various schemes use either (a) the Indian sidereal zodiac, (b) the stars, (c) arbitrary divisions between the constellations, (d) planetary cycles (such as planetary conjunctions in Aquarius in 1962), or (e) calendar dates (such as the year 2000). The complete range of dates given for the beginning of the Age of Aquarius extend from 1457 at the earliest to 3550 at the latest.

Astrological ages were generally ignored by astrologers until they were popularized by Gerald Massey (1828–1907) in the 1880s. They were then adopted by a number of influential writers notably C. G. Jung in the 1910s, and the theosophists

Alan Leo, Alice Bailey (1880–1949), and Dane Rudhyar from the 1910s to 1970s. The Age of Aquarius entered mass culture after it was featured in the musical *Hair* in 1967, but the meaning ascribed to the age has nothing to do with the traditional meaning of the sign Aquarius and is instead adopted from notions of a coming spiritual New Age of peace and harmony.

Nicholas Campion

See also: Apocalypticism; Mundane Astrology; New Age

Further Reading

Campion, Nicholas. 2015. *Astrology and Popular Religion in the Modern West: Prophecy, Cosmology and the New Age Movement*. London: Routledge.
Reid, Vera W. 1944. *Towards Aquarius*. New York: Arco Publishing Company.

AGRICULTURE

Agriculture and astrology have a long, intertwined history. Well before a discipline identifiable as astrology existed, people in many parts of the world began to note correspondences between the movement of the heavens and natural seasonal changes on Earth. This, in turn, led to more detailed observation of the heavens. The advent of agriculture, which occurred in the Fertile Crescent somewhere around the eighth millennium BCE, required intimate knowledge of when to sow and harvest, the timing of which depended on understanding the relationship between the position of the stars and the changing of the seasons. Following the development of astrology into a distinct discipline, various rules emerged governing agricultural practices based not only on these practical relationships but on symbolic ones; as growth came to be associated with the moon, gods and goddesses of planting and harvesting came to be identified with stars corresponding to the time of year for each agricultural activity, and different plants and herbs came to have powers and properties imbued with astrological significance. During the early Christian era, as other forms of astrology came under attack for various theological reasons, agricultural astrology remained insulated due to its innocuous, practical nature. The same expertise garnered from this form of astrology served the church well, for example, in determining canonical hours of prayer and dates for movable feasts such as Easter. During the early modern era, as almanacs developed into one of the most prominent forms of distributing astrological thought, the agricultural component often occupied the most important place. Almanacs have mostly endured to this day as compendia of agricultural information and complementary weather prediction. In short, agricultural astrology was one of the oldest and most enduring forms of astrological practice from prehistory through to the modern era.

Prehistoric observation confirmed that the sun was the source of light and heat on Earth, that the movement of the ecliptic (the sun's path across the sky) was connected to the changing of the seasons, and that the movement of the moon was associated with the tides. Evidence from bone markings on cave walls may indicate basic knowledge of lunar cycles as early as 25,000 BCE, and these cycles eventually provided the basis for some of the first calendars. With the Neolithic agricultural revolution around 8000 BCE, knowledge regarding the synchrony between the rising and setting of certain groups of stars and the change of the seasons allowed ancient farmers to better predict when planting and harvesting needed to take place. It is likely that the origins of the zodiacal constellations and their monthly association arose after these connections were made. By the third millennium BCE, a number of Old World Neolithic cultures had acquired a sophisticated understanding of the movement of the stars, the time and date of the equinoxes and solstices, and the phases of the moon, and many constructed large structures to align with various astronomical phenomena. This was notably done for heliacal risings—or the annual first appearance of stars on the eastern horizon—such as the megaliths at Stonehenge on Salisbury plain in southern England, erected between 2400 and 2200 BCE (Burl 1983, 36–45).

This association between astrology and agriculture had social and religious dimensions. For example, since at least 3300 BCE, the Egyptians had noted that Sirius, the Dog Star, always first appeared on the horizon at or near the summer solstice and presaged the flooding of the Nile River. This was the most important event on the ancient Egyptian calendar as the receding of the waters in that alluvial plain left behind soils rich in nutrients, which made agriculture in an otherwise arid environment possible. Due to the precession of the equinoxes—in which the location of the equinoxes moves slowly westward along the ecliptic against the relative position of the fixed stars in a cycle lasting approximately 26,000 years—this event now occurs on August 10, but Sirius has retained its favorable agricultural connotations.

Agricultural management was essential to the smooth functioning of ancient Near Eastern city-states and the empires that sprung from them. The fusion of practical agricultural knowledge, religious symbolism, and astrological techniques underscores this arrangement. For example, in one of the earliest surviving texts concerning the role of astrology in the administration of the state, *The Dream of Gudea,* from the Mesopotamian city-state of Lagash, agriculture necessitated a proper interpretation of astrology. In this story, written around 2125 BCE, the goddess Nanshe (or Nisaba), who may have been an early version of the Babylonian god Nabu (who was later associated with the Greek god Hermes), is called upon by the people of Lagash to aid them when another god, Enlil, decides to restrict the annual flooding of the Tigris. Nanshe's powers included the ability to measure the heavens and the Earth and the ability to calculate the length and time of the days, seasons, and years with impeccable precision. She was the goddess of grain and the harvest but also of accounting, bookkeeping, and the management of natural resources. She eventually counseled the people of Lagash to build a temple to Ningirsu, the god responsible for the flooding. The connections between these aspects sheds light on the relationship between astronomy, astrology, and agriculture, as well as the importance of a harmoniously functioning state and agricultural plenitude (Campion 2008, 56–57).

The ancient Greeks and Romans also cultivated bonds between astrology and agriculture. The Greek poet Hesiod's (fl. ca. 800–650 BCE) *Works and Days* combined a farming calendar with a comprehensive guide for living in accordance with the expectations of the gods. Written in a straightforward, pragmatic style, *Works and Days* gave advice on how to best maintain harmony with the cosmos and minimize strife by using astrological signs to choose the appropriate moments for various actions. Many of these actions were agricultural in nature, and Hesiod described both seasonal and daily instructions: A shrewd farmer would not begin harvesting until the Pleiades rose with sun (early May) and plough when they set together (November). One should cut and harvest grape clusters when Sirius and Orion reach midheaven (September). Planting was better than sowing on the 13th day of a waning moon. This advice was as practical as it was astrological—the moon would hardly provide much light at that point in the lunar cycle (Campion 2008, 135–136).

Other Greeks and Romans followed in Hesiod's footsteps by either penning their own works further describing the concatenation between astrology and agriculture. Not all were positive. Around 160 BCE, the Roman orator Cato the Elder wrote in *De Agri Cultura* that farmers should never consult foreign oracles or Chaldean astrology on the proper times to plant and harvest. Virgil's (70–19 BCE) *Georgics*, on the other hand, provided an agricultural manual for elites that incorporated some astrological knowledge, while Columella's (4–ca. 70 CE) *Res Rustica* noted that farmers must take account of the "skies" when planting, though he also professed disbelief in astrologers' ability to foretell the future in either human or natural events.

In early Christian Europe, although certain aspects of astrology fell into disrepute, it endured in part because of its practicality. Some early church figures were emphatic about astrology because it took a careful observation of the heavens to calculate the lengths of canonical hours of prayer and to fix the dates of movable religious festivals, church holidays, and, most important, Easter. Some forms that astrology took in the early Middle Ages did not necessarily require precision in astronomical calculation or even a thorough understanding of astrological rules. At the ninth-century Carolingian court, for instance, divinatory astrology predicated on planetary associations with numbers, days of the week, and various plants and herbs for the purposes of medicine and agriculture flourished (Campion 2009, 22). Even Christian critics of astrology, like the Protestant reformer John Calvin (1509–1564), who inveighed against astrology for usurping the power of God, allowed for agricultural astrology because either it did not require what was thought to be demonic magic or divination or its efficacy did not come into question the way that horoscopy and the foretelling of individual futures did (Campion 2009, 113). English philosopher Francis Bacon (1561–1626) claimed that astrology might be useful in horticulture and agriculture to help with determining the appropriate time to "graft, sow, or plant seeds" (Tester 1987, 222).

By the early modern era, astrology and agriculture further fused due to their simultaneous inclusion in almanacs. Short, simple, inexpensive treatises usually written in vernacular languages and directed at literate commoners, almanacs contained annual weather forecasts, planting and harvesting dates for farmers, tidal tables, and astrological predictions. As almanac publishing became more common in the 15th and 16th centuries, many of astrology's processes and concepts were simplified, and basic prognostication became available to those who wished to make rudimentary observations of the heavens. In one of the most popular mid-16th-century almanacs to include weather prediction, Leonard Digges's (1515–1559) *Prognostication Everlastinge of Right Good Effect* included a technical description of positions and movement of the planets and stars but also included many descriptions of what weather to expect based on certain conjunctions. The conjunction of Saturn and the sun in cold zodiacal signs portended dark weather, hail, rain, and cold days. The opposition of Jupiter and the sun meant moisture and heavy winds. The conjunction of Mars and the sun meant drought when it occurred in fire signs like Aries, Leo, or Sagittarius, while it meant thunder and rain in water signs. This type of astrology, known as "astrometeorology," became vitally important for farmers who depended on astrological almanacs for weather prediction (Capp 1979).

Perhaps the most prominent astrometeorologist was John Goad (1616–1686). His major work on the impact of astrology on weather prediction, entitled *Astro-Meteorologia* and published in 1686, compared extant weather records with the angular separation of the planets in order to determine, observationally, what type of weather events occurred when the planets were in certain positions. Goad collected data for nearly 30 years and also compiled records of others' documentation of weather phenomena from the Americas, Europe, East Asia, and the coast of Africa in order check them against his own observations. This research program led Goad to the conclusion that, in fact, there was a correlation between stellar phenomena and weather patterns and events, and, thus, astrology and meteorology were valid and overlapping bodies of knowledge and both were necessary for agriculture (Bowden 1974, 176–195).

In the Anglophone world, there were notable differences between English and North American almanacs. Although the former had highly politicized content, the latter were far more concerned with natural events. Because of the social and environmental fragility of English settlements in North America, the areas of major concern to almanac readers remained weather, agriculture, and husbandry. After all, predicting the weather was tantamount to predicting the possibilities of a good or bad harvest, and, if efficacious, these predictions would be highly prized. Rarely offering the type of specific political predictions of their English counterparts, American almanacs cleaved almost entirely to natural astrological prediction, and, thus, meteorological, medical, and agricultural advice dominated their pages.

In one sense, agricultural astrology managed to hold on by being appropriated and absorbed into the almanac genre. Even as other forms of astrology struggled for legitimacy in the 17th and 18th centuries, agricultural astrology endured under the auspices of predictive almanacs, which combined seasonal weather predictions with agricultural instructions. On the one hand, reforms attempted by natural philosophers since at least the early 16th century allowed astrologers to claim more ground as legitimate scientific practitioners. On the other hand, reformers of horoscopic, horary, and electional astrology ultimately addressed problems that had no definitive solutions. Because of its focus on natural changes, weather, and the planting and harvesting of crops, rather than the fate of humanity, agricultural astrology did not necessarily succumb to the decline of astrology in the later 17th century.

Justin Niermeier-Dohoney

See also: Almanacs; Science

Further Reading

Bowden, Mary Ellen. 1974. *The Scientific Revolution in Astrology: The English Reformers, 1558–1686*. PhD diss. New Haven, CT: Yale University.

Burl, Aubrey. 1983. *Prehistoric Astronomy and Ritual*. Oxford: Shire Archaeology.

Campion, Nicholas. 2008. *A History of Western Astrology, Vol. I: The Ancient World*. London: Continuum.

Campion, Nicholas. 2009. *A History of Western Astrology, Vol. II: The Medieval and Modern Worlds*. London: Continuum.

Capp, Bernard. 1979. *Astrology and the Popular Press: English Almanacs, 1500–1800*. Ithaca, NY: Cornell University Press.

Lindberg, David C. 1992. *The Beginnings of Western Science: The European Scientific Tradition in Philosophical, Religious, and Institutional Context, 600 B.C. to A.D. 1450*. Chicago: University of Chicago Press.

Noonan, George C. 1984. *Classical Scientific Astrology*. Tempe, AZ: American Federation of Astrologers.

Tester, S. J. 1987. *A History of Western Astrology*. Suffolk, UK: Boydell Press.

ALBERTUS MAGNUS (1200–1280)

The German Catholic philosopher and scientist known as Albertus Magnus (Albert the Great), was one of the leading Christian thinkers on the role of astrology in the Middle Ages. Known as the doctor universalis or universal doctor, Albertus set the standards for integrating the new Aristotelianism coming from the Islamic world with Christianity, and his acceptance of astrology as part of this synthesis helped immeasurably in gaining it academic and religious legitimacy. He was a Dominican friar and university professor at a time when the foundations of university learning were being established, making him particularly influential in spreading ideas about astrology as well as many other subjects. He was interested in a broad range of astrological subjects, including electional and mundane astrology as well as the use of astrological talismans.

The introduction of sophisticated mathematical astrology from the Islamic world raised questions of the compatibility of astrological prediction with the Christian doctrine of the freedom of the human will. This was particularly controversial toward the end of Albertus's life, when the bishop of Paris, Etienne Tempier, sought to control the intellectual life of the University of Paris through a set of condemnations, issued first in 1270 and greatly expanded in 1277. These included condemnations of astral determinism. Albertus was then at the University of Cologne, well out of Tempier's jurisdiction, but found himself drawn into the controversy through his connections at Paris. His contributions to this debate include the encyclopedic *Speculum Astronomiae* (*The Mirror of Astronomy*). Such was Albertus's reputation that numerous works were attributed to him that were not his, and some have questioned his authorship of the *Speculum*, but most modern scholars believe it genuinely his. It displays a very wide knowledge of astrological literature and ranges over a variety of astrological topics. Albertus was particularly influenced by Abū Maʿshar whom he regarded as an authority outranking Aristotle in astrology and who grappled with religious problems similar to Albertus's own but in an Islamic context rather than a Christian one.

One reason why Albertus's defense of astrology was so influential is the very high prestige he enjoyed in European intellectual circles, where he was described as a second Aristotle or Avicenna. (He received the designation "Magnus" during his own lifetime.) His expertise on the relation of Christian doctrine and astrology in particular was also widely acknowledged. Astrological references permeate his work throughout his career, and he was familiar with major ancient and Arabic astrological writers including Julius Firmicus Maternus, Ptolemy, and Abū Maʿshar in Latin translation.

Albertus argued that the power of the stars was not deterministic in that it was limited or modified by the power of God, and by the particular circumstances of the individuals or communities on which the stars were exerting their influence. Celestial influences acted directly on the body, not the soul, leaving the soul free in how it responded to these influences or resisted them. (They could also influence the soul through dreams.) Albertus promoted the maxim that the wise man rules his stars. Knowledge of astrology was beneficial in that it enabled the "wise man" to take celestial influences into account, while resisting those that were sinful or otherwise unwise. Knowledge of celestial influences also enabled astrologers to make predictions with a high probability of being accurate, even if absolute certainty cannot be attained. (The inability of astrologers to make accurate predictions was also limited by the complexity of the heavens and the multiplicity of celestial bodies, far beyond the reach of human understanding.) Even if the astrologer made an inaccurate prediction, it might be accurate according to the disposition of the heavens but fail due to actions and conditions on Earth.

In explaining astrological causality Albertus followed the fundamental Aristotelian division between hot and cold and moist and dry. He assigned pairs of these qualities to each planet—the sun, for example, was hot and dry. Celestial influence was then propagated to Earth through light. Albertus believed that the influence of the stars was natural, not magical in any way.

Albertus's advocacy of astrology, however, was not limited to theoretical concerns. He did not regard himself as an astrologer but gave advice on when astrological aid should be invoked. He was a believer in the efficacy of astrological talismans and that they were religiously legitimate. The use of talismans further demonstrated the ability of the wise to harness and control the power of the stars rather than being ruled by them. Albertus also advised that the stars be taken into account when attempting to conceive children, as conception under the wrong stars could result in conjoined or otherwise deformed children. This was true for animal births as well as humans. Albertus also endorsed the practice of medical astrology, believing that physicians should be astrologically aware. Much of the practical application of astrology, including the association of planets with herbs and times of day, is put forward in *The Book of Secrets of Albertus Magnus*. However, this book was not written by Albertus but attributed to him to increase its authority, a common practice in the Middle Ages. It may reflect aspects of his thought as a compilation by a student of Albertus, from different sources, some of which may originate from Albertus.

Albertus's acceptance of astrology was followed by his student Thomas Aquinas, the maker of the most influential philosophical and theological synthesis in the history of Latin Christianity, although Aquinas himself had little interest in the topic. Albertus was also invoked as an authority on the matter by subsequent Christian writers such as Pierre d'Ailly and Marsilio Ficino.

William E. Burns

See also: Abū Ma'shar al-Balkhī; D'Ailly, Pierre; Fate; Ficino, Marsilio; Medical Astrology; Medieval European Astrology; Ptolemy

Further Reading

Best, Michael R., and Frank H. Brightman, eds. 1973. *The Book of Secrets of Albertus Magnus of the Virtues of Herbs, Stones and Certain Beasts, also a Book of the Marvels of the World*. Oxford: Clarendon Press.

Hendrix, Scott. 2016. "From the Margins to the Image of 'The Most Christian Science': Astrology and Theology from Albert the Great to Marsilio Ficino." *Culture and Cosmos* 20: 129–146.

Zambelli, Paolo. 1992. *The* Speculum Astronomiae *and Its Enigma: Astrology, Theology and Science in Albertus Magnus and His Contemporaries*. Dordrecht: Kluwer.

ALMANACS

An almanac is a book or pamphlet containing astronomical and calendrical tables, frequently organized by month. It announces astronomical or astrological events, such as the phases of the moon, solstices and equinoxes, and solar and lunar eclipses. Their main purpose is providing information about the movements of celestial bodies and their astrological effects, but most contain other material, such as medical advice for people and animals, historical facts, calendars of market days, religious holidays, and information on the most favorable days for plantings and other agricultural activities. Almanacs can also be aimed at specific professional groups, such as farmers or sailors. Older almanacs frequently contained prophetic announcements. The earliest documented use of the word *almanac* is in a Latin work of Roger Bacon in 1267. For Bacon, an almanac was a set of tables describing the paths of the celestial bodies. The word's origins are obscure, although the syllable "al" suggests an Arabic origin or possibly a Latin writer making up an Arab-sounding word for prestige value.

Almanacs started as calendars. The earlier texts considered almanacs were found in the Middle East, originating around the middle of the second millennium BCE. The Greek term for these early almanacs was *hemerologies* (from *hēmerā*, meaning "day"). The Greek almanac (*parapegma*) existed in the form of an inscribed stone with movable pegs that indicated the days of the month by being inserted into holes drilled into the stones. The Greeks also had written texts resembling almanacs. Ptolemy wrote a treatise, *Phaseis,* whose full title is translated as "phases of fixed stars and collection of weather-changes," and that has as a central theme a parapegma, a list of dates organized by the solar year and including weather changes, the first and last appearances of stars or constellations at sunrise or sunset, and solstices and equinoxes. The Roman Fasti were early almanacs that included explanations of festival days.

Greeks and Romans, who had great difficulty in devising a calendar year that coincided with a solar year, proposed various cycles, including the Meton Cycle (19 years, or 6,940 days, divided into months). The Meton Cycle, also known as the Lunar Cycle, is reflected in almanacs even today by the "Golden Number" from 1 to 19 that shows the position of the cycle of a given year and is important for determining the date of Easter.

Clogg (or clog) almanacs, also called log almanacs, were introduced in England in the 11th century. The same instruments were called runstocks (or runstaffs) in Scandinavia. These runic almanacs were wooden blocks, decorated and notched on all four sides to denote the day of the year, the seasons, the golden numbers, and the dominical letter. Cloggs were often found attached to staffs, swords, and agricultural implements and were in use to the late 17th century.

Manuscript almanacs are believed to have been prepared in Alexandria as early as the second century CE but none survive. The earliest Christian almanac was written in 354 CE on parchment; reconstructed from fragments, it was published in 1634 and again in 1850. In 1150, Hebrew astronomer Solomon Jarchus created an almanac with many modern features. The first printed almanac may be the so-called Astronomical Calendar (1448), printed by Gutenberg in Mainz. Printed almanacs did not immediately drive out manuscript almanacs, which persisted for centuries after Gutenberg. They also remained ubiquitous in the early modern Islamic world, hungry for astrological information but slow to adopt printing. The first almanac printed in England was *The Shepheard's Kalendar*, published in 1497 by Richard Pynson, who translated the French *Grand Compost des Bergers* (1493). Most English almanacs would continue to be translations of Continental works from France, Germany, and the Low Countries into the 17th century. Michael Nostradamus was probably the most famous almanac maker of the 16th century. He published his first astrological almanac in 1550, and it appeared annually to his death in 1566. His almanac was so popular that it was widely translated, including translations into Italian, English, German, and Dutch. Counterfeit almanacs bearing his name appeared to exploit the market he created.

The heyday of the English almanac was from 1640 to 1700, when almanacs were the most widely circulated genre of printed book. The leading almanac

An Antiastrological Almanac—*Apollo Anglicanus* and Richard Saunder

In 1684 in England, a surveyor and mathematician, Richard Saunder, took over *Apollo Anglicanus*, an almanac formerly written by the astrological physician Richard Saunders who had died in 1675. The following year came King James II's prohibition on astrological predictions in almanacs. Saunder, who would continue to write *Apollo Anglicanus* until 1736, took advantage of this shift to repudiate astrology altogether, making *Apollo Anglicanus* the first English antiastrological almanac. The combination of a serious, technically sound almanac with mockery of astrology was new. In addition to satire and ridicule of failed predictions, Saunder used religious and scientific arguments against astrology. He attacked astrologers, including John Gadbury, as poor and inaccurate astronomers, and suggested that heliocentric astronomy, which he devoted portions of several almanacs to explaining, invalidated traditional astrology. Although Saunder attacked nativities and horary astrology, he was more sympathetic to the idea that the stars and planets might influence the weather. His almanac, which survives in numerous copies, was successful enough that Benjamin Franklin, when he began his famous *Poor Richard's Almanac*, adopted the pseudonym "Richard Saunders." *Apollo Anglicanus* also appeared in numerous still life paintings of letter racks by the Dutch English painter Edward Collier.

writer was William Lilly, whose first almanac, *Merlinus Anglicus Junior: The English Merlin Revived; or, A Mathematical Prediction upon the Affairs of the English Commonwealth, and of All or Most Kingdoms of Christendom, This Present Year 1644*, was published June 12, 1644. This was an immediate best seller. Lilly continued to publish his almanac, which in 1647 became *Merlini Anglici Ephemeris* until 1682, the last one published posthumously. His great astrological and political rival, John Gadbury, also published an almanac series, *Ephemeris*, as did the leading astrologer of the next generation, John Partridge, whose almanac appeared under several titles. Such was the political influence of almanacs that King James II of England barred them from making political predictions in 1685, shortly after his accession, driving Partridge into exile. Leading astrologers such as Lilly, Gadbury, and Partridge all used their almanacs to advance their astrological positions, but almanacs could also be used to oppose astrology, as was the *Apollo Anglicanus* of Richard Saunder. The astrological content of almanacs declined in the 18th century, with one exception being *Old Moore's Almanac*, first published in 1699 by Francis Moore.

Early modern almanacs also contained a wide range of medical advice for human and beast, and some of their authors were medical practitioners ranging from physicians to midwives who used their almanacs to advertise their medical practices. Knowledge of astrology was important in maintaining physical health. By the late 17th century, almanacs were frequently advertising the new-style proprietary commercial medicines. Despite the astrological nature of Paracelsian medicine, many early modern almanac writers stuck to traditional Galenic medicine ignoring Paracelsus's innovations.

In 1639, Stephen Daye printed America's first almanac in Cambridge, Massachusetts. Harvard became the first North American center for the annual publication of almanacs. The earliest American almanacs contained astrological predictions as well as astronomical and meteorological data for the year. Like European almanacs, they often included a miscellany of other information. Almanacs were printed in virtually every American town with a printing press and were among the most commonly owned texts besides the Bible. American almanacs were published in a wide variety of languages including indigenous languages such as Chippewa and Cherokee, and the major European languages spoken in the colonies.

James Franklin began publishing the *Rhode-Island Almanack* in 1728. Five years later, his younger brother Benjamin began publishing *Poor Richard's Almanack* in Philadelphia under the pseudonym "Richard Saunders." Franklin's attitude to astrology was ambivalent; he mocked detailed astrological predictions and borrowed Jonathan Swift's trick of claiming to predict the death of competitors, but saw a role for astrology in agriculture. *Poor Richard* included classical astrological material such as the "zodiac man," an image of a man marked by which zodiac signs governed which parts of the body.

Astrological almanacs underwent a revival in 19th-century England, with the 1821 appearance of *Raphael's Prophetic Almanac*, published to the present day as *Raphael's Astrological Almanac*. Its rival was *Zadkiel's Almanac*, first published in 1832. The popularity of astrological almanacs led the Society for the Diffusion of Useful Knowledge, an organization devoted to popularizing science and opposing astrology, to issue a competing *British Almanac* in 1828. The popular German astrologer, Elisabeth Ebertin (1880–1944), founded a successful astrological almanac, *Ein Blick in Die Zukunft (A Glimpse at the Future)* in 1917. However, many modern almanacs are thick volumes that include an array of worldwide facts and statistical data, but exclude astrological material. The calendar has been relegated to a minor role and astrology omitted completely.

Martin J. Manning

See also: Agriculture; Gadbury, John; Horoscopes; Lilly, William; Medical Astrology; Nostradamus; Partridge, John; Science; Zadkiel

Further Reading

Burns, William E. 2005. "Astrology and Politics in Early Modern England: King James II and the Almanac Men." *The Seventeenth Century* 20: 242–253.

Capp, Bernard S. 1979. *English Almanacs, 1500–1800: Astrology and the Popular Press*. Ithaca, NY: Cornell University Press.

Curry, Patrick. 1992. *A Confusion of Prophets: Victorian and Edwardian Astrology*. London: Collins and Brown.

Curth, Louise H. 2013. *English Almanacs, Astrology and Popular Medicine, 1550–1700*. Manchester, UK: Manchester University Press.

Stowell, Marion B. 1997. *Early American Almanacs: The Colonial Weekday Bible*. New York: Franklin.

Tomlin, T. J. 2014. *A Divinity for All Persuasions: Almanacs and Early American Religious Life*. Oxford: Oxford University Press.

AL-QABĪṢĪ (D. 967)

Abū ṣ-Saqr ʻAbd al-ʻAzīz Ibn ʻUtmān Ibn ʻAlī l-Qabīṣī l-Mawṣilī, commonly known as al-Qabīṣī (Alcabitius) was a professional astrologer who devoted his life and writings to understanding and practicing astrology. Although he wrote numerous books and treatises, his reputation rests on a single work, *The Introduction to Astrology*. This textbook was ranked among the highest astrological works and built al-Qabīṣī's reputation in the Islamic world. In the early 12th century, in or before 1135, the textbook was translated into Latin by John of Seville (fl. 1135–1153), the main translator of works of Arabic in the early days of the Escuela de Traductores de Toledo (Toledo School of Translators). From that point onward the work became established in Western Europe and was the first, often the only, set text in the universities where astrology was taught as part of the curriculum for medicine. Along with Abū Maʻshar (787–886), al-Qabīṣī became known to all as an astrological authority. At least 24 Arabic manuscripts are known, dating from 1191 to 1754, three manuscripts were written in Hebrew script, and over 200 Latin translations define the extent his work reached. Between 1473 and 1521 the text was printed 12 times. His techniques and the astrological house system named after him, which he may have originated, continue to be employed by astrologers today.

Al-Qabīṣī's name indicates a connection with both Mosul (northern Iraq on the bank of the Tigris opposite ancient Nineveh) and Qabisa (unknown location). Little is known of his early life other than that he was a professional astrologer who learned from a teacher in Mosul. Other evidence points most directly to his positon as an astrologer at the court of Sayf al-Dawla al-Hamdani (Sword of Dynasty), the Emir of Aleppo, in Syria from 945–967, to whom he dedicated at least four books, including *The Introduction to Astrology*. Sayf al-Dawla created a court renowned for the quality of the scholars and poets who attended it, including the philosopher al-Farabi (ca. 870–950) and the poet al-Mutanabbi (915–965).

It is clear from the sources that al-Qabīṣī cited in *The Introduction to Astrology* that he owned a personal working library (Al-Qabīṣī 2004, 7). This library contained works by Abū Maʻshar, al-Andarzagar ben Sadi Afraj, one of the first generation of Islamic astrologers, and al-Kindi (ca. 800–after 870). Al-Qabīṣī also quoted from Māshā'allāh Ibn Atharī whose techniques were situated in the works of astrologers such as Hermes Trismegistus and Vettius Valens. Al-Qabīṣī also referred to Dorotheus of Sidon and to Ptolemy's *Tetrabiblos*. Al-Qabīṣī's work is valuable not only for the astrology it contained but also because he copied his sources verbatim, thus showing how astrological traditions were carried through time and history.

Al-Qabīṣī was rigorous in maintaining a high standard for astrologers and recognized that the prince was surrounded by varying levels of astrological competency. In one of the works he dedicated to the prince, *Risāla fī mtiḥān al-munağğimīn mimman huwa muttasim bi-hādā l-ism* (*The Treatise on the Testing of Those Who Call Themselves Astrologers*), he described four groups of proficiency. Al-Qabīṣī described an individual in the first group as a "complete astrologer," the one who was familiar with Ptolemy's *Almagest* and was able to work with first principles in drawing up tables of planetary movements from observing the sky, rather than adapting earlier tables: "He has read the Almagest and demonstrated the movements of the planets, and their forms, sizes, and distances one from another, with rational self-professed astrologers, and he does not need a book or tables" (Al-Qabīṣī 2004, 5–6). The second group were those who were proficient with astrological techniques and skilled in applying the knowledge, but who did not seek the underpinning knowledge necessary to the first group. The third group were the untutored illiterate, who learned astrological information through repetition and routine, "like a blind man," without any comprehension of why they are memorizing the information. Al-Qabīṣī underlined the point that most of the astrologers at the time he wrote this advice fell into this category. The fourth group were the astronomers, those who relied solely on the astrolabe and gave their undivided attention to determining, among other techniques, the direction of the *qibla* in order to preform ritual prayers and had no knowledge of astrological theory and practice. Al-Qabīṣī then proposed a set of 30 questions that allowed the prince to recognize the competency of the astrologers who served him. This list also included trick questions, a further safety net in weeding out ignorance from competence. Because al-Qabīṣī also provided the answers to the questions, he demanded that the prince keep the document secret so that it did not fall into the wrong hands. For if this were to happen, then the ignorant man could learn them by rote and rely on memory when tested, rather than showing true astrological ability and calculating from first principles (Burnett 2002, 203). Such lists were not unusual, for lists of a similar nature belonged to a genre and have been found in the area of medicine. This list of al-Qabīṣī, however, was the first of its kind for astrologers, thus it is important historically for showing the value ascribed to the subject. Indeed, Charles Burnett has noted how al-Qabīṣī, along with Abū Ma'shar, can be considered to be the inheritors of a single tradition of thought, founded on Ptolemy's *Tetrabiblios* and advanced, for the most part, independently of prevailing religious and philosophical beliefs (Burnett 2002, 213). Although *The Introduction to Astrology* began life in the environment of the Islamic court of the 10th century, it became a fundamental text for scholastic learning in the West, complete with glosses and commentaries and deeply embedded in the curricula of the emerging universities wherever the quadrivium was taught (Burnett 2011, 43, 60).

Darrelyn Gunzburg

See also: Court Astrologers; Islamic Astrology; Medieval European Astrology

Further Reading

Al-Qabīṣī (Alcabitius). 2004. *The Introduction to Astrology*, *Warburg Institute Studies and Texts*. ed. and trans. Charles Burnett, Keiji Yamamoto, and Michio Yano. London and Turin: The Warburg Institute and Nino Aragno Editore.

Burnett, Charles. 2002. "The Certitude of Astrology: The Scientific Methodology of Al-Qabīsī and Abū Ma'shar." *Early Science and Medicine* 7, no. 3: 198–213.

Burnett, Charles. 2011. "Al-Qabīṣī Introduction to Astrology: From Courtly Entertainment to University Textbook." In *Studies in the History of Culture and Science: A Tribute to Gad Freudenthal*, ed. Resianne Fontaine and Gad Freudenthal, 43–70. Leiden: Brill.
Burnett, Charles, and Dorian Gieseler Greenbaum, eds. 2015. *From Masha' Allah to Kepler: Theory and Practice in Medieval and Renaissance Astrology*. Ceredigion: Sophia Centre Press.

AMERICAN STARS DEBATE

In 16th- and 17th-century Spain and Spanish America, there was an intense debate over the effects of the stars of the southern sky on the environment and peoples of the south. Much of the southern sky was new to Europeans (the Portuguese had previously encountered southern stars on their voyages along the coast of Africa, but they had kept this information tightly controlled, so it never became the subject of public debate). Generally, European scholars saw the influence of the southern stars as debilitating, while American-identified scholars, whether immigrants to the Americas or American-born Creoles, claimed the stars of the south were particularly beneficent.

The first major natural historian of Spanish America, Gonzalo Fernandez de Oviedo (1478–1557), argued that the southern stars induced cowardice and weakness among those who they ruled. The Franciscan friar Bernardino de Sahagun (1499–1590) argued that the corrupting influence of the stars made Native Americans unfit for the priesthood and weakened Creoles as well. Sahagun and others asserted that the only way of overcoming this heavenly corruption was through a regime of strict discipline, a regime that Sahagun claimed had characterized the preconquest Aztec Empire. This argument, common among Creoles, justified a regime of harsh exploitation that maximized the benefit of coerced Native American labor to Spaniards. The Dominican Gregorio Garcia (d. 1627) argued that the American stars and climate explained how the ancient Carthaginians, who he believed had originally settled the Americas, had degenerated into "slothful," "cowardly" Native Americans.

Beginning around the second quarter of the 17th century, Creoles began to respond with works exalting the benevolent power of the southern stars. The Augustinian Antonio de la Calancha (1584–1684) claimed that the southern sky was full of beautiful stars and that the horoscopes for the major cities of Spanish Peru were all auspicious. One of the leading intellectual lights of Creole Mexico, Diego Rodriguez (1596–1668), holder of the chair of mathematics at the University of Mexico City, linked the Mexican sky with the Virgin Mary, specifically the doctrine of her Immaculate Conception. He linked the path of the comet of 1652 through the Mexican sky with the Virgin's triumph over the dragon of the book of Revelations. The Southern Cross also functioned as a religious symbol of God's care for the Americas for Catholic Spaniards.

Spanish and Creole believers in the favorable southern sky were faced with the problem of justifying the rule of Europeans and European-descended Creoles over Native Americans and Africans who grew up under these benevolent stars.

They accomplished this by proclaiming the innate differences between Native American, African, and European bodies as causing the stars to affect them differently, and they did not challenge the dominant position of European-descended peoples.

William E. Burns

See also: Mundane Astrology

Further Reading

Canizares-Esguerra, Jorge. 2006. "New World, New Stars: Patriotic Astrology and the Invention of Amerindian and Creole Bodies in Colonial Spanish America, 1600–1650." In *Nature, Empire and Nation: Explorations of the History of Science in the Iberian World*, 64–95. Stanford: Stanford University Press.

ANTIASTROLOGICAL THOUGHT

Intellectual opposition to astrology has taken many forms, most of which can be put into four broad categories: the skeptical, attacking astrology's claims to authority and accusing it of internal contradictions; the religious, attacking it for its inconsistencies with religious doctrine and for presenting an alternative to the truth-claims of religion; the political, attacking its purported effects on the body politic; and the scientific, attacking it for its inconsistency with scientific truth. There are many different lines of attack within each group, and elements of the four groups are frequently blended in antiastrological polemic, as they were in the influential Renaissance work, *Disputations against Astrology* (1494) by philosopher Giovanni Pico della Mirandola (1463–1494) or the Elizabethan cleric John Chamber's *Treatise against Judiciall Astrologie* (1601). Not all opponents of astrology have attacked all branches of it—some who objected to natal and horary astrology were willing to accept at least the possibility of predicting the weather through astrology. Astrologers have responded to these criticisms, and their responses have shaped the history of astrology.

Skeptical arguments go back to the Roman Empire, and the skeptical attacks on astrology from Greek philosopher Sextus Empiricus (ca. 200 CE) and Roman philosopher and statesman Marcus Tullius Cicero (106–43 BCE) had a long history. One common skeptical argument was the example of a battlefield, where many individuals with vastly different horoscopes died within a short space of time. The example of twins, born close together but leading vastly different lives and dying at different times, was also frequently invoked. Opponents of astrology pointed out that people's lives and bodies were shaped more by the families and communities into which they were born than by the positions of the stars and planets at their birth. These arguments were frequently repeated in subsequent centuries and are still used by modern opponents of astrology. Ancient skepticism also often rested on a rigidly deterministic interpretation of astrological causation that many astrologers have repudiated.

Cicero Denounces Astrology

The Roman statesman and philosopher Marcus Tullius Cicero's *On Divination*, written around 44 BCE, contains several arguments against astrology. Here, Cicero argues that if we don't think the weather at the time of birth influences our destinies, how can the distant stars:

> But what utter madness in these astrologers, in considering the effect of the vast movements and changes in the heavens, to assume that wind and rain and weather anywhere have no effect at birth! In neighbouring places conditions in these respects are so different that frequently, for instance, we have one state of weather at Tusculum and another at Rome. This is especially noticeable to mariners who often observe extreme changes of weather take place while they rounding the capes. Therefore, in view of the fact that the heavens are now serene and now disturbed by storms, is it the part of a reasonable man to say that this fact has no natal influence—and of course it has not—and then assert that a natal influence is exerted by some subtle, imperceptible, well-nigh inconceivable force which is due to the condition of the sky, which condition, in turn, is due to the action of the moon and stars?

Source: Cicero, Marcus Tullius. 1921. *De Senectute, De Amicitia, De Divinatione,* trans. William Armistead Falconer, 477. Cambridge, MA: Harvard University Press.

Much of the skeptical critique of astrology was an anti-intellectual attack on astrologers rather than the discipline itself. Skeptical approaches took the form of mockery as well as argument. The pretensions of astrologers to understand the stars could be mocked in the same way—and sometimes by the same people—as the pretensions of physicians to understand the human body or philosophers to understand the cosmos. Astrologers were especially vulnerable to such attacks after spectacular failed predictions, individual or collective. The astrological community in England came under fierce attack following the failure of the "Black Monday" eclipse of 1652 to be followed by great events or indeed much of anything—a failure remembered 50 years later. In more recent times, the failed predictions surrounding the "Harmonic Convergence" of 1987 or the "Mayan Apocalypse" of 2012 resulted in widespread satirical mockery. Astrologers' attacks on each other, in a pattern familiar in other areas of thought, could also be exploited by skeptics to attack the validity of astrology in general.

Although attacks on astrology have come from numerous religious positions, by far the most sustained and serious attacks have come from religions in the Abrahamic tradition—Judaism, Christianity, and Islam. Jeremiah 10:2, "Thus saith the LORD, Learn not the way of the heathen, and be not dismayed at the signs of heaven; for the heathen are dismayed at them" (King James Version), has been frequently invoked by Jewish and Christian opponents of astrology. The idea of astrology as related to pagan star-worship can be found in the Bible, and continued partly due to the continued use in the West of the names of Roman gods to designate the planets, as well as the mythological associations of many constellations. By ascribing power to planets with the names of gods, astrologers were accused of carrying on paganism in another form.

There were more deeply rooted theological problems with astrology. For Muslims, Christians, and Jews the idea of the power of the stars seemed to infringe on the omnipotence of God. Muslim critics of astrology argued that by taking power from God, astrology led to atheism. The leading Muslim intellectuals who attacked astrology include the physician and philosopher Ibn Sina (980–1037), known to the West as Avicenna, the conservative theologian and jurist Ibn Tamiyyah (1263–1328), and Ibn Tamiyyah's disciple Ibn Qayyim al-Jawziyya (1292–1350). Ibn Qayyim al-Jawziyya's *Miftāḥ al-sa ʿāda (The Key of Happiness)* is often considered the classic refutation of astrology from an Islamic religious perspective. Muslim opponents of astrology drew a clear distinction between astronomy, a clearly legitimate discipline, and astrology, which they linked with forbidden arts of magical divination. Astrology was also linked with polytheism, which some Muslims believed originated in the worship of the planets.

The most prominent opponents of astrology from a Christian perspective include St. Augustine of Hippo (354–430), the Italian renaissance Dominican preacher Girolamo Savonarola (1452–1498), and the Russian Orthodox monk St. Maximos the Greek (1470–1556). For Christians, for whom human free will was an important doctrine, the power of the stars was frequently identified with a "hard" astral determinism that seemed to deny human beings the ability to choose. This was the reason that astrology was attacked in the famous condemnations by Etienne Tempier, the Bishop of Paris, in 1270 and 1277. He forbade Christians from teaching that the power of the stars overrode human free will. Christians also feared that by ascribing evil impulses to the stars, astrologers made God, who created the stars, ultimately responsible for human sin. Christian astrologers responded by claiming that the stars influenced human choices but did not "force" human beings to do anything. Christian opponents of astrology, and even some astrologers, frequently distinguished between astrology and the legitimate interpretation of unusual celestial events such as comets or novas as divine signs or warnings. Because unusual celestial events could be seen as providential signs or warnings from God with no independent power of their own, they were less threatening to Christian worldviews than the astrological idea of a power inherent in the stars themselves.

Christians had to separate the star of Bethlehem that announced the birth of Christ to the Magi from astrology. This was even more of a problem as the three Magi or wise men were often represented as astrologers themselves. Christians often dealt with this issue by claiming that the star of Bethlehem was a special, miraculous heavenly phenomenon, not the kind of star or planet that astrologers dealt with, or asserting that the Magi gave up astrology after their visit to the infant Jesus.

Politically, astrology has been attacked both as a threat to the established order and as a support to it. Astrology, with its ability to predict the death of monarchs or other major political changes, seemed to threaten the social and political order, often leading to fierce legal repression. Political criticism focused less on the intellectual validity of astrology and more on its consequences. In the period following the English Restoration in 1660, astrology was frequently associated with the preceding civil wars, and marginalizing it was considered part of a project of creating authoritative knowledge that would support a conservative social order.

A new type of political criticism emerged in the 20th century, in the work of Marxist Theodor Adorno of the Frankfurt School (1903–1969). Adorno's leftist criticism focused not on astrology's destabilizing effects but on its stabilizing effect on a political and economic order Adorno though exploitative and wrong. Adorno's attack was focused less on the intellectual tradition of astrology, whose falsity he simply assumed, and more on popular newspaper horoscopes, particularly Carroll Righter's horoscopes in the *Los Angeles Times* to which he devoted a lengthy analysis. He saw these as reinforcing the status quo and reinforcing hierarchical relationships through an appeal to people's psychological needs. Influenced by psychoanalyst Sigmund Freud (1856–1939), Adorno claimed that belief in astrology could even be a way of fulfilling a sexual desire to submit to a force more powerful than oneself, in this case the stars.

The claims of astrologers to know the future via the power of the stars has also been criticized by political ideologies that view other forces as determining human affairs. Some Nazis criticized astrology because it treated the individual's horoscope, rather than their racial bloodline, as determining their destiny. Similarly, astrology was a poor fit for the "historical materialism" and emphasis on economic class of Marxist regimes.

The last major set of criticisms to emerge were the scientific. Although criticisms of astrology based on its incompatibility with natural philosophy date back to the ancient world, and the medieval philosopher Nicholas Oresme (1320–1382) argued that planetary motions were too irregular and uncertain to be the basis for astrology, science and astrology only permanently parted ways in the 17th century. The scientific revolution saw the replacement of astrology as the foremost practical application of astronomy with navigation. Because astronomers could now justify their work to their patrons on the grounds of assisting with navigation and cartography rather than astrology, support of astrology was no longer necessary. One of the earliest major scientists to criticize astrology was the English astronomer John Flamsteed (1646–1719), the first head of the Royal Observatory at Greenwich, although his critique remained unpublished.

An early scientific criticism of astrology, still heard today, is that it reflects a pre-Copernican, geocentric cosmos in which the sun and planets are treated as orbiting the Earth. Another type of scientific criticism focuses on the lack of a physical mechanism to explain astrological influence. More materialist analyses of the universe leave little room for the influence of the stars—which did not prevent astrology from flourishing in the officially "materialist" Soviet Union despite official opposition.

In the 20th century, astrology became for many scientists and believers in scientific rationalism a paradigm case of "unscientific" or "superstitious" thought incompatible with scientific modernity. It was lumped with other forms of magic and divination and often viewed as the purview of intellectually stigmatized groups such as lower-class people and women. Rationalist and skeptical groups such as India's Maharashtra Andhashraddha Nirmoolan Samiti (Maharashtra Blind Faith Eradication Committee) or the United States' Committee for Skeptical Inquiry have campaigned against newspaper horoscope columns and other forms of popular astrology as part of a broad campaign against "superstition." In 1975, "Objections to Astrology," a public statement of 186 leading scientists, including 19 Nobel Prize winners, appeared. It expressed distress over the popularity of astrology and reasserted that it had no scientific basis. The website http://www.astrology-and-science.com/ collects many of the modern skeptical and scientific critiques of astrology.

William E. Burns

See also: Albertus Magnus; Christianity; Enlightenment; Fate; Legal Regulation of Astrology; Politics; Science

Further Reading

Adorno, Theodor W. 1994. "The Stars Down to Earth: The *Los Angeles Times* Astrology Column." In *The Stars Down to Earth and Other Essays on the Irrational in Culture*, ed. Stephen Crook, 34–127. London: Routledge.

Burns, William E. 2000. "'The Terriblest Eclipse That Hath Been Seen in Our Days': Black Monday and the Debate on Astrology during the Interregnum." In *Rethinking the Scientific Revolution*, ed. Margaret J. Osler, 137–152. Cambridge: Cambridge University Press.

Caroti, Stefano. 1987. "Nicolas Oresme's Polemic against Astrology, in His *Quodlibeta*." In *Astrology, Science and Society: Historical Essays*, ed. Patrick Curry, 75–93. Woodbridge, Suffolk, UK: Boydell.

Chevalier, Jacques M. 1997. *A Postmodern Revelation: Signs of Astrology and the Apocalypse.* Toronto: University of Toronto Press.

Curry, Patrick. 1989. *Prophecy and Power: Astrology in Early Modern England.* Princeton: Princeton University Press.

Hunter, Michael. 1987. "Science and Astrology in Seventeenth-Century England: An Unpublished Polemic by John Flamsteed." In *Astrology, Science and Society: Historical Essays*, ed. Patrick Curry, 260–300. Woodbridge, Suffolk: Boydell.

Jerome, Lawrence E. 1997. *Astrology Disproved.* Buffalo, NY: Prometheus.

Michot, Yahya J. 2000. "Ibn Taymiyya on Astrology: Annotated Translation of Three Fatwas." *Journal of Islamic Studies* 11: 147–208.

"Objections to Astrology: A Statement by 186 Leading Scientists." *The Humanist* (September/October 1975): 14–18.

Thomas, Keith. 1971. *Religion and the Decline of Magic: Studies in Popular Beliefs in Sixteenth and Seventeenth-Century England.* London: Weidenfeld and Nicolson.

APOCALYPTICISM

Apocalypticism is the belief that the world is about to undergo a radical transformation. In extreme cases this transformation will result in the end of the material world and its possible replacement by a new final spiritual phase, such as the eternal kingdom of God. The term *apocalypse* is derived from the Greek for revelation, and its use as a description for the end of the world is in turn derived from St. John the Divine's revelation of the end of the world in Revelation, the final book of the Christian New Testament. In common usage the apocalypse is the moment of global transformation. Associated terms include *millennialism* and *millenarianism*, both derived from the Latin for 1,000, the length of historical periods identified in both Revelation and Persian texts. From the early Jewish tradition it was common to link the apocalyptic moment to upheavals in the sky, prompting later astrologers to assume that the end of the world, or at least lesser historical upheavals, could be predicted. Apocalyptic astrology has three forms. In the first, God uses the stars as omens of his intentions. In the second, the mathematical laws of planetary motion, created by God, become instruments of the rise and fall of states, religions, and the entire world. In the third, long-term astronomical shifts and calendar counts separate great periods of history.

Apocalyptic Astrology and Omens

In Western and Christian culture the main influence on apocalyptic thought is Jewish scripture. The key astrological texts are Isaiah 13:10 ("For the stars of the Heavens and their constellations will not give their light; The Sun will be dark at its rising And the Moon will not shed its light") and Amos 8:9 ("And on that day," says the Lord God, "I will make the sun go down at noon, and darken the earth in broad daylight . . . The house of Jacob shall be a fire, and the house of Joseph a flame, and the house of Esau stubble; they shall burn and consume them all . . . and the kingdom shall be the Lord's"). Both are generally interpreted as references to eclipses and were the inspiration for similar passages in the Christian New Testament. Typical is Mark 13:24–27 ("But in those days, after that tribulation, the sun will be darkened, and the moon will not give its light, and the stars will be falling from heaven, and the powers in the heavens will be shaken. And then they will see the Son of man, coming in clouds with great power and glory. And then he will send out the angels, and gather his elect from the four winds, from the ends of the earth to the ends of heaven"). Revelation 6:12–14 combined apparent eclipse imagery with more poetic accounts of upheaval in the sky ("I watched as he opened the sixth seal. There was a great earthquake. The sun turned black like

Astrology in the Book of Revelation: The "Four Beasts"

The role of astrological symbolism in the Book of Revelation in the Christian Bible remains controversial, although few scholars would deny its presence. The "Four Beasts" in chapter 4 are frequently identified with the signs Taurus (the calf), Leo (the Lion), Scorpio (the eagle), and Aquarius (the Man). These signs are equidistant in the Zodiac.

> And the first beast was like a lion, and the second beast like a calf, and the third beast had a face as a man, and the fourth beast was like a flying eagle.
>
> And the four beasts had each of them six wings about him; and they were full of eyes within: and they rest not day and night, saying, Holy, holy, holy, Lord God Almighty, which was, and is, and is to come.
>
> And when those beasts give glory and honour and thanks to him that sat on the throne, who liveth for ever and ever.

Source: Revelation 4:7–9, KJV.

sackcloth made of goat hair, the whole moon turned blood red, and the stars in the sky fell to earth, as figs drop from a fig tree when shaken by a strong wind. The heavens receded like a scroll being rolled up, and every mountain and island was removed from its place").

Such astrological literature was clearly framed in terms of direct omens (warnings) from God. As such it was not included in theological denunciations of the use of astrology as demonic or fatalistic. It also underpinned a tradition, especially strong in medieval Europe, in which any major astronomical event, such as a comet, solar eclipse, or major planetary conjunction could be used as an indicator of the Parousia (Christ's imminent return) and the final battle forecast in Revelation.

Apocalyptic Astrology and Planetary Cycles

A separate tradition evident in classical Greece argued that historical periods were measured by planetary cycles. The earliest extant text is Plato's *Timaeus*, section 39D ("The complete number of Time fulfils the Complete year when all the eight circuits with their relative speeds, finish together and come to a head, when measured by the revolution of the Same and the Similarly-moving"). By the first century CE it was believed that when the seven planets form a conjunction on Cancer the world will be destroyed by fire, and when the conjunction falls in Capricorn it will be destroyed by flood.

The Persian astrologers of the early centuries CE focused the concept of planetary cycles on the slow-moving Jupiter and Saturn, whose total sequence of 20-year conjunctions through the zodiac lasted 960 years, just short of the thousand year periods that divided world history in the Persian religion of Zoroastrianism. After the coming of Islam, in surviving texts from the eighth and ninth centuries composed by Mashāllāh Abū Ma'shar, the conjunctions of Saturn, Jupiter, and Mars "signify the destruction of sects and kingdoms, and the changing of them (and) . . . prophecies" Mashāllāh), "the changes of the Sharias and the Sunnas, the occurrence of important matters, the change of the kingdom, the death of kings and the kinds of occurrence of prophets, revelation, and miracles in religions and dynasties" (Abū Ma'shar). The striking claim about such statements is their relativity. No religion, not even Islam, and no prophet, not even Mohammed, is supreme, and all are subject to the vicissitudes of fate as revealed in planetary cycles: all religions have their place in the unfolding life of God's universe.

From the 12th to the 17th centuries both models, omens and planetary cycles, were merged as a means of predicting either historical crisis or the second coming of Christ. Notable was the conjunction of the sun, Mercury, Venus, Mars, Jupiter, and Saturn in the water sign Pisces in 1524, which was interpreted as a warning of a great flood. Such ideas became marginalized in Europe with the decline of the credibility of astrology, although eclipses and comets continued to exert a prophetic power for millennial Christian groups. In India, astrology was never discredited, and in recent times a multiple conjunction in Aquarius (the water pourer) in 1962 provoked predictions of a great flood, as in 1524.

Long-Term Astronomical and Calendar Counts

A third tradition depends on long-term astronomical changes and calendrical counts. The Indian system of yugas, adapted by the Persians, divides history into periods of thousands or millions of years, separated by apocalyptic upheavals. In the 19th century, the scheme was adopted by Western Theosophists who believed that a coming global crisis was presaged by entry into the kali yuga, the worst of all possible worlds. However, the end of the kali yuga would inaugurate the return to spirituality. Theosophists were also instrumental in developing the belief that the movement (precession) of zodiac signs in relation to the position of the sun at the annual spring equinox (see Age of Aquarius) leads to a spiritual New Age. From the 1970s this prophecy was adapted to the so-called long count of the Maya calendar, from which it was deduced that October 2012 would signify the decisive shift into the New Age. The idea became popular in the Americas where the Maya calendar was seen as an authentic New World basis for prophecy, in contrast to the Aquarian Age, which relied on the Greco-Babylonian zodiac of the Old World. Such technical differences aside, the 2012 prophecies exactly repeated those of Aquarian Age theorists. The so-called 2012 phenomenon attracted intense media interest in the run-up to the key date. However, although the majority of protagonists argued that the date signified an inner transformation that might not be evident in external events, most media attention emphasized the danger of apocalyptic disaster, misrepresenting its character.

Nicholas Campion

See also: Age of Aquarius; Astrotheology; Bible; Christianity; Comets; Indian Astrology; Mesoamerican Astrology; Mundane Astrology; New Age; Pont, Robert

Further Reading

Campion, Nicholas. 1994. *The Great Year: Astrology, Millenarianism and History in the Western Tradition*. London: Penguin.

Campion, Nicholas. 2013. "The 2012 Phenomenon in Context: Millenarianism, New Age and Cultural Astronomy." In *Ancient Cosmologies and Modern Prophets*, ed. Ivan Šprac and Peter Pehani, 15–31. Lubljana: Anthropological Notebooks year XIX, supplement.

ART

Art can be defined as the creation of monuments and artifacts that convey cultural values that engage the senses beyond words. When linked with astrology, defined as "the practice of relating the heavenly bodies to lives and events on earth, and the traditions that have thus been generated" (Curry 1999, 55), art helps us understand how other cultures saw these heavenly bodies and the value they placed upon them. Ancient globes, classical synagogue mosaics, ninth-century Islamic desert bath houses, stained glass windows and sculptural archivolts in medieval cathedrals, frescoes on the walls of medieval private chapels, castles, and palaces, early modern paintings containing mythology, the ceilings of Popes and bankers, and the works of contemporary artists such as Joan Miró (1893–1983), Alexander Calder (1898–1976), and Salvador Dalí (1904–1989), all show the diverse ways cultures have responded to these heavenly bodies.

In Mesopotamia, kudurrus or boundary stones dating as far back as 1350 BCE contained images of the sun, moon, and Venus and some constellations. Kudurrus were stone documents stored in a temple that recorded the land granted by the king to his vassals. The kudurrus were stored in a temple but the vassal would be given a clay copy to be used as a boundary stone as confirmation of legal ownership. The planets engraved on the boundary stones served as witnesses to protect and oversee the contract (Thierens 1935, 25; Bahn 2000, 78).

Images of the constellations in the form of globes in late Hellenistic and Roman pedagogy (Ryan 2012, 122) were based on the work of Aratus of Soli (ca. 315/310–240 BCE) whose poem *Phaenomena* was written for a sky-watching readership. Aratus encouraged the reader to understand the constellations visible from the Northern Hemisphere, as well as how to predict the weather through descriptions that included similes and mythic personifications (Aratus 2010, xvi). As D. Mark Possanza has observed, because it offered "a non-technical exposition of the constellations and celestial sphere in relatively short compass, it was adopted as a kind of guidebook to the heavens and became part of the reading list in the Greco-Roman system of education" (Possanza 2012, 67). Aratus went to great lengths to describe how the zodiac constellations could be seen along the ecliptic in relation to the constellations surrounding them and how they could best be observed as they ascended in the east. Visible depictions within the broader field of the starry dome with constellational relationships made his explanations clearer. On all of the globes the constellations are depicted from the outside looking down toward the Earth. Although only three celestial globes have survived from the classical world—Kugel's Globe, dated to ca. 300–100 BCE, and so named as it was acquired and is still exhibited by the Gallery J. Kugel Antiquaries in Paris; the Farnese Atlas, dated to 117–138 CE; and the Mainz Globe, dated to ca. 150–220 CE and acquired in 1996 by the Römisch-Germanischen Zentralmuseum in Mainz, Germany—fragments from three others have been found (the Salzburg fragment, the Berlin fragment, and the Larissa globe) (Dekker 2012, 52–56). Although there were differences in the style and quality of the images based on how much knowledge the goldsmith or sculptor brought to bear, in all three globes the zodiac constellation images are clearly recognizable and consistently represented.

Elaborate mosaic panels on the pavements of six synagogues in Israel dating from the fourth to the sixth centuries CE—Hammat Tiberias, south of Tiberias on the west bank of the Sea of Galilee; Sepphoris, or Zippori, in the central Galilee, six kilometers north–northwest of Nazareth; Beit Alpha at the foot of the northern slopes of the Gilboa mountains near Beit She'an; Huseifa, on Mount Carmel, south of Haifa; Na'aran, on the West Bank north of Jericho, in Ephraim; and Horvat Susiya, in the Judean hills south of Hebron—depict the zodiac surrounding the central chariot of the sun (a Greek motif). The corners depict personifications of the four "turning points" ("tequfot") of the year, solstices and equinoxes, each named for the month in which it occurs—tequfah of Tishrei, tequfah of Tevet, tequfah of Ni(san), tequfah of Tamuz. The identical designs found in each synagogue offer an insight into Jewish thought and culture after the second Temple had been destroyed (Hachlili 1996, 61; Laderman 2013, 71). Some scholars have suggested the synagogue mosaics affirmed a Jewish belief in an ordered world; others have seen them as calendrical, linking them with the decision by Hillel II (360 CE), the leader of Palestinian Jewry, to reveal the knowledge of the intercalation of the lunar and solar year of the Jewish calendar. These mosaic pavements suggest this was a community that maintained a relationship with the sky visibly emphasized by the images of the zodiac on which they walked.

Representation of the sky is also found in early Islamic architecture in the sand-colored limestone complex of Quṣayr 'Amra, a bath-house located in the desert east of the northern tip of the Dead Sea. Quṣayr 'Amra is one of several hunting lodges and fortresses established in the deserts of Syria and Jordan during the first half of the eighth century and used as desert retreats to escape the pestilence and politics of large cities. The complex is covered in brightly colored frescoes and mosaics. It is, however, the 2.75 meter diameter dome/cupola of the *caldarium* portraying in fresco the night sky with 35 constellations of the Northern Hemisphere and zodiac signs that Emilie Savage-Smith described as the earliest evidence within Islamic culture of painted celestial cartography (Savage-Smith 1992, 12).

In the late 11th century, Muslim Spain and the kingdom of Sicily changed to Christian rule and attracted European translators in search of new learning. These translations changed European astrology. Astrological learning was incorporated into imagery found in ecclesiastical and civic architecture, manuscript illumination, and Books of Hours. In Padua, the Commune, or city government, commissioned Giotto di Bondone (ca. 1267–1337) to implement a monumental fresco scheme for the restoration of the Commune's law courts, the Palazzo della Ragione, in the early 14th century. The fresco scheme of 319 images across three registers on these newly heightened bare walls is filled with astronomical and astrological imagery, informed by the extensive astrological knowledge of Pietro d'Abano (ca. 1250–ca. 1316), who was teaching medicine, philosophy, and astrology at Padua University at the time. Along the walls of the top register of the first floor Salone, restored following the original scheme after fire damage in 1420, are images of heavenly constellations. Images of the zodiac signs are clearly identifiable in the middle register of the scheme. The complete three-register fresco scheme also contains images that represent the Labors of the Month, together with Christian saints, trades and skills exemplified by the Paduan workforce, and theological and liturgical images. The scheme visually reminded the judges who worked in this building of the cosmology in which they lived, an Aristotelian sympathetic cosmos creating the accord that the Commune regarded as important between the order of the celestial realms and the order of life on Earth (Gunzburg 2016, 87–113).

From 1430–1650, Popes, wealthy bankers, and merchants in Italy filled the vaults of their chapels and reception halls with stars, planets, and constellations. Their aim was also to be in accord with the heavens. Via painted imagery, astrology was translated into the visual mythology of antiquity, which underpinned the regeneration and implementation of classical learning. An example is the horoscopic ceiling found in the Sala di Galatea in the Villa Farnesina in Rome, commissioned in ca. 1511 by Agostino Chigi, a Sienese banker and treasurer to Pope Julius II, which depicts the zodiac images portrayed alongside the personifications of the planets but laid out as Chigi's horoscope. A second example, the Sala dei Pontifici (Borgia Apartments) in the Vatican Palace, decorated in 1520–1521 for Pope Leo X (1475–1521, Pope 1513–1521), also depicts the zodiac images portrayed alongside the personification of the planets but this time laid out as the Chaldean order of the planets and their rulerships. A third example, the Sala Bologna, Vatican Palace commissioned by Pope Gregory XIII (1502–1585, Pope 1572–1585) in 1575, shifted away from the personal and employed mapmaking in an effort to understand heavenly space. Emily Urban has argued that Pope Gregory XIII may have been influenced by his close friend Gabriele Paleotti (1522–1597), then Bishop of Bologna, who believed that "a learned viewer who looked at such a painting would not merely see a map or landscape, but would be able to metaphysically contemplate each aspect of the image and comprehend God's presence in everything depicted" (Urban 2016, 157; Paleotti [1582] 1961, 384–385).

Illuminated manuscripts depicted astrology within the calendrical parts of books, each month occupying two pages and accompanied by miniatures of the signs of the zodiac and Labors of the Month. Examples are the Queen Mary Psalter (1310–1320) (Royal MS 2 B VII) or in the *Très Riches Heures* of John, Duke of Berry

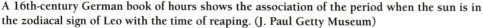

A 16th-century German book of hours shows the association of the period when the sun is in the zodiacal sign of Leo with the time of reaping. (J. Paul Getty Museum)

(1340–1416), created between ca. 1412 and 1416 by the Limbourg brothers and Jean Colombe. In the 17th century, astrological engravings appeared in books written by physicians such as English Paracelsian physician Robert Fludd's *Utriusque Cosmi Historia*, published in Oppenheim, 1617, which depicts a seated man with a square horoscope on the table front of him conversing with a client in *An Astrologer Casting a Horoscope*. They also appear in Dutch poet and engraver Jan Luyken's (1649–1712) *Het Menselyk Bedryf* (*Book of Trades*) (1694) where an etching of *The Astrologer* depicts a man seated by a table containing a globe of the world and an armillary sphere.

Astrology was reflected in early modern and 19th-century painted works that moved away from walls and ceilings, such as Sandro Botticelli's (ca. 1445–1510) *Venus and Mars* (tempera and oil on poplar), thought to be a backboard from a chest or daybed, Johannes Vermeer's (1632–1675) *The Astronomer* (oil on canvas), Jan Brueghel the Younger's (1601–1678) *Children of the Planet Sun* (oil on canvas), Elihu Vedder's (1836–1923) *The Pleiades* (oil on canvas), and Witold Pruszkowski's (1846–1896) *Falling Star* (oil on canvas), among others, showing the continuing meaning and cultural importance of the sky.

In the 18th and 19th centuries, the artistic emphasis was also focused on how to use the heavens as instruments. Thus apertures created in buildings so that they focused light at particular moments of the day for timing or remembrance resulted in meridian lines. An example is in the Basilica of St. Mary of the Angels and the Martyrs in Rome, completed by Francesco Bianchini (1662–1729) in 1702, built along the meridian that crosses Rome at longitude 12° 30' E, which focused light onto the line at solar noon. Its threefold purpose was to check the accuracy of the Gregorian reformation of the calendar, to have at hand a ready tool to predict Easter exactly, and to compete with the meridian line in Bologna cathedral. It was, however, in itself a beautifully created artefact made of bronze surrounded by white and yellow marble. Bianchini also placed holes in the ceiling to mark the passage of stars.

In the 21st century, architect Daniel Libeskind incorporated sunlight, date, time, and place to create his *Wedge of Light* at the National September 11 Memorial in New York. Each year between 8:46 a.m. and 10:28 a.m. on September 11, the sun casts a shaft of light across the plaza in remembrance of the nearly 3,000 people killed in the terror attacks of 2001 at the World Trade Center.

In the 20th century, the close working relationship between American sculptor Alexander Calder (1898–1976) and Spanish painter Joan Miró (1893–1983) resulted in a number of astrological works: Miró's *Constellations,* a series of 23 small paintings on paper painted between 1939 and 1941 and Calder's *Constellations* (1943), 29 tabletop wood and wire constructions. In 1940, after escaping from France to the Spanish island of Mallorca, Miró wrote, "I felt a deep desire to flee. I shut myself deliberately. The night, music and the stars began to play a role in my painting." Between 1955 and 1958 Miró also created the pair of ceramic murals for the UNESCO building in Paris, entitled *Wall of the Sun* and *Wall of the Moon.* In 1967, Salvador Dalí (1904–1989) created a limited edition series of lithographs known as *The Twelve Signs of the Zodiac* suite.

Gustav Holst, *The Planets*

The best-known musical composition animated by astrology and theosophy is the suite of German composer Gustav Holst (1874–1934), the seven linked compositions known as *The Planets* first performed in 1918. (The music was composed earlier, but performance was delayed by World War I.) The seven planets are the astronomical planets known at the time from Mercury to Neptune (excluding Earth) not the seven planets of traditional astrology, which include the sun and moon. Holst was inspired by an interest in theosophy and a friendship with English astrologer and writer Clifford Bax (1886–1962). Immediate inspiration for *The Planets* came from a book by astrologer and theosophist Alan Leo, *The Art of Synthesis* (1912). *The Art of Synthesis* is divided into chapters on each planet, in the same manner as Holst's composition. Many of the elements associated with planets, such as that of Mars with war, are embodied in Holst's music.

Darrelyn Gunzburg

See also: Hellenistic Astrology; Islamic Astrology; Judaism; Medieval European Astrology; Mesopotamian Astrology; Renaissance and Reformation Astrology; Roman Astrology; Zodiacs

Further Reading

Aratus. 2010. *Phaenomena*, trans. Aaron Poochigian. Johns Hopkins New Translations from Antiquity. Baltimore: Johns Hopkins University Press.

Bahn, Paul G. 2000. *The Atlas of World Archaeology*. New York: Checkmark Books.

Cooley, Jeffrey L. 2013. *Poetic Astronomy in the Ancient near East*. Winona Lake, IN: Eisenbrauns.

Curry, Patrick. 1999. "Astrology." In *The Encyclopaedia of Historians and Historical Writing*, 2 vols., ed. Kelly Boyd, vol. 1. London: Fitzroy Dearborn.

Dekker, Elly. 2012. *Illustrating the Phaenomena: Celestial Cartography in Antiquity and the Middle Ages*. Oxford: Oxford University Press.

Evans, James. 2004. "The Astrologer's Apparatus: A Picture of Professional Practice in Greco-Roman Egypt." *Journal for the History of Astronomy* 35, pt. 1, no. 118: 1–44.

Forenbaher, S., and A. Jones. 2011. "The Nakovana Zodiac: Fragments of an Astrologer's Board from an Illyrian-Hellenistic Cave Sanctuary." *Journal for the History of Astronomy* 42: 425–438.

Fowden, Garth. 2004. *Qusayr Amra: Art and the Umayyad Elite in Late Antique Syria*. Berkeley: University of California Press.

Gunzburg, Darrelyn. 2016. "Giotto's Sky: The Fresco Paintings of the First Floor Salone of the Palazzo Della Ragione, Padua, Italy." In *The Imagined Sky: Cultural Perspectives*, ed. Darrelyn Gunzburg, 87–113. Sheffield, UK: Equinox Publishing.

Hachlili, Rachel. 1996. "Synagogues in the Land of Israel: The Art and Architecture of Late Antique Synagogues." In *Sacred Realm: The Emergence of the Synagogue in the Ancient World*, ed. S. Fine, 96–129. New York: Oxford University Press.

Hyde, J. K. 1966. *Padua in the Age of Dante*. Manchester: Manchester University Press.

Künzl, Ernst. 2002. *Ein RöMischer Himmelsglobus Der Mittleren Kaiserzeit (A Roman Celestial Globe of the Middle Imperial Period)*. Studien Zur RöMischen Astralikonographie (Studies of Roman Astral Iconography). Mainz: Mainz Römisch-Germanisches Zentralmuseum.

Laderman, Shulamith. 2013. *Images of Cosmology in Jewish and Byzantine Art: God's Blueprint of Creation.* Jewish and Christian Perspectives. Leiden: Brill.
National Gallery of Art, Washington, D.C.
Paleotti, Gabriele. (1582). 1961. "Discorso Intorno alle Imagini Sacre e Profane." In *Trattati d'Arte del Cinquecento: fra Manierismo e Controriforma*, ed. Paola Barocchi, vol. II, 117–509. Bari: Laterza e Figli.
Possanza, D. Mark. "Review: Aratus: Phaenomena, Translated with an Introduction and Notes by Aaron Poochigian." *Aestimatio* 9 (2012): 68–87.
Ptolemy, Claudius. 1998. *Ptolemy's Almagest*, trans. G. J. Toomer. Princeton: Princeton University Press.
Rochberg, Francesca. 2004. *The Heavenly Writing: Divination, Horoscopy and Astronomy in Mesopotamian Culture.* Cambridge: Cambridge University Press.
Ryan, Sean Michael. 2012. *Hearing at the Boundaries of Vision: Education Informing Cosmology in Revelation 9.* Library of New Testament Studies. London: T and T Clark.
Savage-Smith, Emilie. 1992. "Celestial Mapping." In *History of Cartography: Cartography in the Traditional Islamic and South Asian Societies*, ed. J. B. Harley and David Woodward, vol. 2. Chicago: University of Chicago Press.
Thierens, A. E. 1935. *Astrology in Mesopotamian Culture. An Essay.* Leiden: Brill.
Urban, Emily. 2016. "Mapping the Heavens: The Ceiling of the Sala Bologna in the Vatican Palace." In *The Imagined Sky: Cultural Perspectives*, ed. Darrelyn Gunzburg, 142–162. Sheffield, UK: Equinox Publishing.

ASHENDEN, JOHN

John Ashenden (variously Ashindon, Eschenden, Eschuid, and Eastwood) was a 14th-century English astrologer and the compiler of an important sourcebook of astrological theory. A fellow of Merton College, Oxford, ca. 1337–1355, Ashenden was a member of the "Merton School" of natural philosophy, an influential circle of scholars who wrote on astrology, astronomy, mathematics, and physics.

Ashenden authored a series of tracts making astrological predictions based on eclipses and planetary conjunctions. The earliest of his prognostications involved a lunar eclipse and a conjunction of Mars, Jupiter, and Saturn in March 1345. From these events he forecast chaos, conflict, and "great mortality." A bloody outbreak in the Hundred Years' War, marked particularly by the battles of Crecy and Neville's Cross and the arrival of the Black Death, seemed to confirm Ashenden's predictions. In another composition dating to 1349 he wrote that mortality from the plague would lessen as "dry" celestial forces would soon counteract the "cold-wet" nature of the disease. Two later treatises discussed eclipses and planetary conjunctions occurring in 1357 and 1365, respectively. Ashenden interpreted the 1365 alignment of Jupiter and Saturn as being particularly consequential. He believed celestial influences would favor an English victory over the French, lead to the overthrow of Islam in the Holy Land, cause troubles for the Papacy, and give rise to a new religious sect. He commented on the prospects for religious upheaval but distanced himself from millenarian speculators who attempted to validate their claims through astrology. Ashenden's astrological writings were highly academic in character; there is no evidence that he made predictions in order to attract aristocratic patronage or to win ecclesiastical preferment.

Ashenden's most substantial work, the *Summa astrologiae judicialis de accidentibus mundi*, is a compendium of astrological theories pertaining to large-scale or universal events in the world. Ashenden stated that his goal was to bring together the most authoritative literature; he deemed himself no more than a humble compiler of material from Ptolemy, Abū Ma'shar, Mashāllāh, Abraham Ibn Ezra, Alcabitius (al-Qabi'si), Haly Abenragel (Ali Ibn Abi 'l-Rijal), and Albertus Magnus. Even so, the first part of the *Summa* is noteworthy for its rather original discussion of biblical chronology and the age of the world in the context of great cycles of planetary conjunctions.

The *Summa* achieved wide distribution in manuscript and printed form. English and Dutch translations of the Latin text appeared in the 15th century. Johannes Santritter issued a printed Latin edition in 1489. The *Summa* remained a standard astrological reference through the early modern period. John Dee and William Lilly were among the later practitioners who consulted Ashenden's work. For modern scholars its chief value is as an important witness to the textual foundations of medieval European astrological thought and practice.

Keith Snedegar

See also: Albertus Magnus; D'Ailly, Pierre; Medieval European Astrology; Mundane Astrology

Further Reading

Carey, Hilary M. 1992. *Courting Disaster: Astrology at the English Court and University in the Later Middle Ages*. New York: St. Martin's Press.

Snedegar, K. V. 1988. "John Ashenden and the Scientia Astrorum Meronensis." DPhil diss. Oxford: University of Oxford.

ASHMOLE, ELIAS (1617–1692)

Elias Ashmole was born May 23, 1617, at Lichfield, Staffordshire, England, the only son of a saddler and an impoverished lady. He attended Lichfield grammar school where he was also a chorister of the local cathedral, and at the age of 16 he went to live in London as a page boy with a relative of his mother. Ashmole could thus acquire legal training, which enabled him to become a barrister. In 1638, he began to practice at the Court of Chancery, and in March of the same year he married Eleanor, daughter of Peter Mainwaring in Cheshire. Ashmole's ambition and talent allowed him to have a brilliant career, and in 1641 he was sworn in as attorney at the Court of Common Pleas, and was admitted to Clement's Inn. On the outbreak of the English Civil Wars in 1641 Ashmole took the King's side; in May 1644 Charles I appointed him commissioner for the gathering of the excise in Lichfield. The following year he received the same royal commission for the city of Worcester and later was named "gentleman" equipment manager of the royal garrison of Oxford, with the rank of captain.

Although there is no proof of registration at Brasenose College, Ashmole always proudly claimed Oxford University as his alma mater, to which he later bequeathed an important legacy. The period after the war seems to have marked a turning point in Ashmole's life and interests. Ashmole studied astrology, astronomy, natural philosophy, and mathematics while at Oxford. For the rest of his life, Ashmole devoted much time and energy to astrology, drawing astrological figures to help choose the best times to act. At Oxford he met the astronomer, astrologer, and royalist George Wharton, who had a strong influence on him. In London, Wharton introduced Ashmole to many astrologers and mathematicians. Among his new acquaintances was Puritan astrologer William Lilly. Ashmole became the secretary and benefactor of the Society of Astrologers of London, and he regularly noted in his diary astrologers' dinners.

In 1649, he remarried (his first wife having died in December 1641), this time Lady Mary Mainwaring—a rich widow 20 years his senior. This new wealth allowed him to devote most of his time to his alchemical collections. At the beginning of the 1650s, Ashmole left London. On April 3, 1651, he became the "adopted son" of the famous antiquary and alchemist William Blackhouse of Swallowfield, Berkshire (Josten 1966, II, 567). Ashmole had just bought Blackhouse's cousin's library and was busy collecting books of alchemy and heraldry. During his life Ashmole would assemble an impressive collection of Roman and British coins, English archaeological objects, wax seals, and heraldic paraphernalia. He also amassed a huge library of manuscripts about astrology, medicine, history, and alchemy, as well as thousands of political and religious pamphlets.

While Ashmole published works about alchemy in the 1650s, and helped Lilly with his astrological works, he collected most of his astrological and alchemical manuscripts only much later, in the 1670s and 1680s, mainly thanks to his astrologer friends who died and left him their libraries. In 1682 he acquired Lilly's library. Thanks to the acquisition of Lilly's books, Ashmole's library was enriched with much astrological material.

Ashmole was, like Lilly, a practicing astrologer, but he was above all an antiquary. This is evident in the antiquarian uses to which he put his collection of nativities. A nativity is an astrological scheme in which biographical data of an individual are recorded. He was aware of the usefulness of nativities for prosopographical purposes and in 1676 obtained several volumes of astrological manuscripts from Thomas Napier containing biographical data about hundreds of 17th-century Englishmen and -women. Ashmole bound them with other nativities and in 1681 allowed the antiquary John Aubrey to work on them to extract biographical data for the Oxford antiquary and mutual acquaintance Anthony à Wood. Aubrey also used information that he found in Ashmole's manuscripts for his own prosopographical work, *Brief Lives*.

After the 1679 fire, in which all Ashmole's foreign books perished, Ashmole may have targeted Lilly's library precisely because of its foreign editions. Lilly had owned possibly one of the largest libraries of foreign astrological editions in 17th-century England. Among the earliest astrological works, Ashmole owned the Latin

Kalendarium, written by Johannes de Regiomontanus and published at Augsburg in 1489. His 16th-century European material included several editions of works that were at the same time mathematical and astrological textbooks, as well as early editions of Oriental authors. For instance, MS.Ashm.135 contains Giovanni Pontano's *Commentariorum in Ptolomaei* (Basel, 1531), Alcabitus's *Magisterium iudiciorum astrorum isacoge* (Paris, 1521), Lindhout's *Speculum astrologiae* (Frankfurt, 1608), Abraham Judaeus's *De nativitatibus . . . liber . . . restitutus per I. Dryandrum* (Cologne, 1537), and, appropriately, Johannes Dryander's *Astrolabii canones* (Marpurg, 1538). He also owned Alfraganus's astrological *Compilatio* printed in Ferrara in 1493. An exemplar of late 16th-century astrological work was William Meurerus's *Meteorologia* (Leipzig, 1587). They complemented Ashmole's weather data manuscripts with theoretical texts about the uses of mathematics applied to astrology for weather prognostications. On the other hand, the anonymous treatise *Astrologiae ad medicinam adplicatio brevis* (Strasbourg, 1537) reminds us of Ashmole's interest in the uses of mathematics and astrology in medicine.

Among English astrological material, Thomas Hill's *Almanack* published in London in 1571 is the earliest example of such a work written in the vernacular. Ashmole left to the Ashmolean hundreds of English almanacs, clearly aiming at having a comprehensive collection of English astrological works. They are arranged chronologically, from the 1570s until Ashmole's time, in tens of volumes, and overall comprise hundreds of almanacs. Astrological almanacs and ephemeredes illustrate the formation of an English astrological printing market in the vernacular, and Ashmole's library testifies to the evolution of the uses of English in the transmission of knowledge in print.

Ashmole's loyalty won him the favor of the court at the Restoration and on June 18, 1660, he became Windsor Herald, namely, a significant member of the College of Arms, and courtier (Wagner, 1952, 61, 67). Charles II gave Ashmole back his office as gatherer of the excise. He also received other pensions and the honorary office of secretary of Suriname. On January 2, 1661, Ashmole became a fellow of the Royal Society. In 1658 his second wife had died and he could therefore marry the daughter of the famous antiquary William Dugdale, thanks to whom Ashmole was allowed to read in the library of Sir John Cotton. There he copied several volumes of manuscripts previously owned by John Dee, to whom Ashmole felt close intellectually (Josten, 1966, IV, 1298–1300, 1332–1335, 1371–1373, 1685, 1776, 1843). On January 26, 1679, a fire erupted in his rooms in the Middle Temple, destroying almost all of his foreign books, and many of his volumes of notes. He saved what he could and continued his work until his death. But it was the foundation of the Ashmolean Museum in Oxford in 1683 that earned him great fame, and it was to this institution that Ashmole bequeathed most of his books and manuscripts, as well as his collections of rarities inherited from the gardener and collector John Tradescant. The Ashmolean Museum became the first public museum in England, and a center of scientific studies. Ashmole died on May 19, 1692, and a week later was buried in the church of St. Mary, Lambeth.

Vittoria Feola

See also: Astrological Associations; Lilly, William; Politics; Renaissance and Reformation Astrology

Further Reading

Feola, Vittoria. 2005. "The Recovered Library of Elias Ashmole." *Bibliotheca* 1: 259–278.

Feola, Vittoria. 2008. "Elias Ashmole's Theatrum Chemicum Britannicum (1652): Renaissance Medievalism and the Relation Antiquarianism-Science." In *Renaissance Medievalisms*, ed. Eisenbichler, Konrad. 321–343. Toronto: Toronto University Press.

Feola, Vittoria. 2012. *Elias Ashmole and the Uses of Antiquity*. Paris: STP Blanchard.

Feola, Vittoria. 2012. "Elias Ashmole's Collections and Views about John Dee." *Studies in History and Philosophy of Science* 43, no. 3, pt. A: 530–538.

Hunter, Michael C. W. 2004. "Elias Ashmole." *Oxford Dictionary of National Biography.* Oxford: Oxford University Press.

Josten, Conrad Hermann. 1966. *Elias Ashmole, 1617–1692: His Autobiographical Writings and Historical Notes, His Correspondence, and Other Contemporary Sources Relating to His Life and Work*, 5 vols. Oxford: Clarendon Press.

Parry, Graham. 1995. *The Trophies of Time: English Antiquarians of the Seventeenth Century*. Oxford: Oxford University Press.

Wagner, Anthony Richard. 1952. *The Records and Collections of the College of Arms*. London, Burkes Peerage.

ASTEROIDS

Traditional astrologers knew only seven visible planets—the sun, the moon, Mercury, Venus, Mars, Jupiter, and Saturn. The first "new planet" discovered was Uranus, identified by the German astronomer William Herschel in 1781. Since then, not only have Neptune and Pluto been discovered and attained the status of planets (though this status proved contested and short lived for Pluto), but astronomers have discovered many thousands of smaller celestial bodies in different parts of the solar system. These new bodies have posed many challenges for astrologers but are increasingly accepted in astrological interpretation.

The "asteroid belt" between the orbits of Mars and Jupiter contains over 400,000 asteroids. Some astrologers have incorporated the first four to be discovered, Ceres, Pallas, Juno, and Vesta, into their chart analysis, but many are daunted by the nearly 20,000 other asteroids for which there now exist ephemerides listing their daily zodiacal positions. Nor are asteroids the only small celestial objects found by modern astronomers. Chiron, the first "centaur," was discovered in 1977. Centaurs are defined as small planetary bodies located between the orbit of Jupiter and Neptune—the closest and farthest of the gas giants from the sun—and crossing a planetary orbit. Chiron was located between the orbits of Saturn and Uranus, and it quickly became popular among astrologers. By the 1990s, other centaurs, including Pholus, Nessus, Asbolos, Hylonome, and Chariko were identified. The Kuiper Belt, home to thousands of celestial objects, most prominently Pluto, extends 7 billion miles beyond Neptune. In the first decade of the 21st century, a host of other celestial bodies—Orcus, Haumea, Makemake, Quaoar, Varuna, Ixion, Eris, and Sedna among many others—have been found, icy objects billions of miles even further out.

Asteroid Discovery and Research

In *Mysterium Cosmographicum* (1596) Johannes Kepler speculated about the existence of a planet between Mars and Jupiter. German astronomer and polymath Joseph Daniel Titius (1729–1796) made a detailed study of the distances of planets from the sun and each other, and noted a significant gap between the orbits of Mars and Jupiter. Titius's theory of the spacing of the planetary orbits later became better known as Bode's Law after German astronomer Johann Ellert Bode (1747–1826) although it is not a scientific law in the strict sense but an observed pattern. (It is also known as the Titius-Bode law.) It was initially dismissed as a curiosity, but in 1781 the German astronomer William Herschel (1738–1822) discovered Uranus at the position Bode's Law predicted. This discovery inspired astronomers, observatories, and astronomical societies worldwide to search for the missing fifth planet.

On January 1, 1801, Guiseppe Piazzi (1746–1826), a Sicilian priest and head of the Palermo Observatory, accidently discovered a new celestial body between the orbits of Mars and Jupiter. He was not looking for the missing planet, but correcting errors for a new edition of a star catalog. Piazzi gave his discovery the name Ceres Ferdinandea, after the Roman and Sicilian goddess of grain, whose mythological site was near his observatory, and King Ferdinand IV of Naples and Sicily (1751–1825). However, Ceres proved too small to be classified as a planet, and along with other objects sharing a similar orbital position it received the newly coined term *asteroid*, literally "starlike." (Along with Pluto and a few other celestial objects, Ceres, the largest asteroid, is now classified by astronomers as a "dwarf planet.") Several more asteroids were discovered in the following years: Pallas (1802), Juno (1804), and Vesta (1807), all named after classical goddesses. The location of the asteroids in accordance with the predictions of Bode's Law indicates that they are part of the underlying mathematical and geometrical structure of the solar system, and not random cosmic junk as some astrologers have suggested.

The astronomer who discovered the asteroid had the privilege of proposing a name for it. Most followed Piazzi's precedent of naming asteroids after goddesses from classical myth. Each asteroid is also given a number in chronological order of discovery. About 95 percent of the asteroids have regular orbits between those of Mars and Jupiter, and these have been given feminine names; the remaining 5 percent with irregular orbits were given masculine names. By the late 19th century, there were 450 known asteroids, mostly named after Greco-Roman goddesses or famous women. In the 20th century, asteroids were named after female and male deities from many mythic traditions and religions, as well as countries, cities, rivers, distinguished musicians, artists, writers, intellectuals, and concepts. Some asteroids have received male and female common names in honor of the astronomer's relatives and colleagues.

In the century following their discovery, asteroids received only passing mentions by a few astrologers—James Wilson (fl. 1819), who thought they were too small to have much effect, Alan Leo, and Walter Gorn Old (1864–1929), better known by his astrological pseudonym of Sepharial. No ephemerides for the asteroids were available, so interest was theoretical as well as sparse. Only in 1973 was the first asteroid ephemeris published. It covered the first four asteroids to be discovered, Ceres, Pallas, Juno, and Vesta. The work was published thanks to New York astrologer Eleanor Bach (1922–1995) who convinced an astronomer to calculate these difficult orbits in a time before widely available personal computers made the task relatively easy. Bach proposed tentative astrological meanings for these asteroids derived from the mythology associated with their names. In the next few years, Esther Leinbach (1924–2006) and Emma Bell Donath (1930–1992) investigated asteroids and put forth preliminary findings. Meanwhile, Neil Michelsen (1931–1990) produced more accurate ephemerides and Zipporah Dobyns (1921–2003) began to research these newly known bodies. Al Morrison (1916–1995) put out an ephemeris for Chiron shortly after its discovery in 1977.

Morrison, with the assistance of J. Lee Lehman (b. 1953), ushered in the 1980s with the publication of a dozen more ephemerides of the "minor" asteroids. On the East Coast of the United States, Lehman, Diana Rosenberg (1933–2012), and Nona Gwynn Press made strides in asteroid research, while on the West Coast Michelsen, Dobyns, Batya Stark (b. 1939), and Mark Pottenger pursued further investigations. Lorraine Welsh (1928–2011), Frances McEvoy (1929–2007), Tony Joseph (1946–1986), and Pamela Crane (b. 1943) lectured, taught, wrote articles, and sponsored asteroid-related astrological education at that time. And the first books about the astrological meaning of Chiron by Erminie Huntress Lantero (1907–1992), Richard Nolle (b. 1950), and Zane B. Stein (b. 1951) came out.

The second half of the 1980s saw published works on asteroids by Press, Lehman, Demetra George, and Martha Lang Wescott; Pottenger made available to the public his CCRS asteroid program that generated positions for thousands of asteroids. The still-active National Center for Geocosmic Research Asteroid Special Interest Group was formed. Roxana Muise (b. 1935) instituted a service to provide ephemerides for individual asteroids, which Dave Campbell now continues. Barbara Hand Clow (b. 1943) and Melanie Reinhart (b. 1959) also published on Chiron.

In the 1990s a German astronomer specializing in asteroids, Lutz D. Schmadel (1942–2016), published the *Dictionary of Minor Planet Names* (that has current online and print updates), which served as an inspiration for Jacob Schwartz's *Asteroid Name Encyclopedia* (1995) and software programs. Press and George published books on the minor asteroids, and Ariel Guttman (b. 1949) and Kenneth Johnson gave equal space to the asteroid archetypes in the Mythic Astrology books published by Llewellyn Press. Eric Francis (b. 1964), Martin Lass (b. 1958), and Adam Gainsburg continued research into Chiron. The first decade of the 21st century has seen additional asteroid research as well as investigations into the centaurs and other distant objects in our solar system by Roderick Kidston (1961–2017), Melanie Reinhart, Philip Sedgwick (b. 1950), Dave Campbell, Jonathan Dunn (b. 1961), Brian Clark (b. 1949), Kelley Hunter (b. 1949), Mark Andrew Holmes, and Nick Anthony Fiorenza. Astrological software can now find the zodiacal position of over 20,000 asteroids.

Astrological Interpretation

The multitude of newly discovered and named objects in the solar system raises questions that earlier generations of astrologers, working only with the seven traditional planets, did not have to consider. Should astrologers treat all celestial bodies as bearing interpretive meaning in the astrological chart? If so, how can their significance for human and terrestrial experience be derived?

The arrival of asteroids into the astrological pantheon coincided with the articulation of Carl Jung's psychological theory that gods and goddesses correspond to aspects of human consciousness. One way to apprehend the meanings of planetary archetypes is that images of gods are projections of active psychic forces. Harkening to the ancient Babylonian and Greek astrologers who looked to the characteristics of the deity that shared the name of the planet as a starting point for assembling astrological correspondences, contemporary astrologers proposed the following interpretations for the first four major asteroids.

Ceres the goddess of agriculture whose daughter was abducted to the underworld is associated with the capacity to give and receive nurturing and unconditional love, growing and preparing food, the experiences of loss and separation from loved ones, and tending to the dying. Pallas Athene, goddess of wisdom and war, was a patroness of heroes and artisans and points to intelligence, creativity, artistic vision, courage, strategy, activism, and a desire to excel in worldly achievements. Juno, goddess of marriage, indicates a loyal commitment to a fair and equal relationship in the face of disappointment, betrayal of trust, and power struggles with the other. Vesta, goddess of the hearth fire and vestal virgins, is associated with devotion to an inner spiritual life, purification, a one-pointed focus and dedication to an ideal, and the themes of safety and protection.

The Future

In the 19th and 20th centuries, astrologers were confronted with accepting Uranus, Neptune, and Pluto into their charts and arriving at interpretive meanings. The discovery of more celestial bodies in the solar system has spurred astronomers to reclassify the solar system, and likewise demands that astrologers rethink their rationale concerning the incorporation and interpretation of additional planetary bodies. The mythic approach, whose roots go back to the origin of astrology, has proved fruitful in asteroid study in the past 40 years and provides one way to derive meaning from the myriad gods in the heavens.

Demetra George

See also: Gender; Jung, Carl G.; Science

Further Reading

Dobyns, Zipporah Pottenger. 1983. *Expanding Astrology's Universe*. ACS Publications.
George, Demetra, and Douglas Bloch. 2003. *Asteroid Goddesses: The Mythology, Psychology and Astrology of the Re-Emerging Feminine*. York Beach, ME: Nicolas-Hays; [Enfield: Airlift].

Hunter, Kelly. 2009. *Living Lilith: Four Dimensions of the Cosmic Feminine*. Bournemouth, UK: Wessex Astrologer.
Reinhart, Melanie. 2000. *Chiron and the Healing Journey*, 3rd ed. London: Starwalker Press.

ASTRAL MAGIC

Magic used in the context of astrology is often described as astral magic, the invocation of spirits associated with the planets and other celestial bodies. Although astrological divination seeks to predict the future, astral magic seeks to control or change it. As such, it is found in a variety of astrological traditions. Despite modern conceptions of the irrational and unscientific nature of magic, astral magic usually had a rational purpose from the ancient period until the Enlightenment. Astral magic encompassed medicine, astronomy, and sometimes theology. Magic was also a way of explaining why astrology worked at all.

Astral magic dates to Hellenistic Egypt and was related to theology. Practitioners of astral magic in Hellenistic Egypt did not pursue science. Magicians believed that utterance of a certain word or phrase would allow that thing to come into existence through the influence of spirits associated with the planets. For example, "By speaking the name of Venus or inscribing a symbol representing her, one invokes the planetary deity" (Campion 2012, 172). This approach was embodied in the Hermetic Corpus produced in Egypt in the early Christian era, although in later times many believed it was far older. The work of Ptolemy, which came to dominate the Western tradition of astrology, however, shunned spiritual and magical explanations of the influence of the stars in favor of naturalistic ones.

Early Christians perceived astral magic as demonic and evil. Early Christians also condemned those who practiced astrology and magic as "adherents of false religion" (Hegedus 2007, 141). St. Augustine of Hippo, one of the most influential of the Church Fathers of the Latin tradition, did not endorse the idea that astrology could offer theological or scientific knowledge and supported the claim that astrology was devilish, stating in his *On Christian Doctrine* that "astrology is a system of signs developed by human pride and is therefore a type of vicious contract between demons and human beings" (Hegedus 2007, 142). Augustine firmly denounced any superstitious activities, which included "the magic arts," which according to him "medical science condemns" (Bailey 2013, 20).

Islam also had a complicated relationship with astral magic. In al-Andalus, the mystic Ibn Arabi (1165–1240), often called the Shaykh al-Akbar or "The Great Master," discussed astrology and magic in his esoteric writing. Ibn Arabi claimed that God is the oneness of being or *wujud* and that God is the "archetypal perfect man who has a simultaneously human, cosmic, and divine nature and embodied everything that human beings should strive to achieve" (Campion 2012, 182). This understanding of God was conducive to the perception of magic as theological. Sufism, the tradition of Islamic mysticism, embodied this notion that the universe was sustained through theological knowledge. The dervishes, who were famous Sufis, believed that "astrology is practiced not through the casting of horoscopes but through the imitation of the planets around the Earth" (Campion 2012,

The Sabians of Harran and Astral Magic

The development of the schema linking astral gods, the seven planets, and seven metals is associated with the semilegendary culture of the city of Harran in northern Mesopotamia, where a neo-Platonic system of pagan reverence of the Heavens known as Sabianism survived the coming of Christianity and the initial Islamic conquests into the 11th century. (Harran had a history stretching back to ancient Mesopotamia as a center for the worship of the moon god.) The Sabians were tolerated as "People of the Book" under Islamic rule although the connection between the Sabians mentioned in the Koran and the Sabians of Harran is tenuous. Eminent Sabians include the astronomer, mathematician, and astrologer Thabit Ibn Qurra (826–901). A work on the construction of astrological talismans surviving only in Latin translation, *On Images*, is attributed to Thabit Ibn Qurra, although not all scholars agree on the accuracy of the attribution. Another important Arabic astronomer/astrologer, Al-Battani (858–929) may have been a Sabian or a descendant of Sabians who converted to Islam. Subsequent occultists and astrologers looked to a mythologized version of the Sabian tradition for the transmission of astral magic and hermetism from the ancient to the medieval world.

182). For the dervishes, astral magic involved the pursuit of knowledge. Around the same time, the Kabbalah was developing among Jews, a mystical and magical system in which the magical powers were frequently identified with the planets.

For medieval Europeans, astrology had a theological element in order to understand the place of God, humans, and animals in the world but it also had a scientific element in that astrology embraced astronomical study. Another indication of its magical use was through "the casting of talismans or objects having astrological significance and used for the intention of manipulating the psychic and physical environment and the diagnosis and treatment of disease" (Campion 2012, 16). However, mainstream Scholastic astrology as seen in the work of scholars such as Albertus Magnus tended to treat planetary and stellar influences as natural rather than magical phenomena.

In the late Middle Ages in the kingdom of Aragon on the Iberian Peninsula, astrology was associated with "occult and dark knowledge" because Christians viewed Jewish and Muslim communities as alien and therefore deviant and possessing knowledge derived from "demonic agency" (Ryan 2011, 81). Although Europeans on the Iberian Peninsula distrusted Arabic astral magic, it had a scientific significance in the Arabic text *Ghyat Al-Hakim,* known in the West as *Picatrix* due to its translation into Castilian during the rule of Alfonso X of Castile. In this text, "one learns about the materials that compose the sky and the quality of the celestial spheres themselves." *Picatrix* was also invaluable for "practitioners of astral magic, as the planets' respective characters had a direct influence upon the efficacy of any astral magic conducted in their name" (Ryan 2011, 96–97). Astral magic was widespread in the Middle Ages but was a somewhat underground tradition practiced by marginal figures.

Astral magic was revived in the Renaissance in a Neoplatonic context focusing on the spiritual nature of the universe and the connection between the macrocosm of the universe and the microcosm of humanity in the work of astrologers and magicians such as Marsilio Ficino. Later astrologers such as John Dee and Tommaso Campanella also worked with astral magic. However, the reform of astrology in the late 17th century, whether empirical in the work of John Gadbury or neo-Ptolemaic in the work of Placidus and John Partridge, tended to shun magic in favor of naturalistic explanations of the power of the stars. The tradition of astral magic, like astrology in general, was marginal in the Enlightenment period.

The 19th-century occult revival embodied in such phenomena as Theosophy revived astral magic and the idea of the cosmos as permeated by spiritual forces. This tradition of spiritual and magical astrology continued in small occult groups such as the Hermetic Order of the Golden Dawn active in Great Britain around the turn of the 20th century and in the work of such major 20th-century magicians as William Butler Yeats and Aleister Crowley (1875–1947). Astral magic also influence the 1920s occult frenzy in California in which many cults arose.

For modern Christians, attitudes toward astral magic comes in a spectrum. On one extreme, the use of "horoscopes, magic, and the ascent through celestial spheres" (Campion 2012, 172) is considered valid. On another extreme, the idea that astral magic, and therefore astrology, is demonic in inspiration persists, and astrology is highly discredited. The middle ground is occupied by those who believe astrology is permissible so long as it avoids contact with supernatural agencies. Astrological magic continues to be used for entertainment and for spiritual purposes in contemporary Occultist circles, while many contemporary astrologers see their work as existing within the field of magic.

Isabel Lasch-Quinn

See also: Astrotheology; Bruno, Giordano; Buddhism; Campanella, Tommaso; Dee, John; Ficino, Marsilio; Judaism; New Age; *Picatrix*; Theosophy; Yeats, William Butler

Further Reading

Bailey, Michael. 2013. *Fearful Spirits, Reasoned Follies: The Boundaries of Superstition in Late Medieval Europe*. Ithaca, NY: Cornell University Press.

Campion, Nicholas. 2012. *Astrology and Cosmology in the World's Religions*. New York: NYU Press.

Hegedus, Tim. 2007. *Early Christianity and Ancient Astrology*. New York: Peter Lang Publishing.

Ryan, Michael. 2011. *A Kingdom of Stargazers: Astrology and Authority in the Late Medieval Crown of Aragon*. Ithaca, NY: Cornell University Press.

ASTROLABE

The astrolabe is a device for measuring the positions of stars and the sun over time. Its origins lie in ancient Greece, but it was further developed by medieval Arab astrologers and craftspeople and eventually by Europeans. In addition to its astrological functions, it was used in astronomy, surveying, and timekeeping. The most common astrolabe, the flat astrolabe, is based on a projection of the

This 17th-century Persian astrolabe, the work of Muhammad Zaman al-Munajjim al-Asturlabi, shows the complexity of the astrolabe in a late period of its development. (The Metropolitan Museum of Art/ Harris Brisbane Dick Fund, 1963)

heavens from the point of view of the celestial North Pole onto a flat disk. (There are also straight astrolabes and spherical astrolabes.) Astrolabes varied greatly, but the common element was a stereographic projection of the heavens for a particular location on a disk, set in a fixed disk (the mater) with a raised rim marked with a calendar and other measurements of time, very often including the zodiac. A rotating disk, known as a rete, has arrows that can be aligned with particularly bright stars. A rule, a rigid pointer, rotated around the same central point as the rete. The back of the mater was frequently engraved with charts and tables to add to the usefulness of the device. Astrolabes could be made of wood or metal, although wooden astrolabes had a tendency to warp and become unusable. The most common metal is brass, which has the advantage of not shrinking or expanding much with changes of temperature. Elaborate astrolabes of precious metals were made to be given as gifts. Holy Roman Emperor Rudolf II (r. 1576–1612), known for his interest in astrology and magic, owned eight astrolabes.

For the astrologer, the principal use of the astrolabe was determining the ascendant for a particular time, along with the midheaven, descendant, and imum coeli. Some astrolabes were made specifically to help astrologers divide the celestial houses, but an ordinary astrolabe could be used for that purpose as well. The astrolabe was limited in its astrological uses and could not be used to cast a complete horoscope, as it did not track the positions of the planets. The device had many nonastrological uses, including timekeeping and surveying.

Origins and Spread

The earliest astrolabes are sometimes credited to the Alexandrian Greek astronomer and astrologer Ptolemy (ca. 100–ca. 170), who describes the stereographic projection in his book *Planisphere*. Whether or not he personally had anything to do with the creation of actual astrolabes, they seem to have emerged from the intellectual culture of Hellenistic Egypt during the Roman Empire. A now lost treatise on the astrolabe was written by Theon of Alexandria in the fourth century, and the oldest surviving book on the astrolabe was written by another Alexandrian, John of Philoponus, in the sixth century.

The astrolabe appears to have been widely adopted and improved in the Islamic world during the Abbasid Caliphate, when Islamic elites were cultivating astrology along with other aspects of Greek science. The oldest surviving treatise on the astrolabe in Arabic dates from around 815 CE and was the work of the Jewish astronomer and astrologer Mashāllāh (The oldest surviving astrolabe whose date is known is of Islamic manufacture and dated to 927/928 CE.) Astrolabes were manufactured and used throughout the area of medieval Islamic civilization, from Central Asia to Spain. Astrologers in Islamic art were frequently depicted using astrolabes, which became symbols of their profession.

The Byzantines were also familiar with the astrolabe, and there are several Byzantine treatises on its use, but they do not seem to have produced very many, possibly relying on manufacturers in the Islamic world. Islamic astrolabes were also introduced into India, where the earliest Sanskrit treatise was the work of a Jain monk, Mahandra Suri, around 1370. In the 13th century, when the vast reach of the Mongol Empire was producing an unprecedented degree of cultural contact across Eurasia, astrolabes were introduced into China. However, the Chinese, whose astronomy and astrology were based on different principles, do not seem to have taken up their use very widely.

The Astrolabe in Europe

Knowledge of the astrolabe passed from the Islamic world to Europe probably through Spain around the 11th century. (One possible carrier of the knowledge was Gerbert of Aurillac, a French scholar who studied astronomy, astrology, and mathematics in Spain and became Pope from 999 to 1003 as Sylvester II. A Latin treatise on the astrolabe is ascribed to him.) At first, Western astrolabes were imported from Islamic Spain and adapted to Christian use, with Latin inscriptions added to Arabic ones, although some Islamic makers produced astrolabes with Latin inscriptions for the Christian market. By the 13th century, however, Christian Europe was producing its own astrolabes.

Astrolabes became cheaper, more widely distributed, and more widely used in Europe to the 16th century. Astrolabe treatises were published in both Latin and vernacular languages, and in a variety of formats from the elaborate to the cheap. Although South German makers took advantage of the availability of copper there to lead in the production of brass astrolabes, there were also inexpensive astrolabes made of paper glued to wood. In the 16th century, the center of manufacturing shifted to the southern Netherlands. With the arrival of other instruments in the 17th century, European astrologers lost interest in the astrolabe, but in the Islamic world astrolabes continued to be produced and used by astrologers into the 19th century.

William E. Burns

See also: Chaucer, Geoffrey; House Systems; Islamic Astrology; Mashāllāh; Medieval European Astrology; Mercator, Gerardus; Renaissance and Reformation Astrology

Further Reading

Hayton, Darin. 2012. *An Introduction to the Astrolabe.* E-book. http://dhayton.haverford.edu/wp-content/uploads/2012/02/Astrolabes.pdf

Webster, Roderick S., Marjorie Webster, and Sara Schechner Genuth. 1998. *Western Astrolabes.* Chicago: Adler Planetarium and Astronomy Museum.

Whitfield, Peter. 2001. *Astrology: A History.* New York: Abrams.

ASTROLOGICAL ASSOCIATIONS

There are few precedents for astrologers meeting in groups before the 20th century, but in the past century they have proven to be gregarious, with numerous astrological groups covering different countries, astrological traditions, and functions.

One of the earliest examples of an astrological association is the Society of Astrologers in London that put on annual "Astrologers Feasts." About 40 astrologers representing different astrological and political positions met annually between 1648–1657 for a dinner and a sermon (although the earliest reference is to a "Mathematicall" rather than an Astrologer's feast.) The group included such leading lights as William Lilly, Elias Ashmole, and John Booker. There was a brief revival in the early 1680s.

The modern history of astrological associations begins with Alan Leo and his founding of a series of explicitly theosophical astrological groups, beginning with the Astrological Society founded on January 14, 1896. The group suffered divisions between Leo and others who emphasized Theosophy and more traditional astrologers, and collapsed after Leo resigned as president in 1902. It was followed by a short-lived Society for Astrological Research founded the same year. In 1909 Leo revived the Astrological Society, and in 1912 he founded the Astrological Institute, a smaller group whose membership was intended to be professional astrologers. The final group founded by Leo was both the most Theosophical and the most enduring, the Astrological Lodge of the Theosophical Society founded in 1914. Many British astrological associations can trace their roots to the Astrological Lodge, which under the leadership of Charles Carter placed more emphasis on astrology than Theosophy. The first Irish astrological association, the Irish Astrological Society founded in 1922, also emerged from Theosophical circles and could boast William Butler Yeats as patron at its founding, although it seems to have dissolved by the early 1940s.

The most important British group to emerge out of Theosophy is the Astrological Association of Great Britain, founded in 1958. The principal founders, John Addey and Roy Firebrace, were members of the Astrological Lodge. The Astrological Association exists to the present and is considered the leading British astrological group. It publishes an *Astrological Journal* and sponsors an annual conference.

The year 1915, which saw the founding of the Astrological Lodge, also saw the founding of an early German astrologer's organization, the Kepler Circle. The founder was Friedrich Sieggrün, a German astrologer. It was from the Kepler Circle that the Hamburg School of Astrology emerged. The rising interest in astrology in post–World War I Germany saw a series of German Astrological Congresses. The first was held in Munich in 1922 and the second in Leipzig in 1923. The second is particularly noteworthy for being dominated by debates over the Hamburg School. The period following the second congress saw the foundation of several astrological societies, including the Central Astrological Office and the Academic Society for Astrological Research, the first academic society for astrology. (Membership was limited to PhDs.) The congresses continued annually until 1936. The congress planned for Baden-Baden in 1937 was abruptly canceled on the orders of the Nazi regime, and a small congress held in 1938 at the Bavarian resort of Starnberg was the last.

The oldest surviving American astrological organization, the American Federation of Astrologers (AFA), was founded as the American Federation of Scientific Astrologers at 11:38 a.m. May 4, 1938, in Washington, D.C. (Astrological organizations tend to be precise about the moment of founding, for the purpose of calculating the organization's horoscope.) The AFA emphasizes the maintenance of professional standards through a system of courses, exams, and certification. It has also carried on an active publishing program. The National Council for Geocosmic Research founded in 1971 is a group for astrological research and education. The Association for Astrological Networking (AFAN) is a lobbyist for astrologers fighting anti-astrological laws and ordinances and counteracting negative media coverage. It originally emerged as a splinter group dissatisfied with the direction of the AFA in 1982.

India, a large country with a thriving astrological culture, has a large number of astrological organizations. The Indian Council of Astrological Sciences (ICAS) was founded in 1984 by B. V. Raman to promote astrological education and certification. Unlike most Western astrological organizations, which are secular and restrict their coverage to astrology itself, the ICAS is oriented to Hindus and claims a larger moral mission for the regeneration of society through the teaching of "Vedic" astrology. It offers courses and examinations and is allied with Vedic Astrology organizations outside India, such as the American Council of Vedic Astrology (now known as the Council of Vedic Astrology) founded in 1993. The All India Federation of Astrologers Societies, founded in 2001, has more of a business orientation and teaches other forms of divination such as palmistry as well as astrology.

William E. Burns

See also: Ashmole, Elias; Hamburg School of Astrology; Leo, Alan; Raman, Bangalore Venkata; Theosophy; Yeats, William Butler

Further Reading

Curry, Patrick. 1989. *Prophecy and Power: Astrology in Early Modern England.* Princeton: Princeton University Press.

Curry, Patrick. 1992. *A Confusion of Prophets: Victorian and Edwardian Astrology.* London: Collins and Brown.

Feola, Vittoria. 2012. *Elias Ashmole and the Uses of Antiquity.* Paris: STP Blanchard.
Howe, Ellic. 1967. *Astrology: A Recent History Including the Untold Story of Its Role in World War II.* New York: Walker.

Organizational websites:
All India Federation of Astrologers Societies: http://www.aifas.com/
American Federation of Astrologers: www.astrologers.com
Association for Astrological Networking: www.afan.org
Astrological Association: http://www.astrologicalassociation.com
Astrological Lodge of London: www.astrolodge.co.uk
Council of Vedic Astrology: http://www.councilvedicastrology.com/
Indian Council of Astrological Sciences: www.icasindia.org
National Council for Geocosmic Research: www.geocosmic.org

ASTRONOMY. *SEE* SCIENCE.

ASTROTHEOLOGY

The idea that the sun, moon, fixed stars, planets, comets, and other celestial phenomena carry religious meanings dates to prehistory. The Stonehenge monument in Great Britain is oriented to astronomical phenomena and was probably the site of religious rituals, like many other ancient monuments across the world. The ancient Mesopotamians, the earliest known practitioners of astrology, venerated the planets and identified them with their Gods, an idea the Greeks adopted after Alexander the Great's conquest of the Middle East. The names of the planets in European languages are derived from the Greco-Roman deities they were originally identified with. Many constellations are representations of Greek deities, such as the zodiac constellation Gemini, the Twins, originally the gods Castor and Polydeuces (Pollux in Latin). Virgo, another zodiac sign, is identified with the goddess Astraea, the virginal goddess of justice. The idea of the return of Astraea from the heavens to the Earth as inaugurating a new golden age occurs frequently in literature. Numerous other polytheistic religions have identified heavenly bodies with gods and goddesses. One Chinese view of the planets was as high officials in the celestial bureaucratic hierarchy.

The sun, by far the most prominent of all celestial bodies, is particularly likely to be identified as the chief deity, as in the late Roman cult of Sol Invictus, the unconquered sun. The chief deity of the Japanese Shinto pantheon, Amaterasu, is the sun goddess. In popular Taoism and traditional Chinese religion the sun is seen as the essence of yang, the active force of the cosmos, the moon as the essence of its passive complement, yin. The Hindu Sun god, Surya, appears in the Vedas and has been adopted by some traditions within Buddhism. The Gayatri Mantra, a short verse from the Rig-Veda devoted to the power of the sun, has a long history in Hindu devotion and is commonly recited among modern Hindus. Worship of the sun was also common among Native North Americans and Mesoamericans. The idea of the sun as a unique divine force prompted some early expressions of heliocentric astronomy, as in the case of the followers of Pythagoras and the first heliocentric astronomer, Aristarchus (310–230 BCE).

The classical Greeks and Romans, however, identified the planet Jupiter, the largest of the planets, with their chief God, rather than the sun. Another frequently encountered celestial representation of the chief deity is as the sky, often with a masculine sky deity contrasted with a feminine earth goddess. The term *Dyaus Pita* or *Sky Father* is found in the Vedas and is the root of the names of many Gods in the Indo-European traditions, including Zeus and Jupiter.

An 11th- or 12th-century statue of the Hindu Sun god Surya shows him associated with the solar disk. (The Metropolitan Museum of Art/Samuel Eilenberg Collection, Bequest of Samuel Eilenberg, 1998)

Moon deities are usually female, the exceptions usually occurring in pantheons in which the sun deity is a goddess rather than a god. One reason for this is the linkage between the moon's cycle and the female menstrual cycle. Moon deities do not generally occupy the leading position in a pantheon, one exception being the moon-god Sin in early Mesopotamia.

Classical pagan astrotheology is closely linked to Western astrology, in which the "personalities" and areas of domination of the planets are often those of the deities after which they are named—as Venus governs love and Mars war. The continued influence of pagan astrotheology extended outside astrology proper into other magical realms. For many alchemists and magicians, the seven traditional planets—the sun, Mercury, Venus, Earth, Mars, Jupiter, and Saturn—provided a schema by which phenomena could be divided into groups of seven and the 12 zodiacal signs a system for dividing things into groups of 12.

The monotheistic religions that originated in the Middle East—Judaism, Christianity, and Islam—were careful not to identify their gods with heavenly phenomena, a practice they identified with their polytheistic rivals (although a general identification of God with the sky or "Heaven" as His dwelling-place was common). The seventh century BCE Hebrew prophet Jeremiah exhorted the Jews to "be not dismayed at the signs of the heavens, as the heathen are dismayed" (Jeremiah 10:2). This passage was often used by Christian opponents of astrology, who denounced it as polytheistic. However, the stars and planets could still be revered as the work of God and evidence of his handiwork. The Koran, which refers to pagans as "star-worshippers," also states: "He has made subservient for you the night and the day and the sun and the moon, and the stars are made subservient by His commandment; most surely there are signs in this for a people who ponder" (16:12).

Despite the Christian reluctance to identify God with celestial objects, the idea of the Heavens continued to influence the way that Christians felt about God's dwelling-place. The medieval Christian poet Dante Alighieri (1265–1321) identified the different Heavens in which saved souls spent the afterlife with the spheres that carried the different planets around the Earth in Ptolemaic cosmology.

As well as celestial bodies, celestial events carried religious meanings, and in many cultures religious professionals were among the main practitioners of both calendar making and astrology. Celestial calendars provided the occasions for religious rituals central for linking Heaven and Earth, as the sacrifices made on the solstices and equinoxes by the Chinese Emperor, the "Son of Heaven." Religious holidays like Easter and Eid al Fitr are based on the astronomical cycles. The linkage of religion with timekeeping and calendar making led to close study of the heavenly bodies with an emphasis on their creation by God. Less predictable astronomical events, such as eclipses and comets, were also often viewed as divine signs and warnings. The best-known example in Christianity is the star of Bethlehem, a phenomenon that existed to point out the birth of Christ and disappeared thereafter. Apocalyptic literature, including the Christian Book of Revelation, is replete with strange and disturbing astronomical happenings, which influenced how they were perceived by religious believers. The "night the stars fell," a spectacular Leonid meteor shower on November 13, 1833, was widely interpreted by North American Christians as a divine sign, perhaps of the imminence of the end of the world. Regularly occurring and predictable events like eclipses and great conjunctions of Saturn and Jupiter could also be treated as part of apocalyptic time.

Astrotheology was considered a branch of natural theology by writers who emphasized what the perfection and regularity of the heavens said about God. This kind of astrotheology was particularly compatible with Aristotelianism, which claimed that the heavens beyond the sphere of the moon were perfect, in contrast to the earthly realm of corruption. Aristotelianism dominated Latin Christian natural philosophy from the 12th century to the scientific revolution, and its view was adapted by Christians into a distinction between the perfect realm untainted by sin and earth, corrupted by sin after the fall of man. The perfect heavens were contrasted with hell at the center of the Earth, which for an Aristotelian was also the center of the universe.

The rise of heliocentrism during the scientific revolution, beginning with the Polish astronomer Nicolaus Copernicus (1471–1543), dealt a blow, but not a fatal one, to astrotheology and astrology by ending a sharp division between the heavens and the Earth. The invention of the telescope in the early 17th century and the discoveries it made in the solar system such as the mountains of the moon and the satellites of Jupiter also helped dissolve the idea of celestial perfection. Subsequent advances in science have continued the displacement of the Earth from the center of the universe, eventually relegating it to the position of a small planet circling a

Valentin Weigel, *Astrology Theologized*

German mystic Valentin Weigel's (1533–1588) Astrology Theologized both endorsed the truths of astrology and warned of the danger of not subordinating it to theology. It was translated in the 19th century by Anna Kingsford (1846–1888), one of the first English women to get a medical degree and a leading member of the Theosophical Society:

> Astrology is so called because it ariseth from the stars. As Theology, because it flows from God. To live astrologically is with a pleasing concupiscence to eat of the Tree of the knowledge of good and evil, and to bring death to himself. To live theologically is to eat of the wood and Tree of Life by an intimate abnegation of oneself, and thence to attain to oneself, Life and Salvation.
>
> The Light of Nature in Astrology, with his incitative fruits, is the probatory instrument whereby Man, placed in the midst, that is, between God and the Creature, is proved which way he would direct or convert his free will, desire, love and appetite; whether to God his Creator, by loving Him above all things, with his whole heart, with his whole mind, with his whole soul, and with his whole strength; which should be the Theological life. Or, whether, casting God behind, he would reflect to himself and to the Creature by love of himself, and arrogating of good things received, which was the Astrological life at the Babylonish fornication, as will appear by that which followeth.

Source: Valentin Weigel. 1886. *Astrology Theologized: The Spiritual Hermeneutics of Astrology and Holy Writ,* trans. with an introduction by Anna Kingsford, 50–51. London: George Redway.

star among billions in one arm of one galaxy, thoroughly destroying the traditional picture of the heavens, although astrology, much to the surprise and consternation of some of its detractors, has survived this transformation. However, the rise of the view of God as the great Heavenly lawmaker or divine clockmaker during the scientific revolution led to a new astrotheology that emphasized God's handiwork in making the universe as a whole rather than the perfection of the heavens.

In the 19th century, the term *astrotheology* was often used in the scholarly study of comparative religion, in its early stages as a discipline, to denote the veneration of stars and planets as divine as practiced in the Ancient Middle East. Some argued that Christianity was originally an astrotheological religion based on Jesus as a "solar myth," and there are systems for associating each of the 12 apostles to one of the signs of the zodiac. Although rejected by mainstream scholarship, this tradition has been carried on by astrologers and practitioners of new religions wanting to link Christianity and other monotheistic religions to ancient paganism. The modern religious use of the skies has been influenced by science fiction and the belief in extraterrestrial life that has contributed to such movements as the "Heaven's Gate" cult, which expected to be physically carried away from Earth by a spaceship following in the wake of the Hale-Bopp comet in 1977. Thirty-nine members of the group engaged in mass suicide to do so.

William E. Burns

See also: Apocalypticism; Bible; Buddhism; Christianity; Comets; Islamic Astrology; Judaism

Further Reading

Burkert, Walter. 1972. *Lore and Science in Ancient Pythagoreanism*, trans. Edwin L. Minar Jr. Cambridge, MA: Harvard University Press.

Campion, Nicholas. 2014. *Astrology and Cosmology in the World's Religions*. New York: NYU Press.

Chevalier, Jacques M. 1997. *A Postmodern Revelation: Signs of Astrology and the Apocalypse*. Toronto: University of Toronto Press.

Cumont, Franz. 1960. *Astrology and Religion among the Greeks and Romans*. Reprint. New York: Dover.

Genuth, Sara Schecner. 1997. *Comets, Popular Culture and the Birth of Modern Cosmology*. Princeton: Princeton University Press.

Tester, S. J. 1987. *A History of Western Astrology*. Wolfbridge, UK: Boydell.

B

BIBLE

Both the Hebrew Bible and Christian New Testament are rife with allusions to astrology and astral events. A fundamental tenet of ancient near eastern cosmology holds that everything in the world below is an abstract of the world above. In this cosmology, the Garden of Eden, for example, represented in miniature the entire universe. Two of the trees growing there ("the tree of life" and "the tree of the knowledge of good and evil," Gen. 2:9) represented the upper and lower world or creation. Elsewhere in the Pentateuch, the 12 loaves of the "bread of the Presence" (Exod. 25:30, 35:13), unleavened bread placed on a table in the Jewish tabernacle, correspond to the 12 months of the calendar year. Next to the bread of the Presence was a candlestick with seven branches, representing the seven planets known to antiquity (the five planets visible to the naked eye—Mercury, Venus, Mars, Jupiter, and Saturn—as well as the sun and the moon). There is an interpretive strain in the Hebrew tradition that associates each of the 12 tribes of Israel, named after the sons of Isaac, with one of the 12 constellations of the zodiac. One of these sons, Joseph, claimed to have dreamed that "the sun, the moon, and eleven stars were bowing down to me" (Gen. 37:9).

In the Hebrew Bible, Chaldean astrologers play a significant role in the early chapters of the book of Daniel (second century BCE). The Chaldeans were a Semitic-speaking nation that was absorbed by the Babylonian Empire. They eventually settled near the Euphrates River (in present-day Iraq, the locale of the Babylonian exile and the setting of Daniel). A basic characteristic of Chaldean astrology (which they inherited from the Mesopotamians) is that a spiritual force resides behind natural phenomena. Chaldean astrologers sought guidance through omens, lunar activity, solar eclipses, etc. In their view, events such as crop failures, plagues, wars, and the death of nobility were dependent upon astral events. They divided the years into periods of 90 days, known as astrolabes. At the time of the exile (sixth century BCE), Eastern magi traced the sun along an elliptical path, known as the Way of Anu (the supreme deity of the Mesopotamian pantheon). Anu's throne is seated at the celestial North Pole.

The second chapter of Daniel contains a vignette in which Nebuchadnezzar, the king of Babylon, is troubled by a dream. Nebuchadnezzar summoned magicians, enchanters, sorcerers, and "the Chaldeans" (Dan. 2:2) and demanded that they make known to him both the dream and its interpretation. The Chaldean astrologers remonstrated "there is not a man on earth" (Dan. 2:10) who could satisfy this demand. This remonstrance enraged Nebuchadnezzar, who sentenced the various wise men to death. Daniel, a Hebrew exile, interceded on behalf of the wise men

A Biblical Denunciation of Astrologers

The following passage from the Book of Isaiah talks of astrologers to make the point that they are unable to discern the will of God:

> Let now the astrologers, the stargazers, the monthly prognosticators, standup and save thee from these things that shall come upon thee. Behold they shall be as stubble; the fire shall burn them; they shall not deliver themselves from the power of the flame: there shall not be a coal to warm at, nor fire to sit before it.

Source: Isaiah 47:12–14, KJV.

and was able to recount Nebuchadnezzar's dream and provide an interpretation, thus succeeding where the astrologers failed. As a reward for this service, Nebuchadnezzar made Daniel the ruler over the province of Babylon and chief prefect over its magi (Dan. 2:48). The Hebrew Bible recognizes the presence of astrology but demonstrates that the power of its practitioners is inferior to that of God's prophets. This skepticism toward astrology and its identification with non-Jewish peoples is reflected in the famous line from Jeremiah 10:2, "Be not dismayed at the signs of the Heavens, as the Nations are dismayed," a line that would be frequently invoked by subsequent Jewish and Christian opponents of astrology.

The Christian New Testament contains references to astral events and their interpreters in the Gospel of Matthew and the Revelation to John. The Gospel of Matthew (chapter 2) claims that "wise men" or magi came from the east to worship the new-born Jesus. Hellenistic legends of the time (first century CE) interpreted the discovery of a new star as heralding the birth of a great man (Beare 1981). The individuals who visited the baby Jesus may have been Zoroastrian priests, who were subsequently given the names Melchior (king of Persia), Gaspar (king of India), and Balthasar (king of Arabia). The wise men stated in Matthew's infancy narrative that they had seen a "star in the East" (Matt. 2:2). They came looking for "he who has been born king of the Jews." Matthew's account of the visit of the magi is perhaps the only positive account of astrology in the New Testament. Because of their knowledge of the signs of the zodiac, they recognized the royal lineage of Jesus before the scholars in Jerusalem came to the same realization. It is interesting to note that the Gospel of Luke makes no mention of the Magi or birth star. In place of the Magi, Luke records that shepherds visited the baby Jesus.

The Revelation to St. John contains numerous astrological motifs that linger in the background of this apocalyptic narrative. In Revelation 1:4–2:1, the exalted, resurrected Jesus is accompanied by seven stars. In this passage, John is given a vision of heaven (ch. 4) where he glimpses the figures of a lion, bull, human being, and eagle (corresponding to the zodiac signs of Taurus, Leo, Aquarius, and Scorpio). In the visions of the Seven Seals and Seven Trumpets (Rev. 6–11), stars fall from the heavens, bringing great calamity to the Earth. The Seals and Trumpets are followed by seven mystic figures, which are described as great portents in heaven (Rev. 12:1ff). The finale of the Revelation to St. John depicts the downfall of Babylon, site of the Jewish exile and the home of astrologers, and the ultimate triumph of Jesus Christ and his saints.

Wendell Johnson

See also: Apocalypticism; Astrotheology; Christianity; Judaism; Mesopotamian Astrology

Further Reading

Beare, Francis Wright. 1981. *The Gospel According to Matthew*. San Francisco: Harper and Row.
Claiborne, Arthur. 2017. "Ancient Chaldea." TheSunsetChart.com. http://kaldu.com/chaldea.html.
Hübner, Wolfgang. 2007. "Astrology." *Religion Past and Present: Encyclopedia of Theology and Religion*, vol. 1, ed. Hans Dieter Betz et al., 468–470. Leiden: Brill.
Jeremias, Alfred, C. H. W. Johns, and C. L. Beaumont. 1911. *The Old Testament in the Light of the Ancient East*. Manual of biblical archaeology. London: Williams and Norgate.
Koester, Craig R. 2014. *Revelation: A New Translation with Introduction and Commentary*. New Haven, CT: Yale University Press.

BONATTI, GUIDO (CA. 1210–1290)

Guido Bonatti was among the most famous medieval astrologers, and his *Book of Astronomy (Liber Astronomiae)* represents one of the most complete accounts of Arabic-language astrology available in Latin, in all branches of the art except astrological magic. In an age when generals and kings all hired astrologers as advisers, Bonatti's own life experiences, employment history, and comments about culture and humanity illustrate what it meant to be a high-level, practicing astrologer. Such an astrologer was a valued consultant (but sometimes a victimized sycophant); was a socially responsible individual and opponent of superstition and demagoguery; having a sympathetic view of the human condition, sometimes concealed painful truths so as not to hurt his clients; was an observant social critic; was a therapist whose art helped clients gain perspective on their hopes and fears, instilling a more balanced and realistic approach to life; and enhanced the opportunities of disfavored and poor people.

Based on his own account and those of others, Bonatti was born around 1210 in or around Forlì, Italy, not far from Bologna. His father was a notary for the archbishop in Florence, and Bonatti provides the nativity of a nephew born in early 1268. He was probably studying astrology in Bologna in 1233, as he witnessed the troubling actions of the religious demagogue Brother Giovanni da Schio of Vicenza (John of Vicenza) during that year.

By 1258–1259, Bonatti was working for Ezzelino III, a tyrant and governor of Padua. This violent man had a staff of soothsayers and astrologers, including Salio, the Canon of Padua. Bonatti relates several stories that illustrate the danger of working as an astrologer for powerful men: for example, Ezzelino was holding Salio's own brother as a hostage, to prevent Salio from leaving. As a result, Ezzelino's staff, and Salio in particular, gave pleasing but false reports to their master so as not to make him angry. After Ezzelino's death, Bonatti worked for Count Guido Novello in Florence. He successfully advised Novello to attack the Florentine Guelphs in 1260, and two months later Bonatti is listed as a witness to high-level negotiations that would make Novello the new authority in Florence.

By 1276–1277, Bonatti was assisting the new authority in Forlì, Count Guido da Montefeltro (ca. 1220–1298). He advised Montefeltro on the battle of Valbona in 1276–1277, and near the end of his career he advised Montefeltro in his 1282–1283 defense against the forces of Pope Martin IV (Pope, 1281–1285). Bonatti would have died about 1290. Dante's *Divine Comedy* placed him in the eighth Circle and fourth Ring of Hell, the place of Fortune Tellers and Diviners. There, the damned souls who have tried to divine the future are placed with their heads turned completely around (facing the past, as it were), their eyes blinded with tears.

The *Book of Astronomy*, composed over a long period but finalized after 1277, is especially notable for including charts and interpretations from Bonatti's own practice. In one chart, Guido Novello wanted to capture a castle and asked if he could take it. Bonatti saw in the chart that while Novello could take the castle, his troops were lazy and weak and so would be reluctant to do their duty. So the answer was essentially, "yes, you can, but you won't." Novello proceeded anyway, and Bonatti reports that despite having superior numbers, the army performed poorly. He suggests that the troops' bad morale had partly to do with a serious drought: in the end they asked him to predict the weather, and after he predicted rain in a few days, the army left in good spirits.

Bonatti describes himself as a socially responsible opponent of fear and superstition. In several passages he says he stood up to tyrants and religious frauds who were harming the people—directly counter to the opinion that astrologers are selfish frauds who promote superstition. One example involves a local demagogue in Forlì named Simon Mestaguerra, who was born of a low father but rose to high status. At first the populace was behind him, but he began to terrorize the people for about three years before being exiled. Bonatti claims that he was the only one who really knew what kind of man Mestaguerra was, and stood alone in resisting him (though he does not say how). Some of Bonatti's most interesting social commentary has to do with sexual politics and the delicate position the astrologer is sometimes in. For example, some men ask whether a prospective bride has already had children who have been given up for adoption, because they worry about potential scandal. In cases like these, Bonatti sometimes advised astrologers to smooth things over and not reveal the painful truth: the astrologer is supposed to help people's lives, not ruin them.

As for astrology itself, Bonatti believed that it helps people overcome the forces of fortune, in a world where neither God nor human free will is directly in control of events: for example, some people obey the rules and treat everyone well but ask what is wrong in their lives because they are always mistreated and suffer. So, astrology helps people make practical decisions when they suffer bad fortune through no fault of their own. In addition, astrology's predictive quality provides some critical distance from life, appreciating and preparing for both good and bad with equanimity. For example, many predictive methods define periods of time that will be more favorable or unfavorable for various things, giving a client more reasonable expectations and preparedness concerning what each period means for life as a whole.

Benjamin N. Dykes

See also: Court Astrologers; Horary Astrology; Medieval European Astrology

Further Reading

Alighieri, Dante. 1996. *The Inferno*, trans. John Ciardi. New York: New American Library.
Bonatti, Guido. 2007. *Book of Astronomy, Vols. I–11*, trans. Benjamin N. Dykes. Golden Valley, MN: The Cazimi Press.

BRAHE, TYCHO (1546–1601)

Tycho Brahe was an astrologer and astronomer. He proposed to apply an observational method to astrology, avoiding the vulgar charlatanism and popular beliefs surrounding it. Brahe sought to convert astrology into a practically exact science and thereby improve astronomy. Although some scholars deny this, he cultivated astrology throughout his life.

Born in the Castle of Knudstrup (Scania, then Denmark, now Sweden) into a noble family, he was destined to study law to become a statesman. After learning Latin, he began to study rhetoric and philosophy in 1559. But he was very prone to astrology/astronomy and after the observation of an eclipse of the sun on August 21, 1560, he became even more interested in astrological predictions and horoscopes. After knowing that the eclipse had been exactly predicted, he started to think that astrology has something divine because men could know the motions of the stars so accurately that they could foretell their places and relative positions well beforehand. He remained in Copenhagen for three years learning mathematics and astronomy. However, his tutor insisted he continue his studies of law and he was sent to the University of Leipzig (Germany). He arrived at the university in March 1562. It seems that he did not attend the lectures on law but made some astronomical observations using the "radius" and "cross-staff," instruments of sailors of the time. He also went on to use the sextant and the quadrant later.

He cast horoscopes for his friends and, more importantly, he predicted wet weather. He returned to Denmark in 1565 but visited Wittenberg, Rostock, and Ausburg afterward where he was in touch with the best German astronomers. He resided in Helsingborg from 1570 onward. While in Helsingborg, he devoted himself to alchemy (1570–1572), an essential complement to astronomy because the planets ruled the elemental world and the microcosmos. So, the moon represented silver, Mercury quicksilver, Venus copper, sun gold, Mars iron, Jupiter tin, and Saturn lead. He applied the traditional astrological principle: "as above, so below."

Brahe's year of glory was 1572: he described a new star (*nova stella*) in the constellation of Cassiopeia. This discovery was published in Copenhagen: *De nova stella* (1573). Brahe's writings on the new star included an interpretation of its astrological meaning. As a result of his increased fame, he was invited to teach at the University of Copenhagen. At the same time he was appointed court astronomer to Frederik II of Denmark and commissioned to design horoscopes for the three princes.

In Brahe's first lecture (1574) (*De disciplinis mathematicis*) he gave his opinions about astrology. Brahe advocated the legitimate use of both natural (prediction of the weather) and judicial astrology (foretelling of human events). The prediction of events required many accurate measurements so as to produce correct results. The discussion of natal astrology is divided into sections by topic: infancy, life span, mood, moral dispositions, bodily build, travels, wedding, sons, friends, and death.

He concluded by stating that no prediction is irrevocable because the will of God orders everything. The reference to the will of God was made in order to not contradict the theologians attending the lecture. Brahe was very interested in astro-meteorology and from 1582 onward he kept long records of the weather that were correlated to planetary positions, the appearance of comets, and the moon's phases. But he became increasingly skeptical mainly because of the insufficient accuracy in the calculation of the positions of planets in advance. This was why Brahe worked to improve the accuracy of the observations necessary for a true astrology including weather prediction and nativities. It was necessary for time to be determined correctly and for the position of planets on the astrological chart to correspond with the actual sky. He claimed to have developed an experience-based method, differing from those previously used. But he did not want to inform others about this method.

In 1576, by order of the king, he went to live and make astronomical observations in an observatory on the island of Hven known as Uraniborg, fortress of Urania, muse of astronomy. In 1599, after a quarrel with the new king and a stay in Germany, Brahe went to Prague, under the protection of Emperor Rudolph II, where he died in 1601. These approximately 20 years were the period in which he did his best astrological and astronomical work.

Astrology and alchemy were included in Brahe's's cosmology. In his books *De mundi aetheri phaenomenis* (1588), *Epistolarum astronomicarum* (1596), and *Astronomiae instauratae mechanica* (1598) appear two drawings that bear the meaningful captions *suspiciendo despicio* (by looking up I see downward) and *despiciendo suscipio* (by looking down I see upward). Both pictures show a man in reclining posture and a youth, but in one case the man is looking upward into the sky and leaning on a globe with a pair of compasses in his hands. In the other one, he is escorted by an alchemical instrument, holding a bunch of herbs in his hands and looking downward. In other words astrology is the mirror of alchemy and vice versa: as above, so below. Brahe's observations were inherited by Johannes Kepler, who used them to develop his own astronomy and astrology.

Justo Hernández

See also: Kepler, Johannes; Renaissance and Reformation Astrology; Science

Further Reading

Dreyer, J. L. E. 2014. Tycho Brahe, *A Picture of Scientific Life and Work in the Sixteenth Century*. Cambridge: Cambridge University Press.

Oestmann, G. 2002. "Tycho Brahe's Attitude towards Astrology and His Relations to Heinrich Rantzau." In *Tycho Brahe and Prague: Crossroads of European Science*, ed. John Robert Christianson, Alena Hadravová, Petr Hadrava, and Martin Šolc, 88–94. Frankfurt am Main: Verlag Harri Deutsch.

BRUNO, GIORDANO (1548–1600)

Giordano Bruno, originally named Fillipo at his baptism and later referred to as *il Nolano* after his place of birth, was an Italian philosopher, scholar, and one-time Dominican friar who contributed to metaphysics, cosmology, astronomy, astrology, natural magic, and the art of memory. Perhaps best known for his early adoption of the Copernican heliocentric theory, Bruno also proposed that the cosmos was infinite, that it contained a plurality of worlds, and that beings may exist on these worlds. His complex and highly heterodox cosmology drew inspiration particularly from the Hermetic tradition but also incorporated ideas from Neoplatonism, Averroism, Pythagoreanism, ancient Egyptian religions, and Renaissance natural magic (Rowland 2008, 1–14).

Giordano Bruno was born in Nola, a provincial southern Italian town in 1548. He relocated to Naples, about 30 miles away, in 1565. There Bruno entered the Dominican monastery of San Domenico Maggiore, distinguished himself as an outstanding scholar of metaphysics and theology, and proved quite adept in the mnemonic arts. This latter ability established him as an asset to various noblemen across Europe who recognized the practical value of recalling vast amounts of detailed information. Following an accusation that he had promoted anti-Trinitarianism, Arianism, and possessed forbidden books by Erasmus and others, Bruno unceremoniously withdrew from the Dominican Order in 1576 and became a peripatetic scholar and teacher. Between 1576 and 1591, he traveled throughout much of Europe, including Geneva, Toulouse, Paris, London, and various university towns in Germany and Central Europe including Marburg, Wittenberg, Prague, and Frankfurt, where he lived off teaching and the munificence of various patrons. He briefly converted to Calvinism while in Geneva, though he ran afoul of authorities there and was excommunicated, later unsuccessfully seeking absolution from Catholic authorities in Toulouse. In France, he received the favor and protection of King Henri III. With his approval, Bruno traveled to London as a guest of Ambassador Michel de Castelnau (ca. 1520–1592), where he visited the court of Queen Elizabeth I, and Oxford, where he lectured and reputedly outraged the faculty with his speculative philosophy and pugnacious personality. During his stay in England (1583–1585), he wrote prolifically and produced several works that made his reputation as a scholar, including *La Cena de le Ceneri* (*The Ash Wednesday Supper*), *De la Causa, Principio et Uno* (*On Cause, Principle, and Unity*), *De l'Infinito Universo e Mondi* (*On the Infinite Universe and Worlds*), and *Lo Spaccio de la Bestia Trionfante* (*The Expulsion of the Triumphant Beast*), all published in 1584.

After nearly two decades of itinerant teaching throughout the scholarly centers of Europe, he returned to Italy in 1591 and was supported by the patronage of Giovanni Mocenigo, a minor Venetian nobleman, who endeavored to learn the secrets of the art of memory from Bruno. Unable to master these arts, Mocenigo suspected Bruno of fraud and denounced him to the Venetian Inquisition for various heresies, including a denial of the Trinity, the divinity of Christ, the virginity of Mary, and Transubstantiation, as well as his perceived pantheism. Eventually, the Venetians handed Bruno over to the less forgiving Roman Inquisition, and after a nearly eight-year-long trial, during which he languished in prison, Bruno was burned at the stake as a heretic at the Campo de' Fiori in Rome on February 17, 1600.

Bruno's regard for astrology is difficult to assess. On the one hand, he attacked horoscopic and mathematical astrology in several of his writings throughout his life. On the other hand, he appears to have authored a now-lost work on astrology (*De Segni de' Tempi*), explained various physical phenomena such as the generation and corruption of organisms in astrological terms, accepted stellar causes for many diseases, and used astrological symbols as memory aids in his mnemonic techniques (Spruit 2002, 229). In general, he seems to have had limited knowledge of the technical aspects of astrology, though he was familiar with its rationale, and his esteem for it varied from topic to topic. For example, he referenced the conjunctions of planets in a number of his works as harbingers of great events and spoke on the importance of the heavens in understanding major terrestrial matters. However, he also ridiculed the application of mathematics to astrological prediction, claiming that greater precision in plotting the movement of the planets would not increase the accuracy of astrological prediction, and he argued that there could be no specific interpretation of rare celestial events like eclipses, comets, and novas. Notably, when he was arrested in Venice in 1592, he possessed a hand-copied astrological treatise *De Sigillis Hermetis, Ptolemaei, et alorium* and later mounted a defense of astrology during his trial (Spruit 2002, 243).

Bruno's interest in astrology increased from the early 1580s onward. His most astrologically influenced surviving work, *De rerum principiis*, posits an essential correspondence between the celestial and the terrestrial, arbitrated by a universal spirit that channels stellar influence. In this work, Bruno divided these correspondences into three categories based on the length of the time periods they influenced. The first section on "circumstances and fortunes" covered events that occurred over long periods of time, while the latter two, on stellar influence of the generation and corruption of life, covered seasonal and daily effects, respectively. Bruno's astrology was concerned with the relationship between the public at large (rather than individuals) and celestial events, as well as the potential applications for medicine and natural magic.

Much of the confusion in understanding his position on astrology comes from the varied nature of his criticism. His belief in a sun-centered cosmos and the homogeneity of the heavens and the Earth directly contradicted Ptolemaic and Aristotelian physics, which were his primary targets. Yet he endeavored to unify the heavens and the Earth into one cosmological system, which in no way necessitated a destruction of traditional astrology and in fact might bolster its claims. Rather, he railed against what he called the "superstitious manipulations" of astrological techniques (Spruit 2002, 244). Much of his criticism is directed at mathematical astrology, which he saw as a futile effort to quantify an infinite combination of astral movements that could never be fully determined to make useful, specific predictions.

Justin Niermeier-Dohoney

See also: Astrotheology; Christianity; Renaissance and Reformation Astrology

Further Reading

Candella, Giuseppe. 1998. "An Overview of the Cosmology, Religion and Philosophical Universe of Giordano Bruno." *Italica* 75, no. 3: 348–364.

Couliano, Ioan P. 1987. *Eros and Magic in the Renaissance*, trans. Margaret Cook. Chicago: University of Chicago Press.

Gatti, Hilary. 2002. *Giordano Bruno and Renaissance Science*. Ithaca, NY: Cornell University Press.

Rowland, Ingrid. 2008. *Giordano Bruno: Philosopher/Heretic*. Chicago: University of Chicago Press.

Spruit, Leen. 2002. "Giordano Bruno and Astrology." In *Giordano Bruno: Philosopher of the Renaissance*, ed. Hilary Gatti, 229–249. London: Ashgate.

Yates, Frances A. 1964. *Giordano Bruno and the Hermetic Tradition*. Chicago: University of Chicago Press.

BUDDHISM

Astrology has played a significant role in Buddhism throughout history. Modern Buddhist traditions have differing views on the validity of astrology, though many Buddhists practice it.

Early Buddhism initially discouraged the practice of astrology by monks yet did not reject its validity. Over time Buddhist traditions took an increasing interest in astrology and eventually incorporated it into their religious systems. Buddhist astrology can be divided into two major types: the pre-Hellenistic type and the post-Hellenistic type. The former followed a native Indian model whereas the latter was heavily influenced by Hellenistic concepts. These different systems were transmitted to East Asia and Tibet via Buddhist scriptures. Chinese Buddhist astrology included additional elements from Iranian astrology. Its mature system was transmitted to Japan and Korea in the 9th and 10th centuries. Tibetan Buddhist astrology included both Chinese and late Indian elements.

The extant Buddhist canon indicates that early Buddhists did not actively participate in the development of Indian *jyotiḥśāstra* (a subject encompassing astrology and mathematical astronomy) as it ran contrary to the ideal of renouncing the worldly life. In the *Brahmajāla-sutta*, an early Buddhist scripture, the Buddha criticizes monks who practice divination to receive offerings. The Vinaya (monastic rules) also forbids monks from practicing divination especially for material gain. Although such prohibitions existed, the validity of astrology itself was seldom attacked and Buddhist literature often assumes a passive belief in astrology. Early Brahman society similarly disparaged astrologers but accepted the validity of their art.

The Buddhist *sangha* or monastic community traditionally operated according to the lunar calendar in which the month is divided into two periods composed of 15 days (*tithi*) each: the waxing (*śukla-pakṣa*) and waning (*kṛṣṇa-pakṣa*) periods. Specific days within each lunar phase are regarded as auspicious and community meetings are normally carried out on them. This is additionally connected to a belief in deities descending into the world on these days. Like all Indian traditions, Buddhists throughout history have used different calendars that vary by time period and region. Buddhist astrology uses a system of nine planets

(Sanskrit: *nava-graha*), which include the five visible planets (Mercury, Venus, Mars, Jupiter, and Saturn), sun, moon, Rāhu (the ascending node of the moon), and Ketu (the descending node of the moon).

The earliest known Buddhist text dealing with astrology is the *Śārdūlakarṇāvadāna* (written in the second or third century CE). It teaches an Indian system of predictions based on convergences between the moon and the 28 *nakṣatras* (lunar stations along the ecliptic). There are also prescribed foods and associated Vedic deities for each convergence. The name of each day in a month is derived from the *nakṣatra* in which the moon lodges. This was not formulated by Buddhists, but rather represents an early pan-Indian system of astrology before the introduction of major Hellenistic influences. Although a similar system of lunar stations emerged in ancient China, the *nakṣatras* are indigenous to India and likely come from the Indus Valley Civilization. Their earliest listing in full is found in the *Atharva Veda*. The *nakṣatras* are defined by stars, but they were never universally defined the same way. They were first enumerated starting from Kṛttikā, but later this was changed to Aśvinī to accommodate the precession of the equinoxes:

1. Kṛttikā
2. Rohiṇī
3. Mṛgaśīrṣa
4. Ārdrā
5. Punarvasū
6. Puṣya
7. Aślesā
8. Maghā
9. Pūrvaphālgunī
10. Uttaraphālgunī
11. Hasta
12. Citrā
13. Svāti
14. Viśākhā
15. Anurādhā
16. Jyeṣṭha
17. Mūla
18. Pūrvāṣāḍhā
19. Uttarāṣāḍhā
20. Abhijit
21. Śravaṇa
22. Dhaniṣṭhā
23. Śatabhiṣaj
24. Pūrvabhādrapadā
25. Uttarabhādrapadā
26. Revatī
27. Aśvinī
28. Bharaṇī

Abhijit can be excluded and thus there can be either 28 or 27 *nakṣatras*. Each *nakṣatra* is assigned qualities that determine the personalities of people born under them. Predictions about the harvest and the political situation are also made by seeing which *nakṣatra* the moon is in when the monsoon rains commence.

A rare example of a Buddhist scripture refuting the validity of astrology is the *Saddharmasmṛtyupasthāna-sūtra* (probably written in the third or fourth century CE). It emphasizes that astrology is an inappropriate practice for a monk in addition to arguing that it cannot be true for various reasons. Such arguments, however, are rare in the Buddhist canon. The premise of determinism inherent to astrology runs contrary to Buddhist theories of karma, which assert that suffering and happiness are the result of past negative and positive actions, respectively. One way this contradiction has been approached is to suggest that being born under unfavorable stars is a result of negative karma from past lives, in which case one's fate is still connected to one's own actions albeit before birth. The extant literature, however, seldom recognizes any problem to begin with owing to the normalcy of astrology in ancient Indian culture.

The Mahāyāna tradition that emerged in the first few centuries CE actively encouraged its adherents (bodhisattvas, i.e., those aspiring to achieve enlightenment for the benefit of all beings) to study worldly arts in order to play an active, engaged role in society. This included calendrical science and astrology. From around the fourth century onward, Indian astrology was heavily influenced by Hellenistic astrology and subsequently new elements such as the 12 zodiac signs and seven-day week were introduced. The earlier negative sentiments toward astrologers in Indian society declined and Buddhists also took an increasing interest in astrology. This was paralleled by the new studies of mathematical astronomy, exemplified by figures like Āryabhaṭa (b. 476), though he was probably not a Buddhist. Astrologers in India were increasingly respected and called into courts to advise kings.

In the seventh century a new practice known as Tantric Buddhism emerged, which emphasized proper timing for rituals. It integrated the new foreign elements into an earlier Indian system of *nakṣatras* but continued using a sidereal zodiac. An increasing number of astrological variables had to be considered to determine the opportune time for a ritual. The literature also expresses belief in astrological factors affecting human lives. Indian Buddhists also increasingly studied mathematical astronomy and in the early 11th century a set of texts called the *Kālacakra Tantra* was compiled in which advanced astronomy and the tropical zodiac were incorporated into a complex new religious system. This late Buddhist interest in astronomy is highlighted by the eminent Buddhist astronomer Daśabala (fl. 1055–1058).

Buddhist astrology in East Asia is a mix of Indian, Chinese, and Iranian elements. The *Śārdūlakarṇāvadāna* was translated twice between the fourth and the sixth centuries, though it does not appear Indian astrology was practiced in China in these centuries. Similar works dealing with Indian *nakṣatra* astrology were translated throughout the sixth and seventh centuries, but the Indian system of astronomy was not adequately translated and explained in Chinese. There was moreover little need for Chinese Buddhists to practice astrology until the eighth century when Tantric Buddhism was introduced. The *Mahāvairocana-sūtra*, an early major work of Buddhist Tantra, was translated by the Indian monk

Śubhakarasiṃha (637–735) and the Chinese astronomer monk Yixing (683–727) in 724. The text emphasizes that rituals be performed with due consideration to astrological timing. The subsequent commentary written by Yixing briefly discusses the *nakṣatras*, zodiac signs, and seven-day week but fails to provide any details. This led to the monk Amoghavajra (705–774) compiling an astrological manual in Chinese entitled *Xiuyao jing* that details both electional and natal astrology. It builds on earlier material similar to that of the *Śārdūlakarṇāvadāna* while additionally detailing the seven-day week (each day has astrological features), 12 zodiac signs and a basic system of natal predictions. This text, however, only alludes to advanced horoscopy yet provides no details on it. Between 785 and 805, Persian astronomers working in the capital Chang'an translated a work of Dorotheus of Sidon into Chinese that was widely studied by Chinese astrologers in the following centuries. This work of Hellenistic astrology provided a complete system of horoscopy including aspects and the 12 houses. It also introduced the tropical zodiac into China, though Buddhists for a time continued using a sidereal zodiac. Various elements of Iranian astrology and astrological iconography were adopted by Buddhists and incorporated into their religious practice throughout the ninth century. This led to the development of astral magic in which various spells and rituals were performed to counteract undesirable astrological influences. Astrology became very popular in ninth century China and both Buddhists and Daoists studied it. As in India, Chinese Buddhist astrology also uses nine planets, but Ketu was redefined as the lunar apogee sometime around the year 800 CE.

The mature form of Chinese Buddhist astrology was adopted by Japanese monks. The founder of the Shingon school, Kūkai (774–835), is credited with first bringing the *Xiuyao jing* to Japan in 806 and introducing the new concepts there. The monk Shū'ei (809–884) brought back a different but equally influential text called the *Qiyao rangzai jue* and the aforementioned translation of Dorotheus. These works were studied in the subsequent century, which led to the formation of an influential community of astrologer monks called the Sukuyōdō. The first monk of the lineage is said to be Hōzō (905–969), who actively debated with members of the rival Onmyōdō school who practiced a different system of Chinese astrology. The Sukuyōdō in addition to drafting horoscopes primarily for the aristocracy also practiced astral magic. The community disappeared sometime before the 14th century, but many of their texts survived. In the 20th century there was a popular revival of Sukuyōdō in Japan initiated by Komine Yumiko (b. 1930) who claimed to have received a secret lineage from Iseki Tenkai leading to a large genre of popular astrology works associated with Buddhism.

Astrology was widely studied in other East Asian countries including the Tangut Xixia (1038–1227), Jurchen Jin (1127–1234), Khitan Liao (906–1125), and Korean Koryŏ (918–1392) kingdoms. Korea was believed by some to possess a superior system of astrology. In Korea it was believed that national calamities were caused by the movements of planets and resulting imbalances, but Buddhist divinities could be petitioned to correct these; in particular; Tejaprabhā Buddha, who appears in astrological artwork across East Asia.

This 17th-century Japanese wooden star mandala shows the incorporation of the stars into a Buddhist religious object. (Philadelphia Museum of Art, Gift of the Friends of the Philadelphia Museum of Art, 1978-45-2)

Tibetan astrology is deeply connected to the *Kālacakra Tantra*. The two primary Tibetan calendars are the Tsurphu and Phugpa systems, both of which draw on calculations and methods from the Kālacakra. Most Tibetan electional astrology is from India (*nakṣatras* and the seven-day week), though parts of Tibetan astrology draw on elements from Chinese lore (in particular the trigrams from the *Yijing* and the five elements) and calendrical science plus the indigenous religion of Tibet called Bön. The Tibetan science of calculation (Tiben: *tsi rik*) or astrology is considered a secondary science (i.e., not specifically Buddhist doctrine) and connected to Tibetan medicine. It is still a special subject studied by lamas and monks. It is also studied among several non-Tibetan communities in Nepal.

Modern Buddhist traditions in the wake of Western science's complete rejection of astrology have sometimes publicly rejected astrology or otherwise quietly ignored its long history in Buddhism, though many monks and Buddhist laypeople around Asia still practice it. Astrology is often identified as non-Buddhist and something to be removed in the process of modernizing and purifying Buddhism. Modern Chinese Buddhists no longer have a specifically Buddhist system of astrology and thus those with the interest largely practice Chinese astrology. The Tibetan

Buddhist tradition of astrology is intact and widely taught around the world. The study of astrology as an important component of Buddhist history has often been overlooked by scholars of Buddhism, but relevant research is ongoing.

Jeffrey Kotyk

See also: Chinese Astrology; Indian Astrology; Thai Astrology

Further Reading

Cornu, Philippe. 1997. *Tibetan Astrology*, trans. Hamish Gregor. Boston: Shambala.

Dolce, Lucia, ed. 2007. *The Worship of Stars in Japanese Religious Practice*. Bristol: Culture and Cosmos.

Henning, Edward. 2007. *Kālacakra and the Tibetan Calendar*. New York: The American Institute of Buddhist Studies at Columbia University.

Kālacakra. http://kalacakra.org. Editor: Edward Henning

Mak, Bill M. 2014. "*Yusi Jing*—A Treatise of 'Western' Astral Science in Chinese and Its Versified Version *Xitian yusi jing*." *SCIAMVS* 1: 105–169.

Pingree, David. 1997. *From Astral Omens to Astrology: From Babylon to Bīkāner*. Rome: Ist. Italiano per l'Africa e l'Oriente.

Sørensen, Henrik H. 2006. "Esoteric Buddhism under the Koryŏ in the Light of the Greater East Asian Tradition." *International Journal of Buddhist Thought & Culture* 7: 55–94.

BUREAU OF ASTRONOMY (CHINA)

In ancient China astronomy was managed by the government. This was decided when astronomy emerged in Chinese civilization. The earliest well-documented ruler was King Yao, whose deeds were recorded in the Yao dian chapter in *Shang shu (Book of Documents)*. According to this literature, many of Yao's decrees and institutions were related to astronomy. He commanded two chief astronomical officials Xi and He to "in reverent accordance with the august heavens, to compute and delineate the sun, moon and stars, and the celestial markers (chen), and so to deliver respectfully the seasons to be observed by the people." He also sent four astronomical officials to four places in the four cardinal directions to observe the culminating stars at the two equinoxes and the two solstices and watch the things people should do and the changes in nature. In Taosi Site (ca. 2300–1900 BCE) in Xiangfen County, which is believed to be the site of Yao's capital, remains of an observatory were found constituted by two curved rammed-earth walls facing east with a series of slots and a rammed-earth round center to the west of the walls. The slots on the two curved walls together with the gap between the two walls form in total 12 slots when observing from the center. It is an observatory for observing the rising sun in different seasons. There are two slots exactly positioned for observing the summer solstice and the winter solstice. This large-scale observatory was deliberately designed outside the southeast wall of the Taosi City. It must have been constructed under the organization of the government, which conformed well to the records in the Yao dian chapter and shows that the earliest astronomical observation was managed by the regime.

Before the foundation of the Zhou Dynasty (1046–256 BCE), the Earl of Zhou constructed a high platform, ling tai (spirit terrace), for astronomical observation and obtaining Heaven's will, which was regarded as an announcement to overthrow the Shang Dynasty (ca. 1600–1046 BCE). According to Zhou li (the Rites of Zhou), in the Zhou Dynasty, at least nine officials were concerned with astronomical affairs. Among them the Feng xiang shi, Bao zhang shi, and Qie hu shi were the most important. Feng xiang shi was in charge of the 12 years, 12 months, 12 celestial markers (chen), 10 dates, and the 28 xiu (28 constellations along celestial equator or ecliptic), to make calendar. Bao zhang shi was in charge of astrology; he

> concerns himself with the stars in the heavens, keeping a record of the changes and movements of the stars and planets, sun and moon, in order to examine the movements of the terrestrial world, with the object of distinguishing [prognosticating] good and bad fortune. He divides the territories of the Nine Provinces of the sub-celestial realm in accordance with their dependence on the particular celestial bodies. All the fiefs and principalities are connected with distinct stars, and from this their prosperity or misfortune can be ascertained. He makes prognostications according to the 12 years [of the Jupiter cycle], of good and evil in the terrestrial world. Zhou Li, as quoted in Pankenier 2013, 268.

Qie hu shi was in charge of clepsydra and timing.

In the Spring and Autumn to the Warring States period (770–221 BCE) the court of the Zhou Dynasty was weak while the feudal states were strong. After a long time of observation, astronomical knowledge had accumulated, and astrology was eagerly needed because of the frequent wars. At this time, the traditional Chinese astronomical system was founded, including the 28 xiu and the equatorial system, the naming of stars by Shi Shenfu (or Shi Shen) and Gan De, the maturity of solar-lunar calendar, and the observation of the five planets, and so on. But the astronomical bureaus of the feudal states are not well documented.

The Qin Dynasty (221–207 BCE) began the empire era of Chinese history, with the establishment of what became the traditional administrative system. In the Qin special astronomical institutions had not been set up, but among the officials there was the tai shi ling, which became the name of a special astronomical official in later times. The Qin also had 300 clerks in charge of astronomical observations.

In the early Western Han (202 BCE–8 CE) in the second century BCE the official tai shi ling was not only in charge of astronomy but also the writing of history. The most famous tai shi ling of this time was Sima Qian, a great astronomer and historian. In Eastern Han (25 CE–220 CE), the astronomical bureau was called tai shi, and the chief official was called tai shi ling. The duty of the tai shi ling was restricted to astronomy, including observing the sun, the moon, the five planets, and the stars, making calendars, designing and managing clepsydra, and also the choosing of auspicious dates for important public concerns, such as sacrifices or the funerals of members of the Imperial family. After the Han, every dynasty had an astronomical bureau, though it may have different names.

From the Three Kingdoms (220–280) through the Western Jin (266–316), the Eastern Jin (317–420), the Southern States (420–589), and the Northern States (386–581), the country was not united and the states were often at war. Each government had an astronomical bureau, but not as developed as that of the Han.

In the Sui Dynasty (581–618) the country was united again. Though it lasted only 37 years, it established an administrative system. The astronomical bureau of the Sui was not as large as that of Han, but it began to train specialists in calendar making. In the Tang Dynasty (618–907) the name of the astronomical bureau changed several times, such as tai shi jian, tai shi ju, hun tian jian, and si tian tai. Once it had even more than 800 on staff. In the Song Dynasty (960–1279; Northern Song 960–1127; Southern Song 1127–1279) the bureau was called si tian jian or tai shi ju. During the Northern Song the bureau had about 100 staff. In Northern Song besides the tai shi ju, another astronomical institution was set up, which was the han lin tian wen yuan (astronomical institution in han lin yuan; Han lin yuan was the royal academy of knowledge and arts). Observational results of the han lin tian wen yuan were compared to those of the astronomical bureau.

During the Tang and the Northern Song, management of the astronomical bureau became stricter. In early Han the duty of tai shi ling was not restricted to astronomical affairs, thus the officials were involved in general affairs. But in the Tang and the Northern Song, officials of the astronomical bureau were treated differently. In 840, Emperor Wen of Tang ordered that officials of the astronomical bureau not contact other officials and various kinds of people, and also sent royal supervisors to supervise them. The second emperor of the Song issued a decree soon after he took the throne demanding the states send people who were good at astronomy to the imperial court, and those who hid astronomers would be sentenced to death. These astronomers were then tested in the court, and the prominent ones were sent to work in the astronomical bureau, while the others were tattooed on their faces and exiled to Hainan Island. The fourth emperor of the Song once promulgated an imperial edict prohibiting officials of the astronomical bureau from visiting other officials' homes. Sometimes astronomical officials could be reduced to a lower rank

Foreign Astrologers in Tang China

The Tang Dynasty in China (618–907) was known for its cosmopolitanism, and this applied to astrology as well. Astrologers from India and Persia resident in the Tang capital of Chang-an influenced the development of Chinese astrology by translating foreign works, many of Greek origin, into Chinese. Such astrologers could be essentially bicultural, drawing from Chinese traditions as well as those of their native countries, as did the Sino-Indian astrologer Gautama Zhuan (712–776), whose tomb was discovered in 1977. They were affiliated with the Bureau of Astronomy as "foreign specialists." Gautama Zhuan was succeeded as foreign specialist by a Persian Christian known as Li Su (743–817) who used methods ultimately derived from Hellenistic astrology. Use of Indian and Persian astrologers set a precedent for the Astronomical Bureau's later use of Muslim and Jesuit astronomers.

Source: Kotyk, Jeffrey. 2016. "Indian Astronomers in Sui-Tang China." *The Jyotish Digest* 14: 31–35.

if they failed to predict a solar eclipse precisely or chose a wrong date for an important affair. In Southern Song the restrictions on astronomers relaxed because of war and lack of good astronomers in the astronomical bureau.

The Mongol Yuan Dynasty (1271–1368) had a large astronomical bureau, although astronomy was allowed outside the government. There were three subastronomical bureaus named si tian tai, hui hui si tian tai (the Islamic si tian tai), and tai shi yuan, and these three subbureaus experienced departure and unity. According to literature, the building of tai shi yuan was a magnificent 3-story observatory. It had offices for calculation, observation, and management of clepsydra, a library, a room for star charts. Astronomical instruments such as clepsydra, celestial globe, and water driven celestial globe each had its own room. There was a gnomon of 4 zhang tall (about 9.75 meters) for measuring the sun's shadow at noon, and there was even an office for the workshop in charge of printing calendars. This building no longer exists. The existing Dengfeng Observatory in Henan Province was built under the direction of Guo Shuojing (1231–1316). Guo was a very famous astronomer and hydraulic engineer who was once in charge of the astronomical bureau and made great achievements in instruments building, calendar making, and observation and organized a large-scale geographic survey in preparing for the new calendar. His Shou shi Calendar was one of the greatest calendars in Chinese history. The hui hui si tian tai introduced Arabic astronomy into China.

In the Ming Dynasty (1368–1644) the name of the astronomical bureau changed several times, but its duty was similar as that of the former dynasties, and astronomy as well as astrology were strictly forbidden outside the government again. Under this situation astronomy had little development, and astronomers could not even make a new calendar; the Shou shi Calendar remained in use with a little revision through the Ming. By the end of Ming, Jesuit missionaries came to China and the astronomical bureau began to accept Western astronomy and made a new calendar, the Chong zhen Calendar, which was not used till the end of the Ming.

In the Qing Dynasty (1644–1911) more Jesuit astronomers worked in the astronomical bureau, sometimes as its head. Contemporary Western astronomical works were translated into Chinese and Chinese astronomy gradually merged into modern astronomy.

Xu Fengxian

See also: Chinese Astrology; Legal Regulation of Astrology; Mundane Astrology; Sima Qian

Further Reading

Needham, Joseph. 1959. *Science and Civilization in China, Volume 3. Mathematics and the Sciences of the Heavens and the Earth*. Cambridge: Cambridge University Press.

Pankenier, David. 2013. *Astrology and Cosmology in Early China*. Cambridge: Cambridge University Press.

C

CAMPANELLA, TOMMASO (1558–1639)

Tommaso Campanella was a late Renaissance Italian polymath and astrologer whose work helped pave the way to modern science. Rejecting Aristotelianism, he based science, including astrology, on observation.

Born in Calabria he entered the Dominican order in 1582. He went to Cosenza to study theology in 1588 where he discovered the empiricist natural philosopher Bernardo Telesio (1509–1588) whose physics he preferred to Aristotelianism. Campanella was transferred to the small remote convent of Altomonte.

Undergoing several conflicts, he left Calabria and sailed to Naples. In 1590, he was received as a guest in the house of his friend Mario del Tufo, being preceptor of his sons. He finished the three volumes of *De investigatione rerum*, which would be lost due to confiscation by the Inquisition.

Campanella's friend Giambattista Della Porta (1585–1615), author of *Magia naturalis*, helped introduce him to the magic, which explained that all the things of the cosmos are connected by influences of sympathy and antipathy. The most important part of this natural magic was astrology. As a magician and astrologer Campanella was also influenced by the work of Marsilio Ficino. Astrology was central to Campanella's thought and life. His astrology dealt with the influences of the planets, living things—in accordance to Plato—on both individuals and society. The main principle of astrology is "as above, so below" (i.e., the supralunar world dominates the sublunar world). Campanella's astrology was political. Campanella considered himself a major prophet, able to determine the changes to come.

Campanella studied medicine at the University of Padua. There he wrote the now lost *Della Monarchia dei cristiani* in 1593. This book will be the source of his *De Monarchia hispanica*. He was arrested by the Inquisition and jailed in Rome in 1594 on the charge of disputing about the faith with a converted Jew who returned to Judaism without having reported him to the Inquisition. The Inquisition, after the trial (1595), ordered Campanella to do a public retraction and to remain in the convent of Santa Sabina. Looking for freedom he wrote three letters to the Holy Office. Finally he was moved to Santa Maria sopra Minerva in 1596. Only three months later he was accused of heresy and jailed again. Although he was absolved in this trial, all his writings were forbidden and Campanella went back to the convent of Nicastro (1598).

He was a leader in a failed 1599 plot to raise Calabria in rebellion against Spain to create a communist republic. The timing of the revolt was based on astrology and apocalyptic prophecy. As a friar, Campanella was tried by the Inquisition.

He was imprisoned, tortured, and only liberated 27 years later. Campanella then sailed to Rome under a false name in 1626.

Campanella wrote most of his works in Naples. In 1602 he composed the *City of the Sun*. It is not a Utopia because this town will exist and the stars will announce the moment of its starting up. The sun is represented at the center of the city, which is rounded by seven circles, representing the planets. It is an astrologic cosmovision. Even the procreation of new citizens will be founded on astrology. Coitus should be carried out at the right astrological moments for the production of perfect men and women. The City of the Sun has an important official called "the astrologer," who is consulted to do everything and examine the propitious signs. This shows, according to Campanella, that this town will be converted in the Universal Monarchy, ruled by the Pope.

He wrote *Astronomy* and *Prognosticonastrologicum de his quae mundo imminent usque ad finem* (1603). This last book argues that the astrological events of this year such as the "Great Conjunction" of Saturn and Jupiter will favor the establishment of the *Monarchia Universalis* represented by the Spanish Empire whose supreme authority will be the Pope and, in a second place, the king of Spain.

In Rome, to which he was transferred in 1626, Campanella survived as astrologer, in which capacity he met Pope Urban VIII. The relationship ended soon: Campanella published *Apologia pro Galileo* (1622) and Pope Urban turned against astrology. In 1634, Campanella escaped to France, a country where he was already known.

Once again Campanella's knowledge of astrology opened doors for him, as he was protected by the French leader Cardinal Richelieu. Since the predictions of a Spanish world empire in the *Monarchia hispanica* had failed, he now claimed that this monarchy would be a French one. The queen, Anne of Austria, asked him to cast a horoscope of the heir, the future Louis XIV. Campanella foretold a new golden age with the king under the Pope in a French universal monarchy. Campenella did not live to see if his predictions would be fulfilled, as he died piously on May 5, 1639, at his Dominican convent.

Justo Hernández

See also: Astral Magic; Mundane Astrology; Politics; Renaissance and Reformation Astrology

Further Reading

Ernst, G. 2010. *Tommaso Campanella: The Book and the Body of Nature*. Dordrecht: Springer.
Headley, J. M. 1997. *Tommaso Campanella and the Transformation of the World*. Princeton: Princeton University Press.

CARDANO, GIROLAMO (1501–1576)

Girolamo Cardano was an Italian Renaissance polymath whose areas of expertise included astrology, mathematics, philosophy, chiromancy, physiognomics or physionomy, metoposcopy and oneiromancy). According to Cardano, astrology was only one element of the new and sophisticated practices of divination. All the sciences and disciplines he studied, learned, and cultivated were oriented toward divination: horoscopes (astrology), signs and symptoms, favorable or unfavorable, diseases (medicine), numbers and calculus to predict results of gambling (theory of probabilities), numbers and maps to the horoscopes (algebra and geometry), the rules of nature and morals (philosophy), palm reading (chiromancy), interpreting the look of the body (physiognomics), evaluating the spots in the skin of the face (metoposcopy) and predicting events and phenomena by means of dreams (oneiromancy).

Born in Pavia (now Italy) as an illegitimate child, he was a strange, extravagant, eccentric man who wanted his name immortalized. He studied medicine and mathematics at the Universities of Milan, Pavia and Padua (1522–1525). He got his doctorate in Medicine in Padua (1526). He worked as doctor (1526–1532) in Sacco (near Padua). In 1533, he composed *De fato* (*On prediction*). He became a doctor in the Hospital of Saint Ambrose (Milan) and taught mathematics and other subjects in the *Scuole Piattine* (1534). He wrote *De ludo aleae* (*On gambling*) in 1541. He was appointed professor of medicine in Pavia in 1544 where he would lecture on medicine from 1545 to 1550. In 1545, he published his masterpiece in mathematics: *Ars magna*. He prepared his encyclopedic work *De subtilitate* in 1551, which was published a year later. He traveled to Scotland to help Archbishop John Hamilton whom he cured of his disease in 1552. Afterward, he lived in Milan writing and practicing medicine from 1553 to 1560. In 1554, he published his masterpiece on astrology: a commentary of the *Quadripartito* by Ptolomeus. On April 9, 1560, his first son, Giovanni Battista, was executed for killing his wife. This fact marked Cardano for life. He published his masterpiece on oneiromancy: *Somniorum Synesiorum libri IV* in 1562. He taught medicine in Bolonia (1563–1570). He was arrested by the Inquisition in 1570 on suspicion of heresy and unbelief. He was freed after his retraction. He went to Rome in 1571 where he started working on *De propria vita* in 1575 and where he died the following year.

Cardano restored and renewed traditional astrology. The renovation consisted of preparing complete and exhaustive horoscopes because he included chiromancy, oneiromancy, metoposcopy, physiognomics, and the mood of the subject. Cardano also prepared his own horoscope, showing that he had *harpocratic* or divination-related skills. He also prepared many horoscopes of famous persons: Vesalius, Edward VI of England, Pope Paul III, Erasmus, and Christ. The latter caused an outcry and led to his punishment by the Inquisition. He based his horoscopes on the position of the planets but also on conjectures and intuitions.

Furthermore, with people in political positions, he was very prudent and ambiguous in his favorable horoscopes to gain their goodwill and not to fall into disgrace. However, he failed in the case of Hamilton, because, in spite of giving a good horoscope, the bishop was hanged by his enemies several years later. The same occurs with his own horoscope because he predicted he was going to die at the age of 44, but he died when he was 75.

In the case of interpreting dreams, he affirmed he had a God-given gift of interpretation. Cardano had a dream before marrying in which he following a girl out of a house with a garden. When he reached the girl, the garden gates were closed, and then he could not go back to the house and he had to stay with the girl. Cardano's interpretation of this was that his marriage would not be happy, and it really was so.

On chiromancy, for instance, he predicted the execution of his first son for poisoning his wife. The sign was a red mark like a sword at the bottom of the ring finger on his right hand, which grew all along his finger. Then, at the date in question his son was beheaded.

However, his greatest contribution to astrology in general and horoscopes in particular was his book *De propia vita*. *De propia vita* is the complete horoscope of Cardano along with commentary. So, as a good horoscope it includes fatherland and ancestors, birth, parents, biography, corporal look, health, sport, desires of immortality, predictions, capacity of teaching, mood, friends, enemies, defamations, hobbies, gambling, clothing, way of walking, religiosity, houses, richness or poverty, travels, dreams, and personal defaults.

Justo Hernández

See also: Legal Regulation of Astrology; Medical Astrology; Renaissance and Reformation Astrology

Further Reading

Cardano, G. 2002. *Book of My Life*. New York: New York Review of Books.

Grafton, A. 2001. *Cardano's Cosmos: The Worlds and Works of a Renaissance Astrologer*. Cambridge, MA: Harvard University Press.

CATHOLICISM. *SEE* CHRISTIANITY.

CECCO D'ASCOLI (D. 1327)

Cecco d'Ascoli was born Francesco degli Stabili in Italy in the middle of the 13th century; the exact date is unknown. He was a scholar, scientist, poet, and astrologer who was burned as a heretic in Italy in 1327. He is most well known for his incomplete encyclopedic text, *L'Ascerba*, which expounded scientific theories and information of the time, and his necromantic commentary on *The Sphere of Sacrobosco* by Johannes de Sacrobosco, another astrologer and theorist of the 13th century. His contribution to science may have been limited to a few texts, but his defense of science in the face of persecution was most noteworthy.

The details of Francesco degli Stabili's early life are not particularly well known. He was born in or around Ascoli, Italy, which is reflected in his name, a diminutive version of his given name and his place of birth. He was well educated and became a professor of astrology/astronomy at the University of Bologna in the early 14th century. There Cecco was first censured for heresy by the Inquisition. The Catholic Church's issues with Cecco's teaching and writings lay mainly with his belief that "every man was under the irresistible influence of the stars that presided over his nativity," and even Jesus Christ also fell under their purview (Mariotti 1853, 176).

Cecco's teachings were problematic "not merely in identifying the star of the Magi with an astrological constellation, but in denying the exercise of free will even to Christ" (Thorndike 1934, 323).

As a result of his lectures, he was forbidden to teach and was forced to leave the university. The sentence also came with a heavy fine and a stipulation to attend religious sermons for rehabilitation. Cecco subsequently left Bologna and went to Florence to continue practicing astrology privately and at court, in spite of his condemnation by the Inquisition and their warning him to cease his heretical practices. It was there that Cecco encountered another inquisitor, who brought a second case against him. The Church and the Inquisition were satisfied with the first attempt to silence Cecco and put him back on the righteous path; however, his continued work with astronomy and belief about the powers of nature were not overlooked again. In 1327, he was sentenced to be burned at the stake along with all copies of his published work. The execution was carried out.

Cecco d'Ascoli's notoriety is attributed to his unwillingness to recant his beliefs about astronomy in the face of the Inquisition's threats, torture, and execution. Additionally, the Inquisition attempted to control the flow of Cecco's ideas by burning his writings along with his body and threatening all owners of his works with excommunication. They ultimately failed. Though some copies of his writings were burned with him, others survived. His *L'Ascerba*, left unfinished at the time of his death, was reprinted many times over the following centuries. He was memorialized as a scholar, scientist, and astronomer in 1935 with the naming of the lunar crater Cichus, Latin for "Cecco."

Josianne Leah Campbell

See Also: Christianity; Court Astrologers; Legal Regulation of Astrology; Medieval European Astrology

Further Reading

Mariotti, L. 1853. *A Historical Memoir of Fra Dolcino and His Times: Being an Account of a General Struggle for Ecclesiastical Reform, and of an Anti-Heretical Crusade in Italy, in the Early Part of the Fourteenth Century.* London: Longman, Brown, Green, and Longmans.

Peters, Edward. 1978. *The Magician, the Witch, and the Law.* Philadelphia: University of Pennsylvania Press.

Sharpes, Donald. 2007. *Outcasts and Heretics: Profiles in Independent Thought and Courage.* Lanham, MD: Lexington Books.

Thorndike, Lynn. 1934. *A History of Magic and Experimental Science*, vol. IV. New York: Columbia University Press.

CENTILOQUIUM

The *Centiloquium* (meaning "the one hundred sayings") is a pseudo-Ptolemaic work containing short, pithy aphorisms on astrological traditions and rules. Aphorisms from the *Centiloquium* include information on how to interpret natal charts, rules for determining appropriate times to engage in specific actions, and the relationship between celestial patterns and physical maladies. It embraces the teaching of horoscopes, delineates methods for finding hidden objects, and describes the astrological significance of fixed stars, constellations, and comets.

In the Muslim world, Arabic-speakers referred to the *Centiloquium* as the *Kitāb al-Ṯamara* (*The Book of Fruit*), a translation of the Greek title ***Καρπός*** (*Karpos*—literally "fruit"), which may have signified that the work was meant to be a condensed version of a larger treatise on astrology. It was among the many texts that Western scholars translated from Arabic into Latin, sometimes literally as *Liber Fructus*, during the 12th century. At least four known Latin translations exist from the 1130s and 1140s, including ones by Hugh of Santalla and John of Seville in 1136, Plato of Tivoli in 1138, and John of Spain in 1142 (Tester 1987, 152).

Though originally attributed to Ptolemy during the later Middle Ages by Latin, Hebrew, and Arab scholars, it likely originated in the early 10th century CE. No record of it exists until then, when it appears in a commentary by the Egyptian mathematician Abu Ja'far Ahmad Ibn Yusuf al-Misri (835–912 CE), known in the West as Hametus, during the Tulumid dynasty. Historian Richard Lemay has argued convincingly that Ahmad Ibn Yusuf is the actual author of the work (Lemay 1978, 91–107). Its Ptolemaic origin has been called into question since at least the 1550s, when Gerolamo Cardano noted that it contained astrological elements unknown in Ptolemy's time (Grafton 1999, 137). At various times, Abū Ma'shar al-Balkhī, William of Ockham, and Ali Ibn Ridwan have been suggested as the work's creator.

There is a good deal of evidence to suggest that the *Centiloquium* is non-Ptolemaic in origin. It combines two largely discordant versions of astrology—Ptolemaic, conjectural astrology based on a mathematical understanding of the heavens, and Hermetic astrology, which interpreted stellar influences through the lens of divine prophecy and natural magic. Slightly less than a third of the aphorisms from the *Centiloquium* are non-Ptolemaic in origin and many either directly contradict tenets of Ptolemaic astrology or exhibit characteristics not incorporated until well after the Ptolemy's time. For example, several aphorisms are concerned with ***καταρχή*** (*katarche*—literally "beginning" and usually translated into Latin as *electio*, or "choice"), in which the most astrologically auspicious time for beginning an event or activity is chosen. Similarly, there is an emphasis on houses (aphorisms 35, 59, and 79), decans (95 and 96), the importance of the fixed stars (28, 29, and 36), and the conjunction of Saturn and Jupiter (63), none of which featured prominently in the works of Ptolemy but which played a more important role in later Byzantine and medieval Arab astrology (Tester 1987, 93).

Other works circulated under this title during the Middle Ages, including the *Centiloquium Hermetis* attributed to Hermes Trismegistus and surviving only in the Latin version of Stephen of Messina, and the *Centiloquium Bethem* (i.e., of al-Bittani), which also existed only in Latin translation (Tester 1987, 154).

Justin Niermeier-Dohoney

See also: Cardano, Girolamo; Islamic Astrology; Medieval European Astrology

Further Reading

Campion, Nicholas. 2008. *A History of Western Astrology, Vol. I: The Ancient World*. London: Bloomsbury.

Grafton, Anthony. 1999. *Cardano's Cosmos: The Worlds and Works of a Renaissance Astrologer*. Cambridge, MA: Harvard University Press.

Lemay, Helen. 1980. "The Stars and Human Sexuality: Some Medieval Scientific Views." *Isis* 71: 127–137.

Lemay, Richard. 1978. "Origins and Success of the Kitāb Tamara of Abū Ja'far Ahmad ibn Yūsuf ibn Ibrahim from the Tenth to Seventeenth Century in the World of Islam and the Latin West." In *Proceedings of the First International Symposium for the History of Arabic Science*. Syria: University of Aleppo Institute of Arabic Science.

Tester, S. J. 1987. *A History of Western Astrology*. Wolfbridge, UK: Boydell.

CHAUCER, GEOFFREY (CA. 1340–1400)

Geoffrey Chaucer was born in London, England, around the 1340s; the exact date is unknown. He was a soldier, diplomat, and clerk, serving in numerous royal posts before becoming a writer. He died in London and was the first to be buried in Poet's Corner at Westminster Abbey. Chaucer is known for his use of the English vernacular in his literary works, most famously in *The Canterbury Tales*. However, Geoffrey Chaucer also penned one of the earliest English language scientific manuals, *Treatise on the Astrolabe*, illustrating the practical use of an instrument used in the astronomical and astrological sciences of his time.

Medieval Europeans beliefs about the heavenly bodies and their power varied widely. Some people thought that one's birth day, time, month, season, and year foretold the characteristics that appeared in one's personality or appearance: natal astrology. Some people believed in medical astrology; planets and stars influenced bodily functions and the four humors. Still others understood that judicial astrology could be used to predict the future or fate of a person or institution. "It is not astonishing, then, that the great monuments of literature in the mediaeval period . . . are filled with astronomical and astrological allusions; for these are but reflections of vital human interests of the times" (Grimm 1919, 4). Chaucer alluded to all these beliefs in his poetic works in order to reflect on contemporary culture.

In *The Canterbury Tales*, references to astronomy and astrology appear in relation to every one of the characters. Even the order of the stories is thought to be "a planetary pattern of descent . . . link[ing] the progress of his pilgrims with that of the wandering stars" (Astell 1996, 93). For example, The Wife of Bath's prologue draws on natal astrology in the manner in which the character describes herself ruled by Venus and Mars, and marked by both. She is lusty and ruled by passion and notes that it was in her stars to be so. In the general prologue, the Doctor of Physik is also noted to have wide knowledge of astronomy in order to cure ailments; this seemed to be a positive attribute in the profession, illustrating the belief that it was necessary for a doctor to obtain knowledge of both earthly and heavenly influences on the human body. Though Chaucer alluded to fate within his poetry, he avoided overt references to judicial astrology, which was quite dangerous at the time because it challenged the Catholic Church's views on free will. Recognizing this, he never overtly stated his own belief about astrology in this realm. The varying voices within *The Canterbury Tales* helped to avoid the issue. "This fact may point to a wise caution on his part lest his evident interest in astrology (which was closely associated with magic, and hence, indirectly, with sorcery) might involve him in difficulties with Mother Church" (Grimm 1919, 57). Though interested in astrology and astronomy, Chaucer did not endorse all methods and practices of the science. He disapproved of the "shady observances and quackery connected with its application" (Grimm 1919, 57). No matter what Chaucer may have believed about different practices within astrology, he did recognize its importance in the lives of English people. "His originality in employing astrology for poetic purposes is incontestable and is, perhaps, unrivaled in the entire realm of mediaeval literature" (Wedel 1920, 143).

Chaucer's written work on astronomy and astrology was not limited to poetic expression. "In 1390, he wrote one of the earliest scientific textbooks written in the English language, *The Treatise on the Astrolabe*" (Baker and Cartwright 2005, 15). This book stood apart from his poetry because it was so technical. It reflects a different reason for the discussion of astronomy; it is "a professedly scientific work designed to instruct" (Grimm 1919, 28). Chaucer's personal beliefs are more ambiguous in *The Canterbury Tales*, contributing more to character description and identification of time. But *The Treatise on the Astrolabe* provides "sufficient evidence that he was thoroughly familiar with the technical details of the astronomical science of his day" (Grimm 1919, 28).

Geoffrey Chaucer's works, with their astrological allusions in the English vernacular, are still widely appreciated and studied today. His reputation as a scholar and author was memorialized with the naming of an asteroid, number 2984 discovered on December 30, 1981, by E. Bowell. Additionally, a lunar crater was named after Chaucer.

Josianne Leah Campbell

See also: Astrolabe; Medieval European Astrology

Further Reading

Astell, Ann W. 1996. *Chaucer and the Universe of Learning*. Ithaca, NY: Cornell University Press.

Baker, Brian, and Cartwright, John H. 2005. *Literature and Science: Social Impact and Interaction*. Santa Barbara, CA: ABC-CLIO.

Grimm, Florence M. 1919. *Astronomical Lore in Chaucer*. The Library of Alexandria. Lincoln: University of Nebraska.

Wedel, Theodore Otto. 1920. *The Medieval Attitude toward Astrology: Particularly in England*. New Haven, CT: Yale University Press.

CHINESE ASTROLOGY

Chinese astrology observes irregular phenomena in the sky and predicts the fate of states or groups of people by it. It was rooted in the idea of respecting and observing the heavens. It began in early Chinese civilization and was systemized during the Spring and Autumn (770 BCE–476 BCE) and the Warring States (476 BCE to 221 BCE) periods with the development of astronomy, but after the Han Dynasty (202 BCE–220 CE) with the establishment of the United Empire it began to be restricted and had little development. Annual and diurnal changes of the sky were the rule of the heavens, which people must follow carefully, but only special changes or abnormal phenomena were the objects of astrology. In order to correspond different stars or different areas of the heavens with different regions on the ground, fen ye theory, or field allocation theory, was established, which assigned certain stars or areas of the heavens to certain people or areas on the Earth.

Astrology originated with Chinese civilization. As Sima Qian pointed out: "Ever since the people have existed, when have successive rulers not systematically calendared the movements of the Sun, Moon, stars and asterisms?" Regular change of the sky was the rule of the heavens, while irregular phenomena were regarded as the omen of special things on the ground. The complete Chinese astrological system was established through the Spring and Autumn period to the Warring States period, along with Chinese astronomy.

The 28 xiu system had been established at the latest by the Warring States period. The 28 xiu are 28 asterisms along the celestial equator or the ecliptic divided by ancient Chinese. In fact they are constellations. Some of the 28 xiu may have been created in early Zhou (1046–771 BCE) or even earlier. The 28 xiu were used together with the North Pole to constitute the equatorial coordinate in Chinese astronomy. Their main role in astrology was in the field allocation system.

Another dividing diagram along the celestial equator or the ecliptic was the 12 ci system. Originally the 12 ci were divided in order to delineate the movement of Jupiter. In early times the sidereal period of Jupiter was regarded as 12 years thus 12 ci was created. In the Han Dynasty Liu Xin (died in 23 CE) first realized that Jupiter's sidereal year was not exactly 12 years but had a leap ci every 144 years. Each of the 12 ci had its own name, and, before Liu Xin, Jupiter was regarded as moving one ci each year. In the early stages, the 12 ci were bound to the 28 xiu, 8 of the 12 ci contained 2 xiu each, and 4 of them contained 3 xiu. During the Warring States period, the measuring instrument hun yi, an armillary sphere, came out, and the 12 ci began to be separate from the 28 xiu and were measured according to the position of the sun against the background of stars. The main role the 12 ci played in astrology was in that Jupiter's position among the 12 ci had astrological meaning, especially concerning drought, floods, and harvest; on the other hand, the 12 ci were combined to the 28 xiu system in the field allocation system.

Whether the 28 xiu and the 12 ci were along the celestial equator or the ecliptic is a controversial issue. Chinese astronomy mainly adopted the equatorial coordinate system, as the North Pole was not only important in astronomy but also in Chinese culture. The earliest measurements of the widths of 28 xiu were along the celestial equator. In the first century BCE astronomers began to measure the

28 xiu along the ecliptic. But throughout Chinese history there was no concept of the ecliptic pole, instead, the widths of the 28 xiu in ecliptic were measured along an ecliptic circle on the armillary sphere using the celestial North Pole as the pole.

In the Xia, Shang, and Western Zhou (ca. 2070–771 BCE) times, the kingdoms were united. But in the Spring and Autumn and Warring States periods the kings of the Zhou were weak while the feudal states were strong, and wars happened very often. In this age of chaos, as Sima Qian pointed out, "it was especially anxious to watch the omens and observe the signs in the stars." Astrologers were active in feudal states, observing the sky carefully and diligently. Among them there were two important figures, Gan De and Shi Shenfu (or Shi Shen). Gan De wrote an eight-volume book entitled *Tianwen xingzhan*, *Astronomy and Astrology*, and Shi Shenfu wrote an eight-volume book entitled *Tianwen*, *Astronomy*. These two books are lost now, but much of their content was retained in *Kaiyuan zhanjing*, an astrological book composed by Qutan Xida (Gautama Siddha) in the eighth century CE. Besides Gan De and Shi Shenfu, there was another famous astrologer Wu Xian, whose dates are unknown and who was more like a legendary figure. Observation of stars by Gan De, Shi Shenfu, and Wu Xian constitutes the foundation of traditional Chinese star catalog, and they also observed the five planets and other celestial phenomena carefully. Their works formed the main foundation of Chinese astrology.

Because Chinese astrology aimed to predict the fate of the states or the country by irregular celestial phenomenon, after the Han Dynasty when the United Empire was established, astrology gradually became forbidden to ordinary people and only royal astronomical officials were allowed to learn it. In the Han Dynasty, Sima Qian, a great historian and astronomer, set up a chapter on astronomy and astrology entitled tian guan shu (the Chapter on the Heavenly Offices) in his great history book *Shiji* (*The Grand Scribe's Records*). This chapter was elaborately organized and included almost all aspects of Chinese astrology. After Sima Qian, several other persons added new content to the knowledge of astrology, but they were not professional astrologers, instead they were scholars and their new theories were based on the popular cosmology and philosophy of that time. Jing Fang (77–37 BCE) was most prominent among them. He contributed much to astrology, but his theory was mostly based on the wu xing, or five phase theory, which was one of the dominant philosophical theories not only of the Han but even through Chinese history. After the Han, though, there came several astrological books. They were basically composed from former books by astronomical officials, and astrology had little further development. Sometimes when a special celestial phenomenon appeared, astronomical officials reported the phenomenon with its astrological meanings in astrological books to the royal court. Astrology became secret and even astronomers' astrological practices were seldom recorded.

The Epistemological Foundation and Basic Practice Rule of Chinese Astrology

Chinese astrology was deeply rooted in Chinese cosmology. In ancient Chinese culture there was no supreme God, but heaven was regarded as a supreme being.

The phenomena shown on the sky were called tian xiang, tian means heaven or sky, xiang means image. Ancient Chinese believed that what appeared on the sky was just an expression of the Dao, or Way, of the Heaven. As an official of the Spring and Autumn period explained about a comet: "Things of the heaven were always shown in images." Mature cosmogony from the Warring States period to the Han insisted that Dao, or Way, was the root of everything, its evolution creating everything that had body and shape on the Earth, and creating the images in the sky on the heaven. So the images in the sky and the bodies with shapes on the Earth could interact with each other. *Tian wen zhi chapter in Han shu (Treatise on Astronomy in the History of the Former Han)*, the official history of the former Han (202 BCE–8 CE) composed in the first century CE, summarized this as: "All that clearly documented in astronomical charts and books, permanent inner and outer guan (constellations) and xiu are totally 181, accumulating to 783 stars—they all have the images of states, countries, officials, palaces and various kinds of things." Their irregular changes and appearances of anomalous phenomena are "all the spirits of yin and yang, whose roots are on the ground and rise up into the heaven." So the names of stars contain almost everything. The area near the North Pole was regarded as the royal area, and the stars in this region were named after the royal family and officials, including di, the emperor, taizi, the prince, and so on.

The most important irregular change of stars was the change in lightness, and predictions by them were mostly based on what the stars symbolized.

Eclipses were important objects of astrology. Because the sun was regarded as the symbol of yang, or positive, and among people it was the symbol of the king or emperor, solar eclipses were more important than lunar eclipses. In the Han Dynasty astronomers began to calculate eclipses, and with more and more accurate calculations eclipses became less important in astrology.

Comets were called hui, which meant broom, because the tail of a comet looks like a broom. Because the basic use of a broom is to sweep, the original meaning of comets in astrology was "to sweep the old and arrange the new." Its extending meanings included change of government, military affairs, and so on. Astrology attached great importance to comets. The silk manuscripts unearthed from Mawangdui, in Changsha, buried in 168 BCE contained 29 figures of comets in various shapes, each giving the name of the comet and its astrological meanings. There were 18 different names in total. All the predictions are ominous, such as "there would be military affairs, and the general is going to die," and "there would be disease all over the world."

Ke xing, or guest star, was another kind of irregular star. Most of the ke xing in Chinese literature referred to novas or supernovas. As expressed by its name, ke xing in astrology mainly meant the coming of guests. The guests may be friendly or hostile.

The five planets were also very important. Their colors and rays, their motions, their positions against the background of stars, their relations with the sun and the moon, and the relations between each of them are all the concern of astrology. In early Chinese history people believed that all the five planets had no retrograde motion. During the Warring States period Gan De and Shi Shenfu first realized that Mars and Mercury had retrograde motions. In the Han, it was realized that all five planets had retrograde motions. From the Han on, astronomers explained this as in ancient times there had been a peaceful and prosperous time so all the five planets had no retrograde motion, then came wars and chaos and the planets began to have retrograde motion. Among the five planets, Saturn was a fairly auspicious planet, Jupiter mostly related to harvest, Venus mainly related to war, Mars to chaos and fire, and Mercury to disasters and death, but not very strictly. The Mawangdui silk manuscripts also contained an astrological text concerning the five planets.

Clouds, rainbows, and winds were also objects of astrology. Because clouds change all the time, they could be observed at any time, but only those in special shape were important. The rainbow was beautiful, but its astrological meaning was mostly ominous. Observing the clouds and winds in special dates, such as winter solstice and the first day of a new year, predicted the coming year's harvest.

Fen Ye or Field Allocation: The Scheme of Correspondence between Heaven and the Earth

In predicting good or bad luck for people by special phenomena in the heaven, which place on the Earth was going to be affected by the celestial phenomenon needed to be made clear. Ancient Chinese astrology created the fen ye theory, or field allocation theory. Before the Qin, there had been mainly four kinds of field allocation patterns: the pattern of a single star (or single group of stars), the pattern of 28 xiu and 12 ci, the pattern of the five planets, and the pattern of the Big Dipper.

Sporadic records of the earliest field allocation idea were scattered in classics, according to which it could be seen that this early idea was the pattern of a single star (or single group of stars) allocation. It originated before the Xia Dynasty, and its basic idea was that a clan corresponded to one star or a group of stars. The most famous example was in zuo zhuan (the commentary of Zuo to the Spring and Autumn Annals) in recording the stars of the Xia people and the Shang people. It recorded:

Formerly, Gao Xin had two sons, the eldest was named E Bo and the younger Shi Chen. They lived in Kuanglin but could not get along, daily taking up shield and lance against one another. In the end, Gao Xin could no longer condone it and removed E Bo to Shangqiu to have charge of [the asterism] Chen (Great Fire, α Scopio); the ancestors of the Shang people followed him, therefore Great Fire is the Shang asterism. [Gao Xin] removed Shi Chen to Da Xia to have charge of Shen [Orion's belt], so the people of the Tang followed him, and there served the houses of Xia and Shang. And the story went on that in the beginning of Western Zhou Shuyu was enfeoffed to the territory of Tang and in Spring and Autumn period the state of Jin, who were Shuyu's offspring also took the three stars of Shen [Orion's belt] as their stars.

Gao Xin was a legendary figure who lived before Xia. In the first story, he arranged his two sons in different places and each of them had his own star (or group of stars). In the second story, E Bo not only made sacrifice to his star but also determined seasons by it. This would be the earliest pattern of field allocation. The first story also shows that, though the earliest single star was allocated to a certain tribe, it could be transferred to the territory, then in later times to the state in this territory.

Twenty-eight xiu and 12 ci allocation may have emerged in 11th century BCE at the beginning of Zhou. Zhou li (the rites of Zhou) recorded that in Western Zhou one of the official Bao zhang's duties was to "discern the places of the 9 zhou by star-earth (field allocation scheme); every fief has its own star to observe its ominous or auspicious luck." According to Chinese classics, Da Yu (Yu the Great), the founder of the Xia, divided the whole region under his control into 9 zhou. In the Warring States period, the 9 zhou evolved into 12 zhou or states. Sima Qian said: "The 28 she (means xiu) dominate the 12 zhou, the handle of the Big Dipper works concurrently, it has been a long time." During the Warring State period the field allocation scheme of 28 xiu and 12 ci was completed. Several works of literature recorded this scheme. In this scheme 28 xiu were combined to 12 ci, assigned to all the feudal states of that time.

In the Han when the United Empire had been established, the concepts of 9 zhou or 12 zhou gradually faded, instead, the new concept of zhong guo (the central country, means China) against yi di (means foreign countries) emerged. This also reflected in field allocation theory, especially in the chapter on the heavenly offices in the Grand Scribe's Records by Sima Qian.

The field allocation scheme of the five planets was based on the wu xing, or five phase, theory. The five phase theory divided time, space, colors, virtues, and other phenomena, each into five subcategories, and then assigned each of the subcategories into one of five phases, under the name of wood, fire, earth, metal, and water. People believed that the five of them had the relation of generating, conquering, and replacement. The five planets were combined into the five phase theory, Jupiter corresponded to wood, Mars to fire, Saturn to earth, Venus to metal, and Mercury to water. The astrological text on the five planets from Mawangdui assigned the five planets according to the five phase theory; that is, Mars to the states in the south, Mercury to the states in the north, Saturn to the states in the center, and Venus to the states in the west. Jupiter was lost from the text because of the damage on the silk, but it would be assigned to the states in the east. Sima Qian assigned the five planets to concrete states in his tianguan shu chapter in *Shiji* (the chapter on the heavenly offices in *The Grand Scribe's Records*) as: the territory of Qin to Venus, the territories of Wu and Chu to Mars, the territories of Yan and Qi to Mercury, the territories of Song and Zheng to Saturn, and the territory of Jin also to Mercury. Sima Qian's allocation method obeyed the same rule as the Mawangdui text but substituted directions of states for the concrete names of states.

The field allocation scheme of the Big Dipper was quite simple, but it reflected that in ancient China the Big Dipper was very important.

Yi Xing (683–727), a great astronomer of the Tang Dynasty (618–907), was the only one who constructed a new field allocation scheme after Han. He based his

Chinese and Western "Zodiacs"

The cycle of 12 animals (rat, ox, tiger, rabbit, dragon, snake, horse, goat, monkey, rooster, pig, dog) used in Chinese astrology is often identified as a "zodiac." However, it is both similar to and different from the Western zodiac. The Western zodiac divides the year into 12 parts, while the primary meaning of the Chinese zodiac, particularly in the popularization of Chinese astrology in the West, is identifying a cycle of years. However, Chinese astrologers also apply the Chinese zodiac to months, as well as days and hours, in a fashion similar to the Western zodiac. The Western zodiac is based on constellations, while the Chinese zodiac is not. All of the Chinese signs are animals, while only some of the Western ones are. The Chinese zodiac, often with slight variations, is used widely through East and Central Asia.

scheme on his own understanding of the relation between the structures of the heavens and that of the Earth. His theory was complicated and obscure.

After the Han until the Qing (1644–1911, the last dynasty in Chinese history), field allocation theory became a part of geographic theory rather than astrology, because astrology became secret and beyond the knowledge of ordinary people. Scholars in composing treatises on geography or local chronicles sometimes included the sky area, constellations, or stars of every administrative region, sometimes in even more detailed form, indicating "from what degree of which xiu to what degree of which xiu," but it had little relation to astrology.

See also: Buddhism; Bureau of Astronomy (China); Mundane Astrology; Sima Qian

Further Reading

Cullen, Christopher. 2011. "Understanding the Planets in Ancient China: Prediction and Divination in the Wu xing zhan." *Early Science and Medicine* 16: 218–251.
Nakayama, Shigeru. 1966. "Characteristics of Chinese Astrology." *ISIS* 57, no. 4: 442–454.
Needham, Joseph. 1959. *Science and Civilization in China, Volume 3. Mathematics and the Sciences of the Heavens and the Earth.* Cambridge, MA: Cambridge University Press.
Pankenier, David W. 2013. *Astrology and Cosmology in Early China.* Cambridge, MA: Cambridge University Press.

CHRISTIANITY

Christianity has coexisted with astrology for its entire existence. The relationship between the two has varied, as Christians have tried to synthesize astrology with their religion in various ways, or have opposed it in various ways to varying degrees. In the contemporary world, the bonds between Christianity and astrology have become weaker but still exist. The issues around which this relationship revolves—the power of the stars versus the power of God, the relationship of astral determinism and human free will, and the fear of astrology becoming star-worship—have remained remarkably constant over this long period.

The New Testament and Astrology

Astrology accompanied Jesus, the founder of Christianity, from his birth. An early Christian legend, preserved in the Gospel of Matthew, speaks of a star that marked the birth of Christ and three "wise men" who came from the East to see him. Because the wise men were interpreters of the stars, the Gospel puts astrology near the beginning of the Christian story, and the idea that the wise men were astrologers became widespread. Subsequent Christian defenders of astrology have pointed to the Magi as precedents for God speaking to and through interpreters of the stars. The star itself also has vexed generation of Christian astrologers as to its nature and meaning. Theories have ranged from a conjunction to a comet or an outright miracle.

Another long-standing problem for Christians dealing with astrology was the natal horoscope of Jesu. Drawing a horoscope for Christ implied that he was subject to the stars, at least as a man, and was anathema to many Christians. In the Middle Ages, astrologers were even executed for the crime of drawing Christ's horoscope. The fact that the birthdate of Jesus is disputed adds to the complexity of the problem.

The other great influence of the New Testament on Christian astrologers is the Book of Revelation, whose complicated time scheme, combined with those of the "prophetic books" of the Hebrew Bible such as Daniel, is ripe for astrological analysis, particularly given the books emphasis on the number seven, the number of the days of the week and the seven classical planets including the sun and moon. The connection between the time scheme of Revelation and astrology became stronger with the later development of mundane astrology. Revelation also refers to "signs in the heavens" preceding the last days, relating changes in the sky to changes on Earth, a fundamentally astrological idea.

Astrology and the Early Church

Astrology was deeply linked with pagan religion and the philosophical learning that the early Christians rejected, and it is unsurprising that the early Christian writers had little good to say about it. Christian attacks on astrology begin to appear in

The Three Magi and Astrology

The most famous astrologers in Christianity were the so-called three Magi mentioned in the gospel of Matthew as having visited the infant Christ. Matthew is very vague, even on the number of the visitors who brought precious gifts of gold, frankincense, and myrrh, but elaborate legends have grown up around the three in the subsequent Christian tradition. Because these "wise men" or "magi" from the East as Matthey refers to them, were guided by the star of Bethlehem, it is natural to think of them as astrologers. (The popular idea that the Magi were kings emerged later.) However, many antiastrological Christians have rejected the idea that the Magi were astrologers, asserting that their following the star was a special case that has nothing to do with astrology as practiced.

the literature of the second century CE. The early church fathers who denounced astrology included some of the most influential writers in both the Greek and Latin traditions of Christianity, including among many others Augustine (354–430) for the Latins and John Chrysostom (349–407) for the Greek-speakers. Chrysostom's Sixth Homily on the Gospel of Matthew is specifically directed against astrology, and contains an elaborate discussion of the Magi and the Star, designed to show that their activities bore no relation to those of astrologers and that the Star was a clearly supernatural phenomenon. Augustine, who had sought the advice of astrologers in his youth, combined religious arguments against astrology like its opposition to human free will with traditional skeptical ones like the differing fates of twins born at the same time. The Christian Roman Empire continued to issue decrees against astrology. Christian emperors were following the doctrines of Christianity, but they were also following the traditions of the pagan empire, which had sought to suppress or regulate astrology as a danger to the state.

Astrology in the Byzantine and Orthodox Traditions

The official hostility to astrology of the Greek Fathers was carried on in the Byzantine Empire, where state and church authorities opposed astrology despite the fact that many Byzantines practiced astrology and even emperors consulted astrologers. The church's hostility was a cause of the virtual eclipse of Byzantine astrology during the seventh and eighth centuries. It revived around 800 with a stimulus from the Arabic world.

The hostility to astrology found in the Byzantine Church has continued in the tradition of the Orthodox Churches that emerged from the Byzantine tradition. This opposition is expressed in Orthodox canon, or religious, law. Although the ban on astrology has not prevented astrology from being practiced in Orthodox societies, it has prevented the emergence of the type of synthesis between astrology and Christianity found in the medieval and Renaissance Catholic Church.

The Rebirth of Astrology in Medieval Europe and the Scholastic Synthesis

Astrology had virtually disappeared in the West following the fall of the Roman Empire. The church controlled most calendrical and astronomical knowledge but was more concerned with the calculation of the date of Easter and allied religious problems than with astrology. What changed this was the flood of astrological, astronomical, and natural-philosophical knowledge coming from the Islamic world beginning in the 11th century.

The new astrology posed numerous problems for Christians. One was the nature of astrological causation. If the stars determined human action, that threatened both the omnipotence of God and human free will. Another problem associated with the new astrology was the relation of religion to mundane astrology. Drawing on Persian precedents, Arabic astrologers had worked out a scheme for world history in which the introduction of new religions coincided with particularly significant "Great Conjunctions" of Saturn and Jupiter. Applied to Christianity, this raised the same problem as the nativity of Christ—what was the role of the stars, if any, in the making of the Christian church?

The work of reconciling astrology and Christianity was accomplished by a succession of Christian thinkers mostly working in universities, of whom the most important was the Dominican scholar Albertus Magnus. Magnus's solution, which had precedents, was to view the stars as impelling, but not compelling. Knowledge of astrology could even enable a person to resist when the stars were pushing him or her toward a bad end. This solution was adopted in the "Scholastic synthesis" of Thomas Aquinas (1225–1274), Albertus's pupil and the most influential theologian of the Middle Ages, and was also broadly accepted by Thomas's main rival, Duns Scotus (1266–1308). Numerous clerics and leaders of the church in the Middle Ages either practiced astrology or patronized the work of astrologers, and this was generally not seen as a problem. The Franciscan order was particularly seen to be friendly to astrologers. Some opponents of astrology were found among Christians, such as Nicholas Oresme (1320–1382), but they were not the dominant party.

The Renaissance, the Neoplatonic Synthesis, and the Revival of Opposition to Astrology

The Renaissance saw a revitalization of Christian astrology in an explicitly magical tradition, in part sparked by the rediscovery of the works of Plato and the Hermetic corpus. Christian magi such as Marsilio Ficino, Paracelsus, John Dee, and Tommaso Campanella tried to found a Christian and magical astrology. This was different from the old Scholastic synthesis, although it drew on it, because it was less about the power the stars exerted on the world and humanity and more about the correspondences between the universe as a macrocosm and the individual as a microcosm. The power the planets exerted was conceived of less in physical terms, as had the basically Aristotelian Scholastics, and more in spiritual terms, with each planet seen not so much as a physical object but as the home of a spirit. The practice of this spiritual and magical astrology could help draw the soul closer to God. For Giordano Bruno, astral magic may have taken him away from Christianity altogether, but he was the exception during this period.

The Renaissance also saw a revival of Christian hostility to astrology, often associated with movements for church reform, both Catholic and Protestant. Pico della Mirandola (1463–1494), a disciple of Ficino, wrote a denunciation of astrology that combined religious and skeptical arguments to become a classic of the genre. The Dominican friar and religious reformer Girolamo Savonarola (1452–1498) wrote a more religiously focused work also denouncing astrology. Antiastrological efforts in the Catholic Church led to major condemnations of astrology by Popes Sixtus V (Pope, 1585–1590) and Urban VIII (Pope, 1623–1644). The Council of Trent, which defined Catholic doctrine, had taken a relatively mild position on astrology, only condemning those astrological works that asserted that their predictions were certain, thus infringing on God's sole certain knowledge of the future. These condemnations, however, had as much to do with the potentially destabilizing influence of astrology on the Papacy through astrological predictions of the Pope's death as they had to do with purely theological issues. Sixtus's 1586 decree is known as *Coeli et terrae*. Although it forbade all astrology outside the realms of agriculture and medicine, in practice it was not enforced even after it was reaffirmed by Urban VIII in *Inscrutabilis Judiciorum Dei* (1631) and the laxer standard of Trent continued to hold sway. The newly centralized Inquisition, however, did take note and question astrologers suspected of determinism, such as Galileo Galilei.

The leading Protestant reformers, Martin Luther (1483–1546) and John Calvin (1509–1564), were also hostile although this attitude was far from universal among Protestants. Luther's disciple Philipp Melanchthon (1497–1560) was a supporter of astrology who helped preserve its place in the German universities he was reforming. (And it was German Lutheran universities in this tradition that educated the great astronomer/astrologers Tycho Brahe and Johannes Kepler.) Astrology and Protestantism may even have been allied in some ways, with astrology preparing the way for Protestantism by providing an alternative to the authority of the Catholic Church, while Protestantism, by denying the wonderworking power of the saints and the sacraments, cleared a space for astrology alongside other forms of popular magic. The apocalyptic expectations of early Protestants also contributed to widespread interest in the "great conjunctions" of Saturn and Jupiter in the late 16th century. Protestants usually looked at the new magical astrology with suspicion, however, and supported a naturalistic astrology based on Ptolemy and Aristotle rather than Neoplatonism. Some astrologers coped with religious opposition by flaunting their piety, as did the English protestant William Lilly, whose major astrological textbook was called *Christian Astrology*. Although there is no reason to doubt Lilly's Christian faith, this was in part a defensive maneuver, as many of the Puritan Christian ministers who dominated English religion at that time were opponents of astrology and of Lilly in particular.

Christianity and Astrology Part Ways

The 18th-century Enlightenment saw the decline of astrology as well as the creation of the first intellectual movement to challenge the dominance of Christianity in European thought since the pagan Roman Empire. The question of astrology was far down on the list of challenges the Christian church was facing, and little changed in their relationship.

The revival of astrology in the 19th century did not revive the astrological question as a major issue for Christian churches. Although some astrologers continued to be Christian, astrology was making new religious alliances, such as that with Theosophy, a movement founded in 1875. At the same time, the growing secularization of society in the West made the question of astrology's relationship to Christianity far less urgent.

Christianity and Astrology in the Contemporary World

Christianity and astrology continue to coexist. In the United States, belief in astrology does not vary much between Christians and the general population.

Contemporary Christian fundamentalists, ranging from extremist fringe figures such as Texe Marrs (b. 1944) to the mainstream Southern Baptist Convention, attack astrology as an occult and New Age practice, but as one among many others, with little interest in the technicalities of astrology itself. The extreme fundamentalist view of astrology as part of a magical system, in fact, resembles that of Renaissance magicians such as Ficino, with the exception that fundamentalists view the whole system as satanically inspired. Ironically, hostility to astrology among fundamentalists and evangelicals can go along with an obsessive interest in astrological aspects of the coming apocalypse, as in the recent literature on successions of lunar eclipses known as "blood moons" and their relationship with the End-Times.

The Catholic Church does not see astrology as demonically inspired, but it does forbid it. This position was formally stated in the catechism issued in 1994, which forbade astrology alongside other forms of divination. Some Catholics have interpreted this as forbidding all forms of astrology, while others see it merely as a restatement of the Church's long-held position against astrological determinism and insist that it leaves the door open for a nondeterministic astrology.

William E. Burns

See also: Albertus Magnus; Antiastrological Thought; Apocalypticism; Art; Ashmole, Elias; Astrotheology; Bible; Bonatti, Guido; Brahe, Tycho; Bruno, Giordano; Campanella, Tommaso; Cardano, Giorlamo; Cecco d'Ascoli; Chaucer, Geoffrey; D'Ailly, Pierre; Dee, John; Fate; Ficino, Marsilio; Gadbury, John; Galilei, Galileo; Judaism; Kepler, Johannes; Legal Regulation of Astrology; Lilly, William; Medieval European Astrology; Morandi, Orazio; Mundane Astrology; Nostradamus; Paracelsus; Partridge, John; Placidus; Pont, Robert; Renaissance and Reformation Astrology; Theosophy; Villena, Enrique de

Further Reading

Barnes, Robin. 2015. *Astrology and Reformation.* New York: Oxford University Press.

Campion, Nicholas. 1994. *The Great Year: Astrology, Millenarianism and History in the Western Tradition.* London: Penguin.

Campion, Nicholas. 2014. *Astrology and Cosmology in the World's Religions.* New York: NYU Press.

Chevalier, Jacques M. 1997. *A Postmodern Revelation: Signs of Astrology and the Apocalypse.* Toronto: University of Toronto Press.

Collis, Robert. 2010. "Maxim the Greek, Astrology, and the Great Conjunction of 1524." *The Slavonic and East European Review* 88: 601–623.

Hegedus, Tim. 2007. *Early Christianity and Ancient Astrology.* New York: Peter Lang.

Kjellgren, Martin. 2011. *Taming the Prophets: Astrology, Orthodoxy and the Word of God in Early Modern Sweden.* Lund: Sekel Bokforlag.

Smoller, Laura Ackerman. 1994. *History, Prophecy and the Stars: The Christian Astrology of Pierre d'Ailly, 1350–1420.* Princeton: Princeton University Press.

Southern Baptist Convention. 1988. "Resolution on the New Age." http://www.sbc.net/resolutions/785/resolution-on-the-new-age-movement

Thomas, Keith. 1971. *Religion and the Decline of Magic: Studies in Popular Beliefs in Sixteenth and Seventeenth-Century England.* London: Weidenfeld and Nicolson.

COMETS

The dramatic appearance of comets and their relative rarity when viewed with the naked eye has invested them with astrological and religious meaning in many cultures. Comets were considered to be presages of disaster by ancient Mesopotamian, Indian, Greek, and Chinese civilizations among others. The Romans saw a comet as the sign of the death of an emperor or other great personage. This idea survived the coming of Christianity and was endorsed by many who denied the validity of traditional astrology, although a comet could also be seen as an endorsement of a powerful ruler. Some Christians even claimed that the star of Bethlehem that had presaged the birth of Christ had been a comet. Christians and others also viewed comets, like other unusual celestial phenomena, as possible heralds of the end of the world. In China, a comet was viewed as resembling a broom, coming to sweep away old things. The Hindu astrological classic, the *Brithat Samhita* by Varahamihira, claimed that comets portended great changes and classified them by shape. A comet with three tails and three colors would herald the end of the current phase of the world.

Natural philosophers in the West debated on what comets actually were. The Greek philosopher Aristotle (384–322 BCE) claimed that comets were exhalations of flaming gas from the Earth. This view was followed by the Aristotelians who dominated natural philosophy in the Middle Ages. Comets, which appeared and

Montezuma's Comet

Comets presaged great changes for Mesoamericans as well as other peoples. The following passage shows the Aztec ruler Montezuma afraid of a comet that interpreters fear refers to a foreign invader. Shortly afterward, the Spanish invader Hernando Cortez and his army landed in Mexico. Like other accounts, its ultimate source is Aztecs remembering preconquest days after the conquest, so the connection of comet and invasion may have been clearer in hindsight.

> Montezuma, who was too superstitious to look with indifference on so uncommon a phenomenon, consulted his astrologers upon it; but they being unable to divine its meaning, applied to the king of Acolhuacan, who was reputed able in astrology, and in the art of divination. These kings, although they were related to, and perpetual allies of, each other, did not live in much harmony together, the king of Acolhuacan having put to death his son Huexotzincatzin, as we shall see presently, paying no regard to the prayers of Montezuma, who, as the uncle of that prince, had interfered in his behalf. For a long time past they had neither met with their usual frequency, nor confidence; but on this occasion the mysterious dread which seized the mind of Montezuma incited him to profit by the knowledge of the king Nezahualpilli, for which reason he intreated him to come to Mexico to consult with him upon an event which appeared equally to concern them both. Nezahualpilli went, and after having conferred, at length, with Montezuma, was of opinion, according to the account of historians, that the comet predicted the future disasters of those kingdoms, by the arrival of a new people.

Clavigero, Francesco. 1806. *History of Mexico*, trans. Charles Cullen, 303. Richmond, VA: William Prichard.

disappeared, waxed and waned, were incompatible with the Aristotelian view of the perfect, unchanging heavens. For Aristotelians, the study of comets was part of meteorology, and irrelevant to astronomy or astrology. The opposing view, held by the Roman philosopher Seneca (4 BCE–65 CE) among others, was that comets were heavenly objects like stars and planets. Neither interpretation precluded the idea that comets were divine signs, although the Aristotelian interpretation made it harder to ascribe astrological meaning to comets. In the 16th century, the belief that comets were celestial objects, endorsed by Tycho Brahe among others, began to overcome its rival.

Astrologically, comets could be interpreted like planets and other celestial phenomena, according to sign and house as well as the aspects they formed with other bodies. Other factors, such as the comet's shape, color, and direction of the tail, were more unique to comets. Comets were held to affect (usually adversely) those countries and areas of life governed by the signs they traversed. They might also have bad effects on those areas to which their tails pointed or those under the nucleus. The shape of comets also had meaning, although they were capable of various interpretations. Comets that astrologers saw in the shape of swords, for example, presaged violence. The course of a comet, whether east to west or west to east, was also important, as was the area of the sky in which it first appeared. Among the planets, comets were particularly associated with Mars and to a lesser extent Mercury, a claim going back to Ptolemy.

Thinking about the meaning of comets was transformed in late 17th-century Europe by two events. One was the French protestant skeptic and opponent of astrology Pierre Bayle's *Thoughts on the Comet* (1682) inspired by the comet of 1680. Bayle's widely read and translated work attacked the idea that comets presaged anything along with many other ideas he considered superstitious, including astrology. The other development was the analysis of cometary paths in terms of Newtonian mechanics, which demonstrated that comets returned predictably. In 1705 the English scientist and friend of Newton, Edmond Halley (1656–1742), made the first prediction of a comet's return, claiming that the comet of 1682 would reappear in 1758. The vindication of his prediction after his death was a great triumph of Enlightenment science, and the comet has become known as "Halley's Comet."

The fact that comets were no longer sudden and mysterious visitors did not end their astrological and religious uses. Astrologers were of course used to dealing with periodic phenomena in their work, and if anything the fact that comets were now regular and predictable made them easier to deal with. However, because the discovery of comet regularity coincided with the decline of Western astrology, the new knowledge was not fully incorporated into astrological theory or practice. Even for religious interpreters the comet was less likely to be viewed as a divine sign and more a physical object, even a missile, launched by God and aimed at the Earth or a celestial body. English physicist Isaac Newton (1642–1727) himself believed that comets might play an important role in the apocalypse by plunging into the sun, causing its fire to destroy the Earth. Halley suggested that Noah's Flood could have been caused by a comet crashing into the Earth. The founder of

Methodism John Wesley (1703–1791) warned in a sermon that God might punish human sinfulness by destroying the Earth with a comet, and popular misunderstanding of a paper given at the French Royal Academy of Sciences in 1773 precipitated a panic as French people feared the Earth's imminent annihilation by comet.

Comets continue to play a role in religious belief. Some Christians believe that the destruction of the world by means of a comet is near. New religions have also ascribed religious meaning to comets. The spectacular Hale-Bopp comet of 1997 was treated as a signal for mass suicide by the Heaven's Gate cult, who believed they would be taken to a higher plane of existence by a starship traveling behind the comet. Modern astrologers continue to identify comets with change and disruption, but even though they have been definitively identified as celestial bodies, they play only a minor role in contemporary astrology.

William E. Burns

See also: Apocalypticism; Astrotheology; Mundane Astrology; Politics

Further Reading

Genuth, Sara Schecner. 1997. *Comets, Popular Culture and the Birth of Modern Cosmology*. Princeton: Princeton University Press.

van Nouhuys, Tabitta. 1998. *The Age of Two-Faced Janus: The Comets of 1577 and 1618 and the Decline of the Aristotelian World View in the Netherlands*. Leiden: Brill.

Yeomans, Donald K. 1991. *Comets: A Chronological History of Observation, Myth and Folklore*. New York: Wiley.

COURT ASTROLOGERS

Court astrologers are those astrologers who advise rulers and political leaders. They can be found from ancient Mesopotamia to the corridors of power in the late 20th century.

The proclaimed ability of astrologers to predict the future is a priceless asset for leaders dealing with the uncertainty of events. All of the major branches of astrology can be relevant for a court astrologer. Natal astrology can predict the destiny of a ruler as well as his or her consorts, allies, and enemies. Horary astrology can answer a ruler's specific questions. Electional astrology can help a ruler choose the best time for everything from offering battle to getting married to laying the foundation of a palace. Medical astrology can safeguard the health of the ruler and his or her family, while mundane astrology can help put the ruler's choices in a historical context. In addition to offering astrological advice, the court astrologer could use his or her knowledge to put the actions of the ruler and such occasions as the birth of an heir in the most favorable astrological light, thus serving as an element of the ruler's propaganda.

The origins of astrology in Mesopotamia and China were connected to the desire of rulers to know the future, and astrologers were court astrologers before they took the alternative route of addressing popular audiences. In general, court astrology has risen and fallen along with the prestige of astrology in particular cultures. In some environments the position of court astrologer has been an official one, while in others it has been characterized by informal advice. Many court astrologers have combined astrological advising with other forms of astrological, religious, scientific, or magical work. China took a somewhat different road than Western, Islamic, or Indian societies in bureaucratizing the function of the court astrologer through the Bureau of Astronomy. China was followed along this road by Japan, Korea, and Vietnam. Less is known about astrologers in the Mesoamerican court, but the application of astrology to public affairs seems to have been more the responsibility of a priesthood than of individuals appointed by the ruler. This also seems to have been the case in early Mesopotamia.

In addition to financial compensation, court patrons can be useful in protecting an astrologer against enemies. Although the rewards for a successful court astrologer could be great, there were also risks. A failed prediction of importance could lead to a spectacular fall, although it did not always. The court astrologer faced the risk of being particularly harshly judged if the ruler was a knowledgeable astrologer, as many were. Court astrologers also ran the risk of being drawn into plots against the ruler. In cultures where astrology was considered a branch of magic, court astrologers might attract problematic reputations as sorcerers.

Court astrologers do not exhaust the potential roles that astrology might play at a court. Czar Peter I "the Great" of Russia (r. 1682–1725) did not employ a court astrologer or make much use of astrological advice, but several court poets wrote poems in praise of him that employed dense astrological imagery and some of his public representations employed astrological symbols.

Indian Court Astrologers

In India, court astrologers from the Brahman class played a central role in kingship. Brahmans generally had a monopoly on the written tradition of astrology, and astrological expertise was part of their role as advisers to the king. Rather than being specialists, Brahman astrologers carried out religious functions such as sacrifice in addition to their astrological work. With the expansion of the cultural sphere of India in the ancient and early medieval periods, Indian Brahmans took their astrological expertise to areas in Southeast Asia and Indonesia. Muslim rulers also brought Islamic court astrology into India. The tradition of court astrology persisted into the age of British colonialism and continues to influence Indian astrology today.

Roman and Byzantine Court Astrologers

The rise of astrology following Alexander the Great's conquests in the Middle East may have led the new Hellenistic rulers to seek the assistance of astrologers, but little evidence has survived. There is some evidence that the last Hellenistic monarch, Cleopatra of Egypt (r. 51–30 BCE), had a court astrologer, but there is more information available for the Roman period. The first known Roman court astrologer was Thrasyllus (d. 36 CE?), the astrologer to the second Roman emperor Tiberius (r. 14–37 CE). Thrasyllus, a Platonic philosopher as well as an astrologer, attracted a cluster of legendary stories and wrote some astrological works that survive only in fragments. It is probable that the Babillus who served as astrologer to the Emperors Nero (r. 54–68 CE) and Vespasian (r. 69–79) was Thrasyllus's son. Roman historians tended to treat astrologers as a menace for their catering to Imperial paranoia. Bad emperors are portrayed as seeking those whose horoscopes proclaim them as future emperors and killing them.

Despite opposition to astrology on the part of the early Christian church fathers, it flourished at the court of Byzantium. The defeat of the emperor Constantine VI (r. 780–797) at the Battle of Marcellae against the Bulgars in 792 was widely blamed on the bad advice of his astrologer Pankratios. The emperor Manuel I Komnenos (r. 1143–1180) was such a supporter of astrology that he actually wrote a defense of it against the attacks of theologians. Astrological expertise was viewed with suspicion in Byzantium partly because so much of it was the work of pagan Greeks, Jews, and Muslims, but Byzantine emperors employed Muslim astrologers as their Muslim contemporaries employed Jewish and Christian ones.

Court Astrology in Classical and Medieval Islam

Despite the opposition of some Muslim religious thinkers to astrology, Islamic societies have a rich history of court astrology. The earliest Islamic rulers—the Rashidun caliphs and the Ummayad dynasty—do not seem to have made much use of astrology, although the later Ummayads, in Spain, employed astrologers. The Abbasid caliphs, however, whose rule began in 750, were prominent patrons of astrology. The Abbasids were more influenced by Persian culture than previous Islamic rulers, whose culture was mainly Arab, and they were in part drawing on the astrological traditions of the pre-Islamic Persian Sassanian dynasty. The Abbasids were the first Islamic dynasty to establish an official position for court astrologer. Astrologers determined the date for the founding of the official capital of Baghdad. Such leading astrologers of the Islamic world as Mashāllāh and Abū Ma'shar served the caliphs. Like their Byzantine contemporaries, caliphs were willing to look beyond their own religious community for astrological talent. The great Christian Byzantine astrologer Theophilos of Edessa (695–785) ended his career at the court of the Caliph al-Mahdi in Baghdad. Many court astrologers were part of family dynasties of astrologers, such as the Nawbakht family whose founder was one of the astrologers who cast the date for the founding of Baghdad and whose descendants served the caliphs for the next 200 years.

The tradition of using court astrologers survived the decline of the caliphate beginning in the 10th century. The Turkish sultans who exercised authority over much of the Islamic heartland continued to rely on the counsel of astrologers, including al-Qabīṣī, who served at the court of the Hamdanid dynasty of Aleppo in Syria. (Al-Qabīṣī even composed a text advising rulers on how to screen out astrological charlatans.) The observatories of the Islamic world were founded with astrology as well as calendar making in mind. Like their Christian fellow-professionals, court astrologers in the Islamic world faced the hostility of religious scholars who saw their art as a challenge to the omnipotence of God, but astrology was too useful a science to be shunned for religious reasons.

The Seljuk Turks of Anatolia in the 13th century offer one of the few examples of a woman court astrologer before the 20th century, Bibi Munajjime, who like many successful court astrologers made her reputation by correctly predicting a victory when all seemed lost. According to her son Ibn Bibi, a Seljuk court official and historian, she was amply rewarded for her accuracy by the Seljuk ruler Kayqubad I (r. 1220–1237).

The Decline and Revival of Western Court Astrology in the Middle Ages

Court astrology, like other branches of astrology in the West, suffered from the collapse of learned culture following the fall of the Roman Empire in the fifth century. The revival of court astrology in the West went along with the revival of learning beginning in the 11th century, which brought back learned astrology along with other branches of classical knowledge.

Among the well-known court astrologers of the Middle Ages was Michael Scot (1175–1232), astrologer to the Holy Roman emperor Frederick II (1194–1250). Scot was knowledgeable in Arabic, and Frederick, who had grown up in the Mediterranean culture of South Italy, was an admirer of Arab culture, so it is possible that his role in the emperor's court was based on a conscious imitation of Islamic models. A highly educated man, Scot gratified the curiosity of Frederick, one of the most intellectual rulers of the Middle Ages, on such questions as the construction of the heavens as well as performing astrological services. It is an indication of the newness of the role of the court astrologer that Scot acquired a very bad legendary reputation as a wicked magician. Dante's *Inferno* places him in the circle of hell reserved for wizards. Another astrological adviser to Frederick II, Guido Bonatti, is also depicted as damned. Bonatti served many of the governments of Italy after Frederick's death, including republics as well as monarchies, serving as a kind of court astrologer for hire, particularly valued for his knowledge of military astrology.

Despite Scot's and Bonatti's bad reputations, astrology continued to flourish at European courts. Charles V of France (r. 1363–1380) was a great supporter of astrology and the collector of a vast library of astronomical and astrological books. He established a college of Medicine and Astrology (two closely related disciplines) at the University of Paris in 1371. Products of courtly culture such as the elaborately decorated early 15th-century French manuscript *The Very Rich Hours of the Duke of Berry* are full of astrological images. Even Popes retained the services of astrologers.

Late medieval England was less hospitable to court astrologers, partly because the executions of astrologers Roger Bolingbroke and Thomas Southwell in 1441 for predicting the death of King Henry VI frightened astrologers away from court politics. By the end of the 15th century, however, the Italian-trained Englishman John Argentine (d. 1507) served Edward VI as physician and astrologer, and two Italian astrologers, John Baptista Boerio and William Parron, attended the court

This illuminated initial of a manuscript of Guido Bonatti's *Liber Astronomiae* shows the book being presented to Henry VII of England (r. 1485–1509). (The British Library)

of Henry VII (r. 1485–1509). His son Henry VIII (r. 1509–1547) had another foreign-born astrologer, the German Nicholas Kratzer (1487?–1550).

The Renaissance—Heyday of Court Astrology in the West

The Renaissance was a golden age of court astrologers. Astrological learning, enhanced by contact with the original Greek texts of Ptolemy and other classic astrological writers, was flourishing and even being taught at universities. Many of the skilled astrologers of the period sought employment at court. Many combined astrology with the practice of medicine, considered a kindred art and one that also attracted support from rulers.

Paying too much heed to astrological advice could lead to ridicule, but entirely shunning it would be seen as foolhardy. Some rulers, such as Duke Lodovico Sforza of Milan or the Bohemian general Albrecht von Wallenstein (1583–1634), were particularly notorious for the faith they put in astrology. Wallenstein's astrological counselors included Johannes Kepler. In addition to Kepler, such eminent founders of modern astronomy as Tycho Brahe and Galileo Galilei served as court astrologers. John Dee, astrologer to Queen Elizabeth I (r. 1558–1603) of England, was not paid as a court astrologer by the notoriously parsimonious queen but advised

A Renaissance Politician and His Astrologer—Lodovico Sforza and Ambrogio Varesi da Rosate

For the late 15th-century Milanese ruler Lodovico Sforza (1452–1508) astrology was an indispensable guide in the treacherous circumstances of Renaissance politics. Lodovico was particularly dependent on an astrologer and physician named Ambrogio Varesi da Rosate. Varesi has fallen into obscurity relative to other prominent Renaissance astrologers due to not publishing anything, at least not anything that survives. Varesi determined the best dates for everything including Lodovico's wedding to Beatrice d'Este and the consummation of the marriage. The fact that Beatrice gave birth to a healthy boy a year after the wedding further raised Lodovico's estimation of Varesi's skills. Lodovico continued to rely on Varesi's advice in a wide range of political and military affairs, but the fall of Lodovico led to the fall of Varesi, accused of murdering Lodovico's nephew Gain Galeazzo. Lodovico's ultimate political failure—he died in a French prison—contributed to the ridicule he received subsequently as a man helplessly in thrall to astrology. The greatest Milanese astrologer of the 16th century, Girolamo Cardano, was particularly contemptuous of Lodovico's gullibility. Cardano also condemned Varesi as an ignoramus, a reflection not only of Varesi's failure but also of the differences between Cardano and Varesi as astrologers. Varesi specialized in horary and electional astrology, areas in which Cardano had little interest but which were extremely useful in Renaissance courts such as Sforza's.

Source: Azzolini, Monica. 2013. *The Duke and the Stars: Astrology and Politics in Renaissance Milan.* Cambridge, MA: Harvard University Press.

on electional astrology. He was able to broaden his position into one of general scientific adviser. Lucas Gauricus (1475–1558) served as the astrological adviser to several Popes, receiving an appointment as bishop. He was most famous for allegedly predicting the death of Henry II in a tournament in 1559, which indeed came to pass. Pope Leo X thought highly enough of the potential uses of astrology to found a chair of astrology at the University of Rome. Astrologers served many Holy Roman emperors. Rudolf II, a skilled astrologer himself, was particularly known for his patronage of astrologers, including Dee, Brahe, and Kepler.

Court Astrology in the Early Modern Islamic Empires

In the early modern period, much of the Islamic world was dominated by stable empires, the Ottomans in the Balkans, Asia Minor, the Middle East and North Africa, the Safavids in Persia, and the Moguls in northern and Central India. All incorporated astrology into rulership.

In the Ottoman Empire, court astrology was in the hands of a permanent official, the Munajjim-bashi, a position established in the reign of Sultan Bayezid II (r. 1481–1512), a particularly avid patron of astrology and other occult arts. The Munajjim-bashi commanded a staff of astrologers who prepared calendars and determined the "auspicious hour" for the sultan's various enterprises, ranging from the departure of armies to throwing banquets. The calendars, or "taqwims," carried a set of astrological predictions for conditions throughout the year.

A Munajjim-bashi could be involved in court intrigue and some suffered spectacular falls, such as Taqi-ad-Din, who established the last traditional Islamic observatory, or Huseyin Effendi (d. 1650), who was strangled by order of the Sultan for his political intriguing. Although astrology became less central to the Munajjim-bashi's role as Western science affected it in the 19th century, the position lasted until the fall of the empire in 1923.

A similar official was found at the court of the Persian Safavid dynasty. Court astrologers in Persia and Mogul India, more influenced by the Timurid tradition (Timur, the Central Asian conqueror and ancestor of the Moguls, was referred to as the "Lord of the Conjunction" due to a Jupiter–Mars conjunction at the time of his birth) and Sufi mysticism than the Ottoman Court, spent much of their energy in adducing astrological evidence for the special spiritual status of the ruler. The Moguls were perhaps the most astrologically inclined of all Islamic dynasties, and visitors remarked on the omnipresence of astrologers at the Mogul court. The Moguls, like previous Indian Islamic rulers, drew from both mainstream Islamic astrology and the Hindu Sanskrit astrological tradition, employing Brahman astrologers as well as Muslim ones at their court and sponsoring the translation of Sanskrit texts.

Enlightenment and 19th-Century Decline in the West

The general decline of predictive astrology in the European Enlightenment was accompanied by a decline in court astrology. Seen as an archaic and superstitious discipline, astrology was regarded as having no place in the modern state or in the courts of "Enlightened" rulers.

The revival of Western astrology in the 19th century did not lead to a widespread revival in court astrology. The new astrology was either esoteric, appealing to a small number of mystically or magically minded initiates, or popular, appealing to the ordinary person who wanted to know what the stars foretold for his or her personal life. In neither guise was it of much interest to statesmen, who mostly came from the educated class that, except for a few eccentrics, disdained astrology.

Court Astrologers in Modern Times

Although astrology is viewed by many in the intellectual and cultural elite as superstitious, court astrologers have by no means disappeared even in the most modern societies. The late 19th- and 20th-century revival of astrology contributed to a modest renewal of court astrology. A well-known example is Nazi Germany where astrologers advised not Adolf Hitler, who had little interest in the stars, but SS leader Heinrich Himmler and other leading Nazis.

The opening of astrological knowledge to women in the 20th century led to a new prominence for the female court astrologer. Two famous cases where prominent leaders in Western democracies received astrological advice from women are those of Joan Quigley, in the Ronald Reagan White House, and Elizabeth Teissier (b. 1938), astrological adviser to the president of France, Francois Mitterand

(1916–1996). In both cases, the fact that the leader was receiving advice from an astrologer was treated as discrediting. The Quigley case was a minor scandal in America, and Teissier's connection to Mitterand, hushed up until she went public years after his death, was treated as a blow to his reputation.

One place where a strong connection between political leaders and astrology continues to flourish is India and those areas of South and Southeast Asia influenced by it. Although astrology is no longer a monopoly of the Brahmans, connections between Indian astrologers and politicians are numerous. In Sri Lanka, astrologer Sumanadasa Abeygunawardena (b. 1943) was an influential adviser to President Mahinda Rajapaska (b. 1945). A more traditional court astrology is also found in areas where traditional Indian-influenced monarchies have persisted, such as Nepal until the abolition of the monarchy in 2008 and Bhutan and Thailand today.

William E. Burns

See also: Abū Ma'shar al-Balkhī; Al-Qabīṣī; Bonatti, Guido; Brahe, Tycho; Buddhism; Bureau of Astronomy (China); Campanella, Tommaso; Dee, John; Electional Astrology; Galilei, Galileo; Indian Astrology; Islamic Astrology; Kepler, Johannes; Mashāllāh; Medical Astrology; Medieval European Astrology; Mesoamerican Astrology; Mesopotamian Astrology; Nazism and the Third Reich; Politics; Quigley, Joan; Renaissance and Reformation Astrology; Roman Astrology; Sima Qian; Thai Astrology

Further Reading

Azzolini, Monica. 2013. *The Duke and the Stars: Astrology and Politics in Renaissance Milan.* Cambridge, MA: Harvard University Press.

Carey, Hilary M. 1992. *Courting Disaster: Astrology at the English Court and University in the Later Middle Ages.* New York: St. Martin's Press.

Collis, Robert. 2011. "Using the Stars: Astrology at the Court of Peter the Great." In *Astrologies: Plurality and Diversity: The Proceedings of the Eighth Annual Conference of the Sophia Centre for the Study of Cosmology in Culture, University of Wales, Trinity Saint David, 24–25 July 2010*, ed. Nicholas Campion and Liz Green, 125–150. Ceredigion: Sophia Centre Press.

Hayton, Darin. 2015. *The Crown and the Cosmos: Astrology and the Politics of Maximilian I.* Pittsburgh: University of Pittsburgh Press.

Ilhan, Baris. *The Astrology of the Ottoman Empire.* http://www.academia.edu/5016755/The_Astrology_of_the_Ottoman_Empire

Moin, A. Azfar. 2012. *The Millennial Sovereign: Sacred Kingship and Sainthood in Islam.* New York: Columbia University Press.

Parry, Glyn. 2011. *The Arch-Conjuror of England: John Dee.* New Haven, CT: Yale University Press.

D

D'AILLY, PIERRE (1350–1420)

The prominent French churchman Pierre d'Ailly's astrological interests focused on mundane astrology, particularly the effects of Jupiter/Saturn conjunctions and other infrequent events on human history. He believed that history, particularly religious history, followed the pattern of such conjunctions, particularly the great cycle of 960 years between times the conjunction appeared in the first degree of Aries, the position the two planets had occupied at their creation. D'Ailly believed that the relationship between conjunctions and significant historic events was complex in that sometimes a conjunction could herald events decades in the future. D'Ailly also drew on theories of historical astrology that placed particular emphasis on a cycle lasting roughly 300 years based on 10 revolutions of Saturn. He put conjunctions and Saturn cycles in an apocalyptic context. He drew heavily on Abū Ma'shar, whom he read in Latin translation. Other astrologers who influenced d'Ailly include Roger Bacon (ca. 1219–ca. 1292), John Ashenden (d. 1368?), and Rabbi Abraham Ibn Ezra (1089–1167).

In his defenses of astrology, d'Ailly generally followed the Scholastic line that the stars affected the body but not the soul, and therefore the strong-willed individual could rule his or her stars rather than be ruled by them. However, he had little interest in astrology as it applied to individuals as opposed to historical cycles.

Although d'Ailly wrote about astrology throughout his career, his interest vastly increased in the last decade of his life, due to his preoccupation with the Great Schism of the Catholic Church. At this time, there was one line of popes in Rome, and another in the southern French city of Avignon, both claiming to be the true head of the Church. Like many other Western Christians, d'Ailly initially saw the Schism as a sign of the approaching apocalypse. He turned to astrology to cast light on the nature and timing of the apocalypse, perhaps hoping for something with a more solid grounding than the ambiguities of prophecy. D'Ailly's studies of astrology, however, seemed to have played a role in convincing him that the apocalypse was not inevitable and that human action could heal the Schism and delay the end of the world. (D'Ailly was one of the leaders of the Council of Constance [1414–1418] that did resolve the Schism and reunify the Church.) He included astrological evidence and arguments in a letter he wrote to one of the papal claimants, "John XXIII" (now considered an anti-pope). D'Ailly came to project the apocalypse around the year 1789, based principally on the Saturn cycle. This date seems to have originated with d'Ailly.

William E. Burns

See also: Abū Ma'shar; Albertus Magnus; Apocalypticism; Medieval European Astrology; Mundane Astrology

Further Reading

Smoller, Laura Ackerman. 1994. *History, Prophecy and the Stars: The Christian Astrology of Pierre d'Ailly, 1350–1420*. Princeton, NJ: Princeton University Press.

DECANS

The decans, 36 divisions of the ecliptic, are the preeminent ancient Egyptian contribution to astrology. Their history in Egypt may be roughly divided into three periods. First, lists of 36 star names appear on coffin lids as early as the Ninth Dynasty (2160–2130 BCE). These early decans mark the star that rises on the eastern horizon for each hour of the night throughout the year. (The nocturnal and diurnal halves of the ecliptic each have 18 decans, but three morning and three evening decans passed unseen due to twilight.) Next, related lists of decans by star names appear in royal monuments, including the cenotaph of Seti I (ca. 1279 BCE) and the tomb of Ramesses IV (ca. 1150 BCE). These intermediary decans report the star that transited the zenith for each hour of the night throughout the year. This measurement of nocturnal hours with culminating stars may survive into the Arabic folk-astronomy described by al-Farisi and others, wherein the culminating star at the break of dawn is noted. Finally, sometime after the conquest of Alexander the Great (332 BCE), the decans were assimilated into the zodiac as equal subdivisions of the zodiacal signs. These subordinate decans with Egyptian names entered the Hellenistic astrological tradition.

Throughout these stages of evolution, no single Egyptian word for the decans is immediately obvious. The early decans on the coffin lids occasionally appear alongside captions that refer to "the 36 gods of the sky" or "stars of heaven." At this time, the decans may not have composed a distinct category to Egyptians: the star names vary, the stars themselves may vary, and some decans seem to form parts of larger constellations. The decans may simply have been a practical subset of fixed stars useful for measuring time. The tomb of Osorkon II (850 BCE) refers to the decans as "living fates(?)" and the pronaos (forecourt) (ca. 50 CE) of the Esna temple mentions "living souls" in the sky, but whether these references included planets or other astral bodies is not certain. The *Book of Nut* (second century CE) describes the decans as "workers," a set of stars that "work" for certain hours. When the decans entered Hellenistic astrology, probably through the now-lost *Salmeschiniaka* (300 BCE[?], cited by Porphyry [third century CE], Iamblichus [third century CE], and Hephaistio of Thebes [late fourth century CE]), their terminology standardized somewhat. The Greek and Latin words *dekanoi* and *decani*, respectively, derive from the fact that each of the 36 decans remains in use for 10 days before the next star marks the nocturnal hours.

Greco-Roman astrologers used the decans in three ways. First, the Egyptian tradition survives with descriptions of decans as a third of each zodiacal sign. Astrologers who report this method often include an attempt at phonetically rendering the Egyptian star lists as divine names, occasionally of a specific figure with a particular iconography. Teucer of Babylon (first century CE?), Antiochus of Athens (first or second century CE), Anubio (second or third century CE), Firmicus Maternus, Hephaistio of Thebes (fifth century CE), Rhetorius (sixth or seventh century CE), and the *Liber Hermetis* report Egyptian-style decans. Teucer describes the decans almost analogously to the cardines of the house system, emphasizing the importance of the rising decan to the character of the native, much like the ascendant. Anubio eschews the term *decan*, preferring *hour-regulators* or *ministers*, perhaps translating an Egyptian word. Firmicus associates the Egyptian-style decans with diseases and their cures. Hephaistio (citing the *Salmeschiniaka*) develops the association of decans and the houses, seemingly approximating the cardines by discussing the decan at the eastern horizon, crossing the midheaven, setting on the western horizon, and most hidden by the Earth. These Egyptian-style decans also appear on tables used by astrologers to display planetary positions.

A second, more abstract, tradition of decanic faces (*prosōpa* in Greek, *facies* in Latin) associates the divisions of the zodiacal signs with a specific planet, using the reverse order of the days of the week. This method can be found in citations from Teucer, but also appears in Antiochus, Paul of Alexandria (fourth century CE), Firmicus Maternus, and the *Liber Hermetis*. Paul of Alexandria suggests that the faces arose from an association of decans with planets. The *Liber Hermetis* presents the Egyptian-style decans and the decanic faces together in the same discussion but a curious rule seems to separate the decans and the decanic faces: no presentation of decanic faces associates them with illnesses. Additionally, although neither Ptolemy nor Vettius Valens mention decans, both discuss the "faces" of a planet. Ptolemy (and perhaps Valens) declare a planet to be "in its face" if it has the same relationship to the sun or moon as the planetary house has to the house of the sun or moon. This technique may relate in some way to decanic faces.

Finally, Manilius presents a similarly abstract but idiosyncratic arrangement that assigns each decan a zodiacal sign according to a straightforward progression. Thus, Aries rules the first decan, Taurus rules the second decan, Gemini rules the third decan, and so on, until three zodiacal cycles produce 36 associations.

The decans enjoyed a surprisingly fertile legacy. They entered Indian astrology through the *Yavanajataka* and from there resurfaced in Arabic astrology. In these practices, a fourth tradition relates the decans to the triplicities, with the first decan taking the zodiacal sign itself and the following decans taking signs of the same element. This fourth tradition was adopted in the modern era by Alan Leo and Isabel Hickey but references to decans abound in medieval works. Representations of the decans appear unexpectedly in the frescoes of the Salone dei Mesi (Hall of Months, 1476–1484 CE) of the Palazzo Schifanoia by Cosimo Tura (15th century CE), which follows decan iconography from a variant of Abū Ma'shar (787–886 CE). The Persian Abū Ma'shar derived his images from India, which struggled to interpret the Greek account of Egyptian images in the *Yavanajataka*.

Even though William Lilly numbered the decans among his "five essential dignities" in 1647, their interpretive value was limited. Even in antiquity, their use was uncommon. Neugebauer and Van Hosen collected four examples of their use, and a mere six horoscopes from Oxyrhynchus use decans as the last element of the chart.

Micah T. Ross

See also: Zodiacs

Further Reading

Abry, Josèphe-Henriette, ed. 1993. *Les tablettes astrologiques de Grand (Vosges) et l'astrologie en Gaule romaine*. Collection du Centre d'Etudes Romaines et Gallo-Romaines, Nouvelle Série. 12. Paris: De Boccard.

Clagett, Marshall. 1995. *Ancient Egyptian Science. Vol. 2: Calendars, Clocks, and Astronomy*. Memoirs of the American Philosophical Society. 214. Philadelphia: The American Philosophical Society.

Neugebauer, Otto, and Henry Bartlett van Hoesen. 1959. *Greek Horoscopes*. Memoirs of the American Philosophical Society. 48. (Addenda 1964, reprinted 1987). Philadelphia: The American Philosophical Society.

Warburg, Aby. 1999. "Italian Art and International Astrology in the Palazzo Schifanoia, Ferrara." In *The Renewal of Pagan Antiquity*. Los Angeles: Getty Research Institute for the History of Art and the Humanities, 563–592.

DEE, JOHN (1527-1609)

John Dee was Elizabethan England's leading astrologer and prominent in many other branches of magic and science.

From a Welsh background, Dee was educated at St. John's College Cambridge and the University of Louvain in the Spanish Netherlands. Louvain offered the opportunity for more advanced mathematical training than anything available in England, to which Dee added further in a visit to Paris in 1550. (In the Netherlands, Dee's associates included Gerhard Mercator.) Dee applied the sophisticated mathematics he had learned at Louvain to astrology. He returned to England in 1551. He began his career as a courtier, serving as an occasional consultant on geography and natural philosophy to the young King Edward VI. He also began to keep a weather diary, hoping to establish the influences of the stars on the weather. This document eventually broadened into an astrological diary in which Dee recorded the events of his life in relation to the stars. These included times of sexual intercourse with his wives, as Dee believed that celestial influences at the moment of conception as well as of birth influenced later life.

Edward died in 1553, and was succeeded by his Catholic sister Mary I. Dee attempted to ingratiate himself with Mary and even became a Catholic priest, but he was arrested for having cast horoscopes of Mary, her husband King Philip of Spain, and her sister and presumptive heir, Elizabeth, at Elizabeth's behest. Dee managed to escape severe punishment. He continued to work as an astrologer and mathematician in London.

Dee's influence was at its height after the accession of Elizabeth on Mary's death in 1558, although like others of Elizabeth's servants his rewards were limited by the queen's notorious stinginess. She did, however, honor Dee by visiting his house at Mortlake outside London on multiple occasions. It is a mark of his rising status that he married Jane Fromoundes, a court lady, in 1578 after the death of his first wife, Katheryn Constable, in 1575.

This portrait of John Dee emphasizes his mathematical skills, showing him holding a set of dividers. (Wellcome Collection)

Dee's aptitude for mathematics and Continental training made him one of the most advanced mathematicians and astrologers in England, where mathematics was not well developed. Dee hoped to advance the cause of mathematics in English, making it available to English people who did not know Latin. He contributed a poem and mathematical material on fractions to the 1561 edition of Robert Recorde's mathematics textbook *The Ground of Artes*. Dee's preface focused on the many uses of mathematics in advancing human activities including astrology and astronomy as branches of mathematics. Dee's expertise in astronomy also led him to advise the Elizabethan court on the adoption of the recently created Gregorian calendar, which was rejected despite his support.

As a court astrologer, Dee drew horoscopes for great occasions such as Elizabeth's coronation and provided interpretations of unusual celestial events such as supernovas and comets. His astrology was an eclectic mix, drawing on mathematics, the Kabbalah, and legend. Like many in the 16th century, he associated astrology with prophecy, drawing on astrological evidence to argue that the end of the world was near. Although he never published a treatise specifically devoted to astrology, his most important magical work, *Monas Hieroglyphica* (1564), drew on astrology as well as Kabbalism, alchemy, and religious mysticism to present a complex system that supposedly revealed the secrets of the universe. Dee believed that the stars exerted their influence through "rays" that could be analyzed through the science of optics. He also believed that alchemy was a "terrestrial astrology," based on the influences of the stars on substances on Earth. Dee treated the symbols of the planets used by astrologers and astronomers as having a hidden meaning, even dividing the planets into a "lunar" and "solar" group depending on the presence or absence of a the semicircle in their symbols.

Dee shared the common excitement about the great conjunction of Jupiter and Saturn in the first sign of the zodiac, Aries, in 1583. The belief that all the planets had lined up in conjunction in Aries at the creation made this conjunction particularly significant. Along with his associate, the alchemist Edward Kelly, Dee left for the European continent that year, perhaps hoping to be at the scene of the great apocalyptic events that many astrologers thought the conjunction presaged in Eastern Europe. Dee hoped to acquire the Holy Roman emperor Rudolf, a leading supporter of astrologers, astronomers, and alchemists, as a patron, and spent some time in Rudolf's capital Prague. However, these hopes came to nothing.

Dee and his family, but not Kelly, returned to England in 1589, broke. Although he and Jane were able to move back into his house at Mortlake and even received a few favors from Elizabeth, late Elizabethan England was much less sympathetic to his magical and prophetic astrology. Under the recently appointed archbishop of Canterbury, John Whitgift (1530–1604), the Church was cracking down on magic. Dee managed to use his alchemical skills and the usefulness of his prophesying for certain political agendas to make a modest comeback, but his last years were hard. Disappointed of more lucrative and secure appointments, he was made warden of Manchester College, a penurious institution far from the centers of power in London and Westminster. Many of his remaining court connections were lost after the death of Elizabeth in 1603 and the subsequent accession of James I (r. 1603–1625). Dee died in London on March 26, 1609.

William E. Burns

See also: Ashmole, Elias; Astral Magic; Court Astrologers; Mercator, Gerardus; Politics; Science

Further Reading

Clulee, N. H. 2001. "*Astronomia Inferior:* Legacies of Johannes Trithemius and John Dee." In *Secrets of Nature: Astrology and Alchemy in Early Modern Europe*, ed. William R. Newman and Anthony Grafton. Cambridge, MA: MIT Press.

French, Peter. 1989. *John Dee: The World of an Elizabethan Magus.* New York: Dorset Press.

Parry, Glyn. 2011. *The Arch-Conjuror of England: John Dee.* New Haven, CT: Yale University Press.

DOROTHEUS OF SIDON (FL. FIRST CENTURY CE)

Dorotheus of Sidon wrote an astrological poem in Greek, known as the *Carmen Astrologicum* or *Pentateuch* (because the extant version is in five books). Now in modern-day Lebanon, Sidon was an important Phoenician city. Evidence points to Dorotheus as living in the first century CE: nativities cited in his work predominantly date to the first century (some are later interpolations). Only fragments remain of the original Greek version, many excerpted by the fourth/fifth-century CE astrologer Hephaestio of Thebes (b. 380, fl. 415 CE). Dorotheus's work primarily exists in a ca. 800 CE Arabic translation by 'Umar Ibn al-Farrukhān al-Ṭabari (Omar Tiberiades), said to be from a third-century Pahlavi translation (Dorotheus 1976, vii).

Of the books comprising the *Pentateuch*, the first four cover natal astrology, while the fifth examines katarchic astrology, the astrology of determining the best time to begin an action (election), or interpreting the time in which a question was asked about something (interrogation or horary).

Dorotheus is an important source for the early delineation of Hellenistic astrological doctrines and practices, some of which may derive from the ancient pseudonymous astrological authorities, Nechepso and Petosiris (Heilen 2010, 131–138). Book I outlines the basic principles and mechanics of natal astrology. It discusses the native's parents and siblings, how he (the standard viewpoint in Hellenistic astrology assumes the native is male) is raised, and his fortunes and misfortunes. Book II moves to his marriage and children in chapters 1–13 (chapter 3 delineates marriage from a female perspective), and the relationships of planets by aspect in chapters 14–17. Chapters 18–33 are each devoted to the effects of a single planet and its relationships. In Books I and II, the technique of lots is prominent. These are interpretive points that take the arc between two planets (usually) and project it from the ascendant.

In Book III, Dorotheus examines life span, determining longevity from "governing" planets that will provide certain numbers of years to a life. This is a twofold process. First, the "indicator" (*haylāj*) is found (this corresponds to the Greek *aphetēs*), to be either the sun, moon, ascendant, or Lot of Fortune. The "governor" (*kadhkhudāh*, Greek *oikodespotēs*) is the term-lord (the planet ruling specific sets of degrees [terms] in a zodiacal sign) of this planet. Dorotheus illustrates this (Book III, chapter 2, 19–25) with an example where the ascendant is the *haylāj* and the *kadhkhudāh* is its term-lord, Mars, in a nativity Pingree dates to 281 CE (Dorotheus 1976), but it is more persuasively dated by James Holden (1996, 34n83) to October 2, 44 CE.

Book IV discusses the predictive technique of profections. It also contains a section on the body, chronic illness, and death. Book V, in 43 chapters (not all are genuine Dorotheus, e.g., chapter 41), covers all forms of katarchic astrology, including elections and interrogations. Many facets of human experience are covered: runaway slaves, the condition of a sick person, the recovery of lost items, and when to build, begin a journey, or marry.

Dorotheus's work was known in the Byzantine period and to Arabic writers such as Mashāllāh in the Middle Ages.

Dorian Gieseler Greenbaum

See also: Buddhism; Electional Astrology; Hellenistic Astrology; Horary Astrology; Lots; Natal Astrology Mashāllāh

Further Reading

Barton, Tamsyn. 1994. *Ancient Astrology*. London: Routledge.

Dorotheus of Sidon. 1976. *Carmen Astrologicum*, ed. David Pingree. Leipzig: B. G. Teubner. http://www.skyscript.co.uk/dorotheus1.pdf (Book 1); http://www.skyscript.co.uk/dorotheus3.pdf (Book 3).

Heilen, Stephan. 2010. "Anubio Reconsidered." *Aestimatio* 7: 127–192.
Holden, James Herschel. 1996. *A History of Horoscopic Astrology from the Babylonian Period to the Modern Age*. Tempe, AZ: American Federation of Astrologers.
Pingree, David. 1973. "The Horoscope of Constantine VII Porphyrogenitus." *Dumbarton Oaks Papers* 27: 217, 219–231.

E

ELECTIONAL ASTROLOGY

In its most sophisticated form, electional astrology is based on the astrological figure (also referred to as a horoscope, chart, map, or scheme), a two-dimensional, schematic drawing of the three-dimensional planetary configurations at a specific moment. The election might be viewed as a subset of the type of figure known as an inception (Hand 2014, 48). The latter is cast for the moment that something happens (or begins to happen), without being chosen astrologically. It is the application of astrology to the analysis of beginnings, such as the founding of a city or building. In the astrological guide of Simon Forman, we find an inception cast for the time at which a woman entered the baths, 9:45 a.m., June 12, 1602, and subsequently died (Forman 1606, 85).

The moment for casting the election, however, is chosen *intentionally*, its function to identify an astrologically propitious moment for the beginning of an action, deed, or event in the future. In the case of Forman's client, the same woman might have requested an astrologically propitious point in time at which she should venture to the baths. The election might invoke one or more of the 12 houses of the figure and thus has an extensive range of application: choosing the time for a marriage, the founding of a city, the start of a battle, or the preparation and administering of remedies/treatments for patients.

The election was not covered at all by Claudius Ptolemy, whose work was exceptionally important for later practitioners. Yet, the election is well represented in pre-Arabic material such the work of Dorotheus (Hand 2014, 48–49). Electional astrology is also revealed in the work of medieval Latin astrologers such as Guido Bonatti. Theoretical evidence of early modern electional astrology is found in the astrological guides of practitioners such as Forman, Richard Saunders (1613–1675), and William Salmon (1644–1713). Evidence of the practical application of electional astrology is revealed, inter alia, in the manuscripts and papers of Forman, Richard Napier (1559–1634), and William Lilly.

A less sophisticated electional astrology invokes various planetary locations and rulerships rather than the figure. In terms of taking a medicine for diarrhea, for example, the commencement of this is best, according to Dorotheus, when the moon is in Libra or Scorpio (Dorotheus 1976, V 38). Lunar movements were important in the medical practice of medieval and early modern physicians, in particular the identifying of a propitious time to commence phlebotomy. Henry Coley (1633–1704) confirms that in the hour of Venus "tis good to Court women"; in the hour of Mars "it is ill to take a Journey." Coley points out that planetary hour rulers are useful, but they are not "of that Efficacy as well-grounded elections, from an apt positure of the heavens" (Coley 1676, 272). Indeed, practitioners such as Richard Saunders tended to combine an analysis of the planetary hour ruler with an analysis of the figure. Saunders invokes this model when "Giving the First Medicine to the Sick," or "Of Going to the Sick" (Saunders 1677, 60, 68).

Yet, the work of various authors, such as Dorotheus and the medieval astrologers, reveals a blurring of classification between the election and the interrogation, both grouped together under the label katarchic, derived from the Greek for beginning (Hand 2014, 48–49). Eugenio Garin, citing the *Speculum Astronomiae*, attributed to Albertus Magnus (1200–1280), clarifies the distinction: The interrogation is concerned with a "radical intention," in other words, whether the thing should be accomplished or not. The election, however, is the matter of choosing "a praiseworthy hour to start some task" (Garin 1976, 37–38). In the early modern texts this classification is seldom blurred and the distinction is more obvious.

In the identification of a propitious, elected, moment for the casting of a figure, it is best if the *Fortunes*, Venus and Jupiter, are emphasized (angular) and the *Infortunes*, Mars and Saturn, are tucked away (cadent). We find a wonderful description of an election in *The Book of Instruction in the Elements of the Art of Astrology* by Al Biruni, Abu'l-Rayhan Muhammad Ibn Ahmad (1029) (Ramsey-Wright, 1934). Al-Biruni (973–1048), one of the greatest scholars of the medieval Islamic era, tells us that when selecting

> a suitable time for carrying out some business [an Election] . . . the astrologer must . . . insure the presence of fortunes and the absence of infortunes, just as we protect ourselves on the surface of the earth from the rays of the sun, by selecting northern aspects, and shady spots and using moistened punkahs and ice-houses. (Ramsay-Wright 1934, 331)

Forman sets out his understanding of the function of *Electiones* in his guide *Astrologicalle Judgmentes of Physic and Other Questions* (Forman 1606, 6). Forman's particular concern is the "tyme medicin should be made," or when and what time it should be given (Kassell 2005, 58). Of the seven elections in *Judgmentes* we find one each for Richard Staunton and Agnes Farewell for the administering of the first preparative. In terms of Farewell's election, Forman is very clear about the moment for its casting: "The figure of the instante when she tooke the first draught of her preparative" (Forman 1606, 84, 85, 86). We also find an election for the production of the philosopher's stone, a gold sigil to help with the "falling evill" and two copper rings (sigils), for attracting love and friendship (Forman 1606, 41, 143–144, 160). Forman's casebooks from 1596 to 1603 reveal just 24 elections.

William Lilly's *Christian Astrology* (1647) contains no information relating to elections, although Lilly notes that there could be no "ingenious Astrologian that having studied or well entred into this my Book shall not be able . . . to frame his owne Figure of elections" (Lilly 1647, "To the Reader"). Yet, there is evidence of Lilly's practical application of electional astrology in an election for Charles II concerning an astrologically propitious moment to deliver his speech to Parliament on October 27, 1673, mediated to the king by Elias Ashmole. However, the time constraints specified for an election might preclude the choice of the most propitious moment. Even for a king, Parliament would not assemble in the favorable early hours of the morning, such as those astrologers frequently invoked for the commencement of the production of sigils, talismans, and amulets (Kitson 1989, 191).

William Ramesey (1627–1676?), astrologer and physician-in-ordinary to King Charles II (r. 1660–1685), devoted particular attention to the election in his principal work, *Astrologia Restaurata, or, Astrologie Restored: Being an Introduction to the General and Chief Part of the Language of the Stars* (London, 1653). Among the topics suitable for elections are the "Weaning of Children," "cutting of Hair," "borrowing and lending of money," "Of selling to advantage," "Of making of friendship," "Of Building of Churches," "Of . . . Marriage." A section devoted to propitious times for delivering babies, for conceiving and circumcising includes an interesting note: "Arabians and Ancient Authors, not used to christenings, were deficient in those elections" (Ramesey 1653, 132–202). Ramesey also includes the less sophisticated electional astrology in the form of a table of lunar aspects to the six planets. If, for example, the moon makes a conjunction with Jupiter, this is "a fortunate day, go to noble men, Judges, and Prelates, and sue for they right, and take councel." If the moon makes a conjunction with Saturn it is "an unfortunate day, take no journey, speak not to Princes nor old men, avoid the company of husbandmen" (Ramesey 1653, 129).

In keeping with the astrological tradition, Ramesey emphasizes the importance of cross-referencing the election with the nativity in order to harness the most favorable planetary energies. Coley confirms that it is a "vain and foolish thing" for an election to be drawn without knowledge of the nativity. Indeed, parents and parish clerks should be careful to record the time of birth, rather than the time of the christening, which might be two or three weeks later (Coley 1676, 276). William Salmon (1644–1713), invokes a further set of requirements: the planet, cusp, and house in the nativity corresponding to the matter inquired about should be identified and observed in relation to the transits and directions at the time of the proposed election. The election should not be cast if the testimony in the nativity is weakened. If this advice is ignored, there may be some "accidental good," but it can never overcome the power of an "Essential or Radical Evil" (Salmon 1679, 306). Thus, the fortune anticipated from a propitiously timed election depends ultimately upon the testimony of the nativity, which no promising election can override.

The importance of a good beginning is a very powerful concept, generating hopes of an auspicious outcome. Underpinning electional astrology, indeed all astrology, is the relationship between the celestial bodies and lives and events on Earth: an epistemology of signatures and sympathies, in which "individual objects on earth . . . contain the signature of the heavenly bodies to which they . . . correspond" (Osler 2010, 32). Perhaps the interpretative skill relating to the election is less than that required of the interrogation, yet a mastery of these correspondences was, and continues to be, essential to the astrological judgment of all figures.

Barbara Dunn

See also: Bonatti, Guido; Court Astrologers; Dorotheus of Sidon; Forman, Simon; Lilly, William; Sex and Love

Further Reading

The Casebooks Project: A Digital Edition of Simon Forman's and Richard Napier's Medical Records 1596–1634. http://www.magicandmedicine.hps.cam.ac.uk/

Coley, Henry. 1676. *Clavis Astrologiae Elimata, or A Key to the Whole Art of Astrology, New Filed and Polished.* London.

Corredera, V. 2015. "Faces and Figures of Fortune: Astrological Physiognomy in Tamburlaine Part 1." *Early Modern Literary Studies* 18: 1–26.

Dorotheus of Sidon. 1976. *Carmen Astrologicum*, ed. David Pingree. Leipzig: B. G. Teubner.

Forman, Simon. 1606. *The Astrologicalle Judgmentes of Phisick and Other Questions*. MS Ashmole 389. Oxford: Bodleian Library. http://dev.magicandmedicine.hps.cam.ac.uk/view/text/normalised/TEXT5

Garin, Eugenio. 1976. *Astrology in the Renaissance: The Zodiac of Life*. London: Routledge.

Hand, Robert. 2014. "The Use of Military Astrology in Late Medieval Italy: The Textual Evidence." Unpublished diss., Catholic University of America.

Kassell, Lauren. 2005. *Medicine and Magic in Elizabethan London: Simon Forman: Astrologer, Alchemist, and Physician.* Oxford: Oxford University Press.

Kitson, Annabella. 1989. "Some Varieties of Electional Astrology." In *History and Astrology: Clio and Urania Confer*, ed. A. Kitson, 171–199. London.

Lilly, William. 1647. *Christian Astrology Modestly Treated of in Three Books.* London: Thomas Brudenell for John Partridge and Humphrey Blunden.

Osler, Margaret. 2010. *Reconfiguring the World: Nature, God, and Human Understanding from the Middle Ages to Early Modern Europe.* Baltimore, MD: Johns Hopkins University Press.

Ramesey, William. 1653. *Astrologia Restaurata, or, Astrologie Restored: Being an Introduction to the General and Chief Part of the Language of the Stars.* London: Printed for Robert White.

Ramsay-Wright, R. ed. and trans. 1934. *The Book of Instruction in the Elements of the Art of Astrology by Al Biruni, Abu'l-Rayhan Muhammad Ibn Ahmad (1029).* London: Luzac.

Robbins, Frank E., ed. and trans. 1940. *Ptolemy: Tetrabiblos.* Cambridge, MA: Harvard University Press.

Salmon, William. 1679. *Horae Mathematicae, or, Urania the Soul of Astrology.* London: Thomas Dawks.

Saunders, Richard. 1677. *The Astrological Judgment and Practice of Physick. Deduced from the Position of the Heavens at the Decumbiture of the Sick Person.* London: L. C.

Zambelli, Paolo. 1992. *The* Speculum Astronomiae *and Its Enigma: Astrology, Theology and Science in Albertus Magnus and His Contemporaries.* Dordrecht: Kluwer.

ENLIGHTENMENT

The European Age of Enlightenment, approximately from the late 17th century to the end of the 18th century, has long been considered by historians to possess a straightforward stance on astrology. Notably, the spirit of Enlightenment, as expressed in its final stages by German philosopher Immanuel Kant (1724–1804), was deemed incompatible with belief in celestial influence on terrestrial affairs. Research in recent decades, however, has shown Enlightenment thinkers to be more ambivalent. For modern scholars, whether astrology played a role in

Enlightenment thinking depends on one's definition of astrology. If ideas are considered to be astrological only when they are explicitly framed as being astrological, they are definitely not part of Enlightenment thinking after the first decades of the 18th century. If, however, every theory implicating celestial influence is judged astrological, astrology figures in some key Enlightenment works. These works are often characterized by implicit or explicit denunciations of practices labeled as "astrology," but at the same time elaborate extensively on solar, lunar, planetary, and cometary influence on the Earth and even human lives. Among these, the celebrated *Encyclopédie, ou dictionnaire raisonné des sciences, des arts et des métiers* (1751–1772), edited by Denis Diderot (1713–1784) and Jean le Rond d'Alembert (1717–1783), stands out.

The *Encyclopédie* is generally believed to express the central tenets and principles of Enlightenment thinking, and might well be considered as an example of the commonplace stance on astrology of 18th-century intellectuals. Edme-François Mallet (1713–1755), the *Encyclopédiste*, who largely copied his entry on astrology from the one in Ephraim Chambers's *Cyclopaedia* (1728), reproduces the ancient distinction between condemned judicial astrology on the one hand, and the laudable natural version on the other. Here, however, there is a significant twist compared with earlier centuries. The word *astrology* was considered no longer applicable to medical or physical research on celestial influences. Studies of these influences should be labeled as contributions to medicine or natural science. Astrology is now left to contain only those beliefs and practices deemed vulgar and unworthy of receiving the attention of men of learning. Following this pattern, Mallet declares predictions about people's character, people's life, or the fate of nations unscientific and illegitimate and, therefore, "astrological." Quite the opposite is true for Mallet's assessment of predictions regarding natural phenomena like the weather, winds, floods, or earthquakes. Research on those subjects is considered to bear the possibility of bringing forth truthful results and is consequently classified as a branch of physics. Mallet praises Robert Boyle (1627–1691), a prominent member of England's famous Royal Society of London for Improving Natural Knowledge, for encouraging investigation of the impact of celestial phenomena on terrestrial air and atmosphere. Richard Mead (1673–1754), a friend of Isaac Newton (1643–1727) and vice president of the Royal Society, receives comparable praise for his advocacy of integrating celestial influences into medical theory and practice.

Before and after the publication of the *Encyclopédie*, intellectuals and scientists undertook efforts similar to the *Cyclopaedia* and the *Encyclopédie*, denouncing or ignoring the word *astrology* in their works while defending celestial influences. In physics and astronomy, it was mostly comets that made thinkers ponder the possibilities of celestial influence. Comets were not only a likely subject for the study of celestial influence because of their rapidly changing appearance in the sky. Study of comets was also boosted because Newton's *Philosophiae Naturalis Principia Mathematica* (1687), the foundational work of 18th century physics and astronomy, endowed them with an important role in sustaining terrestrial life. This cometary role in renewing earthly life was among others defended by David Gregory (ca. 1659–1708) in his *Astronomiae Physicae et Geometricae Elementa*, by

Henry Pemberton (1694–1771) in his *View of Sir Isaac's Newton's Philosophy*, and on numerous occasions by the well-known astronomer and friend of Newton and Mead, Edmund Halley (1656–1742). Comets were not only considered to produce beneficial effects, but they were often thought to have the capacity to bring about enormous maleficent and deleterious events. These included the destruction of all human life. Halley repeatedly suggested the scriptural deluge might have been caused by cometary impact, and investigated the possible consequences of a comparable collision in the future. Similar approaches to comets can be found throughout 18th-century England, sometimes explicitly portraying them as divine means to punish mankind. At the very end of the century, the opinion that the deluge could have been caused by cometary effects was still upheld by writers like Adam Walker (1731–1821), an exponent of the Midlands Enlightenment. The study of cometary effects on earthly life was far from limited to the British Isles, and went much further than exploring the consequences of direct collision. Continental proponents of far-reaching cometary influence include Pierre Louis Moureau de Maupertuis (1698–1759), the first president of the Prussian Academy of Science; the Swiss naturalist and geologist Elie Bertrand (1712–1790), one of a group of thinkers inspired by the Lisbon earthquake of 1755 to contemplate cometary influence on such disastrous natural events; and the French mathematician and astronomer Joseph Jérôme Lefrançois de Lalande (1732–1807). The latter illustrates how Enlightenment astronomers could have a societal impact as profound as astrologers in earlier centuries. A wrongly interpreted paper of Lalande caused many inhabitants of Paris and its surroundings to believe the end of the world was pending.

Some scientists of the Enlightenment, however, claimed that celestial influences went far beyond comets. The Italian astronomer and physicist Giuseppe Toaldo (1717–1797) wrote an extensive, observation-based, and much translated book on the influence of heavenly bodies on the weather (1770). Toaldo's work was conceptualized as a contribution to navigation, agriculture, and, importantly, medicine. Historical research in the first decade and a half of the 21st century has pointed out that the study of celestial influence might have been stronger in Enlightenment medicine than in astronomy or physics. Influential doctors and medical theorists of the early Enlightenment like Friedrich Hoffmann (1660–1742) and Georg Ernst Stahl (1659–1734) wrote works exclusively devoted to celestial influence. Hoffmann's dissertation on the influence of the stars on the human body (1706) did not even shy away from the positive use of the word *astrology*; neither did Stahl's work on weather forecasting. Hoffmann's dissertation remained important throughout at least the first part of the 18th century. It was recycled as the entry on "astronomia" in the *Medical Dictionary* (1743–1745) of the English physician Robert James (1703–1776), which was translated into French by the *Encyclopédistes* Diderot, Marc-Antoine Eidous (1724–1790), and François-Vincent Toussaint (1715–1772). The English and French translators made one important adjustment to Hoffmann's original text, reflecting the ever-increasing negative Enlightenment stance on the word *astrology*: wherever Hoffmann writes positively of the use of *astrology* in medicine, the word is translated as *astronomy*.

Ehrenfried Walther von Tschirnhaus's (1651–1708) experiments in which the moonlight was denied any warmth, cold or moisture were often cited by both critics and apologists of celestial influence. They did not, however, cause doctors to rule out lunar interference in the human body, as some Enlightenment physicians explicitly based their defense of celestial influence on Newton's laws of gravitation. Mead's often republished and expanded treatise on solar and lunar influence of 1704 is the first-known example of such works but has counterparts on the continent like the dissertations of Christian Gottlieb Kraztenstein (1723–1795) in Halle, and of Franz Anton Mesmer (1734–1815) in Vienna. In the second part of the 18th century, some physicians and medical associations tried to prove planetary, solar, and lunar influence on the weather—and consequently on the human body—by keeping records of celestial constellations and meteorological changes. The Dutch doctor Iman Jacob van den Bosch (1731–1788) and his kindred spirits in the *Natuur-en Geneeskundige Correspondentie-Societeit* are clear-cut examples. Another category of medical professionals, physicians who worked in the European East and West Indies, produced a significant amount of treatises on lunar and solar influences on disease. This was in line with the common belief that the effects of sun and moon were stronger in tropical areas. The work on this subject of—among many others—James Lind (1716–1794), most famous for his discovery of a cure for scurvy, and Francis Balfour (before 1755–after 1807), whose work on celestial influence was commissioned by the British East India Company in 1794, was read and elaborated upon at some European universities. A summary of the work on celestial influences of selected Europe-based and colonial physicians can be found in Evert Jan Thomassen à Thuessink's (1762–1832) *Waarnemingen* (1789). Apart from the works specifically devoted to celestial influences, the effects of heavenly bodies figured in passing and in different degrees of elaboration in countless medical works of authors based in different corners of Enlightenment Europe, like Herman Boerhaave (1668–1738) in the Dutch Republic, Nils Rosén von Rosenstein (1706–1773) in Sweden and Erasmus Darwin (1731–1802) in England.

Arno Rombouts

See also: Agriculture; Antiastrological Thought; Comets; Medical Astrology; Science

Further Reading

Harrison, Mark. 2000. "From Medical Astrology to Medical Astronomy: Sol-Lunar and Planetary Theories of Disease in British Medicine, c. 1700–1850." *British Journal for the History of Science* 33: 25–48.

Roos, Anne Marie. 2000. "Luminaries in Medicine: Richard Mead, James Gibbs, and Solar and Lunar Effects on the Human Body in Early Modern England." *Bulletin of the History of Medicine* 74, no. 3: 433–457.

Schaffer, Simon. 1987. "Authorized Prophets: Comets and Astronomers after 1759." *Studies in Eighteenth Century Culture* 17: 45–67.

Schaffer, Simon. 2010. "The Astrological Roots of Mesmerism." *Studies in History and Philosophy of Biological and Biomedical Sciences* 41: 158–168.

F

FATE

Astrologers consider that their lives are linked to the orderly movement of the planets and stars. This order of the heavens instills a level of fate into their lives, where fate is some form of external influence on one's life. Today, the classical and medieval arguments about fate have disappeared from academic discourse, as fate is now considered an obsolete concept. One of the dilemmas within philosophy, however, is how one maintains the possibility of free will in light of the modern notion of inevitable and universal determinism. Within these modern debates various positions are adopted including: that there is only free will (libertarianism), that humans are separate or can control determinism (a form of dualism), that there is only determinism (hard-incompatibilism), and that there is a way to have free will within determinism (compatibilism). Despite the diversity and, at times, complexity of these modern arguments about free will and determinism, fate, as accepted by astrologers, is ignored. The outsider astrological literature views the concept of fate within astrology as a belief in an inevitable future (hard-incompatibilism). This is, however, in contrast to the evidence of the insider astrological literature of the 20th century. Astrologers have, in fact, varying views about fate some of which are that fate is a blind force that can be manipulated (a dualistic argument), that fate is inevitable, (hard-incompatibilism), that fate does not exist (libertarianism), and that one can live and work with fate (compatibilism). This diversity of opinions, which loosely parallels the philosophical debates on free will, indicates that, rather than being a simplistic adoption of hard-incompatibilism, fate is instead the more complex phenomenon of an individual's personal dialogue with the inevitability of the Newtonian solar system.

In the earliest astrological writings from the Assyrian period in the seventh century BCE, fate was viewed as a blind law of nature that could be manipulated by trickery or ritual (Rochberg-Halton 1982, 363). A difficult planetary omen could be nullified by prayers, drum beating, or even using a substitute king. The Greeks, however, developed many different views on the nature of fate. One view was to personify fate as the *Moirae*, the three fates that handled the thread of life, Clotho who spun it, Lachesis who measured it, and Atropos who cut it. By the first century CE the authors known as Pseudo-Plutarch, in the *De Fato*, defined it as *heimarmene*, a divine law that penetrated the whole cosmos. In contrast to these views of fate, Plato (ca. 428–423 BCE) considered that fate influenced the material realm but that the human soul could choose to rise above this and eventually reunite with the divine. This is a dualist model of fate, where the world was made of two types of substances, the one influenced by fate, and the other, containing the soul, free from fate. In direct contrast to Plato's dualism was the Stoic model of fate. Stoicism was a philosophical movement that arose in the third century BCE in Athens. The Stoics considered that everything was influenced by fate, even the soul; however, the mind was free to decide to be happy or sad at one's fate (Epictetus trans. 2004, 4). The Middle Platonist Calcidius (fl. ca. fourth century) believed however that humanity could create chains of fate, which, once started, could not be stopped (Calcidius 1970, paragraph 151). In Calcidius's model, humanity was a fate-maker, and it was important to use astrology to find the correct moments to take action in order that the fate that was being cast was beneficial.

The most influential definition of fate, however, came from the Roman senator Marcus Tullius Cicero (106–43 BCE). He defined fate as, "Now by Fate I mean . . . an orderly succession of causes, wherein cause is linked to causes and each cause of itself produces an effect." He described how fate worked by stating that "things which are to be do not suddenly spring into existence, but the evolution of time is like the unwinding of a cable: it creates nothing new and only unfolds each event in its order" (Cicero [1923] 2001, I lv.125, and I lvi 27). With this definition of fate, the events of any moment were deemed to be predetermined as a causal chain since the beginning of time. Cicero criticized astrology, which linked human life to fate, and therefore, according to Cicero, removed human free will (Cicero [1923] 2001, II vii 18). Thus Cicero viewed the horoscope as inevitable, containing only one possible life. Cicero's views on fate were adopted across the Western world and thus the inevitability of fate became the foundation of most major criticisms leveled at astrology. The arguments of different destinies, two people born at the same time living different lives, and common destinies, people with different birth times all dying at the same time in an accident, are both classical criticisms of astrology (Hegedus 2007, 43) based on Cicero's definition of fate.

Arguments about fate continued after the Roman Empire's adoption of Christianity. Fate was dismissed by Saint Augustine (354–430) who claimed that all was dictated by divine providence. According to Augustine, it was invalid to assume that a person could be involved with the expression of one's fate, or to use the planets as intermediaries, as all was dictated by God. With fate eliminated from Christian views by the late Middle Ages, the concept of fate was placed into the natural sciences and thus transformed from a human dialogue with the heavens to a causal, naturalistic, and deterministic system. The idea of fate as a part of the natural sciences was, however, finally discarded in the 17th century when the science of nature became separated from theology (Faivre and Voss 1995, 48). In its place was a nondivine cause eventually defined as determinism, which was seen as universal and thus applicable to all organic and inorganic objects. Consequently, the idea of fate, viewed as belonging to the religious or esoteric realms, was dismissed from scientific and philosophical thought and generally held in contempt. Astrologers, however, could not disregard the fate that heavenly movements placed into their lives and thus astrologers and their subject became increasingly marginalized. In this environment, new polemics emerged. In the 1950s the philosopher Theodor Adorno (1903–1969) claimed that astrologers must be maladjusted for, by accepting fate, they gave up all notions of free will, as they allowed their life to be dictated by the stars. Adorno, like Cicero 2,000 years before him, considered

A Shakespeare Villain Critiques Astrology

This passage from William Shakespeare's tragedy King Lear is often quoted as a critique of astrology as encouraging moral evasion and passivity in the face of fate. However, it should be remembered that the speaker, Edmund, is a villain. He is also ignorant of astrology, as Ursa Major is a nonzodiacal sign, hence a nativity could not be under it:

> This is the excellent foppery of the world, that, when we are sick in fortune, often the surfeit of our own behaviour, we make guilty of our disasters the sun, the moon, and the stars; as if we were villains on necessity; fools by heavenly compulsion; knaves, thieves, and treachers by spherical pre-dominance; drunkards, liars, and adulterers by an enforc'd obedience of planetary influence; and all that we are evil in, by a divine thrusting on. An admirable evasion of whore-master man, to lay his goatish disposition to the charge of a star! My father compounded with my mother under the Dragon's Tail, and my nativity was under Ursa Major, so that it follows I am rough and lecherous. Fut! I should have been that I am, had the maidenliest star in the firmament twinkled on my bastardizing.

Source: Shakespeare, William. *King Lear* Act I, Scene 2, ll. 442–454.

that fate in astrology was inevitable and that it could proscribe only one possible meaning for any astrological combination—an inevitable fate led to an inevitable horoscope.

In stark contrast to this outsider literature, Cicero's version of fate is not supported by the astrologers. From some of the earliest astrological writings fate was not considered to be inevitable. The first-century polymath Claudius Ptolemy seemed to directly argue against Cicero when he discussed the fate of astrology, stating that "nor is it to be thought that all events are shown to proceed from one single inevitable fate, without being influenced by the interposition of any other agency" (Ptolemy 1969, Book I.III.). More recently astrological literature published in the 20th century reveals a variety of views on fate. For example, Alan Leo (1860–1917) promoted spiritual astrology and voiced Plato's argument that the soul was free. Some 60 years later in the 1970s, Jungian astrologer Liz Greene (b. 1946) promoted what can be viewed as a neo-Stoic approach suggesting that humanity is largely fated but our minds are free. Horary astrologers have, from the classical period to the current day, promoted a view of fate aligned with Calcidius where the astrologer is a fate-maker.

Today there are three views on fate. The everyday use of the word *fate* is to speak of a person meeting their fate, death, or dire consequences. For the critic of astrology, fate is viewed as the belief in an inevitable force that removes all control from the individual's life. For the astrologer, fate is their personal dialogue with the heavens, and the strength of that dialogue varies from one astrologer to the next. In short, fate in astrology is a phenomenon generated by the experiences of living in an ordered world of apparent cycles and patterns.

Bernadette Brady

See also: Albertus Magnus; Antiastrological Thought; Christianity; Leo, Alan; Natal Astrology; Ptolemy; Stoicism

Further Reading

Adorno, Theodor, W. 1994. "The Stars Down to Earth: The *Los Angeles Times* Astrology Column." In *The Stars Down to Earth and Other Essays on the Irrational in Culture*, ed. Stephen Crook, 34–127. London: Routledge.

Calcidius. 1970. *Calcidius on Fate*, trans. J. den Boeft. Leiden: Brill.

Cicero, Marcus Tullius. (1923) 2001, repr. *De Divinatione*, trans. W. A. Falconer. Loeb Classical Library. Cambridge, MA: Harvard University Press.

Dilman, lham. 1999. *Free Will: An Historical and Philosophical Introduction*. London: Routledge.

Epictetus. 2004. *Discourses Books 1 and 2*, trans. P. E. Matheson. New York: Dover Publications.

Faivre, Antoine, and Karen-Claire Voss. 1995. "Western Esotericism and the Science of Religions." *Numen* 42, no. 1: 48–77.

Greene, Liz. 1984. *The Astrology of Fate*. London: George Allen and Unwin.

Hegedus, Tim. 2007. *Early Christianity and Ancient Astrology*. New York: Peter Lang.

Ptolemy, Claudius. 1969. *The Tetrabiblos*, trans. J. M. Ashmand. Mokelumne Hill, CA: Health Research.

Rochberg-Halton, Francesca. 1982. "Fate and Divination in Mesopotamia." *Archiv für Orientforschung, Beiheft* 19: 363.

Willis, Roy, and Patrick Curry. 2004. *Astrology Science and Culture, Pulling Down the Moon*. New York: Berg.

FEMINIST ASTROLOGY

The later 20th century saw the development of feminist astrology, often associated with the New Age movement and like transpersonal and other forms of humanist astrology emphasizing the spiritual and psychological aspects of astrology rather than the predicting of future events. Feminist astrologers see themselves as challenging a male-dominated Western astrological tradition as feminists have challenged male intellectual and cultural authority in other fields. The fact that astrology is marginalized by the male-dominated scientific and intellectual establishment also makes it a natural ally for women, a marginalized population, for some feminist astrologers. Feminist astrologers also start from the knowledge that in Western societies, astrology is more commonly consumed by women than by men, making it an aspect of "female culture."

Feminist astrologers such as Geraldine Hatch Hanon (1947–2011) associated both astrology and women with cyclic time rather than the linear time of the patriarchy, particularly the time scheme of the Abrahamic religions Judaism, Christianity, and Islam from creation to apocalypse. In particular, they correlate the lunar cycle with the menstrual cycle, arguing that women are particularly attuned to celestial rhythms and therefore particularly suited to astrology. Feminist astrology is often associated with goddess spirituality, and some have identified the origin of astrology in early goddess-oriented cultures.

The Three Faces of Lilith

Feminist astrology has contributed to a desire to identify more celestial objects as female. Feminist astrologers want celestial representation of a broader range of female roles and possibilities than the traditionally feminine planets of the moon and Venus. In addition to the planets and asteroids discovered in modern times, many feminist astrologers use a concept known as "Lilith" named after the first wife of Adam in Jewish legend. Lilith was punished and exiled from the Garden of Eden for her refusal to submit to Adam. Outside astrology, Lilith has become a symbol of women's resistance to patriarchy as seen in such phenomena as the Lilith Fairs of women's music. The most common astrological interpretation of Lilith is that it is the focus of the moon's elliptical orbit not occupied by the Earth, also known as the "Dark Moon." Lilith can also refer to an asteroid named Lilith discovered and named in 1927 or a mythical "black moon" that orbits the Earth at a distance farther than the moon. (The asteroid was given the name to honor a French composer named Lili Boulanger rather than the Jewish mythological figure.) The fact that Lilith has three separate meanings is often linked to the concept of the triple goddess. In all her forms, Lilith is held to embody a more assertive, dangerous concept of female energy than the moon or Venus.

One aspect of the feminist critique of the astrological tradition is its view of gender. Because traditional astrology is highly gendered, with each planet and sign categorized as male or female, part of the work of the feminist astrologer is to deconstruct this binary, and in particular to broaden the astrological possibilities of the feminine. Feminist astrologers have tried to redefine traditionally male planets such as the sun as androgynous. Asteroids and newly discovered dwarf planets such as Eris, discovered in 2005, and named after the Greek goddess of discord the following year, are often gendered female. They are particularly useful for feminist astrologers looking for female archetypes other than those represented by the traditionally feminine astrological planets, Venus and the moon. The discovery of these celestial bodies is often associated with a reemergence of female spiritual energy. Feminist astrologers who address a broader public, rather than writing for other astrologers, view their work as a tool for social change and consciousness-raising, and their work often appears in feminist and woman-oriented periodicals and websites. Although the work of popular feminist astrologers such as the "Astrotwins" (Tali Edut and Ophira Edut, b. 1972) is expressed in the traditional sun sign format and covers the same personal and relationship issues as mainstream sun sign columns, it is often phrased in a feminist-inspired rhetoric of self-actualization and self-empowerment.

William E. Burns

See also: Asteroids; Gender; Information Technology; New Age; Sex and Love; Transpersonal Astrology

Further Reading

Edut, Ophira. "Sisterhood and the Stars: My Disjointed Life as a Feminist Astrology Columnist." http://www.feminist.com/ourinnerlives/features_ophira_edut_astrology.html

George, Demetra, and Douglas Bloch. 2003. *Asteroid Goddesses: The Mythology, Psychology and Astrology of the Re-Emerging Feminine*. York Beach, ME: Nicolas-Hays; [Enfield: Airlift].
Hanon, Geraldine Hatch. 1990. *Sacred Space: A Feminist Vision of Astrology*. Ithaca, NY: Firebrand Books.
River, Lindsay. 1987. *The Knot of Time: Astrology and the Female Experience*. New York: Harper and Row.

FICINO, MARSILIO (1433–1499)

Renaissance Platonic philosopher Marsilio Ficino was a leader in adapting the basically Aristotelian astrology of the Middle Ages to the revival of Platonism and Hermeticism in the 15th century. His astrology was thoroughly integrated into a magical view of the universe. Ficino was particularly influential due to his position in Florence, the center of the Italian Renaissance and his key role as a translator of Greek works, including the complete writings of Plato, into Latin. He was the head of an informal body of scholars investigating the newly available Greek works known as the Platonic Academy of Florence.

Ficino strongly identified with the planet Saturn, in the ascendant in Aquarius at the time of his birth. (Aquarius was a sign believed to be ruled by Saturn.) He accepted the traditional association of Saturn with melancholy but also believed that as the outermost of the planets it was physically closest to divinity, being the outermost planet, and that it called him to study and wisdom. He consulted the stars before beginning a new book or publishing one and advised that the all types of actions including sex in the hope of children should take place at astrologically chosen times. Although not a professional consulting astrologer, he gave astrological advice. Ficino's letters are full of astrological language.

Ficino was familiar with ancient and medieval astrological writers including Manilius, Firmicus Maternus, Abū Ma'shar, and Albertus Magnus. However, his approach to astrology was more Neoplatonic and magical than Aristotelian. He was greatly influenced by the ancient Neoplatonic philosopher Plotinus (204–270 CE), whose *Enneads* he translated into Latin along with a range of other ancient Neoplatonic writers, pagan and Christian. He was also influenced by the Hermetic Corpus, a body of ancient Greek magical texts that he and others thought were several millennia old, even though they actually date from the first centuries of the Common Era. He was the first to translate the Hermetic Corpus into Latin, a task he took up at the request of his patron, the ruler of Florence Cosimo de Medici. He did not believe that the stars exerted a force that directly influenced people and things as the dominant Aristotelian school thought so much as that human life corresponded to the movements of the stars in a harmonious cosmos. Planets and other celestial bodies were divine spiritual beings obedient to God, and the fact that they represented earthly changes did not mean that they caused them. The sun was particularly important, being the physical analogy to God. The planets were also associated with spiritual entities called "daemons" that functioned as personal guardians. This led to a generally positive outlook on the planets, and Ficino had little interest in the traditional astrology that classified Mars and Saturn as purely "malevolent." The signs were also governed by spirits associated with the most prominent star in their constellations. Like other Christian writers, Ficino strongly opposed the idea of astrological determinism and defended the freedom of the will. Given the excellence of the planets as spiritual beings created by God, it was particularly problematic for astrologers to blame them for crimes and disasters.

Ficino's *Three Books on Life* (1489) set forth a system of maintaining health and prolonging life through astrology. The book was extremely popular and stayed in print for many years. In the third book, Ficino endorsed the creation and use of astrological talismans and discussed how to make them. When made under the right circumstances, talismans could share in the qualities of the celestial entities they were meant to represent. Ficino was clearly worried about responses to this endorsement of magical images and included an unconvincing statement that he was not actually supporting them but merely giving the view of Plotinus. The powers of the planets could also be invoked by music, which could heal. Influenced by Pythagoreanism, Ficino believed that the "harmonious" movements of the planets were analogous to musical harmonies.

Ficino's views of astrology were not always consistent. He was always much more dubious about using astrology for prediction than he was about elective astrology. (He blamed Ptolemy for much of this.) In 1477 he wrote a book against judicial, or predictive, astrology, *Disputation against the Judgement of the Astrologers*, although he did not publish it. In the last decade of his life, when hostility to astrology was becoming more prevalent in both his home of Florence and in Rome, he published a work denouncing it. He was close friends with the much younger Giovanni Pico della Mirandola (1463–1494), an opponent of astrology. Ficino believed he had a particular bond with Pico in that both had Saturn in Aquarius. Much of Pico's antiastrological classic, *Disputations against Astrology* (1494), is based on Ficino's earlier work, although Pico went much further and condemned the magical astrology Ficino supported as well as the predictive astrology based on cause and effect that he condemned.

Despite the growing hostility to astrology in late 15th-century Italy, Ficino wrote and published a book of astrological mysticism, *The Book of the Sun* (1494), which used description of the sun's path through the zodiac to direct the reader's attention to the sun as an image of God, or even in some allegorical sense as God. This solar mysticism had ancient roots going back to Pythagoras. As a Christian, Ficino describes the sun not solely as a unit but also in terms of threes—its three properties of fecundity, light, and heat, for example—connecting it to the concept of God as a Trinity found in the dominant Christian traditions. Fecundity he links with the Father, light with the Son, and Heat with the Holy Spirit. The sun stands as the ruler of the planets (with the moon his consort or queen, according to the traditional gendering of sun and moon) as does God the ruler of the universe.

In the subsequent centuries, Ficino's Platonic, magical, and spiritual astrology was largely eclipsed by the Ptolemaic tradition that viewed the stars and planets as actually exerting power on the Earth and the task of the astrologer as prediction but the astrological revival of the 19th and 20th centuries saw the return of some of Ficino's concepts in Theosophy and transpersonal astrology.

William E. Burns

See also: Antiastrological Thought; Christianity; Electional Astrology; Medical Astrology; *Picatrix;* Pythagoras of Samos; Renaissance and Reformation Astrology; Theosophy; Transpersonal Astrology; Zodiacs

Further Reading

Ficino, Marsilio. 1989. *Three Books on Life*; a critical edition and translation with introduction and notes by Carol V. Kaske and John R. Clark. Binghamton, NY: Medieval and Renaissance Texts and Studies in conjunction with the Renaissance Society of America.

Kaske, Carol V. 1982. "Marsilio Ficino and the Twelve Gods of the Zodiac." *Journal of the Warburg and Courtauld Institutes* 45: 195–202.

Moore, Thomas. 1982. *Planets Within: Marsilio Ficino's Astrological Psychology.* Lewisburg. PA: Bucknell University Press.

Voss, Angela, ed. 2006. *Marsilio Ficino.* Berkeley, CA: North Atlantic Books.

FIRMICUS MATERNUS, JULIUS (FOURTH CENTURY CE)

Julius Firmicus Maternus, a Roman aristocrat, wrote the longest surviving Latin astrological text from the ancient world, *Mathesis*, probably written around 334. (*Mathesis* roughly translates to "branch of knowledge.") Although he does not seem to have been a creative or innovative astrologer, Firmicus Maternus's work is of considerable value in recording ancient Hellenistic and Roman astrological theory and for Firmicus Maternus's discussion of the social and legal role of astrologers and astrological practice.

Mathesis is dedicated and addressed to an eminent Roman politician and friend of Firmicus Maternus, Lollianus Mavortius, and divided into eight books. It covers a standard range of astrological topics, including zodiac signs, houses and decans, planets and their aspects, and the ascendant. *Mathesis* includes one of the most extensive discussions of lots from any ancient source. He also mentions the rarely expounded doctrine of myriogenesis, the use of subdivisions of the degrees of the ascendant arc. Firmicus referred to lost "Books of Myriogenesis" by "Asclepius," claiming that the meanings of individual minutes of ascendant arc can explain an entire nativity. Other rarely mentioned astrological procedures and doctrines include full and empty degrees, so distinguished according to whether or not certain groups of stars appear in them. Firmicus Maternus's sources include Manilius, Dorotheus of Sidon, and Ptolemy. (He does not specifically refer to Manilius, but shows knowledge of his work. This silence was probably motivated by his claim to be the first Latin astrological writer.) Many of the sources he draws from are lost, making *Mathesis* a particularly valuable source for astrology in the Hellenistic and Roman periods. As an educated aristocrat, he would have known Greek as well as Latin and been able to read the Hellenistic astrologers, although like other ancient writers he regards the true sources of astrology as Egypt and Babylon and its ultimate source as the wisdom handed down from the god Mercury to humanity. His expositions of astrological principles are not always clear, reflecting the difficulties of translation from Greek to Latin, and sometimes inconsistent, often reflecting a failure to reconcile his diverse sources. However, he is not a mere copyist and his work is full of terminology characteristic of fourth-century Rome, including the titles of public officials. He also mentions his previous career as a lawyer, and the text shows familiarity with the law and courts.

Mathesis begins with a defense of astrology against its skeptical and other critics. Firmicus Maternus saw astrology as a branch, the highest branch, of divination. The primary focus of the work is natal astrology, although it also deals with medical astrology and other branches of astrology. *Mathesis* focuses on the meaning of the stars rather than the calculations necessary to draw up a horoscope, making it essentially useless without a background in mathematical astronomy. Firmicus Maternus was influenced by Stoic philosophy and accepted the idea of human beings as a microcosm of the macrocosm, the universe. Like other Stoic diviners and astrologers, he took a strongly deterministic attitude to the influence of the stars. This meant that precision was necessary, as even a slight difference in the horoscope could mean a completely different fate for its subject. (He expounded the different fates according to which degree of the ascendant sign was actually ascendant at the moment of birth, a technique that would have been impossible to apply in most cases given the lack of records for precise moments of birth.) However, as was common among Roman astrologers, he insisted that the emperor was not subject to the power of the stars but only to the power of God, a way of avoiding the ever-dangerous practice of predicting the emperor's death or misfortune. He warned astrologers against such illegal questions.

Firmicus Maternus's depiction of individual fates tends toward the sensational, with horoscopic phenomena either leading to great success or to catastrophe including violent death at the hands of murderers or the public executioner. His interest in extreme fates has been linked to his study of rhetoric, an essential part of a late antique education and one particularly linked with lawyers like Firmicus Maternus. He shows a great interest in sexual matters, taking a typically Stoic puritanical attitude.

For Firmicus Maternus, it was not just astrological expertise that defined the astrologer, but a specific way of life. He stated that the astrologer should fit the pattern of Stoic virtue, requiring little luxury and adhering to a strict code. A reputation for goodness is an important qualification for an astrologer. A reputation for being money-grubbing is a particular handicap, and an astrologer must not be greedy for money. Sexual restraint is also very important. Rather than being marginal figures, astrologers should be solidly rooted in their communities, married, and with friends among the social elite. Astrological consultations should be carried out in public in part to clear astrologers from accusations of secret divination. However, the astrologer should not be an informer, a class that Firmicus Maternus, like many Roman writers, viewed as a plague on society.

At the time when he wrote *Mathesis*, Firmicus Maternus seems to have been, like many Stoics, a philosophical monotheist. He lived during the time when the Roman Empire, or at least its elite, was becoming Christian. Sometime after he wrote *Mathesis*, he converted to Christianity and wrote his second surviving book, *The Error of Pagan Religions*, a denunciation of the worship of pagan gods and a call for its extirpation. There is no evidence in the text, which never mentions astrology, that his conversion had turned him against it.

Except for one doubtful fifth-century reference, *Mathesis* disappeared from sight after publication. References to Firmicus Maternus first appear in the literature of the 11th century, the same time as the oldest surviving manuscripts. (About 10 percent of the original work has been lost.) He was viewed in the Middle Ages as an authority on astrology, the only Latin rival of the great Greek and Arabic astrologers. His reputation fell with the introduction of major Greek and Arabic astrologers like Ptolemy and Abū Ma'shar in Latin translation, but Firmicus Maternus was never entirely displaced from the Western astrological canon. (He appears as one of only three ancient authorities in the bibliography of William Lilly's *Christian Astrology*, the others being Manilius and Ptolemy.) *Mathesis* received its first printed edition in 1501.

William E. Burns

See also: Hellenistic Astrology; Lots; Manilius, Marcus; Roman Astrology; Stoicism

Further Reading

Firmicus Maternus, Julius. 2011. *Julius Firmicus Maternus: Mathesis*; ed. and trans. James Herschel Holden. Tempe, AZ: American Federation of Astrologers.

Holden, James H. 2006. *A History of Horoscopic Astrology*. Tempe, AZ: American Federation of Astrologers.

Sogno, Cristiana. 2005. "Astrology, Morality, the Emperor and the Law in Firmicus Maternus' 'Mathesis.'" *Illinois Classical Studies* 30: 167–176.

Tester, S. J. 1987. *A History of Western Astrology*. Wolfbridge, UK: Boydell.

FIXED STARS

The fixed stars have had a checkered history in astrology. At the dawn of astrology in the Mesopotamian period, the stars fulfilled a vital role as they contributed qualities to the planets based on the part of the constellation image that the star defined. These qualities were assigned by the rising or setting of stars with planets or the visual phenomenon of the planet moving close to a star. Later, however, in the Hellenistic period, the stars were projected onto the ecliptic, which gave rise to the stars represented as a two-dimensional table of degrees, rather than their earlier role of populating the heavenly dome. These tables, designed for astronomical use, led to a new method in astrology of blending all the stars, north or south, onto the ecliptic independent of their constellations and assigning the different zodiac degrees different star meanings. This methodology dominated astrology from the end of the classical period right through to the late 20th century. The result of this disconnect between a star and its place in the heavens eventually led to a simplification of the role of stars in astrology and they became reduced to simple keywords. Consequently, most 20th-century astrologers rejected the use of fixed stars, seeing them as antiquated, simplistic, and unsuited to modern life. With the advent of the personal computer, however, astrologers have revisited stars in astrology and some have returned to the older, observational methods, all of which have contributed to a revival of the role of fixed stars in astrology in the late 20th and early 21st century.

The stars, known as fixed stars in astrology, have since antiquity been grouped into patterns recognized as constellations. The actual constellations may vary from one cultural group to another. In astrology, however, in both the east and the west, the constellations that are used are the Mesopotamian/Hellenistic constellations recorded in the fourth century BCE by Aratus. The first use of fixed stars in astrology was at the dawn of astrology in the Mesopotamian period. At this time astrology was the body of knowledge that saw the sky as a continuous sky narrative where the planets represented the king and members of his royal court as they moved among the stars of the zodiac constellations. In the letters written by the Assyrian priests to their king in the seventh century BCE, the different stars were assigned different qualities that contributed to the ongoing sky narrative. The importance of a star was not based on its brightness (magnitude) but rather on its location within a particular constellation and the nature of that constellation. Thus the star that marked the lion's heart (Regulus) was linked to the success of the king, while the star called the Fish star in Capricorn was linked to plentifulness of fish and birds (Hunger 1992 no. 29, 73). This first use of stars in astrology, where meaning is based on the star's contribution to the image of a constellation rather than its magnitude, remains the principal way meaning is assigned to particular stars. Hence small dim stars can be considered just as important as bright stars. In this tradition, although there are over a thousand named stars in the heavens, astrologers worked with a far shorter list of 15 to 60 stars.

The method used by the Assyrian priests was direct observation, watching how the planets moved among the stars, as well as the rising, setting, or culminating of stars and planets with each other. This methodology is known as working with the paranatellonta, abbreviated to parans, and is evident in the astrological work written by an anonymous author in 379 CE, *The Treatise on Bright Fixed Stars*. In this work, the author allocates qualities to the bright stars and brings these qualities to bear in a person's life if the star is on a "pivot point" (the points rising, culminating, setting, or on the lower culmination) at the time of birth, while also allocating a time of life when the star's influence will be felt based on the particular angle occupied by the star (Anonymous 1993, 1–2).

All this was about to change, however. By the late Hellenistic period the rate of precession, the slow movement of stars against fixed points like the equinox due to the wobble of the Earth's axis, was of vital interest. To address this question, Claudius Ptolemy devised a method where he took the poles of the ecliptic and, using ecliptical longitude, drew a line from pole to pole through 1022 stars and noted the place where each star-line crossed the ecliptic. From this Ptolemy compiled a star-ecliptic degree catalog. This catalog formed part of Ptolemy's *Almagest*, his astronomical work, and was undertaken so that future researchers could remeasure the ecliptical position of the 1022 stars and thus finally establish the rate of precession. In that regard Ptolemy is attributed with discovering the rate of precession. Ptolemy's star catalog, however, with its convenient list of ecliptical degrees, was far easier for astrologers to use than direct observations of risings, culminatings, and settings of the stars and planets and thus it offered an alternative method for working with fixed stars. The astrologer could take a horoscope and check Ptolemy's list of stars for a degree matching with the natal planets and luminaries to see which fixed stars need to be considered in that horoscope's interpretation.

Because precession slowly moved the stars along the ecliptic, Ptolemy's list needed to be constantly updated. Thus it was, over the next thousand years, a slowly changing table being constantly recalculated by astronomers or astrologers. By the 15th century, in seeking to create accurate star maps, the astronomer Regiomontanus (1436–1476) turned to the poles of the equator for his projections, rather than using Ptolemy's poles of the ecliptic. This shift of poles effectively changed the ecliptical degree of every star. Nevertheless, because astrologers were used to this table of fixed stars slowly changing, this shift of pole, with its new listing of ecliptical degrees for the stars, was accepted without apparent question. So dominant was this method of using a simple table of degrees for stars that even Galileo Galilei in his astrology worked in this manner. In writing about Algol, a star in the northern constellation of Perseus, Galileo noted that, if a planet was in the ecliptical degree that was the listed degree for the fixed star Algol, known as the "head of the gorgon," then that planet was damaged. This was independent of the fact that he would have known that Algol was located over 22° north of the ecliptic.

Other influential astrologers also worked in this manner. Earlier in the 14th century, Guido Bonatti used fixed stars projected onto the ecliptic in his horary astrology. So did William Lilly who used 16 stars, all allocated to particular ecliptical degrees, to help with his horary interpretations. As the fixed stars in astrology became disconnected from their constellation and thus their mythological meanings, slowly they became reduced to simplistic statements so that, for example, Zosma, a star in the back of the constellation Leo, which, according to Hellenistic mythology, was linked with the overthrowing of an older order, became simplified to mean disgrace, melancholy, fear of poisons, and a shameless and egotistical nature (Robson 1984, 219). Consequently, by the 20th century, fixed stars in astrology tended to be only used in horary astrology and were generally considered to be of little value in natal chart interpretation.

By the latter half of the 20th century, with the new movement of humanistic astrology promoted by Dane Rudhyar, the individual degrees of the ecliptic were allocated unique meaning, not from the fixed stars but from the psychically derived Sabian Symbols of Marc Edmund Jones (1888–1980). Astrologers who wished to consider the uniqueness of a particular degree could now turn to these nonmoving (not subject to precession) and modern symbols, rather than what was considered the archaic and inappropriate meanings of the fixed stars. The result could have been the end to the role of fixed stars in astrology. Having been disregarded as the shining lights of the heavens in the Mesopotamian period and reduced to just points on the ecliptic by the late Hellenistic period, now too those very points were being replaced by new symbols. In the late 20th century, however, the fixed stars saw a revival.

With the advent of the personal computer it became possible for astrologers to return to the earlier technique of parans by reconstructing the whole dome of the heavens for the moment of birth and observing if a star and planet moved simultaneously onto any one of the four angles on the date of birth. In 1998 the Australian astrologer Bernadette Brady, working with this original method, published a revision of all the astrological fixed star meanings as a way of bridging the cultural and historical vacuum between the meanings suggested by the anonymous author in 379 CE and life in the late 20th century. Later the U.S. astrologer Diana Rosenberg published her revision of meanings, choosing to maintain the later model of stars projected to ecliptical degrees. Both these works have revitalized the role of fixed stars, with astrological software now providing astrologers a choice of both techniques. Such is the return of stars to astrology that the online Swiss company Astrodienst, now offers fixed star computerized reports using the original paran method of working with fixed stars.

Bernadette Brady

See also: Galilei, Galileo; Hellenistic Astrology; Mesopotamian Astrology; Zodiacs

Further Reading

Allen, Richard Hinckley. 1963. *Star Names Their Lore and Meaning*. New York: Dover Publications.

Anonymous, of 379. 1993. *The Treatise on the Bright Fixed Stars*. Berkeley Springs, WV: Golden Hind Press.

Brady, Bernadette. 1998. *Brady's Book of Fixed Stars*. York, ME: Samuel Weiser.

Brady, Bernadette. 2008. *Star and Planet Combinations*. Bournemouth, UK: Wessex Astrologer.

Robson, Vivian E. 1984. *The Fixed Stars and Constellations in Astrology*. York, ME: Samuel Weiser.

Rosenberg, Diana. 2012. *Secrets of the Ancient Skies*, vols. 1–2. New York: Ancient Skies Press.

FORMAN, SIMON (1552–1611)

Simon Forman was an English astrologer and medical practitioner who collected and employed astrological knowledge primarily for practical purposes.

Forman was born in Quidhampton, Wiltshire. He lived in many places throughout his life. In the 1590s he had a successful medical practice in London, and he died in Lambeth (London Borough) where he is buried. Poorly educated, he attended Magdalen College in Oxford for a year. In 1603, in response to the accusations by the College of Physicians of him being an unskillful and ignorant practitioner, he obtained a doctorate in physics and astronomy and a license to practice medicine from Jesus College in Cambridge. The hostility from the regulatory authorities he faced throughout his life—including several imprisonments—was due to the fact that Forman relied on mystical knowledge of the universe in his practices rather than rational knowledge.

Forman was a tireless learner. His library included staple works in astrology and astronomy, as well as collections of works in alchemy and magic, including Cornelius Agrippa's *De Occulta Philosophia* and an Arabic magical compendium from the 11th century, *Picatrix*. As did many practitioners of his time, Forman attempted to use the energy of the planets to cure illnesses or affect human affairs. He desired to connect the forces of spiritual realms with the material world, summoning natural powers that were beyond ordinary perceptions.

Forman considered astronomy as the principal science with five constituents: astronomy, astrology, astromagic, geomancy, and alchemy. For him, astronomy was the science of the heavens, and astrology interpreted the significance of the moving celestial bodies in human life. Astromagic was a practice-oriented part of astronomy that involved capturing the powers of the stars in physical objects. Forman himself created rings, images, and amulets that his patients would use to influence events in their lives. Geomancy was a kind of judicial astrology and a form of divination that used abstract symbols (instead of planets and stars) to establish a cosmic model, where each figure contained within in it a distribution of the four elements. However, Forman was most interested in alchemy: a sacred science that blended mysticism, philosophy, chemistry, and medicine, and aimed at finding the philosopher's stone, an object that could prolong life indefinitely, transmute metal into gold, and help resolve the riddles of the universe.

Forman was more a medical practitioner than a scholar, and he also was a consultant on human affairs (such as stolen property, missing people, or prospects for journeys). The study of alchemy provided him knowledge for making potions and elixirs. He used astrology to diagnose and treat people. For example, he would calculate astrological or geomantical figures at the time of consultation to understand the cause or outcome of a disease, as well as the kind of treatment he ought to use. Using the patients' horoscopes and the knowledge of the disposition of the planets, Forman would predict the astrologically appropriate treatment time.

Only one of Forman's works was published during his life time: *The Groundes of Longitude* (1591). He did produce, however, a detailed autobiography, many papers including a treatise in astrological medicine (*The Astrologicalle Judgmentes of Phisick and Other Questions*, drafted around 1594), and three volumes of his transcriptions of over 100 alchemical texts.

Thomas Gosart and Ulia Popova

See also: Lilly, William; Medical Astrology; Renaissance and Reformation Astrology

Further Reading

The Casebooks Project: A Digital Edition of Simon Forman's and Richard Napier's Medical Records 1596–1634. http://www.magicandmedicine.hps.cam.ac.uk/

Kassell, Lauren. 2005. *Medicine and Magic in Elizabethan London: Simon Forman: Astrologer, Alchemist, and Physician.* Oxford: Oxford University Press.

Traister, Barbara Howard. 2001. *The Notorious Astrological Physician of London: Works and Days of Simon Forman.* Chicago: University of Chicago Press.

G

GADBURY, JOHN (1627–1704)

John Gadbury was the premier politically conservative astrologer in late 17th-century England, the political and astrological adversary first of his former instructor William Lilly and then of his former friend and student John Partridge.

From a family of Oxfordshire yeomen, Gadbury started his public career around 1650 as a very radical Protestant but rapidly moved to the right in the following decade. After the English monarchy was restored in 1660 he lavished praise on the new King Charles II, claiming that the stars portended good fortune for king and kingdom. He edited the works of Sir George Wharton, the best-known royalist astrologer of the civil war period, as *The Works of that most excellent Philosopher and Astronomer, Sir George Wharton, bart* (1683) as part of an effort to succeed Wharton as the most important royalist astrologer.

As an astrological reformer, Gadbury believed that an improved astrology would emerge from the gathering and examination of a large number of nativities, aligning himself with the "Baconian" empirical movement inspired by English philosopher Francis Bacon (1561–1626). Baconianism attracted the interest of several English astrologers in the late 17th century, including Gadbury, Joshua Childrey (1625–1670), and John Goad. *Collectio Genituarum* (1662), a collection of hundreds of natal horoscopes was Gadbury's major contribution to the project. He

John Gadbury Discovers Astrology:

In this passage from one of his astrological treatises, Gadbury remembers how he became interested in astrology by reading Robert Burton's *Anatomy of Melancholy*:

> In the year 1650, as I well remember, I was one night reading in my bed (as it was my custom then to do, in some book or other) in the *Anatomy of Melancholy*: and coming to this passage of the author, that I have just now cited, viz. of his having Jupiter in the sixth house, which made him a physician, I was really non-plust, and Planet-struck for that bout, and forced to lay aside my book, being unwilling to read what I could not understand. I then endeavoured to go to my rest, but in vain, my active genius was watchful, and constantly solicited me, even in my dreams, to enquire, and discover if I could, what Jupiter in the Sixth house meant. . . . I had then . . . some small acquaintance with the learned Dr. Nicholas Fisk . . . who presently gave me such satisfaction in the Point as I was then capable of receiving.

Source: Gadbury, John. 1684. *Cardines Coeli*, London, 59.

published numerous books on astrological subjects ranging from celestial prodigies to the importance of the cardinal points of the horoscope.

As a working astrologer, Gadbury was a consultant and almanac writer. His almanac first appeared for 1656, eventually settling on the title *Ephemeris, or a Diary Astronomical, Astrological and Meteorological*. He also published a less astrologically sophisticated almanac, *Calendarium Astrologicum*, under the pseudonym Thomas Trigge. Gadbury became the best-known English astrologer after Lilly, to the point where "Gadbury" became a generic term for astrologer. He was particularly prominent in the great crisis late in Charles II's reign, when it had become clear that Charles and his queen, Catherine of Braganza, would have no children and the king would be succeeded by his openly Roman Catholic brother James, duke of York. Some—the "Whigs" or exclusionists—tried to exclude James from the succession on the grounds of his religion or put limitations on him, while the "Tories" supported James's succession to the full rights of kingship. Charges and countercharges of plots and conspiracies filled the air, and many looked to the next great conjunction of Saturn and Jupiter, in 1683, as portending great changes in politics or even the end of the world. Gadbury lent his astrological support to the Tories, and suffered for it. When the government of London was controlled by the Whigs, Gadbury spent a brief spell in the Gatehouse prison, charged with plotting.

Gadbury's Toryism was unusual, because most political astrologers supported the Whigs. Among the most passionate of the astrological Whigs was Partridge. Partridge and Gadbury had actually worked together on a few projects, including a horoscope of France's King Louis XIV. (Gadbury and the French king both had Scorpio as an ascendant. Gadbury spent much ink trying to rescue "Scorpionists" bad reputation.) The Exclusion Crisis wrought a bitter and permanent division between them. This division would be expressed in struggles over astrological technique as well as politics.

This division would sharpen in the reign of James II (r. 1685–1688). Drawing from the experience of the exclusion crisis, the new government of James II lost no time in banning the publication of astrological predictions. Most astrologers quietly dropped predictions from their almanacs. Partridge fled the country to Holland, where many English and Scottish opponents of the king were going, and Gadbury loudly obeyed the new decree, while sneaking in overwhelmingly flattering predictions about the greatness that awaited the new reign. He adulated the new monarch in servile terms, suggesting that October be renamed Mensis Jacobi, Latin for "month of James." Gadbury began to include Catholic Saints' Days in the calendar portion of his almanacs, and eventually openly avowed his Catholicism. Despite his close alignment with the regime, however, Gadbury was not a court astrologer, and there is no evidence that he gave astrological advice to the monarch directly. Partridge, from his safe haven in Amsterdam, took particular aim at Gadbury's religion and politics while Gadbury attacked Partridge as both seditious and a bad astrologer.

Gadbury lost his leading position in English astrology through a combination of astrological failure and political catastrophe. He did correctly predict the birth of a son to James's young wife, Mary of Modena, in early 1688. Because James's children by his previous marriage were daughters (and Protestants), the new son, also named James, jumped ahead of them in the line of succession. Because the boy would be raised as a Catholic, the Catholic succession to the British throne seemed assured. Rejoicing, Gadbury sent his almanac for 1689 off to the printers filled with praise of the infant prince and his father and hopes and predictions that the future "James III" would restore the country to Catholicism. In November, James's Protestant son-in-law William of Orange ruined Gadbury's predictions by invading England and exiling James, with Partridge following in William's wake by returning to England shortly thereafter. Despite Gadbury's increasingly frantic demonstrations that the stars opposed this endeavour, William took over the country, eventually becoming king along with his wife as William III and Mary II, and Partridge took over the leading role in English astrology.

As Lilly had after the Restoration, Gadbury suffered some legal trouble after the change of regime and was briefly imprisoned. *Ephemeris* continued to appear, but Gadbury's last few almanacs indicate that the failure of his hopes caused him to doubt, although never deny, the usefulness of astrology itself. *Ephemeris* continued for many years after his death but never regained the verve or popularity it had when Gadbury wrote it.

William E. Burns

See also: Almanacs; Ashmole, Elias; Lilly, William; Partridge, John; Politics; Science

Further Reading

Bowden, Mary Ellen. 1974. *The Scientific Revolution in Astrology: The English Reformers, 1558–1686*. New Haven, CT: Yale University Press.

Burns, William E. 2005. "Astrology and Politics in Early Modern England: King James II and the Almanac Men." *The Seventeenth Century* 20: 242–253.

Capp, Bernard S. 1979. *English Almanacs, 1500–1800: Astrology and the Popular Press*. Ithaca, NY: Cornell University Press.

Curry, Patrick. 1989. *Prophecy and Power: Astrology in Early Modern England*. Princeton: Princeton University Press.

GALILEI, GALILEO (1564–1642)

Galileo Galilei, the physicist, engineer, and mathematician who played a central role in the scientific revolution was also a leading Italian astrologer. His most notable astrological clients were the Medici family but earlier in his life he was a jobbing astrologer doing consultations to supplement his household income. His astrological work is preserved within his notes titled *Astrologica nonnulla* and held in the first volume of the sixth part of Galileo's Manuscripts at the Biblioteca Nazionale in Florence. His astrology was that of the day, traditional medieval astrology informed by the Islamic algebraic approach of almutens and directions. His approach to the mathematics used in these techniques, however, reveals his innovative approach to time and motion.

Galileo probably encountered astrology around 1582 when, at the age of 17, he became a student of medicine at the University of Pisa. Galileo did not finish his medical training, however, as he transferred his study to mathematics and by 1589, at the age of 24, he was appointed professor of Mathematics at Pisa. In 1592 he moved to Padua University and remained professor of Mathematics until 1610. One of his duties at Padua was to teach astrology to the medical students (Rutkin 2005, 112). While occupying this position Galileo supplemented his teaching income by taking on astrological clients (Favaro trans. 2003, 13). However, he held a genuine interest in astrology, evidenced by the long-standing correspondence with Ottavio Brenzoni, a professional astrologer in Verona with whom he discussed horoscopes and sought astrological opinions during his time in Padua. This correspondence is preserved in Brenzoni's letters to Galileo (Part VI. Tome VII Biblioteca Nazionale in Florence). It was during this time that Galileo first encountered difficulties with the law. In 1604 one of his servants reported him to the Inquisition for using astrology to foretell the future. It was a widely conducted practice at the time for university employed mathematicians to earn additional income casting horoscopes, however, Galileo, according to the servant, had "maintained that his prediction was certain and would inevitably come to pass" (Antonino Poppi's translation of Venezia Archivio di Stato 1604 fliza 26). Galileo was found guilty of heresy but his position at the university meant that he was only given a reprimand. He did, however, continue to cast horoscopes, evident by his correspondence with Brenzoni, but with greater caution in his language (Poppi 2003, 51). The heresy in his action was his attempt to make exact predictions. This conflicted with the Church's Aristotelian cosmology as exactness could only exist in the supra lunar realms of the divine (Poppi 2003, 54). The trial of 1604 reveals that in this period Galileo, through his astrological practice, was already challenging the prevailing cosmology of his day.

Central to the understanding of Galileo's use of astrology are his astrological notes and chart collection, which he named the *Astrologica nonnulla.* These notes were his personal collection of horoscopes of family members and friends that he maintained and annotated for his own use. They comprise some 50 pages of horoscopes and supporting astrological calculations in Galileo's own hand and are composed of 27 horoscopes, a partial horoscope, notes, drawings, and random calculations. Of these horoscopes, 19 consist of a single chart with or without planetary calculations, and eight are charts accompanied by *Dominus Geniturae* tables, tables designed to reveal the planet that held rulership over the individual's character. Of these eight charts, two have additional pages of predictive work. The dates of the charts range from 1505 to 1603, with a single charted dated to 1624. Two of the horoscopes are of Galileo's daughters, Virginia and Livia, and contain his brief notes on the interpretation of their horoscopes. Another horoscope was that of his friend Giovanfrancesco Sagredo, which was accompanied by tables of profections and primary directions. The final horoscope was constructed for the birth of a child named Augusta on August 6 (July 27, Old Style) 1624 at 2:35 a.m. (Local Mean Time) for a location in northern Romania (48N00, 24E30). This chart was drawn up by Galileo when he was 60 years of age and suggests that he maintained his interest in astrology throughout his life. Galileo's own horoscope is also among these papers and his birth data is recorded as February 15, 1564, Pisa at around "22 of the dial," which translates into the modern calendar and time keeping as February 26, 1564 at 15:30.

Galileo used the Regiomontanus house system, the known planets and luminaries, and a single lot, the Part of Fortune, calculated in the Ptolemaic manner. He also used the standard medieval essential dignities of rulership, exaltation, triplicity, terms, and face. However, his allocation of triplicity rulership is unique, as he used a combination of both Dorothean triplicities, as used by the 13th-century Italian papal and military astrologer, Guido Bonatti, together with the paired triplicities of Claudius Ptolemy, which were later used by William Lilly. Galileo also used the Egyptian terms that Ptolemy strongly criticized in the *Tetrabiblos*, (Ptolemy, book I, chapter XXIII), an argument with which Galileo would have been familiar but evidently rejected.

What is revealed in Galileo's papers is a predominantly Islamic astrology, based on the quantification of astrological qualities. Such quantification is represented in almuten tables, where a number value is assigned to a particular planet, based on its horoscopic attributes of dignity, aspects, and house. These assignments were combined into *Dominus Geniturae* tables, where the quantification could be arithmetically handled to find the planet with the highest score in order to reveal the planet with the greatest influence over the person's life. One of the unique features of Galileo's tables is that he placed a strong emphasis, via a higher score, on any planet that was moving faster than its daily average speed, and a larger than normal negative score for planets moving retrograde. This was against the conventions of the day, which valued a planet's essential dignity above speed and hence gave it greater importance. In addition, Galileo also worked with astrological directions for his predictive work. These directions were constructed in tables where he moved a planet at a fixed velocity, measuring the time it would take to form an exact relationship to a natal point. This astrological technique was commonplace in European medieval astrology; however, in his astrological notes Galileo sketched arcs of projection, showing his mind moving between the dynamic time and motion techniques within astrology and the problems he was seeking to solve in dismantling Aristotelian cosmology in order to find the laws of time and motion in physics. In this regard it has been argued that Galileo's astrology aided his inspirational thinking in time and motion (Brady 2015).

Bernadette Brady

See also: Fate; Legal Regulation of Astrology; Renaissance and Reformation Astrology; Science

Further Reading

Brady, Bernadette. 2015. "Galileo's Astrological Philosophy." In *From Masha' Allah to Kepler: Theory and Practice in Medieval and Renaissance Astrology*, ed. Charles Burnett and Dorian Gieseler Greenbaum, 77–100. Lampeter, UK: University of Wales, Sophia Centre Press.

Campion, Nicholas and Nick Kollerstrom, ed. 2003. *Galileo's Astrology, Culture and Cosmos, A Journal of the History of Astrology and Cultural Astronomy* 7, no 1.
Favaro, Antonio. trans. 2003. "Galileo, Astrologer." In *Galileo's Astrology*, ed. Nicholas Campion and Nick Kollerstrom, 9–19. Bristol, UK: Cinnabar Books.
Poppi, Antonino. 2003. "On Trial for Astral Fatalism: Galileo Faces the Inquisition." In *Galileo's Astrology*, ed. Nicholas Campion and Nick Kollerstrom, 49–58. Bristol, UK: Cinnabar Books.
Rutkin, H. Darrel. 2005. "Galileo Astrologer: Astrology and Mathematical Practice in the Late-Sixteenth and Early-Seventeenth Centuries." *Galilaeana* II: 107–43.
Swerdlow, N. M. 2004. "Galileo's Horoscopes." *Journal for the History of Astronomy* 35, pt. 2, no. 119: 135–141.

GAUQUELIN, MICHEL (1928–1991) AND FRANÇOISE GAUQUELIN (1929–2007)

A French statistician, Michel Gauquelin, is responsible for some of the most influential and controversial scientific research into natal astrology in the 20th century. Gauquelin's research focused on the relation of ascendant planets at birth and career path. His work is based on statistics, and much of the debate on Gauquelin and astrology has focused on statistical methodology. Although the work appeared under Michel Gauquelin's name, much of it was the work of his wife, Françoise Gauquelin, and as is often the case with husband–wife teams, we do not always know the precise division of labor between the couple, although Michel originated the project as a whole. The couple separated in 1982, although they remained friendly, and collaborated until 1985. Françoise carried on independent research into astrological effects until around 1997 and edited a journal, *Astro-Psychological Problems* from 1982 to 1995. The books of the Gauquelins were published in French, but widely translated.

Michel Gauquelin was interested in astrology from his childhood. He became interested in the statistic evaluation of astrological claims through the work of German-Swiss astrologer Karl Ernst Krafft (1900–1945) and the French astrologers Paul Choisnard (1867–1930) and Leon Lasson (1901–1989). Krafft, Choisnard, and Lasson had all attempted to put astrology on a sound scientific footing by collecting large numbers of horoscopes and examining them for common factors, although Gauquelin came to see their statistical knowledge as weak and their work as fundamentally valueless. He graduated from the Sorbonne with a degree in statistics in 1949, and together with Françoise, a Sorbonne-educated psychologist, he determined to create the first large-scale, mathematically rigorous investigation of astrological claims.

The key resource for Gauquelin's research was the birth records held by the French state. The gathering of birth information presented difficulties partly because the midwives and others who recorded the time of birth were not always precise. It also involved days and days of tedious work just to gather and transcribe the information, before the work of statistical analysis could even begin.

Gauquelin's first book, *The Influence of the Stars*, appeared in 1954. It was an examination of the charts of hundreds of people eminent in particular fields. Gauquelin's empirical research led him to deny the worth of many procedures of traditional astrology including zodiacal signs and planetary aspects. However, what attracted attention and came to define Gauquelin's work was his argument for the influence of planetary position at birth with later career, a theory requiring relatively precise data as to time of birth. He did not use a traditional house system but divided the sky into 36 "Gauquelin sectors." The planets that had a discernable effect were Mars, Jupiter, Saturn, the moon, and Venus. (The moon and Venus were added later and *The Influence of the Stars* focused on Mars, Jupiter, and Saturn.) The sun, Mercury, and the outer planets had no discernible effect. His statistics demonstrated, he claimed, that athletes and military leaders were particularly likely to have Mars in the ascendant or midheaven (this is sometimes referred to as the Mars effect). Jupiter favored actors, and Saturn scientists—claims reconcilable with traditional astrological thought about the nature of these planets. This effect is restricted to the ascendant and midheaven, and noteworthy only among the leaders of these professions. Although statistically verifiable according to Gauquelin it is still rather weak. The effect is also irrelevant for the large number of people, whatever their occupation or eminence, born when no significant planets occupy the so-called key sectors.

In the following years Michel and Françoise gathered information for European countries other than France to see if this effect could be replicated. Subsequent work demonstrated that similar effects could be found in these other countries. In the 1960s, the Gauquelins broadened their research by examining whether significant planetary positions were heritable. They found that the same five planets in the same significant areas were heritable, although not always in the same area—Michel claimed that his mother was born with Jupiter in the ascendant, and he with Jupiter near the midheaven, and considered this a case of planetary heredity. The results were published in *Planetary Heredity* (1966). These effects had the advantage of applying to a far broader range of people than the eminent who had been the subject of Gauquelin's earlier research. In terms of the effect of the planets, Gauquelin focused on personality rather than occupation.

Considering the statistical correlations established, Gauquelin faced the problem of how the planets affected individuals. He ruled out the concept of celestial influence, which he believed would have had to take effect during conception rather than birth. Rather he believed that there might be a genetic predisposition for being born when certain planets were in significant positions. He found that the effect disappeared for births after 1950, and speculated that the increased prevalence of Caesarian deliveries and artificially induced births had destroyed this connection. However, subsequent attempts to replicate the heritability study were less successful than the study of the professions, and evaluating personality traits had a subjective element that led to accusations of bias. Françoise Gauquelin's *Psychology of the Planets* (1982) was an attempt to evaluate the merits of astrology directly by extracting key character traits associated with each planet and associating them with the professions of those people born with those planets in significant positions. She found a correlation resembling that of their earlier work, but it remained controversial.

The Gauquelins published numerous other books, but these mostly repeated and elaborated their basic arguments. Skeptics of astrology have generally acknowledged that the Gauquelin's work is the most formidable of all of the empirical efforts to find an empirical basis for astrology and that it revolutionized the statistical study of astrological effects. It has been the subject of statistical inquiries and analyses from astrologers, statisticians, and astrological skeptics alike since its publication. However, skeptics have found it unconvincing, while astrologers have emphasized the Gauquelin's support for the influence of some of the planets while downplaying the fact that they rejected the rest of traditional astrology.

William E. Burns

See also: House Systems; Natal Astrology; Science

Further Reading

Dean, Geoffrey. "The Gauquelin Work: A Concise History with Photographs." http://www.astrology-and-science.com/g-hist2.htm

Gauquelin, Michel. 1991. *Neo-Astrology: A Copernican Revolution*. London: Penguin.

GENDER

Gender in astrology can be considered in at least two different aspects. The first is to recognize that the very structure of astrology, zodiac signs, and planets, are shaped by being assigned genders. The origins of these gender assignments lie primarily in the Hellenistic period where the components of astrology were classified into a system ordered around principles of masculine and feminine, with the masculine focused on power and the feminine representing a lack of power. The second form of gender issue in astrology lies in the 20th century's cultural shift from a largely male dominated study of the subject focused on the material world and issues of power to a female-dominated study of the subject embracing the inner or spiritual world of the individual. However independent of this shift, the gender labels applied to the zodiac signs and planets have been consistently maintained since their inception and today are generally defined within a psychological framework, rather than their original focus on outer world success or failure.

The earliest known assignment of gender in astrology was in the seventh century BCE when the Assyrian priests saw Venus as feminine, while all the other planets plus the two luminaries were seen as masculine. The moon was the god Sin, and his role and power was equal to that of the sun. Venus was considered feminine, possibly because it was, at times, a bright light in the sky, yet as an inferior planet it is always tied to the horizon and thus never able to culminate and sit in the throne of heaven (Cooley 2013, 195–196). Instead Venus's power, which was considerable, was seen in its ability to give support or blessing to another planet or constellation (Hunger 1992, 16, 143). This imbalance of gender, with both luminaries and all the other planets being masculine, gives an insight into the role of women in the royal Assyrian court of the seventh century BCE. Rather than holding power, they bestowed power. This particular feminine role was defined within the larger Assyrian context of an astrology designed as a political tool, created to be of use in maintaining a kingdom, rather than maintaining a household.

Table 1 Duality of the Zodiac Signs and Planets

Zodiac sign	Gender	Element	Diurnal	Old rulership
Aries	Masculine	Fire	Day	Mars
Taurus	Feminine	Earth	Night	Venus
Gemini	Masculine	Air	Day	Mercury
Cancer	Feminine	Water	Night	Moon
Leo	Masculine	Fire	Day	Sun
Virgo	Feminine	Earth	Night	Mercury
Libra	Masculine	Air	Day	Venus
Scorpio	Feminine	Water	Night	Mars
Sagittarius	Masculine	Fire	Day	Jupiter
Capricorn	Feminine	Earth	Night	Saturn
Aquarius	Masculine	Air	Day	Saturn
Pisces	Feminine	Water	Night	Jupiter

It was not until the Hellenistic period that astrology began to be codified so that it could be used for information about an ordinary individual. Ptolemy placed Aristotelian cosmology into the zodiac and, in so doing, extended gender to the zodiac signs. In this new cosmological framework, the world was made up of the qualities of hot, cold, wet, and dry. To each of the 12 zodiac signs Ptolemy assigned two qualities that then merged to form an element. Thus the element fire was hot and dry, air was wet and hot, earth was dry and cold, and water was cold and wet. The 12 zodiac signs were then ordered as six masculine and six feminine signs "arranged in alternate order, one after the other, as the day is followed by the night, and as the male is coupled with the female" (Ptolemy Book I, chapter, XV). The masculine was defined as elements of fire or air and were linked to the day, while the feminine signs consisted of the elements of earth and water and linked to the night (see Table 1).

The gender of the planets was also revisited. Venus retained its feminine attributes but in order to maintain the symmetry of signs and rulership, the moon was transformed to a feminine principle. This gave the symmetry of the sun and the moon ruling one sign each, one masculine (the sun ruling Leo) and one feminine (the moon ruling Cancer), while the planets ruled two signs each, one masculine and one feminine. Masculinity was also assigned to the day and femininity to the night, thus the planets had one rulership of a night sign and one rulership of a day sign. Nevertheless, even though a planet ruled both a masculine and feminine sign, those planets or luminaries deemed to be largely moist, by Aristotelian logic, were allocated to the feminine (the moon and Venus), while those that were largely dry were considered masculine (sun, Mars, Jupiter, and Saturn). Mercury was reclassified as common to both genders, at times being masculine while at other times feminine. Because it was an inferior planet, like Venus, and tied to the horizon but was only fleetingly visible, Mercury was not free in its orbit in the same way as the masculine planets.

Taurus, the Gender-Ambiguous Bull?

In Western astrology, zodiac signs are assigned gender in alternation, each feminine sign preceded and followed by a masculine. Since the first two signs represent masculine animals, the Ram and Bull, that means one masculine animal must be considered a feminine sign. Thus the bull, ordinarily considered a classic icon of masculinity, is ruled by the female planet Venus and has been assigned a feminine gender. Most astrologers would not see this as a problem, as what the constellations represent is of minor importance in considering the meaning of a zodiacal sign.

This genderization of astrology was still interpreted within the framework of the Assyrian approach, which viewed astrology as an instrument that described political power or material efficacy. It was the Hellenistic reform of astrology that emphasized the focus onto the individual, rather than the state, and, in particular, to how well the individual could engage with, control, or make use of political power. Ptolemy, for example, wrote of judging the Rank of Fame within the horoscope, the level of status that an individual could acquire. He described the planetary pattern, which would show that the individual could achieve kingship or god-like status, but warned if "both luminaries may not be found in masculine signs as aforesaid, but the Sun only in a masculine and the Moon in a feminine sign . . . the person about to be born will then become merely chieftains" (Ptolemy, book IV, chapter III). Hence worldly power and material success primarily belonged to the masculine planets and signs and the role of astrology was to measure the individual against the standards of success or failure defined by the masculine world.

In the history of natal astrology, the gender orientations of the signs and planets have been consistent. Johannes Schöner (1477–1547), a German polymath who was one of the central figures of European astrology at the end of the 15th century, used the same gender assignment, which carried the identical Hellenistic meanings. Schöner stated that the sun was debilitated if it was "descending in its circle, in a cadent house, in a feminine sign, degree or quarter, in the dignities of the infortunes, with infortunes elevated above him" (Schöner 1994, 55) thus equating the feminine as weakening the power of the sun to perform in the material world in a similar manner to other depleting features. The moon, however, being the feminine luminary, was deemed fortunate in a feminine sign, though notably not weakened by being in a masculine sign.

With the discovery of the new planets of Uranus (discovered 1791), Neptune (discovered 1846), and Pluto (discovered 1930), the number of masculine planets increased for the new planets were assigned the characteristics of the Greek gods for which they were named. They were, however, also allocated sign rulerships. Uranus was allocated the masculine sign Aquarius, and the feminine signs of Pisces and Scorpio were allocated for Neptune and Pluto, respectively. Hence the older balance of each planet ruling two signs, one masculine and the other feminine was disrupted.

Additionally, in the early 20th century Alan Leo placed the theosophical spirituality of Madam Helena Blavatsky (1831–1891) into astrology, which shifted its focus from power and material success to spiritual wholeness (Campion 2009, 231). For Leo, the material world was the fated world that needed to be transcended. In this regard he redefined the feminine qualities of astrology as belonging to the body and the sensual needs. This alternative spirituality that astrology offered meant that women increasingly took an interest in the subject so that today, overwhelmingly, women outnumber men as practitioners and consumers of astrology (Campion 2012, 2). This shift has changed astrology. In the past, planets and signs were used to define power and success; now these same planets and signs are used to clarify the inner world of an individual, their emotional outlook, and relationship issues. Such a use of astrology had existed in a minor way since the medieval period; however in the 20th century, it moved into mainstream astrological thinking. It was refined by the humanistic astrology of Dane Rudhyar, then found psychological direction in the Jungian-inspired astrology of Margaret Hone (1892–1969) and Liz Greene. Consequently, the gender of signs, but not planets, has become redefined. Within psychological astrology the masculine signs represent the personality traits of the extrovert and the feminine signs those of the introvert, neither of them being viewed as negative nor positive. By the late 20th century, the gender labels of signs and elements no longer revealed one's ability to gain or not gain power and material success but instead spoke of one's psychological qualities.

Along with the shakeup in sign rulerships, in 1986 Demetra George and Douglas Block published *Asteroid Goddesses*, which presented the asteroid to astrologers as additional components of the solar system that could be inserted into their horoscopes. The asteroids as fragments of a destroyed planet were viewed as carrying the Greek goddess mythology and through their use, George and Block sought, by using the asteroids, to place the feminine myths into astrology. This drive to insert the feminine voice continues today. Different movements that attempt to challenge the gender makeup have developed in astrology in the early part of the 21st century. Feminist astrology, loosely driven by either Earth-based religions or Wicca, is at times a desire to use astrology to develop a female centered spirituality while other astrologers use it to define an astrology that seeks to empower women. In terms of academic gender studies, the emergence of the Queer Astrology conferences sought to explore the gender debates within the subject. The first of these was held on July 20–21, 2013, in San Francisco, California. Papers published from this first conference, however, focused on finding ways to bring the language of the LGBT community into the consulting room. The work of attempting ways of deconstructing astrology to explore the possibility of removing or understanding the gender issues within the system lies in such work, for example, that confronts the hegemony of the ecliptic. Using the rising and setting of the stars for fixed star work rather than their projected ecliptical degrees or thinking about the sky in terms of visual astrology, which uses the full dome of the heavens, breaks up the dominancy of the sun-defined ecliptic. The work of deconstructing astrology to explore ways of removing or understanding gender issues within the astrological system will continue as long as society continues to explore the consequences of gender issues for humanity.

Bernadette Brady

See also: Asteroids; Feminist Astrology; Goodman, Linda; Medical Astrology; Sex and Love; Theosophy; Zodiacs

Further Reading

Brady, Bernadette. 2014. *Cosmos, Chaosmos and Astrology*. London: Sophia Centre Press.

Campion, Nicholas. 2009. *A History of Western Astrology Volume II*. London: Continuum Books.

Campion, Nicholas. 2012. *Astrology and Cosmology in the World's Religions*. New York: NYU Press.

Campion, Nicholas, and Liz Greene, eds. 2011. *Astrologies, Plurality and Diversity*. Ceredigion: Sophia Press, University of Wales Trinity Saint David.

Cooley, Jeffrey L. 2013. *Poetic Astronomy in the Ancient near East: The Reflexes of Celestial Science in Ancient Mesopotamian, Ugaritic, and Israelite Narrative*. History, Archaeology, and Culture of the Levant. Winona Lake, IN: Eisenbrauns.

George, Demetra, and Douglas Bloch. 2003. *Asteroid Goddesses: The Mythology, Psychology and Astrology of the Re-Emerging Feminine*. York Beach, ME: Nicolas-Hays; [Enfield: Airlift].

Hunger, Herman. 1992. *Astrological Reports to Assyrian Kings*. Helsinki, Finland: Helsinki University Press.

Hone, Margaret E. 1973. *The Modern Text-Book of Astrology*. 5th ed. London: Fowler.

Leo, Alan. 1974. *Astrology for All*. 4th ed. London: Fowler.

Schöner, Johannes. 1994. *Opusculum Astrologicum*, trans. Robert Hand. Project Hindsight, Latin Track, vol. IV, Berkeley Springs, WV: Golden Hind Press.

GHAYAT AL-HAKIM. SEE *PICATRIX.*

GOODMAN, LINDA (1925–1995)

Linda Goodman was one of the most successful sun sign astrologers of the late 20th century and the first person to demonstrate the power of astrology in the North American book market with an astrology book that made the *New York Times* best-seller list.

Goodman was born Mary Alice Kemery. The name Linda came from a radio show she hosted, *Letters from Linda*, and Goodman from her second husband Sam Goodman. Goodman's first book, *Linda Goodman's Sun Signs* (1968), stayed on the *New York Times* best seller list for six months and is often credited with the American astrological boom of the seventies. Follow-up volumes appeared about every 10 years, *Linda Goodman's Love Signs: A New Approach to the Human Heart* in 1978 and *Linda Goodman's Star Signs: The Secret Codes of the Universe* in 1988. (The selling power of Goodman's name can be seen in its incorporation into the titles of her books.) By the time of her death, the books together had sold over 30 million copies and were still selling at the rate of 200,000 a year. They had also been translated into over a dozen languages. She also published three books of poetry, *Gooberz* (1972), an autobiographical epic poem, the astrologically inspired collection *Venus Trines at Midnight* (1973), and *Linda Goodman's Love Poems* (1980).

Goodman's astrological writings focused on relationship advice directed to heterosexual women. The dominant theme was describing the characters associated with each sun sign and examining the compatibility between people of different signs. Describing character, not making predictions, was her mission as an astrologer. *Sun Signs* helped inaugurate the burgeoning genre of astrological relationship advice, which was a major form of astrological publishing in the late 20th and 21st centuries. Goodman was also increasingly interested in New Age mysticism and nonastrological forms of occultism such as numerology. The broadening of her interests was particularly marked in *Star Signs*, which was advertised as a "Practical Guide for the New Age."

Goodman's personal life was marked by tragedy. Her daughter Sarah committed suicide in 1973 at the age of 18. Goodman never accepted this, partly because her interpretation of Sarah's astrological chart did not allow for it. She spent much time and money searching in vain for her daughter, who she believed kidnapped. She was also generous to charitable organizations and friends. Despite the millions of dollars she had received for her books, Goodman died broke. *Linda Goodman's Relationship Signs* (1998), a guide to constructing astrological charts, appeared posthumously. Goodman leads a vigorous afterlife on the Internet in sites constructed by fans.

William E. Burns

See also: New Age; Sex and Love; Sun Signs

Further Reading

Goodman, Linda. 1968. *Linda Goodman's Sun Signs*. New York: Taplinger.

Holden, James H. 2006. *A History of Horoscopic Astrology*. Tempe, AZ: American Federation of Astrologers.

Linda-Goodman.com

Thomas Jr., Robert. 1995. "Linda Goodman, Writer Turned Astrologer, Dies." *New York Times*, October 25, 1995. http://www.nytimes.com/1995/10/25/us/linda-goodman-writer-turned-astrologer-dies.html

H

HAMBURG SCHOOL OF ASTROLOGY

The Hamburg School of Astrology, founded in Germany in 1925, comprises a suite of innovations to the technical practice of astrology including hypothetical planets, a revision and expansion of midpoint systems, and new dial charts and dial tools. Founder Alfred Witte (1878–1941) worked as a surveyor for the city of Hamburg before World War I. In 1911, he began learning astrology from Karl Brandler-Pracht (1864–1939). Witte applied mathematical skills from surveying to what he was learning. During combat service in World War I, he postulated the existence of an undiscovered planet beyond the orbit of Neptune (a "trans-Neptunian" planet, or TNP), which he named Cupido. Between 1913 and 1924, Witte wrote frequently for astrological periodicals and his innovations stirred controversy at astrological conferences. Witte held his first public lecture in 1919 at the Kepler circle (*Keplerzirkel*), which was founded in 1915. In 1925, Witte, along with fellow Kepler circle astrologers Friedrich Sieggrün (1877–1951) and Ludwig Rudolph (1893–1982), officially founded the Hamburg School. Sieggrün is credited with coming up with the group's name (Holden 2012, 660).

Witte remained the head of the school until his suicide in Hamburg in 1941. After Witte's death Rudolph took his place as the head of the Hamburg School. Udo Rudolph (1921–2008) became head of the Hamburg School in Germany after his father's death in 1982.

Eight hypothetical planets, which are now understood to be "energy points," form a hallmark contribution of the Hamburg School to astrological technique. Witte discovered Cupido, Hades, Zeus, and Kronos. Sieggrün found Apollon, Admetos, Vulkanus, and Poseidon. These hypothetical planets have their own glyphs and ephemerides. Due to their proposed distance beyond Neptune (actually, even Pluto), they move extremely slowly through the zodiac. Witte's TNPs follow noncircular orbits, more akin to actual celestial bodies than the circular orbits proposed for most hypothetical points (Hand 1981, 95).

Witte devised complex systems of midpoints, which he termed *planetary pictures*. Planetary pictures are formed out of two or more stellar factors aligned around an axis. Although the technical literature features many ways to construct them, in general, planetary pictures are created by adding and subtracting longitudes of planets and other chart factors (ascendant, midheaven, the Aries point, lunar nodes, hypothetical planets). They often involve three stellar factors that make a fourth point a "sensitive point." The system incorporates natal configurations, as well as transits, directions, and the charts of others (synastry). Specific interpretations arise out of the combinations of the factors. Astrological houses are not used to construct planetary pictures, but they may be optionally used to interpret their effects.

Two dial systems are also fundamental to the Hamburg system: the 360-degree dial and the 90-degree dial. The innovation of the 90-degree dial is that it enables an astrologer to easily identify hard aspects (0, 45, 90, 135, 180), which makes it easier to see planetary pictures and midpoints, among other things.

The first major technical manual for Hamburg School techniques, *Rulebook for Planetary Pictures* (*Regelwerk für Planetenbilder*), was published in 1928. In the mid-1920s, Witte began delineating planetary pictures for his students during lectures. The idea arose that he should release these interpretations in book form. Witte assigned the tasked to Ludwig Rudolph, who organized the publication of the book in 1928 through his newly established press, Witte Verlag, which continues operations today.

Witte intended the brief interpretations of planetary pictures as inspirations to be expanded upon, rather than definitive statements. The first through third editions contain no reference to the four hypothetical planets discovered by Sieggrün. In 1932, the second edition of *Rulebook* doubled the page count. The third edition of the *Rulebook* (3,000 copies) appeared in 1935, but in 1936 the text was officially banned and the press's entire stock was burned by the Nazis. This came as a serious blow to the Hamburg School in general, and to the Rudolph family and the press directly. After the war, the ban on the book was lifted. In 1946, Hermann Lefeldt (1899–1977), student of Rudolph since 1931, helped Ludwig Rudolph incorporate both Pluto and Sieggrün's trans-Neptunian planets into the fourth edition of the *Rulebook*. This edition received mixed reviews, especially from Witte's widow, Gertrud, who held that her husband's work should remain as he left it.

German astrologer Reinhold Ebertin (1901–1988) was an early follower of Witte's techniques, but he branched off and established cosmobiology. Cosmobiology does not implement the TNPs or any house system (although it utilizes ascendant and midheaven points), and it has a simplified version of the midpoint systems employed by the Hamburg School. The historical enmity between cosmobiologists and Hamburg School astrologers stems ostensibly from the publication of Ebertin's enduring, *Combination of Stellar Influences* (1950), which promoted Witte's techniques in an extremely simplified form.

American astrologer Richard Svehla (1878–1942) created an authorized translation of Witte's *Rulebook* in 1939, and wrote about the methods and applications of Hamburg School astrology for an English-speaking audience. After 1948, astrologer Curt Knupfer (1907–1978) translated the Witte-Lefeldt version of the *Rulebook* and other Hamburg School publications into English. Hans Niggemann (1891–1985), a German-born American astrologer who worked with Witte before he emigrated, taught Hamburg School techniques in New York City under the term *Uranian astrology*, which he claims to have coined (Holden 2006, 259). Niggemann had disputes with Ludwig Rudolph and in 1959 produced an unauthorized translation of the *Rulebook*. Like Witte, he was negatively disposed to cosmobiology (Holden 2012, 527). Many organizations, conferences, and publications have emerged around Uranian astrology since Niggemann's time, including a new appellation, *Symmetrical astrology*.

Jennifer Zahrt

See also: Astrological Associations; Nazism and the Third Reich

Further Reading

Hand, Robert. 1981. *Horoscope Symbols.* Rockport, MA: ParaResearch.
Holden, James H. 2006. *A History of Horoscopic Astrology.* Tempe, AZ: American Federation of Astrologers.
Holden, James Herschel. 2012. *Biographical Dictionary of Western Astrologers,* Tempe, AZ: American Federation of Astrologers.
Witte-Verlag, http://www.witte-verlag.com/

HELLENISTIC ASTROLOGY

The term *Hellenistic astrology* generally refers to the astrology of the Mediterranean world from, roughly, the second century BCE to the seventh century CE. Hellenistic in this context does not refer to the period beginning with the conquest of the Persian Empire by Alexander the Great (323 BCE) and ending around 30 BCE with the conquest of Egypt by Rome but to the development and amalgamation of Western astrology under the vector language of Greek, the lingua franca for the exchange of ideas in the Mediterranean area during the centuries surrounding the turn of the millennium from BCE to CE. After Alexander's conquest of India, Indian astrology reflects some Hellenistic astrological concerns through the use of Greek loan words in Sanskrit for some Greek astrological terminology.

The Origins and Milieu of Hellenistic Astrology

Hellenistic astrology did not arise in a Greek vacuum but depended on practices developed in Mesopotamia and to a lesser extent Egypt. Astronomical and astrological practices from both these cultures combined with Greek natural, philosophical, and religious doctrines and mathematics to produce Hellenistic astrology.

In Mesopotamia, which was particularly suited geographically to observe the sky, there was a strong tradition of astral omens. The sky was seen as the Earth's mirror image, and the connection between celestial phenomena and human events was articulated from a very early period (probably beginning in the late third millennium BCE). Beginning in the Persian period (ca. 500 BCE), the zodiac, as a circular band of 12 equal divisions of the sky based on constellations, was introduced in Mesopotamia and correlated with previous astral omen texts and other divinatory material such as hemerologies (lucky and unlucky days). The earliest extant birth chart dates to 410 BCE. First a prerogative only of kings, astrological prediction later became available to nonroyalty, as can be seen in the corpus of Babylonian horoscopes. This is one of the practices that entered the Hellenistic astrological milieu.

In Egypt, astronomical concerns can be found in the Old Kingdom (ca. 2700–2100 BCE). Decans—constellations that rose on the horizon at 10-day intervals (hence the name)—were an important concept from the Ninth or Tenth Dynasty (ca. 2100 BCE). In Hellenistic astrology, Egypt is likely responsible for the introduction of the ascendant (the sign and/or degree rising on the eastern horizon at the time of birth) and midheaven (the sign and/or degree culminating at the meridian), as well as the 12 "places" (*topoi*) into which the birth chart was divided. All these derive from Egyptian practices. None exist in Babylonian charts.

In the Hellenistic and Greco-Roman periods, astrology found a particular locus of development in Alexandria, the city in Egypt founded by Alexander the Great. Even before the city's founding, Babylonian astrological doctrines were adapted to an Egyptian milieu (Ross 2006). Egyptian astrological practices expanded within temple culture. Particularly rich Egyptian sites for remains of astronomical/astrological artifacts are Oxyrhynchus and Medinet Madi, the ancient city of Narmouthis. Ancient astrological texts, now only extant in fragments, were ascribed to the Egyptian king Nechepso and his priest Petosiris. Hellenistic astrology also spread to Rome, where it became an important topic for both commoners and nobility. Hellenistic astrology included all of the major branches of Western astrology: natal, mundane, and katarchic. Katarchic astrology, literally the astrology of "beginnings" (*katarchē*), includes events, electional, horary, and parts of medical astrology.

Mechanics of Hellenistic Astrology

Data in Hellenistic astrological charts include an ascendant and midheaven (and their opposites, the descendant and lower midheaven, respectively). These four points were called *kentra* (centerpins) or cardines (from Latin *cardo*, hinge), and are known as angles in modern astrology. They also include 12 places (*topoi*), modern "houses." Each place is connected with a particular area of life.

The components of the chart included the seven classical planets: sun and moon, called the luminaries, and the five visible planets Saturn, Jupiter, Mars, Venus, and Mercury. The zodiacal positions of these celestial bodies were calculated for each chart. The zodiacal signs are Aries, Taurus, Gemini, Cancer, Leo, Virgo, Libra, Scorpio, Sagittarius, Capricorn, Aquarius, and Pisces.

Planets and Signs Arranged in Various Schemes

Triplicities

Signs of the same element are called triplicities (they are not only composed of three signs but they are in trine [triangular] aspect to each other).

Fire signs: Aries, Leo, Sagittarius
Earth signs: Taurus, Virgo, Capricorn
Air signs: Gemini, Libra, Aquarius
Water signs: Cancer, Scorpio, Pisces

Table 1 The Sect of the Planets

Day Sect		Night Sect
Sun (leader)		*Moon (leader)*
Jupiter	← *Mercury* →	*Venus*
Saturn		*Mars*

Quadruplicities

Signs were also divided into groups of tropical/solsticial (modern cardinal), solid (modern fixed), and double-bodied (modern mutable):

Tropical signs: Aries, Cancer, Libra, Capricorn
Solid: Taurus, Leo, Scorpio, Aquarius
Double-bodied: Gemini, Virgo, Sagittarius, Pisces

Gender

Signs and planets were grouped by gender:

Masculine signs: Aries, Gemini, Leo, Libra, Sagittarius, Aquarius
Feminine signs: Taurus, Cancer, Virgo, Scorpio, Capricorn, Pisces
Masculine planets: Sun, Saturn, Jupiter, Mars, Mercury
Feminine planets: Moon, Venus

Sect (hairesis)

Planets were placed into day and night groups: the sun leading the day sect and the moon the night. Mercury's sect depended on its location ahead (diurnal) or behind (nocturnal) the sun. A planet's effects were seen as positive or negative based on its sect. For example, a day planet in a day chart (where the sun is above the horizon) offered more positive outcomes than a night planet in a day chart. The same rationale applied for night planets in night charts (the sun below the horizon) and the reverse.

Benefic and Malefic

Some planets were considered favorable (benefic) or unfavorable (malefic). Mars and Saturn were malefic, Venus and Jupiter benefic, and Mercury could be either depending on where it was placed. The sun and moon were not classified in this scheme.

Aspects

Planets and luminaries also made aspects—geometrical relationships—with one another and with the ascendant and midheaven (less frequently with the other cardines/angles). Only five aspects were used: conjunction, sextile, square, trine, and opposition. If planets did not make any of these aspects to each other, they are called "averse" (*apostrophos*) or "unjoined" (*asyndetos*). Signs were also considered in aspect to each other, or averse.

Table 2 Planetary Triplicity Rulers Based on Sect and Elements, according to Dorotheus of Sidon

Fire	Earth	Air	Water
(Day) Sun	(Day) Venus	(Day) Saturn	(Day) Venus
(Night) Jupiter	(Night) Moon	(Night) Mercury	(Night) Mars

Note: Degrees in Table 3 and Table 4 are given as ending longitudes, and are exact, e.g. 6°00'00.00"

Table 3 The Terms of the Planets, according to the Egyptians

Aries	Jup **6**	Ven **12**	Merc **20**	Mars **25**	Sat **30**
Taurus	Ven **8**	Merc **14**	Jup **22**	Sat **27**	Mars **30**
Gemini	Merc **6**	Jup **12**	Ven **17**	Mars **24**	Sat **30**
Cancer	Mars **7**	Ven **13**	Merc **19**	Jup **26**	Sat **30**
Leo	Jup **6**	Ven **11**	Sat **18**	Merc **24**	Mars **30**
Virgo	Merc **7**	Ven **17**	Jup **21**	Mars **28**	Sat **30**
Libra	Sat **6**	Merc **14**	Jup **21**	Ven **28**	Mars **30**
Scorpio	Mars **7**	Ven **11**	Merc **19**	Jup **24**	Sat **30**
Sagittarius	Jup **12**	Ven **17**	Merc **21**	Sat **26**	Mars **30**
Capricorn	Merc **7**	Jup **14**	Merc **22**	Sat **26**	Mars **30**
Aquarius	Merc **7**	Ven **13**	Jup **20**	Mars **25**	Sat **30**
Pisces	Ven **12**	Jup **16**	Merc **19**	Mars **28**	Sat **30**

Dignities

Other schemes, called "dignities" in the medieval period (Bezza 2007), assigned planets as rulers of various portions of the zodiac. The major categories of dignity are by domicile, exaltation, triplicity, term, and face.

In chart interpretation, certain places confer ability to act (operative), namely the cardines, 5th and 11th places, while others are considered ineffective and/or producing ill effects, especially the 6th, 8th, and 12th places.

Doctrines and Techniques

The mechanics described briefly above were employed in chart interpretation and combine with various doctrines that enabled an astrologer to advise a client about life issues. These could include concerns about length of life, marriage, children, career, and wealth, not dissimilar to client concerns in modern astrology. Vettius Valens and Ptolemy described techniques to determine longevity. Finding a ruler or rulers of the chart (called an *oikodespotēs*) by various methods could determine a planet governing particular areas of life or the life in general.

Other techniques allowed astrologers to look ahead over years, using the natal chart combined with methods to move it forward in time. These include profections, annual revolutions, and primary directions. Other techniques assigned

Table 4 The Faces of the Planets

Aries	Mars 10	Sun 20	Venus 30
Taurus	Mercury 10	Moon 20	Saturn 30
Gemini	Jupiter 10	Mars 20	Sun 30
Cancer	Venus 10	Mercury 20	Moon 30
Leo	Saturn 10	Jupiter 20	Mars 30
Virgo	Sun 10	Venus 20	Mercury 30
Libra	Moon 10	Saturn 20	Jupiter 30
Scorpio	Mars 10	Sun 20	Venus 30
Sagittarius	Mercury 10	Moon 20	Saturn 30
Capricorn	Jupiter 10	Mars 20	Sun 30
Aquarius	Venus 10	Mercury 20	Moon 30
Pisces	Saturn 10	Jupiter 20	Mars 30

"chronocrators," time lords (planetary or zodiacal) to various periods of life, and the condition of such time lords allows prediction of what that period will be like.

The doctrine of lots (*klēroi*, misnamed *Arabic parts* in modern astrology) was widely used in Hellenistic astrology. Lots are interpretive points in a chart, derived from taking the arc between two points (usually planetary positions) and projecting it from a third point (usually the ascendant). Lots feature, like planets, in some of the techniques described above.

Astrological Authors

Dorotheus, Ptolemy, and Vettius Valens are among the preeminent authors within the Hellenistic astrological tradition, but others are also important. The earliest authors cited in astrological texts are the pseudonymous Nechepso and Petosiris (mentioned above), who wrote in verse (Nechepso and Petosiris 1892; Heilen 2011). "Hermes Trismegistus" (or just "Hermes") is another early pseudonymous author.

Among writers in Latin, Manilius wrote an astrological poem, *Astronomica*, in five books (ca. 10 CE). Julius Firmicus Maternus (fl. ca. 338 CE), a Sicilian lawyer, wrote the *Mathesis* in eight books. Greek writers include Antiochus of Athens (ca. second century CE) who wrote a *Thesaurus* (Treasury) and an *Introduction*. Manetho the Astrologer (b. 80 CE) wrote an *Apotelesmatika* (*Astrological Outcomes*) in verse. Teucer of Babylon in Egypt (possibly first century CE), wrote particularly on the co-risings (*paranatellonta*) of decans and constellations. Paul of Alexandria wrote an *Introduction to Astrology* in 378 CE (Greenbaum 2001; Paul of Alexandria 2012), which received a *Commentary* from the Neoplatonist Olympiodorus the Younger in 564 CE (Greenbaum 2001). Hephaestio of Thebes (b. 380 CE, fl. 415 CE) wrote his *Apotelesmatika* in prose, particularly important for including passages from both Dorotheus and Ptolemy (Hephaistio of Thebes 1994 and 1998; Hephaistion of Thebes 2013). Finally, the Egyptian compiler Rhetorius

A representation of the constellation Leo from the monumental tomb of King Antiochus I of Commagene (r. 70–38 BCE) at Nimrud Dagh in modern-day Turkey. The culture of the area combined Hellenistic, Iranian, and Armenian elements. (Ancient Art and Architecture Collection Ltd./Bridgeman Images)

(sixth–seventh century CE) wrote a *Compendium* on astrology containing many earlier doctrines (Rhetorius 2009).

Documentary and Material Evidence of Hellenistic Astrological Practices

In addition to astrological manuals in Greek, Latin, and demotic Egyptian, evidence for Hellenistic astrology includes ancient horoscopes written in Mesopotamian languages, Greek, Latin, Demotic Egyptian, Coptic, Hebrew, and Arabic.

Many astrological artifacts survive from the period, including:

- The *Lion Horoscope* from Nimrud Dagh. This is a stone relief built to show an astrological moment in the reign of Antiochus I of Commagene (r. 70–38 BCE).
- The Tyche Zodiac from Khirbet et-Tannur. This sculpture is an important relic of the Nabataean religious site. The zodiac is unique in that it has Aries and Libra at the top, each moving down the left and right sides, respectively, to Virgo and Pisces. The zodiac in combination with Tyche emphasizes the connections between the zodiac and fortune.
- The Mithraic "Housesteads Monument" from Hadrian's Wall, Northumberland. This shows the god Mithras being born from an egg, surrounded by a zodiac. The zodiac begins at the bottom left with Aquarius, moving up clockwise to Cancer and Leo at the top, then down to Capricorn on the lower right.

- The Grand Tablets, astrological boards (*pinakes*) on which planetary markers could be laid to show a client his or her chart. These come from Grand, Vosges, France, from a healing shrine dedicated to Apollo Grannus.
- Numerous astrological gems.
- A gold horoscope ring depicting the planetary and ascendant positions for a birth on August 17, 327 CE, probably belonging to a physician (a signet-bust of Asclepius and the word *hygia*, health, decorates the top of the ring).

Dorian Gieseler Greenbaum

See also: Art; Dorotheus of Sidon; Electional Astrology; Firmicus Maternus, Julius; Horary Astrology; Indian Astrology; Lots; Manilius, Marcus; Medical Astrology; Mesopotamian Astrology; Mundane Astrology; Natal Astrology; Ptolemy; Roman Astrology; Valens, Vettius

Further Reading

Bezza, Giuseppe. 2007. "The Development of an Astrological Term—from Greek *hairesis* to Arabic *ḥayyiz*." *Culture and Cosmos* 11: 229–260.

Evans, James. 2004. "The Astrologer's Apparatus: A Picture of Professional Practice in Greco-Roman Egypt." *Journal for the History of Astronomy* 35: 1–44.

Gordon, Richard. 2013. "'Will My Child Have a Big Nose?' Uncertainty, Authority and Narrative in Katarchic Astrology." In *Divination in the Ancient World: Religious Options and the Individual*, ed. Veit Rosenberger, 93–137. Stuttgart: Franz Steiner Verlag.

Greenbaum, Dorian Gieseler, trans. and annot. 2001. *Late Classical Astrology: Paulus Alexandrinus and Olympiodorus with the Scholia from Later Commentators*. Reston, VA: ARHAT.

Greenbaum, Dorian Gieseler. 2016. *The Daimon in Hellenistic Astrology: Origins and Influence*. Vol. 11, Ancient Magic and Divination. Leiden: Brill.

Greenbaum, Dorian Gieseler, and Micah T. Ross. 2010. "The Role of Egypt in the Development of the Horoscope." In *Egypt in Transition: Social and Religious Development of Egypt in the First Millennium BCE*, ed. Ladislav Bareš, Filip Coppens, and Kveta Smolarikova, 146–182. Prague: Faculty of Arts, Charles University in Prague.

Heilen, Stephan. 2011. "Some metrical fragments from Nechepsos and Petosiris." In *La poésie astrologique dans l'Antiquité*, ed. Isabelle Boehm and Wolfgang Hübner, 23–93. Paris: De Boccard.

Hephaistio of Thebes. 1994 and 1998. *Apotelesmatics Book I; Apotelesmatics Book II*, trans. Robert H. Schmidt. Berkeley Springs, WV: Golden Hind Press.

Hephaistion of Thebes. 2013. *Apotelesmatics Book III: On Inceptions*, trans. Eduardo J. Gramaglia. Minneapolis, MN: Cazimi Press.

Holden, James Herschel. 1996. *A History of Horoscopic Astrology from the Babylonian Period to the Modern Age*. Tempe, AZ: American Federation of Astrologers.

Jones, Alexander, ed., trans., and commentator. 1999. *Astronomical Papyri from Oxyrhynchus*. 2 vols. Philadelphia: American Philosophical Society.

Jones, Alexander. 2007. "Astrologers and Their Astronomy." In *Oxyrhynchus: A City and Its Texts*, ed. A. K. Bowman, R. A. Coles, N. Gonis, D. Obbink, and P. J. Parsons, 307–314. London: Egypt Exploration Society.

Jones, Alexander, ed. 2016. *Time and Cosmos in Greco-Roman Antiquity*. Institute for the Study of the Ancient World at New York University. Princeton: Princeton University Press.

Nechepso and Petosiris. 1892. *Fragmenta magica*. In *Philologus*, ed. E. Riess, suppl. vol. 6, pt. 1.

Neugebauer, Otto. 1943. "Demotic Horoscopes." *Journal of the American Oriental Society* 63, no. 2: 115–127.

Neugebauer, Otto, and Henry Bartlett Van Hoesen. (1959) 1987, repr. *Greek Horoscopes*. Philadelphia: American Philosophical Society.

Paul of Alexandria. 2012. *Paul of Alexandria: Introduction to Astrology*, trans. James Herschel Holden. Tempe, AZ: American Federation of Astrologers.

Pingree, David. 1997. *From Astral Omens to Astrology: From Babylon to Bīkāner*. Rome: Istituto italiano per l'Africa e l'Oriente.

Rhetorius. 2009. *Rhetorius the Egyptian: Astrological Compendium Containing His Explanation and Narration of the Whole Art of Astrology*, trans. James H. Holden. Tempe, AZ: American Federation of Astrologers.

Ross, Micah T. 2006. "Horoscopic Ostraca from Medînet Mâdi." PhD diss. Providence, RI: Brown University.

Ross, M. 2007. "A Continuation of the Horoscopic Ostraca of Medînet Mâdi." *Egitto E Vicino Oriente* 30: 153–171.

HORARY ASTROLOGY

The theory and practice of horary or interrogational astrology is underpinned by the astrological figure (also referred to as a chart, horoscope, map, or scheme), a two-dimensional, schematic drawing of the three-dimensional planetary configurations at a specific moment. There are four figures, each of which corresponds to the classifications of astrology variously found in classical, medieval, and early modern texts: the nativity, revolution, election, and interrogation (horary). A fifth division of the text, the *Introductorium*, foundational to the four, provides the entire syntax, grammar, and basic methodology essential to astrology. The function of the interrogation is to provide judgments for specific and immediate inquiries, rather than those relating to an entire lifetime or "generall fate of the Native," which invoke the nativity (Lilly 1647, opening page).

The interrogation, a most important part of the medieval corpus, is not discussed by Ptolemy, an important source for later Arabic, Latin, and early modern astrologers. Nor is interrogational astrology well represented in other Greek texts. Scholars continue to debate whether interrogations were part of Greek astrology at all (Hand 2014, 45–47). Yet, interrogational material is found in a range of Arabic era sources, such as the Egyptian Jewish astrologer Mashāllāh, and the Persian Abū Ma'shar, the "Prince of Astrologers." Horary astrology is also found in the work of the Latin Guido Bonatti, as well as later Western practitioners such as Simon Forman and William Lilly, the acknowledged master of interrogational astrology in 17th-century England. Bonatti's transmission from Arabic astrology is a primary source for later European interrogations (Cornelius 1994, 116).

The theory and application of interrogational astrology is well illustrated by early modern English astrological guides and casebooks, in particular Lilly's *Christian Astrology Modestly Treated of in Three Books* (1647) and Forman's *The Astrologicalle Judgmentes of Physick and Other Questions* (1606). In Forman's opening pages

Guido Bonatti on the Horary Astrologer and the Client

In 1676, eminent English horary astrologer William Lilly published a translation from Guido Bonatti, *Anima Astrologiae or a Guide for Astrologers Being the Considerations of the Famous Guido Bonatus.* Bonatti warns that the inquirer take the process seriously:

> The Second Consideration is . . . the method or manner everyone ought to observe that inquires of an astrologer; which is, that when he intends to take an artist's judgement of things past, present, or to come, he should, first, with a devout spirit, pray unto the Lord, from whom proceeds the success of every lawful enterprise, that he would grant him the knowledge of those things of the truth of which he would be resolved; and then let him apply himself to the astrologer with a serious intent of being satisfied in some certain and particular doubt, and this not on trifling occasions, or light sudden emotions, much less in matters base or unlawful, as many ignorant people use to do; but in matters of honest importance, and such to have possessed and disturbed his mind for the space of a day or night or longer; or else in sudden accidents which admit not of delay.

Source: Lilly, William. 1676. *Anima Astrologiae or A Guide for Astrologers, Being the Considerations of the Famous Guido Bonatus, faithfully rendered into English.* London: B. Harris. 4.

he sets out his understanding of the interrogation: *Instanti Respondere ad omnem Questionem interrogatam*, the immediate response to all questions asked (Forman 1606, 6). In response to an inquiry, the astrologer performs complex calculations, draws the figure and formulates the judgment in accordance with a rigorous set of astrological principles relating to the 12 houses of the figure. The latter correspond to or "signify" every area of human concern, including health, finance, children, sickness, marriage, journeys, and career.

There are no precise statistics available for Lilly's casebook figures, but of the 38 figures in *Christian Astrology* 36 are interrogations. Forman's casebooks from 1596 to 1603 reveal 10,047 interrogations, while his guide, *Judgmentes*, is devoted almost entirely to "Questiones" (interrogations). Among the range of Forman's and Lilly's clients we find servants, yeoman, clergymen, and merchants, as well as aristocrats such as the countess of Hertford in 1597, John Whitgift, archbishop of Canterbury, in 1601, and King Charles II in 1673. The interrogation was deployed in response to all areas of human concern: "Where an absent brother was"; "A lady, if marry the Gentleman desired"; "If bewitched" (Lilly 1647, 196, 385, 468). Medical inquiries made up the majority of inquiries in both Forman's practice and that of the clergyman-astrologer Richard Napier (1559–1634). Particularly common inquiries concerned the prospects for life or death of a relative "utrum vivit aut moritur" (MS Ashmole 226 f.260 r). For Lilly, one question would stand out: "Quid agendum?"—"What is to be done?" (Thomas 1971, 373).

Despite the fivefold classification of the figures found in the astrological guides and manuscripts, interrogational astrology is classified rather differently by historians. Indeed, a persistent historical generalization appears to have taken hold in the form of two divisions: "Natural" astrology, the forecasting of mass behavior, natural events, and changes in humoral physiology (considered to have been acceptable).

"Judicial" astrology (which includes the interrogation), the prediction of events concerning individual persons (considered unacceptable). Perhaps the fact that practitioners themselves frequently invoked the same division has prompted historians to adopt the two as if they were unambiguous. A well-known polemic relating to judicial astrology, for example, was that of John Chamber in 1601 and a subsequent defense by Sir Christopher Heydon in 1603 (Dunn 2009, 53–67). Yet, the distinction was neither clear nor consistent. The application of astrology to medicine, for example, does not fall neatly into either division. Indeed, "medical astrology" invoked the interrogation extensively, yet enjoyed relative orthodoxy in early modern England. As Robin Barnes points out, "Where was one to draw the line between the general and the particular? This very broad grey area was the ground upon which countless debates played out" (Barnes 2016, 9).

The critically important matter of the moment for casting the interrogation has been given little attention by historians. Yet this "moment" underpins methodology and practice. In *Christian Astrology*, Lilly claims that the "time the Astrologer should take for the ground of his Question" is disputed. For the "Arabians" this moment might be when the querent first enters the house or closet, or when the querent first "salutes the Artist." In accordance with reason and experience, however, Lilly rejects these moments in preference to the moment when the astrologer *perceives the intention* of the querent, at which time Lilly casts an interrogation and makes an "Astrologicall Judgment" (Lilly 1647, 166). Forman's "moment," defined under "Rueles and observances before youe give Judgment," appears to be "the directe oware [hour] and Juste Instante time that the question was moved in" (MS Ashmole 240 f.12r). In practice, however, Forman appears to invoke a variety of moments for casting the interrogation, including the arrival of a client, the arrival of urine in a medical inquiry, and the moment of falling sick (usually invoked in casting a Decumbiture).

But what is the likely origin of the interrogational moment? Albertus Magnus, suggests that if births are "natural things," then interrogations are "like natural things." Eugenio Garin, summarizing Albertus, suggests that "the initial influence is not placed and concentrated solely at birth" but distributed in the successive moments of life (Garin 1976, 38). Thus, the interrogation can be substituted for the nativity, because its testimony is related to that of the nativity (Lilly 1647, 135–142, 177–181). Coley suggests that the nativity provides a much "surer Foundation" for an astrological judgment, but in its absence, an interrogation is acceptable "being as it were a second Birth, viz. The Birth or motion of the mind" (Coley 1676, 131). Similarly, John Gadbury, on the opening page to his guide confirms that if the details of a nativity are unavailable, an interrogation "is sufficient to inform any one of all manner of Contigencies necessary to be known" (Gadbury 1658). Yet, Lilly makes it very clear that no promising interrogation can contradict the testimony of the nativity, upon which good fortune ultimately depends (Lilly 1647, 240).

Having cast the interrogation, the first requirement is to establish the presence or otherwise of astrological "warnings" (Dunn 2009, 229–239). This is unique to the interrogation and not required for any other figure. The presence of such warnings reveals that the interrogation is not radical (invalid), and advises caution in judgment, or warns against proceeding with judgment. These warnings might indicate, inter alia, danger to the practitioner, or displeasing the querent. At best, the reliability of the judgment is undermined. In a nativity, radicality has been established at the moment of birth, thus the nativity is a valid starting point for any inquiry relating to the owner of that nativity. Another figure, however, such as the interrogation, may only be termed *radical* if it also qualifies as a valid starting point (Schmidt and Hand 1996, IV 2).

A further issue in terms of radicality is related to "intention": the querent's intention must be serious and not arise from a wish to test or deceive the astrologer. If the astrological testimony reveals that the querent's intention is dishonest, the interrogation is not radical. Lilly does not explicitly discuss the matter of intent but is careful to observe the astrological warnings, which guarantee seriousness of motive. Bonatti's rules relating to validity appear to underpin Lilly's 11 "Considerations before Judgment," to which Lilly adheres closely, in order to ensure that the figure is "radicall and capable of judgment" (Lilly 1647, 121–123, 298). Forman's, "Rueles and Observances," also appear to be underpinned by Bonatti's rules (Forman, f.12r). Forman was keen to address the matter of intent and honesty in *Judgmentes*, yet in practice, Forman's casebooks consistently reveal figures containing unheeded warnings.

Societies, clients, and settings were very different for the astrologers of ninth-century Baghdad, medieval Europe, and 17th-century England, yet they were informed by the same astrological principles. These principles rest upon an ancient body of learning, Babylonian Hellenistic, Persian, Arabic, and Medieval Latin in origin, an unbroken tradition since the Babylonians, the major elements of which were in place by about 800 CE. Interrogational astrology provided practitioners with a means of addressing, with precision, almost any area of human concern. The revival of horary astrology in the 20th century owes much to Olivia Barclay (1919–2001) and the republication of Lilly's *Christian Astrology* by Regulus Publications in 1984.

Barbara Dunn

See also: Forman, Simon; Gadbury, John; Horoscopes; House Systems; Lilly, William; Medical Astrology; Zodiacs

Further Reading

Abū Ma'shar al-Balkhī. 1994. *The Abbreviation of the Introduction to Astrology*, ed. and trans. Charles Burnett, Keiji Yamamoto, and Michio Yano. Leiden: Brill.

Barclay, Olivia. 1990. *Horary Astrology Rediscovered: A Study in Classical Astrology.* West Chester, PA: Whitford Press.

Barnes, Robin. 2016. *Astrology and Reformation.* New York: Oxford University Press.

The Casebooks Project: A digital edition of Simon Forman's and Richard Napier's medical records 1596–1634. http://www.magicandmedicine.hps.cam.ac.uk/

Chamber, John. 1601. *A Treatise against Judicial Astrologie.* London: John Harison.

Coley, Henry. 1676. *Clavis Astrologiae Elimata, or a Key to the Whole Art of Astrology, New Filed and Polished.* London: Benjamin Tooke and Thomas Sawbridge.

Cornelius, Geoffrey. 1994. *The Moment of Astrology: Origins in Divination.* London: Arkana.
Dunn, Barbara. 2009. *Horary Astrology Re-Examined: The Possibility or Impossibility of the Matter Propounded.* Bournemouth, UK: Wessex Astrologer.
Forman, Simon. 1606. *The Astrologicalle Judgmentes of Phisick and Other Questions.* MS Ashmole 280, Bodleian Library. http://dev.magicandmedicine.hps.cam.ac.uk/view/text/normalised/TEXT5
Forman, Simon. "Rueles and Observances before Youe Give Judgment." MS Ashmole 240, Bodleian Library.
Forman, Simon. Simon Forman Casebook (Vol II 20 February 1597–20 February 1598): MS Ashmole 226, Bodleian Library.
Gadbury, John. 1658. *The Doctrine of Nativities, Containing the Whole Art of Directions, and Annual Revolutions.* London.
Garin, Eugenio. 1976. *Astrology in the Renaissance: The Zodiac of Life.* London: Routledge.
Hand, Robert. 2014. "The Use of Military Astrology in Late Medieval Italy: The Textual Evidence." Unpublished diss. Catholic University of America. http://cuislandora.wrlc.org/islandora/object/etd%3A260
Heydon, Christopher. 1603. *A Defence of Judicial Astrologie.* Cambridge: University of Cambridge.
Lilly, William. 1647. *Christian Astrology Modestly Treated of in Three Books.* London: Thomas Brudenell for John Partridge and Humphrey Blunden.
Schmidt, R., ed., and Robert Hand, trans. 1996. *Guido Bonatti: Liber Astronomiae Part IV On Horary, First Part.* Berkeley Springs, WV: Golden Hind.
Thomas, Keith. 1971. *Religion and the Decline of Magic: Studies in Popular Beliefs in Sixteenth and Seventeenth-Century England.* London: Weidenfeld and Nicolson.
Zambelli, Paolo. 1992. *The* Speculum Astronomiae *and Its Enigma: Astrology, Theology and Science in Albertus Magnus and His Contemporaries.* Dordrecht: Kluwer.

HOROSCOPES

The horoscope has undergone many expressions in its two and a half thousand-year history. It began in Mesopotamia as a simple list of planets and zodiac signs. Later in the Hellenistic period it was cast onto boards with movable pieces and then removed once read. In the medieval period it took on a more permanent form, being drawn on paper or parchment, which can be recognized as what is now considered a horoscope. In essence, it is a representation of the orientation of the heavens around an individual at their birth and as such it binds the life of the astrologer to the movement of the solar system. In this regard, the horoscope is both an icon of astrology, as it has over its long history maintained its central place in the practice of astrology, but it is also the astrologer's personal instrument of fate.

The horoscope provides the astrologer with a symbolic view of themselves or another individual through the lens of the position of the heavenly bodies at their moment of birth. The resulting diagram is called the natal horoscope. In the 16th century, horoscopes were also called figures while today astrologers call them charts. A horoscope can be constructed to examine any moment in time and place, be that for the birth of a person, country (mundane astrology), or any difficult or auspicious event. Additionally, a horoscope can be cast for the time of asking a question (horary astrology) in the hope of finding an answer or a horoscope can

Elaborate horoscopes were associated with rulers and princes. This is a detail from *The Book of Birth of Iskandar,* the horoscope of the Central Asian Muslim prince Mirza Iskandar (1384–1415). (Wellcome Collection)

be created for choosing a time in the future for a wedding, opening of a business, or commencing any sort of activity. In this way, the horoscope is the central instrument of astrology.

The actual horoscope itself is constructed for a specific place, converted to its longitude and latitude, with the level of accuracy of the time of the birth or event required to be within a few minutes. There are, however, many techniques for creating partial horoscopes where the time is unknown or known only within a few hours. In Western astrology, the zodiac used is generally not associated with the actual physical constellations but instead is one that is mathematically derived. For example, one of the major zodiacs used in the past 2,000 years is known as the tropical zodiac, which is based on the seasons. The 12 equal zodiac signs are reset every year to commence from the point on the ecliptic as it crosses the equator. The sun is at this point at the vernal equinox (around March 21) and that point is deemed to be the 0° Aries point of the tropical zodiac.

In the construction of a horoscope the first point to be determined is the orientation of the zodiac band to the local horizon for the time of the birth or event. With that in place the planets can be introduced by placing them in their current positions within the zodiac being used. The individual, or place of the event, is located in the center of the diagram with the eastern horizon placed to the left.

Additional notation is generally added, such as the planets' angular relationships to each other, known as aspects. The 360° of space around the individual (in the case of a natal horoscope) is also divided into 12 sections, which are known as the houses. Each of these houses represent an area of the individual's life and are numbered 1 to 12 commencing from below the eastern horizon and moving in an anticlockwise direction. In this manner, the horoscope becomes a complex of planets in zodiacal degrees, aspects, and houses making any given horoscope unique. The resulting horoscope provides the astrologer with a distinctive diagram that establishes, what astrologers believe to be, the individual's personal relationship to the cosmos.

The first horoscopes came from Mesopotamia and they were list maps, a text-based list of the planets and their zodiac signs, with the earliest known being dated from 410 BCE (Rochberg 1998, 3). By the Hellenistic period horoscopes were laid out on horoscopic boards on which the planets were markers to be arranged as required (Greenbaum 2016, 208). Thus such horoscopes were ephemeral and according to J. Thomann (2008, 98) the notion of a horoscope drawn on paper or parchment remained scarce in the West until Arabic influences in the 12th century. However, once the horoscope, as a drawn diagram, was established, whether it was represented as a square diagram or in its later 19th-century version of a circular form, it has maintained its dominant position in astrology as the central motif of the subject.

The location of the person in the center of the horoscope reveals the historical link between the horoscope and the astrolabe. The astrolabe was used to quickly determine the orientation of the zodiac band to the horizon and, according to Al-Biruni, an 11th-century Iranian polymath, it could also quickly produce the mathematical divisions of time or space to construct the 12 houses within the horoscope (1934, 205). Hence both the astrolabe and the horoscope are orientated in a similar manner with, in the case of the astrolabe the user being located in the center of the instrument while facing south with east on their left, while in a horoscope the individual was also located in the center of the diagram with east on their left. In the Northern Hemisphere, the ecliptic is located south of the observer so this orientation allowed for the planets and zodiac band to culminate overhead on the meridian. This movement of the heavens from left (east) to right (west) is now defined as clockwise motion. In a world without mechanical clocks or standardized calendars the astrolabe represented a time-finding instrument, since it could accurately use the heavens to find the time of the day or night, while the horoscope was a time-holder, as any horoscope held the exact time and place in its combination of planets, horizon line, and zodiac, which could be read retrospectively.

This union between the astrolabe and the horoscope led to the assumption that the horoscope was in principle a simplified map of the heavens. Hence today astrologers can be criticized for what are considered to be errors between the actual heavens and its representation in their horoscopes. Astrologers are often accused of being simplistic or ignorant about the nature of the solar system with its heliocentric (sun-centered) structure, as they maintain their Earth-centered, or rather individual centered, view of the heavens. Additionally, with the different seasonal or mathematical zodiacs, astrologers are criticized for not knowing the true location of the planets among the stars of the zodiac constellation. Yet such criticisms are based on the assumption that the horoscope is a simple map of the sky. This assumption is not supported by the history of astrology nor is it supported by how astrologers themselves view their horoscopes.

In the late 18th and early 19th century with the Western colonization of parts of the Southern Hemisphere, European astrologers began to cast horoscopes for Southern Hemisphere locations. The astrolabe, having been replaced by the mechanical clock, had already been put to one side as the major instrument of time and astrologers relied solely on sets of printed tables known as Tables of Houses to construct charts. However, to use these tables in the Southern Hemisphere a different methodology was required. In the Southern Hemisphere, the sun moves in an anticlockwise direction across the sky and the point of culmination of the planets is in the north. As astrologers juggled their tables to produce Southern Hemisphere horoscopes, they maintained the concept of the east being located to the left of the horoscope. This, however, created a problem, for in the Southern Hemisphere the ecliptic is located to the north of the individual, and hence the place of culmination, the meridian, is in the north. Technically, therefore, with north in the upper part of the horoscope, the east needed to be located to the right of the chart. However, instead of making this correction, astrologers chose to maintain the east in its historical left position. Consequently, the normal order of the 360° of the compass bearings of east (left)–south (above)–west (right)–north (lower) shifted in Southern Hemisphere horoscopes to east (left)–north (above)–west (right)–south (lower). In fact, there is no visual difference between horoscopes cast for the Northern Hemisphere to those of the Southern Hemisphere. In both cases the sun is assumed to move from left to right—clockwise. Hence the requirement that the horoscope maintain a level of loyalty to the actual sky is questionable.

This mismatch between sky and horoscope stems from its medieval roots. The medieval approach to maps is described by Evelyn Edson and Emilie Savage-Smith (2000, 21) as "world maps were philosophical rather than practical, providing a cosmic overview rather than information for some mundane journey." Here the map is being expressed as a union between space and spirit willingly sacrificing the necessities of topography for the needs of the soul. Mircea Eliade ([1957] 1987, 42–45, 52) also described such maps; for him they were traditional sacred maps. He called these maps *imago mundi* and defined their features as maps divided into quadrants by the cardinal points, which placed the sacred or known world in the center and enabled the individual to communicate with the transcendental world by a ritual iteration of the moment of birth or origin of the world. It is evident from historical examples that the astrologer's map, the horoscope, is largely unchanged in its layout and concept since the Hellenistic period, and consequently it is logical to assume that it shares more with the symbolic, spirit-space maps of the medieval period and Eliade's concept of an *imago mundi* and personal orientation than with the desire for accuracy of modern cartography.

The actual view that many astrologers take of their own natal horoscope varies greatly; many, however, do see it as a symbolic map. They believe that this personal map establishes their uniqueness in the world, providing them with a unique

Elongations

Because Mercury and Venus are closer to the sun than to Earth, and their orbits are inside Earth's, they never appear too far from the sun in the sky as viewed from Earth. This phenomenon was apparent to astrologers long before it was explained by the heliocentric system. The distance between the sun and one of these "inferior planets" along the ecliptic is called the "elongation." The maximum elongation of Mercury is 28 degrees. Venus's is 47 degrees. That means that neither can form an aspect with the sun greater than the semisextile (30 degrees) for Mercury and the semisquare (45 degrees) for Venus. It also means that they form conjunctions with the sun very frequently and, therefore, that these conjunctions are less astrologically meaningful than those formed by the sun and the "outer planets" beyond Earth's orbit.

chronology (Brady 2011). Indeed, in the same way as Eliade described the need to return to the point of origin by revisiting the birth of the world, each astrologer constantly revisits their personal moment of creation, returning to their birth horoscope for guidance, timing, and understanding. In the light of such evidence, Patrick Curry (Willis and Curry 2004, 62) argued that "surely a horoscope is a symbolic map of someone's psyche . . . a soul-map," supporting the idea that the horoscope for astrologers shows greater loyalty to spirit than to the necessity of the sky.

Today, horoscopes are rarely calculated by hand, as computers and now apps are the instrument of choice for constructing an astrological chart. Indeed, such was the need of astrologers to generate horoscopes that they were among the early adopters of personal computers. In 1980, when the personal computer was on the verge of being launched by IBM, Michael Erlewine pioneered astrological software by producing a computer programming manual for astrologers so that individual astrologers could code their own software applications (Holden 1996, 224). Finally, in the latter half of the 20th century a level of pluralism arrived into astrology and horoscopes today may contain many other heavenly bodies, in addition to the planets of the solar system and the two luminaries, while some astrologers have even experimented with the heliocentric, sun in the center, horoscope, although this has not been generally accepted. The horoscope itself has proved to be the consistent instrument of astrology and thus a horoscope drawn today could be recognized and read by an astrologer from a thousand years ago.

Bernadette Brady

See also: Astrolabe; Electional Astrology; Horary Astrology; House Systems; Medical Astrology; Mundane Astrology; Natal Astrology; Zodiacs

Further Reading

Al-Biruni. 1934. *The Book of Instruction in the Elements of the Art of Astrology.* London: British Museum.

Brady, Bernadette. 2011. "The Horoscope as an 'Imago Mundi': Rethinking the Nature of the Astrologer's Map." In *Astrologies, Plurality and Diversity*, ed. Nicholas Campion and

Liz Greene, 47–62. University of Wales Trinity Saint David. Lampeter, UK: Sophia Centre Press.
Edson, Evelyn, and Emilie Savage-Smith. 2000. "An Astrologer's Map: A Relic of Late Antiquity." *Imago Mundi* 52: 7–29.
Eliade, Mircea. (1957) 1987. *The Sacred and the Profane: The Nature of Religion.* Harcourt: London.
Greenbaum, Dorian Gieseler. 2016. *The Daimon in Hellenistic Astrology, Origins and Influence.* Leiden: Brill.
Gunzburg, Darrelyn. 2011. "How Do Astrologers Read Charts." In *Astrologies, Plurality and Diversity*, ed. by Nicholas Campion and Liz Greene, 181–200. University of Wales, Trinity Saint David. Lampeter, UK: Sophia Centre Press.
Holden, James Herschel. 1996. *A History of Horoscopic Astrology.* Tempe, AZ: American Federation of Astrologers.
Rochberg, Francesca. 1998. *Babylonian Horoscopes.* Philadelphia: American Philosophical Society.
Thomann, J. 2008. "Square Horoscope Diagrams in Middle Eastern Astrology and Chinese Cosmological Diagrams: Were These Designs Transmitted through the Silk Road?" In *The Journey of Maps and Images on the Silk Road*, ed. P. Forêt and A. Kaplony. Leiden: Brill.
Willis, Roy, and Patrick Curry. 2004. *Astrology, Science and Culture: Pulling Down the Moon.* New York: Berg.

HOUSE SYSTEMS

House systems refer to the different spherical astronomical methods used to divide the ecliptic into 12 sections, known as the houses. Because the house system used to create a horoscope will greatly influence the actual reading of that horoscope, astrologers have developed many methods. The different systems are defined by which circle of the celestial sphere is used to divide into 12 sections, how these divisions may be projected back to the ecliptic, and whether these circles are divided by time rather than space. Over the past 2,000 years, different systems have risen and fallen in popularity. Today a house system tends to be associated with a particular branch of astrology or school of astrology. Through astrological software packages, astrologers today have access to the full range of systems.

The oldest house system, first used in the Hellenistic period, is Whole Sign houses which uses the zodiac signs on the ecliptic to define the 12 houses. The zodiac sign that rose over the horizon at the chosen moment of time was used to define the first house; the other 11 zodiac signs then create the other houses moving in an anticlockwise direction from the rising sign, the sign rising over the horizon in the east. Each house, therefore, begins and ends with the boundaries of the zodiac signs and is 30° in size. This is a nonquadrant house system as it does not acknowledge the role of the midheaven (MC, the point where the ecliptic crosses the prime meridian), nor the ascendant (the point where the ecliptic cuts the eastern horizon) to act as house-defining axes in the horoscope. A variation of Whole Sign house system is known as the Equal House system. It is similar to Whole Sign houses except that the degree of the ascendant is noted and the 1st house is then defined from this rising degree. Thus if a horoscope had 10° Taurus rising, then the first house would be the area from 10° Taurus to 10° Gemini. In this manner each house, as with Whole Sign houses, contains 30° of the ecliptic and thus all houses are equal in size. However, in the Equal House system the personal point of the degree of the ascendant is emphasized as the defining feature that dictates the remaining 11 houses cusps. This concept is also used to construct house systems based on a chart point, planet, or luminary. Solar Houses, for example, are those created by placing the sun on the ascendant and then allowing all the houses to be generated as in the Equal House system. This provides a way of constructing a horoscope for an individual with an unknown birth time. Both of these nonquadrant house systems have solid support among contemporary astrologers.

Most house systems, however, are quadrant systems. In quadrant house systems the ascendant/descendant defines the first and seventh house cusps, as with the Equal House system but additionally the midheaven is used to define the cusp of the 10th house while its opposite point, that of the I.C (Imum Coeli), defines the cusp of the fourth house. This creates four zones or quadrants within the circle of the ecliptic. The earliest quadrant house system is known as the Porphyry house system, named after the third century CE Neoplatonist, Porphyry, although he was probably not its creator. In the Porphyry system the span of the ecliptic contained within each quadrant is trisected to produce three houses. Because the number of ecliptical degrees between the ascendant and the MC will vary with the latitude of the location, time of the day, and season, the quadrants are not of equal size. Hence the three houses in the rising-to-culminating quadrant (houses 12, 11, and 10) will be a different size than the three in the culminating-to-setting quadrant (houses 9, 8, and 7). This difference is reflected diagonally across the horoscope into the houses below the horizon.

The astrolabe, however, provided an alternative method of dividing the quadrants by using the prime vertical, the circle perpendicular to the horizon that links the due east and due west points on the horizon. The prime vertical is reflected on the latitude plate of the astrolabe as the circles of unequal hours. In the 11th century the Islamic scholar Abū Rayḥān Muḥammad Ibn Aḥmad Al-Bīrūnī, known today as Al-Bīrūnī, described how to use the astrolabe to construct the 12 houses. It was not until 1495, however, when Joseph and Matthew Campanus published this system as a set of easily referenced tables that it gained the name of the Campanus house system. It maintained popularity in astrology as it divided equally the local space around an individual and represented this spatial division on the ecliptic. The Campanus house system was promoted in the 20th century by U.S. astrologer Dane Rudhyar who considered it the most suitable system for his work in humanistic astrology, which viewed the horoscope as the seed potential of an individual.

A variation of the Campanus system was promoted in the 15th century by Johannes Müller von Königsberg (1436–1476). Müller rejected the prime vertical as the foundation of a house system and instead developed a house system based on the equator, which drew on the work of Abenmoat, Abū Abd Allāh Muhammad Ibn Mu'ādh al-Jayyānī (989–1079), the Islamic scholar who wrote the first-known treatise on spherical trigonometry (North 1986, 35–38). Similar to Campanus houses, Müller also used the house circles to project his divisions back to the ecliptic. This method became known as Regiomontanus, after Müller's Latin epithet and, through the mass production of its tables, it grew in popularity. William Lilly used Regiomontanus houses for his horary work and to this day students of Lilly continue to use this system. A variation of Regiomontanus known as the Morinus house system is named after Jean-Baptiste Morin the 17th-century reformer of astrology. His system is a nonquadrant system and he focused on the point due east for the time of birth, rather than the degree of the ecliptic on the horizon. Like Regiomontanus, he divided the equator into 12 divisions but projected these divisions onto the ecliptic by means of circles of equal longitude, the great circles that pass through the ecliptical poles. The resulting first house is the due east point, rather than the ascendant, and the 10th house cusp is 90° from the east point. Hence the ascendant and midheaven float in the horoscope. As a result, the Morinus house system never gained popularity among astrologers.

Another approach was to use the diurnal circles, the small circles parallel to the equator that mark the path that any heavenly body will take as the Earth rotates. There are several different house systems based on the diurnal circles, one of which is named after the Islamic scholar, Abū ṣ-Saqr 'Abd al-'Azīz Ibn 'Utmān Ibn 'Alī l-Qabīṣī l-Mawṣilī, commonly known as Al-Qabīṣī (Alcabitius) (d. 967). Using an astrolabe, he measured how long it took for the degree rising to become the midheaven, then trisected that time. Using the diurnal path of the ascendant he then found the degree on the ecliptic at one-third and two-thirds of the time to give the different house cusps. Its popularity was maintained for, like Campanus, it was easy to generate these house cusps directly from the astrolabe and it was the preferred house system used by Guido Bonatti. Another system that used the diurnal circles was developed by the Italian monk Placido de Titis, known as Placidus, who published *Primum Mobile* in 1657. Placidus was critical of both the Campanus and Regiomontanus spatial house systems and returned to a temporal system, which he believed was linked to Ptolemy. He avoided projection and worked directly with the degrees of the ecliptic to find the diurnal circles that the ecliptic intersected one-third and two-thirds of the distance from the meridian to the horizon and similarly in the lower quadrant. These points of intersection formed the house cusps. Because this method is easily tabulated and these tables have been published since 1820 in *Raphael's Almanac*, the Placidus house system is probably the most widely used house system today.

In the 20th century, different house systems have been promoted, for example the Meridian system of David Cope in the early 1900s another nonquadrant system, and the Topocentric House system of 1964, developed by Wendel Polich and A. P. Nelson Page, which gives similar results to that of Placidus. The most recent house system was put forward in 1971 by Walter Koch, which claimed to combine both time and space by using the diurnal small circles but projecting the division back to the ecliptic by lines parallel to the horizon. This became known as the Koch house system, and although popular in the United States in the early 21st century, it appears to be declining in use.

Bernadette Brady

See also: Al-Qabīṣī; Astrolabe; Gauquelin, Michel, and Françoise Gauquelin; Horoscopes; Morin, Jean-Baptiste; Placidus

Further Reading

Evans, James. 1998. *The History and Practice of Ancient Astronomy*. New York: Oxford University Press.

Lorenz, Dona Marie. 1973. *Tools of Astrology: Houses*. Topanga, CA: Eomega Grove Press.

North, J. D. 1986. *Horoscopes and History*. London: Warburg Institute, University of London.

Webster, Roderick S., Marjorie Webster, and Sara Schechner Genuth. 1998. *Western Astrolabes*. Chicago: Adler Planetarium and Astronomy Museum.

INDIAN ASTROLOGY

The Indian astral sciences, known collectively as *jyotiḥśāstra* or *jyotiṣa/jyautiṣa* and including elements of astral divination, date back at least to the late Vedic period of approximately 1000–500 BCE. The early divination was based largely on the lunar phases and on the moon traversing 27 or 28 asterisms (*nakṣatra*), one for each day of the sidereal lunar month. These factors—used for determining the proper times for sacrifices and other rituals, but also to some extent for personal predictions—partly survived in later Indian astrology, where the asterisms were normalized as 27 equal divisions of the ecliptic (that is, the path of the sun, rather than that of the moon). But the discipline of horoscopic astrology proper, known by the Greek loanword *horā*, was introduced into India from the northwest in two main waves of transmission, although the memory of the first transmission in particular was eventually replaced with a mythologized history that had astrology originate with a number of semidivine sages. This entry deals only with the astrological tradition resulting from the first transmission; for the second, see "Tājika Astrology."

The Hellenistic origins of classical Indian astrology are clear from the many Greek technical terms employed in its foundational texts. Such terms are more

Table 1 Astrological Terminology in Sanskritized Greek

Sanskrit form	Greek origin	Meaning of Greek
kendra	*kentron*	angle
paṇaphara	*epanaphora*	succedent
āpoklima	*apoklima*	cadent
trikoṇa	*trigōnon*	trine
horā	*hora*	hour, ascendant
meṣūraṇa	*mesouranēma*	midheaven
jāmitra	*diametron*	opposition
dyūna	*dunon*	descendant
hibuka	*hupogeion*	subterranean [midheaven]
drekkāṇa	*dekanos*	decan
anaphā	*anaphēs*	separation
sunaphā	*sunaphē*	application
durudhurā	*doruphoria*	spear-bearing
kemadruma	*kenodromia*	being void of course

numerous in the earlier sources, but for a number of important concepts, no indigenous vocabulary was ever developed. In addition to names for the planets and zodiacal signs, astrological terminology in Sanskritized Greek (the orthography of which may vary considerably) includes the terms in Table 1.

The transmission of Greek-language astrology to India appears to have taken place at some point in the early centuries of the Common Era, although David Pingree's deceptively precise dating to 149–150 CE has now been convincingly refuted. Because classical Indian astrology employs the same system of 7 planets, 12 signs, and 12 places or houses as Hellenistic astrology, this article will focus on the points where the Indian system differs from the Hellenistic or has developed in other directions.

Hellenistic Elements Not Present in Classical Indian Astrology

Some technical elements of Hellenistic astrology appear to have been lost en route to India, while others were simplified or did not retain their original significance. Elements entirely absent from Indian astrology include, most importantly, the concept of sect (*hairesis*), dividing planets into two groups—one solar or diurnal, the other lunar or nocturnal—and the use of mathematically derived points known as lots (*klēros*). The grouping of the 12 signs into triplicities (four sets of three signs each, the signs in any set forming an equilateral triangle within the zodiac) does survive in India to some extent, but the system of rulerships connected with the triplicities does not, nor are triplicities included in the schemes of planetary dignities. (A special dignity known as *mūlatrikoṇa*, literally "root triangle," may perhaps represent a version of triplicities; but the *mūlatrikoṇa* signs, always identical with a planet's domicile or exaltation, agree with the standard Hellenistic scheme in only four out of seven cases.) A subdivision of each sign into five unequal parts known as *triṃśāṃśa* ("thirtieth-parts") and assigned to the rulership of the nonluminary planets likewise survives; this is obviously a form of terms (Greek *horia*, but often called simply *moirai* "degrees," that is, thirtieths of a sign), though not an exact match for any of the several systems of terms found in extant Greek sources. Unlike the Hellenistic terms, the *triṃśāṃśas* also have rather few practical uses.

The perhaps most striking difference between Indian and Hellenistic astrology, however, concerns the aspects of the planets. In the Indian system, the only full aspect common to all planets is the opposition, which is not considered inherently bad or difficult; indeed, all aspect angles are neutral in themselves, so that an aspect becomes good or bad solely depending on the nature and state of the planet emitting the aspect. Aspects are reckoned from sign to sign, counting inclusively, so that the opposition is called a seventh-sign aspect. In addition, the three superior planets have two full aspects each: Mars, on the fourth and eighth signs from itself; Jupiter, on the fifth and ninth; and Saturn, on the third and 10th. Other planets cast the same aspects with varying fractions of strength. The origin of these aspect doctrines is not known. Another important feature of the Indian aspects is that they are static or frozen in time: the distinction between applying and separating aspects, conceived by the Greek authors and developed in great detail in the Arabic era, is entirely lacking from classical Indian texts.

Other Technical Differences and Considerations

The seven celestial bodies ("planets") are the same in Indian and Hellenistic astrology and have largely the same functions, with some adaptations to the Indian social and religious environment. Although the perception and worship of the planets have been influenced to a certain extent by the Indian mythological characters with whom they were identified, their astrological significations remain more or less intact. Thus, for instance, the planetary deities are all conceived of as male, and several have one or more female consorts, but, in a horoscope, the moon and Venus still signify female persons. Over the centuries, Indian astrologers also began to include the lunar nodes among the planets, first as a single entity and eventually as two separate ones, known as Rāhu (north node) and Ketu (south node), respectively—although the original meaning of "comet" and similar phenomena for Ketu (typically named in the plural) is still evident in some texts. The resulting *navagrahas* or "nine planets" are commonly worshipped as a group in Hindu temples, especially in South India, with Rāhu and Ketu depicted iconographically as two halves of a serpentine eclipse demon. Some astrological texts and practitioners also include so-called minor planets (*upagraha*), which are really mathematically derived points, in a horoscope; but the practice appears rather late, and not widespread.

With regard to the zodiac, the Indians, like the Persians, have preserved the sidereal definition of the zodiac, although there is some disagreement over the precise fiducial star or the exact offset of 0° Aries from the equinoctial point. Tropical values are used for some calendric purposes, but astrology proper is always done using sidereal positions. The 12 zodiacal signs are the same as in Greek sources, and the Indians have preserved the subdivisions of the signs, if not always their uses: in addition to the terms or *triṃśāṃśa* discussed above, these include the decan or *drekkāṇa* (with variants) and the 12th-parts (Greek *dōdekatēmoria*, Sanskrit *dvādaśāṃśa*), also known as the "micro-zodiac." However, the Indian assignment of planetary rulers to the decans rather follows the order of triplicities (so that, for instance, the three decans of Aries are assigned in turn to the domicile rulers of Aries, Leo, and Sagittarius), suggesting that these two "groupings of three" may have been conflated at some point. For the 12th-parts, two parallel models of calculation have existed since Babylonian times, one of which actually results in 13 divisions to a sign (the last being a repetition of the first). Both models are present in Sanskrit as well as Greek sources.

More important in practice than these divisions, however, is the ninth-part of a sign or *navāṃśa*, which may be indigenous to India, and which is identical with the division of the 27 lunar asterisms into four quarters each (9×12 = 4×27). By either definition, the zodiac is divided into 108 parts, a number of great significance in Indian religious speculation. The ninth-parts were later introduced, through Persia, into Arabic-language astrology, and from there into Europe, although they remained an exotic and little-used astrological technique. Indian authors gradually added more subdivisions of a sign, each with its own set of planetary rulers; the most comprehensive scheme is called the group of 16 divisions (*ṣoḍaśavarga*), the smallest of which comprises half a degree of ecliptical longitude. Later and more speculative works of the genre known as *nāḍi* even speak of a division of each sign into 150 parts, or 1,800 for the zodiac as a whole, in a vision of astrological fate calculation that recalls the *myriogenesis* doctrine alluded to by Firmicus Maternus in the fourth century.

Although most Indian astrological works are silent on the technical topic of house division, and many seem to presuppose a scheme where the houses are identical with or at least equally distributed throughout the zodiacal signs, a system of quadrant houses (popularly named after, but certainly predating, the 11th-century astrologer Śrīpati) is also known and widely used. This system, which trisects the ecliptical arc between horizon and meridian and considers the resulting points as the centers rather than the beginnings of the respective houses, is in fact identical with that propounded by the third-century Hellenistic astrologer Pancharius (as later reported by Hephaestio of Thebes); whether and how it was transmitted to India is not known.

One often noted feature of Indian astrology is the importance given to *yogas* or predefined combinations of astrological factors present in a horoscopic figure. Such combinations range from the simple and generic, such as a planet occupying an angle while simultaneously in its sign of exaltation or domicile, to combinations so complex as to appear more or less unique to a single nativity. Indian texts contain hundreds of *yogas*, some named after their supposed outcomes, but many with fanciful names of uncertain derivation.

With regard to the timing of events, Indian astrology relies chiefly on schemes dividing a human life into blocks of time, each block being assigned to a planet (or, occasionally, a zodiacal sign) and divided in a fractal-like manner into subperiods. Such a period may be called the "maturation" (*pāka*) or "allotment" (*dāya*) of a planet but is most often known as a *daśā*, literally "condition" (also used of nonastrological divisions of life, e.g., the "condition of childhood"). Of the *daśā* systems presented in the earliest Indian texts, probably derived from Hellenistic sources, some are fixed and identical for all, while others depend on the arrangement of the planets in the angular, succedent, and cadent places of the individual horoscope, taking the sun, moon, or rising degree as the starting point. In the medieval period, however, systems based on the position of the moon with respect to the indigenous 27 asterisms became popular, and they are still prevalent today. The most well-known of these systems is the *viṃśottarī daśā*, based on a cycle of 120 years (the theoretical maximum life span of a human being), but there are many others, including the *aṣṭottarī*, *kālacakra*, and *yoginī* systems. Common to all is the lack of the sense of motion (whether astronomically based or purely symbolic) inherent in many Hellenistic astrological procedures. No point is "sent out" to move around the horoscope; rather, the *daśās* are fixed or static, just like the Indian aspects.

Differences in Outlook and Special Developments

This static perspective may be seen as one characteristic feature of Indian astrology. Another such feature is a marked predilection for calculation and quantification.

Although the tendency to reduce qualitative assessments to numerical values is also found in non-Indian astrology, it is probably fair to say that it has been carried here to its furthest extreme. As a result, Indian astrology includes numerous techniques of varying complexity for calculating the exact strength of a planet, a house, or the transit of a planet through a sign. The last method, known as *aṣṭakavarga*, appears to have begun as a qualitative description of the results of a transit from the vantage point of each of the planets but was soon reduced to a binary system of good or bad, symbolized by points and dashes (*bindu, rekhā*) not unlike the noughts and ones of computer code.

A more explicit philosophical difference concerns the framework of *karma* theory within which Indian astrology is placed. From its inception, astrology has comprised both a predictive aspect, presupposing a certain degree of determinism, and a prescriptive aspect, similarly presupposing a certain freedom of choice. As the doctrine of *karma* represents a middle path between freedom and determinism, it does fit this dual nature of astrology particularly well, which has probably contributed to the widespread and long-standing acceptance of astrology within Indian culture. The belief in *karma* also ties in closely with the practice of propitiating the planets (*grahaśānti*) to avoid or mitigate an evil fate, which is often seen by practitioners and clients alike as the chief practical purpose of astrology.

Although Indian horoscopic astrology (*horā*) is typically divided into the branches of genethlialogy or natal astrology (*jātaka*), interrogations or horary astrology (*praśna*), and catarchic or electional astrology (*muhūrta*), other forms of divination have been subsumed under astrology as well, and several hybrid forms have emerged. These include, for instance, the highly ritualized forms of interrogations known as *aṣṭamaṅgala-praśna* and practiced particularly in Kerala, as well as the phenomenon known in South India as *nāḍi* and in the North as *Bhṛgusaṃhitā*: a cross between astrology and bibliomancy, where horoscope readings supposedly written long before a client's birth are claimed to describe his or her life—sometimes, several lives—in minute detail.

Indian Astrologers, Society, and Modernity

Like other traditional knowledge systems in India, astrology was typically practiced by members of hereditary communities who preserved it as their intellectual property, as indicated by family names like Joshi or Jois (from *jyotiṣī* "astrologer") still current today. Although astral divination and its practitioners were generally censured by religious authorities in ancient India, they were deemed necessary in some areas of life, particularly to rulers, and the *Arthaśāstra* of Kauṭilya (third century CE) lists diviners as functionaries of the court alongside spies and counselors. With the introduction of horoscopic astrology, the status of astrologers appears gradually to have increased, and in the sixth century, Varāhamihira argued passionately that when even Greek (*yavana*) foreigners were honored like sages for their knowledge of astrology, a Brahman astrologer should be even more so. He also stressed the importance of astrologers not only for the king, but for everyone, even ascetics who had renounced life in the world. In practice, hereditary guilds of astrologers eventually formed *jātis* ("castes") whose social standing was often below

Astrology is big business in India, from famous astrologers to roadside astrologers like this one, shown consulting a young couple. (Sajjad Hussain/AFP/Getty Images)

that of other Brahmans, as they polluted themselves by performing paid work and necessarily associated with clients of lower status. In these respects astrologers were similar to temple priests, with whom they were sometimes considered to be connected as a mixed *jāti*.

This traditional structure began to change in the late 19th century, when the Theosophical Society set up its headquarters near Chennai in South India. The society was strongly linked to the emergence of a modernized Western astrology around the same time, brought about largely by Alan Leo, and many of its members took a lively interest in Indian astrology. Along with the technology facilitating the mass printing and distribution of books and magazines, this interest led to a wave of publications on the subject, chiefly in English.

While the modernizers of Western astrology explicitly strove to transform their art from "fortune-telling" (punishable under British law) into a vehicle of esoteric spiritual symbolism, and later of depth psychology, the Indian modernizers were happy for astrology to retain its traditional predictive and prescriptive functions. The modernization process in India related chiefly to shifts in the medium and intended audience: printed manuals in English and the Indian vernaculars were available to anyone who could afford their modest price. In the place of privileged oral instruction, modern authors offered a reconstructionist astrology based on classical texts, coupled with an experimental and sometimes innovative approach.

Jahangir's Zodiac Coins

The coins minted by Islamic rulers generally featured calligraphy or other abstractions, in line with the Islamic prohibition on images. There were exceptions, and one was a series of coins minted by Jahangir (r. 1605–1627), the Mogul ruler of India. The "Zodiac coins" were first minted in 1617. This series of 12 coins each featured a sign of the zodiac. They were to be minted throughout the year, each during the time when the sun was in that sign. The obverse would carry the date and the name of the mint along with a short inscription in Persian. The finest were the gold coins or "mohurs," but silver and copper zodiac coins were minted as well. In the subsequent reign of Shah Jahan many of these coins were melted down as blasphemous because they carried the images of living things, and they are quite rare today.

These developments produced a new type of astrologer, typically of the professional middle class and practicing astrology as an avocation.

Without question, the most important voice in the formulation of this modern Indian astrology was that of B. V. Raman, who, in addition to his many books and frequent lectures, served for over 60 years as chief editor of *The Astrological Magazine*—perhaps the single most influential medium prior to the Internet for disseminating Indian astrological ideas. Raman had been trained in astrology by his grandfather B. S. Rao, one of the pioneers of the astrological revitalization movement, which also coincided with burgeoning Hindu nationalism and struggle for Indian independence. Like many of their peers, Rao and Raman were fiercely patriotic and disinclined to accept a foreign origin for any aspect of Indian astrology, attitudes that still persist today even among its non-Indian practitioners.

Although inspired by Western developments, early English-language publications on Indian astrology were not targeted at a Western audience and enjoyed very limited circulation in the West. The real turning point in this regard came only in the 1980s, most likely as a result of the increased presence of Indian forms of spirituality in the West on the one hand, and of a growing dissatisfaction among practitioners with the one-sidedly psychological orientation of modern Western astrology on the other. The latter factor was similarly of importance for the reemerging interest in traditional astrology around the same period. At some point during the 1980s, the phrase "Vedic astrology" came into use in North America as a preferred synonym of "Indian/Hindu astrology," possibly coined by several persons independently of each other. Although the misnomer "Vedic" for anything traditionally Indian (including music, architecture, and even cooking) has become common in popular discourse, even when the phenomenon so described bears no discernible relation to the Vedic corpus and may date no further back than the Mughal or even colonial era, the phrase "Vedic astrology" is perhaps unique in having been successfully reexported to India, where it has been in frequent use since the 1990s. Under the nationalist government of the early 21st century, "Vedic astrology" was made an academic discipline at Indian universities.

Martin Gansten

See also: Astrological Associations; Astrotheology; Hellenistic Astrology; Indian Cinema; Raman, Bangalore Venkata; Tājika Astrology; Thai Astrology; Theosophy; Varāhamihira

Further Reading

Kropf, Marianna. 2005. *Rituelle Traditionen der Planetengottheiten (Navagraha) im Kathmandutal: Strukturen—Praktiken—Weltbilder*. Published electronically. Heidelberg: Südasien-Institut, Universität Heidelberg.

Mak, Bill. 2013. "The Transmission of Greek Astral Science into India Reconsidered: Critical Remarks on the Contents and the Newly Discovered Manuscript of the Yavanajātaka." *History of Science in South Asia* 1, 1–20. http://dx.doi.org/10.18732/H2RP4T

Markel, Stephen. 1995. *Origins of the Indian Planetary Deities*. Studies in Asian Thought and Religion 16. Lewiston: Edwin Mellen Press.

Pingree, David. 1981. *Jyotiḥśāstra: Astral and Mathematical Literature*. A History of Indian Literature 6, no. 4. Wiesbaden: Harrassowitz.

Pingree, David. 1997. *From Astral Omens to Astrology: From Babylon to Bīkāner*. Serie orientale Roma 78. Roma: Istituto italiano per l'Africa e l'oriente.

The Yavanajātaka of Sphujidhvaja. 1978. Ed., trans., and commented on by David Pingree. Cambridge, MA: Harvard University Press.

INDIAN CINEMA

In India, where people from all walks of life consult astrologers, there are astrological specialties, just like medical specialties. Medical or health astrology, for example, is an ancient and well-known branch. More recently, and given India's preoccupation with cricket and cinema, there are "cricket astrologers" who specialize in reading the horoscopes of cricket stars and aspirants and astrologers who cater to those in the entertainment business or those who want to enter the film world. An online search yields numerous advertisements for "celebrity astrologer" or "Bollywood astrologers" or even "World famous Bollywood astrologer."

Filmmaking everywhere is a high-risk enterprise where investments are massive and uncertainty shapes the fate of any film. Film business insiders seek various ways of reducing risk. In India consulting astrology is one way of addressing unknowns in filmmaking. There is no stage of filmmaking immune to the influence of astrology. Directors and producers may consult astrologers, some of whom are also numerologists and psychics, before launching a film project. The first shot of a film called the *muhurat* or *muhurtam* shot is timed to take place at an auspicious time and place determined by astrologers or Hindu priests either on an auspicious day in the calendar, or a day and time based on the producer, director, or star's horoscope. A film's title may be determined based on how lucky it is for the director and maybe the result of consultation with astrologers or other soothsayers. Bombay filmmakers Rakesh Roshan and Karan Johar are known to have titled several of their films with words beginning with the letter "K" for good luck. Even a film's release may be timed at an astrologically auspicious time. It is reported that Rakesh Roshan sought the help of his astrologer for the release of his film *Kaabil* (2017) after he learned that Shah Rukh Khan's *Raees* was to be released on the same day.

Considerations of auspicious dates and times may even play a role in the routine release of films on Fridays and festival days. Thursdays are thought to be inauspicious, yet when a particular Friday is deemed inauspicious, films are moved to a Thursday release date. Release of the film *Iru Mugan* (2016) release was set for a Thursday, September 8, as Friday the ninth was inauspicious, being *Ashtami*, the eighth day of the moon's cycle, associated with Saturn and considered inauspicious for beginning a new project, starting a journey, and certain rituals. Sources within the industry also cited the number eight as being the star, Vikram's, lucky number. Similarly, Priyanka Chopra's film *Sarvann* (2017), scheduled for a December 9 release, was postponed due to the demonetization crisis. The makers decided to move the release of the film to the auspicious date of the *Lohri* festival, January 13.

Fans want to know what the year holds for their matinee idols and celebrity astrologers are happy to oblige with public predictions. A 24-hour astrology channel on television offers advice on how to navigate planetary effects for the day and includes predictions about Bollywood liaisons. Astrologers predicted 2016 would be a great year for mega star Rajinikanth's career because of the influence of Jupiter and Mars. The star was even predicted to win an award. However, another star passing through a Venus–Saturn phase would not do well but suffer no serious setbacks. The Saturn period might also endanger his health. Even the box-office fate of individual films are forecast based on the horoscopes of the stars and directors and the start and completion times of the film. A well-known celebrity astrologer predicted Bombay heartthrob Hritik Roshan's film would do better than his competitors release due to the influence of Venus.

Film hopefuls may have their horoscopes seen by astrologers to determine whether they stand a chance. Astrologers have identified certain *yogas* (planetary placements and combinations) for success in film as well as planets and planetary combinations that favor actors and directors. The moon is thought to be very important for a career in film as the moon sways the masses. Similarly, Venus, Jupiter, and sun must be strong. The sun and Venus determine charisma and looks, Jupiter governs money and finances. The sun's placement also determines leadership according to some, so Jupiter and the sun must be strong for a director, moon for the actor, Mars for editing, Mercury for distribution, Venus for music and advertisements, and so on even down to the lunar nodes Rahu, which governs overseas rights and foreign travels, and Ketu, which is important for fight sequences and stunts. Planets even govern the type or genre of movie a director makes. Filmmakers and stars' beliefs extend to gemstone astrology, and they are seen wearing rings of particular precious or semiprecious stones to ward off negative planetary energy.

Stars, directors, and other industry insiders consult astrologers about their career. A Bombay movie star whose career had faltered after he was imprisoned is said to have turned to astrology when he was keen to reenter the film industry. South Indian filmmaker Dinesh Baboo was told by his astrologer that he would never do well in his place of birth. In an interview Dinesh Baboo confirmed that he had found success after leaving his home state. Tamil film icon MG Ramachandran is described as being a firm believer in God and in astrology. His protégé Jayalalitha was known to have consulted a Kerala astrologer who in 2001 had predicted her becoming chief minister. It is said that Dravidian Progress Federation Party leaders were so pleased with the astrologer's forecast that they gifted him 10 lakh rupees. Jayalalitha is reported to have consulted him regularly from then on. Even the time of her cremation and funeral procession was set by astrology.

Celebrities may consult astrologers for other, more mundane matters. Newspapers report stars seeking out astrological help to determine when they might start a family or purchase a house, just like their audiences might. Astro-architect Neeta Sinha is reported to have advised Shah Rukh Khan to rename his house to a name beginning with "M" when heritage societies presented obstacles to his redoing his home, hence the name "*Mannat*" for his iconic Bombay residence. She advised Amitabh Bachchan to change the name of his home from "*Mansa*" to "*Jalsa*" and soon after he signed up as host for the television show, "*Kaun Banega Crorepati,*" which went on to become a hit. Akshay Kumar was advised to put his real name "Rajeev Bhatia" on the property papers for his home to avoid astrological dangers and Hritik Roshan and his then wife Suzanne were told to move out of their bedroom to another room in their home to avoid problems in their relationship.

But what is reported as the most spectacular story involving film and astrology was Bombay star and former Miss World Aishwarya Rai's ritual marriage to a banana tree following her engagement to Amitabh Bachchan's son, the actor Abhishek Bachchan, sometime in 2007, a report denied by the Bachchan family. The story goes that Rai's horoscope indicated she was a *manglik* an astrological combination and *dosha* that forecasts marital discord and the ill health of the spouse, and so the precaution of being wedded to a tree was to divert the planetary energies to the unfortunate plant. In a case of film imitating life the plot device in *Phillauri* (2017) has the groom who is a *manglik* being wedded to a tree only to find that it houses a tree spirit who believes she is married to him. Chaos ensues.

Lakshmi Srinivas

See also: Indian Astrology

Further Reading

Srinivas, Lakshmi. 2016. *House Full. Indian Cinema and the Active Audience.* Chicago: University of Chicago Press.

INFORMATION TECHNOLOGY

Information technology is a phrase typically used to refer to computer systems, but it also encompassing other electronic media like television and telephones. It has featured astrological content in many forms. The telephone has long been used to communicate commercial personalized astrology readings through services advertised in print, radio, television, and Internet. Since the mid-20th century, television and radio have promoted and featured astrologers through call-in or talk show style programming where people may receive advice from professional astrologers on air. Additionally, television broadcasts have represented astrology through investigative journalism and dating shows. Newer forms of media, such as computers and mobile Internet devices from the 1990s onward, have also been a locus for the interchange of astrologically related content and have dramatically shifted the nature of astrology as a communication practice.

Because of shifts in networking, distribution, and production, digital media and the Internet have revolutionized astrology publishing. Some scholars have argued that the Internet as a form of decentralized communication has actually increased the prevalence of noninstitutionalized religious and spiritual practice—particularly those associated with New Age and occult beliefs.

As astrology became part of Internet-based digital media communications, and people became networked in ways not limited to material reproduction or geographic location, access to astrology services, products, images, and texts increased. At the same time, astrological content has diversified because of this change. People who practice astrology disseminate their work to a broad audience with greater ease because of the Internet's ability to transfer and reproduce data. Additionally, new tools for the production of image, text, and video through digital software create new modes for astrology's transmission. Changes in media have also produced audiences attuned to visual aesthetics, and the astrologer's personality and performance.

With widespread computer and Internet access, mediated astrology practices have become more complex. Contemporary popular astrology—as a tradition, practice, and form of communication—is produced and consumed in a range of forms including personal websites, forums, social media, ebooks, images, videos, and apps. In addition to the increased access to many written texts on astrology, including published books digitized through sites like Google Books, and consumption of commercial products via Internet shopping, there are many novel modes of astrology praxis online.

Consumption of Astrology Online

Commercial and professional astrological texts and readings are bought and sold online, and amateur practitioners and enthusiasts share user-produced content through a range of networks and sites. Soon after the Internet became accessible for commerce, personal entertainment, and expression in the early 1990s, astrology content emerged. Personal websites were among the first modes of communication on the Internet and have been used by both independent amateur and professional astrologers. As early as 1995, books with directories for accessing content on the "World Wide Web" reference astrology sites. Personal astrology pages dating back to the mid-1990s are still accessible in 2016. Some early sites were informational, presenting general knowledge along with personal anecdotes, while others were personal sites from professional astrologers selling readings.

As newspapers began to migrate to the Internet, standard newspaper–style horoscope columns also emerged online. The astrological content on professional news sites and curated media sites are typically aimed at a general audience, and mostly represent the "low" forms of astrology associated with sun sign astrology, like that of mass-distributed print media. As in women's interest magazines in print media, women's interest sites often have an astrology section.

More advanced astrology, or more esoteric traditions, are often published on text-based sites, which allow for sharing longer forms of writing and the expression of metaphoric language. Personal sites and blogs allow specialized knowledge to be publicly accessible via web searches or communities, while maintaining the potential for anonymity, as the user may choose whether or not, and to what degree, they present themselves.

Forums and Communities

Another important means of communicating astrology online is the forum, which can connect astrology practitioners and enthusiasts as a community that is not geographically bound. On forums, and in other specialized communities within social media such as blog rings and Facebook groups, communal knowledge about astrology is shared and debated. Forums and other networks that share specialized knowledge construct what Robert Glenn Howard has described as a new vernacular authority pertinent to religious and spiritual practices. Astrology-centric groups display varying levels of expertise and practice with astrology. Some forums or social media groups may be general and provide opportunities for socializing with others who share interests in astrology, while others are organized around members who share sun or rising signs or practice very specific methods of astrology.

Image-Sharing Networks

Social media brings additional interactive properties, where people can create and distribute astrological content to a range of audiences. Tumblr and Instagram, for instance, are networks that encourage the sharing of images, in particular, and feature many astrology-related posts. Oftentimes astrology is communicated through pictures on these sites, with text embedded in the images or accompanying them as captions. The astrology images are often not associated with any particular astrologer or professional but may be watermarked by the user to show authorship. Many images combine recycled material in the quotes and text with a new image that adds an aesthetic component and allows for easy transmission and legibility. Imagery used in astrology content often references established symbols associated with the zodiac, such as using a cartoon picture of a bull to represent Taurus. There is some user-produced original astrology imagery shared online, as well as widespread bricolage that alters and repurposes existing images and characters.

Astrology images shared online typically reference general sun sign astrology and do not require specific knowledge or expertise. Quotes from astrologers, print media, and other websites are common, as are general aphorisms that represent popular contemporary understandings of zodiacal astrology. Notably, astrology images do not typically feature daily or weekly horoscopes and are instead focused

Astrological Software

The late 20th century witnessed a revolution in astrological practice caused by the rise of astrological software. In the space of a few years, the elaborate mathematical calculations of traditional astrology became obsolete as computers could do them with incomparable speed and accuracy, freeing astrologers to concentrate on interpreting charts rather than generating them. Astrological software can also store charts and search a database of charts for specific features such as planets in houses or aspects. Astrological software has grown increasingly elaborate over the following decades and can also perform operations such as solar and lunar returns, as well as many other formerly arduous tasks. Software packages also generate basic astrological interpretations based on the positions of planets in signs and houses.

The earliest astrological software programs date from the late 1970s. Initially, many working astrologers were suspicious of the new technology, but it soon came to be accepted by most. Software exists for both Western and Indian astrological systems. There are also programs for astrologers working with the techniques of a particular historical period, such as Hellenistic or medieval programs. Some of the most powerful and successful commercial astrological software packages include Solar Fire, Sirius (formerly Kepler), AstrolDeluxe, and the Indian or "Vedic" program Shri Jyoti Star. There are also astrology apps for smartphones.

on character traits associated with signs, or specific celestial occurrences, like Mercury in retrograde.

Digitally Mediated Divination

Various web-based and mobile applications provide birth charts and astrology readings or divinations online. Some of these are based on programmable content, while others distribute original readings for daily or on-demand consumption through mobile apps. Additionally, video technologies are used to produce astrological interpretations and horoscopes and personal webcam readings. YouTube is a platform that allows users to practice the verbal forms of astrology divination and interact with their audience to some extent. There are many different practices, as users are able to record personal meditations and interpretations. YouTube, like blogs and personal sites, allows professional astrologers to expand their services to a new audience and advertise themselves.

Many amateur astrologers gain followers through social media platforms, and then attempt to monetize their services through purchasable personalized readings. According to one study of the orientation of New Age rhetoric (including astrology) toward entrepreneurialism, new media technologies encourage the commodification of self via personal branding, in order to be competitive in the labor market of neoliberal society. No longer are astrologists limited to their geographic location. They are able to reach out to clients and customers across the world. Successful online personalities manage to establish dedicated fans using the tools available online that showcase performance, originality, and simulated interpersonal relationships.

Perspectives on Expressions of Astrology, New Age, and Occultic Practices Online

New media and folklore scholars have noted the proliferation of vernacular belief practices that fall under the broad category of "new age" and "occult" traditions, as an alternative to institutional religions. Although there has, to this point, been little analysis of astrology in digital cultures, the use of the Internet for the personalization of traditions, not tied to geographic location or ethnic identity, has been a noted effect of new media. Folklore scholars have studied the changes in networks of belief and the formation of social groups based around religion online. Like the rise in vernacular variations of Christian traditions observed by Robert Glenn Howard, the Internet may also allow for the vernacular expression of astrology and new traditions. Experts on the rise of astrology in mass-distributed print media have noted the pressure on astrologers to conform to norms in order to appeal to the broad public in a profitable way. With the low overhead cost for distribution of content online, astrologers may be less beholden to popular beliefs and local traditions.

Annamarie O'Brien

See also: New Age; Sun Signs

Further Reading

Blank, Trevor J., and Robert Glenn Howard. 2013. *Tradition in the Twenty-First Century: Locating the Role of the Past in the Present*. Logan: Utah State University Press.

Campion, Nicholas. 2012. *Astrology and Popular Religion in the Modern West: Prophecy, Cosmology, and the New Age Movement*. Farnham, Surrey, UK: Ashgate.

Darian-Smith, Kate. 2014. "In the Stars: Astrology, Psychic Powers and the Australian Media." *Media International Australia* 150: 89–95.

Fehérváry, Krisztina. 2007. "Hungarian Horoscopes as a Genre of Postsocialist Transformation." *Social Identities* 13, no. 5: 561–576.

Nederman, Cary J., and James Wray Goulding. 1981. "Popular Occultism and Critical Social Theory: Exploring Some Themes in Adorno's Critique of Astrology and the Occult." *Sociological Analysis* 42, no. 4: 325–332.

Tandoc, Edson C., Jr., and Patrick Ferrucci. 2014. "So Says the Stars: A Textual Analysis of Glamour, Essence and Teen Vogue Horoscopes." *Women's Studies International Forum* 45: 34–41.

ISLAMIC ASTROLOGY

At its early inception in the Islamicate world, astrology, relating celestial phenomena to terrestrial events, was known as *ʿilm aḥkam al-nujūm* (lit. the science of the judgments of the stars). It is the qualitative aspect of the more general study of *ʿilm al-falak* (lit. the science of the [celestial] sphere) or *ʿilm al-nujūm* (lit. the science of the stars). Astronomy, the quantitative aspect, was known as *ʿilm al-hayʾa* (lit. the science of [celestial] conditions). Five main branches constituted the practice of astrology: genethlialogy or natal astrology, which describes the lives of individuals on the basis of their natal charts; historical astrology, which describes the

This early-17th-century drawing, from Muslim-ruled India, is a classic image of the learned Muslim astrologer, surrounded by the tools of his trade, including an astrolabe, zodiac tables, and an hourglass. (Werner Forman/Universal Images Group/Getty Images)

fortunes and misfortunes of dynasties and religions; catarchic or electional astrology, which guides its followers with choosing propitious times for initiating activities (*ikhtīārāt*); interrogations or horary astrology, which provide answers to queries addressed to the astrologer (*masā'il*); and iatromathematics, which applies astrological doctrine to medical practice.

The pre-Islamic inhabitants of the Arabian Peninsula practiced a local form of astrological/astronomical observations that related astral phenomena to agricultural events. Crude techniques were employed to observe the passage of the sun and the moon through the zodiac, and special importance was given to the progression of the moon through 28 mansions (*manāzil*), a concept of Indian origin. Predictions based on the lunar mansions constituted the traditional Arabic *ʿilm al-anwāʿ*. Babylonian omen knowledge was known to a small extent as evinced by the *Apocalypse of Daniel*, preserved only in a Greek translation made by Alexius of Byzantium in 1245. He reports that the Arabic manuscript he translated was discovered by Muʿāwiyah (r. 661–80).

Persian influences were fundamental to the development of Islamicate astrology. The oldest treatise on genethlialogy surviving in Arabic is *Kitāb al-mawālīd wa aḥkāmihā* (*The Book of Nativities and its Principles*), which was translated from Avestan script to Pahlavi in 637 and into Arabic in the middle of the eighth century. It introduced astrological concepts such as *haylağ* (prorogator of life) and *kadhkhudāh* (lord of the significant luminary's term). One of the most significant Persian contributions is the doctrine of the revolution of the world–years based on the conjunctions of Jupiter and Saturn, which is known as historical astrology. It is epitomized in the Islamicate world by *Kitāb al-milal wa al-duwal* (*Book of Sects and Dynasties*) by the Persian astrologer Abū Ma'shar al-Balkhī (787–886), *Kitāb al-qīrānāt wa al-adyān wa al-milal* (*Book of Conjunctions, Religions, and Sects*) by the Persian Jewish astrologer Mashāllāh Ibn Atharī (ca. 740–815), and *Kitāb al-qirānāt wa tahāwīl sinī al- ʿālam* (*Book of the Conjunctions and the Revolutions of the Years of the World*) by Abū Saʿīd Aḥmad b. Muḥammad al-Sijzī (ca. 945–ca. 1020). In fact, astrologers in the Abbasid period were mostly Persian. Early Persian astrologers include ʿUmar al-Farruḫān al-Ṭabarī (d. 815) who translated Dorotheus's *Pentateuch* (*Kitāb al-Khamsa*) from Pahlavi, al-Fazarī (d. 777), and Nawbakht (d. ca. 777), all of whom, with Mashāllāh, chose the astrologically propitious moment for the founding of Baghdad at the year 758 by the Abbasid Caliph al-Manṣur (r. 754–775).

Court patronage played a crucial role in the efflorescence of astrology in Islam. Caliphs employed astrologers: the Maronite Christian astrologer Theophilus of Edessa (known in Arabic as Thawfīl Ibn Tūma) served at the court of al-Mahdī (r. 775–785); al-Wāthiq (r. 842–847) had an astrologer at his deathbed; al-Mu ʿtaḍid employed a Persian astrologer called al-Nayzirī; al-Muktafī (r. 902–908) consulted an astrologer concerning the selection of his heir; and al-Rāḍī (r. 934–940) granted a commander a gift at a precise astrological moment. Harūn al-Rashīd (r. 786–809) fostered astrology and employed chief astrologers including Abū Sahl b. Faḍl b. Nawbakht, ʿAbd Allāh b. ʿUbayd al-Asnī, Abū al- ʿAbbās al-Faḍl b. Sahl al-Sarkhasī, and Kanaka al-Hindī. However, it is in the reign of al-Maʾmūn (r. 813–833) that astrology reached a peak. He chose a solar eclipse as the suitable moment to enter Baghdad after the civil war with al-Amīn. It has been argued by Damien Janos that al-Maʾmūn's interest in astrology and the employment of Persian astrologers "was part and parcel of a wider social phenomenon that led to the persianisation of the Abbasid culture and administration and which was chiefly triggered by the policies endorsed by the ruling elite and al-Maʾmūn in particular, who took the Sasanian imperial legacy as a model on which to fashion court etiquette" (Janos 2014, 414–415). Two families of Persian descent made their mark at the Abbasid court as astrologers: the Nawbakhts, two who are mentioned above, and the Banū al-Munajjim (*munajjim* meaning astrologer). The ancestor of al-Munajjims, Abū Manṣūr al-Munajjim, was a Zoroastrian astrologer—as was Nawbakht—who worked under the caliph al-Manṣūr. His son Yaḥya worked for al- Maʾmūn and reportedly converted to Islam. Interest in astrology continued in his descendants but they were also known for their contributions in poetry, music, and law.

The Abbasid translation activity, especially under Harūn al-Rashīd and al-Maʾmūn, introduced seminal Greek astrological texts such as Ptolemy's *Tetrabiblos* translated into Arabic by Yaḥyā Ibn al-Biṭrīq (d. ca. 798–806) and commissioned by the aforementioned ʾ ʿUmar al-Farruḫān al-Ṭabarī, and Ptolemy's *Almagest* by Isḥāq Ibn Ḥunayn (ca. 830–ca. 910) then again by the mathematician, astronomer, and astrologer Thābit Ibn Qurra (ca. 830–ca. 901) who also wrote *Kitāb ṭabāʾiʿal-kawākib wa taʾthnīrahā* (*The Book of the Natures of the Planets and their Influences*). This was not a passive reception but rather critical. These texts were subject to theoretical scrutiny, which resulted in a number of works revising Ptolomaic theories, including *Shukūk ʿala Baṭlīmūs* (*Casting Doubt on Ptolemy*) by Ibn Haytham and *al-Istidrāk ʿala Baṭlīmūs* (*Recapitulations regarding Ptolemy*) by an anonymous Andalusian astronomer/astrologer.

In addition to their revisionist efforts, astrologers of the Islamicate world recast astrological knowledge by producing a practical and comprehensive body of astrological literature in the form of introductions and handbooks that were very influential in the Arabo-Persian world and the Latin West: the most prominent of these texts is *Kitāb al-madkhal al-kabīr ilā ʿilm ahkām al-nujūm* (*The Great Introduction to Astrology*) by Abū Maʿshar al-Balkhī (787–886) which was translated twice in the 12th century, once by John of Seville in 1133 and another by Hermann of Carinthia in 1140. He also composed an abridged version known as *Kitāb al-madkhal al-sag̱īr* (*The Minor Book*). Abū al-Saqr ʿAbd al-ʿAzīz b. ʿUthmān al-Qabīsī (d. 967) wrote *Kitāb al-madkhal ilā ṣināʿat ahkām al-nujūm* (*The Introduction to the Art of Astrology*), which he dedicated to the Hamdanid ruler of Aleppo Sayf al-Dawla (r. 945–967). He is known in the Latin West as Alcabitius and this introduction was translated in 1144 by John of Seville. Ibn Hibinta (d. after 929) composed *al-Mug̱nī fī ahkām al-nujūm* (*The Ultimate [Guide] to Astrology*). We must add to the list *Kitāb al-tafhīm li awāʾil ṣināʿat al-tanjīm* (*The Book if Instruction on the Elements of Astrology*) by Abū al-Rayḥān al-Bīrūnī (973–1048), and *Kitāb al-bari* ʿby Abū al-Ḥasan ʿAlī b. Abī al-Rijāl, astrologer of the Zirid ruler of Ifrīqyā al-Mu ʿ izz b. Bādīs (r. 1016–1062). Known in the Latin West as Haly Abenragel, his work was first translated into Castillian by Yehuda Ibn Moshe for Alfonso X in 1254 and a Latin translation was made in 1485.

The most unique contribution of Islamicate astrologers was devising theoretical and philosophical justifications for the practice, something the Greek sources lacked. The most prominent Arabic text that provides an extensive justification of astrology is Abū Maʿshar *Kitāb al-madkhal al-kabīr*. Therein, he assigns a causal role to the celestial bodies. Adopting the Aristotelian theory of generation and corruption and concepts of causality, he argues that the celestial bodies constitute the efficient cause of generation and corruption and that variation of species and members is determined by the star. As a result of these generative connections, everything has planetary correspondences. Though not known as an astrologer, Abū Maʿshar contemporary and mentor Ya ʿ qūb Ibn Isḥāq al-Kindī (801–873) wrote two epistles concerned with the nature of astral influences: *al-Ibāna ʿan al-ʿilla al-fāʿila al-qarība li al-kawn wa al-fasād* (*On the Explanation of the Proximate Cause of Generation and Corruption*) and *al-Ibāna ʿan sujūd al-jurm al-aqsā* (*On the Explanation of the Bowing of the Outermost Body*), which is addressed to the son of the Caliph al-Mu ʿtaṣim as a response to the latter's question regarding the meaning of the Koranic verse, which states that the stars and the trees bow down (K. 55:6). In these two texts, he also presents the celestial bodies as causes of generation. The unique formulation of astrological theory and the composition of user-friendly astrological texts perhaps account for the successful reception and translation in the Latin West of texts such as Abū Maʿshar's, al-Qabīsī, and Abū al-Rijāl.

In Mamluk Syria and Egypt, astronomy thrived. Both Cairo and Syria in the 13th and 14th centuries were centers of activity. Astronomers engaged with theoretical and computational astronomy, spherical astronomy, and timekeeping. The vocation of the astronomer was associated with that of the *muwaqqit* who was responsible for ascertaining the *qibla* (the direction of the Kaʿ ba in Mecca toward which Muslims face during prayer) and regulating times at which the *muezzin* calls for prayer. However, very little Mamluk literature on astrology survives; but we know of a treatise by al-Marrakūshī surviving in a single fragment; another supposedly composed in Cairo in 1358 by Ibrahīm al-Ḥāsib al-Malikī al-Nāṣirī; another work also composed in Cairo by Ibn al-ʿArabānī in 1425; and a treatise by Aḥmad Ibn Timurbāy. The astronomer al-Ḥamzāwī from Aleppo wrote a treatise that contains a series of horoscopes for several Mamluk campaigns against the Ottomans near Adana ca. 1495. We also hear from the Egyptian historian Ibn Abī al-Faḍāʾil that the Sultan al-Nāṣir Muḥammad Ibn Qalāwūn consulted astrologers and geomancers when he became ill. This sparsity has been explained by the requirement of orthodoxy in the vocation of astronomer-*muwaqqit*, the exclusion of astronomers and astrologers from the court in the 14th and 15th centuries and an evident animosity against astrology by traditionalists and religious scholars. Ibn al-Ukhuwwa the *muhtasib* banned the astrologers in Egypt and Syria from practicing publicly on main streets and byways in the year 1341. There was a precedent for this in the 10th century when al-Muʿtaḍid's (r. 892–902) administration forbade astrologers and fortune-tellers from practicing in the streets or in the Friday mosque, though the Caliph himself had a court astrologer (see above).

Systematic attacks on astrology in the Abbasid period were few; the prose author and theologian al-Jāḥiẓ (776–ca. 868) condemned it, but the most prominent and influential voices of rejection came later from the Ḥanbalī scholar Ibn Taymiyya (1263–1328) in a number of *fatwas*, and his pupil Ibn Qayyim al-Jawziyya (1292–1350) in his *Miftāh al-saʿāda* (*The Key of Happiness*). They both emphasize that astrology is forbidden, akin to magic, and a form of idolatry.

In the Mamluk period the divinatory practice of geomancy (ʿilm al-raml) was widespread. Astrological elements permeate the geomancy, rendering it a "terrestrial" form of astrology. Many Islamic geomantic texts (from the Mamluk period onward) claim that this art was revealed to the Prophet Idrīs (Hermes) and in other texts it is the Prophet Daniel. It was associated with the Indian Sage Ṭumṭum al-Hindī whose teachings were transmitted to Khalaf al-Barbarī (d. 634) and from him to a series of practitioners and disciples, reaching the father of Islamic geomancy, according to many Islamic medieval and early modern sources, Abū ʿAbd Allāh Muḥammad Ibn ʿUthmān al-Zanātī (fl. before 1230) from the North African Berber tribe of Zanāta, which thrived in Tunis and Morocco. He supposedly learned the art directly from Abū Saʿīd al-Ṭarābulsī to whom *Thamarat al-fuʾād al-muhaddith* is attributed. Many of the texts that have become seminal were attributed to al-Zanātī but they are mostly printed treatises from the late 19th and early 20th centuries, though some manuscripts are preserved of geomantic treatises attributed to al-Zanātī. This science also thrived in the Persianate world; the philosopher and astronomer Naṣīr al-Dīn Ṭūsī (d. 672/1274) and founder of the Maragha Observatory wrote *al-Kāfī fī ʿilm al-raml* (*The Sufficing [Book] on Geomancy*) and *al-Sulṭāniyyafī al-raml*. Other Persian authors include Ḥaydar b. Muḥammad Rammāl-i Isfahānī (fl. 1252–1281) who wrote *Kashf al-asrār* (*The Exposition of Secrets*), and Nāsir b. Ḥaydar Rammāl-i Shirāzī (fl. 13th century).

The status of astrology in al-Andalus, Muslim Spain, was more precarious than in the Eastern regions of the Islamicate world. Furthermore, awareness of eastern works on astronomy and astrology was limited. Nonetheless, it is reported that Umayyad rulers appointed court astrologers. Though skeptical, the amir Hāshim I (788–796) summoned the astrologer al-Ḍabbī from Algeciras to Cordoba immediately after his succession in order to gain knowledge into the future of his reign. The skepticism of sovereigns in al-Andalus is exemplified in an anecdote involving the poet-astrologer Ibn al-Shamir and the amir ʿAbd al-Raḥmān II (822–852). The latter invited the astrologer into one of the rooms of his palace and asked him through which of its doors would he exit. After casting a horoscope, Ibn al-Sahmir wrote down his answer and put it inside an envelope that was then sealed. The amir then ordered a new door to be created and exited through it. This was exactly what Ibn al-Shamir had predicted and written down.

Nevertheless, astrology held a respectful status in the ninth century particularly under ʿAbd al-Raḥmān II who sponsored a circle of astrologers in his court at Cordoba. This is perhaps as a result of the "acculturation of Abbasid civilization in the Umayyad court." After his death a period of hostility against astrology was initiated by the amir Muḥammad (r. 852–886) who dismissed all court astrologers. His reasons were primarily religious, reflecting Ibn Saʿ īd al-Maghribī's remark that in al-Andalus generally "whenever people say about a man 'so and so reads philosophy' or 'he works in astrology,' he will be considered a heretic." More specifically, the case of amir Muḥammad reflected the Maliki reaction against astrology as witnessed in the antiastrology work by Ibn Ḥabīb (d. 853) called *Risālafī al-nujūm* (*Epistle Concerning Astrology*). During the reign of ʿAbd al-Raḥmān III (r. 912–961) astrology was marginalized even further, arguably due to the support of traditionalists to the Umayyad dynasty and their efforts to legitimize it. It was part and parcel of the strict policy of clamping down on heterodoxy.

Astrology flourished under the caliphate of al-Ḥakam II (r. 961–975) who employed a court astrologer known as Aḥmad Ibn Fāris, the author of the *Mukhtaṣar min al-anwāʿ* (*The Concise Book on Anwā ʿ*). It was under the Caliph Hishām II that the prominent Maslama al-Majrītī (d. ca. 1007) was active. He was the foremost authority on astronomy and mathematics in al-Andalus and the first Andalusian to make his own astronomical observations. Al-Majrīṭī's major work in astronomy was an adaptation he made with his disciple Ibn al-Ṣaffār of Khwārizmī's *Sindhind zīj*. Zījs were the earliest Islamic works of mathematical astronomy based on Indian and Sasanid works, differing from later Islamic astronomical material, which depended on the *Almagest*. As an astrologer, al-Majrīṭī predicted a change of dynasty and disasters such as slaughter and famine from the Saturn–Jupiter conjunction of 1006–1007. This prediction can also be found in the Alphonsine *Libro de las Cruzes*, which warned that the conjunction signaled the end of Arab rule of Spain.

Once al-Manṣūr (967–1002) ascended to power, astrology was persecuted. Astrology and philosophy particularly were extremely censored due to the strict religiosity that al-Manṣūr assumed in order to buttress the legitimacy of his de facto usurpation of power with the support of religious scholars. He ordered the burning of heterodox books in the library of al-Ḥakam II, including works on astrology. When the reign of al-Manṣūr and his heirs ended in 1009, astrology was revived in the court of the Umayyad rulers. Ibn al-Khayyāṭ, pupil of Maslama, was known as the astrologer of Sulaymān al-Musta ʿ īn (r. 1009–1016). He also practiced medicine. Another famous astrologer of that time is Abū Marwān ʿAbd Allāh Ibn Khalaf al-Istijī whom Sa ʿīd al-Andalusī, in his *Ṭabaqāt al-umam*, claims to have not known "anyone in al-Andalus, past or present, who has known all the secrets and marvels of this science as well as he." Al-Istijī wrote *Tasyirāt wa maṭāriḥ al-shu ʿā ʿāt* (*The Directions and Projections of Rays*), a work on historical astrology. He deals with the astrological periods known as *intihā ʾāt* (the ends), which last 1000, 100, 10, or 1 years. He was also interested in nativities, interrogations, and elections. He was critical of the work of other astrologers of his time who made projections on the equator rather that direct computation of the direction and projection of rays on the ecliptic, which he considered to be more accurate. He also criticized their reliance on inaccurate zījs. After the collapse of the Umayyad dynasty in 1031, the influence of traditionalists diminished and the science of astrology held again a more respectable status; however, it was not fully accepted and institutionalized in the way we see in the eastern regions. The Ṭawa'if period (ca. 1035–1085) has been seen by some historians as the "golden age of astronomy and astrology" as a result of the redevelopment of patronage. Toledo was the center of astronomical and astrological activities. There worked astrologers such as Yusuf Ibn ʿUmar Ibn Abī Thalla (d. 1043). Yaḥya I al-Ma ʾmūn (1043–1075) employed the astrologer Yaḥyā Ibn Aḥmad b. al-Khayyāṭ who previously worked for al-Musta ʿīn.

Under the Almoravid and Almohad dynasties astrology was once more censured by religious scholars and less and less cultivated. Although we know of active astrologers such as Ibn al-Hā ʾim who dedicated his *al-Zīj al-kāmil fī al-ta ʿālīm* (*The Complete Zīj*) to the Almohad Caliph al-Nāṣir (1199–1213) whose own physician was the astrologer Abū Muḥammad ʿAbd al-Malik al-Shadhūnī. The Nasrid period of Granada witnessed a renewal of patronage, particularly under Yusuf son of Muḥammad I and his successor Muḥammad II (1273–1302). Royal interest in astrology continued into the 14th century. Muḥammad VI (1360–1362) hearkens the words of the astrologer Aḥmad Ibn Muḥammad b. Yusuf al-Anṣārī in electing the moment of the rebellion against Muḥammad V (1354–1359, 1362–1391). He also predicted the moment Muḥammad V would recover his throne in 1362.

In the 15th century, astrology and astronomy were fervently cultivated; a deep interest exemplified by the celebrated Sultanic Astronomical Tables of the Timurid Central Asian ruler Ulugh Beg (1393–1449) and the prominence of his observatory in Samarqand. This was helped by the fact that divinatory sciences were revived and systematically utilized in the political life and fortunes of rulers and courtly life in the 15th and 16th centuries.

In the Ottoman Empire, the cultivation of the "calendars" known as *taqwīms* was characteristic. Composed mostly by court astrologers (*munajjims*), they give detailed predictions and guidance for the coming year. The earliest complete examples date from the reign of Meḥmet the Conqueror (r. 1451–1481), though the earliest *taqwīm* featuring the autograph of a *munajjim* is from the reign of Murād II (r. 1421–1444). They ultimately imply the prophetic reign of the Ottoman House as indicated by the heavens themselves. For example, a *taqwīm* composed for Selim I (r. 1512–1520) and presented at Nowruz (New Year) on March 10, 1513, indicated the troubled accession of a sultan and the unsettled state of his power. This led Selim to march against the Safavid shah Ismāʿīl, whom he defeated at the plain of Chaldrian below Mount Ararat in 1514. Another Ottoman use of astrology was as verification of Messianic claims, particularly in the 15th and 16th centuries, a period characterized as a "Messianic Age." For instance, Muḥammad Nūrbakhsh (d. 1464), referred to Ptolemy and Naṣīr al-Dīn Ṭūsī to support his claim to be the Messianic saviour (*Mahdi*). This interconnection between politics and the justification of rule (implying divine favor) and astrology is an ancient concept and concern that is perhaps the incentive of the patronage and development of the science of astrology from the early Abbasid period.

Sultan Bāyezīd II's (r. 1481–1512) patronage of astrology is notable because surviving payment registers show the contrast between the royal use of astrology under his reign and his immediate predecessors. There were more astrologers working for him with higher salaries. After him, astrology in the court seems to have declined, with fewer astrologers and lower salaries.

The gradual loss of patronage certainly dealt a blow to the status of astrology and its formal recognition as a useful science. This is perhaps a consequence of economical unburdening, but it is also connected to the permeation of the Enlightenment's paradigms of reason and empiricism that demoted astrology as "superstition," seriously affecting the respectability of the practice and diminishing its visibility. So nowadays, astrological services in Muslim societies are sought in private and often underground businesses on the "street" level; a persisting and ubiquitous phenomenon that has always been active parallel to formal patronage on

Taqi-al-Din and the Istanbul Observatory

The story of the last attempt to establish a major state-sponsored observatory in the premodern Islamic world, the Ottoman Empire's Istanbul Observatory, contemporary with Tycho Brahe's observatory at Hven, is an example of the disasters that could follow failure at high-stakes astrological prediction. The head of the Observatory, Taqi al-Din (1526–1585), had been a captive in Italy and incorporated some Western instruments into the observatory although it remained predominantly influenced by the Islamic tradition. It had only a short life from 1577 to 1580. It was founded in a time of apocalyptic expectations encouraged by several significant appearances of conjunctions, comets, and solar eclipses. Shortly after the founding of the observatory, the comet of 1580 appeared in the night sky. Taqi claimed that it augured good fortune for the sultan Murad III, who was about to embark on an invasion of Persia. Unfortunately, for the observatory, the prediction was followed by a devastating plague in the empire. This strengthened the hand of the observatory's opponents in the religious establishment of the empire, contributing to its destruction at the sultan's command in 1580.

"court" level. On the other hand, cultural globalization, accelerated by the Internet, introduced and revived a type of astrological consultation incorporated into New Age and Self-Help programs and other related spiritual services.

Liana Saif

See also: Abū Ma'shar al-Balkhī; Al-Qabīṣī; Astrolabe; Court Astrologers; Mashāllāh; Medieval European Astrology; *Picatrix*; Politics; Tājika Astrology

Further Reading

Bezza, Giuseppe. 2015. "Saturn–Jupiter Conjunctions and General Astrology: Ptolemy. Abū Ma'shar and Their Commentators." In *From Mashā'allāh to Kepler: Theory and Practice in Medieval and Renaissance Astrology*, ed. Charles Burnett and Dorian Gieseler Greenbaum, 5–48. Ceredigion: Sophia Centre Press.

Blake, Stephen P. 2014. *Astronomy and Astrology in the Islamic World.* Edinburgh: Edinburgh University Press.

Charette, Francois. 2003. *Mathematical Instrumentation in Fourteenth-Century Egypt and Syria: The Illustrated Treatise of Najm al-Dīn al-Miṣrī.* Leiden: Brill.

Ekmeleddin, İhsanoğlu, ed. 2011. *Osmanlı astroloji literatürü tarihi ve Osmanlı astronomi literatürü tarihi zeyli (History of Ottoman astrology literature and supplement to the history of Ottoman astronomy literature)*, vol. I. Beşiktasş, İstanbul: İslâm Tarih, Sanat ve Kültür Arasştırma Merkezi.

Fleischer, Cornell. 2009. "Ancient Wisdom and New Sciences: Prophecies and the Ottoman Court in the Fifteenth and Early Sixteenth Centuries." In *Falnama: The Book of Omens*, ed. Massumeh Farhad and Serpil Bağcı, 232–243. London: Thames and Hudson.

Forcada, Miquel. 2015. "Astrology in al-Andalus during the 11th and 12th Centuries: Between Religion and Philosophy." In *From Mashā'allāh to Kepler: Theory and Practice in Medieval and Renaissance Astrology*, ed. Charles Burnett and Dorian Gieseler Greenbaum, 149–176. Ceredigion: Sophia Centre Press.

Janos, Damien. 2014. "al-Ma'mūn's Patronage of Astrology." In *The Place to Go: Contexts of Learning in Baghdad, 750–1000 C.E.*, ed. Jens Scheiner and Damien Janos, 389–454. Princeton: Darwin Press.

Kennedy, Edward S. 1998. *Astronomy and Astrology in the Medieval Islamic World.* Aldershot, UK: Ashgate.

King, David A. 1983. "The Astronomy of the Mamluks." *Isis* 74: 531–555.

King, David A. 1990. "Astronomy." In *Religion Learning and Science in the 'Abbasid Period*, ed. M. J. L. Young, J. D. Latham, and R. B. Serjeant, 274–289. Cambridge: Cambridge University Press.

Michot, Yahya J. 2000. "Ibn Taymiyya on Astrology: Annotated Translation of Three Fatwas." *Journal of Islamic Studies* 11: 147–208.

Pingree, David. 1987. "Astrology and Astronomy in Iran." *Encyclopedia Iranica*, vol. II, ed. E. Yarshater, 858–871. New York: Routledge and Kegan Paul.

Pingree, David. 1990. "Astrology." In *Religion Learning and Science in the 'Abbasid Period*, ed. M. J. L. Young, J. D. Latham, and R. B. Serjeant, 290–300. Cambridge: Cambridge University Press.

Saliba, George. 1996. "Arabic Science and the Greek Legacy." In *From Baghdad to Barcelona: Studies in Islamic Exact Sciences in Honour of Prof. Juan Vernet*, 2 vols., vol. II, ed. Josep

Casullera and Julio Samsó, 19–38. Barcelona: Instituto "Millás Vallicrosa" de Historia de la Ciencia Arabe.

Saliba, George. 2004. "The Role of the Astrologer in Medieval Islamic Society." In *Magic and Divination in Early Islam*, ed. Emilie Savage-Smith, 341–370. Aldershot, UK: Ashgate Variorum.

Samsó, Julio. 1979. "The Early Development of Astrology in al-Andalus." *Journal for the History of Arabic Science* 3: 228–243.

Samsó, Julio. 2007. "A Social Approximation to the History of the Exact Sciences in al-Andalus." In *Astronomy and Astrology in al-Andalus and al-Maghrib*, 519–530. Aldershot, UK: Ashgate Variorum.

Şen, Ahmet Tunç. 2016. "Astrology in the Service of the Empire: Knowledge, Prognostication, and Politics of the Ottoman Court, 1450s–1550s." PhD diss. Chicago: University of Chicago Press.

Şen, Ahmet Tunç. 2017. "Reading the Stars at the Ottoman Court: Bāyezīd II (r. 886/1481–918/1512) and His Celestial Interests." *Arabica* 64: 557–608.

J

JAPANESE ASTROLOGY. *SEE* BUDDHISM.

JOHN OF SAXONY (14TH CENTURY)

John of Saxony (also known as John Dank or John Danekow of Saxonia) was probably born in Germany and was active in astronomy 1327–1335. John of Ligneres, who wrote on mathematics, astronomy, and astronomical instruments (particularly the astrolabe) was among the most prominent Parisian astronomers of his time and his fame drew John of Saxony to Paris (where he also worked with John of Meurs).

John of Saxony's best-known writings are his canons on the Alfonsine Tables (1327). It is difficult to overemphasize the importance of the Alfonsine Tables for medieval astronomy and astrology. The Alfonsine Tables (compiled at the request of King Alfonso X, 1221–1284, of Leon and Castile) were the first set of astronomical tables prepared in Christian Europe and permitted the calculation of eclipses and positions of the planets at any given time. They were particularly useful for plotting syzygies, the straight-line configuration of three celestial bodies in a gravitational system (such as the position of the sun, moon, and Earth during an eclipse). The tables were based on Ptolemy's view that the Earth was at the center of the universe. They were an important source of information for Christopher Columbus (who used them as navigational aids) and Nicolaus Copernicus (before his own work on heliocentric astronomy superseded them).

Astronomers and astrologers used John's canons to derive planetary positions (longitudes) for a given time and place. To begin, the user calculated the length of time between a base year and the year in question, divided this figure by the mean figure(s) of the planetary orbits, added or subtracted values to account for the differences in time and place (between Toledo and Paris, for example) and then noted the difference in latitude for the location in question. John's canons were often accompanied by corresponding sexagesimal multiplication tables (a base 60 numerical system still used for measuring time and geographic coordinates).

John also wrote a commentary on *Introduction to the Art of Astrology* by al-Qabīṣī, a highly esteemed textbook on the fundamental principles of genethlialogy (the system of astrology that contends that an individual's personality can be determined by constructing a natal chart for the date and location of that individual's birth). John's commentary on *The Art of Astrology* accompanied most Latin translations of al-Qabīṣī's work until the middle of the 16th century.

Medieval manuscripts (and some modern scholars) have attributed numerous astrological and astronomical texts to John of Saxony. Many of these manuscripts are extracts of the Alfonsine Tables or other tables of eclipses; for others, authorship is suspect.

Wendell G. Johnson

See also: al-Qabīṣī; Medieval European Astrology

Further Reading

Kremer, Richard L. 2003. "Thoughts on John of Saxony's Method for Finding Times of True Syzygy." *Historical Mathemetica* 30, no. 1: 263–277.
Kusukawa, Sachiko. 1999. Astronomical Tables. *Starry Messenger*. http://www.hps.cam.ac.uk/starry/tables.html
Pingree, David. 1973. "Al-Qabisi." *Dictionary of Scientific Biography*, ed. Charles C. Gillespie. New York: Charles Scribner's Sons.
Poule, Emmanuel. 1973. "John of Saxony." *Dictionary of Scientific Biography*, ed. Charles C. Gillespie. New York: Charles Scribner's Sons.

JUDAISM

Judaism has a complex understanding of astrology. Although the Rabbinate and mainstream religious leaders strongly disapproved of it, ordinary Jews developed a strong astrological tradition. Astrological signs in Judaism correspond to the 12- to 13-month Jewish calendar. Referred to as *Mazzaroth*, the astrological symbols were borrowed by the non-Jews of the Middle East. In Kabbalah, Jewish mysticism, the *Mazaloth*, or astrological signs of the zodiac, are considered the symbols of fortune. They are used to create astrological charts to determine the favorability of arranged marriages and courtships. Also, they determine when in the year a Jew should perform several actions. Lawsuits, battles, and other forms of conflict can be determined by the Mazaloth as good or bad depending when they fall on the Jewish calendar year.

The Rabbinic Position

Rabbinic disapproval starts with the fact that idol worshippers were referred to in the Talmud and Mishna as Servants of the Stars. To perform a horoscope was anathema. The religious concept behind this resistance to astrology was the idea that the destiny of Jews, unlike that of non-Jews, is not rooted in the zodiac, or Mazzaroth. The other, pagan religions and cultures of the ancient Near East, put great stock in astrology, leading to Jewish opposition.

This resistance was not universal among Jews. It was the particular opinion of the rabbis who taught and otherwise led Jewish communities. Among Jewish commoners, there was an interest in both the zodiac and astrology, which would lead to the development of a Jewish approach to interpreting the astrological signs in Kabbalah.

However, the mainstream use of astrology was to break up the calendar year into 12 (13 in a leap year) months. These are the signs of Mazzaroth used for each month of the Jewish year.

Nisan–Taleh (Lamb)

Nisan is the first month of the Jewish calendar year. It's the chronological marker for each year of the rule of each King of the Jews. During the height of the Jewish kingdom of Israel, every King was anointed in Nisan, and his rule was counted from each subsequent Nisan. Its sign is the lamb, because it corresponds with the rituals of the spring festival of Passover; which includes eating a paschal lamb.

Iyyar–Shor (Ox)

Iyyar is the second month. Its sign is the ox. It corresponds with Taurus. It is the month where traditionally the Jews brought the wave offering of wheat, where farmers would bring a measure of new freshly harvested wheat each day of the month. In recognition of this offering, the Jews count the Omer, which commemorate the 49 days of the wave offering of new wheat.

Sivan–Teomim (Twins)

Sivan is the third month. It marks the festival of Shavuot, wherein the ancient Jews brought the first fruits as a sacrifice to the Temple. It corresponds with Gemini.

Tammuz–Sarton (Crab)

Tammuz is the fourth month. It marks the start of the Roman siege of Jerusalem, which led to the destruction of the Second temple. It corresponds with Cancer.

Av–Aryeh (Lion)

Av is the fifth month. It marks the destruction of both the first and second temple on the 9th day of the month, which serves as a national day of Jewish mourning. It corresponds with Leo. It's considered the least fortunate month in the Jewish calendar year. Traditionally the 15th of Av was a date to starting courting people for marriage purposes.

Ellul–Betulah (Virgo)

Ellul is the sixth month and is dedicated as the month of forgiveness and atonement. Its sign is the virgin woman, or Virgo. Ellul is the month to prepare for the high holy days.

Tishrei–Moaznayim (Libra)

Tishrei is the seventh month, and it's the culmination of the Festival Cycle of each calendar year. Appropriately, its sign is that of the scales of justice, or Libra. This is the month where Jews experience the high holy days of Rosh Hashanah (Head of the Year), the New Year for the entire world, and Yom Kippur, the Day of Atonement. There are multiple new years marked in the Jewish calendar, but this is the significant one. The scales of justice mark the notion that each year, between Rosh Hashanah and Yom Kippur, Jews are judged for the actions and misdeeds or sins over the past year.

Cheshvan–Angkrav (Scorpion)

Cheshvan is the eighth month. Its sign is the scorpion, better known as Scorpio. It is well regarded by the Jews as a month of no religious observances.

Kislev–Keshat (Sagittarius)

The ninth month of the Jewish calendar year. Its sign is that of Keshat, the centaur. Also known as Sagittarius. In this month the Jews commemorate the uprising of the Maccabees against the Hellenistic government of the Seleucid Empire. The minor holiday of Hanukkah is observed in this month.

Tebet–Gedi (Capricorn)

Tebet is the 10th month. Its sign is that of the goat, and it is meant to replace the food horn of Capricorn, which is a pagan symbol. In this month, on the 10th day, the Jews mark the siege of Jerusalem started by the Babylonians.

Shvat–Dali (Aquarius)

Shvat is the 11th month. Its sign is the Water pourer, or Dali and is an analog for Aquarius. In this month, the Jews commemorate their version of Arbor Day. It's called the 15th of Shvat (Tu B'shvat), and it's the New Year of Trees.

Adar–Dagim (Pisces)

Adar is the 12th month of the Jewish Calendar Year, and its sign is the fish, which is also referred to as Pisces. In leap years, the Rabbis decided to make two Adars rather than add more days to prior months. This means ever few years, the Jewish calendar has an Adar I and Adar II. In this month the minor holiday of Purim (Lotteries) is observed, wherein the Jews commemorate their legendary triumph over the Persian statesman Haman, who sought to exterminate the Jews.

For mainstream Judaism astrology is simply a means to chronicle the years, and organize what observances occur in a particular month. Kabbalists, however, have found more practical uses for it.

Kabbalah

Kabbalah views astrology as a tool to be harnessed for holy purpose, rather than a pagan magic to be scorned. Kabbalah embodies various forms of holy symbolic magic. Astrology, numerology, and power words are the three main foci of Kabbalah.

Rather than serving as signs, Kabbalah refers to the Zodiac as the Mazaloth (Fortunes). There are several Kabbalistic uses of astrology; such as forecasting the possible future outcomes of personal choices. The most commonly known one is to augur, or determine, a good match for marriage. For example, when two Jewish young people meet, date, and fall in love, they may schedule an appointment with a Kabbalist, or mystical scholar. He then charts the astrological charts of both young persons and determines by these star charts if the match is favorable. If it is, they marry.

Astrology in Judaism is a tool. Although mainstream Judaism chooses not to use it, Kabbalah finds it very useful for several purposes including matchmaking.

Benjamin Franz

See also: Astrotheology; Bible; Mashāllāh

Further Reading

Budge, E. A. Wallis. 1978. *Amulets and Superstitions*. Oxford: Oxford University Press.

Freudenthal, Gad, ed. 2011. *Science in Medieval Jewish Cultures*. Cambridge: Cambridge University Press.

Halevi, Zev Ben Shimon. 1978. *The Astronomy of Fate: Astrology and Kabbalah*. London: Arkana, Penguin Books.

Ibn Ezra, Abraham. 1939. *The Beginning of Wisdom: An Astrological Treatise by Abraham Ibn Ezra*, ed. R. Levy and F. Cantera. Baltimore, MD: Johns Hopkins University Press.

JUNG, CARL G. (1875–1961)

Carl G. Jung was a Swiss psychiatrist, the founder of analytical psychology, and a prolific writer and thinker whose interests ranged not only to psychology but also to religion, Western and Eastern philosophy, Gnosticism, mythology, alchemy, and astrology. Born in Kesswil, Switzerland, to Paul Achilles Jung, a pastor in the Swiss Reformed Church, and Emilie Preiswerk, the daughter of a wealthy Swiss family, Jung spent his childhood in various Swiss towns including Laufen, Kleinhüningen, and Basel. He attended the University of Basel and studied medicine, though he ultimately gravitated toward psychiatry, as he believed it combined his two greatest interests—biology and spirituality—in equal measure. Jung went on to develop some of the most novel and well-known concepts in psychology, including the theory of archetypes, the collective unconscious, the psychological complex, the anima/animus relationship, introversion and extroversion, and synchronicity. Astrology had a profound influence over Jung, and Jung cast a reciprocal influence over its practice in the second half of the 20th century.

Psychologist Carl Jung in his study. (Bettmann/Getty Images)

Between 1907 and 1912, Jung developed a professional relationship with the eminent psychoanalyst Sigmund Freud (1856–1939) after much of his work confirmed Freud's theories. After several fruitful years of collaboration, their association ended over Jung's refusal to dogmatically uphold Freud's theories of sexuality and his continued emphasis on the importance of the occult in understanding the human psyche. The earliest and most direct influence Freud exerted over Jung was the concept of the unconscious, which in Freudian terminology referred to mental processes of which individuals were largely unaware and which acted as a repository for repressed ideas and potentially dangerous psychological complexes. Jung's major addition to this theory was the "collective unconscious," which he defined as the shared, inherited structure of the human mind that accounted for shared instincts, morals, and, most important, archetypes—universal symbols such as the hero, the trickster, or the flood, which repeatedly manifested themselves in world mythology and religion.

Jung began investigating astrology in earnest around 1910 or 1911. In letters to Freud, Jung claimed that he studied it daily. He argued that it "represents the summation of all the psychological knowledge of antiquity" and could provide psychological insight into the human condition (Jung 1954–1979, 56). Although Jung seems not to have believed that astrology necessarily had any objective scientific merit, he nevertheless supported efforts to submit it to comprehensive statistical analysis. Jung's analytical psychology was individually focused in a way that placed the thoughts, dreams, and experiences of the patient at the heart of the healing process. Consequently, Jung used the interpretive techniques and historical symbols of astrology to identify themes and patterns within the human psyche that he saw stretching back to the ancient world and existing in various forms across cultures from around the globe throughout history. For example, Jung observed possible correlations between various archetypes and deities or mythological motifs associated with planets and zodiacal signs, arguing that these associated figures had originally been inspired by projections of the collective unconscious.

Jungian astrologers have since reinterpreted the idea of the archetype as the influence of stars and planets, so that, for instance, Saturn is equated with the *senex* or "wise sage" archetype, Venus with the feminine *anima*, Mars with masculine *animus*, and so on (Campion 2009, 253). Among these astrologers, the psyche was no longer thought of as a static object directly influenced by the stars. Rather, it became a dynamic process where the aim was not prediction but self-understanding. Through an analysis of a patient's dreams, memories, conversations, and even paintings, Jung began to believe that fundamental symbols existed within the minds of individuals and that astrology could act as a therapeutic tool to aid in individuation, the process whereby a person becomes aware of their unconscious mind. Today, Jungian astrologers often discuss psychological complexes in ways that dovetail with astrological interpretations of heavenly influences on personality types and individual motivations (Campion 2009, 256).

Beginning in 1932, Jung collaborated with Nobel Prize–winning physicist and early quantum theorist Wolfgang Pauli. With Pauli, who was also his patient, Jung developed the concept of synchronicity, which he defined as "temporally coincident occurrences of acausal events" that linked the objective world of physics with the subjective world of the psyche (Jung 1954–1979). First proposed in the late 1920s while Jung was experimenting with the Chinese oracular system the *I-Ching*, Jung argued that synchronicity provided an explanation for the "meaningful coincidences" that people often experienced. By extension, the correlation between the positions of the heavenly bodies and events in an individual's life could be regarded not as a causal relationship but as a synchronistic one. Furthermore, in the same way that observation could change experimental results in quantum mechanics, Jung asserted that there was no objective astrological meaning apart from that created by an astrologer and their client. This interpretation of astrology has influenced many astrologers—including Dane Rudhyar and Alexander Ruperti, two of the most prominent from the 1970s through the 1990s—both of whom have argued that there is no independently existing "astrology with a capital A," only astrologers attempting to understand the relationship between individuals and the cosmos through astrological techniques and symbols (Campion 2009, 256).

Perhaps the most enduring influence that Jung's interpretation of astrology has had on modern psychology is through the Myers-Briggs Type Indicator (MBTI), one of the most widely used personality tests, which was developed in the 1940s. American educators Katherine Cook Briggs and Isabel Briggs Myers designed the test by adapting Jung's typological theories from his work *Psychological Types* (1921). Jung had speculated that four broad categories existed to describe how people experienced the world—sensation, intuition, thinking, and feeling—which he based on the correspondences between the four classical elements and temperaments of the ancient Greeks and their associated zodiacal signs. Thus, the sensation typology corresponded to the sanguine temperament and the Air zodiacal signs, intuition to the melancholic and Earth signs, thinking to phlegmatic and Water signs, and feeling to choleric and Fire signs (Campion 2009, 259). Although no longer directly associated with Jung, the MBTI clearly owes a debt to Jung's investigations into astrology.

Justin Niermeier-Dohoney

See also: Gender; New Age; Rudhyar, Dane; Transpersonal Astrology

Further Reading

Begg, Ean. 1999. "Jung, Astrology, and the Millennium." *The Astrological Journal* 41, no. 6: 21–27.

Campion, Nicholas. 2009. *A History of Western Astrology, Vol II: The Medieval and Modern Worlds*. New York: Continuum.

Jung, Carl G. 1954–1979. *The Collected Works of C.G. Jung*, 20 vols. Princeton: Princeton University Press.

Jung, Carl G. 1965. *Memories, Dreams, Reflections*. Recorded and ed. Anila Jaffé and trans. Richard and Clara Winston. New York: Vintage Books.

Samuels, Andrew. 1985. *Jung and the Post-Jungians*. London: Routledge.

Stern, Paul J. 1976. *C.G. Jung: The Haunted Prophet*. New York: George Braziller.

Wehr, Gerhard. 1987. *Jung: A Biography*. Boston: Shambhala.

K

KABBALAH. *SEE* JUDAISM.

KEPLER, JOHANNES (1571–1630)

As an astronomer, Johannes Kepler (1571–1630) is well known for his three laws of planetary motion, astronomical work on the planet Mars, and the "new star" (the supernova of 1604). Far less known is his involvement with astrology and astrological practice from his student days at the University of Tübingen. Throughout his life Kepler calculated charts for family, friends, and clients—possibly the most famous being the Bohemian count and soldier, Albrecht Wallenstein (1583–1634). He was the court astrologer for the Holy Roman emperor Rudolf II (1552–1612). He wrote astrological calendars containing successful predictions, and treatises on both theoretical and practical astrology. In the Kepler Archive are well over 900 horoscopes cast by him, for 800 discrete individuals, which in 2009 finally merited inclusion in his collected works (*Gesammelte Werke* (*GW*) vol. 21, 2.2). The frequent assertion that Kepler only cast horoscopes for the money is belied by this collection, including hundreds of astrological charts cast for himself, his family, and his friends (presumably without payment).

Kepler was born at Weil-der-Stadt, Germany, on December 27, 1571 (January 6, 1572, in the Gregorian calendar). He was the premature son of Heinrich and Katharina (née Guldenmann) Kepler. Sickly as a child and small for his age, he was bullied at school but excelled in academic work. He was given a scholarship to the University of Tübingen, after schooling in Württemberg, Adelberg, and Maulbronn, the preparatory school for the university. He had intended to be a theologian, but his ability in mathematics and then astronomy, awakened by his teacher Michael Maestlin (a private admirer of Copernicus's theories), caused him to change these plans. After his graduation from Tübingen in 1591, he was appointed as a mathematics teacher in Graz, Austria in 1594. On April 27, 1597, Kepler married Barbara Müller (1573–1611). Their first son, Heinrich, was born in February 1598, but died shortly after birth. His poignant correspondence with Maestlin about this and the death of Maestlin's son examined the astrology of these events (Greenbaum 2015).

In 1600, Kepler became an associate of Tycho Brahe, and eventually the inheritor of his work, as well as replacing him as imperial mathematician (court astrologer) for the Emperor Rudolf II. He served Rudolf in this capacity until the emperor's abdication in 1612. In the meantime, he published *De stella nova* (*On the New Star*) and *Astronomia nova* (*The New Astronomy*) among others. Barbara Kepler died in 1611, and in 1612 Kepler moved to Linz, Austria, with his family, and married Susanna Reuttinger (1589–1636) in 1613. *Harmony of the World* was published in 1619, and the *Rudolphine Tables* in 1627. Kepler died in Regensburg, Austria, on November 15, 1630.

Kepler's work was infused with a deeply spiritual sensibility. Though much of his writing concerned the physical nature of the universe, he also recognized its metaphysical components. To understand the heavens was to better understand God and the human soul's relationship to God. Kepler was a Platonist: this is evident in treatises like the *Mysterium Cosmographicum* (*A Cosmographic Mystery*, 1596), which uses the Platonic solids as a means for understanding the movements of the planets. His inspiration for writing this work displays his mystical leanings. He had a vision, on July 19, 1595, about inscribing regular polygons on the orbits of the planets: "I believe it was by divine ordinance that I obtained by chance that which previously I could not reach by any pains; I believe that so much the more readily because I had always prayed to God to let my plan succeed, if Copernicus had told the truth" (Caspar [1959] 1993, 62).

This spurred him to calculate the birth charts of many family members and friends, including the above-mentioned Michael Maestlin and his family. His correspondence with David Fabricius, a Lutheran pastor with a keen interest in astrology, contains many astrological discussions, including practical as well as theoretical astrology. As a professional, Kepler delineated the nativities of Rudolf II and his family (translations in Greenbaum 2010, 79–121). Between 1595 and 1624 (though not every year), he published at least 15 astrological calendars containing both weather predictions and upcoming political events. He used the doctrine of Jupiter–Saturn conjunctions to predict worldly events. He also made a prediction about Albrecht Wallenstein that has been widely interpreted as a prediction of his death: in 1634, especially in March, "terrible disorders in the country might coincide with the native's fortune" (Analysis of Wallenstein's Nativity, 1625, *GW*, vol. 21, 2.2, 470) Wallenstein was murdered on February 25, 1634. Kepler was not alive to witness the event, having died in 1630, so we have no way of knowing whether he indeed intended a death prediction.

In his personal astrological practice, Kepler calculated nativities, directions, and solar returns for himself and his immediate family, including his grandparents, father and mother, wives, and children. He also studied historical horoscopes, such as those of Augustus, Mohammed and Martin Luther.

Kepler was interested not only in astrological practice, but also its theoretical foundations. He was a passionate advocate for its reform, considering "popular astrology" a "tragic illusion" of what it could be (Letter to an unnamed official, April 3, 1611, Greenbaum 2010, 118). His published attempts to improve it appear in *On the Sounder Fundamentals of Astrology* (1601), *De stella nova* (*On the New Star*) (1606), *Tertius Interveniens* (*Third Man Intervening*) (1610), and *Harmony of the World* (1619). But his unpublished (during his life) correspondence with men such as Maestlin, David Fabricius, Herwart von Hohenburg, Thomas Harriot, and others also honed his arguments.

For example, in a correspondence with David Fabricius in 1602, the two discussed numerous astrological techniques, whether they work and, if so, why. In them we clearly see that Kepler desired to emphasize a physical basis for astrology, to put it on a sounder and more precise, predictable footing. Because of this he rejected signs, profections, houses, and systems of dignity, finding no physical basis for them. But he accepted aspects, directions (today called secondary progressions), and solar revolutions (solar returns) because they had a basis in nature, especially through geometry and harmonics. Yet the physical supported the metaphysical. In Kepler's eyes, "The image of the heavenly disposition, present at the moment of birth, sticks to the spirit or genius of the newborn child" (*On Directions*, 1602, Greenbaum 2010, 237).

Kepler called astrology "the foolish daughter" of "wise mother" astronomy (*De stella nova*, chapter XII; *Tertius Interveniens*, Thesis 7). But he also warned not to "throw the baby [astrology] out with the bathwater" (*Tertius Interveniens*, title page). Can these two statements be reconciled? Thesis 7 goes on to say that there would be no astronomy without astrology's impetus in wanting to learn future things from the sky. And to David Fabricius: "What I wrote to you about astrology, take seriously . . . I have shown from teachings and examples that I am not dismantling the whole [of it]" (Greenbaum 2010, 273; *GW*, vol. 14, 323). By making a better astrology, he sought a truer understanding of how the heavens work together with an ensouled and responsive Earth (Boner 2013, 5–7).

Dorian Gieseler Greenbaum

See also: Brahe, Tycho; Court Astrologers; Renaissance and Reformation Astrology; Science

Further Reading

Baumgardt, Carola. 1951. *Johannes Kepler: Life and Letters*. New York: Philosophical Library.

Boner, Patrick J. 2013. *Kepler's Cosmological Synthesis: Astrology, Mechanism and the Soul*. Leiden: Brill.

Caspar, Max. (1959) 1993, repr. *Kepler*, ed. and trans. C. Doris Hellman, introduction and references by Owen Gingerich. New York: Dover Publications.

Field, J. V. 1984. "A Lutheran Astrologer: Johannes Kepler." *Archive for History of Exact Sciences* 31: 189–272.

Greenbaum, Dorian Gieseler, ed. 2010. "Kepler's Astrology." Special double issue. *Culture and Cosmos* 14.

Greenbaum, Dorian Gieseler. 2015. "Kepler's Personal Astrology: Two Letters to Michael Maestlin." In *From Māshā'allāh to Kepler: Theory and Practice in Medieval and Renaissance Astrology*, ed. Charles Burnett and Dorian Gieseler Greenbaum, 177–200. Ceredigion, Wales: Sophia Centre Press.

Kepler, Johannes. 1938–2017. *Gesammelte Werke*, ed. Max Caspar, Franz Hammer, Volker Bialas et al., 21 vols. Munich: C. H. Beck. http://www.kepler-kommission.de/

Kepler, Johannes. 2009. *Manuscripta Astrologica, Manuscripta Pneumatica*, ed. Friedericke Boockmann and Daniel A. Di Liscia, vol. 21, 22, *Johannes Kepler Gesammelte Werke*. Munich: C. H. Beck.

Methuen, Charlotte. 1998. *Kepler's Tübingen: Stimulus to a Theological Mathematics*. Aldershot, UK: Ashgate.

Negus, Ken. 2008. *Kepler's Astrology: The Baby, the Bath Water, and the Third Man in the Middle. The First Complete English Translation of Tertius Interveniens*. Amherst, MA: Earth Heart Publications.

KOREAN ASTROLOGY. *SEE* BUDDHISM.

L

LEGAL REGULATION OF ASTROLOGY

Astrology has been regulated—or sometimes even banned—for many purposes, including preventing coups or revolutionary political action, suppressing blasphemy or heresy, or protecting people from fraudulent divination.

In a society where the belief that astrologers can predict the future is widespread, astrological predictions can threaten the political order. In ancient China, astrological knowledge was treated as a state monopoly, but more commonly a private astrological sector is politically regulated. One of the most politically and legally dangerous forms of astrology was casting the natal horoscope of the ruler, which could encourage plotting by persuading people that they knew the day of the ruler's death. Despite the first Roman emperor, Augustus's, political exploitation of his horoscope, this was forbidden in the Roman Empire, where it became official dogma that the emperor was not subject to the stars. This principle was later extended to other figures, including kings and Popes. One of the many examples of how astrologers were punished for this crime is the two astrologers executed for plotting the murder of Henry VI of England in 1441. Astrologers were punished for violating this prohibition into the 17th century, when Orazio Morandi was tortured and imprisoned for predicting the death of Pope Urban VIII. The assassination of Indian prime minister Indira Gandhi in 1984, an event that had been predicted by Indian astrologers, was followed in 1987 by a harsh law forbidding astrologers and other diviners from predicting the death of any public official who had taken an oath to the constitution, although this law proved ineffective.

The mass political influence of astrology with the rise of print in the early modern period led to it being subject to censorship. Astrology's mass audience meant that censors were less concerned with the traditional worries over elite plots against the ruler's life and more concerned with the role of astrological propaganda in delegitimizing an entire regime. Even in societies where astrology was broadly accepted, a single prediction could get an astrologer into trouble, as William Lilly was summoned to appear before Parliament for having allegedly predicted the Great Fire of London in 1666. One example of the concern astrology caused political authorities is James II of Great Britain's (r. 1685–1688) sweeping ban on published astrological prediction in 1685, a reaction to the prominent role astrological propaganda had played in stirring up opposition to the Crown during the reign of his brother, Charles II (r. 1660–1685). The Nazi crackdown on astrology was also in part motivated by fear of its popular influence. (In a revival of earlier concerns, the Nazis were also concerned that people not draw adverse conclusions from Hitler's natal horoscope.)

With the rise of monotheistic religions ascribing omnipotence to God, astrology's claims for the power of the stars could result in legal trouble if it touched on fundamental religious issues. In medieval and Renaissance Western astrology, it was forbidden to cast the natal horoscope of Christ, because that would carry the implication that he was subject to the stars. Among the astrologers who faced legal punishment for doing so were Cecco d'Ascoli, who was executed, and Girolamo Cardano, who was imprisoned by the Inquisition. Arguing for the certainty of astrological predictions was also dangerous, as it implied that God was unable to overrule the power of the stars. This was the crime that led to Galileo's first encounter with the Inquisition in 1604. The Catholic Church could also regulate religiously or politically subversive astrology through the Index of Forbidden Books, a list of texts that Catholics were forbidden to own or read. The work of several astrologers including Placidus could be found there, although enforcement of the Index was patchy.

In the 19th and 20th centuries, when a vigorous astrological tradition coexisted with elite denial of its worth, astrology was increasingly regulated as fraudulent and astrologers persecuted for violating antifraud statutes. In 19th-century Britain, the principal tool for persecuting astrologers was the Vagrancy Act of 1824, which forbade taking money for astrological predictions and usually resulted in a short sentence of a few months. (The law was extended from England and Wales to Scotland in 1871 and applied to Canada and other British dominions as well.) In the United States, where astrology has never been regulated at the federal

Legalizing Fortune-Telling: *Spiritual Psychic Church v. City of Azusa*

The Supreme Court of California in Spiritual Psychic Church v. City of Azusa (1985) established that fortune-telling, including astrology, was protected as free speech in California whether or not it was given in return for payment.

We are unable to subscribe to Bartha's broad characterization of fortune-telling as an exclusively commercial activity, and to the theory that it therefore can be indiscriminately regulated, or, in this instance, wholly prohibited. [1] The essence of the issue whether an activity falls within the constitutional protection of "speech" is whether the "speaker," by engaging in the activity, is communicating information of any sort. For example, in *Powers v. Floersheim* (1967) 256 Cal.App.2d 223 [63 Cal.Rptr. 913], the defendant urged that printed forms used in collecting debts were constitutionally protected, and thus their distribution could not be regulated. The Court of Appeal determined that the forms did not constitute a type of speech: "No opinion, thought expression, or other form of information is contained in the forms under discussion. They are merely tools of a trade, much as a hammer is a tool of the trade of carpentry. The purchaser seeks no information from the form, and the designer seeks to convey none." (Id. at p. 233.)

Fortunetelling is different. It involves the communication of a message directly from the fortuneteller to the recipient. That words are used is not critical; the key is that the words convey thoughts, opinions and, sometimes, [39 Cal.3d 509] fiction and falsehoods. fn. 3 This communication between persons, however, is at the very core of what is known as speech. That fortunetelling consists of speech does not of itself determine what level of protection it must be afforded under article I, section 2, of the Constitution, but it does establish that fortunetelling is not a "mere commercial activity."

level, the matter was left to state and local governments. Among the leading 19th- and 20th-century astrologers facing legal persecution as frauds were Evangeline Adams, prosecuted under a New York State law against fortune-telling, and Alan Leo, prosecuted under the Vagrancy Act. Adams was acquitted, Leo convicted, although only required to pay a small fine. Fear of persecution was one reason Leo emphasized astrology as character analysis as opposed to making predictions. A far harder line was taken in the Soviet Union, where astrology along with other forms of "occultism" was strictly forbidden, and astrologers could find themselves packed away to asylums with a state-imposed diagnosis of mental illness.

A milder process involves the banning of astrology from certain communications media in an updated version of the Index. In the United States, the National Association of Radio and Television Broadcasters adopted a Television Code in 1952 that, among other things, banned astrological programs, along with other divination techniques such as palmistry, from the television airwaves. Although this was not legal regulation in that the NARTB was a private entity, it was done in the hopes of forestalling government regulation of the airwaves. Many fans of astrological TV blamed the government, and wrote angry letters to the FCC to no avail.

The tendency in most Western countries in the past few decades has been away from bans on astrology. Professional astrological organizations press for removal of laws against astrology and provide their members with legal assistance. Although the Vagrancy Act of 1824 remains on the statute books in Britain, the controlling legal authority over astrologers in Britain today is the Consumer Protection Act of 2008. This is often interpreted as requiring professional astrologers to give a disclaimer before engaging with a client, stating that their predictions are not being presented as certainties. In California, a hotbed of astrological activity since the early 20th century, the 1985 California Supreme Court decision *Spiritual Psychic Science Church v. City of Azusa* wiped out local prohibitions on taking money for astrology or other divinatory practices as a violation of the state constitution.

William E. Burns

See also: Adams, Evangeline; Cardano, Girolamo; Cecco d'Ascoli; Christianity; Fate; Galilei, Galileo; Leo, Alan; Lilly, William; Morandi, Orazio; Nazism and the Third Reich; Placidus; Politics; Righter, Carroll; Zadkiel

Further Reading

Burns, William E. 2005. "Astrology and Politics in Early Modern England: King James II and the Almanac Men." *The Seventeenth Century* 20: 242–253.

Cramer, Frederick H. (1954) 1996, repr. *Astrology in Roman Law and Politics*. Chicago: Ares Publishers.

Curry, Patrick. 1992. *A Confusion of Prophets: Victorian and Edwardian Astrology*. London: Collins and Brown.

Dooley, Brendan. 2002. *Morandi's Last Prophecy and the End of Renaissance Politics*. Princeton: Princeton University Press.

Jacobs, Jayi. "The Law and Astrology." http://www.afan.org/inside/legal/the-law-and-astrology/

Jaramillo, Deborah L. 2015. "Astrological TV: The Creation and Destruction of a Genre." *Communication, Culture and Critique* 8: 309–326.

LEO, ALAN (1860–1917)

Alan Leo was an influential English astrologer, sometimes considered the founder of modern astrology, who promoted an approach to astrology based on sun signs and the analysis of character rather than making predictions.

William Frederick Allan was born on August 7, 1860 (he later changed his name to Alan Leo to reflect his nativity). His father was a former British soldier serving in India who was discharged after suffering an injury. On his return to England he met Alan's mother. A devout Puritan, she raised their children in a strictly Christian household after Alan's father left when he was nine.

Alan struggled to reconcile his mother's religious convictions with what he saw as unjust inequalities of 19th-century Britain. As a young man working various jobs at a grocery store, a sewing machine factory, and as a traveling salesman, Leo was exposed to the poverty of the London slums. He pondered why it was that people were born into social conditions that were beyond their making and why some were given the gift of wealth but others made to suffer in poverty. The Christian God, he concluded was either unjust or in need of replacing.

Leo found his solution in two different philosophies: astrology and reincarnation. Astrology explained the order and influence of the cosmos while reincarnation and karma reinterpreted social conditions through cosmic justice and evolution. Alan Leo joined a Platonic astrological tradition that accommodated both determinism and free will. However, his embrace of Eastern religious tradition reflected movements in Victorian Britain, specifically Theosophy. At the turn of the century, Europe had undergone tremendous technological and social change. For some British people, a spiritual transformation was required to not only combat materialism and atheism but also overcome the limits of traditional religion to meet the needs of modern life. The twin pillars of science and spirituality were part of a greater truth, they reasoned, and they believed that the world was on the brink of a new era of crisis and rejuvenation. It was within this context that Alan Leo made his mark.

Leo's astrological work began in 1890 when he and F. W. Lacey founded *The Astrological Magazine* (*Modern Astrology* after 1895). A monthly magazine of 24 pages, the journal was meant to introduce astrology to a wider audience and create a network of like-minded people. The contents included lessons to novices, basic terminology and methods, horoscopes of notable people, and writings from astrologers. Free horoscopes were given to annual subscribers and others were sent through mail for one shilling. Although past astrologers had failed to establish a lasting readership with such ventures, Leo and Lacey succeeded. Leo's print innovations, especially the so-called shilling horoscope based on the sun sign, had a lasting legacy on modern astrology and popular culture.

Astrologer Alan Leo depicted as a respectable Victorian gentleman, an image he cultivated to help win astrology the acceptance he thought it deserved. (Fine Art Images/Heritage Images/Getty Images)

Around the same time that he began editing *The Astrological Magazine*, Leo became involved in Theosophy, which became crucial to his astrological worldview. Like many other occultists in the late 19th and early 20th centuries, Leo believed that the world needed to spiritually prepare for the coming World Teacher who would usher in a new age as prophesied by Helene Blavatsky, founder of Theosophy. More fundamentally, Leo's astrology was esoteric, in contrast to the more familiar "exoteric" astrology concerned with prediction. Esoteric astrology emphasized individual character, spiritual development, and philosophy. It was internal and subjective as much as it acknowledged the external influence of the stars or precise mathematics.

In approaching astrology from esotericism, Leo borrowed heavily from Blavatsky. Like Blavatsky, he believed the sun was at the center of the spiritual universe. The physical sun that occupied the center of the solar system and exerted its influence on the movement of the planets was but a manifestation of the spiritual sun (the supreme intelligence) that gave the breath of life. Each planet was in turn conscious and guided by its own intelligence but ultimately acted as a "messenger" or "agent" to carry out the will of the supreme intelligence, exerting influence on individual characters through the zodiac

The other key aspect of Theosophical thinking in Leo's astrology was the adaptation of Eastern mysticism to Western traditions (in this case astrology). Given that the planets were the messengers of the supreme intelligence's will, conditions at birth were purposeful and one's nativity was a window into past lives. Further understanding of astrology could facilitate spiritual development, as greater knowledge of one's character and environment could illuminate the purpose behind one's present state, thus repaying karmic obligations incurred in a previous life or gaining experience necessary for progress. Knowledge brought freedom; the wise man ruled his stars rather than obeying them.

Historians have noted this emphasis on sun-centered nativity and character as a shift in the history of astrology. First, it necessitated an update of the zodiac, virtually unchanged for centuries, to better reflect the challenges of the modern self. Second, at the time of Leo's career, astrology was devoted primarily to outward concerns, event prediction, and fortune-telling. Unfortunately, Alan Leo failed to escape the shadow of the very predictive astrology he denounced. On July 16, 1917, he was found guilty of "pretending and professing to tell fortune" and fined £5 with £25 costs. He died suddenly shortly after in August 1917.

Kyle Falcon

See also: Astrological Associations; Legal Regulation of Astrology; Sun Signs; Theosophy

Further Reading

Campion, Nicholas. 1994. *The Great Year: Astrology, Millenarianism and History in the Western Tradition.* London: Penguin.

Campion, Nicholas. 2009. *History of Western Astrology, Volume II: The Medieval and Modern Worlds.* New York: Continuum.

Curry, Patrick. 1992. *A Confusion of Prophets: Victorian and Edwardian Astrology.* London: Collins and Brown.

Leo, Alan. 1989. *Esoteric Astrology.* Rochester, VT: Destiny Books.

Leo, Alan. (1912) 2003, repr. *How to Judge a Nativity*. Whitefish, MT: Kessinger Publishers.

Leo, Alan. (1912) 2010, repr. *The Art of Synthesis*. Whitefish, MT: Kessinger Publishers.

Leo, Bessie. 1919. *The Life and Work of Alan Leo, Theosophist-Astronomer-Mason.* London: "Modern Astrology" Office.

Owen, Alex. 2004. *The Place of Enchantment: British Occultism and the Culture of the Modern.* Chicago: University of Chicago Press.

LILLY, WILLIAM (1602–1675)

William Lilly was the best-known astrologer of 17th-century England, a master of astrology in all its branches. He published in a variety of astrological fields, including a popular almanac series, a textbook, and pamphlets focusing on events of the day both political and celestial as well as carrying on a thriving practice as a consulting and medical astrologer and teaching astrology.

Lilly was born into a family of yeomen. Frustrated of early ambitions of attending university, he moved to London, where he married a wealthy widow. After his wife's death in 1633, he devoted himself to astrology, a subject in which he was largely self-taught. Lilly was by far the most prominent of the astrologers who supported the Parliament against King Charles I in the British Civil Wars (1642–1649), although it took some time for him to fully commit to the Parliamentarian side. The first edition of his almanac, *Merlinus Anglicus Junior*, appeared in 1644. He was still a moderate at that time, hoping for a reconciliation between king and Parliament, and the defeat of the crypto-Catholic conspirators around the king—the "evil counselors"—who were responsible for the country's woes. Lilly moved further toward the Parliamentarian side in the following months and years, producing horoscopes that hinted at the death of the King—a very risky move. (Casting the royal horoscope had been a felony in England since the reign of Elizabeth I in the 16th century.) Lilly's *England's Propheticall Merline* (1644) used the recent great conjunction of 1642–1643 and the comet of 1618 to argue that a change of dynasty in Britain was imminent, along with a great disaster to the house of Stuart. Although Lilly did not flatly assert that the king's death would be soon, the implication of his writing was obvious. He was called up before Parliament twice to be questioned about his predictions. Lilly attracted much admiration with his astrological prediction of Parliamentary victory at the battle of Naseby in 1645, one of the turning points of the civil war. Lilly's prediction was particularly dramatic because it appeared the morning of the battle itself. Lilly's principal opponent as a political astrologer was the Royalist George Wharton (1617–1681), who he frequently denounced as incompetent. Lilly also interpreted Sibylline and other traditional "ancient prophecies" in this period, mingling prophetic interpretation with astrology. He believed in the power of astrological talismans, prizing one he claimed was created by Simon Forman to defend against evil spirits, although he sold it for 32 shillings, a substantial amount of money at the time.

Although many of the Parliamentarians appreciated Lilly's services, he was no man's puppet. He denounced people on the Parliament's side, including greedy, tax-raising committeemen and power-grubbing Presbyterian ministers, and showed some sympathy for King Charles when he was imprisoned by the Parliament. Lilly was even briefly imprisoned himself after the revolution by the Rump Parliament, England's new rulers, after he denounced them in an almanac. Like other astrologers of the time, Lilly shared English xenophobia, denouncing the Scots, the Continental foreigners, and above all the Irish. When English soldiers invaded Scotland, passages from Lilly were read aloud to encourage them. Lilly's almanac, now called *Merlinus Anglicus*, continued to dominate the market, reaching a peak in sales of approximately 30,000 copies a year by the 1650s.

As England's most prominent astrologer, Lilly was the target of much antiastrological mockery. "Black Monday," the solar eclipse of 1652 that disappointed astrologers and other prognosticators by not leading to much of anything, let alone the dramatic events many predicted, led to much published scorn of Lilly. However, he continued to be England's leading astrologer throughout the interregnum period (1649–1660). He was a leading figure in the short-lived London Society of Astrologers, one of the earliest attempts to form an astrological association, and one that brought together Parliamentarian astrologers like Lilly and Royalists like his close friend Elias Ashmole. The late interregnum saw the opening of Lilly's feud with his former disciple John Gadbury, which would continue for the rest of Lilly's life.

One thing Lilly did not predict was the restoration of Charles I's son, Charles II, in 1660. Although he suffered the confiscation of some of his property and a brief spell of imprisonment at the Restoration, as well as the embarrassment of having failed to predict it, Lilly got away comparatively lightly—partly because he had stayed friends with influential Royalists like Ashmole. (He was the subject of savage satire from the Royalist poet Samuel Butler [1613–1680], who ridiculed him in his mock-epic *Hudibras* under the name Sidrophel.) He was summoned before Parliament yet again after the Great Fire of London in 1666, when an earlier ambiguous prediction of Lilly's relating fire to Gemini, the sign held to rule London, aroused suspicion. Nothing came of it, however, and the government continued to let him alone. Lilly continued to produce almanacs, although their sales dropped considerably. He abjured politics except for the obligatory profuse expressions of loyalty to the king. He supported himself partly by the practice of astrological medicine and obtained a license to practice medicine.

As a working astrologer, Lilly was known for his mastery of horary astrology, which gave him a very active practice as an astrological consultant independent of his political work. Lilly's most influential text in astrology was *Christian Astrology* (1647), the first major astrological synthesis in English and a book that influences astrologers in the English-speaking tradition to the present day. It is partially based on the work of the French astrologer and physician Claude Dariot (1533–1594), whose work had previously appeared in English translation as *The Judgements of the Starres* (1598) as well as other continental authors but incorporates much of Lilly's own astrological experience. He also published translations of astrological work from Guido Bonatti and Girolamo Cardano. Lilly saw astrology as a unified tradition stemming from Ptolemy, and invoked the authority of ancient, Islamic, medieval, Renaissance, and contemporary astrologers without excluding any particular group or school—differently from the next generation of English astrologers led by Gadbury and John Partridge, who would view the astrological tradition in need of reform. His astrology was also more magical in its orientation than subsequent English astrologers, viewing the stars as occult rather than natural causes.

Black Monday

After the victory of Parliament over the king during the English Civil War (1642–1649) astrologers, led by William Lilly, were riding high. Most had supported Parliament. What challenged their position was the total solar eclipse of March 29, 1652. This widely anticipated eclipse was already the object of dispute between astrologers, who interpreted it as indicating great changes, and Puritan ministers, who agreed about the changes but saw the eclipse as a direct sign from God not to be interpreted astrologically. One Parliamentarian astrologer, Nicholas Culpepper, placed the eclipse in an apocalyptic context, predicting the emergence of the prophesied "Fifth Monarchy." Sources aligned with the government minimized the importance of the eclipse, emphasizing its regular and predictable nature.

The failure of the eclipse to be as spectacular as promised or to usher in any remarkable change, let alone the end of the world, led to a torrent of ridicule, much of it directed at astrologers. Lilly complained in his almanac for 1653 of having been denounced in two dozen pamphlets and 30 sermons, as well as ballads and newssheets. Black Monday would be invoked by opponents of astrology in England until the early 18th century—Jonathan Swift's 1708 Bickerstaff hoax would prophesy the death of another famous English astrologer, John Partridge, on another Monday, March 29.

Source: Burns, William E. 2000. "'The Terriblest Eclipse that hath been seen in Our Days': Black Monday and the Debate on Astrology during the Interregnum." In Rethinking the Scientific Revolution, ed. Margaret J. Osler, 137–152. Cambridge, UK: Cambridge University Press.

Lilly spent the last few years of his life in retirement at Hersham outside London, although he continued to produce an almanac. Lilly's student Henry Coley (1633–1704) took over his almanac after Lilly's death, but although more mathematically skilled than Lilly, Coley did not have the astrological talent or reputation to replace Lilly at the head of English astrology.

William E. Burns

See also: Almanacs; Ashmole, Elias; Astrological Associations; Forman, Simon; Gadbury, John; Horary Astrology; Medical Astrology; *Picatrix*; Politics

Further Reading

Capp, Bernard S. 1979. *English Almanacs, 1500–1800: Astrology and the Popular Press*. Ithaca, NY: Cornell University Press.

Curry, Patrick. 1989. *Prophecy and Power: Astrology in Early Modern England*. Princeton: Princeton University Press.

Geneva, Ann. 1995. *Astrology and the Seventeenth Century Mind: William Lilly and the Language of the Stars*. Manchester: Manchester University Press.

Halbronn, Jacques E. 1987. "The Revealing Process of Translation and Criticism in the History of Astrology." In *Astrology, Science and Society: Historical Essays*, ed. Patrick Curry, 197–217. Woodbridge, UK: Boydell.

LOTS

Lots, or Parts (known in modern astrology, incorrectly, as "Arabic parts"), are an important astrological doctrine and technique with a long history. Lots have been used, with more or less frequency, since the beginning of the practice of Hellenistic astrology around the second century BCE. For example, the Lot of Fortune, arguably the most important and certainly most employed lot throughout astrology's history, appears in textual fragments of the earliest Greek astrological authors, documentary and literary horoscopes, and astrological manuals. In interpretation, lots are used to supplement and enhance other astrological doctrines.

The lot is not a physical body but an imaginary point, unlike, for example, planets, which are physical bodies correlated to the ecliptic, a zodiacal sign and degree. Simply defined, a lot is formed from the arc between two bodies (or even other lots), which is projected from a third point, usually the astrological ascendant.

The direction from which this arc is projected is based chiefly on whether the chart in question is diurnal or nocturnal (see "Sect (*hairesis*)" in Hellenistic Astrology). (Strictly speaking, the lot arc is projected in the same direction [counterclockwise], but the length of the arc changes based on which formula, diurnal or nocturnal, is being used.) For example, the day formula of the Lot of Fortune uses the arc from the sun to the moon, but the night formula uses the arc from the moon to the sun. In the above illustration of the Lot of Fortune in a day chart, the arc from the sun to the moon is 32°, which yields a position of 7° Sagittarius for the Lot of Fortune. (In a nocturnal chart the arc would be from the moon to the sun,

Table 1 Formulas for the Lots of Fortune and Daimon

	Day Formula	Night Formula
Lot of Fortune	Asc + Moon – Sun	Asc + Sun – Moon
Lot of Daimon (a.k.a. Spirit)	Asc + Sun – Moon	Asc + Moon – Sun

Table 2 Formulas for the Lots of Love and Necessity, according to Vettius Valens

	Day Formula	Night Formula
Lot of Love (Eros)	Asc + Daimon – Fortune	Asc + Fortune – Daimon
Lot of Necessity	Asc + Fortune – Daimon	Asc + Daimon – Fortune

Table 3 Formulas for the Planetary Lots, according to Paul of Alexandria (chapter 23)

	Day Formula	Night Formula
Lot of Fortune (Moon)	Asc + Moon – Sun	Asc + Sun – Moon
Lot of Daimon (Sun)	Asc + Sun – Moon	Asc + Moon – Sun
Lot of Necessity (Mercury)	Asc + Fortune – Mercury	Asc + Mercury – Fortune
Lot of Love/Eros (Venus)	Asc + Venus – Daimon	Asc + Daimon – Venus
Lot of Courage (Mars)	Asc + Fortune – Mars	Asc + Mars – Fortune
Lot of Victory (Jupiter)	Asc + Jupiter – Daimon	Asc + Daimon – Jupiter
Lot of Nemesis (Saturn)	Asc + Fortune – Saturn	Asc + Saturn – Fortune

Table 4 Popular Lots, according to Dorotheus, *Carmen Astrologicum*

	Day Formula	Night Formula
Lot of Father (*CA* I, 13)	Asc + Saturn – Sun	Asc + Sun – Saturn
Lot of Mother (*CA* I, 14)	Asc + Moon – Venus	Asc + Venus – Moon
Lot of Siblings (*CA* I, 19)	Asc + Jupiter – Saturn	Asc + Saturn – Jupiter
Lot of the Wedding (*CA* II, 2)	Asc + Venus – Saturn	Asc + Saturn – Venus
Lot of Marriage, Female (*CA* II, 3)	Asc + Saturn – Venus	
Lot of Children (*CA* II, 10)	Asc + Saturn – Jupiter	Asc + Jupiter – Saturn

328°, and the Lot of Fortune would fall at 3° Libra.) The formulas for most lots follow this day/night distinction.

The earliest extant mention of lots appears in fragments attributed to Nechepso and Petosiris, eponymous authors writing in Greek verse. Fragments 19, +12a and +12b (Riess 1892; Heilen 2011) mention the Lot of Fortune, and provide circumstantial evidence for the Lot of Daimon (Heilen 2015, II 1162–1164, 1172–1179; Greenbaum 2016, 332–335). Manilius's *Astronomica* (ca. 10 CE) describes a system

Table 5 Examples of Lots Used in Crop Prediction and Sales (al-Bīrūnī, *Book of Instruction*, section 479)

	Day Formula	Night Formula
Lot of Watermelons	Asc + Mercury – Jupiter	Asc + Jupiter – Mercury
Lot of Chickpeas	Asc + Sun – Venus	Asc + Venus – Sun
Lot of Sesame, Grapes	Asc + Venus – Saturn	Asc + Saturn – Venus
Lot of Olives	Asc + Moon – Mercury	Asc + Mercury – Moon

using the Lot of Fortune as an ascendant ("Circle of Athla"). In addition to the Lots of Fortune and Daimon, other lots in early use (first century CE, by Dorotheus of Sidon) are the Lots of Love (Eros), Necessity, father, mother, siblings, children and marriage. Documentary evidence of lots in horoscopes shows primarily the Lots of Fortune and Daimon, but others as well.

By the fourth century, the doctrine of lots was well established and was discussed in detail by Firmicus Maternus in his *Mathesis*, and by Paul of Alexandria (fl. 378 CE) in his *Introduction to Astrology*. By the sixth century (564 CE), Paul's commentator Olympiodorus the Younger listed more than 100 lots (in various recensions of the text). In the sixth or seventh century, the Egyptian Rhetorius's *Compendium* contained an important section on lots in astrological interpretation ("The Fifth Consideration, on Lots").

The medieval period saw even more proliferation of lot doctrine and techniques, the most important by Abū Ma'shar, Al-Qabīṣī, and al-Bīrūnī (fl. 11th century). Book 8 of Abū Ma'shar's *Great Introduction to Astrology* systematized and discussed 97 lots. Sections 475–480 of al-Bīrūnī's *Book of Instruction in the Elements of the Art of Astrology* (1029) mentioned many lots, even providing for their mercantile use (e.g., the Lot of Watermelons to predict harvest yields). Al-Qabīṣī's *Introduction* devotes chapter 5 to lots. Guido Bonatti (ca. 1210–ca. 1296) covered them in his *Liber astronomiae*, Tractate 8 Part 2.

In the later Renaissance and early modern period, only the Lot of Fortune (now "Part of Fortune" from its Latin name *pars fortunae*) was calculated in nativities, probably because of the continuing influence of Ptolemy (who used only the Lot of Fortune) and the waning influence of Arabic sources. The Lot of Fortune appeared in the chart collections of Gaurico (1475–1558) and Kepler, and William Lilly used it in *Christian Astrology* (1647).

By the 18th and 19th century, with the decline of astrology, lots fell out of favor. Not until the late 20th century did they make a comeback among traditional astrologers like Robert Zoller, whose *The Arabic Parts in Astrology* (1989), reintroduced the technique.

Historically, the Lot of Fortune is the most used, followed by the Lot of Daimon (a.k.a. Lot or Part of Spirit). Other popular lots were those of father, mother, siblings, and marriage.

The Lots of Fortune and Daimon are constructed so that they form a mirror image from the ascendant with each other.

The Lot of Fortune represents the body and material fortune. The Lot of Daimon represents the soul and the mind. In medieval Arabic astrology it is called the Lot of the Hidden or Absent (*pars celati* or *absentiae*), and the Part of Future Things (*pars futurorum*).

Two different traditions involving these lots are evident in Hellenistic astrology, and associated with the concept of "planetary" lots. One tradition emphasizes the Lots of Fortune, Daimon, Love, and Necessity, constructing them in such a way that the Lots of Love and Necessity become mirror images of the Lots of Fortune and Daimon.

The second tradition supposes a system of "planetary lots," each assigned to one of the seven classical planets, and representing topics associated with each of those planets. This tradition, said to be from a Hermetic text called *Panaretos* ("All-Virtuous"), is described by Paul of Alexandria (chapter 23) and Olympiodorus (chapters 21 and 22), using different formulas for the lots of Love and Necessity, and adding lots for the other planets. It becomes garbled and conflated with the first tradition in the medieval period (e.g., in Abū Ma'shar and Bonatti, following Abū Ma'shar).

Other lots frequently mentioned by Hellenistic and medieval astrologers are those of the Father, Mother, Siblings, Marriage, and Children.

In Arabic astrology, lots could have a mercantile application, as seen in al-Bīrūnī:

Dorian Gieseler Greenbaum

See also: Abū Ma'shar al-Balkhī; Al-Qabīṣī; Bonatti, Guido; Dorotheus of Sidon; Firmicus Maternus, Julius; Hellenistic Astrology; Islamic Astrology; Kepler, Johannes; Lilly, William; Manilius, Marcus; Roman Astrology

Further Reading

al-Bīrūnī. 1934. *The Book of Instruction in the Elements of the Art of Astrology*, trans. R. Ramsay Wright. London: Luzac.

Greenbaum, Dorian Gieseler, trans. and annot. 2001. *Late Classical Astrology: Paulus Alexandrinus and Olympiodorus with the Scholia from Later Commentators*. Reston, VA: ARHAT.

Greenbaum, Dorian Gieseler. 2008. "The Lots of Fortune and Daemon in Extant Charts from Antiquity (First Century BCE to Seventh Century CE)." *MHNH* 8: 173–190.

Greenbaum, Dorian Gieseler. 2016. *The Daimon in Hellenistic Astrology: Origins and Influence*, vol. 11. Ancient Magic and Divination. Leiden: Brill.

Heilen, Stephan. 2011. "Some Metrical Fragments from Nechepsos and Petosiris." In *La poésie astrologique dans l'Antiquité*, ed. Isabelle Boehm and Wolfgang Hübner, 23–93. Paris: De Boccard.

Nechepso and Petosiris. 1892. *Fragmenta magica*. In *Philologus*, ed. E. Riess, suppl. vol. 6, pt. 1. Göttingen.

Neugebauer, Otto, and Henry Bartlett Van Hoesen. (1959) 1987, repr. *Greek Horoscopes*. Philadelphia: American Philosophical Society.

Rhetorius. 2009. *Rhetorius the Egyptian: Astrological Compendium Containing His Explanation and Narration of the Whole Art of Astrology*, trans. James H. Holden. Tempe, AZ: American Federation of Astrologers.

Zoller, Robert. 1989. *The Arabic Parts in Astrology: A Lost Key to Prediction*. Rochester, VT: Inner Traditions International.

M

MACHIAVELLI, NICCOLÒ (1469–1527)

Niccolò Machiavelli was one of the most notable political philosophers of the Renaissance, whose influence is still felt today. His work marks the starting point of modern political thought, a pragmatic politics completely independent of any moral question. He saw politics as an autonomous art and he proposed a strong united state ruled by the prince, like the first modern states in Europe (i.e., Spain, France, and England). He tried to apply this thinking to Italy, composed of many small republics and monarchies, but was unsuccessful.

However, a deeper study of Machiavelli reveals another discipline that supports his political system: astrology. In Renaissance Italy, astrology was considered a true science. Machiavelli founded his political construct on the astrological natural philosophy. In fact, till the universal gravitation law of Newton, the universal natural astrological law would rule the world. Therefore, most intellectuals in the Renaissance would divide the world in three parts: the natural (philosophy), the supernatural (religion), and the occult (astrology). It is not possible to understand the early modernity of the thought of Machiavelli except by means of the occult science. He had an astrologic-political worldview and proposed an astrology-based policy.

Machiavelli was born in Florence to a not particularly well-off middle-class family. He studied Latin and rhetoric and was appointed secretary of the second chancellery of the Republic of Florence in 1498. Around this time, the Medici family was expelled from Florence when the town was controlled by the friar Girolamo Savonarola. His first official visit to France was crucial for his intellectual development. He stayed in the court of France for six months and in 1502 he participated in the negotiations with Cesare Borgia.

He went on several diplomatic missions while he wrote his first printed work *Decennale primo* (1506) where he states that the decadence of Italy is mainly in the military. While he was being promoted in the chancellery, he prepared the materials (*Dell'ordinare lo Stato di Firenze alle armi* and *Sopra l'ordinanza e milizia fiorentina*) for his future book *Arte della Guerra* (1519–1520). In 1507 he was sent on new missions to Germany, Switzerland, and Tirol and Leo X sought his advice about the League of Cambrai (1508). He wrote *Decennale secondo* (1509) and *Rapporto delle cose d'Alemagna* (1512).

The Medici returned to power in Florence in 1512 and the Republic of Florence ended. As a result Machiavelli fell into disgrace and was imprisoned for a year. However, the election of Leo X in 1513 led to his release and he retired to his country house. This new period was fruitful. He wrote his masterpiece *Il Principe* in 1513, the *Discorsi sopra la prima Deca di Tito Livio* between 1513 and 1519, the *Vita di Castruccio* in 1520, other history books (*Storia Fiorentina*), as well as *La Mandragola* (1518) and *Cligia* (1525). Niccolò Machiavelli died in 1527 shortly after the restoration of the Republic of Florence.

All Machiavelli's work had an astrologic-political aim. Astrology even influences the *mixed bodies* (states, Church, religions) by means of conjunctions of planets, propitious signs, calamities, and even astrology-based prophecies. It is also useful to elaborate the horoscopes of republics, religions, princedoms, and so on. There is a celestial causality or fate that affects the political history of countries. Therefore, in this astrological way, he was concerned about the sad disunity and feebleness of Italy, a mere battlefield of France and Spain. In this respect, his key idea was to create a united statist system for Italy ruled by a prince. The prince is an exceptional person, protected by the *fortuna* (favorable astrological chance) and endowed with a rare *virtù* (not moral, but a capability, valor and energy, connected with the motion of planets), able to enact superior political aims, the *necessità*, a concept that states the modern state has its own autonomous, not moral, goals; the mission of the prince is to serve these aims, thereby following the raison d'état. Both men and the state, are influenced by the heavens (astrological signs, conjunctions, and motion of the planets). They may be sick because of the bad quality of their humors. Then the new *prince* is the doctor who has to treat with energy (violence) and cure the politic body by means of purges and bloodlettings. Therefore, the prince, according to Machiavelli, as a great doctor is above ordinary morality, the religious one, because his moral duty, as prince not as man, is to serve by all means the aims of the state. Any means, immoral or not, could be needed to maintain the health of the state.

Machiavelli saw politics as a play of wills, passions, persons, whose forces are constantly colliding (i.e., the interaction of the diverse and many humors of the political body). This way of thinking has been described as a natural organic mentality, which led Machiavelli to conceiving of the state as a human "political" body whose doctor was the prince. Such a mentality could even resort to murder if necessary. The astrological thinking of Machiavelli justifies murder in the same way as a doctor eliminates a bad humor. So, the prince eliminates the head of a party or another person if convenient.

The state has to concern itself with earthly things and its reason (i.e., astrological influences), and it has its own morals to maintain the health of the public body. Moreover, his astrological worldview shows there is no sovereign God who rules the world and, then, there is no moral at all. Divine providence is replaced by naturalistic astrological providence. But the agnostic and amoral nature of his political thinking that led to the secularization of politics was based on his astrological philosophy.

Justo Hernández

See also: Mundane Astrology; Politics; Renaissance and Reformation Astrology

Further Reading

Parel, A. J. 1992. *The Machiavellian Cosmos*. New Haven, CT: Yale University Press.

MANILIUS, MARCUS

Marcus Manilius survives only through his didactic Latin poem, *Astronomicon*. Although the *Astronomicon* is the earliest surviving Latin work on astronomy and astrology, no contemporary sources cite it or relate biographical details of its author. A reference to the Battle of the Teutoburg Forest reveals its composition to have been after 9 CE, but modern scholars disagree whether he wrote under the emperor Augustus (r. 27 BCE–14 CE) or Tiberius (r. 14–37 CE). Because of his idiosyncratic Latin, scholars further disagree whether Manilius was a Greek-speaking foreigner or Roman, even though he refers to Latin as "our" language and regularly refers to Roman politics and poets.

As befits the earliest surviving Latin work on astral sciences, Manilius declares himself the first to have addressed the topic in verse although his opening lines (Book 1.1–2) lifts the topic of "stars knowledgeable of fate" from the Roman poet Virgil's *Aeneid*. Moreover, the astronomical section of the *Astronomicon* follows lines 19–558 of Aratus's *Phaenomena* (ca. 315–240 BCE), particularly the extant fragments of the Ciceronian translation. Manilius echoes Pythagoras in describing the Milky Way as the abode of dead heroes and the music of the spheres (Book 1.22–23) but the proximate source for these ideas may have been the *Republic* by the Roman philosopher and poet Marcus Tullius Cicero (106–43 BCE). Some cosmological details, such as four elements, indicate a familiarity with Stoicism but Manilius's cosmology also recalls Hermetic doctrines. Among astrological authors, Manilius particularly resembles Teucer of Babylon (fl. ca. 1 CE), but the priority of the two authors cannot be stated with certainty.

As the earliest surviving Latin astrologer, the idiosyncrasies of Manilius attract the attention of historians of astrology but whether these peculiarities represent innovations, vanished traditions, or errors in the received text cannot be stated. For example, in his astronomical passages, Manilius introduces an apparently novel detail that the Antarctic constellations never seen in the Northern Hemisphere parallel the circumpolar stars, which never set—two bears divided and encircled by a serpent (Book 1.451–453). However, he also commits astronomical errors in declaring that lunar eclipses are first seen in the east and later in the west. Moreover, this error is particularly irreconcilable with another error that the Southern Hemisphere experiences night when the Northern Hemisphere experiences day (Book 1.243–245). Whether they be errors or innovations, Manilius introduces seven unique astrological doctrines. First, Manilius does not consider quartile signs to have a negative relationship. Second, Manilius assigns a divinity to each zodiacal sign. Manilius may import this arrangement from the same Mesopotamian source that informed Diodorus Siculus but the strategy of assigning astrological elements, particularly those associated with planets, to zodiacal signs constitutes a recurring theme in the *Astronomicon*. Third, when dividing signs into masculine and feminine, Manilius is unique in describing pairs as loving, with the possibility of treachery. Fourth, Manilius identifies the dodecatemoria (that is, the subdivision of each zodiacal sign into 12 2.5° sections) with zodiacal signs, not planets. Fifth, Manilius propounds a "circle of 12 athla" (which he also called *sortes* or *labores* as the meter of the poem required), whereby the lot of fortune is taken as the ascendant and the 12 houses are distributed sequentially. Sixth, Manilius presents two systems of chronocrators, again preferring zodiacal associations over planetary periods. Seventh, Manilius associates the decans with zodiacal signs.

Manilius also omits common astrological themes. Marriage and children have little role in Manilius. Moreover, he does not discuss in detail the calculation of astrological houses or places, perhaps because he uses "whole sign" houses, which renders the allocation of astrological houses simple once the ascendant has been determined. More importantly, Manilius omits any detailed discussion of planetary influences. Manilius admits that planets moving through the 12 astrological houses can affect their powers. Likewise, he concedes that planets affect the lots, zodiacal aspects, and the dodecatemoria, harmful degrees of the zodiac, but comparable discussions from other astrologers overwhelm the thin information provided by Manilius. For Manilius, perhaps the most important role of the planets is in the determination of the length of life. One possible explanation for this lack (and the general replacement of planetary associations with zodiacal influences) is that Manilius simply followed Aratus, who curtailed his discussion of planets to eight lines. Another is that their omission rendered the work harmless under the Augustan ban on astrological divination in 11 CE. This limited utility confounds modern notions of didactic poetry.

In keeping with Stoic tendencies, Manilius adopts a strongly determinist philosophical stance but offers little advice for accepting or manipulating fate. He proposes no scientific mechanism and many of his conclusions take the form of direct analogies. For example, the rising of Auriga spawns charioteers; the rising of Ara produces priests.

Micah T. Ross

See also: Fate; Hellenistic Astrology; House Systems; Roman Astrology

Further Reading

Goold, George P., ed. and trans. 1977. *Astronomica*, rev. 1997. Loeb Classical Library 469. Cambridge, MA: Harvard University Press.

Green, S. J. 2014. *Disclosure and Discretion in Roman Astrology: Manilius and His Augustan Contemporaries*. Oxford: Oxford University Press.

Green, S. J., and Katharina Volk, eds. 2011. *Forgotten Stars: Rediscovering Manilius' Astronomica*. Oxford: Oxford University Press.

Housman, A. E., ed. 1903–1930. *M. Manilii Astronomicon Libri*. 5 vols. London: Richards.

Volk, Katharina. 2009. *Manilius and His Intellectual Background*. Oxford: Oxford University Press.

MASHĀLLĀH IBN ATHARI (740–815)

Mashāllāh Ibn Athari was a Persian Jewish astrologer and Kabbalist. At the height of his fame, he served as the court astrologer for the Abbasid Caliph Al Mansur (r. 754–775). He served as part of the team of Abbasid astrologers who helped determine the date for founding the city of Baghdad. He penned several notable books on astrology and taught many students, some of whom became acclaimed astrologers in their own right. The name Mashāllāh is one he took for himself and is Arabic for "that which god intends." He proposed that there are 10 worlds in the spheres of existence, 2 more than Aristotle's 8, which would lead to the Kabbalistic notion of sephiroth. Although his writings were all in Arabic, they have been translated into several different languages, including Latin, Hebrew, and Greek. He remains a spectacular personality in Kabbalistic astrology.

Mashāllāh was born in the Babylonian town of Basra. Ibn Nadim suggests his name when he was born was Misha, the Persian equivalent of Jethro. Babylon and Persia were ruled by the Islamic Abbasid Caliphate. Having been classically trained as a boy, he turned to astrology and astronomy as his subjects of research.

One of his first accomplishments, in 762, was to assist then preeminent astrologer Naubakht the Persian to create the horoscope for the founding capital city of Al Mansur. Along with several other astrologers, they called for the founding of a new town, which would augur a positive fate for the Abbasid dynasty. This city was Baghdad, the modern capital of Iraq.

After the successful founding of Baghdad, Mashāllāh was installed as the court astrologer for Al Mansur. He would continue to serve the caliphate through the reign of Caliph Mamun. During his tenure as court astrologer, Mashāllāh trained many young men to serve as astrologers through the Islamic Empire. He also worked on astronomical research and was most fascinated by the astrolabe. He wrote 22 works, many of which were translated into scholarly languages including Latin. He died in 815 CE, and we do not know how he died; only that his work in astrology and Kabbalah remains of interest to this day.

Mashāllāh is credited with writing one of the first works concerning the astrolabe. Mashāllāh, among others, used it in his readings of the stars for astrological star charts. He was most interested in cosmology. His writings explored the mystical nature of the universe. This influenced Maimonides, Abraham Ibn Ezra, and other later Jewish scholars to seriously consider his. He was the first Jewish scholar to seriously consider the stars and astrology, thus his work was the basis of future Kabbalistic astrological texts.

Mashāllāh wrote several treatises concerning astronomy. He also prepared several works on the philosophical theories of Aristotle. Aristotle suggests the universe fits into eight orbs of influence. These are spheres that allow philosophers and astrologers to determine the actions of people, countries, and so on. Mashāllāh suggested rather than eight orbs, there are 10 orbs.

These orbs were of great significance to the astrologers, astronomers, and cosmologists of the middle ages. Each orb represented a pattern of movement for the celestial bodies, particularly other planets. It was through the calculations of the number of orbs, and their specific rates of movement that horoscopes, star charts, and navigations were achieved. Kings also used the star charts to determine ideal locations and times to build their capital cities. With the introduction of the 10th orb, Mashāllāh was expanding the reach of astrological predictions and astronomical observation of stars, planets, and comets. He was also influential in the adoption of the Persian theories of the importance of Jupiter–Saturn conjunctions in mundane astrology. Many of Mashāllāh's writings were focused on determining the exact orbits of Jupiter and Saturn.

For medieval Jewish astrologers and astronomers such as Abraham Ibn Ezra (1089–1167), a philosopher and astronomer, or Moses Maimonides (1135–1202), a philosopher, rabbi, and court doctor of the Islamic kingdom of Egypt, Mashāllāh was the source they translated from Arabic into Hebrew, Latin, and other scholarly languages. Mashāllāh's writings were the basis for much of the Kabbalistic learning done concerning the Sefer Yetzirah, or the book of essence. Mashāllāh cemented himself as a notable figure in the golden age of Islam and left behind a wealth of information for astrologers to this day.

Benjamin Franz

See also: Astrolabe; Islamic Astrology; Judaism; Medieval European Astrology

Further Reading

Freudenthal, Gad, ed. 2011. *Science in Medieval Jewish Cultures*. Cambridge: Cambridge University Press.

Pingree, David. 2001. "From Alexandria to Baghdād to Byzantium: The Transmission of Astrology." *International Journal of the Classical Tradition* 8, no. 1: 3–37.

Pingree, David. 2006. "The Byzantine Translations of Māshā'allāh on Interrogational Astrology." In *The Occult Sciences in Byzantium*, ed. Paul Magdalino and Maria Mavroudi, 231–243. Geneva: La Pomme d'or.

Sela, Shlomo. 2012. "Maimonides and Mashallah on the Ninth Orb of the Signs and Astrology." *Aleph: Historical Studies in Science and Judaism* 12, no.1: 101–134.

MEDICAL ASTROLOGY

Astrology and medicine have been intertwined in a multitude of cultures for millennia. The professions of physician and astrologer were often combined from the ancient world to the Renaissance, and a modicum of astrological knowledge was considered necessary for medical professionals and even for laypeople concerned about their health. Major Greek and Roman astrological writers, including Ptolemy, Manilius, and Firmicus Maternus wrote about the medical uses of astrology. Ptolemy claimed the ancient Egyptians, revered for their wisdom, had entirely merged medicine and astrology, thus perfecting both sciences. In those medieval universities where astrology was taught, it was principally taught as an aid to physicians, and many court astrologers doubled as court physicians. In the early modern period, physician-astrologers used their almanacs and other writings to advertise their medical as well as astrological practices. Even those few women who wrote almanacs were frequently identified as midwives. Although in medieval and early modern Europe, the authority of ancient physicians supported the connection of astrology and medicine, medical rebels such as Paracelsus who denigrated the ancients and their Islamic and Christian disciples also supported the importance of astrology for the physician. Some astrological physicians would in turn become Paracelsians, but many would not, as astrology retained its relevance for a broad range of medical philosophies. Astrological medicine was not restricted to a medical or astrological elite but was employed by a variety of practitioners, learned and unlearned. Consulting astrologers who did not claim medical expertise still dealt with the medical questions brought by their clients, sometimes employing the techniques of horary astrology to do so. Medicine and astrology were also closely allied in non-Western astrological systems, including those of India and Tibet.

The applications of astrology to medicine were legion, from the classification of diseases and medicines, the treatment of the sick, and even public health. Examination of the natal horoscope could reveal the patient's proclivity for certain diseases. The ability claimed by many astrologers to determine the time of death from the natal horoscope was also obviously relevant to medicine, although the death might have nonmedical causes. Astrology could even be used for forensic medicine, to determine the cause of death when the evidence was unclear or ambiguous. Outside the realm of health and sickness, astrology could also be used to answer such questions as the gender of a child in the womb, as long as one knew the time of conception. Because it dealt with the body and not the mind, and because astrological factors were generally viewed as interacting with other factors affecting health rather than determining the course of a disease by themselves, medical astrology was less deterministic than other branches of astrology and raised fewer religious problems.

Astrology and Disease

One of the most important skills for the astrological physician was the ability to take and interpret horoscopes of particular moments in the course of an illness. The concept of "decumbiture," taking the horoscope of the moment when a patient took to his or her bed, dated to the Hellenistic era and continued through the early modern era. Another possibility was taking the horoscope of the moment the patient presented his or her urine to the physician, an important part of the diagnostic process, or when the patient first sought the physician's aid, although not all physicians agreed that these moments were medically relevant.

Many medieval and early modern Western and Islamic physicians and astrologers believed that there were certain "critical days" in the course of an illness that could be interpreted astrologically. The concept of critical days, counted from the onset of the illness, was part of the legacy of ancient medicine, particularly Galenism, the doctrine named after the ancient Greek physician Galen (130–210 CE). Galenism was the dominant school of medicine in the Islamic world and medieval Europe into the late 17th century. (Despite its usefulness in an astrological context, the theory of critical days was independent of astrology. Renaissance philosopher and opponent of astrology Pico della Mirandola believed in critical days but attacked the theory that they were determined astrologically and was followed by several Renaissance humanist physicians.) The onset and course of a disease could follow that of planets though the zodiac. Girolamo Cardano and other astrologer-physicians produced elaborate case histories relating every change in the condition of the sick person with the corresponding change in the heavens. The lunar cycle was often thought to be particularly influential on the course of a disease. Galen himself had endorsed the idea of the moon's influence on health.

Epidemics presented a problem for astrologers in that they could clearly not be based on individual horoscopes as thousands of people born at different times were dying in a short span of time. However, baneful movements of the stars could affect large numbers of people and epidemics have been incorporated into mundane astrology. When the medical faculty of the University of Paris were asked to explain the Black Death that struck Europe in 1347, they ascribed it to a conjunction of Saturn, Mars, and Jupiter in Aquarius in 1345 compounded by the effects of a lunar eclipse. Mars and Saturn, malefic planets, were particularly strongly associated with plagues, as were the rare "Great Conjunctions" of Jupiter and Saturn. Unusual celestial events, such as comets and eclipses, could also have adverse impact on the health of both humans and animals.

Astrology and Treatment

In Western medical astrology, the different parts of the body were governed by different signs of the zodiac. The division begins with Aries governing the head and ends with Pisces governing the feet. The visual representation of this division is known as the zodiac man (the figure was assumed to be male). References to the zodiac man can be traced to the Hellenistic period although the earliest surviving image dates from the 11th century. By the 13th century it was appearing in almanacs and it became extremely common in 16th- and 17th-century English almanacs, disappearing only in the late 18th century.

The importance of the ruling sign for treatment was that operations on a particular part of the body should be avoided depending on what planets were in the ruling sign at the time. The presence of the moon in the ruling sign of a particular part of the body, for example, was a strong contraindication for a medical or surgical procedure affecting that body part. The administration of medicine or the letting of blood, a common medical procedure in medieval and early modern Europe, should take place at a favorable astrological moment. (This principle was not restricted to humans; the position of the moon also influenced favorable or unfavorable times for castrating male animals.) Talismans prepared at a particularly propitious moment and incorporating astrological symbolism were also thought useful for medical problems.

Many illnesses were treated with herbs. Medical herbs were associated with planets and signs. Many astrologers, such as Nicholas Culpepper (1616–1654), were also herbalists. Culpepper was the author of the *English Physitian* (1652), an encyclopedic guide to the medicinal herbs of Britain, which emphasized their connections to the planets and signs. (He also wrote a work on decumbiture.) Culpepper believed that the first step in treatment was to identify the planet responsible for the disease. The proper treatment would be to administer herbs associated with the "opposite" planet, as Mercury was opposite to Jupiter. However, in some cases herbs associated with the planet causing the disease were the appropriate treatment.

Astrological talismans and even astrologically inspired music could also preserve or restore health. Astrological treatments were the subject of Marsilio Ficino's *Three Books on Life*.

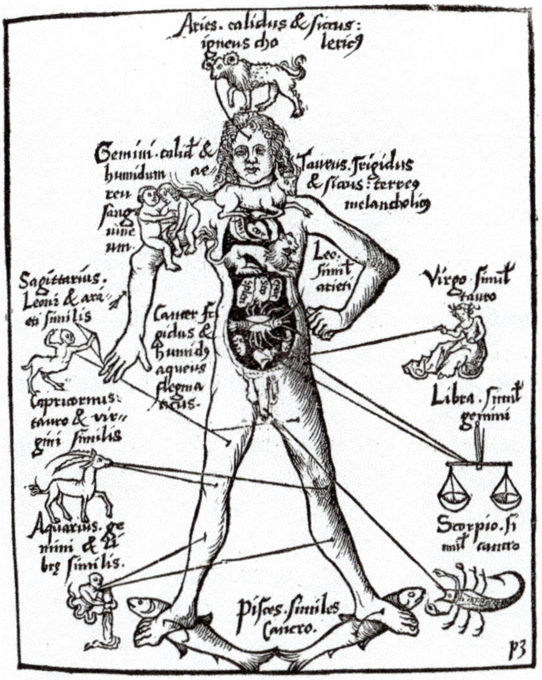

An early printed example of the "zodiac man," associating zodiac signs with parts of the body. These images would proliferate in early modern Europe, particularly in almanacs. (Wellcome Collection)

Decline and Survival of Medical Astrology

The decline in the intellectual prestige of astrology in the West from the mid-17th century on led to a decline in medical astrology, as physicians separated themselves from a practice widely viewed as superstitious. Although during the 18th-century Enlightenment physicians studied what they believed to be the influence of the sun and moon on the body and its illnesses, they did not call what they did astrology, nor did this research program continue into the 19th century. The self-image of modern physicians as supporters of science and rationality has separated them from astrology, although some physicians and other medical professionals are astrological believers.

Medical astrology survives into the present era primarily as a specialty within astrology, although in countries where medical authority is tightly regulated, astrologers, like other "alternative" and New Age practioners, take care to distinguish between their work and "medicine," the legal monopoly of physicians and others trained and licensed by the state or professional associations. The tradition of using astrology to give general health advice to a broad population also persists, as in the numerous astrological diet books. However, the emphasis on character analysis in much modern astrology has diminished interest in medical astrology. In India, where astrology remains a mainstream and extremely popular practice, medical astrologers operate much more openly, sometimes even with state sponsorship.

William E. Burns

See also: Albertus Magnus; Almanacs; Cardano, Girolamo; Court Astrologers; Dorotheus of Sidon; Electional Astrology; Enlightenment; Ficino, Marsilio; Gender; Horoscopes; Islamic Astrology; Lilly, William; Medieval European Astrology; Mesoamerican Astrology; Mundane Astrology; Natal Astrology; Nostradamus; Paracelsus; Ptolemy; Science; Sex and Love; Sibly, Ebenezer; Zodiacs

Further Reading

Barton, Tamsyn. 1994. *Power and Knowledge: Astrology, Physiognomics and Medicine under the Roman Empire.* Ann Arbor: University of Michigan Press.

Curth, Louise Hill. 2007. *English Almanacs, Astrology and Popular Medicine.* Manchester, UK: Manchester University Press.

Grafton, A. 2001. *Cardano's Cosmos: The Worlds and Works of a Renaissance Astrologer*. Cambridge, MA: Harvard University Press.

Kassell, Lauren. 2005. *Medicine and Magic in Elizabethan London—Simon Forman: Astrologer, Alchemist, and Physician.* Oxford: Oxford University Press.

Traister, Barbara Howard. 2001. *The Notorious Astrological Physician of London: Works and Days of Simon Forman.* Chicago: University of Chicago Press.

Williams, Gerhild Scholz, and Charles D. Gunnoe Jr., eds. 2002. *Paracelsian Moments: Science, Medicine and Astrology in Early Modern Europe.* Kirksville, MO: Truman State University Press.

MEDIEVAL EUROPEAN ASTROLOGY

The medieval period in Europe is usually considered to stretch from the overthrow of the last Western Roman emperor in 476 CE to the fall of Constantinople to the Ottoman Turks in 1453. The astrology prevalent at the beginning of this period was Hellenistic astrology, largely shaped by Claudius Ptolemy who took the Mesopotamian visual descriptions of the heavens and married them with Aristotelian physics. Yet as the Roman legions disappeared, so too did the rigor of astrology in the Latin west, which retained only enough astrological knowledge to understand weather and farming, and to calculate the dates of Easter. Astrology in Europe only became revitalized in the late-12th century through European scholars seeking new knowledge in the translation centers of Spain and Sicily. Texts previously only known in Arabic or Greek, were avidly translated into Latin sometimes through the filters of Hebrew and Castilian or Catalan. Although the language in which astrology was transmitted has changed over the millennia, its content remained steadfast, whatever the techniques used. Rabbi Avraham Ibn Ezra (1089–1164) a Jewish scholar and astrologer from Spain, described astrology as "the interpretation of the laws of heaven according to the rules as practiced by the ancients, generation after generation" (Ibn Ezra, trans. Epstein, 19981, 1). Aptly, this underlines the essence of medieval astrology—tradition.

As the Greco-Roman world disintegrated in the fifth century, astrology all but disappeared in the Latin west. At the start of the seventh century, the works of Ptolemy were thought to have emanated from the Ptolemaic kingdom in Egypt (323 BCE–30 BCE), which was named after the dynasty of its Greco-Macedonian rulers, not the astrologer. This confusion showed how far astrological historical knowledge had slipped from memory. Furthermore, early medieval Latin astrology lacked the mathematical and astronomical precision of classical astrology. Works such as that of Isidore of Seville (ca. 560–636) in his *Etymologies* and the English monk Bede (d. 735), writing on the computus, revealed what might be termed a simplistic astrology, one that identified the constellations, planets, and signs of the tropical seasonal zodiac, and instructions on how to calculate the liturgical year.

In the Islamic Middle East, however, astrology underwent a revitalization, after the fall of the Roman Empire, beginning in the late seventh century. This period was marked by a genuine and systematic emphasis on the value of knowledge, starting with the Abbasid caliphs who came to power in Baghdad in 750, and particularly in the reign of al-Ma'mun (813–818), who established the Bait al-Hikma, the House of Wisdom. This venture successfully brought together Muslin and non-Muslim scholars to translate Greek, Syriac, Persian, and Sanskrit works into Arabic and exchange ideas about the cosmos. This melting pot of cultures recognized the authority of Ptolemy and, like Ptolemy, divided the "science of the stars" ('ilm al-nuj um) into the science of movements ('ilm al-falak) and the science of judgments of the stars ('ilm ahk am an-nuj um). They combined Ptolemy's astrology with Indian number theory and developed algebra from which was established a complex algorithmic astrology that could describe life from the practical expressions of its length, or profession, consider future periods of a person's life governed by a different planet or luminary (the al Firdaria), or explain a person's soul (the almuten of the chart). Islamic astronomers also refined the astrolabe, originally developed by the Greeks, by adding angular scales as well as circles representing horizon azimuths. Astrolabes allowed morning prayers to be scheduled by ascertaining the times of sunrise and the rising of fixed stars. More importantly, astrolabes played a vital role in carrying astrology to the Latin west because they easily enabled the calculations, and hence construction, of the horoscope.

Astrologers of the Islamic world also connected astrology with medicine and those whose technical treatises would become essential to the thinking of medieval European astrology included Mashāllāh Ibn Atharī (ca. 740–815), a Jew born in Basra (modern Iraq) whose *Introductorium in astronomiam* became a standard in medieval Europe; Abū Ma'šar (787–886), a student of Mashāllāh, born in Balkh (modern Afghanistan), one of the best-known astrologers of the Middle Ages in both the Islamic world and Christian West, equated in rank with Mashāllāh and Ptolemy; Abu Yūsuf Ya'qūb Ibn 'Isḥāq aṣ-Ṣabbāḥ al-Kindī (ca. 801–873) known as "the Philosopher of the Arabs," born in Kufah, a major center for Arabic learning and culture and who was thought to have brought classical Greek to the Islamic world; and Al-Qabīṣī (Alcabitius) with *The Introduction to Astrology*. Two philosophers—Abū 'Alī al-Ḥusayn Ibn 'Abd Allāh Ibn Sīnā (Avicenna) (980–1037) and Ibn Rushd (Averroës) (1126–1198)—were not practicing astrologers, but they did lay the foundations for the reconciliation of sacred scripture with classical philosophers, particularly Aristotle. For several centuries, the language of astronomical learning was Arabic.

In the late 11th century, Muslim Spain changed to Christian rule, as did the kingdom of Sicily, and both places became centers of translation filled with European translators in search of the new learning. Men such as John of Seville (fl. 1135–1153) and Gerard of Cremona (1114–1187) in Toledo, Plato of Tivoli (1110–1145) in Barcelona, and Hermann of Carinthia (ca. 1100–ca. 1160) working with Robert of Ketton (ca. 1110–ca. 1160), archdeacon of Pamplona, translated Arabic texts of astronomy, astrology, mathematics, and medicine into Latin, including the astrolabe and astronomical tables (Burnett 1977, 62–63). These translations filtered into the Latin west and changed European astrology. Because astrology described the physical world, it continued to be a tool for weather predicting and farming. Islamic scholarship also coupled astrology with medicine through the Aristotelian temperaments that connected the health of the body with the elements, fire, water, earth, and air, and which, in turn, were related to body organs, fluids, and treatments. Medical men already trained to see the body of man (microcosm) as corresponding with the greater whole of the natural world (macrocosm) and seeking new knowledge with which to cure their patients, recognized this practical function of astrology.

The most common form of astrological text that cascaded into Europe was the "introduction," which described the fundamental and necessary components of astrology, such as the signs and the planets. These components formed the fundamental framework for the prevailing uses of astrology: nativities, which offered a consideration of the individual's horoscope based on the time, date, and place of birth; revolutions, a horoscope drawn up for the Aries Ingress, the entry of the sun into the first degree of Aries and from which could be read such predictions as the weather, the state of politics, agricultural conditions, commodity prices, and the possibility of the outbreak of disease and epidemics; elections, a horoscope erected for the most propitious time for events to take place, which included coronations and marriages, but could also be used for more commonplace acts such when to cut one's hair, take medicine or offer a prison visit; and interrogations, casting a horoscope for the time a question was asked.

Astrology became part of the emerging culture of universities through the quadrivium, where astrology and astronomy were synonymous, and through the increasing need for medical practitioners to have a thorough knowledge of astrology. As Roger French observed, the Greek word *physis* (nature) became the root of the word *physician* (French 1996, 452, 456). In this way the works of Aristotle, and his theory of reality—his physics, psychology, and metaphysics—entered the West complete with Arabic commentaries. Thus astrology became a part of the discourse in philosophy, medicine, and cosmology.

In the late 13th century these Aristotelian ideas were taught in the universities of Western Europe. It was Saint Thomas Aquinas (1225–1274), however, who as a result of embracing Aristotle's natural philosophy, reconciled astrology with Christianity. Understanding that a healthy body was critical in serving God and that medical astrology could sustain that health, in his writings Aquinas stated that celestial influences affect the body but not the soul, which was answerable to God (Aquinas 1975, 40). Astrology flourished as the world system with major teachers and writers of astrological textbooks that included Michael Scotus, Guido Bonatti, Ramon Lull (1232–1316), Pietro d'Abano (ca. 1250–ca. 1316), and Antonius de Montulmo (fl. late 14th century). Astrology also moved into the royal courts. Michael Scotus, who worked in Toledo and lectured in Bologna, was employed by Emperor Frederick II. Guido Bonatti, who lectured at the University of Bologna, was employed by Emperor Frederick II, Ezzelino da Romano III, Guido Novello da Polenta, and Guido I da Montefeltro, all Ghibelline supporters of the Holy Roman emperor in conflict with the Guelphs and the Papacy. Astrology's importance in the culture meant that astrology also ricocheted into the literature, such as Geoffrey Chaucer's (1343–1400) *Canterbury Tales*, art, sculpture, and theological commentaries.

For astrologers from the 13th through the 15th century, Ptolemy's *Tetrabiblos* was a standard text, with its model of causation connecting Aristotelian mechanics with planetary influences and sympathetic movements, an understanding of the Chaldean order of the planets, the use of epicycles rather than retrograde motion, and the employment of essential dignities, the system of assigning strength to the zodiac and a planet's ability to perform its function as it traversed it. This quality was reflected in the medieval hierarchical structure of life (Ptolemy 1969, 43; Bonatti 1998, 47). Other tools in the medieval astrologer's toolkit included the ability to judge profession, marriage, wealth, and length of life from the chart as well as levels of eminence or slavery, and prediction via planetary periods (al Firdaria), profections, revolutions, and directing by triplicity, a central tenet in Arabic astrology. It also contained the ability to recognize the individual's definition of God, spiritual purpose, and attitude to religions. These tools are insightful for understanding the rich and deep approach astrologers were able to offer to an elite individual who could afford to employ them.

Universities continued to teach astrology and records for the early 15th century list the curriculum that arts degree students at the University of Bologna undertook: in the first and second years, knowledge of basic astronomy, the ability to read the Alfonsine tables, and to use the astrolabe; in the third year, Al-Qabīṣī's *The Introduction to Astrology* and the *Centiloquium,* falsely ascribed to Ptolemy; and in the fourth and final year, Ptolemy's *Tetrabilbos* and William of England's *De urina non visa* (Thorndike 1944, 281–282).

By the 17th century many medieval astrological techniques were no longer being used. In 1992, however, a new wave of translations undertaken by practitioners of astrology and beginning with Project Hindsight (Golden Hind Press 2004) has seen these medieval techniques reemerge into contemporary astrology.

Darrelyn Gunzburg

See also: Albertus Magnus; Ashenden, John; Astrolabe; Bonatti, Guido; Chaucer, Geoffrey; D'Ailly, Pierre; Islamic Astrology; John of Saxony; *Picatrix*

Further Reading

Aquinas, Thomas. 1975. *Summa Contra Gentiles, Book Three: Providence Part II*, trans. Vernon J. Bourke. London: University of Notre Dame Press.

Bonatti, Guido. 1998. *Liber Astronomiae*, trans. Robert Zoller. Brisbane: Spica Publications.

Burnett, C. S. F. 1977. "A Group of Arabic-Latin Translators Working in Northern Spain in the Mid-12th Century." *Journal of the Royal Asiatic Society of Great Britain and Ireland* 1: 62–108.

Carey, Hilary M. 2010. "Astrology in the Middle Ages." *History Compass* 8, no. 8: 888–902.

French, Roger. 1996. "Foretelling the Future: Arabic Astrology and English Medicine in the Late Twelfth Century." *Isis* 87, no. 3: 453–480.

The Golden Hind Press. 2004. "The Early History of Project Hindsight." http://www.projecthindsight.com/archives/history.html

Greenbaum, Dorian Gieseler. 2005. *Temperament, Astrology's Forgotten Key*. Bournemouth: The Wessex Astrologer.

Hartner, Willy. 1967. "Qusayr 'Amra, Farnesina, Luther, Hesiod. Some Supplementary Notes to A. Beer's Contribution." *Vistas in Astronomy* 9: 225–228.

Ibn Ezra, Abraham. 1939. *The Beginning of Wisdom: An Astrological Treatise by Abraham Ibn Ezra*, ed. R. Levy and F. Cantera. Baltimore, MD: Johns Hopkins University Press.

Ibn Ezra, Avraham Ben Meir. 1998. *The Beginning of Wisdom (Reshith Hochma)*, ed. Robert Hand, trans. Meira B. Epstein. Reston, VA: ARHAT Publications.

North, John David. 2008. *Cosmos: An Illustrated History of Astronomy and Cosmology*. Chicago: University of Chicago Press.

Ptolemy. 1969. *Tetrabiblos*, ed. J. M. Ashmand. Mokelumne Hill, CA: Health Research.

Thorndike, Lynn. 1944. *University Records and Life in the Middle Ages*. New York: Columbia University Press.

MERCATOR, GERARDUS (1512–1594)

Gerardus Mercator, originally Gerard de Kremer or de Cremer, was best known for being the first cartographer to construct a world map showing sailing courses with a constant bearing using straight lines. In 1537, Mercator established his reputation with his first solo map: the Holy Land, which he researched, worked on, and produced himself. It detailed the Exodus route from the Red Sea. This was followed, a year later, by a map of the world; in 1539/1540, he drew a map of Flanders, and in in 1541, he compiled a terrestrial globe. Three years later, Mercator was brought up on charges of heresy for being sympathetic to Protestant beliefs and for taking numerous trips that seemed suspicious. There were also implications that the Catholic theologians of the University of Louvain were concerned about: possible astrological symbols Mercator allegedly placed in his Holy Land map, which the authorities did not really understand. Mercator was investigated for writing "suspicious letters" and was imprisoned in the castle at Rupelmonde for seven months, then all charges against him were dropped.

Mercator worked in astrology and cosmographical instrument making. This element is most clearly distinguished in the astrological volvelle that Mercator developed in May 1551. This unique instrument complemented the famous celestial globe that Mercator published in April 1551. His intention was to adapt this instrument not just to astronomy but to astrology. For the purpose, Mercator produced an isagogical instrument for making judgments out of Ptolemy, al-Qabīṣī, Joannes of Seville, Cardano, and some other astrologers.

Mercator's volvelle, or astrolabes, was a compact instrument used to observe the position of celestial bodies before the invention of the sextant. The instrument, one of a kind, is often linked with John Dee's work at Louwain between 1548 and 1550. The instructive functionality of the instrument indicates the interplay between astrological theory and practice in Mercator's work, which clearly intended to associate his notions of "astronomy" and "astrology" with the scholastic traditions of astrological *theorica*: astronomical theory and astrological physics. This interpretation was confirmed by the vocabulary of Mercator's further instructions. Although his astrological instrument offered little more than a novel presentation of popular astrological textbooks, Mercator consistently referred to its lists of significations as "natures." With this concern, Mercator let it be known that he equated astronomy and astrology.

Mercator was also one of the first people to connect the dates of historical solar and lunar eclipses with Julian dates calculated from Mercator's own understanding of the movements of the sun, moon, and Earth. Mercator took these calculated dates and linked them to dates of other events from the Babylonian, Greek, Hebrew, and Roman calendars in relation to the eclipses. The time origin was fixed from the genealogies of the Bible as 3,965 years before the birth of Christ. European scholars lauded this as Mercator's greatest achievement. The Catholic Church, however, placed Mercator's printed work on the *Index Librorum Prohibitorum* (List of Prohibited Books).

Martin J. Manning

See also: Astrolabe; Dee, John; Renaissance and Reformation Astrology

Further Reading

Broecke, Steven Vanden. 2013. *The Limits of Influence: Pico, Louvain, and the Crisis of Renaissance Astrology.* Leiden: Brill.

Crane, Nicholas. 2003. *Mercator: The Man Who Mapped the Planet.* New York: Henry Holt.

MESOAMERICAN ASTROLOGY

Nearly all of the literature of the indigenous cultures of Mexico and Central America was lost or destroyed in the Spanish conquest of the 16th century. However, enough remains, supplemented by archeological evidence and anthropological studies among contemporary Native Americans, to draw conclusions about the central role of the sky in their culture. Mesoamerican cultures were characterized by complex and accurate astronomically based calendars as well as a desire for society to mirror a cosmic order.

The identification of the political and social order with the cosmic order led to a highly state-centered astrology that took the form of elaborate buildings with astronomical orientations and imagery and rituals related to the calendar. This type of astrology was principally the concern of a political and religious elite whose power rested on the accurate reckoning of days and performance of rituals at the correct time. These rituals were related to the agricultural year, and much of their purpose was to ensure a good harvest. Astronomical time was viewed as a matter of interlocking cycles, with the greatest of cycles being that of the periodic creation and destruction of the world. (Although the date December 21, 2012, marked the end of a calendrical cycle, the Mayans did not believe it would see the destruction of the world, and the belief commonly held in New Age circles that they did rested on a fundamental misunderstanding of the Mayan calendar.) The solar year of 365 days, which was very accurately measured, coexisted with a "day-count" of 260 days, which was used for divinatory purposes. (Thirteen and 20 were both numbers of great significance for the Mayans, and 13 x 20 = 260.) Another cycle was the synodic period of 584–587 days between conjunctions of Venus and the sun. Venus was particularly important to many Mesoamerican cultures, and the Mayan building known as the "Palace of the Governor" in the city of Uxmal in present-day Mexico (probably dating from the 9th and 10th centuries CE) is oriented to the northern- and southernmost rising points of Venus and covered with glyphs representing Venus. The zodiac played less of a role for Mayans than for Europeans and other Afro-Eurasian astrologers. In one of the few surviving Mesoamerican representations it has 13 signs.

In addition to a keen awareness of the predictable and cyclic nature of the skies, however, Mesoamericans were also believers in the significance of celestial portents, including those of an unexpected and disruptive nature. Aztecs who survived the Spanish conquest remembered the invasion as having been preceded by disastrous signs such as a comet and a flaming column in the air. Eclipses, although predictable, were also considered heralds of disaster, and eclipse prediction was an important goal of Mesoamerican calendrical science.

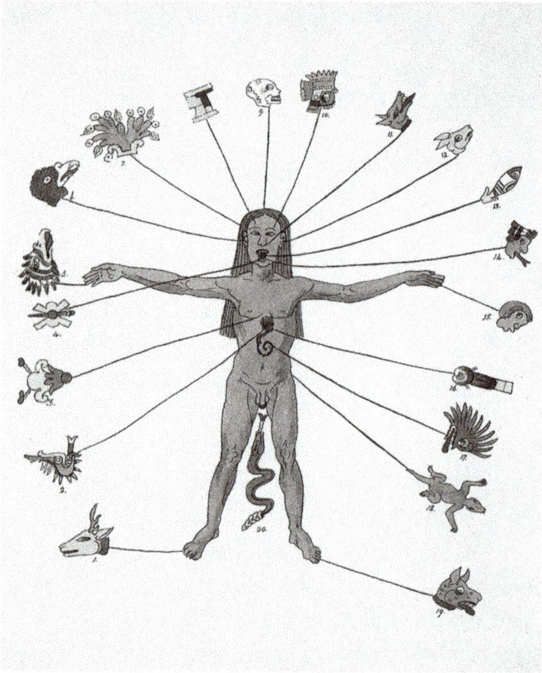

In a striking example of parallel development, an Aztec "zodiac man" displays many similarities to the European version. (Wellcome Collection)

Like other societies that practiced astrology, Mesoamericans linked astrology and medicine. The Aztecs viewed the body as a microcosm of the universe, with the heart playing the role of the sun, the diaphragm the Earth, and the skull the vault of heaven. Organs played similar functions in the microcosm as their complements did in the macrocosm; the heart gave heat to the body as the sun gave heat to the Earth. Because gold was related to the sun, and thus the heart, it was used as a treatment for heart pain. The day and time a person was born and the positions of the celestial bodies at that time influenced health as well as other aspects of her or his destiny. The day and time when an illness first manifested itself was also astrologically significant.

Although the main focus of Mesoamerican astrology was the welfare of the community as a whole and its harmony with the cosmos, there is also evidence that people similar to the consulting astrologers of Europe practiced in pre-Colombian Mesoamerica, giving advice to individuals on the basis of their interpretation of the skies. The evidence for this relies largely on the accounts of Spanish and other post-Conquest chroniclers, as the notebooks that these "calendrical shamans" carried with them did not survive the conquest. After the conquest, some Maya became interested in European astrology along with other aspects of the culture of the invaders. The so-called *Books of Chilam Balam*, 17th- and 18th-century compilations of European and indigenous materials for a Maya audience, some translated and some in their original languages, included European astronomical and astrological works.

William E. Burns

See also: Comets; Mundane Astrology; New Age

Further Reading

Aveni, Anthony F. 2001. *Skywatchers.* Austin: University of Texas Press.

Campion, Nicholas. 2012. *Astrology and Cosmology in the World's Religions.* New York: New York University Press.

George-Hirons, Amy. 2015. "Yokol Cab: Mayan Translations of European Astrological Texts and Images in the *Book of Chilam Balam of Kava.*" *Ethnohistory* 62: 525–552.

MESOPOTAMIAN ASTROLOGY

Mesopotamian astrology lies at the root of the Western astrological tradition. In fact, any astrological system that refers to the zodiac owes some debt to Mesopotamia. As an element of one of the earliest literary traditions, Mesopotamian astrology predates most other astrological traditions. From there, the astrological techniques of Mesopotamia entered other cultures with remarkable ease, adapting to the scientific, philosophical, and social contexts of new cultures. Nevertheless, Mesopotamian astrology philosophically differs from other Mediterranean astrological traditions, even when those systems build on citations from Mesopotamian sources. Although ancient sources never fully satisfy modern curiosity, sufficient Mesopotamian literature has survived to outline the function of astrologers in Mesopotamian culture, the religious context of astrology in Mesopotamia, its internal logic, and social practice.

The earliest Mesopotamians to leave a written record were the Sumerians (3000–2000 BCE). Although Sumerians took an interest in calendars, nothing among their writings constitutes astrology. Instead, the first Mesopotamian astrological omens date to the Old Babylonian period (ca. 1830–1531 BCE). These early omens were carefully structured to consider the effects of eclipses in different months, on several days, at specific times. Additionally, the omens considered eclipses of varying magnitudes, impacting and clearing in particular directions, and lasting for several periods of time. The development of a schematized structure considering many variables (including astronomical impossibilities) provided the foundation of the preeminent astrological composition, *Enūma Anu Enlil* ("When Anu and Enlil," ca. 720 BCE). Not only did *Enūma Anu Enlil* build upon the Old Babylonian eclipse omens, but it incorporated and integrated other Mesopotamian astrological compositions. For example, tablet 63 of *Enūma Anu Enlil* preserves "The Venus Tablet of Ammiṣaduqa (reigned 1646–1626 BCE, or 1582–1562 BCE)." This tablet reports the horizon phenomena, that is, earliest and latest visibilities, of Venus during the reign of a First Dynasty Babylonian king. These reports are paired with astrological predictions related to statecraft: scarcity of barley and straw, downfall of a large army, kings sending messages of hostility and reconciliation. The fact that the astronomical data in "The Venus Tablet of Ammiṣaduqa" precedes the compilation of *Enūma Anu Enlil* clouds the date of the composition, but the predictions invite philosophical speculations. According to one interpretation, "The Venus Tablet of Ammiṣaduqa" may record the astrological advice received by Ammiṣaduqa, but another explanation suggests that the tablet was the result of coupling astronomical observations with historical records.

The degree to which Mesopotamian astrology embraced empiricism remains an open question. Mesopotamians certainly did not believe themselves to engage in an empirical coordination of celestial occurrences with terrestrial events. To these ancient people, the gods had revealed the astrological arts to mankind. Modern scholars operating outside the Mesopotamian context have noted traces of omens based on empirical observations. At one extreme, Peter Huber has hypothesized that Mesopotamian astrology arose as a response to a series of spectacular eclipses that appeared before (and perhaps precipitated) dynastic changes in government. Although this hypothesis fits well with the importance of eclipses in Mesopotamian astrology, it cannot be as easily reconciled with the eclipse omens which defy astronomical possibility but appear in omen literature. For example, because Mesopotamians used lunar months that began at conjunction (new moon), solar eclipses should occur at the very beginning or end of the month; lunar eclipses should fall at opposition (full moon), but some texts considered the possibility of an eclipse on any day of the month. Furthermore, some sets of astrological predictions collectively reveal an internal logic by associating different countries with different directions. Despite the composition of omens according to unstated astrological rules, some portion of Mesopotamian astrology, the so-called historical astrology, coordinates celestial events with the historical tradition as Mesopotamians understood it. For example, an appendix to the *Enūma Anu Enlil* called the "assumed 29th *Ahû* (strange) tablet" seems to couple the results of Alexander the Great's victory at Gaugamela (331 BCE) with an astronomical description of the eclipse that preceded the battle.

To understand further the sources of Mesopotamian astrology, a summary of Mesopotamian astrological genres beyond the Old Babylonian eclipse omens and the *Enūma Anu Enlil* is useful. Such a summary depends in part on a distinction between astrology, astronomy, and ritual texts. The Old Babylonian omens focus on eclipses of the sun and moon, with these prognostications being adopted by neighboring countries. Only six Mesopotamian astrological texts date from the Middle Babylonian and Middle Assyrian periods. These texts mainly treat eclipses. The *Enūma Anu Enlil* as codified in the neo-Assyrian (911–609 BCE) period contains a mythological introduction, lengthy sections about the moon and sun, meteorological omens on thunder and winds, and a final set of omens on the stars and planets. The *Enūma Anu Enlil* is preserved in fragments and many portions have yet to be edited and translated. These gaps may occasionally be filled by two genres of excerpts, the first of which respects the order of the original composition and the second of which assembles omens from the entire text of the *Enūma Anu Enlil* and which relate to an observation or a particular topic. Modern understanding of this central text is augmented by three associated genres of commentaries. The first of these explains substitutions that allow omens to be reapplied to new situations; the second explains the meanings of words and phrases in the *Enūma Anu Enlil*. Finally, a separate composition *Šumma Šin ina tāmartišu* ("If the Moon in its Appearance") combines excerpts and commentary. In addition to these canonical sources, several copies of a *Diviner's Manual* from the seventh century BCE list the titles of astrological works and address the question of when omens might be invalid or negated. To these literary works, documentary evidence for Mesopotamian astrology appears in the *Letters* and *Reports* from the neo-Assyrian and neo-Babylonian Empires. The *Letters* to the king were written by scribes in one column on tablets longer than they were wide. The *Reports* contained observations and excerpts from other astrological texts on horizontal tables. In the fifth century BCE, Mesopotamian astrology expanded from statecraft to the lives of individuals. To this end, Mesopotamian astrologers composed *Horoscopes*, and several miscellaneous texts detailed their techniques of interpretation.

In order to navigate the lengthy *Enūma Anu Enlil* and its array of commentaries, the Mesopotamian court maintained a network of scribes skilled in astrological interpretation. Astrology constituted a specialized practice, often described as "secret" (pirištu) or "protected" (niṣirtu). Whether astrologers were privy to a "trade secret" or had mastered an "occult science," they were known as "Scribes of *Enūma Anu Enlil.*" Some "Scribes of *Enūma Anu Enlil*" signed their names to the *Letters*, and these individuals also appear executing other scribal or priestly duties (both divine and clerical) under other titles, appropriate to the specific task. These celestial scribes worked in collaboration with scribes learned in other methods of divination, such as examining the entrails of sacrifices, and with temple personnel charged with performing rituals designed to negate or mitigate negative omens. In some cases, the same individual may have filled multiple roles. The functions ascribed to these Scribes of *Enūma Anu Enlil* may have varied in the neo-Assyrian (911–609 BCE), neo-Babylonian (626–529 BCE), and Achaemenid (538–330 BCE) Empires, but their expertise was never limited strictly to celestial divination. Typically, these scribes occupied intersecting roles in the priestly and scribal culture of Mesopotamia.

This Assyrian limestone stela depicts the Moon god Sin, associated with lunar crescents. (Archaeological Museum, Aleppo/DeAgostini/Getty Images)

Mesopotamians considered the scribes of *Enūma Anu Enlil* copyists, archivists, and interpreters of divine wisdom, but an ancient bibliographic reference revealed the author of *Enūma Anu Enlil* by recording that the work came "from the mouth of Ea," a major water deity of the Babylonian pantheon. Not only was Ea the author of the means by which omens were interpreted, but Mesopotamians considered their gods the authors of ominous celestial phenomena. As the (Sumerian) mythological introduction of *Enūma Anu Enlil* relates,

> When An, Enlil, and Enki, the great gods, in their firm counsel established the boat of Sin (crescent moon) as the great eternal order of heaven and earth, they established the waxing of the crescent moon, the renewal of the month, and the signs of heaven and earth.

As divine attempts to communicate with humanity, these signs were messages with an intended recipient and a purpose. According to Mesopotamian theology, the gods sent unprovoked celestial omens to all humanity, but only scribes with knowledge of divinely authored astrological literature could understand these communiqués. After performing the specialized task of interpretation, these scribes returned the divine communication to religious contexts by notifying the king and priests who focused on the gods' purpose in communication. Positive messages constituted confirmations; negative messages warned the king. In the context of Mesopotamian astrology, a bad omen was not a dire pronouncement of unalterable doom but rather an opportunity to heed the message of the gods, who advised delay, purification, or other actions under the direction of theological authorities.

Copious *Letters* from Assyrian and Babylonian scholars describe the social context of Mesopotamian astrology. These *Letters* detail the practical concerns of Mesopotamian astrologers: observations and their differences due to cloudy skies or ignorant observers, citations of favorite passages from *Enūma Anu Enlil*, the proper scheduling of rituals to dispel baleful omens, coordination of astrology with other modes of divination. Although the manipulative soothsayer has become a literary trope, the *Letters* do not suggest connivance. Like most royal Mesopotamian correspondence, the *Letters* contain flattering descriptions of the king's wisdom, but the scribes still invite the king to make his own observations, deny ominous import to predicted phenomena that did not occur, and err on the side of caution in performing rituals. Even the most dire of predictions could be avoided by appointing a "substitute king." In some cases, particularly terrible eclipse omens prompted the king to appoint a substitute and assume the title of "Farmer." Despite this temporary abdication, the scholarly network maintained correspondence with the true king. When the omen and its effects were deemed to have passed, the "Farmer" chose the time of execution of his hapless usurper. With the doom having been visited on the scapegoat king, the true king returned to power. Most of these rituals (known as *namburbū*) were not as disruptive as the "substitute king ritual" but rather entailed playing drums at night or sacrificing at certain altars or chanting specific prayers.

Through such observances, the king heeded the "decisions," "judgments," and "decrees" of the gods, for the *Letters* described the omens in legal metaphors. Not only did Mesopotamians metaphorically link celestial phenomena to the words of the gods, but they could interpret the astral bodies under observation metaphorically. The sun, moon, and Venus shared names with the Mesopotamian divinities Šamaš, Sin, and Inanna, but personification of the celestial bodies enabled a range of metaphorical interpretations. Thus, omens addressed the conditions that the sun "closed its eyes" (became dark or eclipsed?), the moon "disappeared in distress" (set during an eclipse), or Venus "wore a beard" (became radiant). These omens not only rely on the personification of the celestial bodies as gods, but they also draw on the metaphors and multilayered readings of cuneiform signs and wordplay inculcated through the tradition of scribal education. Just as the existence of *namburbū* rituals indicates that the Mesopotamians did not consider the celestial phenomena to be the cause of terrestrial events, the extensive use of metaphor in omen lists establishes that the gods communicated through Mesopotamian idioms.

In this way, Mesopotamian astrology integrated with and depended on culturally specific religious and scribal traditions. As a fundamentally Mesopotamian method of interpreting divine communications, astrology seems too bound to Mesopotamian culture to allow easy cultural transfer to foreign contexts. Nonetheless, eclipses constitute one of the most awe-inspiring phenomena of the natural world, and neighboring cultures were impressed with the Mesopotamian art of interpretation. In the Old Babylonian period, Syrians in Mari, Hittites in Ḫattuša, Amorites in Emar, and other Mesopotamian city-states adopted eclipse omens. Sometime after the Persian conquest of Egypt in 525 BCE, Egypt also adopted eclipse omens from Mesopotamia. In fact, the Greek writers of late antiquity, Hephaestio of Thebes (415 CE) and John of Lydus (560 CE), ascribe to Egypt several eclipse omens for which astonishingly close parallels maybe found in the *Enūma Anu Enlil*. In many cases, these non-Mesopotamian astrological traditions introduced a causal relationship between the celestial event and events within the human sphere. Without the possibility of *namburbū* rituals to negotiate divine edicts, astrology took a potentially deterministic turn. Moreover, Mesopotamian astrologers enabled the diffusion of astrology when they transferred astrological interpretation from the realm of statecraft to the domain of the individual. In the late fifth century BCE, proto-horoscopes (lacking any reference to the ascendant or houses) connected the individual with stars. The presence of Greek names in the proto-horoscopes has been interpreted as evidence that personal astrology constituted a cultural product for foreign mercenaries. Against this interpretation, post-Alexandrian Mesopotamians often used Greek names. The shift from mundane astrology to personal astrology in the late fifth century BCE created a rising interest in Mesopotamian astrology by foreigners, and while the complex network of Mesopotamian mundane astrology could not be replicated in foreign contexts, certain astrological doctrines could be profitably exported.

Most obviously, the zodiacal signs originated in Mesopotamia. Likewise, the division of the planets into benefic and malefic began in Mesopotamia, albeit somewhat differently. For example, whereas Hellenistic astrology defines Venus as generally benefic, Mesopotamian omens indicate that Venus was benefic as a morning star and malefic as an evening star. Beyond the planets and the division of the sky, Mesopotamia also produced astrological doctrines of the Western tradition. When William Lilly structured astrological interpretation in the 17th century, he acknowledged five "essential dignities," three of which ultimately derived from Mesopotamia. First, the triplicities began as a relationship between months but extended to zodiacal signs. Second, the exaltations began as *bīt niṣirti* (secret houses). Third, the terms also seem to have originated in Mesopotamia, although the exact date remains unclear. Only the domiciles, or house rulerships, which depend on a Greek cosmology and the explicitly Egyptian decans did not hail from Mesopotamia. Authors in the Greek (and Sanskrit) tradition adopted Mesopotamian elements, which have permeated astrology worldwide. Although these authors attempted to rationalize astrology into a scientific and deterministic system of causality, the elements of their analysis issued from the Mesopotamian tradition of decoding divine revelations.

Micah T. Ross

See also: Hellenistic Astrology; Mundane Astrology; Politics

Further Reading

Brown, David. 2000. *Mesopotamian Planetary Astronomy–Astrology*. Groningen: Styx.
Hunger, Hermann, ed. 1992. *Astrological Reports to Assyrian Kings*. State Archives of Assyria 8. Helsinki: Helsinki University Press.
Koch-Westenholz, Ulla. 1995. *Mesopotamian Astrology*. CNI Publications 19. Copenhagen: Museum Tusculanum Press.
Reiner, Erica. 1995. *Astral Magic in Babylonia*. Transactions of the American Philosophical Society n.s. 85.4. Philadelphia: American Philosophical Society.
Rochberg-Halton, Francesca. 1988. *Aspects of Babylonian Celestial Divination*. Archiv für Orientforschung Beiheft 22. Horn, Austria: Ferdinand Berger und Sohne Gesellschaft.
Rochberg-Halton, Francesca. 2004. *The Heavenly Writing*. New York: Cambridge University Press.
Rochberg-Halton, Francesca. 2010. *In the Path of the Moon*. Leiden: Brill.

MORANDI, ORAZIO (1570–1630)

Orazio Morandi was a monk of the Vallombrosan order and a correspondent of Galileo. He is best known for an astrological prediction in 1630 regarding the death of Pope Urban VIII, which landed him in jail (where he died) and which likely helped trigger the 1631 bull *Contra astrologos iudiciarios* (Against Judicial Astrologers) condemning astrology and especially the dissemination of astrological predictions. After obtaining his degree in both canon and Roman law at the University of Rome, he undertook an ecclesiastical career in the Grand Duchy of Tuscany. In Florence he became a fixture of the local cultural scene before finally attracting the attention of Don Giovanni de' Medici, the natural son of Grand Duke Cosimo I. In the company of Don Giovanni, he studied natural philosophy and practiced alchemy and astrology. His abilities as an astrologer helped cement his connections with the Medici family, to whom he, like Galileo, apparently gave astrological consultations. Eventually, Medici patronage gained for him a transfer to Rome as abbot of the monastery of Santa Prassede and the generalship of his order.

In the years following his arrival in Rome in 1613, he enriched the library of the monastery with many texts, printed and manuscript, including those regarding occult matters, and opened it up as a lending library to high-level ecclesiastics and their associates, whose patronage likely prevented excessive scrutiny from the authorities. Although he and the other monks provided astrological consultations to the local community, they began compiling a comprehensive astrological encyclopedia for in-house consultation. Apart from chapters dedicated to such technical subjects as solstice points, the aspects, and the theories of the houses and directions according to both Ptolemy and Regiomontanus, they planned to compare a vast array of natal charts to the fortunes of their subjects–somewhat along the lines suggested by Francis Bacon in *De Augmentis Scientiarum* (3:4). Monks were delegated to look into the parish records when they could not get oral testimony. The results would be divided into subsections on good fortune and ill fortune, with a detailed catalog of catastrophes. In February 1630, Morandi divulged his results regarding the nativity of Urban VIII in the form of a letter dated from Lyon that circulated far and wide. According to his account, the dangerous presence of Mars and the moon was indicated already at birth. Venus, though favorably situated, was no match for these evil planets, especially because it in turn was blocked by the opposition of Saturn in the eighth house. Progressing these directions to 1630, he predicted that the solar eclipse due to occur in June in the sign of Gemini, in the vicinity of Mars, the planetary ruler of late middle age, Urban's current stage of life, would be highly significant. And the fact that Rome was under Taurus, a whole sign away from Gemini, where the eclipse would be occurring, was not enough to save Urban's life. The pope, already inclined to give credence to astrological predictions, if emanating from authoritative sources, ordered the governor of Rome to take action. Morandi, jailed and tortured, soon succumbed to the harshness of his confinement.

Brendan Dooley

See also: Christianity; Galilei, Galileo; Legal Regulation of Astrology; Politics; Renaissance and Reformation Astrology

Further Reading

Dooley, Brendan. 2002. *Morandi's Last Prophecy and the End of Renaissance Politics.* Princeton: Princeton University Press.

Germana Ernst. 1993. "Scienza, astrologia e politica nella Roma barocca: La biblioteca di don O. M." In *Bibliothecae Selectae, da Cusano a Leopardi*, ed. Eugenio Canone, 217–252. Florence: Olschki.

Stefano Tabacchi. 2012. "Orazio Morandi" *Dizionario Biografico degli Italiani* 76.

MORIN, JEAN-BAPTISTE (1583–1656)

Jean-Baptiste Morin was born in Villefranche-sur-Saône in the French province of Beaujolais on February 23, 1583, at 8:33 a.m. local apparent time according to his report of his own nativity. He studied philosophy at Aix and later medicine at Avignon, earning his medical degree in 1613, but was also a talented mathematician and astronomer. In 1630 he was appointed professor of Mathematics at the Collège Royal; in 1638 he was present to record the birth of the future Louis XIV (the Sun King). Morin's first, short work on astrology appeared in 1623, but his magnum opus, the *Astrologia Gallica* in 26 books, was published only posthumously in 1661, by Queen Marie Louise of Poland (1611–1667), whose nativity is discussed in it.

Morin sought to restore the intellectual position of astrology at a time when it was losing ground on the European Continent, and was frequently at odds with his contemporaries. The most well-known objects of his attacks include Galileo Galilei, René Descartes (1596–1650), and Cardinal Richelieu (1585–1642). Morin considered Richelieu to have robbed him of his fair reward for solving the problem of longitude in navigation, and in his work he often returns to this and other grievances. Morin also engages with earlier critics of astrology, including Pico della Mirandola (1463–1494), noting with satisfaction that as soon as Pico had completed his famous refutation of astrology, he had died at a time predicted to him by three different astrologers.

The *Astrologia Gallica* attempts to present a rational and internally coherent system of astrology based on a limited number of axioms. Although Morin's views on individual points of astrological doctrine frequently clashed with those of his junior contemporary Placidus, the two men were united by a wish to purge astrology of everything "fictitious" or merely symbolical and establish it firmly on the basis of natural philosophy and physics.

Morin's method of chart interpretation is based on the concept of *determinations*, which proceed from the celestial houses: a planet occupying a house (or, in the case of an empty house, the one opposite), or ruling one of the signs falling in it, is thereby determined toward the matters signified by that house, so that its natural qualities and *celestial state*—that is, its dignity or debility by virtue of zodiacal position and aspects with other planets—will find expression in the corresponding area of life. Planets have no fixed or universal significations (such as the sun always signifying honors), although they do possess a natural *analogy* with certain phenomena. If the sun in good celestial state is determined toward honors by occupying the 10th house, it will thus manifest honors more fully and easily than Saturn similarly placed, because the sun has greater analogy with honors; but both planets will nevertheless bestow distinctions on the native, whereas the sun not determined toward honors by any connection with the 10th house or its rulers will not do so.

The house system used by Morin was that of the 15th-century astronomer Regiomontanus (not the so-called Morinus system, which Morin had devised solely to complement Regiomontanus houses at extreme latitudes). Again like Placidus, Morin also used a single method for dividing the houses and for primary directions, which are the cornerstone of his elaborate system of predictive techniques. According to Morin, Regiomontanus was the first astrologer properly to have understood Ptolemy's method of direction, incorrectly applied even by Ptolemy himself! Rejecting Ptolemy's use of the sun and moon as universal significators, Morin preferred to direct all planets as significators according to their determinations in the radix or birth chart.

Having further rejected the "fictitious" profections, Morin made revolutions the second most important part of his predictive system, giving them an intermediate position between the radix and its directions on the one hand and transits on the other. Revolutions of both the sun and the moon should be cast for the place at which the native finds himself at the time, and directions calculated from both kinds of figure. Despite the faith Morin had in this method, his lunar revolutions were often significantly miscalculated, largely due to imperfect tables. Transits, the final link in this chain of prediction, were to be examined in the light of the radix and its directions as well as the solar and lunar revolutions. If this prospect was daunting, Morin maintained that the methods of "the old or common astrology" were no less so.

As shown by this last comment, Morin wanted to reform astrology, chiefly by purging it of elements that he and other astrologers of his time mistakenly regarded as Arabic inventions, though Morin did not shrink from criticizing even Ptolemy. Apart from what was said above, Morin also rejected the terms, decans, and other subdivisions of the signs, as well as the entire hyleg doctrine; he formulated a new system of triplicity rulerships, and added the semisextile (30°) and quincunx (150°) to the traditional aspect angles. Even so, his reformatory zeal was moderate compared to that of such contemporaries as Placidus and Kepler. In matters of natural philosophy and cosmology, Morin was fairly conservative, adhering to a scholastic Aristotelianism and favoring the geocentric Tychonic system over Galileo's heliocentrism.

In the late 19th century, as renewed interest in astrology spread from Great Britain to the Continent, the *Astrologia Gallica* was rediscovered and studied in France and Germany. Morin's system was the subject of a book published in 1897 by Henri Selva (pseudonym) and was further discussed, nearly half a century later, by his student Jean Rozières (writing under the name Jean Hieroz). The prominent German astrologer Erich Carl Kühr (1899–1951) was greatly influenced by Morin, but preferred Placidus house division and directions to the Regiomontanus system. During the second half of the 20th century, the Morin method was brought to the attention of the English-speaking world through the astrologer Zoltan Mason (1906–2002) from present-day Slovakia and his American students, the most well-known of whom is Robert Zoller (b. 1947). Since the 1970s, English translations of several volumes of the *Astrologia Gallica* have appeared.

Martin Gansten

See also: House Systems; Natal Astrology; Placidus; Renaissance and Reformation Astrology

Further Reading

Morin, Jean-Baptiste. 1974–2010. *Astrologia Gallica Books 13–19 and 21–26*, trans. James H. Holden, Pepita Sanchís Llacer, Anthony Louis LaBruzza, and Richard S. Baldwin. 10 vols. Tempe, AZ: American Federation of Astrologers.

MUNDANE ASTROLOGY

Mundane astrology aims to analyze and understand history, and manage and predict political affairs. As defined by Charles Carter (1887–1968), the most prominent British astrologer of the mid-20th century, "The aim then of Political Astrology is the study of all that pertains to the life of politically incorporated body, or nation. It must comprehend the cultural and intellectual life, the religious life, the economic, and so forth" (*An Introduction to Political Astrology*, 13).

The term *mundane astrology* is derived from the Latin *mundus* meaning "world." The Latin term Mundi was used to describe the application of astrology to the matters of political and collective significance from the 11th-century onward (the first medieval Latin astrological text was the *Liber Planetis at Mundi Climatibus*). In the European Middle Ages mundane astrology was usually known as the study of "Revolutions"—i.e., the revolutions of Jupiter and Saturn around the Earth, which together were seen as the main timers of history. The use of the word *revolution* to apply to political upheavals is derived from the astrological usage.

In the Western tradition mundane astrology is recognized as one of the four forms of judicial astrology but the other three may still be used for political purposes. Politicians may turn to astrologers to have their birth charts cast (natal astrology), select auspicious moments to launch new enterprises (electional astrology), or answer specific questions (horary astrology). Astroeconomics and financial astrology may also be bracketed as mundane, while having their own specialities, while meteorological astrology also has mundane consequences. In the broad sense, then, any form of astrology can be used for political purposes. In the narrow sense mundane astrology is the branch of astrology that deals specifically with the analysis of history, society and politics.

Bearing in mind the blurring between the personal and professional, it may not always be possible to decide when astrology is mundane and when it is not. For example, if relationships are political when they involve power relations between men and women, or between adults and children, then the comparison of the birth charts of people in relationships is political. Traditionally mundane astrology has two main functions; first, to understand the past and, second, to predict the future. Both are contained within a greater purpose: to manage the present. This aspiration can also be divided into two. First, within the context of millennial and apocalyptic fears of political disintegration or global catastrophe, and the lesser, but still disruptive, significance of planetary aspects, its task is to preserve peace, order, and stability. Second, it can provide political advantage over one's rivals. Advantage in turn can be gained in one of two ways: either by manipulating time and space, or by harmonizing the institutions of state with universal cosmic principles.

It is clear that all cultures that assume a relationship between terrestrial and celestial affairs use the stars and planets for general social and political purposes; some form of political astrology is practiced in most premodern cultures, if not all. Such uses focus around the timing of significant political and religious rituals, most often in connection with the key points in the solar and lunar cycles (solstices and equinoxes, and new and full moons, respectively).

The earliest known astrology in ancient Mesopotamia, where the technical basis was laid for both Western and Indian astrology, was mundane in nature, being concerned exclusively with affairs of state. Most of our written evidence dates from the Assyrian period of the eighth to seventh centuries BCE and indicates that the astrologers task was first to predict likely developments in view of planetary movements and then advise the king accordingly. The emphasis was on the management of the state by averting crises and taking advantage of auspicious moments.

Theory

The notion of a cosmic state in which the human society is intimately connected to the celestial world was adopted by two of the most important Greek philosophers, Plato and Aristotle. Plato developed a model in which the institutions and administration of the ideal state should be harmonized perfectly with the mathematical and geometrical operation of the universe, and the flow of time as embodied in the motions of the stars and planets. Aristotle explained time and change through a series of causes and influences in which all things in the universe, including stars and state, are intimately related through mutual interconnections. The Stoics added a grand scheme in which all things were related through their underlying sympathies, the essential inner nature of things. In what has been termed the Great Chain of Being, all things from the smallest to greatest were interrelated. For example, politically, kings connected to the sun, Leo, and gold because they were, in their underlying sympathy, essentially the same. If, for example, events were arranged with the sun and Leo were prominent, the king would benefit.

The system locked each planet into a series of interconnections with both every other planet and every zodiac sign, allowing for the precise prediction of the future together with the management of political stability and advantage. The scheme spread to India, adapting to the existing calendar and polytheism, surviving intact to the present day, whereas in Europe its use at the highest level of politics came to an end in the latter part of the 17th century.

The major technical and philosophical reform of the system was undertaken in the 17th century by Johannes Kepler, who rejected almost the entire structure of medieval and classical astrology, replacing it with a scheme based on planetary cycles and aspects, with only a minimal role preserved for the zodiac, and a maximum role for free choice and effective management of the state. Kepler adopted Plato's geometrical conception of the universe in which astrology is an effective tool for political prediction and management because individuals, states, and planets are an integrated part of the same system. Therefore, as the planets move, so do people, and the movement of people can be seen in the movement of the planets. Kepler's system was never adopted in European politics, although the notion that one set of laws underpins planetary motions, political change, and individual life became the theoretical basis for the development of sociology by Auguste Comte (1798–1857). Comte reasoned that if sufficient data could be gathered, sociology would be able to demonstrate how the laws of planetary motion were expressed in collective affairs, fulfilling Kepler's hope that society might then be better managed for the collective good. Keith Thomas concluded that "in [the astrologers] confident assumption that the principles of human society were capable of human explanation, we can detect the germ of modern sociology" (Thomas 1971, 386–387).

Kepler's work is the foundation of modern mundane astrology. It was updated by C. G. Jung, who revived the Platonic theory of archetypes, locating them in the collective unconscious. Society is seen as fundamentally unable to take free choices and therefore dominated by eruptions of the archetypes into the collective unconscious. Individuals may separate themselves from such pressures by developing self-awareness, and politicians (like Babylonian kings) may better manage society by anticipating and averting future crises.

It is generally accepted that crowds find it more difficult to take free choices than do individuals and that mundane events, such as revolutions, may be more fated. However, being used to manage national affairs and gain political advantage, mundane astrology necessarily assumes a level of freedom of choice. It therefore generally rejects the "lazy" or "idle" argument, according to which a predicted outcome will eventuate regardless of human action. Instead politicians must act to change the future. In cases in which the future does seem to be preordained, for example in the case of apocalyptic prophecies, Karl Popper argued that it became paradoxically necessary for the faithful to work to make the predetermined outcome come about, a philosophy he termed "activism." Stripped of its astrological features this idea survived in 20th-century revolutionary Marxism.

The Planets

For political purposes the classical scheme had a number of key features. First was the interpretation of horoscopes, using the zodiac signs, planets, and houses. Each planet had a political function that was then exercised according to the rules of horoscopic astrology. The principles were set out in Vettius Valen's *Anthology* (first century) and Claudius Ptolemy's *Tetrabiblos* (second century) According to this system each planet has a set of associations as follows:

Sun: kings, leaders, leadership
Moon: queens, cities, crowds, homes
Mercury: intellectuals, teachers, communication
Venus: love, peace, diplomacy, the arts
Mars: generals, war, violence
Jupiter: judges, justice, alliances, freedom, benefits
Saturn: administrators, austerity, restriction, delays, endings

This system has survived intact to the present day, with the addition of the three commonly accepted modern outer planets, Uranus, Neptune and Pluto, which had been assigned a broadly destabilizing significance.

Uranus: idealism, revolution, technological innovation
Neptune: visionaries, mystics, muddle, confusion, corruption
Pluto: deep, underground passions and forces, the influence of the past, confrontation

The planets are then interpreted in line with the standard techniques of horoscopic astrology, operating according to the zodiac signs within which they are placed, and applied to areas of life represented by the 12 houses.

The Houses

The meanings of the houses have not changed substantially since the formulation of horoscopic astrology in the last centuries BCE. As adapted in 20th-century texts their meanings are as follows:

First: the state; the myths, identity, and image of the state
Second: financial resources

Third: education and transport; propaganda; the media
Fourth: property and material resources; opposition to the government
Fifth: the arts and creative life; children
Sixth: civil service; health and medical services
Seventh: foreign policy
Eighth: international economic relations
Ninth: religion, ideology
Tenth: the executive government, monarch, head of state
Eleventh: legislature
Twelfth: subversion; intelligence services

Until the 17th century the rules of interpretation were the complex ones inherited from Hellenistic astrology. For example the condition of the monarch could be shown by the planet ruling the zodiac sign containing the cusp of the 10th house. That planet may then in turn be involved in a chain of further associations, and so on ad infinitum. Modern astrology is technically simpler. In contrast to medieval astrology, the presence of a planet in the tenth house is broadly enough to indicate the condition of the monarch: for example, Mars is confrontational and may indicate an aggressive heard of state and Venus would suggest a diplomatic one (given that planetary meanings will still be moderated by their zodiacal position). A transit over a one of these planets will then coincide with either confrontational or diplomatic tendencies.

Ingress Horoscopes

In the Ptolemaic system the casting of horoscopes for the sun's annual ingress (entry) into Aries provides the most important analysis of the coming year, along with horoscopes for the sun's ingress, or revolution, into the three other cardinal signs (Cancer, Libra, and Capricorn), which provide more short-term detail. Horoscopes could also be cast for less frequent events, including predictable ones such as eclipses (which occurred at either new or full moons, but endowed them with greater power), and unpredictable ones such as comets. Horoscopes for non-eclipsed new and full moons provided further information between these major events, together with daily planetary transits. The purpose of mundane horoscopes is invariably event-oriented and concerned with such general events as political upheavals, economic fortunes, harvests, and health.

Archaeoastronomy: Horoscopes for Towns and Cities

The application of mundane astrology in archaeoastronomy (the inclusion of astronomical symbolism, alignments, or orientation in monumental architecture) is a means of harmonizing society with the sky and cosmos. For example, Stonehenge's orientation to the solstices and the Great Pyramid's to the cardinal points (north, south, east, and west) turned both into sites of profound ritual significance at which state and society met the cosmos. In India, China, and Mesoamerica, it also became customary to align great cities and temples with the cardinal axis, or key points in the solar calendar, in order to maximize political stability.

The casting of horoscopes for auspicious moments for the foundation of towns and cities is a development of the principles of archaeoastronomy. There are traditions that some of the great cities of the ancient and early medieval world were founded at astrologically auspicious moments, including Persepolis, Seleucia, Constantinople, and Cairo. However, a rare one for which firm evidence survives is Baghdad, founded on July 30, 762. In recent times it is reported that the city of Naypyidaw was founded as the new capital of Myanmar in 2005 on astrological advice.

National Horoscopes

There is a long tradition of the astrological foundation of cities and coronation of monarchs dating back to the first millennium BCE. Horoscopes for coronations were cast from classical times, in order to choose an auspicious moment to begin a reign (the earliest extant example dates to the coronation of Antiochus of Commagene in 109 BCE). With the emergence of the nation state came the development of the idea of the national chart, the horoscope cast for a politically significant moment such as independence or the inauguration of a new regime. The first major example is a horoscope cast for the independence of the American colonies in 1776 and published in 1787, combining astrological positions on July 4, 1776, with that year's Cancer ingress. The idea of horoscopes for states was not promoted until the latter part of the 20th century by Charles Carter. A spate of chart collections were published in the early 1980s as a result of which national charts have become a standard tool in mundane astrology.

Planetary Cycles

Planetary movements can be understood without any reference to a horoscope, and when taken in pairs this leads to the concept of the planetary cycle; the movement of any two planets from conjunction to opposition and back to conjunction. The rationale, which appears to have been developed in Persia around the first century, was that the slower moving planets, chiefly Jupiter and Saturn, relate to long-term historical developments. Jupiter's orbit of the sun takes around 12 years, Saturn's is around 29 years, and every 20 years the planets meet in a conjunction. The whole series of conjunctions rotates through the zodiac in a period of around 960 years, within which there are subperiods created by conjunctions in the elements—the fire, earth, air, and water signs, respectively. Each conjunction relates to political and religious upheaval, with the first conjunction in a new element being more important and the first in an entirely new cycle the most important. The range of possibilities might therefore increase in magnitude from riots and unrest, to a change of dynasty or a new world prophet.

The scheme was codified in various forms, giving rise to the notion of the historical period. For example, Abū Ma'shar created the following scheme of six successive chronological phases in world history, characterized by shifts in religious history:

1. Jupiter conjunct Saturn = Judaism
2. Jupiter conjunct Mars = Chaldean Religion
3. Jupiter conjunct Sun = Egyptian Religion
4. Jupiter conjunct Venus = Islam
5. Jupiter conjunct Mercury = Christianity
6. Jupiter conjunct Moon = Antichrist

Franciscus Florentinus (b. ca. 1420), dean of the College of Theologians in Florence, imagined seven phases.

1. Jupiter conjunct Saturn: dominated by Saturn, men were savage and lived by agriculture.
2. Jupiter conjunct Saturn: dominated by Jupiter, development of Judaism and morality.
3. Jupiter conjunct Saturn and Mars: dominated by war.
4. Jupiter conjunct Saturn and the sun: rise of Egypt, solar religion and magnificent civilizations.
5. Jupiter conjunct Saturn and Mercury: science, austerity, the Greek philosophers, Christianity.
6. Jupiter conjunct Saturn and Venus: The current age; Islam, luxury, decadence.
7. Jupiter conjunct Saturn and the moon: The future age, the Antichrist.

This scheme was modified in the late 20th century when the three new outer planets (Uranus, Neptune, and Pluto) were added, mainly by the French astrologers Joseph Gouchon and Andre Barbault. Jupiter and Saturn are then relegated to a minor role and the cycles (particularly conjunctions, squares, and oppositions) of the new planets are said to relate to revolutionary moments, such as the social upheavals in the 1960s, the fall of the Berlin Wall in 1989 and the Arab Spring of 2011.

Cosmic Geography

Cosmic geography relates the sky to locations on the surface of the Earth. The Mesopotamian astrologers used correspondences between the stars, planets, and places to determine where astrologically predicted events are likely to take place. In the second century, Claudius Ptolemy systematized the scheme to produce 72 regions, each ruled by one zodiac sign, a model that has only recently begun to fall into disuse. Until the late 20th century, for example, an astrological event in Aries would be routinely related to France, Germany, or Britain, all of which were in an Arien zone. Since the 1980s Ptolemy's scheme has been largely replaced by astrocartography, in which zodiac signs are ignored and instead the locations at which each planet is either rising, culminating, or setting, at any particular moment, are connected by lines that indicate significant places. If, for example, Mars is rising at

Washington then one might expect martial developments both there and (Washington being the capital city) in the entire United States.

The Great Year and Astrological Ages

The idea of great periods of history (so-called great years) defined by planetary conjunctions, appears first in Plato, who argued that history reaches a critical point and begins again when all seven planets and the stars simultaneously return to their locations at the creation. The concept of periodic destruction and renewal influenced ideas that planetary cycles bring critical points in history, together with apocalyptic prophecies. Eugenio Garin, who argued that Renaissance astrology constituted "a precise philosophy of history based on a conception of the universe, and characterised by a consistent naturalism and a rigid determinism" (Garin 1976, 16). He added, "As one can see, the theme of 'newness,' of a new life, a new age, new worlds, new heavens, new earths—which would run so eloquently through the centuries of the Renaissance . . . was originally nothing more than an astrological commonplace" (Garin 1976, 18).

The modern theory of astrological ages characterized by zodiac signs is attested in astrological literature from the 19th century and became a standard feature of mundane astrology in the 20th, largely as a result of Theosophical influences. The theory holds that the roughly 2,000-year periods during which the sun rises in a sidereal zodiac sign or constellation, measured by the precession of the equinoxes, relates to the character of the times. There is no consensus on the dates or duration of the ages, and the idea of the coming Aquarian Age has been blended with Theosophical millennial predictions of a rise in spiritual awareness associated with the transition to the New Age.

Calendars

Calendars perform two functions of relevance to mundane astrology. First, they provide annual moments at which events of religious or political significance can be commemorated or celebrated. The repetition of such events year after year binds the community around shared customs and loyalties, harmonizing society with the stars. One class of such calendar festivals is clearly based on astrologically significant moments. For example, the Roman festivals of Saturnalia and Sol Invictus and Christian Christmas all equate to the winter solstice. The Buddhist festival of Wesak is held at the full moon in Taurus and Jewish Pesach (Passover) and Christian Easter coincide with the full moon following the spring equinox. Second, festivals can be suitable moments to ascertain astrological predictions for the coming year, as was the Akitu, or Zagmug, the Mesopotamian version of the spring equinox festival.

Practice

Astrology aided political decision making in any culture in which its principles were accepted. In Central America the Aztecs aligned their monumental architecture with the sky, and the Maya developed a complex divinatory calendar. Both cultures timed their military adventures in accord with movements of Venus. Probably in the latter part of the first millennium BCE the Chinese developed a complex system of astrology that was entirely political in intent, and in which the emperor was the embodiment of the Heavenly Lord Di, and both were represented in the north celestial pole, the point at which the entire sky revolves for an observer in the Northern Hemisphere. The emperor's astrologers formed a state bureaucracy and it was understood that the emperor must be obeyed because everything in society revolved around him, just as the stars revolved the pole. Pharaonic Egypt evolved a similar cosmology from the third millennium, in which the Pharaoh's political authority derived from his theological identification with the sun. The Pharaoh's Solar identity was reinforced by his role as a representative of the star *spdt*, or Sopdet (Greek Sothis, modern Sirius), itself identified with the god and mythical king Osiris. Egyptian notions of the solar state were inherited in Rome, where emperors from Nero onward explicitly identified themselves with the sun and frequently incorporated astrological advice in their decision making. Such traditions were continued by the Persian kings and adopted in India from around the second century CE. The Islamic caliphs adopted astrology in the eighth century, one of their most notable actions being al-Mansur's use of a team of astrologers to select the most auspicious moment for the foundation of Baghdad in 762.

Medieval European kings often relied on astrologers, frequently the leading scholars of their day. For example, Michael Scot in the early 13th century was employed specifically as astrologer to the Holy Roman Emperor Frederick II, in a tradition that continued to the 17th century was practiced at court, and except for medical purposes, it had a mundane character. The demand for prophecy led to the popularization of mundane astrology; in the late 15th century the invention of printing by movable type allowed astrologers to address themselves to a mass market by issuing annual prognostications for the coming year. Typically, such almanacs included predictions on weather, the harvests, the price of food, and medical matters, as well as politics, along with general nonastrological information; they were the first mass media.

The use of planetary cycles and mundane horoscopes raises an issue of individual forecasting, as to which horoscope takes priority, the mundane or the personal. Carter resolved this question according to the doctrine of subsumption, according to which horoscopes with a narrower remit are contained within ones with a wider relevance. The horoscope for an individual is contained within that for the family, the wider community, the city, the country, and, if such a horoscope could be identified, the world. For example, the death of individuals at Hiroshima is signified by the dropping of the atom bomb, rather than their individual horoscopes. Individual destiny is therefore contained within more general destiny, and indications from a mundane chart may overrule those from a natal chart.

In the 21st century astrology is practiced as a matter of state only in India, Sri Lanka, and parts of Southeast Asia. For example, the times for the independence of Burma and the proclamation of the republic of Sri Lanka were chosen by astrologers. Elsewhere astrology is used only by individual politicians privately and usually unknown to their colleagues, as by President Francois Mitterand (1916–1996) in France and President Ronald Reagan (1911–2004) in the United States. In the modern West the number of professional practitioners is tiny; for example, Elizabeth Teissier (b. 1938) for President Mitterand and Joan Quigley who advised President Reagan. Among students of astrology interest in mundane astrology has grown considerably as a result of the coincidence of outer planet cycles with global upheavals since the end of the Cold War, although it remains a minority pursuit.

Nicholas Campion

See also: Age of Aquarius; Almanacs; American Stars Debate; Apocalypticism; Comets; D'Ailly, Pierre; Machiavelli, Niccolò; Politics

Further Reading

Baigent, Michael, Nicholas Campion, and Charles Harvey. 1992. *Mundane Astrology: An Introduction to the Astrology of Nations and Organisations*, 2nd ed. London: Harper Collins.

Campion, Nicholas. 1994. *The Great Year: Astrology, Millenarianism and History in the Western Tradition.* London: Penguin.

Campion, Nicholas. 2008, 2009. *A Cultural History of Western Astrology*. 2 vols. London: Bloomsbury.

Carter, Charles. 1951. *An Introduction to Political Astrology.* London: Fowler.

Garin, Eugenio. 1976. *Astrology in the Renaissance: The Zodiac of Life.* London: Routledge.

Thomas, Keith. 1971. *Religion and the Decline of Magic: Studies in Popular Beliefs in Sixteenth and Seventeenth-Century England.* London: Weidenfeld and Nicolson.

N

NATAL ASTROLOGY

Natal astrology rests on the idea that information on the lives of individual human beings may be obtained through examining a horoscope for their date, time, and place of beginning, which is usually considered to be birth but might also be conception. The earliest surviving example of such a horoscope originates from fourth century BCE Egypt and natal astrology is still used today, giving it a history of over 2,000 years. In that time, despite its journey through many cultures and innovations, its essence remains unchanged; it relies on an image inspired by the sky at the time considered to represent an individual's beginning of life and interpretations are then made from this image concerning a person's character and destiny.

Arguably, the cosmology of Plato (428/427 BCE–348/347 BCE) underlies natal astrology, particularly that demonstrated in his *Timaeus* and in Book Ten of *The Republic*. In the *Timaeus*, Plato asserts that the cosmos is infused with soul and in *The Republic* that each human soul begins in the realm of the fixed stars, descending to incarnation through the planetary spheres (1937, X.614–621). Although Plato did not develop the astrological implications of these ideas, it is easily seen that his philosophy provides a rationale within which natal astrology, which assumes the soul has a relationship with the stars and planets, might arise. The idea that the soul has an innate relationship to the stars was also assisted by two further concepts found in the classical world. The first is the idea of cosmic sympathy, that everything in the universe is linked together by powers or energies that resonate in sympathy with each other. For example, the planet Mars resonates with soldiers, anger, and action. The doctrine of sympathies, or correspondences, thus allows a link to be inferred from the placing and condition of the planet Mars in an individual's horoscope to such things as aggressive action or a career as a soldier. The second concept is that of humanity being a microcosm of the macrocosm. This means that each human being may be conceived as a miniature version of the cosmos. If this is the case, then it is natural to look to the patterning of the stars and planets for guidance as to the meaning and course of human lives. This idea may be found in the work of first-century astrologer Marcus Manilius and is alive and well in modern astrology, for example, in the works of Dane Rudhyar and Stephen Arroyo (b. 1946).

Despite the Platonic nature of natal astrology's founding rationale, it developed along strongly Aristotelian lines through the work of Claudius Ptolemy who presented a naturalistic theory of astrology in his *Tetrabiblos*, the foundation of much of later astrology. Ptolemy derived the planets' natures from properties such as the combination of hot, cold, dry, and moist qualities and related the signs of the zodiac to the seasons in the Northern Hemisphere. This presented natal astrology as a form of celestial causation and paved the way for its conception as a form of early natural science.

Horoscopic astrology, of which natal astrology is one variety, underwent significant decline in Western Europe following the end of the Roman Empire in the fifth and sixth centuries. It survived, however, in Persia and the Islamic World and was reintroduced into Europe in the 11th century, when Greek and Arabic texts were translated into Latin. The Renaissance in the 15th century brought another wave of translation, particularly from Greek texts. Instrumental in the translation process was astrologer Marsilio Ficino. Ficino's astrology, heavily inspired by Platonic and Neoplatonic thought, may be contrasted with that of Ptolemy. Ficino's natal astrology sees the chart as a signature of the soul of the individual, with individual reflection playing an important part in how each planet expresses in an individual life. The purpose of such an astrology is to assist with healing and balancing the soul, thereby foreshadowing much of the psychological astrology of the 20th century. However, despite the efforts of such leading astrologers as William Lilly, John Gadbury, and Jean Baptiste Morin natal astrology declined again in the 17th century as astrology and astronomy were separated as disciplines and astrology was rejected as unscientific.

The revival of modern natal astrology is usually taken to begin with Alan Leo, a devoted theosophist, who integrated his belief in universal wisdom with astrology, in particular stressing the importance of karma and reincarnation in understanding the reasons why some birth horoscopes were easier than others. Leo promoted the idea that character is destiny and moved away from event oriented astrology partly on philosophical grounds and partly due to necessity, having been prosecuted for fortune-telling in 1917. A second boost to modern natal astrology was given by the psychologist Carl Gustav Jung, an enthusiast of astrology himself, whose esoterically influenced ideas produced a psychology that could clearly be applied to the natal horoscope. This was enthusiastically taken up by astrologers, notably Dane Rudhyar, Stephen Arroyo, and Liz Greene (b. 1946–).

The natal horoscope, also commonly referred to as a natal or birth chart, is derived from a mixture of astronomical and symbolic components. It consists of the positions of the planets at birth, including the sun and moon, that are placed within a zodiac usually divided into 12 signs, with each sign often taken as a set of qualities that modify a planet's expression, and further within a framework of 12 houses, which represent spheres of experience and life, and which are often related to two key astronomically derived points in the chart, the ascendant and midheaven. The planets are then read within the natal chart within the context of their zodiac sign, house position, and the relationships made to other planets or significant points within the chart. For example, a modern interpretation of the sun in the zodiac sign of Capricorn placed in the seventh house of the chart, but opposing Mars in Cancer in the first house, might be read as a clash between an authoritative (Capricorn) partner (seventh house), or more psychologically, the perception of the partner, who is central to the person's life (sun) and the individual's emotional outbursts (Mars in Cancer) which are a strong personality trait (first house). Further nuances might result from considering the planets ruling the first and seventh houses of the chart, or from other planets making aspects to either one of these. The orientation and time period of the astrologer would also influence the style of interpretation and the range of techniques used.

In addition to using the natal chart to assess the character and life of an individual, natal astrology includes forecasting techniques, which use the orderly and predictable motion of the celestial bodies to assess when particular components of the natal chart will manifest in the individual's life. Those without deep understanding of astrology often assume that natal astrology presupposes an exact fate. It is rare to find such a view among astrologers, however; even Ptolemy's naturalistic presentation allowed for some causative factors beyond the stars and planets. Instead, for most astrologers the planets are seen as representing principles or archetypes that have a variety of possible expressions. For example, the movement of Pluto to the position of natal Venus might symbolize a transformation in love. For one person this could mean a deep change in attitude to love relationships; for another, a decision to end a painful marriage; and for another, entry into a connection that takes the individual into personal metamorphosis.

Throughout its long history, natal astrology has been criticized with several recurring arguments. The first is that twins, born very close together, have different characters and lives. This is sometimes refuted by psychological astrologers as a case of unconscious collusion in splitting the psychological dynamics portrayed in the natal chart, whereby each twin lives out certain sections of the chart in question. The "twins argument" also presupposes that the horoscope signifies just one possible life, rarely the view taken by astrologers. Another critique relates to disasters or wars, when many with different horoscopes die at the same time. Responses to this argument often admit that whatever the merits of natal astrology, sometimes the life of an individual is subsumed into wider collective currents. Both science and religion have also critiqued natal astrology, with both often assuming that regardless of the façade of rationality, it is actually a form of magic at home in an animistic cosmology. Because science often starts from the principle that such a cosmos is impossible, natal astrology becomes unscientific and invalid. In the case of some monotheistic religions, such as Christianity and Islam, natal astrology is condemned as a divinatory practice potentially involving supernatural entities, which contradicts the supreme authority of the one God. Some astrologers partially agree, as least as regards the nature of natal astrology, identifying it as a divinatory practice, operating within an 'as if' framework that occasionally produces the right conditions for the cosmos to guide the individual. Such a view sees astrology as part of a postmodern, reanimated cosmos.

Laura Andrikopoulos

See also: Horoscopes; House Systems: Sun Signs; Zodiacs

Further Reading

Arroyo, Stephen. 1984. *The Practice and Profession of Astrology*. Reno, NV: CRCS Publications.
Campion, Nicholas. 2008. *The Dawn of Astrology*. London: Continuum.

Ficino, Marsilio. 2006. *Marsilio Ficino*, ed. Angela Voss. Berkeley, CA: North Atlantic Books.
Manilius. 1997. *Astronomica*, trans. G. P. Goold. Cambridge, MA: Harvard University Press.
Ptolemy, Claudius. 1940. *Tetrabiblos*, trans. F. E. Robbins. Cambridge, MA: Harvard University Press.

NAZISM AND THE THIRD REICH

The claim that Nazi dictator Adolf Hitler used astrology in his rise to power is a lingering myth. Though Hitler was interested in astrology, there is no clear evidence that he used astrology or allied phenomena like the prophecies of Nostradamus for personal, political, or military decisions. However, he never publicly denied the claim that he did so, and that the occult was responsible for most of his early political and military successes. Hitler's nondenial only fueled speculation, something that Hitler was well aware of. Many high ranking Nazis, including Rudolf Hess (1894–1987), Hitler's Deputy Reichsführer from 1933 to 1941, and SS Leader Heinrich Himmler (1900–1945), did consult astrologers, which led people to assume that Hitler did so as well.

The first recorded association of astrology with Hitler came in 1924, when his oratory was beginning to attract the cheering crowds that became an important part of the Nazi myth. A female fan sent Hitler's chart to Hamburg astrologer Elisabeth Ebertin (1880–1944), a regular contributor to *Zenit*, one of Germany's top astrological periodicals. Although she claimed she had no knowledge of him, Ebertin wrote a mostly accurate account of Hitler. During the mid-1920s, the future Fuhrer was hardly known outside of Bavaria yet Ebertin described his personality and future activities, such as the times of his arrests.

After taking power in 1933 the Nazi leader became the major focus of German astrological publications. In 1934, the Ministry of Propaganda made it illegal to publish any predictions concerning Hitler or the Third Reich. Much of this was an attempt by propaganda minister Josef Goebbels (1897–1945) to craft a more positive image for Germany's new leader. His wife Magda Goebbels (1901–1945) first introduced her husband to a claim in a 1921 book by a German postal worker who described the predictions of Nostradamus when passages in his Prophecies (II.24, IV.68, V.29, VI.49) with the name "Hister" were believed to foretell the rise of Adolf Hitler. Hitler's propaganda machine also made use of Nostradamus (Prophecies III.57–58, VI.51, X.31). Verse III.57 that allegedly predicted that there would be a crisis in Poland in 1939, the year of the Nazi invasion of that country.

On May 10, 1941, Hess, partially inspired by astrological predictions, flew an ME110 fitted with auxiliary gas tanks from Augsburg to Scotland, then landed by parachute south of Glasgow where he was captured and held in comfortable imprisonment. Hitler was not pleased as he was concerned as to how much intelligence Hess might release to the British about "Barbarossa," the projected German invasion of Russia. Hitler's first reaction at what he consider Hess's betrayal was to order his immediate execution upon his return to Germany, but later Hitler made no effort to have Hess rescued or killed and even spoke of him as a loyal but misguided "Old Comrade." Hitler was aware of astrology's influence on Hess. He claimed that the influence of astrologers and other "charlatans" surrounding Hess had led to his "insanity." Hitler and other opponents of astrology within the Nazi leadership, such as Goebbels and Reinhard Heydrich, responded to Hess's flight with the "Aktion Hess," ordering the Gestapo to arrest over 600 astrologers and other occultists.

Although it was never officially made public, a few German astrologers predicted that autumn 1942 would be the turning point of the war, and that Germany needed to win before this date. Hess was aware of these predictions as far back as 1937 when the claim was first made by the famous Swiss astrologer, Karl Ernst Krafft (1900–1945). Krafft was a Swiss astrologer of German descent who participated in tests by the German parapsychologist Hans Bender (1907–1991) in 1937; in 1939, he was introduced to the German Propaganda Ministry by the astronomer and astrologer H. H. Kritzinger (1887–1968), who had worked on interpretations of the famous Nostradamus prophecies. Krafft became highly regarded after he made a successful prediction of the attempt on Hitler's life in November 1939. Krafft warned Hitler of danger from bombing in the period November 7–10, 1939. On November 8 of that year, Hitler spoke at a celebration of his 1923 Beer Hall putsch when a bomb exploded. There were many injuries but the perpetrators missed the real target, Hitler, who left the assembly in the hall a few minutes before the explosion. This prophecy was so remarkable that Krafft was interrogated by the Gestapo, who thought he might have had a hand in the plot.

After this 1939 prediction, Goebbels put Krafft to work adapting Nostradamus prophecies for use in propaganda, mostly astrological material that predicted a Nazi victory, could be "imported" to magazines around the word, most notably to the United States, to influence public opinion and sympathy. Krafft enjoyed some success. In May 1940, the Luftwaffe dropped pamphlets over Belgium and France containing faked prophecies by Nostradamus, announcing that flying machines would bring heavy destruction (Verse VI.34) but that southeastern France would be spared. Civilian populations could then flee in that direction, leaving open both the approaches to Paris and the channel ports, which would then be less congested when the German armies began to move in French territory. This would keep French forces in these areas from getting to the areas under attack. Among his other correct predictions, Krafft foresaw that General Bernard Montgomery would be chosen to take over British operations in North Africa. Krafft was arrested by the Gestapo during "Aktion Hess" on June 12. He was exploited to draw up horoscopes for propaganda, but eventually his mental condition deteriorated. He died enroute to Buchenwald concentration camp on January 8, 1945.

Just after the 1940 German victories in Denmark and Norway, Ludwig (Louis) de Wohl (1903–1961), learned through a friend that Krafft was in Berlin working for the German High Command. De Wohl was a German-born astrologer of partially Jewish descent who escaped to Britain and played a prominent part in the British psychological warfare campaign. In *The Stars of War and Peace* (1952), De Wohl claimed that in 1935 he was invited to be an astrological adviser for the Nazis. He escaped to Britain as a refugee in the same year, where he practiced as an astrologer and wrote books on the subject. De Wohl convinced British intelligence that Krafft was Hitler's astrologer, and was therefore responsible for the German miltary's swift victories. The British High Command took this seriously, mainly because they had been beaten in Norway, where the Germans arrived only one week before the British planned to do so. Also, the stereotype of Germans as astrological believers helped De Wohl convince British High Command that Hitler was using it for the German war effort De Wohl then persuaded British intelligence to hire him, not to work on any astrological plans for the Allies, but to report on what astrological advice Krafft might be giving Hitler. De Wohl was also recruited by British intelligence to participate in psychological warfare projects that used astrology. One was a fake edition of the prophecies of Nostradamus, which spread subversive rumors in Germany. During the war, De Wohl disseminated anti-Nazi astrological propaganda in Germany and then-neutral America. After the war he became a devout Catholic and writer of religious fiction.

Martin J. Manning

See also: Court Astrologers; Legal Regulation of Astrology; Nostradamus; Politics

Further Reading

Cavendish, Richard, and Brian Innes, eds. 1997. *Man, Myth and Magic: The Illustrated Encyclopedia of Mythology, Religion, and the Unknown*. New ed. New York: M. Cavendish.

Howe, Ellic. 1965. *Nostradamus and the Nazis: A Footnote to the History of the Third Reich*. London: Arborfield.

Howe, Ellic. 1972. *Astrology and Psychological Warfare during World War II*, rev. and condensed ed. London: Rider.

Kurlander, Eric. 2017. *Hitler's Monsters: A Supernatural History of the Third Reich*. New Haven, CT: Yale University Press.

Partridge, Christopher, ed. 2015. *The Occult World*. New York: Routledge.

NEW AGE

The term *New Age* is used in two senses. First, the New Age is a coming period of history, a utopia usually characterized by spiritual enlightenment, and sometimes conflated with the coming Age of Aquarius. Second, New Age is a culture that generally adopts ideas, beliefs and practices outside of the Western religious and scientific mainstream, and which may or may not be specifically related to belief in the coming period of history.

New Age as a Historical Period

The term *New Age* first appeared in the late 18th century and was used in the sense of a coming spiritual period by the poet William Blake (1757–1827) in the 1790s. The term was then popularized by the followers of the Swedish prophet Emmanuel Swedenborg (1688–1782), who had claimed that humanity had entered the spiritual kingdom of Christ in 1752: Swedenborg's church was known as the New Church and his followers began to call the new spiritual era the New Age. The term owes its modern popularity to the theosophical teacher Alice Bailey (1880–1949) who used it widely as a synonym for the coming Age of Aquarius. Indeed, the prophecy that the Aquarian Age will be one of heightened spirituality is largely due to Bailey. In turn, astronomically derived dates for the beginning of the Aquarian Age are applied to the beginning of the New Age, which is therefore seen as a definite historical period, rather than a vague expectation of a future utopia. Bailey wrote about the New Age widely from the 1920s to the 1940s and her followers, such as George Trevelyan (1906–1996), David Spangler (b. 1945), and William Bloom (b. 1948) promoted it in the 1970s and 1980s. Although Rudolf Steiner (1861–1925), the theosophist and founder of Anthroposophy, described the coming period as the Age of Michael, many of his followers have followed Bailey's New Age/Aquarian Age synthesis.

In its broad outline, the ideas of historical evolution that underpin the New Age are set out in *Isis Unveiled* (1877), the major text written by H. P. Blavatsky (1831–1891), the founder of Theosophy. In turn, Blavatsky's work has deep roots in Neoplatonic concepts of true reality as consisting of consciousness rather than physical matter. In Bailey's version, individuals may work to raise their own levels of spiritual awareness at the same time as babies are born who already possess a heightened spirituality. As the astrological Age of Pisces shifts into Aquarius cosmic law will increase the trend toward greater spirituality until the spiritual New Age is reached. To be spiritual in this sense means a lot more than an awareness of spiritual dimensions, though. Rather, physical matter will itself gradually disappear leaving existence as composed of pure spirit. Eventually individual humans will also disappear and be absorbed into the pure spirit of the universe.

Politically, New Age thought is revolutionary, countercultural, antistate, and anticapitalist. It adheres to a version of globalization in which current economic and political structures are destined to collapse. Its leading activists were involved in shaping countercultural notions in the 1960s and its religious assumptions are theosophical in the sense that all world teachers are respected as manifestations of, or messengers from, the One. The approach of the Aquarian Age/New Age is often said to be marked by a rise in Christ Consciousness and the appearance of the "Cosmic Christ," the spiritual version of the historical Jesus.

New Age as a Culture

In the 1980s it was common to talk about the New Age movement, although it is clear that there was no single organized movement. It is now usual to talk of New Age as a network or culture rooted in ideas and practices generally drawn from outside the Western mainstream, or from overtly mystical traditions in other religions. Most New Age practices are based in Platonic Idealism, claiming that consciousness is more important than matter, and therefore that individual and collective life can be altered by the power of the mind. Kabbalah, Neoplatonism, Gnosticism, Hermeticism, esoteric Christianity, and spiritual forms of astrology are all also favored, along with eastern philosophies such as Sufism, Buddhism, and Hinduism. With the rapid spread of such ideas from the late-1960s to mid-1980s, a wide range of other practices were added, including feng shui, transcendental meditation, so-called Native American spirituality and a variety of practices from alternative and complementary medicine, such as homeopathy, acupuncture, aromatherapy, reflexology, and reiki. The result is a spread of activities that might be practiced by people who believed that the New Age was coming, but equally might not. The idea of a wider New Age culture with no necessary connection to belief in a literal, coming spiritual era was therefore widely acknowledged.

New Age Astrology

The most obvious application of astrology in New Age thought is the use of the Aquarian Age as a timer for the New Age's beginning. In addition, deliberate reforms in astrology have been undertaken by astrologers who believed that astrology must be adapted in order to assist individuals who were spiritually evolved and ready to work for the coming of the New Age. Such arguments are found chiefly in the works of two theosophists, Alan Leo and Dane Rudhyar, himself a student of Alice Bailey. Like New Age thought in general, New Age astrology emerged from Neoplatonic and Hermetic currents and is broadly known as esoteric, after its emphasis on inner change. It asserts that astrology should be devoted to spiritual development and/or psychological self-understanding and freedom from fate. Deterministic character readings and prediction are regarded as suitable only for individuals who have not achieved self-awareness and are therefore still subject to fate. For example, the self-aware person would no longer be unconsciously living out a fate defined at birth but consciously developing their higher selves, becoming more evolved.

Rudhyar introduced the terms *humanist* and *person-centered* to denote an astrology in which individual concerns took priority over the laws of astrological interpretation, and "transpersonal," to emphasize the integration of the individual into the spiritual transformation of the whole universe. Leo's astrology was heavily influenced by eastern currents in Theosophy and places great emphasis on reincarnation and the law of karma. According to this model, reading the birth chart leads to an understanding of one's current incarnation and an escape from karmic bonds. Rudhyar also incorporated recent developments in depth psychology, notably from C. G. Jung, into his astrology, leading to a greater emphasis on psychology rather than spirituality. Drawing on Neoplatonic and Hermetic currents, the astrological planets are redefined as either archetypal energies or symbols of archetypes in the unconscious, and interpretation of the horoscope moves away from the literal reading of exact and often deterministic character descriptions or external circumstances, toward an attempt to explore the dynamics of the personality. In a consultation each astrological factor is seen as a symbol that should be interpreted in terms of the client's needs and circumstances.

Although New Age astrology is invariably esoteric, we can identify two main currents: spiritualization and psychologization. Astrologers who are concerned with spiritual evolution may have little interest in psychology and psychological astrologers may regard an interest in spirituality as a manifestation of an archetypal

The Harmonic Convergence 1987

The Harmonic Convergence of August 16–17, 1987, was an astrological event that led to a New Age meditation event that some hoped would usher in global transformation. It was inspired by a combination of Mesoamerican calendrics and Western astrology. In *Quetzlcoatl: Lord of the Dawn* (1971) New Age writer Tony Shearer put forth an interpretation of the Aztec calendar by which the date of the convergence would mark the end of a "hell cycle" that had begun with the Spanish conqueror Cortez's invasion of Mexico in 1519. The date was also marked by a "Grand Trine" with the sun, moon, Mars, and Venus, with Mercury nearby forming one point of an equilateral triangle, Jupiter another, and Saturn and Uranus the third. Many astrologers, however, viewed this event as not particularly significant. The principal promoter of the event was American New Age author José Argüelles (1939–2011), a student of Dane Rudhyar. Arguelles brought in the Mayan calendar and linked the 1987 event with the alleged "Mayan apocalypse" of 2012.

The Harmonic Convergence aroused widespread interest, as well as mockery. Many expected that the world would enter a new period of peace and harmony. Millions gathered at mountaintops and others areas designated as "power points," where "spiritual energy" was supposed to be concentrated for group meditation, making this the first global meditation event. However, no dramatic events followed the Harmonic Convergence, and the event itself soon faded from popular memory.

pattern. Further, neither spiritual nor psychological astrologers may any longer have an interest in the literal coming of the New Age, and in this sense the term New Age astrology describes a kind of astrological culture directed toward self-understanding and aiming toward freedom from fate.

Nicholas Campion

See also: Age of Aquarius; Apocalypticism; Goodman, Linda; Jung, Carl G.; Leo, Alan; Mundane Astrology; Rudhyar, Dane; Theosophy; Transpersonal Astrology

Further Reading

Campion, Nicholas. 2015. *Astrology and Popular Religion in the Modern West: Prophecy, Cosmology and the New Age Movement.* Abingdon: Ashgate, 2012; London: Routledge.

Campion, Nicholas. 2015. *The New Age in the Modern West: Counter-Culture, Utopia and Prophecy from the late Eighteenth Century to the Present Day.* London: Bloomsbury.

Hanegraaff, Wouter J. 1996. *New Age Religion and Western Culture.* Leiden: Brill.

York, Michael. 1995. *The Emerging Network: A Sociology of the New Age and Neo-Pagan Movements.* London: Rowan and Littlefield.

NEWSPAPERS

Since the 1930s, many newspapers have featured regular astrology columns. These columns have had a continuous presence in local and national newspapers, tabloids, and women's interest magazines. Generally appearing as daily, weekly, or monthly horoscopes, columns are composed of brief predictions for each of the

12 signs of the zodiac. This form of serialized horoscope is produced for mass consumption, at times attributed to specific professional astrologers, though many are authored by anonymous writers on the publication staff. Many studies of contemporary cultural attitudes toward astrology have examined newspaper horoscopes, as they are thought to shape popular engagement with astrology in the United States, Australia, and many European nations. The newspaper horoscope has become a generic form with many consistent thematic and stylistic traits translated into other media including astrology blogs and video horoscopes.

The first newspaper astrology columns were likely published in the United States and the United Kingdom in the early 1930s. British astrologer R. H. Naylor provided a forecast for the birth of Princess Margaret Rose in the *Sunday Express* in 1930, and a horoscope column appeared in 1931 in the *Boston Record*. Before this, astrology forecasts were printed in publications like almanacs but focused more on agricultural and weather forecasts than interpersonal advice. By the mid-1930s, astrology forecast columns were published in the *Los Angeles Times* and the *New York Post*, and the 12-paragraph horoscope form became the norm. Although the decline in newspapers since the advent of the Internet and digital media signals a potential shift in this genre, horoscope columns continue to proliferate online in news-oriented sites.

Production and Consumption

The widespread distribution and sustained popularity of horoscope columns in newspapers and magazines has been noted in scholarship on astrology, as well as the popular press. Since the rise of newspaper astrology columns in the 1930s and 1940s, experts have noted a growth in the general audience for astrology. By the late 1960s, newspaper horoscopes were exceedingly common, and according to one study, it was estimated that "1200 of the 1750 daily newspapers" in the United States had astrology columns (Truzzi, "Occult Revival," 19). Another study of newspaper content found that 85 percent of dailies had astrology features at least once a week in 1987 (Bogart 1989, 197). In the early 21st century, many American newspapers (aside from the more prestigious publications like the *New York Times*) still feature horoscopes, including the *Chicago Tribune, Los Angeles Times, New York Post*, and *Washington Post*. Horoscope columns are also published in many British and Australian newspapers and, according to one study, are part of "all women's magazines in the UK" (Campion 2012, 4). Horoscopes are also published in newspapers in India, China, South Korea, and post-Soviet Eastern Europe.

Although men and women of all ages and many racial and ethnic backgrounds are found to be consumers of astrology, some studies have shown that women and marginalized people tend to be the primary audience. Readers of newspaper horoscopes often have a casual interest in astrology, in comparison with those who are more engaged with astrology and seek out more in-depth discourses. The authors of astrology columns include popular figures and professional astrologers, though many publications feature uncredited columns. Popular astrologers who have authored horoscope columns include Linda Black, Fred Davies, Roger Elliot, Shelley von Strunckel, Linda Goodman, psychic Jeane Dixon, and academic Nicholas Campion.

General Characteristics of Newspaper Horoscopes

The newspaper astrology column has become a particular genre with consistent formal and literary attributes. Typically, these columns consist of 12 brief paragraphs, with a paragraph directed toward each of the 12 signs of the zodiac. Often there is a heading for each paragraph, indicating the paragraph is meant for readers based on their sun sign, as determined by their birthdays. The signs are bolded and the dates associated with each sun sign are often also articulated explicitly. Although some columns may merely provide information about the personality traits of each sign, most provide forecasts for the upcoming day, week, month, or year (depending on the frequency of publication).

The 12-paragraph horoscope column, first attributed to Paul Clancy in the early 1930s, emerged in the United States through newspapers and astrology publications. The style was influenced strongly by the work of Alan Leo who is credited with producing simplified birth charts based on sun signs.

Horoscope Content

Newspaper columns typically focus on personality traits and general proclivities associated with the zodiac signs to produce character analysis readings and forecasts. The understandings of the zodiac signs often follow the norms of sun sign descriptions established by Leo. Although astrology columns occasionally focus on just describing the personality and habits of the sun signs, more frequently the traits are included with predictions, rather than set apart.

The textual content of astrology columns has been analyzed in a range of scholarship, and featured prominently in the work of Frankfurt School Marxist Theodor Adorno (1903–1969). Themes in horoscope columns include work, family, love, health, and finances. Adorno notes in his analysis of the *Los Angeles Times* astrology column, that there is great consistency in the words used as well as in the forecast and advice. Language includes abstract, yet commonplace terms like *problems*, *battles*, *situations*, *energy*, *stress*, *relationships*, *work or school*, *intuition*, *path*, and *resolution*. Adorno identified the use of general terms as necessary to maintain focus on day-to-day reality while remaining ambiguous.

Typically, horoscopes are centered on the personal and mundane, featuring a description for each sign of the upcoming day or week with regard to home and work. Advice about how to deal with these events is given, incorporating the characteristics of the particular sign. Information about the particular locations and arrangements of celestial bodies during that time period is sometimes included, though daily newspaper columns tend to allude to them without using advanced language.

Public Discourse about Astrology Columns

The mass distribution of newspapers across various locations and demographics reached a much larger audience than printed books or magazines devoted to astrology. For success with the audience, astrological content needed to be comprehensible and applicable to a broad population, while still varying according to the date of publication. The audience is addressed in horoscopes through commonsense advice about how to manage oneself based on cultural norms, occasionally incorporating spiritual or occult language.

The commercial aspects of newspaper horoscopes made them especially suspect to cultural critics like Adorno, and the subject of science-based critiques. Professional astrologers who practice a "higher" or more advanced and elite form of astrology were also often harsh critics of newspaper columns. However, there were astrologers, including some authors of horoscope columns, who defended the practice and felt that accessibility was important for reaching a broader public.

Alongside the rise of popular consumption of horoscopes through newspapers were strong critiques that regarded astrology as a fraudulent pseudoscience. Some public intellectuals, like Richard Dawkins, denounced horoscopes, while scientific and quantitative studies "disproved" astrology predictions, or highlighted the gullibility of its consumers. Government institutions in the United States, Canada, and the United Kingdom also sought to regulate astrology in print and broadcast media.

Effects on Astrology

According to Campion, newspaper columns directly influenced the rise of sun sign astrology (Campion 2012, 69–70). The horoscope form was also characterized by the new centrality of personal divinations, which appealed to many without particular interest in astrological techniques or traditions. With the mass distribution of horoscopes and less technical language came apparent growth of casual, popular interest in astrology outside of the esoteric, occult traditions. The widespread consumption of astrology in newspapers may have helped spur the explosion of interest in New Age and countercultural movements of the 1960s and 1970s.

Interpretations and Discussions

Scholars have suggested that the turn to horoscopes as a form of divination results from modernity's call for the repression of irrational, traditional, and mystical beliefs. Horoscopes have been positively interpreted, as an opportunity for people to reflect and commune spiritually in a consumerist and progress-oriented society. Newspaper horoscopes have also been negatively portrayed as resulting from industrial capitalism's need to control and pacify the workforce, distracting the population from systemic inequality. The expansion of astrology into newspapers coincided with the shift toward personality analysis, patterned on cultural rhetorics of psychology, self-help, and self-improvement.

Annamarie O'Brien

See also: Omarr, Sydney; Righter, Carroll; Sex and Love; Sun Signs

Further Reading

Adorno, Theodor, W. 1994. "The Stars Down to Earth: The *Los Angeles Times* Astrology Column." In *The Stars Down to Earth and Other Essays on the Irrational in Culture*, ed. Stephen Crook, 34–127. London: Routledge.

Aphek, Edna, and Y. Tobin. 1989. *The Semiotics of Fortune-Telling*. Foundations of Semiotics. Amsterdam: John Benjamins.

Bogart, Leo. 1989. *Press and Public: Who Reads What, When, Where, and Why in American Newspapers*. Hillsdale, NJ: Lawrence Erlbaum.

Campion, Nicholas. 2012. *Astrology and Popular Religion in the Modern West: Prophecy, Cosmology, and the New Age Movement*. Farnham, Surrey, UK: Ashgate.

Campion, Nicholas. 2014. *Astrology and Cosmology in the World's Religions*. New York: New York University Press.

Curry, Patrick, Angela Voss, and Geoffery Cornelius. 2007. "From Primitive Mentality to Haecceity: The Unique Case in Astrology and Divination." In *Seeing with Different Eyes: Essays in Astrology and Divination*, ed. Patrick Curry and Angela Voss. Newcastle, UK: Cambridge Scholars.

Darian-Smith, Kate. 2014. "In the Stars: Astrology, Psychic Powers and the Australian Media." In *Looking Forward, Looking Back*, ed. Sue Turnbull, Bridget Griffin-Foley, and Gerard Goggin. St. Lucia: University of Queensland.

Feher, Shoshanah. 1992. "Who Looks to the Stars? Astrology and Its Constituency." *Journal for the Scientific Study of Religion* 31, no. 1: 88.

Fehérváry, Krisztina. 2007. "Hungarian Horoscopes as a Genre of Postsocialist Transformation." *Social Identities* 13, no. 5: 561–76.

Kim, Andrew Eungi. 2005. "Nonofficial Religion in South Korea: Prevalence of Fortunetelling and Other Forms of Divination." *Review of Religious Research* 46, no. 3: 284–302.

Lawrence, Marilynn. 2007. "A Phenomenological Approach to Astrology: Thinking of Astrology at the End of Metaphysics." In *Seeing with Different Eyes Essays in Astrology and Divination*, ed. Patrick Curry and Angela Voss. Newcastle, UK: Cambridge Scholars.

Nederman, Cary J., and James Wray Goulding. 1981. "Popular Occultism and Critical Social Theory: Exploring Some Themes in Adorno's Critique of Astrology and the Occult." *Sociological Analysis* 42, no. 4: 325–332.

Rogers, Paul, and Janice Soule. 2009. "Cross-Cultural Differences in the Acceptance of Barnum Profiles Supposedly Derived from Western versus Chinese Astrology." *Journal of Cross-Cultural Psychology* 40, no. 3: 381–399.

Truzzi, Marcello. "The Occult Revival as Popular Culture: Some Random Observations on the Old and the Nouveau Witch." *The Sociological Quarterly* 13, no. 1 (1971): 16–36.

Wuthnow, Robert. 1976. "Astrology and Marginality." *Journal for the Scientific Study of Religion* 15, no. 2: 157.

NOSTRADAMUS (1503–1566)

Michel de Notre-Dame or de Nostredame (*Nostradamus* in Latin) is one of the best-known astrologers and prophets in history. His main vocation and occupation was prophesying but he also worked as a physician. This ability to see the future was based not only on astrology and horoscopes but also on divine inspiration, which, according to Nostradamus, was a gift of God. The influence of his father, Jaume, and grandfather Émile who were both born into the Jewish faith but later converted to Roman Catholicism was crucial.

The legend of Nostradamus (1503–1566) persisted long after his death. (Wellcome Collection)

Nostradamus was born in the small French village of Saint Remy de Provence. Fascinated by astrology from his adolescence he went on to study humanities in Avignon and medicine at the University of Montpellier. The plague broke out in Provence while he was a student and although many doctors fled, Nostradamus stayed to help the sick and prepare special drugs for them. This service to the poor gave him both medical and popular prestige in that region. When the plague ended in 1529, he went back to Montpellier where university documents show his attendance. When he began to practice medicine he changed his French family name to *Nostradamus*. Name changes were common among intellectuals of the Renaissance to show their social position. However, he always rejected academic medicine and chose drugs not recommended by official doctors.

Although it is not clear whether he did his doctorate, Nostradamus was fortunate enough to teach medicine in the Medical Faculty of the University of Montpellier, but the academic environment did not suit him. He preferred to learn from experience and astrology. He considered himself touched by God because he was born on Christmas Eve, a propitious day.

He left Montpellier in 1532 and became a traveling doctor. It was on his travels when he met the great intellectual and physician Julius Caesar Scaliger (1484–1558), who helped him to stay in Agen, a small town halfway between Avignon and Marseilles, where he married and became the father of two children. However, he did not get on with Scaliger because he defended the medicine of the time, which was dogmatic and bookish. Nostradamus chose astrology, his own experience, freedom, and occult wisdom and when the Inquisition arrived in Agen, he decided to leave. His fear of the Inquisition never left him. Unfortunately, when he returned to Agen so did the plague, which killed his family. He then went back to being a traveling physician. When the plague ravaged Aix-en-Provence for the second time, the stricken city persuaded him to help fight the dreaded disease in 1546 and, in gratitude for his labors, awarded him a pension for life. He settled in Salon in 1547, and married a wealthy widow, who bore him six children. His domestic and family life in Salon brought him happiness. There was a telescope on the top floor of his house where he observed the moon and wrote most of his predictions.

Nostradamus wrote an astrological almanac beginning in 1650 and lasting until his death. He wrote *Prophesies* of future events with great success, which were later published as the famous *Centuries*, a compendium of hundred quatrains, in 1555, 1557, and 1558. The complete work includes 10 *Centuries* with 942 quatrains. The numerous allusions to heavily veiled persons, places, and events were strewn about in no discernible arrangement, either chronological or geographic. These deliberately vague forebodings, promulgated in a France trembling on the verge of a religious civil war, were an instantaneous success. Nostradamus was promptly summoned to the capital in 1556 to cast the horoscopes of the royal children. Encouraged by such favorable responses Nostradamus was appointed astrologer to Queen Catherine de' Medici. On October 17, 1564 the young king Charles IX sought out the seer at Salon. In the last years of his life, he lost most of his inspiration and became a more or less complete charlatan. He died at home in Salon of a heart attack.

As regards Nostradamus's method of prophesying, he wrote the *Centuries* during states of grace. He had a natural instinct to foretell, a prophetic spirit, and this came to him suddenly as a mighty virtue to prophesy in the form of instinctive intelligence and automatic irrational writing. He was convinced that this was a question of religion because he felt his inspiration to foretell was mainly god-given. This moving principle is one of the bases of his prophecies but not the only one. The incident that happened to him one night is quite revealing in this respect. Nostradamus explains that one night, when he was alone, a little flame came to him from this loneliness and he then developed these visions. It was in such a setting that he waited for the gift from God. He also adapted texts from the Bible and other famous books to modern and future times (bibliomancy). Nostradamus projected events of the past in the future, describing them in such a way that they become unrecognizable. He was also careful about what he wrote for fear of the Inquisition. Furthermore, he used ambiguous and obscure words from other languages (Latin, old French, Provençal, etc.). Therefore, because they are long-term prophecies, it is easy to see either the truth or the falseness of the sentences. There is also a measured dose of charlatanism (i.e., of possible probabilities). In this way, he probably used one principle of prediction: to make many predictions, waiting till one of them came true, and giving it a disproportionate emphasis while ignoring the rest. As a result of this ambivalence, the adversaries of Nostradamus have to this day denounced him as a charlatan who predicted such portentous crises as the French Revolution and World War II.

Justo Hernández

See also: Almanacs; Medical Astrology; Nazism and the Third Reich; Politics; Renaissance and Reformation Astrology

Further Reading

Gerson, Stephane. 2012. *Nostradamus: How an Obscure Renaissance Astrologer became the Modern Prophet of Doom*. New York: St. Martin's Press.

Lemesurier, P. 2010. *Nostradamus, Bibliomancer: The Man, the Myth, the Truth*. Prompton Plains, NJ: Career Press.

O

OMARR, SYDNEY (1926–2003)

In the second half of the 20th century, Sydney Omarr's widely distributed newspaper sun sign column, many astrological books, and frequent media appearances made him the public face of popular astrology in the United States.

Omarr was born Sidney Kimmelman in Philadelphia. He changed his name as a youth, mostly for numerological reasons. (Numerology, the study of the occult properties of numbers, was his first love, and he turned to astrology partly because he could not support himself as a numerologist.) He continued to practice astrology in the Army, where he had a radio show. After the war, he became a reporter for CBS radio in Hollywood, where he began to cultivate the connections with celebrities that would serve him well.

At its height, Omarr's astrology column appeared in over 200 newspapers. He also had a radio show and operated a pay telephone service offering horoscopes. Omarr published an extremely popular series of annual astrological guides, offering day-by-day predictions for each of the 12 zodiac signs. He engaged in public debates with opponents of astrology, including leading scientists like Linus Pauling and Carl Sagan, Omarr also wrote numerous astrological books outside the series. Among the most popular were *My World of Astrology* (1965), an introduction to the subject; a cookbook, *Cooking with Astrology* (1969); and *Sydney Omarr's Astrological Revelations about You* (1999). He was also the author of a relationship guide, *Sydney Omarr's Astrology, Love, Sex and You* (2002). His works have been translated and reprinted and sold over 50 million copies.

Like other 20th-century American astrologers, Omarr had close connections with the Hollywood community and was referred to as "astrologer to the stars" (a title he shared with his rival astrological columnist, Carroll Righter). He gave lavish dinners and parties at his Los Angeles home. (Leo was his sun sign, and he was frequently described as a typical gregarious Leo.) His connections and vivid personality made him a frequent guest on television talk shows, including those hosted by Merv Griffin, Mike Douglas, and Johnny Carson. Omarr corresponded with American novelist and avid follower of astrology Henry Miller, the subject of his short study *Henry Miller: His World of Urania* (1960).

In 1971, Omarr was diagnosed with multiple sclerosis, a disease that eventually blinded and paralyzed him. Although his increasing ill-health forced him to cut back on entertaining, he continued to carry on his astrological work. Like many popular astrologers, Omarr's name did not disappear with his death. "Sydney Omarr" remained a valuable brand, conveying an image of astrological expertise and authority. His column is carried on as "Omarr's Astrological Forecast" by astrologer Jeraldine Saunders, who had been briefly married to Omarr in 1966 and remained a close friend. His annual guides continued to appear as *Sydney Omarr's Day-by-Day Astrological Guide* authored by astrologers Trish MacGregor, Carol Tonsing, and Rob MacGregor, with the last set of books appearing in 2014.

William E. Burns

See also: Newspapers; Righter, Carroll; Sex and Love; Sun Signs

Further Reading

Omarr, Sydney. 1990. *My World of Astrology.* Los Angeles: Wilshire Book Company.

P

PARACELSUS (1493–1541)

Philippus Aureolus Theophrastus Bombastus von Hohenheim, better known as Paracelsus, was a Swiss-born, German polymath who contributed to natural philosophical disciplines such as alchemy, iatrochemistry (the treatment of disease with chemical substances), medicine, and astrology and had a major influence on 16th-century theology, cosmology, and occult studies. He is perhaps best known for his deep distrust of orthodox thought; his relentless criticism of classical knowledge, its Scholastic successors, and his contemporaries in natural philosophy, with whom he often disagreed; and for the controversies that surrounded his ideas. Paracelsus's philosophical outlook was a complex one that combined empirical investigation of nature and the human body as the source of knowledge with a natural magic influenced by Neoplatonism, Hermeticism, Pythagoreanism, Cabala, and various medieval alchemical and astrological traditions.

Paracelsus was born in the town of Einseideln in the Swiss canton of Schwyz, as an illegitimate son to Wilhelm Bombast von Hohenheim, a Swabian physician of minor nobility, and an unknown bondswoman attached to the Benedictine abbey in the town. In 1502, after the death of his mother, he and his father moved to Villach, Carinthia (in modern-day Austria), where his father worked as a physician and began Paracelsus's education in medicine and other areas of natural philosophy. Paracelsus likely attended the monastery schools of St. Paul and St. Andrae near Klagenfurt before studying medicine at the University of Basel. He eventually obtained his doctorate from the University of Ferrara in 1515. His "humanist" name Paracelsus, which he gave to himself around this time, likely means "beyond Celsus," referring to the second-century CE Greco-Roman writer on medicine, who may not have even been a physician (Ball 2006, 70).

Despite a university education, he did not lead the life of the elite, and he spent much of his intellectual energies refuting what he believed to be erroneous medical, philosophical, and cosmological thought among both the ancients and his contemporaries. For example, he publicly ridiculed the medical authority of Galen and Avicenna and regularly wrote and lectured in German instead of Latin, as he hoped to reach a more popular audience. He earned a reputation as a bombastic and uncompromising thinker who often invoked the ire of his fellow physicians. Paracelsus led an unconventional, peripatetic life between 1517 and 1524 largely working as an itinerant physician, and traveling throughout Italy, France, Spain, Portugal, England, Croatia, Poland, Russia, Hungary, and the Near East, where he visited Rhodes and Constantinople, and possibly traveled to Egypt as well (Goodrick-Clarke 1999, 15). As a military surgeon in the employ of the

Venetian army in 1522, he attended to various wounds and illnesses that informed his medical theory and supported his assertion that local conditions and individual idiosyncrasies affected the form that treating and healing particular ailments should take. After 1524, he lived in Salzburg, Strasbourg, Basel, and a number of smaller towns in southern Germany, Austria, and Switzerland, where he worked as a physician and wrote a number of texts, especially on medicine and alchemy, including the *Paragranum* and the *Opus Paramirum* (both on medical theory), *Die grosse Wundarznei* (on surgery), *Prognostications* (containing political and religious predictions), and his great philosophical synthesis the *Astronomia Magna, or the whole Philosophical Sagax of the Great and Little World*. In the *Astronomia Magna*, he counted astrology as one of the nine major divisions of his philosophy. He died on September 24, 1541, in Salzburg after suffering a stroke three days earlier (Goodrick-Clarke 1999, 22).

Paracelsus's attitude toward astrology was complex, and he appears to have altered his opinion of it throughout his life, though it remained a major influence over his practice. On the one hand, his cosmology was, in many ways, a continuance of Ptolemy's in that he saw a hierarchical chain of celestial influences that included not only the motion of the stars and planets but also the geography, climate, nationality, and culture of the individual whose fate was being investigated. So, while Paracelsus accepted that a correspondence between planets and bodily organs existed (e.g., the sun relates to the heart, the moon to the brain, Saturn to the spleen, Venus to the kidneys), he claimed this was not a permanent arrangement, and the course of a person's life and their local conditions had just as great an effect. This is why empirical observation was necessary for Paracelsus, because every individual was different, and medicine could only be practiced on a case-by-case basis. On the other hand, he argued that the stars and planets had no direct, causal influence over people and saw the stellar correspondences of traditional astrology as signs better found distributed across the natural world (Campion 2009, 117).

Central to this theoretical framework was Paracelsus's macrocosm–microcosm analogy, which argued via the Hermetic and Neoplatonic traditions that as things were above in the heavens, so too were they below on Earth. However, unlike in various astrological traditions, Paracelsus did not place the priority on the heavens. Instead he saw two kinds of "stars," the heavenly (macrocosmic) and the earthly (microcosmic), which existed within every person, plant, animal, and mineral. With a proper application of astrological and medical knowledge, the microcosm was stronger than the macrocosm. Thus, if a part of the body associated with Mars needed treatment, one could construct a talisman based on the properties of Mars (Campion 2009, 118). In his *Astronomia Magna*, Paracelsus provided instructions on constructing talismans for each sign of the zodiac.

This was contrary to Galenism, the prevailing medical theory in the 16th century. In Galenic medicine, all disease was considered to be an imbalance of the four humors (blood, phlegm, black bile, and yellow bile), and like was treated with unlike. So, if one had a surplus of phlegm, its treatment involved administering a substance associated with its humoral opposite, yellow bile. In Paracelsian medical theory, diseases were caused by "astra" or rogue external elements that ultimately derived from God, but corrupted in the material world by mixing in the four "wombs" (essentially equivalent to the four classical elements of fire, earth, air, and water but with subtly different properties) with his *tria prima*, or "three principles" of mercury, sulfur, and salt. Like was treated with like, and astrological (macrocosmic) correspondences helped determine what treatment to use (Goodrick-Clarke 1999, 27–28).

Justin Niermeier-Dohoney

See also: Astral Magic; Christianity; Medical Astrology; Renaissance and Reformation Astrology

Further Reading

Ball, Phillip. 2006. *The Devil's Doctor: Paracelsus and the World of Renaissance Magic and Science.* New York: Farrar, Strauss, and Giroux.

Campion, Nicholas. 2009. *A History of Western Astrology, Vol II: The Medieval and Modern Worlds.* New York: Continuum.

Debus, Allen G. 1966. *The English Paracelsians.* New York: Franklin Watts.

Goodrick-Clarke, Nicholas, ed. 1999. *Paracelsus.* Berkeley, CA: North Atlantic Books.

Pagel, Walter. 1982. *Paracelsus: An Introduction to Philosophical Medicine in the Era of the Renaissance.* Basel, Switzerland: Karger.

Webster, Charles. 2008. *Paracelsus: Medicine, Magic, and Mission at the End of Time.* New Haven, CT: Yale University Press.

Williams, Gerhild Scholz, and Charles D. Gunnoe, Jr., eds. 2002. *Paracelsian Moments: Science, Medicine, and Astrology in Early Modern Europe.* Kirksville, MO: Truman State University.

PARTRIDGE, JOHN (1644–1715)

John Partridge was the most famous English astrologer from the late 17th to the early 18th century. He was a zealous supporter of the Whig faction in English politics and anti-Catholicism in religion, attitudes that shaped and were shaped by his astrological program. Like many astrologers of his time, Partridge saw himself as a reformer out to purge astrology of its superstitious and magical elements. Unlike his older contemporary, collaborator, and detested rival John Gadbury, Partridge did not seek to use the techniques of the new science of the 17th century to reform astrology but rather called for a return to the "pure" astrology of Ptolemy. He attacked the subsequent "Arab" additions to astrology. His own astrology, however, was largely derived from his contemporary Placidus, ironic considering his fierce anti-Catholicism.

Partridge's Whig political credentials were impeccable. From a working-class background (his early career as a shoemaker was frequently invoked by his detractors) he was largely self-taught. He first came to the attention of the public with a burst of astrological publications in 1678 and 1679. He began publishing an almanac beginning in 1681, at first with the title *Mercurius Coelestis.* He eventually settled on *Merlinus Liberatus* a title harkening back to William Lilly's *Merlinus Anglicus*.

Partridge was an active pamphleteer during the late 1670s when the terms *whig* and *tory* first became used for political factions. He fled the country for Amsterdam following the accession of the Catholic ruler and opponent of the Whigs, King James II, in 1685. (Partridge claimed to have received a medical degree from the University of Leiden during his stay in the Netherlands, and like many astrologers combined medical practice with astrology.) From Amsterdam, he waged pamphlet war against both James and Gadbury, James's foremost astrological advocate. Partridge denounced Gadbury as a crypto-Catholic and boldly predicted the king's death. In addition to anti-Catholicism, Partridge's Whiggism was also based on a contractarian analysis of royal power. James had permanently forfeited the crown due to his breaking of his oaths to the English people. Partridge viewed the political role of the astrologer as being a check on despotism. He was no political dilettante but part of a radical movement that at its most extreme dreamed of overthrowing the monarchy entirely, a goal Partridge sympathized with.

Partridge viewed the Revolution of 1688 in which James was overthrown by the Protestant William of Orange as a repetition of the English Civil War of the midcentury, both caused by a "great conjunction" of Saturn and Jupiter. (Despite Partridge's self-proclaimed Ptolemaic fundamentalism, he employed non-Ptolemaic conjunctionary mundane astrology.) Partridge's continued championing of the Whig cause in the 1690s after his return from exile was also expressed in his ongoing feuds with Gadbury and with the up-and-coming Tory astrologer George Parker (1654–1743) who he accused of wife-beating. In his role as the self-appointed regulator of English astrology, he also attacked magical and talismanic astrology, something he proclaimed too low even for Gadbury.

Although Partridge's political radicalism mellowed after the establishment of a Protestant dynastic line, and he even enjoyed a court appointment as physician to William's Queen, Mary II, he remained a firm Whig and a frequent target of Tory polemicists. The most significant of these attacks was the "Bickerstaff hoax," the work of the Tory satirist Jonathan Swift (1667–1745). Taking the persona of a fictional astrologer, Isaac Bickerstaff, Swift predicted the exact time and date of Partridge's death in *Predictions for the Year 1708*, published toward the end of 1707. (Partridge himself regarded the prediction of the time of death as one of the supreme tests of an astrologer.) The hoax proved very popular, and Swift added to it by rebutting Partridge's indignant denials of his own death by claiming that the author was an impostor taking the name of the dead Partridge. Even Whigs supported "Bickerstaff" against Partridge. The Bickerstaff hoax is often taken as marking the end of serious belief in astrology among elite English people. However, the Bickerstaff hoax, whatever its popularity or Swift's expectations, did not end or even seriously damage Partridge's career. Partridge was actually more threatened by a feud with the Stationer's Company, the organization of London printers that controlled almanac printing in England over his payment for his almanac, the company's best seller. This led to the almanac not appearing from 1710 to 1712. A new agreement between Partridge and the Stationers led to its reappearance in

1713, and it was popular enough for the Stationers to continue many decades after Partridge's death. Partridge's Ptolemaic and Placidean astrology was carried on into the 19th century by his admirer, the Lincolnshire astrologer John Worsdale (1766–ca. 1828).

William E. Burns

See also: Almanacs; Gadbury, John; Placidus; Politics

Further Reading

Burns, William E. 2005. "Astrology and Politics in Early Modern England: King James II and the Almanac Men." *The Seventeenth Century* 20: 242–253.

Capp, Bernard S. 1979. *English Almanacs, 1500–1800: Astrology and the Popular Press*. Ithaca, NY: Cornell University Press.

Curry, Patrick. 1989. *Prophecy and Power: Astrology in Early Modern England*. Princeton: Princeton University Press.

McTague, John. 2011. "'There Is No Such Man as Isaack Bickerstaff': Partridge, Pittis and Jonathan Swift." *Eighteenth-Century Life* 35: 83–101.

PICATRIX

One of the most influential works of astral magic in medieval and Renaissance Europe was an originally Arabic treatise usually known by its Latin title of *Picatrix*. *Picatrix* is a guide to magic focusing on the invocation of celestial spirits associated with the planets, signs, and stars. It is marked by a combination of Neoplatonic philosophy and a very pragmatic approach to using magical techniques to get what the user wants. It describes how to make talismans incorporating astrological symbolism to cure particular ills or carry out other functions such as ingratiating the maker with the authorities. For each talisman, there is a right time for its manufacture depending on the positions of the planets and the ascendant. There are also numerous other magical recipes and descriptions of how and when to carry out magical rituals to win aid from planetary spirits. Decans and lunar mansions also play an important role in *Picatrix*'s astrology. The references to the invocation of spirits to work magic made the *Picatrix*, like other magical texts, religiously dangerous. The spells invoking the planetary spirits were difficult to distinguish from pagan prayers to the gods for whom the planets were named, who the Church identified with devils.

The original author of the *Picatrix* is unknown. Scholarly attributions vary from the 10th to 11th centuries, although there is a consensus that the author worked in Islamic Spain. The original Arabic title, *Ghayat al-Hakim* translates as "Goal of the Wise." (A copy of the original Arabic version was not identified until 1920.) The author or compiler describes the theoretical background of astral magic, drawing from Aristotle, Hellenistic astrology and Abū Ma'shar as well as Neoplatonism. The work also shows influence from India, mediated through Persian-language sources, and the Sabians of Harran. The author endorses the idea of correspondences between the celestial bodies and earthly inhabitants and emanations of divine power from God, their ultimate source, to the planets, in typically Neoplatonic fashion.

The work was translated into Spanish in 1256 (Spain, with its history of Muslim rule, was a hotbed of translation from Arabic) at the behest of Alfonso X of Castile, a ruler known for his interest in astronomy and Arabic thought. *Picatrix* was translated into Latin sometime later. There are different theories about the meaning of the title word *Picatrix*, mostly having to do with the actual or purported author. The influence of the *Picatrix* was limited in the Middle Ages, but it was widely circulated and referred to in the Renaissance and the 17th century. Such eminent astrologers and magicians as Marsilio Ficino and William Lilly were students of the *Picatrix*. The reputation of *Picatrix* remained dangerous enough that no printed edition or translation appeared until the 20th century. Several editions and translations have appeared in the past few decades as part of the revival of interest in the astrological and magical tradition.

William E. Burns

See also: Astral Magic; Astrotheology; Decans; Islamic Astrology; Renaissance and Reformation Astrology

Further Reading

Maxwell-Stuart, P. G. 2012. *Astrology: From Ancient Babylon to the Present Day.* Stroud, Gloucestershire, UK: Amberley.

Saif, Liana. 2015. *The Arabic Influences on Early Modern Occult Philosophy*. Basingstoke, UK: Palgrave Macmillan.

PLACIDUS (1603–1668)

Placido de Titi, known by his Latin name of Placidus, was one of the greatest reformers of astrology in the 17th century. From an Italian noble family, Placidus became a member of the Olivetan monastic order and a professor of Mathematics at the University of Pavia. Placidus called for a return to an astrology based on Ptolemy, with a rejection of many subsequent developments. He famously stated that his only guides in astrology were "Ptolemy and Reason." However, his devotion to Ptolemy was not uncritical. He elaborated many terse passages in Ptolemy, and criticized some aspect of Ptolemaic astrology. He also introduced non-Ptolemaic innovations, basing them on strained interpretations of Ptolemy.

Placidus was a voluminous writer who published many books during his lifetime. *Three Books of Physiomathematical Questions* (1650), generally known by the title of the posthumous second edition *Physiomathematics or Celestial Philosophy* (1675), is usually considered his central astrological work setting forth his system. Other important works are *Tables of Primary Motion* (1657), and *Commentaries on Ptolemy* (1658). All of his major works were in Latin, addressed to a learned audience. As was the case for most of the Catholic academic establishment in that time, Placidus believed in a basically Aristotelian natural philosophy building on the work of the Scholastic writers of the Middle Ages and accepted the Church's rejection of heliocentric astronomy. His astrology firmly repudiated magical influences. He regarded light as the force that underlay astrology, which led him to devise new techniques for dealing with the sun, which is unlike any other astrological planet in that its light persists for a time even when it is no longer visible.

One of Placidus's most important influences on the subsequent development of astrology was the "Placidus House System," which has become very widely used and is often viewed as the standard in Western astrology. Placidus claimed to find this system in Ptolemy, but this required a great deal of interpretation and extrapolation. He rejected the commonly used technique of solar returns but was a strong proponent of primary directions.

Placidus's relationship with the Church during his lifetime was ambiguous. The Olivetan Order did not block his astrological publishing, but astrology remained condemned by Papal decree. One reason Placidus was able to work publicly as both Catholic monk and astrologer was his relation with a powerful patron, Archduke Leopold-Wilhelm Habsburg of Austria (1614–1662), the brother of the Holy Roman emperor. Placidus dedicated *Tables of Primary Motion* to him and served as an astrological consultant.

Ironically, the immediate and long-term impact of Placidus's astrology would be greatest not in Catholic Europe but in Protestant England. The Catholic Church remained suspicious of astrology, and put Placidus's *Physiomathematics* on its Index of Forbidden Books in 1687, repeating the prohibition in 1709. In England, however, Placidus's Ptolemaic fundamentalism was taken up by John Partridge, the leading astrologer of the late 17th century. Partridge, firmly anti-Catholic, was, however, reluctant to credit Placidus by name. The astrologers John Bishop and Richard Kirby published *The Marrow of Astrology* (1689), an adaptation of Placidus's *Tables of Primary Motion* into English, without crediting him. Placidus continued to influence late 18th- and early 19th-century English astrologers including Ebenezer Sibly (whose brother Manoah published a translation of *Tables of Primary Motion* as *Astronomy and Elementary Philosophy* in 1789, claiming the work as his own) and John Worsdale (1766–1826?). (Worsdale, like Partridge, combined a dependence on Placidus with an anti-Catholic refusal to even name him.) Another British Placidean was James Wilson, the author of an influential *Dictionary of Astrology* (1819). In transmission, Placidus's teaching was shorn of some of its complexity. It was also treated as a system of rules rather than a natural philosophy, separated from its basis in Aristotelianism and its light-based theory of astrological causality. In this simplified form, it influenced the 19th-century English astrological revival and modern Western astrology.

William E. Burns

See also: House Systems; Morin, Jean-Baptiste; Partridge, John; Primary Directions; Ptolemy; Sibly, Ebenezer

Further Reading

Gansten, Martin. 2011. "Placidean Teachings in Early Nineteenth-Century Britain: John Worsdale and Thomas Oxley." In *Astrologies: Plurality and Diversity: The Proceedings of the Eighth Annual Conference of the Sophia Centre for the Study of Cosmology in Culture, University of Wales, Trinity Saint David, 24–25 July 2010*, ed. Nicholas Campion and Liz Green. Ceredigion: Sophia Centre Press.

Holden, James Herschel. 1996. *A History of Horoscopic Astrology from the Babylonian Period to the Modern Age*. Tempe, AZ: American Federation of Astrologers.

POLITICS

Any discussion of aspects of astrology, such as its relationship with politics, raises chronological difficulties. On the one hand, astrological lore can be traced back from cuneiform tablets through to Byzantine collections, thus spanning millennia of highly similar material. On the other hand, astrology has shown a remarkable ability to reinvent its rules, thereby making it tricky to identify clear elements defining its development through time. It is important, therefore, to remember that a written astrological corpus began well after the development of an astronomical written corpus. There is no evidence of any complete astrological tract from before the first century CE, while we do own many fragments of papyrus, ostraka, and other material, from well after that time. This is relevant as far as the misleading similarities between divinatory practices by celestial omens and documented political uses of astrology. Traces of the relationship of astrology to politics could be found in many cultures and civilizations around the world since well before the first century CE. Yet, such traces may be misleading and force us to carefully discriminate between phenomena that resembled each other without, however, being one and the same. A history of astrology with special reference to its relationship to politics may indeed include some episodes from classical antiquity, particularly from the time of the Roman Empire; on the other hand, it may not legitimately tell a holistic story without the risk of oversimplifying a complex phenomenon lacking much written evidence.

Astrology shares the same origin with divination by omen, by portents, by bird-flight observation, by animal-guts extraction and observation, and the likes. Such practices can be documented for many cultures worldwide. Likewise, ancient astronomy in the sense of star-gazing, identifying constellations, calculating the courses of certain planets, and so on, is a practice most ancient and which can be documented for many cultures and civilizations worldwide. Astrology is defined as the craft of studying the influence of the stars on human events on the basis of a set of theories about celestial bodies around the sun, the zodiac with its 12 constellations, or signs. The earliest linguistic distinction between astrology and astronomy is recorded in sources dating back from the seventh century CE, in Isidore of Seville's *Etymologies*.

Various forms of astronomical investigation and divination by omen are attested in many cultures worldwide, from the Mayas to the Chinese, from the ancient Egyptians to the Greeks who learned much from them, and from ancient Persia to the Celts. In all these cultures divination by star-gazing also implied the establishment of the figure of the adviser(s) to the ruler(s) akin to the early modern court astrologer. In ancient Rome, for instance, *auguri* made political predictions on the basis of both star-gazing as well as by observing birds' flying routes, also reading the future into extracted organs from dissected fowl. Celts are thought to have arranged a number of stone sites according to astrological considerations and for the purpose—among others—of star-gazing. The role of the Celtic druid, who could discern medicinal herbs and read the stars, was at times also a political one of adviser to the community, if we are to believe Julius Caesar's *Commentaries*, thereby testifying to the political uses of astrology in Celtic lands. But the lack of proper, written evidence, makes Caesar's account more an interesting anecdote than firm ground for historical analysis. Maya society, like other pre-Colombian cultures, shares much with the Celts and Romans in how they built sites and entrusted astronomers with the right to advise rulers. Yet, as for the Celts, written evidence is just not there to allow us to speculate on links between astrology and politics.

"Chinese portent astrology, with its view that heaven's intentions are made manifest by the stars (among other things), held fast to a motivation similar to that of the ancient Mesopotamian astrologers who compiled collections of celestial omens to keep the king informed of potential disasters or successes in the near term" (Pankenier, 343). It is important to distinguish between practices, such as the Chinese ones, which related much more to divination and astronomy, from those political uses of astrological publications that seem to be an historical phenomenon unique to the Roman Empire first, and, above all, to early modern Western Europe, where they were closely linked to the printing revolution in its interactions with the Reformation and the rise of the State on one hand, and the rise of science on the other.

The main and most conspicuous tool of the astrologer is the horoscope, from the Greek horoscopos, or "ascendent," namely, the highest point in which a star or planet can be seen on the horizon at a given time, thereby allowing the astrologer to produce a map of celestial influences—positive, negative, or neutral ones—which must be at work at a given time, typically, at birth. In ancient times, in Medieval Muslim Spain, and in Western Europe until the end of the 17th century at least, it was possible to cast a horoscope to work out the most propitious time for erecting a building or founding a new city, or simply for taking some particular action. In the Renaissance, calculations for the most propitious time for a given action became highly fashionable, and the fashion spread from the upper classes down to whoever could afford consulting an astrologer. Thus, "horary" or "elective" (i.e., relating to the time for choosing to carry out an action) astrology became a widespread feature of Western European culture from the beginning of the 16th century to the end of the 17th century.

Forms of horary astrology with explicit political uses can first be documented properly in relation to the Roman Empire. Although Babylonians, Mayas, Aztecs, Incas, ancient Chinese, all practiced various forms of divination by omens as well as early astronomical observations, if we stick to the definition of astrology given above, we can only really describe conscious political uses of astrology starting with the new figure of the accompanying astrologer that emerged subsequent to the fall of the Roman Republic. Although republican Rome had seen politicians rely on traditional forms of divination by omen, under Augustus, the first Emperor, things changed dramatically. He ordered the minting of new coins with his zodiacal sign, Capricorn. He ordered the erection of a huge meridian in order to celebrate the association of Capricorn with the rebirth of the sun, thereby exploiting the visual mythology of the returning golden age associated to his empire. Astrology became a propaganda tool in Augustan Rome. Court poet Marcus Manlius composed the *Astronomica* around the 9–15 CE. It is the first-known tract on astrology—despite its name—written in the form of a poem about the heavens. It is the first such work in the Latin language, in which the link between astrology and monarchy is clearly spelled out, contrary to contemporary Greek-language works of a similar vein, yet of a different political orientation. Astrology acquired a political role that it never enjoyed before. Subsequent Roman emperors issued legislation against astrologers who dared to cast horoscopes on the best times for people to conjure against the emperor. Ancient sources agree that many astrologers did indeed face persecutions, and even executions, for calculating the times of attempted coups. Tacitus (55–120 CE) recalled that in the year when four different claimants disputed the imperial crown, each was surrounded by astrologers.

With the collapse of the Western Roman Empire and the ascent of Christianity the political role of astrology changed considerably. Church Father Augustine firmly condemned astrology as an illicit practice that aimed to substitute natural necessity for God's will. One cannot find evidence of any political role for astrology in Western Europe until the Renaissance. The printing press, which acted as "an agent of change" in so many spheres, also revolutionized the uses of astrology in relation to politics. Astrology's link with politics reached its climax after the Reformation, when astrology became a weapon for or against religious ideas, which, in turn, meant ecclesiological settlements and, therefore, different ways of sharing power between Church and State.

In early modern Europe, political astrology reached its climax before disappearing from the political scene at the beginning of the 19th century during the Napoleonic Wars. Although the role of astrology in the history of science has been attracting attention from historians of science, its political uses are best understood here in the contexts of Church–State relations on one hand, and of expertise and the early modern State on the other hand. The two issues are intertwined. This was the time in which historians of political thought locate the genesis of the modern state. Crucial was the state's claim to full sovereignty, which could only be achieved when no foreign prince or religious authority encroached onto the power of the sovereign ruler. This process led to civil wars, for example, the French wars of religion (during which the astrological-political works of Michel de Notre dame, best known as "Nostradamus" played an important role in the political debates), the English Civil Wars, the Glorious Revolution, and the subsequent Jacobite wars; the Revolt in the Low Countries; the Venetian interdict question; and many other internal turmoils. The big issue at stake was to find new settlements for Church–State relations. Ecclesiology, the branch of the law that regulates Church–State relations and their balance of powers, was a major ideological and military battlefield.

European libraries keep vast collections of early modern astrological publications whose content can be defined as broadly political, and whose targeted readership can be identified as politically interested before being astrologically minded. In England, the Thomason Tracts Collection in the British Library, London, is made up of some 30,000 pamphlets documenting the upheavals of the Civil Wars, the Commonwealth under Oliver Cromwell, and the Restoration of the Monarchy. The Thomason Tracts were mostly printed in London between 1640 and 1661. Although one could not call the Thomason Tracts astrological, one could surely use them to define the categories and subjects of the English political discourse in the years 1640–1661. The same subjects can be found in astrological almanacs printed in the same years that forecast both the weather and political trends. There were almanacs published by astrologers who were Royalist soldiers, such as Captain George Wharton. There were Independent or Puritan-leaning astrologers publishing almanacs. The most famous astrologer of 17th-century England was indeed the Puritan William Lilly. Antiquary and astrologer Elias Ashmole amassed the biggest and most comprehensive collection of 17th-century English astrological material, which is kept today in the Bodleian Library, Oxford. Indeed, the astrological collections in Ashmole's library can serve us as a useful case study about the relationship of astrology and politics.

Astrological prognostications from the 1650s often dealt with current political and religious affairs. It would be wrong to classify such works as Lilly's Parliamentarian almanac *Merlinus Anglicus* or Wharton's royalist *Astrological Judgement* as purely astrological or natural philosophical material. It would be misleading to regard his almanacs from the 1650s and those dating from the 1680s as only astrological texts. Pamphlets, such as the anonymous *Answer of a Letter . . . on Some Remarks on the Late Comet* (1681), contained astrological discussions of comets, which is actually a pretext for speaking of European politics. The production of knowledge in early modern Europe, and the uses that early modern people made of specific genres for tackling issues that could also be debated in publications, might seem more obviously relevant to us, living centuries later and used to different styles of intervention in the political discourse. From the point of view of an antiquary-astrologer like Ashmole, it seems fair to consider the astrological works in his Oxford library as both astrological publications (especially those which are more general treatises on the rules of the art) and as historical documents relevant to the political and religious issues of Ashmole's time. This is evident in, for example, Ashm.62, which contains English almanacs spanning the years 1571–1598, thus documenting the dawn of astrological publishing in the vernacular in the British Isles. Ashm. 65 spans the years 1612–1617. Ashm.68 covers the years 1629–1631. Ashm.74 contains 15 different almanacs for the year 1643, thus showing the spectacular rise of the astrological press during the civil wars and mirror contemporary English political debates. Ashm.92 contains 24 almanacs for the year 1654 and is an example of astrological publishing from the time of the Commonwealth. Ashm.267 contains 13 almanacs for the year 1662; it is an example of the Restoration astrological market. Ashm.310 contains mostly almanacs for the years 1675–1684. They reflect contemporary worries about Louis XIV's aggressive foreign policy. Ashm.610 contains a rare almanac printed in Boston, New England, in 1683. By the early 1700s, almanacs became more and more devoid of political overtones. The Hanoverian settlement after 1714, while far from undisputed, was strong enough to eject astrology from the political press.

There was a comparable phenomenon in France. Collections of almanacs like Ashmole's can only be found until the settlement of the Huguenot question in the 1640s. Once the French religious wars were practically over, astrology in France lost its connection to the political discourse. This raises the question of the decline of astrology in relation to science on the one hand and on to sovereignty on the other hand. Although it is indisputable that post-Newtonian astronomy was a blow to the theoretical bases of astrology, it seems likely that the political uses of astrology in early modern Western Europe were far more related to the fortunes of the strengths of sovereignty. The heyday of political astrology in the 16th and 17th centuries was made possible by the exploitation of the printing press, which, in times of civil wars or otherwise state troubles, could break free from effective censorship. Astrology was therefore intimately related to the rise of the modern sovereign state in early modern Western Europe.

Vittoria Feola

See also: Almanacs; Ashmole, Elias; Chinese Astrology; Court Astrologers; Gadbury, John; Legal Regulation of Astrology; Lilly, William; Mundane Astrology; Nazism and the Third Reich; Nostradamus; Partridge, John; Quigley, Joan

Further Reading

Barton, Tamsyn. 1994. *Ancient Astrology*. London: Routledge.

Dhombres, J. 2007. "L'astrologie et les savoirs en Europe et dans le monde arabe." In *Culture arabe et culture européenne. L'Inconnu au Turban dans l'album de famille, Histoire et Perspective Méditerranéennes*, ed. Malika Pondevie Roumane, François Clément, and John Tolan, 37–57. Paris: L'Harmattan.

Drévillon, H. 1996. *Lire et écrire l'avenir. L'astrologie dans la France du grand siècle (1610–1715)*. Champ Vallon: Seyssel.

Feola, Vittoria. 2012. *Elias Ashmole and the Uses of Antiquity*. Paris: STP Blanchard.

Feola, Vittoria, ed. 2014. *Antiquarianism and Science in Early Modern Urban Networks*. Paris: STP Blanchard.

Gager, J. G. 1999. *Curse Tablets and Binding Spells from the Ancient World*. Oxford: Oxford University Press.

Pankenier, David. 2009. "The Planetary Portent of 1524 in China and Europe." *Journal of World History* 20, no. 3: 339–375.

PONT, ROBERT (1524–1606)

Robert Pont, a founding father of the Scottish Protestant Reformation, played a major role in both church and state as a minster who served repeatedly as the moderator of the General Assembly and a senator of the College of Justice, Scotland's highest civil court. Pont was also a significant humanist scholar. His authority even with King James VI allowed him unique freedom to address unacceptable topics, extending to that most dangerous of predictions, the death of monarchs.

Pont's central intellectual project concerned the periods and cycles in scripture that showed an underlying coherence to both the biblical past and the prophetic future the bible projected. This logic or rhythm to biblical chronology fit the Protestant master narrative—the story of the early church's decline, the medieval rise of the papal Antichrist, and the current confrontation preceding the Last Judgment at the end of time. Scriptural time sequences also connected with patterns in world history. By creating a chronology of human experience, it became possible to anticipate great historical changes in both religion and politics. The key to understanding these changes was astrology. Astrology not only confirmed scripture and validated prophecy; it also naturalized them.

Pont's naturalism not only upheld, powerfully, the Protestant historical vision, it also ensured that the universe possessed a coherent purpose. Pont was much exercised by the Epicurean cosmos ruled by contingency and chance as set forth by the Roman poet Lucretius in his *De Rerum Natura*. Pont's integration of the universe not only confronted papal misconceptions and the Vatican's cynical manipulation of idolatry and superstition but also responded to potentially far more devastating "Epicurean" ideas of a purposeless universe recovered from the classical era.

Although Pont firmly rejected any hint of "Pythagorical superstition," he had no doubt that "many great hid mysteries" were contained in the number seven. These "mysteries" manifested themselves in the sets of sabbatical years devised by his parishioner, the mathematician, engineer, and biblical exegete John Napier of Merchiston in the recently published *A Plaine Discovery of the Whole Revelation* (Edinburgh 1593). Napier had used his numerical insight, most notably the core periodization of 490 (7 x 70) years, as the basis for reading the Book of Revelation. Pont adopted Napier's numbers to project biblical history back to the beginning of time. In this way he identified the year in which the world began and discovered that it agreed with Joseph Scaliger's conclusions in his *De emendatione temporum* (1583). From this Pont went on to work out what he regarded as a fully grounded world chronology. Pont followed Scaliger's integration of classical history with the histories of other ancient peoples and Jewish history. He commented on ancient peoples' methods for measuring time and defining epochs. Pont sought to integrate prophecy, chronology, and astrology into a massive cyclical narrative that nevertheless described and embodied the ultimately progressive trajectory of the Protestant historical vision. This integration promised to achieve an astral sociology that could account for religious change as well as the rise and decline of states in harmony with natural processes.

Crucial to this undertaking was astrology. To ascribe social decline simply to "the corrupt manners of men" struck Pont as patently inadequate. Men's attitudes were continuously changing, and consequently such explanations were inherently "uncertain" and threw explanation back onto chance and fortune. Rather, there needed to be "a concurrente cause" that proceeded "from a high grounde": the astral influence that proved at once predictive and causal. With astrology introduced into the new chronology, human experience and even nature itself could at last become genuinely intelligible.

But there was a problem. "Vulgar prognosticators" almost always made incorrect predictions bringing astrology into contempt. Hack astrologers went wrong, in part, because the skies had changed since the days of the Chaldeans, Arabs, and other ancient astrologers. Most notably, the solar ecliptic had shifted some 27 degrees, 15 minutes since antiquity, now intersecting Aries at a different point. Sky charts based on the past could only get things wrong.

Astrology's potential was enormous, and Pont hoped to realize it. Pont—who saw himself in the tradition of great academic astrologers like Johann Stoeffler (1452–1531), Caspar Peucer (1525–1602), and Erasmus Rheinholt (1511–1553)—looked to a firmly rational astrology manifesting the great expansion of human knowledge at the end of days.

Astrology, even fortified with prophecy and history, could not as yet make confident large-scale predictions or foresee specific alterations in government or mutations in religion. Nevertheless, Pont expected enormous transformations following 1600. If Napier and Pont's periodization did not project the Last Judgment until the later 18th century, Pont and many of his contemporaries still thought it likely that time would be foreshortened for sake of the elect. John of Patmos's seventh trumpet, Pont came to believe, had begun its blast in 1541: the conclusion of the latter days could not lie far ahead. All the signs, both natural and political, indicated the moment. Yet certainty about historical redemption was simply not available.

Pont's 1599 *Newe Treatise on the Right Reckoning of Yeares, and Ages of the World* was written in haste, and in the vernacular for a popular audience rather than Latin. Its immediate purpose was to show that the announced 1600 papal jubilee at Rome bore no connection whatever to the jubilees of ancient Israel and the markers found in scripture. Papal Jubilees were a fraud invented no more than 300 years earlier by that most tyrannous of medieval popes, Boniface VIII, solely to bilk the credulous. Pont provided an outline of his chronology and synthesis to underwrite his claims.

Greater confidence existed on a less grand level, including the lives of rulers. In 1603 Pont announced Queen Elizabeth of England's death to her heir, King James, before word had reached Edinburgh from England. Pont insisted he was no seer; he denied any special abilities. His knowledge derived from his astrological skills, techniques available presumably to any educated person. That points to a political transformation Pont anticipated for the years after 1600: James's accession to the English crown and the creation of a new British state, supplanting the kingdoms of England and Scotland. Pont, a passionate supporter of the British project, noted the philosopher Cratippus's observation at the fall of the Roman republic that there were periods fatal to governments. The years after 1600 were clearly such. At the same time, the prospect of a new Britain carried eschatological implications for many, both English and Scots.

Pont lived to be 82, yet never saw the publication of his magnum opus, the *De sabbaticorum annorum periodis chronologica a mundi exordio ad nostra usque secula et porro digestio*. Only in 1619, 13 years after his death, was it printed in London. We have no record of its reception or any later commentary on it, though the reprinting in 1626 suggests some audience. In *De sabbaticorum* Pont detailed the periodization described in the *Newe Treatise*, and promoted the grand synthesis he had proposed—supporting it with truly formidable erudition including a striking familiarity with rabbinic sources.

Pont was one of the significant late 16th-century intellects for whom astrology provided intelligibility to both the sacred drama and the natural world, offering a rational and accessible basis for human knowledge.

Arthur Williamson

See also: Apocalypticism; Christianity; Mundane Astrology; Renaissance and Reformation Astrology

Further Reading

Galloway, Bruce, and Brian Levack, eds. 1985. *The Jacobean Union: Six Tracts of 1604*. Edinburgh: Scottish History Society.

Grafton, Anthony. 1983, 1993. *Joseph Scaliger, a Study in the History of Classical Scholarship*. 2 vols. Oxford: Oxford University Press.

Williamson, Arthur. 1994. "Number and National Consciousness: The Edinburgh Mathematicians and Scottish Political Culture at the Union of Crowns." In *Scots and Britons*, ed. R. A. Mason. Cambridge: Cambridge University Press.

PRIMARY DIRECTIONS

Primary directions, known up to the 17th century simply as directions, are a prognostic technique with Hellenistic roots. The English name comes from the Latin *directio*, translating the Arabic *(at)-tasyīr*; in medieval times the latter was sometimes simply Latinized as *athazir* (with variants). Another synonym derived from the Latin is prorogation; the original Greek term is *aphesis*. All these words share the basic sense of "sending out" or "extending," referring to the symbolic release of a planet or other point to move around the nativity, passing through subdivisions of the zodiacal signs and encountering other planets, aspect points, and so on. The qualifying adjective "primary" was added by Placidus to distinguish the earlier technique from his newly invented "secondary directions," generally known today as secondary progressions.

Historical Origins and Technical Foundations

Directions seem to have begun in the second or first century BCE as a counting of the time taken by any zodiacal sign to rise in a given clime or zone of geographic latitude, each equatorial degree or "time" (corresponding to some four minutes of clock time) being equated with one year of life. Eventually, these rising times began to be treated as symbolic numbers of years associated even with signs not rising in the nativity, and ecliptical distances between points in the horoscope were converted into time using such numbers. Because a zodiacal sign or degree requires different amounts of time to rise, set, culminate, or cross some intermediate point, such a procedure no longer corresponded to astronomical reality.

In the classical and more sophisticated form taught by Ptolemy and practiced into modern times, directions are based on the natural apparent motion of the celestial bodies across the sky, caused by the rotation of the Earth around its axis in just under 24 hours. This motion, sometimes called the "primary motion," has given the technique its modern name (Placidus's secondary directions are similarly based on the planets' proper or "secondary" motion). As each degree of the zodiac is carried clockwise across a stationary point of reference (such as the eastern horizon or ascendant), that point is envisaged as moving counterclockwise through the zodiac. Motion toward the horizon is measured by oblique ascension; toward the midheaven or meridian, by right ascension; and toward any point not placed exactly on either of these circles, by a sliding scale known as mixed ascensions or proportional semiarcs. When a moving point has reached the same relative distance to both horizon and meridian as the reference point, the two are considered to be conjunct.

Terminology and Usage

The starting point for any direction is the identification of a significator: a planet or other point signifying the matter under consideration, such as life, actions, fortune. The significator can be moved symbolically either forward through the zodiac (known as direct motion) or backward (converse motion). In a direct direction, typically considered more powerful, the significator is the fixed reference point across which the apparent rotation of the celestial sphere is measured; in a converse direction, the significator itself is moved with the celestial sphere.

As a significator is directed through the zodiac, it passes through the unequal subdivisions of a sign known as terms (Latin *termini*; Greek *ὁρία*), each ruled by one of the five visible planets (excluding the sun and moon). The ruler of the terms through which the significator is directed is known in English and Latin as the divisor, translating the Arabic *al-qāsim*, or as *algebuthar* (with variants), a Latinization of the Perso-Arabic *al-jār baḫtār*, which in turn translates the Greek *χρονοκράτωρ*, *chronokrator* or "ruler of the time." Depending on the extension of the terms and the latitude of birth, a divisor may rule over a period of life lasting many years.

Within each such segment of the zodiac, the significator may encounter one or more planets by body or aspect, as well as fixed stars. Such a planet or star is known as a promissor (or promittor). Authors differ on the relative importance of the divisor and promissor in affecting the area of life represented by the significator according to their nature and position; Ptolemy favours the promissor.

Although directions may be used for prognostication of any type of event, the technique has always been particularly associated with determining the length of life. For this purpose, a special significator of life is identified, often called the *apheta* or *hyleg* (with variants), from the Greek *ἀφέτης* or its Persian translation *hīlāg*, both meaning "releaser." When the hyleg is directed under certain conditions to a sufficiently malefic promissor (known as the abscissor, "cutter-off," or *anareta*, from the Greek *ἀναιρέτης*, "killer"), death is expected to occur at the corresponding age from causes signified by the nature and location of the anareta.

Later Developments

Technical developments of directions were made by some medieval Arabic astrologers, notably by replacing the method of mixed ascensions with that of position circles—a form of artificial horizon intersecting the fixed point of reference in a direction, motion toward which is measured by oblique ascension. The same innovation was introduced in 15th-century Europe, where it was promoted by Regiomontanus. Two centuries later, Placidus championed a return to the Ptolemaic method, but simultaneously introduced numerous innovations of his own, including so-called minor and mundane aspects and a hybrid of the semiarc and position-circle methods of calculation. In the late 17th century, Placidean teachings were disseminated in English, primarily by John Partridge; but with the general decline of astrology during the following century they were largely forgotten, and as the art was gradually revived during the 19th century, only some of Placidus's ideas were reintroduced.

The 20th century saw a sharp drop in the knowledge of primary directions among astrological practitioners, particularly following World War II. The few who continued to use the technique typically transformed it by the inclusion of new planets, the reinterpretation of converse directions to imply a reversal of the primary motion, and the exclusion of the terms. For most, only the directions of the angles remained, as part of the "progressed horoscope," a new hybrid technique introduced by Alan Leo.

Martin Gansten

See also: Hellenistic Astrology; Islamic Astrology; Placidus; Ptolemy

Further Reading

Bouché-Leclerq, Auguste. 1899. *L'astrologie grecque*, 411–421. Paris: Ernest Leroux.

Gansten, Martin. 2009. *Primary Directions: Astrology's Old Master Technique*. Bournemouth: The Wessex Astrologer.

Gansten, Martin. 2011. "Placidean Teachings in Early Nineteenth-Century Britain: John Worsdale and Thomas Oxley." In *Astrologies: Plurality and Diversity*, ed. Nicholas Campion, 109–124. Lampeter, UK: Sophia Centre Press.

Gansten, Martin. 2012. "Balbillus and the Method of *aphesis*." *Greek, Roman and Byzantine Studies* 52: 587–602. http://grbs.library.duke.edu/article/view/14581/3799

Holden, James Hersche. 1996. *A History of Horoscopic Astrology*. Tempe, AZ: American Federation of Astrologers.

Robbins, Frank Eggleston. 1940. *Ptolemy: Tetrabiblos*. Loeb Classical Library 435. Cambridge, MA: Harvard University Press.

PROTESTANTISM. *SEE* CHRISTIANITY.

PTOLEMY (SECOND CENTURY CE)

Claudius Ptolemaeus (Greek: *Κλαύδιος Πτολεμαῖος*), or simply Ptolemy, was an Egyptian of Greek descent known for his scientific work in mathematics, geography, music, optics, astronomy, and astrology. Though his birthplace is unknown, most available evidence suggests that he was born in or around Alexandria in the Roman province of Egypt between 90 and 100 CE and lived his entire life there, dying around 168 or 170 CE (Campion 2008, 209; Taub 1993, 7). The 14th-century Byzantine astronomer Theodore Meliteniotes claimed that he was born in Ptolemaïs Hermiou in Upper Egypt, but no other source confirms this and most historians have not treated this as credible. A number of scholars during the Renaissance presumed that he came from the Egpytian city of Pelusium at the far eastern end of the Nile Delta, but this is likely due to a mistranslation of "Phelud(i) ensis," often appended to his name in medieval Latin commentaries on his work. This, in turn, was a mistranslation of the Arabic "qalūdī," itself a misinterpretation of his Greek name *Klaúdios* (Toomer 1970, 186–187). Almost no information about Ptolemy's life has survived and essentially everything known about him has been gleaned from his writings.

Ptolemy authored several important scientific works including the *Geography*, the *Almagest*, and the *Tetrabiblos*, all of which exerted profound influence on geography, astronomy, and astrology in the Byzantine, Arabic, and European scientific traditions from the second century through the early modern era. The *Geography* served as an atlas, a mathematical treatise on cartographic techniques, and a compendium of the geographic knowledge extant in the second-century Roman Empire. Ptolemy originally intended it to be an updated version of a now-lost atlas by Marinus of Tyre, though he eventually added much that was original. Numerous medieval and Renaissance mapmakers based their own works upon Ptolemy's *Geography* (Toomer 1970, 198).

Ptolemy's best-known work, the *Almagest* is an astronomical and mathematical treatise describing the apparent motion of the stars and planets as observed from the Earth. Written in Koine Greek and originally titled *Μαθηματικὴ Σύνταξις* (*Mathēmatikē Syntaxis*, literally "Mathematical Treatise"), it became known in the West as the *Almagest*, a Latinization of the Arabic *al-majisṭī*, which derived from the Greek *μεγίστη* (*megíste*, or "greatest"). It remained perhaps the most influential astronomical text in the Arab, Byzantine, and Western scientific traditions for nearly a millennium and half until its geocentric system was displaced by the heliocentric system first propounded by Nicolaus Copernicus in his *De Revolutionibus* of 1543 (Campion 2008, 209). In the *Almagest*, Ptolemy described a cosmos borrowed, in part, from Aristotle, where an immobile, spherical Earth occupied the center of the universe around which the sun, moon, planets, and fixed stars moved in perfect circles. It provided a thorough mathematical architecture for understanding the complex movements of the planets, which would undergird astrology as a mathematical science.

Ptolemy's most important contribution to astrology was the *Tetrabiblos*. The *Tetrabiblos* is a treatise on the techniques of mundane and horoscopic astrology, a synthesis of Greco-Roman natural philosophy and Babylonian and Hellenistic astrological thought, and a spirited defense of mathematically grounded astrology against its detractors, such as Cicero and Carneades. Its title means "the four books" after its principal divisions, though it was originally titled *Ἀποτελεσματικά* (*Apotelematiká*, or "effects") and is sometimes known by its Latin translation the *Quadripartitum*. It endured as a robust bulwark of astrological authority throughout Late Antiquity and the Latin Middle Ages and developed a wider audience in the West after Plato of Tivoli translated it from Arabic into Latin in 1138 (Tester 1987, 152). Ptolemy expounded on the general rules for interpreting the influence of the heavenly bodies over events on the Earth and elucidated which changes could be predicted by a mathematical understanding of the movement of the heavens. In this sense, he seems to have intended the *Tetrabiblos* as a complement to or as a natural extension of the work he had done in the *Almagest*: the latter allowed one to determine with precision and accuracy the motion, direction, and position of the planets and stars, while the former gave one the tools for interpreting the influence those movements had over the terrestrial world (Toomer 1970, 198).

Within the *Tetrabiblos*, like several of his other works, Ptolemy began with the general and worked his way to the particular. Book I commences with a defense of astrology and a definition of astrology as a mathematical science, even if it is, like medicine, conjectural at best. It offers procedural rules and techniques for prognostication, describes the movement of the planets and stars in a largely nontechnical summation of details to be found in the *Almagest*, and includes guidelines for understanding the results. Book II deals with various collective facets of astrology that are generally applicable to large groups of people or nations (mundane astrology) and explains the astrological impact on physical events, such as weather and natural disasters. This section served to explain why people born at the same time often experienced different fates. Climate, geography, and nationality could all affect astrological influence. Books III and IV together explain with more specificity the effects of the stars on individuals based on a person's horoscope. In Book III, Ptolemy describes how one's time, date, and place of birth (nativity) establishes certain characteristics of that person, while in Book IV, he expands upon how the heavens affect various major events in a person's life, such as getting married, having children, amassing wealth, and dying (Taub 1993, 130). Notably, Ptolemy does not discuss *katarche* (the selection of favorable moments for embarking on new endeavors) or horary astrology (the casting of horoscopes at the moment a particular question is asked), though Ptolemy's system could easily be adapted to incorporate either.

Although earlier astrological traditions, such as the Babylonian, had developed disciplinary rules for astrology, Ptolemy sought its natural causes. He stressed that the predictability of the movement of the heavens and their physical effects on Earth—such as the relationship between the movement of the sun across the ecliptic and the changing of the seasons or the connection between the moon and the tides—mirrored the effects of the stars on people. For Ptolemy, the position of the celestial bodies, and in particular the order of the planets and their distance from the Earth, sun, and one another, determined their influences. In keeping with the four qualities of Aristotelian thought, therefore, Mars was hot and dry, Venus was hot and moist, and Saturn was cold and dry (Campion 2008, 210). Ptolemy's rationale was that Saturn's qualities were due to its distance from the sun, while Mars's was due to its close proximity. Venus received its heat from the sun but derived its moisture from its nearness to the Earth and moon. The various combinations of these qualities and their associate temperaments, in conjunction with when and in which zodiacal signs they appeared, explained astrological influence (Taub 1993, 131).

Several scientific, philosophical, and religious traditions influenced Ptolemy. Second-century CE Alexandria was a cosmopolitan city full of Gnostics, Hermeticists, Platonists, Jews, Christians, Greco-Roman pagans, and members of various mystery cults, all of whom jostled with one another to define and direct astrological thought. These, of course, were not mutually exclusive categories, and Ptolemy is representative of someone whose philosophical inclinations drew from many sources. According to Liba Chaia Taub, the philosophical and religious climate in the city of Alexandria—and in Ptolemy's mind—is best described not necessarily as "eclectic," but as "syncretic," and various schools of thought intermingled to create unified, harmonious philosophies even more so than they sought to distinguish themselves from one another (Taub 1993, 10).

Ptolemy is sometimes uncritically regarded as a Stoic—a philosophical school whose determinism and fatalism attracted many astrologers in the ancient world. However, Ptolemy incorporated Aristotelian, Platonic, and Pythagorean thought in his natural philosophy and astrology as well. For one thing, Ptolemy argued that if the stars truly determined everything, then astrology was pointless because knowing one's unchangeable fate was worthless. Although he did write that foreknowledge of a preordained event could calm the soul, his astrology allowed for contingency in human life and he seemed to believe that destinies were, in general, changeable (Campion 2008, 211).

Ptolemy adapted from Aristotle the geocentric model of the cosmos and added to it mathematical rules governing the movement of the sun, moon, stars, and planets about the Earth. He also adopted the Aristotelian position, contra Plato, that the material world matters and can be investigated rationally through observation, and he may have held in quasireligious reverence the Aristotelian idea of a prime mover (*primum mobile*) as the ultimate, first cause in the universe. From Plato, Ptolemy maintained an orthodox position concerning the human soul (a tripartite structure with logical, spirited, and appetitive motivations), which he argued were each affected differently by the stars. There are also hints of Pythagoreanism in his astrology. Part of Ptolemy's purpose in writing the *Tetrabiblos* was the hope that by giving astrology a rational, mathematical foundation, and he would consciously distance it from the religiously inflected astrology of the Hermeticists and the Mithraists, even as his interpretation of astrology was itself as a codified

Ptolemy in China: The *Tianwen Shiyong*

There is a long history of Chinese translations and adaptations of Western works on astronomy and astrology going back to the Tang Dynasty. In 1644, the Jesuit scholar Adam Schall von Bell published a work of Western astrology in Chinese, the *Tianwen Shiyong*. Jesuit missionaries at the time were trying to ingratiate themselves with the Chinese state through their mastery of Western astronomy. Jesuits had submitted an astronomical globe to the Chongzhen Emperor in 1637, arousing interest in Western knowledge among court officials. Schall von Bell was ordered to produce a work on Western astrology. The *Tianwen Shiyong* is a translation of a section of Ptolemy's *Tetrabiblios* dealing with the influence of the stars on the Aristotelian physical properties of heating and cooling, drying and moistening. No further translations appear to have been produced as part of this project, but the *Tianwen Shiyong* was instrumental in introducing some Chinese scholars to Western astrology and was also known in 18th-century Japan.

Source: Han Qi. 2011. "From Adam Schall von Bell to Jan Mikolaj Smogulecki: The Introduction of Western Astrology in Late Ming and Early Qing China." *Monumenta Serica* 59: 485–490.

divinatory practice based on the abstract, quasidivine, mathematically ordered cosmos as originally described by Pythagoras (Campion 2008, 213).

Justin Niermeier-Dohoney

See also: Fate; Hellenistic Astrology; Medical Astrology; Placidus; Primary Directions; Pythagoras of Samos; Roman Astrology; Science

Further Reading

Barton, Tamsyn. 1994. *Ancient Astrology*. London: Routledge.

Campion, Nicholas. 2008. *A History of Western Astrology, Vol. I: The Ancient World*. London: Bloomsbury.

Lloyd, G. E. R. 1973. *Greek Science after Aristotle*. New York: Norton.

Robbins, Frank Eggleston. 1940. *Ptolemy: Tetrabiblos*. Loeb Classical Library 435. Cambridge, MA: Harvard University Press.

Taub, Liba Chaia. 1993. *Ptolemy's Universe: The Natural Philosophical and Ethical Foundations of Ptolemy's Astronomy*. Chicago: Open Court.

Tester, S. J. 1987. *A History of Western Astrology*. Wolfbridge, UK: Boydell.

Toomer, G. J. 1970. "Ptolemy." *Dictionary of Scientific Biography*, ed. Charles C. Gillispie. New York: Charles Scribner's Sons.

PYTHAGORAS OF SAMOS (CA. 570–490 BCE)

Little reliable contemporary information exists about the Greek philosopher Pythagoras, and what is known comes from the school of disciples that gathered around him in Croton, Italy. Pythagoras became a legendary figure in the centuries after his death, and much of what is known of him is of doubtful authenticity.

According to legend, Pythagoras traveled widely in Greece, Phoenicia, Babylonia, and Egypt (where he learned Babylonian and Egyptian mathematics). While in Egypt, he became acquainted with local practices. The Egyptians used geometry and astronomy to measure the rise and fall of the Nile River. Pythagoras saw that the location of the pyramids was relevant to determining the solstices, equinoxes, and helical rising of stars, which accurately described the river at any particular time.

Pythagoras is counted among the Ionian philosophers including Thales, Anaximander, Anaximenes, and Heraclitus, many of whom studied celestial phenomena. Pythagoras's contribution to astrology traces back to his astronomical system. This system, developed in detail by Pythagoras's adherent Philolaus (also from Samos) posited that the Earth, sun, and planets orbited in giant spheres around a "central fire." During their orbits, the planets rubbed against each other, creating celestial harmonies (later termed the *Music of the Spheres*). People could not hear this music because they were accustomed to its constant presence. Legend also credited Pythagoras as the first person to recognize that the planet Venus that appeared in the morning was the same orb as the planet Venus that appeared in the evening. In addition, Pythagoras was a forefather of numerology, the study of the mystical significance of numbers and their relationship to events. He used numbers to explain cosmic harmony. Of particular importance was the decad, which contains the basic ratio 1 + 2 + 3 + 4 = 10. Pythagoras has influenced philosophy since the time of Plato (d. 348 BCE) and Aristotle (d. 322 BCE) who both refer to "the Pythagoreans." Copernicus (1473–1543) took inspiration from the Pythagoreans when he developed his idea of a heliocentric universe. Perhaps the last great Pythagorean was Johannes Kepler who believed that the orbits of the planets corresponded to the ratios governing musical chords. Pythagorean philosophy, with its emphasis on cosmic harmonies and correspondences, has been frequently adopted by astrologers.

Wendell G. Johnson

See also: Ptolemy; Science

Further Reading

Baker, Howard. 1972. "Pythagoras of Samos." *The Sewanee Review* 80, no. 1: 1–38.

Heninger, S. K. 1961. "Renaissance Versions of the Pythagorean Tetrad." *Studies in the Renaissance* 8: 7–35.

Huffman, Carl. 2014. "Pythagoreanism." Stanford Encyclopedia of Philosophy. http://plato.stanford.edu/entries/pythagoreanism/

Shibli, Hermann. 1997. "Pythagoras." In *Routledge Encyclopedia of Philosophy*, ed. Edward Craig, vol. 5, 855–857. London: Routledge.

Q

QUIGLEY, JOAN (1927–2014)

Joan Ceciel Quigley, of San Francisco, California, was an astrologer born in Kansas City, Missouri who gained notoriety when she advised the Reagan White House during the 1980s.

Most Americans would never have heard of Quigley until she was revealed (but not by name) in in 1988 by former chief of staff Donald Regan. In his book, *For the Record: From Wall Street to Washington*, Regan mentions Quigley, who he refers to as the Friend, never by her real name, as the astrologer whom Nancy Reagan called several times a week to determine the best days for her husband to carry out certain presidential duties, such as give speeches, or holding press conferences. Nancy Reagan called on her after John Hinckley Jr. attempted to assassinate President Ronald Reagan in 1981, then retained an informal, "secret" position as the White House astrologer.

This portrait of Joan Quigley shows her in a feminine and domestic setting, exemplifying the feminization of popular astrology in the 20th century. Note the contrast between this photo and that of Evangeline Adams, which is much more somber and businesslike. (Yann Gamblin/ Paris Match via Getty Images)

Donald Regan's revelations were used by the media to rail against astrology and the president. In *For the Record*, an angry Regan addressed the many accusations from both the media and from his political colleagues that he felt cast a shadow over his integrity during his terms as Reagan's treasury secretary and chief of staff. According to Regan, astrology was used on a daily, sometimes hourly basis in determining President Reagan's schedule to the extent that, as Donald Regan saw it, it placed the president's life and the American people in Quigley's less-than-capable hands.

In her defense, Quigley claimed that out of respect for the Reagans, she was reluctant to talk about her relationship with the first lady until Nancy Reagan's own book, *My Turn*, appeared in 1989; she left out much about her use of astrology. To respond to this book and to her many critics who ridiculed her, Quigley published *What Does Joan Say* (1990), which overstated the astrologer's role. She claimed credit for most of the Regan's successful ventures, claiming that they were acting on her advice when President Reagan stopped referring to the Soviet Union as the "Evil Empire."

Quigley's practice emphasized electional astrology: the art of discerning the exact moments to take specific actions. Her relationship with the Reagans raised the broader issue that astrology was made famous by individuals who read the stars in order to support powerful political officers.

Martin J. Manning

See also: Court Astrologers; Electional Astrology; Horoscopes; Politics; Righter, Carroll

Further Reading

Quigley, Joan. 1990. *What Does Joan Say? My Seven Years as White House Astrologer to Nancy and Ronald Reagan*. Secaucus, NJ: Birch Lane Press.

Reagan, Nancy. 1989. *My Turn: The Memoirs of Nancy Reagan*. New York: Random House.

Regan, Donald. 1988. *For the Record: From Wall Street to Washington*. San Diego: Harcourt Brace Jovanovich.

R

RAMAN, BANGALORE VENKATA (1912–1998)

B. V. Raman was the most important Indian astrologer of the 20th century, the leader in the revival of Indian astrology in India and the world and a leading promoter of the idea that Indian astrology was purely Indian. He was the grandson of Bangalore Suryanarain Rao (1856–1937), the founder of the Indian *Astrological Magazine* and the man who established Indian astrology as a cultural and nationalist movement.

Raman published an immense amount, including dozens of books, many of which have been translated into English and other non-Indian languages, and an astrology column. He edited the *Astrological Magazine*, the most important periodical in Indian astrology, from its revival in 1930 to his death. Raman was immensely learned in Indian astrological traditions and published on several esoteric topics within Hindu astrology as well as issuing annotated translations of Hindu astrological classics. His books include *Planetary Influences in Human Affairs* (English translation, 1992), *Ashtakavarga System of Prediction* (1962), and *Astrology in Forecasting Weather and Earthquakes* (1992). Raman's *A Manual of Hindu Astrology: Correct Casting of Horoscopes* went through many editions and translations. He recounted some of his early American travels in *A Hindu in America* (1969).

Raman established a reputation in India for accurate predictions of public events including several during World War II. Closer to home he was credited with predicting Indian independence, the Sino-Indian war of 1962, India's three wars with Pakistan, and Prime Minister Indira Gandhi's declaration of a state of emergency in 1977. In addition to public events, Raman was keenly interested in using astrology to predict the weather and natural disasters such as earthquakes. (He claimed to have predicted the disastrous Iranian earthquake of 1978 10 months in advance.) Despite the high regard in which he was held by many Indian politicians, Raman believed that the Indian government was not making sufficient use of astrology in its decision making. In 1984, he established the Indian Council of Astrological Sciences, with a view to creating a standardized system of astrological education and certification throughout India.

Raman's attitude toward astrology was that it was an unjustly stigmatized science, although unlike some rival Indian astrologers he did not claim that it was rigidly deterministic or offered a complete knowledge of the future. He believed this knowledge available only to Brahman. Astrologers he thought could determine the tendencies of future events. He had a degree in science and maintained scientific interests, being appointed a Fellow of the Royal Astronomical Society in 1947. Raman quoted Western scientific thinkers in his astrological writings, but pointed out that Western science was incomplete and needed to be complemented by the more spiritual Indian tradition.

Like his grandfather, Raman was a staunch Indian cultural nationalist who asserted that Indian astrology was of purely Indian origin, denying the importance of Hellenistic or Islamic influences. He also wanted to promote Indian astrology outside of India, frequently touring and speaking outside the subcontinent and introducing Indian astrology to many Western astrologers. He gave a lecture at the United Nations in New York in 1970 on "The Relevance of Astrology in Modern Times." Although he did not originate the use of the term "Vedic" to describe the Indian astrological tradition, Raman encouraged the formation of the American Council of Vedic Astrology in 1993 and the British Association for Vedic Astrology in 1996. He gave the keynote address at the first International Symposium on Vedic Astrology in San Rafael, California, in 1994. After Raman's death, his daughter Gayatri Devi Vasudev and his son Niranjan Babu Bangalore took over control of the *Astrological Magazine.* However, the magazine closed down in 2007. Vasudev now runs the *Modern Astrology Magazine* and Bangalore an Internet publication, *The Astrological eMagazine.* Both claim to be the successor publication to the *Astrological Magazine* and to be carrying on the tradition of B. V. Raman.

William E. Burns

See also: Astrological Associations; Indian Astrology

Further Reading

Astrological eMagazine website: http://www.astrologicalmagazine.com/
Modern Astrology Magazine website: http://modernastrology.co.in/wp/
Raman, Bangalore Venkata. 1992. *My Experiences in Astrology*. Bangalore: Raman.

RENAISSANCE AND REFORMATION ASTROLOGY

During the Renaissance and Reformation eras (roughly the late-14th through mid-17th centuries), astrology reached an apogee in terms of prestige, cultural power, and credibility. Despite a continued barrage of attacks from both secular and religious authorities, astrology maintained a high status among elites and commoners alike. The efforts of Renaissance humanists to rediscover ancient texts and incorporate classical Greco-Roman works into their philosophy spurred an interest in the traditions, mechanics, rules, and practices of ancient astrology. After the sacking of Constantinople by the Ottomans in 1453 and the fall of the Byzantine Empire, Greek scholars and texts from the Eastern Mediterranean flooded into Italy and the scholarly centers of Western Europe. A flurry of translation followed, and Latin and vernacular translations of several hitherto unknown works of Plato, the early Neoplatonists (such as Plotinus, Porphyry, and Iamblichus), Hermetic writings from various anonymous second-century CE Greeks, and Cabalisitic texts inundated Western Europe (Shumaker 1975, 16). Astrology persisted in popularity and influence even if the specific ability to predict the future was suspected as fraudulent and remained controversial. Astrologers believed that an understanding of the heavens would give them the tools to better understand the terrestrial world. By the Renaissance era, many universities offered study in astrology or at least incorporated astrological knowledge into the study of ancillary fields such astronomy, mathematics, and medicine.

Just as humanist scholars revived the literature and rhetoric of classical Greeks and Romans, so too did they resuscitate ancient sciences and natural philosophy, including astrology. Although Aristotle had been the dominant intellectual force for much of the Middle Ages, and remained prominent well into the 17th century, Platonism came to exert a similarly strong pull starting in the 15th century. Before the Ottoman sack of Constantinople, several Renaissance scholars such as Francesco Petrarch and Poggio Bracciolini had scoured the libraries of Europe in search of lost Greek texts, but the rise of humanistic, Platonic thought accelerated after the 1450s. At the forefront of this movement was the Italian humanist philosopher Marsilio Ficino. Under the generous patronage of Lorenzo de' Medici, Ficino set about translating all known works by Plato to Latin and developed a Neoplatonic philosophy that attempted to incorporate Plato's concept of the soul into the theory of astrological influences. Ficino pushed the relationship between Christianity and astrology even further than his predecessors. Although Augustine of Hippo had denounced horoscopic astrology as heretical, Thomas Aquinas had endeavored to reconcile and synthesize Aristotelian thought and Christianity—in the process conferring legitimacy on horoscopic astrology so long as it pertained to the body and not the soul (Allen 1941, 7–8). With the revival of Platonism, Ficino pointed to Plato's concept of a tripartite soul—the logical, spirited, and appetitive—and asserted that while the logical part of a person's soul was not subject to the influence of the stars, the others were, and this opened the door for a number of new interpretations and directions for a religiously sanctioned astrology bolstered by ancient authority (Campion 2009, 86). While horoscopic, horary, electional, and other traditional forms of astrology remained important, the influence of Neoplatonism meant that synchronizing one's physical and spiritual well-being with the heavens developed just as influential a role as prediction.

Not all Renaissance philosophers unquestioningly accepted astrology. Perhaps the most vehement critic was Giovanni Pico della Mirandola (1463–1494). Pico focused his attack primarily on "judicial" astrology (the foretelling of human events via the stars) rather than natural astrology (the use of astrology to study natural occurrences) but he asserted that improper definitions for astrology were among its greatest problems. Rather than attack astrology on theological grounds, which was one of the more common modes of criticism, Pico instead took issue with astrologers on scientific and mathematical grounds. He argued that Renaissance-era astrologers took no heed of stellar measurements and instead relied on an amorphous set of traditions handed down from the time of Ptolemy onward, appropriating countless techniques and rules from various incarnations of Arabic, Persian, Greek, and Babylonian astrological traditions, all of which contradicted one another. He called astrologers of his own time "lazy" because they were content to work with "almanacs and ephemerides . . . [and] believe that a planet is at a cardinal point when it is not, or that it is not when it is," instead of observing the heavens for themselves (Shumaker 1975, 20). Rather than point out these errors of astrology in order to generate interest in an astrological reformation, Pico simply used these examples as reason to dismiss judicial astrology altogether.

In what historian Stephen Vanden Broecke has called "the crisis of Renaissance astrology," many astrologers recognized that reform was necessary to maintain astrology's hard-won legitimacy (Vanden Broecke 2003, 11). The Ficino-Pico debate had caused a split among practicing astrologers and a number of schools of thought emerged to confront the problem. Nicholas Campion has argued that there were two main camps of Renaissance and Reformation-era astrologers—the conservatives and the reformers. Some among the former group, such as Giovanni Gioviano Pontano (1426–1503), simply ignored Pico's criticisms, claimed that horoscopic astrology in no way specified deterministic futures, and went about practicing astrology unfazed (Campion 2009, 105–106). Others, emboldened by Ficino's work and the rise of humanistic studies, acknowledged that there were mathematical difficulties in casting horoscopes but argued these were unimportant because the spiritual and divinatory natural magic derived from Neoplatonic and Hermetic astrology better characterized its nature.

Among the reformers, there were also a variety of positions. By and large, however, all agreed with Pico's criticisms. Where they differed from him was their belief that, through reform, they could rectify these errors and set astrology on a path of greater accuracy. How to accomplish this was up for debate. Some astrologers, perhaps following in their humanistic colleagues' lead, sought to restore astrology to a "textual correctness" based primarily on the original works of Ptolemy. Due to the accretions of various traditions within Western astrology since the time of Ptolemy, however, this was essentially impossible, as it was difficult to cleanly excise non-Ptolemaic elements from ancient and medieval texts that combined them with Babylonian, Persian, Chaldean, and Egyptian. More effective and numerous were the reformers who sought to reinforce astrology with greater mathematical and technical precision in charting the positions of the stars, which they asserted would in turn lead to better accuracy in prognostication. For example, Pico's comprehensive criticism of the failure of astrology to properly order the planets and accurately identify their positions spurred Nicolaus Copernicus, in part, to devise a new system that accounted for their apparent motion. Similarly, Francis Bacon, no friend of occult studies, wrote that astrology was "so full of superstition, that scarcely anything sound can be discovered in it. Notwithstanding, I would rather have it purified than rejected altogether" (Bowden 1974, 164). Perhaps the greatest exponent of astrological reform was Johannes Kepler who hoped for astrology to become closely intertwined with astronomy, while he regarded popular prophesying, which relied on no mathematical knowledge whatsoever, as simply superstitions (Campion 2009, 136–137). Kepler recognized that astrology required serious reform if it were to be regarded as legitimate, and he suggested an adherence to empirical observation, mathematical quantification, and meticulous data gathering as the path to achieving this. In short, he proposed submitting astrology to the same rigors as other fields of natural philosophy to determine its scientific efficacy.

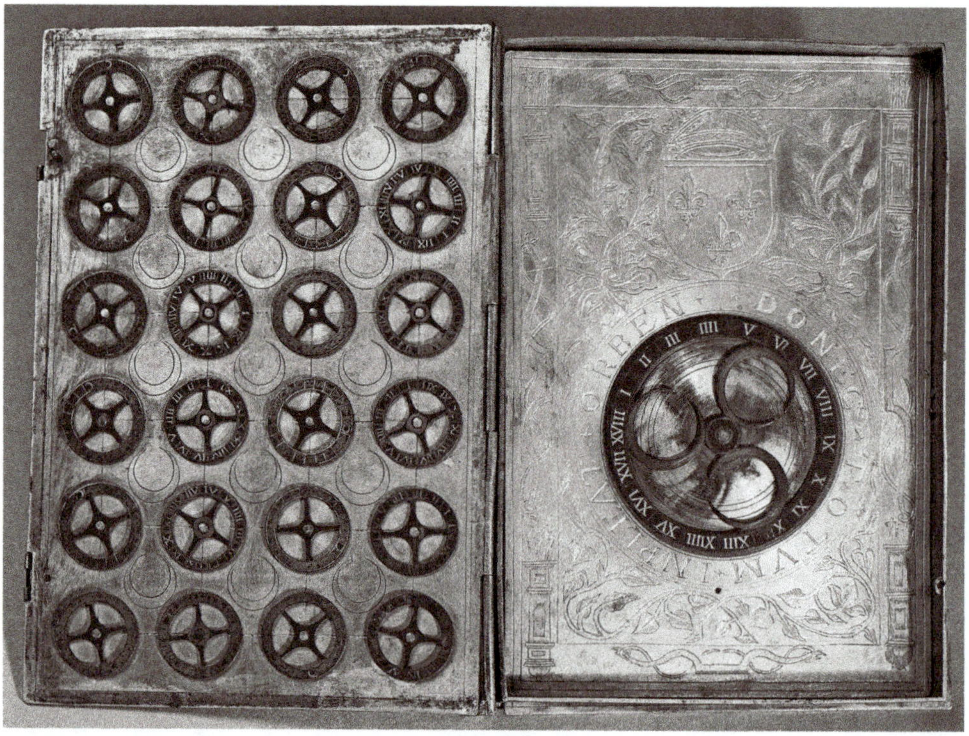

The Renaissance saw the development of new astrological techniques and technologies, such as this instrument for calculating horoscopes. At one point it was the property of Henry II of France (1519–1559). (DeAgostini/Getty Images)

Astrology's success in the Renaissance and Reformation eras was also a political success, and it commanded great respect among many early modern leaders. Several kings, queens, princes, and popes between the 14th and the 17th centuries were major proponents of astrology including Richard II of England, Charles V of France, Frederick II of the Holy Roman Empire, and Ezzelino III da Romano of the March Treviso, as well as several Renaissance popes such as Innocent VIII, Leo X, Paul III, and Urban VIII (Tester 1987, 197–201). The degree to which they accepted it and the manner in which they thought it should be practiced varied from person to person, but many either employed astrologers at their courts or patronized astrological writers. When Giovanni di Lorenzo de' Medici became Pope Leo X in 1513, he brought his personal astrologer with him to the Vatican. England's Elizabeth I relied on astrologer and occult philosopher John Dee to determine the most auspicious moment for her coronation, while Charles II used electional astrology to determine when to give important speeches to Parliament (Braudel 2007, 72). Catherine de Medici hired the famed diviner and astrologer Michel de Nostredame (Nostradamus) to confirm predictions made by her personal astrologer in 1555 that her husband, the French King Henri II, would die a violent death, and she later made him counselor and physician to her son, the future King Charles IX. Nevertheless, there were a number of reasons for early modern rulers to be wary of unchecked astrological practices. Negative connotations accompanied astrology including an association with demonic magic, the conjuring of evil spirits, and suspicious occult activities, even if the actual practice consisted of little more than the drawing up of nativities and the casting of horoscopes. More importantly, though, was the fact that there was a perceived political danger in allowing negative fortunes to be cast for a sitting monarch (Allen 1941, 102).

Astrology was important in courtly life in the Renaissance, but it was important for common people as well. The study of the stars, beyond the potential to predict future events, was important for timekeeping and maintaining calendars, the creation of medicines, the appropriate times for planting and harvesting, and so on, and astrologers and pro-astrological scholars argued for its importance based on practical concerns. Consequently, almanacs, broadsides, newspapers, and other short treatises aimed at common audiences emerged as important texts containing simple, astrological interpretations of natural events such as comets and eclipses, but also practical knowledge such as weather prediction and simple, astrologically inflected medical advice for people and animals. In 17th-century England, these small, otherwise harmless works also became political tools. The English Civil War contributed to a sort of almanac warfare between astrologers who were Parliamentarians and those who were Royalists. At their height in the late 1650s, astrological pamphlets and almanacs accounted for as much as one-third of all English book sales, and after the Bible, were reportedly the most widely read works in all of England (Thomas 1971, 342).

The Protestant Reformation also had a profound effect on astrology. The Reformation began in 1517 when Martin Luther (1483–1546) supposedly nailed his famous 95 theses to the door of the Wittenberg Church, which criticized the perceived abuses and corruption of the Catholic Church. This ushered in a new era of reform, in which religious figures such as John Calvin (1509–1564) and Ulrich Zwingli (1484–1531), advocated doctrinal changes to Church positions on faith, scripture, sacraments, and rules governing ecclesiastical hierarchy, among other things. There was, of course, a long history of Christian opposition to astrology. Though criticism of astrology in the early modern era more often was made on technical rather than theological grounds (e.g., Pico), traditional religious disapproval of the topic remained.

There was concern over the usurpation of the power of an all-knowing, omnipotent God with astrological prediction of preordained events; a problem with the pagan origins of astrology; and the incompatibility of astrology with free will. Given these objections, it is interesting that many Calvinists argued against astrology *because* they were strict determinists, but believed that only God had foreknowledge of preordained events. Thus, any attempt to uncover that hidden knowledge for oneself was both futile and tantamount to blasphemy. In any case, they argued, any knowledge about the future at all derived not from God but from congress with Satan. Nevertheless, there was no official Protestant opinion regarding astrology: Luther and Calvin both condemned it, though Luther's earliest and most vociferous supporter, Phillip Melanchthon (1497–1560) not only supported it but practiced it himself (Campion 2009, 113–115). Some radical reformers attempted to reconcile the prophetic elements of scripture—from the Book of Daniel to Revelation—with astrological prognostication, using the study of great historical events to pinpoint important planetary conjunctions in an effort to predict significant future events during the end times up to and including the Second Coming of Christ. This boldness was not restricted to Protestants. Believing that God used the stars as signs, some argued that the star of Bethlehem had been an astrological omen, and Girolamo Cardano went so far as to cast a horoscope for Jesus Christ, an act that only two centuries earlier had condemned astrologer Cecco d'Ascoli to be burned at the stake.

Similarly, many Catholic authorities asserted that reliance on astrology bordered on the heretical or at least commandeered rightful authority from the Church. Despite having a number of astrological proponents among them, nearly every 16th-century pope issued proclamations against at least some aspects of astrology. Even popes sympathetic to astrology, such as Pope Urban VIII (Pope, 1623–1644), who, for time, was a practicing astrologer, issued edicts forbidding predictive astrology. Several astrologers had predicted his death in the 1620s and 30s, which caused a great deal of civil unrest in Rome, and his papal bull *Inscrutabilis* claimed that God's will and judgment was not subject to human understanding and it was arrogant to think otherwise (Braudel 2007, 74).

Justin Niermeier-Dohoney

See also: Ashmole, Elias; Brahe, Tycho; Bruno, Giordano; Campanella, Tommaso; Cardano, Girolamo; Christianity; Court Astrologers; Dee, John; Ficino, Marsilio; Forman, Simon; Gadbury, John; Galilei, Galileo; Kepler, Johannes; Lilly, William; Machiavelli, Niccolò; Morandi, Orazio; Morin, Jean-Baptiste; Nostradamus; Paracelsus; Partridge, John; Placidus; Pont, Robert; Villena, Enrique de

Further Reading

Allen, Don Cameron. 1941. *The Star-Crossed Renaissance: The Quarrel about Astrology and Its Influence in England.* Durham, NC: Duke University Press.

Azzolini, Monica. 2013. *The Duke and the Stars: Astrology and Politics in Renaissance Milan.* Cambridge, MA: Harvard University Press.

Barnes, Robin B. 2016. *Reformation and Astrology*. Oxford: Oxford University Press.

Bowden, Mary Ellen. 1974. *The Scientific Revolution in Astrology: The English Reformers, 1558–1686*. PhD diss. New Haven, CT: Yale University Press.

Braudel, Hans Peter. 2007. "Astrology." In *Renaissance and Reformation*, ed. James A. Patrick. New York: Marshall Cavendish.

Campion, Nicholas. 2009. *A History of Western Astrology, Vol. II: The Medieval and Modern Worlds*. London: Continuum.

Dooley, Brendan, ed. 2014. *A Companion to Astrology in the Renaissance.* Leiden: Brill.

Garin, Eugenio. 1983. *Astrology in the Renaissance: The Zodiac of Life*, trans. Carolyn Jackson and June Allen. London: Routledge and Kegan Paul.

Shumaker, Wayne. 1975. *The Occult Sciences in the Renaissance.* Berkeley: University of California Press.

Tester, S. J. 1987. *A History of Western Astrology*. Wolfbridge, UK: Boydell.

Thomas, Keith. 1971. *Religion and the Decline of Magic: Studies in Popular Beliefs in Sixteenth and Seventeenth-Century England.* London: Weidenfeld and Nicolson.
Vanden Broecke, Stephen. 2003. *The Limits of Influence: Pico, Louvain, and the Crisis of Renaissance Astrology*. Leiden: Koninklijke Brill.

RIGHTER, CARROLL (1900–1988)

Carroll Righter was one of mid-20th-century America's best-known astrologers whose work was widely circulated in a variety of media including newspapers, books, and television.

Righter traced his interest in astrology to a childhood meeting with Evangeline Adams, who claimed the young Righter had the perfect chart for an astrologer. He began to take up astrology seriously after he moved from his childhood home in Philadelphia to Los Angeles. Closely connected to the Hollywood community, Righter was known as the "astrologer to the stars," a title he shared with several other southern California astrologers. He entertained regularly and reveled in the nickname "the gregarious Aquarius" after his birth sign. In addition to his sign parties, which might include an animal representing the sign, he held weekly astrological meetings in his home on Tuesday nights. These meetings continued after his death under the auspices of the Carroll Righter Astrology Foundation.

A gay man, Righter built much of his influence through close relationships with leading Hollywood women. He frequently told the story of how he advised Marlene Dietrich not to go to the studio one day and how she had broken her ankle after disregarding his advice. The most controversial of these relationships was with Nancy Reagan, wife of President Ronald Reagan. The extent to which the Reagans were taking astrological advice in the White House was controversial, and although the astrologer the controversy centered on was not Righter but Joan Quigley, Ronald Reagan did mention Righter as a friend in his autobiography *Where's the Rest of Me?* (1965) and said after Righter's death that he read his column every day. Righter refused to comment when asked if he was advising the Reagans. One of the major services Righter provided for his clients was elections, selecting the ideal times both for business matters such as signing contracts and for personal events such as weddings. Movie star Glenn Ford and Cynthia Hayward were married on September 10, 1977, at a date and time suggested by Righter. (The couple divorced seven years later.)

Righter was most widely known as the author of one of the country's most popular sun sign newspaper columns which began in 1951 and continued until his death. At its height, the column was carried in over 300 newspapers, although by the time of his death, the number had fallen to 166. Righter's column was the subject of the famous critique from Frankfurt School Marxist Theodor Adorno, "The Stars Down to Earth: The *Los Angeles Times* Astrology Column." Adorno attacked the column as an example of "authoritarian irrationalism" although he did not attack Righter personally. Righter was also one of the pioneers of astrological television with his program *Star Gazing*, aired on Los Angeles station KLAC beginning in October 1949. The success of *Star Gazing* was a major factor leading the National

Association of Radio and Television Broadcasters to ban astrological programming from television in 1952. Righter vigorously protested to the Federal Communications Commission, as did some of his celebrity fans such as Gloria Swanson along with dozens of ordinary people, but to no avail as the FCC had no authority over the NARTB. Later, Righter frequently appeared on television talk shows, including those of Merv Griffin and Mike Douglas. He appeared on the cover of Time Magazine on March 21, 1969.

Righter promoted the renaming of Cancer as an astrological sign as "Moon Children," asserting that the primary meaning of cancer as a disease made it unsuitable to designate a sign or the people born under it. The saying "The stars impel, they do not compel. What you make of your life is largely up to you" appended to his daily column has roots going back to the Middle Ages.

Righter's books focused on practical astrological advice and include *Astrology and You* (1956), *Your Astrological Guide to Health and Diet* (1967), *Astrological Guide to Marriage and Family Relations* (1969), and *Dollar Signs: How to Increase Your Personal Wealth through Astrological Forecasting* (1971).

William E. Burns

See also: Adams, Evangeline; Electional Astrology; Newspapers; Quigley, Joan; Sun Signs

Further Reading

Adorno, Theodor, W. 1994. "The Stars Down to Earth: The *Los Angeles Times* Astrology Column." In *The Stars Down to Earth and Other Essays on the Irrational in Culture*, ed. Stephen Crook, 34–127. London: Routledge.

Jaramillo, Deborah L. 2015. "Astrological TV: The Creation and Destruction of a Genre." *Communication, Culture and Critique* 8: 309–326.

ROMAN ASTROLOGY

Roman astrology is the astrology associated with Rome and ancient Italy during the Republic, the Empire, and Late Antiquity (not including the impact of Christianity). It is, in its origin and development, not fundamentally different from the astrology of the Mediterranean region between the second century BCE and the seventh century CE, generally known as Hellenistic astrology. What may separate "Roman" astrology from the general astrology practiced in this region, in this time frame, is how it was adapted to Roman conditions and Roman culture. It is, perhaps, more overtly political than astrology practiced elsewhere. However, as the historian Tamsyn Barton remarks, "It is striking that astrology in any form was marginal to Roman elite politics until the late Republic" (Barton [1994] 2002, 33).

Only two strictly astrological texts survive in Latin from this period, in contrast to texts written in Greek, the vector language of Hellenistic astrology (even if its techniques may have derived from areas other than Greece, mainly Mesopotamia and Egypt). This article focuses on the strictly Roman and Latin aspects of ancient astrology. This includes evidence, if any, for an indigenous Italian astronomy/astrology as practiced by the Etruscans and the growth of astrology in the Roman Republic and Empire. It also considers the two astrological texts written in Latin, the *Astronomica* of the first century CE Roman poet Manilius and the *Mathesis* of the fourth-century Sicilian lawyer, and later Christian convert, Julius Firmicus Maternus, in addition to astrological content in the Roman writers Censorinus, Macrobius, and Martianus Capella.

Etruscan Skies and Divination

A purely Etruscan astrology is elusive. However, an Etruscan cosmology can be discerned from artifacts, in particular the model of a bronze liver, found at Piacenza, Italy, in 1877. This model is crucial for present understanding of the Etruscan concept of the heavens, its relationship to Earth, and the practice of liver divination. The Etruscan practice of liver divination (hepatoscopy), in turn, has commonalities with Mesopotamian hepatoscopy (Bakhouche 2002, 29–30; Annus 2010, 11). The Piacenza liver is divided into 16 sections, each correlated with a divinity and a portion of the sky. It demonstrates the connection between liver divination and celestial divination, especially through lightning, an Etruscan specialty. Only the Etruscans divided the sky into 16 portions. In an astrological context, the divinities of certain regions correlate with places in the "Circle of Athla," a doctrine outlined in Manilius (Bouché-Leclercq 1899, 298n2; Greenbaum 2016, 294–296). In his *Marriage of Philology and Mercury*, Martianus Capella (ca. 420–490) speaks of 16 regions linked to divinities, in a list that has been shown to have both Etruscan and astrological connotations (Weinstock 1946). Thus indications of indigenous Etruscan astral practices thread through both strictly astrological works and works that incorporate astrological/astronomical themes.

The Rise of Astrology in Rome

As what became Hellenistic astrology developed, beginning around the Alexandrian conquest (ca. 323 BCE), Rome was slow to take it up. Bakhouche notes that the Romans were not necessarily innovators, but synthesizers of astrology with Roman culture, combining elements of Greek thought, Etruscan religion, and the Hellenistic-era "science of the stars" (Bakhouche 2002, 34). However, some doctrines described by Roman writers are unique.

Astrology in Rome had modest beginnings as a lower-class popular, not elite, practice (Barton 1994, 33–34). It is mentioned sporadically in the third century BCE, by the playwright Plautus (ca. 253–184 BCE) and the soldier-poet Ennius (239–169 BCE) (Cramer [1954] 1996, 45–46, 48; Barton 1994, 32–33). The elites denigrated astrology in the second century BCE, not because they considered it fraudulent but because it was a form of divination not controlled by the state (augury was the preferred state divination) and practiced by the lower classes, and therefore dangerous (Green 2014, 66). Around 160 BCE Cato the Elder, for example, warned that farm overseers should not consult astrologers (called "Chaldeans," after the Mesopotamians who brought astrology to prominence as a divinatory practice) (Cato, *De re rustica*, 1.5.4; Barton 1994, 32–33; Green 2014, 65). But astrology achieved a more important status during the late Roman Republic. In the turmoil of the first century BCE in Rome, astrology could be used more easily for individual predictions, especially for those in positions of power (Barton [1994] 2002, 38).

Another cause for the increasing popularity of astrology was the rise of Stoicism in second- and first-century BCE Rome. For elite thinkers who embraced Greek philosophy, Stoicism was attractive, and had doctrines that fundamentally supported an astrological worldview. Though Stoics disagreed about whether astrology was truly fatalistic (with an immutable fate decreed by the stars), by the middle of the first century BCE, Stoics such as Posidonius (ca. 135–ca. 51 BCE), under whom the famous orator Cicero studied, embraced astrology as an example of the workings of "cosmic sympathy." The universe (macrocosm) and the sublunar world (microcosm) are linked, and parts of each have "sympathy" with one another. Thus the sun in the sky has sympathy with the sunflower on Earth. Whatever affects the macrocosm is reflected in the microcosm. Coupled with the popularity of Stoicism, the use of astrology as a political tool also became more prevalent.

Political Astrology

Augury (observing the movements of birds) was the state-sanctioned form of divination in Rome. Also popular was haruspicy: examining the entrails of animals, divining by thunder and lightning, and prodigies (originally Etruscan practices). As practiced by the state, such divinations benefited the population as a whole. But, as the first century BCE dawned, the emergence of political leaders and generals with armies and their own plans for power coincided with a divinatory practice more amenable to a sole ruler, and here astrology fit the bill, based as it was on an individual's natal chart with the planetary and zodiacal positions at the time of birth (Barton 1994, 38; Barton [1994] 2002, 37–38).

In 87 BCE the consul Octavius, supported by the general Sulla (138–78 BCE), was killed by his colleague Cinna (supported by his own general, Marius). According to Plutarch, his body was found with a "Chaldean diagram" assuring his safety (Plutarch, *Life of Marius*, 42.4–5; Cramer [1954] 1996, 61; Barton 1994, 39). Sulla also was said by Plutarch to have consulted astrologers (Plutarch, *Life of Sulla* 37.1).

Astrologers made predictions about the lives of Pompey, Crassus, and Julius Caesar (members of the First Triumvirate), though Caesar was said to be skeptical of such divination. However, he unwittingly opened the door for astrology as a political tool. When Caesar was assassinated in March 44 BCE, after being warned about the Ides of March by the haruspex Spurinna (who likely used astrological methods), the appearance of a comet during his funeral games (called the "Julian star" and "Caesar's comet") was interpreted as a sign of Caesar being taken up to the stars. This allowed his great nephew and adopted son Octavian (later the emperor Augustus) to subsequently associate the comet with Caesar, dedicating a bronze statue of Caesar fitted with a star on its head at the temple of Venus. Julius Caesar was formally deified on January 1, 42 BCE.

Octavian himself was the subject of two probably apocryphal stories of the brilliance of his natal chart, one made by the renowned Roman astrologer Nigidius Figulus (d. 45 BCE) on the occasion of his birth in 63 BCE (Suetonius, *Augustus*, 94, 5; Cassius Dio, 45, 1.3–5; Cramer [1954] 1996, 63). The other, in 44 BCE (Suetonius, *Augustus*, 94, 5), relates how the astrologer Theogenes flung himself at Octavian's feet after inspecting his nativity. As emperor, Augustus was well known for his own astrological interests and put the sign of Capricorn (probably his moon or ascendant sign) on coins. The combination of astrology and rulers, though, could be dangerous; astrologers learned to be circumspect about their imperial clients. There were also periodic expulsions of astrologers from Rome (Cramer [1954] 1996, 233–248; Ripat 2011). Astrology's popularity, however, can be seen in a valuable marble board used to describe a horoscope to a client. The Tabula Bianchini (76 x 78 cm) was found in 1705 in Rome but clearly is a Greco-Roman relic (Evans 2004).

Nigidius Figulus was famed as both astrologer and philosopher. A friend and ally of Cicero, though not as politically astute, he died in an exile ordered by Caesar. As an advocate of Posidonius and an avowed Pythagorean, his now lost works presented views of the universe, the gods, divination, meteorology, geography, animals, and, most important for astronomers, the heavenly spheres (*sphaera graecanica* and *sphaera barbarica*). Philosopher and grammarian M. Terentius Varro (116–27 BCE) was as renowned as Nigidius. Varro eventually came to support astrology (Cramer [1954] 1996, 65–66): he asked the astrologer Tarutius of Firmum to compute the birth chart of Romulus and the chart for the founding of Rome (Heilen 2007). Such "birth charts" of cities could be used to determine its subsequent events.

Finally, attention must be given to Marcus Tullius Cicero (January 3, 106–December 43 BCE). Though a friend and ally of Nigidius, his position on astrology

Augustus and Capricorn

Augustus, the first Roman Emperor (r. 27 BCE–14 CE), was particularly strongly identified with the sign of Capricorn. There is something of a mystery about this, since at his birth the sun was in Libra. One possibility is that the identification comes from the fact that the sun was in Capricorn at his conception nine months earlier. Another is that the connection stems from the fact that the moon was in Capricorn at his birth. The whole problem is not helped by the chaos of the Roman calendar before the reforms of Julius Caesar, Augustus's great-uncle and adoptive father. In any event, Augustus used the image of the Capricorn goat in many of the artifacts produced during his reign, including coinage. He also received the title of "Augustus," or "the increasing," from the Roman senate on January 13, when the sun was in Capricorn. Capricorn was associated with Saturn, and in Roman mythology Saturn was the ruler of the Golden Age that Augustus claimed to be restoring. Capricorn the goat was also sometimes represented in Augustan imagery as a world ruler, with the globe between his forelegs.

was distinctly opposed. His treatise *On Divination* (2.89) mounted a blistering attack on astrology (which he asserted was hard deterministic, if not fatalistic) on philosophical grounds. Even though he was a member of the college of augurs, he was skeptical about divination. However, he softened this position in *On Fate* (Green 2014, 87–89). From total denial of astral influence on humans, he allowed that the stars may affect some parts of human life, but not all (*On Fate*, 7–8) (de facto making astrology less deterministic). There may be political reasons for this, chief among them the appearance of "Caesar's comet." After Octavian's embrace of Caesar's astral apotheosis, Cicero would have been acutely aware of its political implications and, given his relationship with Octavian, reasonably found a way to satisfy his own philosophical demands without dismissing Octavian's position.

Latin Astrological Literature in the Empire and Late Antiquity

The first important astrological text from ancient Italy is the *Astronomica*, a didactic poem, in five books, of the poet Marcus Manilius (fl. 10 CE). Written during the reigns of Augustus and Tiberius, the text strongly shows the Stoic leanings of its author. Manilius makes some deviations from standard Hellenistic astrology. For example, the names he uses to describe the astrological places (now called houses in modern astrology) are iconoclastic and may show Egyptian influence. The doctrines covered in the *Astronomica* are mostly standard astrological practices, but in some places Manilius either gives a unique version of a technique or provides what might be called a Roman version of it. One example is the way he organizes the decans, 10-degree portions of a zodiacal sign. His version assigns each third of a sign to the rule of another sign, beginning in Aries, assigning the first decan to Aries, and going in sign order. No other Hellenistic astrologer does this.

Manilius melds Hellenistic and Roman practices in Book 3.50–155. He uses the astrological Lot of Fortune (*pars fortuna*) as the ascendant of a "Circle of Athla," creating a new way to interpret a chart. Other Hellenistic astrologers (prominently Vettius Valens) also used the Lot of Fortune as an ascendant, but Manilius's practice is unique. As noted above, Manilius's descriptions of some of these lot places strongly link to the 16 regions of the liver in Etruscan divination.

In 238 CE, Censorinus wrote a little book *On the Birthday* (*De die natali*); in chapter 8 he outlines basic astrological principles.

Table 1 The Unique System of Decans in Manilius

Sign	Decan			Sign	Decan			Sign	Decan		
	1	2	3		1	2	3		1	2	3
A	A	B	C	E	A	B	C	I	A	B	C
B	D	E	F	F	D	E	F	J	D	E	F
C	G	H	I	G	G	H	I	K	G	H	I
D	J	K	L	H	J	K	L	L	J	K	L

This Roman floor mosaic from the second century CE incorporates a zodiac wheel surrounding Aion, the god of eternity, along with other imagery connoting the passage of time and the changing of the seasons. (PHAS/UIG via Getty Images)

Julius Firmicus Maternus is another significant presence in astrology in Italy (in this case, Sicily). His *Mathesis* in eight books covers the main topics of Hellenistic astrology; it includes some obscure techniques rarely covered in astrological books, such as full and empty degrees and myriogenesis, the use of minutes of the ascendant arc. His discussion of antiscia (II, 29) uses a case study to illustrate the practice: the historical horoscope of Ceionius Rufus Albinus (b. March 14, 303). He also mentions the horoscope of the general Sulla (VI, 31.1).

Also important for astronomical and astrological content are the previously mentioned Martianus Capella and Macrobius (fl. fifth century), known for his *Saturnalia* and his *Commentary on the Dream of Scipio*. Although not an astrologer, astrological content in his books shows that knowledge of basic astrological cosmology was common in his era. The *Commentary on the Dream of Scipio*, in particular, contains descriptions of the heavens, including the planets and zodiac (I, chapters 19–21). An important passage on the soul's descent through the spheres of the planets (I, chapter 12.14) describes obtaining reasoning and intelligence from Saturn, the power of acting from Jupiter, boldness from Mars, perception and imagination from the sun, desire from Venus, speaking and interpreting from Mercury, and the power of growth from the moon.

Dorian Gieseler Greenbaum

See also: Comets; Decans; Fate; Firmicus Maternus, Julius; Hellenistic Astrology; Manilius, Marcus; Politics; Stoicism; Valens, Vettius

Further Reading

Annus, Amar. 2010. "On the Beginnings and Continuities of Omen Sciences in the Ancient World." In *Divination and Interpretation of Signs in the Ancient World*, ed. Amar Annus, 1–18. Chicago: University of Chicago Press.

Bakhouche, Béatrice. 2002. *L'Astrologie à Rome*. Bibliothèque d'Études Classiques. Louvain, France: Peeters.

Barton, Tamsyn. 1994. *Ancient Astrology*. London: Routledge.

Barton, Tamsyn S. (1994) 2002, repr. *Power and Knowledge: Astrology, Physiognomics, and Medicine under the Roman Empire*. Ann Arbor: University of Michigan Press.

Bouché-Leclercq, Auguste. 1899. *L'astrologie grecque*. Paris: E. Leroux.

Censorinus. 2007. *Censorinus: The Birthday Book*, trans. Holt N. Parker. Chicago: University of Chicago Press.

Cramer, Frederick H. (1954) 1996, repr. *Astrology in Roman Law and Politics*. Chicago: Ares Publishers.

Evans, James. 2004. "The Astrologer's Apparatus: A Picture of Professional Practice in Greco-Roman Egypt." *Journal for the History of Astronomy* 35: 1–44.

Firmicus Maternus, Julius. 2011. *Julius Firmicus Maternus: Mathesis*, ed. and trans. James Herschel Holden. Tempe, AZ: American Federation of Astrologers.

Green, Steven J. 2014. *Disclosure and Discretion in Roman Astrology: Manilius and His Augustan Contemporaries*. Oxford: Oxford University Press.

Greenbaum, Dorian Gieseler. 2016. *The Daimon in Hellenistic Astrology: Origins and Influence*. Leiden: Brill.

Heilen, Stephan. "Ancient Scholars on the Horoscope of Rome." In *The Winding Courses of the Stars: Essays in Ancient Astrology*, ed. Charles Burnett and Dorian Gieseler Greenbaum. Special double issue of *Culture and Cosmos* 11 (Spring/Summer and Autumn/Winter 2007): 43–68.

Hübner, Wolfgang. 2005. "Sulla's Horoscope? (Firm. math. 6,31,1)." In *Horoscopes and Public Spheres: Essays on the History of Astrology*, ed. Günther Oestmann, H. Darrel Rutkin, and Kocku von Stuckrad, 13–35. Berlin: Walter de Gruyter.

Manilius, Marcus. (1977) 1997, repr. *Astronomica*, ed. and trans. George P. Goold. Loeb Classical Library. Cambridge, MA: Harvard University Press.

Pandey, Nandini. 2013. "Caesar's Comet, the Julian Star, and the Invention of Augustus." *Transactions of the American Philological Association* 143: 405–449.

Ripat, Pauline. 2011. "Expelling Misconceptions: Astrologers at Rome." *Classical Philology* 106, no. 2: 115–154.

Stevens, Natalie L. C. 2009. "A New Reconstruction of the Etruscan Heaven." *American Journal of Archaeology* 113, no. 2: 153–164.
van der Meer, L. Bouke. 1987. *The Bronze Liver of Piacenza: Analysis of a Polytheistic Structure*, vol. 2, Dutch Monographs on Ancient History and Archaeology. Amsterdam: J. C. Gieben.
Weinstock, Stefan. 1946. "Martianus Capella and the Cosmic System of the Etruscans." *Journal of Roman Studies* 36, nos. 1, 2: 101–129.

RUDHYAR, DANE (1895–1985)

Dane Rudhyar, born Daniel Chennevière in Paris, was a French American astrologer, musician, writer, and artist. His emigration to the United States in 1916 and change of name in 1918 aptly symbolize his quest to leave behind older Western traditions in favor of the modern, with his chosen name Rudhyar having associations with radical transformation (Ertan 2009, 3). His modernizing zeal and philosophical vision are evident in his attempts to reform Western astrology, which were particularly inspired by the work of Carl Gustav Jung. Rudhyar's vast astrological output and inspiring poetic style had a tremendous impact on later Western astrologers including Stephen Arroyo (b. 1946), Darby Costello, and Melanie Reinhart (b. 1959), and he is often credited with establishing a new psychological version of astrology in the English-speaking world.

Rudhyar first encountered astrology around 1920 through his association with the Theosophical Society in America, and 10 years later his interest was stimulated through his contact with the work of astrologer Marc Edmund Jones (1888–1930). It was, however, the work of Jung that really awoke Rudhyar's passion for astrology, as in it he recognized the psychological concepts that could assist him in creating a connection, through astrology, between psychology and the cosmos. This led to the publication of his influential 1936 book, *The Astrology of Personality*, often considered a founding text of humanistic astrology.

Determined to find a philosophical justification for astrology palatable to modern thought, Rudhyar advanced a theory of astrology as the algebra of life (Rudhyar 1991, 16). This meant recognition of astrology as a formal system of symbolism based on the planetary pattern that could, as a whole, be applied to other wholes, such as the human personality. Astrology was not therefore an empirical science, which has nothing to say on the quality of wholeness or the essence of time, but akin to qualitative algebra with the symbolic meaning of each component making sense within the system as a whole. The psychological meaning of the planet Saturn, for example, is valid to the extent it makes sense within the context of Saturn's position in the planetary system. As Saturn is the most distant and slow-moving of the traditional planets, and the last planet visible to the naked eye, its meaning in human psychology should reflect this. It is thus associated with boundaries, limits, slow and steady development and measured emotions. In fact, for Rudhyar, any astrological system is valid to the extent its symbolism is consistent and makes sense within the whole. This view allowed him to regard modern Western astrology as just one of a variety of possible astrologies, each of which develops relative to the surrounding culture.

Rudhyar viewed the birth chart as a symbolic portrait of an individual's "celestial name" (Rudhyar 1979, 63). The birth chart is an individual mandala, a set of coded instructions, and reveals the order of the sky at the heart of each human being. It can be read as a guide to both conscious and unconscious factors within the human psyche and assist the individual in their journey of individuation—Jung's concept for the maturation and growth of the personality. Although the type of astrology Rudhyar advocated in his early writings had a psychological goal, it placed this within a wider relationship to the cosmos. Each human being, by taking up the instructions contained in their birth chart, has the opportunity to connect with something greater than themselves while also maturing psychologically into the person the universe has destined them to be. The birth chart shows only the blueprint and the potential and is never a guide to fated external events but instead may indicate the timing of psychological development.

In seeing astrology as a means to apply a humanistic type of psychology, Rudhyar rejected older astrological ideas about malefic planets or some zodiac signs or birth charts being more favorable than others. For Rudhyar, all birth charts hold equal potential for good, being a means through which the individual can harmonize their personality with the heavens and live in tune with the universe. Rudhyar was never afraid to question established astrological lore, finding it difficult, for example, to accept the notions of dignity and debility that labeled certain planets as particularly weak or strong within a birth chart.

The practice of astrology was a serious pursuit for Rudhyar. Once an individual had begun to study their birth chart and was faced with symbols that spoke to their unconscious, the door had been opened and could not again be closed. According to Rudhyar, the birth chart, seen as an archetype of the unconscious, becomes a vital factor in the individual psyche, and what it symbolizes becomes more strongly emphasized than was previously the case (Rudhyar 1976, 111–112). The study and practice of astrology therefore comes with dangers and pitfalls; in reaching for fuller consciousness, both good and bad elements of the psyche are stimulated. Astrology thus requires a certain amount of maturity and ego formation if it is not to do more harm than good in an individual's life.

Although inspired by Jung's writings and those of humanistic psychologists such as Abraham Maslow (1908–1970), Rudhyar identified important differences between psychology and astrology. Although psychology looks for specific commonalities in order to develop a theory of the psyche, and as a science proceeds by a principle of exclusion, astrology starts from universal principles that are then applied to the individual, which is a principle of inclusion. In addition, a psychologist confines their work to the psyche of an individual, whereas an astrologer deals with mysterious entities such as Mars and Jupiter, which go well beyond the confines of the human personality and relate the individual to the wider cosmos.

In later work, Rudhyar came to believe that his earlier humanistic astrology had helped to foster an astrology that was mainly descriptive or informative (Rudhyar 1980, 21). This led him to stress that astrology is a vehicle for transformation with a crucial transpersonal dimension. The purpose of the transformation that can be attained through astrology is to prepare individuals for a new age in humanity's history. This perspective places greater emphasis on the birth chart as a means of reading karma, which is then worked through in this lifetime for the purpose of preparing for the new age to come.

Laura Andrikopoulos

See also: Jung, Carl G.; Theosophy; Transpersonal Astrology

Further Reading

Ertan, Deniz. 2009. *Dane Rudhyar: His Music, Thought, and Art.* Rochester, NY: University of Rochester Press.

Rudhyar, Dane. 1969. *Astrological Timing.* New York: Harper Colophon.

Rudhyar, Dane. 1976. *Astrology and the Modern Psyche.* Vancouver, WA: CRCS Publications.

Rudhyar, Dane. 1979. *Astrological Insights into the Spiritual Life.* Santa Fe, NM: Aurora Press.

Rudhyar, Dane. 1980. *The Astrology of Transformation.* Wheaton, IL: The Theosophical Publishing House.

Rudhyar, Dane. 1991. *The Astrology of Personality.* Santa Fe, NM: Aurora Press.

S

SCIENCE

The relationship of science and astrology is complicated and has changed greatly over time. At different moments astrology has been the great support of science or its despised rival.

The Ancient Mediterranean

Astrology and science emerged together, as both of them were attempts to understand the natural world and its significance for humanity. Astrological prediction would be impossible without some understanding of the science of the sky. The greatest astronomer of the ancient world, Ptolemy, was also its greatest, or at least most influential, astrologer. No one at the time thought this to be a contradiction.

Not all natural philosophies in the ancient world were compatible with astrology. Epicureanism, the doctrine that the world was composed of hard, indivisible bits of matter called atoms, circulating endlessly in empty space, was not, in that it offered no mechanism for the stars to affect humanity. However, Epicureanism was a doctrine followed only by a small number of the elite, and it had little impact on the popularity of astrology. Most natural philosophies were either compatible with astrology, or, as in the case of Stoicism, actively encouraged it. The rise of Christianity did not materially affect this relation, as Christians suspicious of pagan astrology were often suspicious of pagan science as a whole.

The Middle Ages and Renaissance

The period following the fall of the Roman Empire in the West saw both astrology and science in eclipse, for the same reason: the decline of learning and written culture and the dominance of religious issues in what intellectual life remained. To the extent that astronomy was practiced, it had less to do with astrology than with calendrical science, particularly the vexed question of establishing the date of Easter.

In those areas where the tradition of ancient science was carried on, astrology continued to be an important part of it. In the early Middle Ages, this was most true in the Islamic world. The adoption of much Arabic science, as well as ancient Greek science through Islamic intermediaries, beginning in the 11th century, led to the revival of Western astrology. By promoting the idea that the universe could be understood through reason astrology gave medieval interest in science a theoretical grounding.

Although a few opponents of astrology, such as Nicholas Oresme (1320–1382), made objections to it based on the science of the day, these were of very minor importance as the debate over astrology took place mainly in the field of religion. These debates, did, however, sharpen the distinction between astronomy, religiously permissible, and astrology, religiously questionable.

Nonetheless, astrology and astronomy continued the close relationship established in the ancient world. This was not just true on an intellectual but also on an institutional level. Astrology provided astronomy with a justification for funding. The great observatories of the Islamic world, culminating in the Maragha and Samarkand observatories, were built largely for the purpose of accumulating accurate observations for astrological purposes. Even Tycho Brahe's observatory at Hven, the last great pretelescopic observatory, was dedicated to astrological as well as astronomical reform. Astrology was also taught in late medieval and Renaissance universities, often as part of the medical curriculum.

The Scientific Revolution and Enlightenment

The scientific revolution of the 17th century began the process by which astrology was defined as nonscientific, or even antiscientific. This was not necessarily due to the ideas of scientists themselves—two of the major scientists of the 17th century, Johannes Kepler and Galileo Galilei, were practicing astrologers. Both were Copernicans and demonstrated that the Copernican belief in a sun-centered cosmos was not incompatible with the practice of traditional astrology that used an Earth-centered model of the universe. Defenders of astrology such as Sir Christopher Heydon (1561–1623), author of *A Defence of Judiciall Astrologie* (1603), were familiar with the advanced science of their day and able to deploy it against astrology's critics.

A bigger problem than Copernicanism for astrologers emerged by the mid-17th century—the rise of mechanical philosophies that reduced the universe to matter and motion. Mechanical philosophers, some of whom revived the ancient atomism of Epicurus and some of whom followed the new philosophy of Rene Descartes (1596–1650), rejected the idea that the stars could exert forces that acted at the vast distances between them and Earth. The revival of action at a distance in the new natural philosophy of Isaac Newton toward the end of the century, however, does not seem to have benefited astrology significantly.

Some hoped to reform astrology along the lines of the new science. A group of English astrologers—Joshua Childrey (1625–1670), who tried to create a heliocentric astrology; John Gadbury; and John Goad (1616–1689)—adopted a "Baconian" program of basing astrology on a mass of systematic observations and data. This effort, inspired by the works of English philosopher of science Francis Bacon (1561–1626), produced such works as Gadbury's *Collectio Genituarum* (1662), a massive collection of nativities designed to provide the empirical basis for a reformed astrology, and Goad's *Astro-Meteorologica* (1686), an attempt to correlate 30 years of weather observations with planetary positions.

The institutional problem the scientific revolution presented to astrology was the rise of alternative pragmatic uses of astronomy. By far the most important of

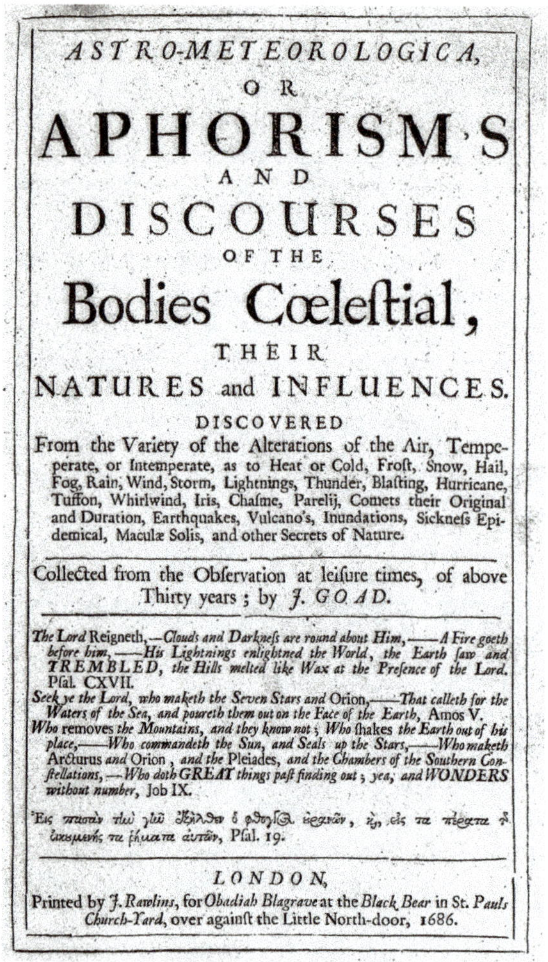

ASTRO-METEOROLOGICA,
OR
APHORISM'S
AND
DISCOURSES
OF THE
Bodies Cœleſtial,
THEIR
NATURES and INFLUENCES.
DISCOVERED
From the Variety of the Alterations of the Air, Temperate, or Intemperate, as to Heat or Cold, Froſt, Snow, Hail, Fog, Rain, Wind, Storm, Lightnings, Thunder, Blaſting, Hurricane, Tuffon, Whirlwind, Iris, Chaſme, Parelij, Comets their Original and Duration, Earthquakes, Vulcano's, Inundations, Sickneſs Epidemical, Maculæ Solis, and other Secrets of Nature.

Collected from the Obſervation at leiſure times, of above Thirty years; by *J. GOAD.*

The Lord Reigneth,—*Clouds and Darkneſs are round about Him*,——*A Fire goeth before him*,——*His Lightnings enlightned the World*, *the Earth ſaw and TREMBLED*, *the Hills melted like Wax at the Preſence of the Lord*. Pſal. CXVII.
Seek ye the Lord, *who maketh the Seven Stars and* Orion,——*That calleth for the Waters of the Sea*, *and poureth them out on the Face of the Earth*, Amos V.
Who removes *the Mountains*, *and they know not*; *Who* ſhakes *the Earth out of his place*,——*Who commandeth the Sun*, *and Seals up the Stars*,——*Who maketh* Arcturus *and* Orion, *and the* Pleiades, *and the Chambers of the Southern Conſtellations*,—*Who doth* GREAT *things paſt finding out*; *yea*, *and WONDERS without number*, Job IX.

Εἰς πᾶσαν τὴν γῆν ἐξῆλθεν ὁ φθόγγος αὐτῶν, καὶ εἰς τὰ πέρατα τῆς οἰκουμένης τὰ ῥήματα αὐτῶν, Pſal. 19.

LONDON,
Printed by *J. Rawlins*, for *Obadiah Blagrave* at the *Black Bear* in St. *Pauls Church-Yard*, over againſt the Little North-door, 1686.

The frontispiece to John Goad's *Astro-meteorologica* proclaims the author's research program. Goad correlated weather changes with celestial phenomena. (Wellcome Collection)

these was navigation. The rise of long voyages across open water in the Atlantic and Pacific in the 16th century had made navigation a central concern of many European governments. The major observatories built in the late 17th century—the Greenwich Observatory and the Paris Observatory—were the first major observatories for which astrology was simply irrelevant. More accurate stellar and planetary observation now served different masters—cartography and navigation. The first Astronomer Royal of Great Britain and master of the Greenwich Observatory, John Flamsteed (1646–1719), was an opponent of astrology, although he kept his opposition quiet and actually took a horoscope of the establishment of the observatory.

Thomas Sprat's *History of the Royal Society* (1667), often viewed as the manifesto of the new science in 17th-century England, denounced astrology by name. Although astrology was rejected in the later phases of the scientific revolution and throughout the 18th-century Enlightenment, there were efforts to absorb parts of it into science, mostly having to do with the impact of celestial bodies on the weather or on the human body. There was an excellent "scientific" precedent for this in the form of the influence of the sun and moon on the tides. It was important, however, that this knowledge be kept separate from the illegitimate "judicial" astrology of nativities, horary questions, and elections. This astrology went into a steep decline in the 18th century.

The 19th Century

By the 19th century, when the revival of judicial astrology was beginning, the relationship of astrology and science was clearly oppositional. The Enlightenment program of tracking celestial influences had produced no solid results and was quietly abandoned.

Astrologers began to exalt the magical and irrational elements in their discipline to carve out a space independent of science. In the early 19th century, astrologers exploited the Romantic reaction against the dominance of mechanistic science. By the end of the century many astrologers were members of or strongly allied with the Theosophical movement, which saw the fundamental reality of the universe as spiritual rather than material and Western science as crudely reductionist. As an "occult" discipline in the modern sense, astrology was not so much antiscientific as it treated science as altogether irrelevant.

Meanwhile, astrology was defined not just by scientists but by much of the Western intellectual and cultural elite as incompatible with scientific modernity. The 19th-century West was marked by a strong distinction between the "scientific" beliefs of a small, predominantly male elite in Western countries, and the "superstitious" beliefs of most women, the lower classes, and non-Western societies. Astrology was firmly located in the latter camp. Organizations for the popularization of science and the enlightenment of the masses, such as England's Society for the Diffusion of Useful Knowledge, were fierce opponents of astrology.

The 20th and 21st Centuries

The 20th century saw a rash of efforts to either scientifically demonstrate astrology or conclusively prove its valuelessness. In a revival of the "Baconian" project of the 17th century, astrologers and skeptics gathered information on hundreds or even thousands of cases. The 1977 New York Suicide Study gathered information on 311 suicides in New York City and was unable to find any common astrological factor that explained them. In 1985, the Shawn Carlson double-blind test was published, which saw astrologers performing no better than chance. Other studies have been more ambiguous or even favorable to astrology. The most famous of these are the studies associated with Michel and Francoise Gauquelin correlating planetary positions and career paths. This has contributed to a split within astrology itself, between those who define themselves as "scientific" astrologers and aspire for astrology to join the ranks of recognized sciences, and those who view astrology as fundamentally a discipline that can never be assimilated to the physical sciences. (The American Federation of Astrologers, the oldest American astrological organization, was founded in 1938 as the American Federation of Scientific Astrologers.) The New Age movement, with its emphasis on the subjective nature of reality, has contributed to moving astrology further away from science, as has the emphasis on character analysis over prediction.

Whatever the impact of the Gauquelin and other studies, there is no doubt that the scientific mainstream remains marked by a profound opposition to astrology. No prominent scientist is publicly identified as a believer in astrology, and many scientists who occupy a position in the public eye strongly denounce it. In 1975, in an attempt to present a united front against astrology, 186 scientists, including

Shawn Carlson's Double-Blind Test of Astrology

"A Double-Blind Test of Astrology" a peer-reviewed article by a young graduate student, Shawn Carlson, appeared in the December 5, 1985, issue of the American science magazine *Nature.* The part of the experiment that attracted the most attention tested the ability of astrologers to match psychological profiles produced by the California Personality Inventory with the natal horoscopes of the subjects. Astrologers from the National Council for Geocosmic Research participated in the design of Carlson's test. The astrological advisers also selected astrologers for the test. In total, 30 astrologers participated. A natal horoscope was presented to an astrologer along with three psychological profiles, including the one of the subject of the natal horoscope. In matching the horoscope with the correct profile, the astrologers performed no better than chance. Carlson concluded that astrology had been experimentally refuted. The Carlson experiment is considered the gold standard in much of the skeptical literature, and continues to be frequently invoked by opponents of astrology. Astrologers have strongly attacked the experiment's design, execution, and in some cases Carlson's personal integrity as well as publishing proastrological interpretations of Carlson's experimental data.

19 Nobel Prize winners, issued a statement entitled *Objections to Astrology.* Popular belief in astrology is often used as an example of the ignorant, unscientific nature of most people as it was in the 19th century. However, many ordinary people with no extensive background in science consider astrology "scientific."

William E. Burns

See also: Antiastrological Thought; Brahe, Tycho; Enlightenment; Gadbury, John; Galilei, Galileo; Gauquelin, Michel and Françoise Gauquelin; Kepler, Johannes; Medical Astrology

Further Reading

Allum, Nick, and Paul Stonman, "Stars in Their Eyes? Beliefs about Astrology in Europe." http://privatewww.essex.ac.uk/~nallum/AllumandStoneman2011.pdf

Barton, Tamsyn. 1994. *Power and Knowledge: Astrology, Physiognomics and Medicine under the Roman Empire.* Ann Arbor: University of Michigan Press.

Bowden, Mary Ellen. 1974. *The Scientific Revolution in Astrology: The English Reformers, 1558–1686.* New Haven, CT: Yale University Press.

Curry, Patrick, ed. 1987. *Astrology, Science and Society: Historical Essays.* Woodbridge, UK: Boydell.

Curry, Patrick. 1989. *Prophecy and Power: Astrology in Early Modern England.* Princeton: Princeton University Press.

Curry, Patrick. 1992. *A Confusion of Prophets: Victorian and Edwardian Astrology.* London: Collins and Brown.

Curth, Louise Hill. 2007. *English Almanacs, Astrology and Popular Medicine.* Manchester: Manchester University Press.

Jerome, Lawrence E. 1977. *Astrology Disproved.* Buffalo, NY: Prometheus.

SEX AND LOVE

Throughout the world, for thousands of years, traditions and beliefs about love and sex have incorporated aspects of astrology through calendrical readings and astrological divination. Examples of the use of astrology in the mediation of love and sex include (1) the use of calendrical astrology and auspicious dates in wedding rituals, (2) the concept of fated love and divination, and (3) practices and beliefs about compatibility based on natal astrology. Societal beliefs and practices regarding love, sexual activity, and reproduction draw upon notions of normative sexuality and gender and are often negotiated through spiritual beliefs and institutions like religion. Because scholars have found that religious and spiritual beliefs help shape intimate and romantic relationships, they also influence attendant astrological rituals. Many religions, including Christianity, Hindu traditions, Confucianism, Islam, and Judaism, have integrated aspects of astrology or allowed for astrology in vernacular practice. Like other unofficial or "occult" practices involving vernacular use of magic or rituals to influence love, astrology is sometimes used to supplement official religious practice. The widespread acceptance of astrology is demonstrated partly through the documented use of astrological readings in matrimony ceremonies, as well as the conceptualization of love and matchmaking as ruled by fate.

Marriage Rituals, Calendrical Astrology, and Auspicious Dates

One way societies incorporate astrological beliefs and practices into life is through rituals associated with courtship and rites of passage like marriage. In anthropology, the use of rituals to mark events in the life cycle is frequently considered to produce meaning and unity in a society. Among these rites of passage, celebrations of matrimony are accompanied by the most elaborate rituals and are nearly universal.

Astrology's association with ritual and tradition may be reason for its incorporation into courtship and marriage practices as a way of highlighting and honoring the transition from youth to adulthood, and courtship to marriage. The planning of weddings according to astrologically auspicious dates is common across societies and throughout history. Astrological consultations and calendrical prognostications have influenced the arrangement of marriages in ancient Greece, 15th-century England, and 18th-century North America and are still a part of wedding planning for many in contemporary India, South Korea, and Japan, among many other times and places.

In agricultural and preindustrial societies the seasons are vital for planning major life events, including those affiliated with reproduction and marriage. For instance, in the United States in the 18th century, almanacs cataloged favorable times of year for weddings, conceptions, and births based on seasonal weather and solar and lunar aspects. Planning based on the calendar is especially important when life depends on the natural world, but it is also seen in the planning of marriages according to holy days and religious calendars as well as secular dates of import. Because humans are not bound to particular times of the year for bonding behavior or mating, these behaviors and marriages become cultural events, and, unlike birth and death, times for marriage can be chosen.

In the contemporary world, wedding planning continues to rely on calendrical divination in the attempt to exert positive influence on an important life event. For instance, popular South Korean belief in auspicious days influences the scheduling of important events like weddings, associated with love and reproduction, leading people to "seek the advice of a fortune-teller to learn about those propitious days before embarking on something important" (Kim 2005, 289). On October 27, 1991, a day believed to be extremely lucky in South Korea, "wedding halls and churches were bursting with weddings, and hospitals were practically overflowing with pregnant women wanting to deliver their babies, quite often resorting to the Caesarean operation" (Kim 2005, 289).

Destiny and Fated Love

The concept of romantic love as a predestined, fated phenomenon is also represented in popular astrological discourses about intimate relationships. The notion of fated love and romantic attraction being part of a larger cosmic narrative is articulated in metaphors and phrases in the English language, such as "written in the stars" or "star-crossed lovers," as well as many popular texts.

Although aspects of astrological discourse change to accommodate cultural norms regarding sex and love, it is also important to consider the role of commercial media in producing contemporary practices and beliefs. Modern horoscopes and sun sign astrology in commercial media is dedicated to the discussion of love and romance. Advice about romantic relations is identified as a central theme in many content analyses of Western horoscopes as well as South Korean and Chinese astrological fortune-telling. These popular horoscope discourses typically circulate traditional advice for readers about pursuing love and romance, demonstrating the potential role of astrology in providing authority in the negotiation of intimate relationships.

Sun Sign Compatibility

In popular forms of Western and Chinese astrology personality traits are considered to be influenced by the time of one's birth or zodiac sign. The attributes associated with a Leo sun sign in the United States, or someone born during the Dragon year in China, are common knowledge in their respective cultures and are represented in courtship rituals, compatibility tests, and matchmaking in vernacular discourse. There is widespread use of zodiac signs in conversation and flirtation, evinced by the cliché pickup line "what's your sign?" as well as on popular dating websites, like Match.com, which include the user's zodiac sign on the profile wall.

Popular books about astrology often include guides to dating, love, and sex based on sun sign and natal astrology compatibility. In 1968, astrologer Linda Goodman published *Linda Goodman's Sun Signs*, the first astrology book to make it onto the

New York Times best seller list, which introduced sun sign compatibility to many in the general population. This was followed by *Linda Goodman's Love Signs*, which focused more exclusively on compatibility in romance and still enjoys enormous popularity. Both appeared in Google's list of top-selling ebooks on astrology in early 2017. Innumerable books about zodiac signs and love compatibility have followed that contain advice on topics like "how to bond with an Aquarius," "seduce any sign of the zodiac," or to reveal the "heavenly sex life you were born to have." Mentions of zodiac signs are not uncommon in popular music including "No Matter What Sign You Are" by Diana Ross and the Supremes (1969), and a successful Spanish language dating television show, "12 Corazones" (2004–2013), is based on audience familiarity with zodiac astrology in dating and matchmaking. There are also astrological guides to romance aimed at subpopulations such as African Americans. A unique aspect of contemporary astrological culture in the West is the plethora of books and articles devoted to romantic advice for gay men and lesbian women.

Critiques of Love-Focused Popular Astrology

Various sociological and cultural studies' critiques of popular astrology have argued that the centrality of love and fate in horoscopes is potentially harmful. In an analysis of the horoscope column in the *Los Angeles Times*, Frankfurt School Marxist cultural theorist Theodor Adorno (1903–1969) describes the use of love and personal relationships in astrology as indicative of the need to adjust to economic forces and labor relations (as well as a means of sublimating Oedipal impulses). Adorno's critique of popular astrology's focus on mundane, personal aspects of life, like relationships, saw horoscopes as a means of quelling anxieties and precluding struggle against systemic oppression and exploitation. The concept of the fated personal life is important in popular astrology as it represents a way of telling consumers to "take things as they are, since you are fated for them anyway" (Nederman and Goulding 1981, 327). Astrology's construction of love, health, and wealth as the subjects of fate, according to this critique, downplays the material reality of "earthly" forces in their allotment as many are unable to "avoid sickness, debt and loneliness; those who do are among the privileged" (Nederman and Goulding 1981, 327).

Love and Gender Norms in Popular Astrology

The metaphorical nature of horoscopes and astrological discourses may be particularly effective in communicating gender norms and indirect instructions for dealing with intimate relationships. Conceptions of fated love and sun sign–based compatibility narratives in popular astrology have been criticized for reliance on traditional expectations based on heteronormativity and procreative marriage. The contemporary use of love and sex as themes in women's magazine horoscopes in particular can also be considered with regard to the social construction of gender norms.

According to a rhetorical analysis of the horoscope content in women's magazines by Edson Tandoc and Patrick Ferruci, the fixation on love and relationships

Astrology and Teen Girl Culture: Cathy Hopkins's *Zodiac Girls*

In modern Western society, astrology is often associated with teenage girls. Several cultural phenomena have emerged to take advantage of this association. One example is *Zodiac Girls*, a series of novels aimed at midteen girls by British writer Cathy Hopkins. The teenage protagonists spend a month as "Zodiac Girls" depending on their charts. (In a characteristically 21st century touch, the girls get magic phones.) They receive astrological assistance from characters personifying the planets to deal with their family, social, and psychological issues. The girls are characterized by their sun signs, which also play a major role in the story. The first in the series, *From Geek to Goddess*, about a Gemini, appeared in 2007. Seven more books appeared over the next two years, although Hopkins abandoned plans to produce 12 books, one for each sign, after a split with her publisher.

in these texts reveals how horoscopes play on existing stereotypes to reinforce normative roles for women. The themes regarding love in the study tend to suggest that women be dependent on men, putting up with their faults because not having a man would make life incomplete. According to this article, horoscopes about love demonstrate social norms and values according to gender and race. These represent the conditions of preexisting patriarchal, racial, and capitalist power structures under which horoscopes are produced.

Therapeutic Functions and Astrological Counseling

Alongside explicitly predictive aspects of astrology, some scholars have recognized astrology readings as a form of counseling or self-help, offering emotional support to people during times of need or of particular import. The overlapping traditions of astrology with courtship rituals and cultural institutions like marriage that are associated with love and sex reflect the importance of these concerns in society and demonstrate the desire to understand and shape relationships that play a vital role in one's personal life. Like other popular divination practices the use of astrology in contemporary contexts reveals "the wish to learn about the best course of future action to ultimately fulfill one's wishes" (Kim 2005, 286). Astrological and divination rituals in love and sex continue to be used as tactics for communicating with others, connecting the individual to his or her community while negotiating major life events.

Annamarie O'Brien

See also: Gender; Goodman, Linda; Omarr, Sydney; Sun Signs

Further Reading

Aphek, Edna, and Y. Tobin. 1989. *The Semiotics of Fortune-Telling*. Foundations of Semiotics. Amsterdam: John Benjamins.

Campion, Nicholas. 2012. *Astrology and Popular Religion in the Modern West: Prophecy, Cosmology, and the New Age Movement*. Farnham, Surrey, UK: Ashgate.

Cressy, David. 1999. *Birth, Marriage, and Death: Ritual, Religion, and the Life-Cycle in Tudor and Stuart England.* Oxford: Oxford University Press.

Diana Ross and the Supremes. 1969. *No Matter What Sign You Are.* Motown.

Fehérváry, Krisztina. 2007. "Hungarian Horoscopes as a Genre of Postsocialist Transformation." *Social Identities* 13, no. 5: 561–576.

Goodman, Linda. 1968. *Linda Goodman's Sun Signs.* New York: Taplinger.

Jha, J. C. 1976. "The Hindu Sacraments (Rites De Passage) in Trinidad and Tobago." *Caribbean Quarterly* 22, no. 1: 40–52.

Kasak, Enn. 2000. "Ancient Astrology as a Common Root for Science and Pseudo-Science." *Folklore : Electronic Journal of Folklore* 15: 84–104.

Kim, Andrew Eungi. 2005. "Nonofficial Religion in South Korea: Prevalence of Fortunetelling and Other Forms of Divination." *Review of Religious Research* 46, no. 3: 284–302.

Miller, Laura. 2014. "The Divination Arts in Girl Culture." In *Capturing Contemporary Japan: Differentiation and Uncertainty*, ed. Satsuki Kawano, Glenda Roberts, and Susan Long. Honolulu: University of Hawaii Press.

Nederman, Cary J., and James Wray Goulding. 1981. "Popular Occultism and Critical Social Theory: Exploring Some Themes in Adorno's Critique of Astrology and the Occult." *Sociological Analysis* 42, no. 4: 325–332.

"Popular Ebooks in Astrology." https://play.google.com/store/search?q=astrology&c=books

Tandoc, Edson C., Jr. and Patrick Ferrucci. 2014. "So Says the Stars: A Textual Analysis of Glamour, Essence and Teen Vogue Horoscopes." *Women's Studies International Forum* 45 (July): 34–41.

Thomas, Robert, Jr. 1995. "Linda Goodman, Writer Turned Astrologer, Dies." *New York Times*, October 25. http://www.nytimes.com/1995/10/25/us/linda-goodman-writer-turned-astrologer-dies.html

Tomlin, T. J. 2010. "'Astrology's from Heaven Not from Hell': The Religious Significance of Early American Almanacs." *Early American Studies: An Interdisciplinary Journal* 8, no. 2: 287–321.

Trachtenberg, Joshua. 2012. *Jewish Magic and Superstition: A Study in Folk Religion.* Philadelphia: University of Pennsylvania Press.

"12 Corazones," November 15, 2004. http://www.imdb.com/title/tt0450347/

SIBLY, EBENEZER (CA. 1750–1799)

Ebenezer Sibly was one of the most prominent astrologers in 18th-century England, and is still recognized as a skilled astrologer and the collector of a valuable library of Renaissance astrology. Much of this is, however, fable. His most important contribution to astrology was actually the publication of *An Illustration of the Celestial Science of Astrology*, which fostered the early 19th-century audience for astrology.

Sibly was born in London into a family of Nonconformists. His father Edmund was a shoemaker who trained sons Ebenezer, Manoah, and Job in the craft as well. In the 1770s all four Siblys became booksellers before expanding into a variety of related occupations, including writing, publishing, translating, and taking shorthand. Ebenezer and Manoah moved into esoteric circles, with both carrying occult works in their shops and publishing books on astrology.

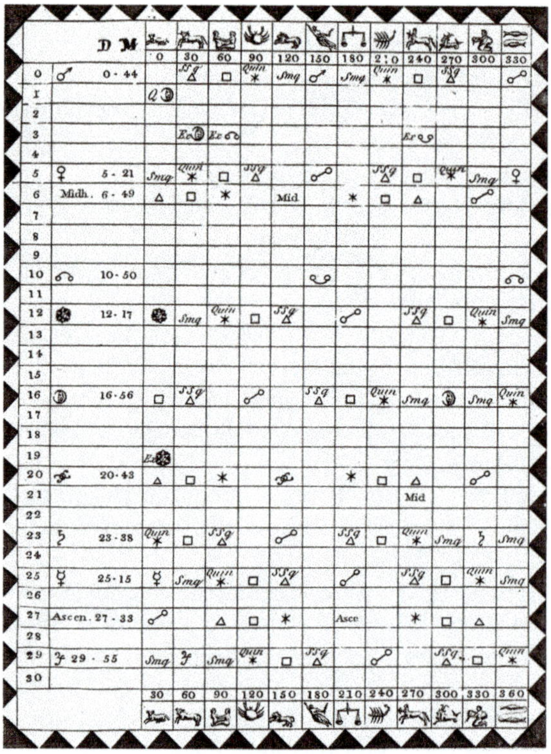

A table, or compilation, of the aspects the celestial bodies formed at the birth of the astronomer George Witchell in 1728, from Sibly's *Illustration of the Celestial Science of Astrology*. (Ann Ronan Pictures/Print Collector/Getty Images)

Sibly was peripatetic, changing locale, wives, and occupation frequently. He was married first in London, in 1770, and went on to marry twice more, though his first wife, Sarah Wainwright, was still living and they did not divorce. Sibly left Sarah and London in the late 1770s when he moved to Portsmouth, Hampshire. There he was initiated into freemasonry and opened a bookshop. From then on freemasonry remained an important part of his esoteric life, and he joined lodges wherever he found himself. He was also active in writing masonic rituals, and during the 1790s he joined his patron Thomas Dunckerley (1724–1795) in organizing at least two new orders: The Masonic Knights Templar and the Ancient Masons of the Diluvian Order, or Royal Ark and Mark Mariners.

In 1784, Sibly relocated to Bristol where he added storefront astrological consulting to selling books. About the same time he also began publication of his most significant astrological work, *An Illustration of the Celestial Science of Astrology*, which was published in installments over the next several years, and was completed in 1790. Its 1,200-odd pages cover the gamut of Early Modern esoterica, ranging from astrology and herbal medicine to animal magnetism, practical magic, spiritualism, and talismans. In addition, Sibly incorporates references to current scientific and medical discoveries, leading scholars like Patrick Curry and Allen Debus to identify him as a significant Enlightenment synthesizer of late Renaissance arcana and modern science.

Sibly's career in Bristol ended in 1786 when lottery tickets sold at his bookshop proved fraudulent. He returned to London where in 1788, along with masonic brothers Stephen Freeman and John Bell, he attempted to establish a College for Instruction in Elementary Philosophy. Despite offering instruction in animal magnetism, astrology, and transmutation of metals, the college failed to attract sufficient subscribers and the scheme was abandoned. From there Sibly once again changed tack, moving to Ipswich, Suffolk, to manage the 1790 parliamentary campaign of John D'Oyly. By this time Sibly knew little of politics but was an experienced freemason, and as a result his largely successful electoral strategy involved creating a pseudomasonic order, the Royal Ark Masons or Good Samaritans.

With the proceeds of his electioneering stint, Sibly returned to London. Joining the already swollen ranks of London quack doctors he purchased an MD from King's College, Aberdeen, in 1792, and patented *Dr. Sibly's Re-animating Solar Tincture* in 1795. For the rest of his life Sibly worked to build up his share of the burgeoning health care market, developed the *Lunar Tincture* for women, and published books and pamphlets puffing his medicines. The latter include *A Key to Physic* (1792), *The Medical Mirror* (1794), and *Observations on the Virtues and Efficacy of Dr. Sibly's Reanimating Solar Tincture* (1794). The formulation and naming of Sibly's medicines look back to 17th-century sol-lunar and planetary theories of disease, and utilize a traditional herbal pharmacopeia to concoct therapies based at least in part on astrology.

Sibly died in 1799 without becoming rich. However, he left a lasting mark on the history of astrology. Sibly has long been recognized as amassing a valuable library of late Renaissance esoteric works, which then provided a substantial part of the foundation for the 19th-century occult revival. As it turns out, he did not. A complete probate inventory, together with a partial reconstruction of his "library," reveals that while he copied and collected manuscripts concerning magic, alchemy, and astrology, none were particularly rare, and he left neither a collection of bound texts nor any indication that he had owned one. Moreover, while Martin Gansten's analysis of the only known surviving nativity Sibly erected on commission, the Wellcome Library's "Horoscope of an unknown lady," reveals him to have been a competent astrologer who used eclectic neo-Placidean techniques, Gansten concludes Sibly was weak on mathematical ability and reliant on an inaccurate planisphere.

Sibly's real importance was as a repopularizer of astrology in the late 18th century. In Britain, astrology had steadily lost favor and fashion as Newtonian science gained acceptance and prominence. As Roy Wiles observes, when books of substantial length and cost were sold in inexpensive installments it stimulated readership, creating demand where none existed before. Thus Sibly reintroduced astrology and affiliated arcana through his attractive and affordable *An Illustration of the Celestial Science of Astrology*, which appeared under various titles and through several editions. This work, richly illustrated with engravings and charts, and sold in 60 installments, encouraged a wide popular readership and cultivated an expanded interest in astrology, as demonstrated by both the mythology that has accrued to Sibly's memory, and the wide survival of his publications—despite the fact that they were indeed almost entirely plagiarized from other writers on astrology and magic, including Reginald Scot (1538–1599), Méric Causabon (1599–1671), John Whalley (1653–1724), William Lilly, John Gadbury, and John Partridge, as well as from contemporary natural philosophers and physicians.

Susan Mitchell Sommers

See also: Enlightenment; Medical Astrology; Placidus

Further Reading

Curry, Patrick. 1989. *Prophecy and Power: Astrology in Early Modern England*. Princeton: Princeton University Press.

Debus, Allen. 1982. "Scientific Truth and Occult Tradition: The Medical World of Ebenezer Sibly (1751–1799)." *Medical History* 26: 259–278.

Sommers, Susan Mitchell. 2018. *The Siblys of London: A Family on the Esoteric Fringes of Georgian England*. Oxford: Oxford University Press.

Wiles, Roy. 1957. *Serial Publications in England before 1750*. Cambridge: Cambridge University Press.

SIMA QIAN (CA. 145–87 BCE)

Sima Qian was a great historian and astronomer of the Western Han Chinese dynasty (202 BCE–8 CE). *Shi ji*, or the *Grand Scribe's Records*, is his best-known work. According to the last chapter of *Shi ji*, his autobiography, he was a descendant of Chong and Li, two ancient astronomers in primitive times who "regulated the heaven and the earth generation after generation," and in the Zhou Dynasty his ancestors became historians as well as astronomers. His father Sima Tan had been a tai shi ling during the reigning period of Emperor Wu (140–87 BCE) in Western Han. The tai shi ling was an official in charge of history and astronomy at that time but then became a special official only in charge of astronomical bureau later. As a youth Sima Qian traveled collecting historical materials. His dying father enjoined him to be a tai shi ling to resume his ancestors' mission. In the third year after his father's death, 108 BCE, Sima Qian became tai shi ling. As tai shi ling he promoted an important calendar reform, namely the Tai chu calendar reform (104 BCE). In 98 BCE he was sentenced to castration for an argument with a general who had surrendered in a battle. Though he accepted a lower rank later, he did not care for politics anymore; instead, he concentrated on writing *Shi ji*, finishing the great book in 91 BCE.

Shi ji has 130 chapters recording history from very ancient times to Sima Qian's own age. This book initiated the tradition of writing an official history for the former dynasty, which formed 24 official histories from Han to Ming (1368–1644), the second to last dynasty in Chinese history whose official history was written under the Qing (1644–1911), the last dynasty. *Shi ji* contributed eight chapters to record decrees and institutions, including *tian guan shu*, the *Chapter on the Heavenly Offices*, and *li shu*, the *Chapter on Calendar*. This also set a model for later official histories, while in later official histories the chapters on astronomy are usually entitled *tian wen zhi*, *treatise on astronomy*, and the chapters on calendar entitled *li zhi*, *treatise on calendar*, with some histories the chapters on calendar are combined with that on temperament and entitled *lü li zhi*, *the treatise on harmonics and calendar*. With the chapters on astronomy and calendar in these official histories, the main development of astronomy as well as the reform of calendars of every dynasty in Chinese history are well documented.

The *tian guan shu* chapter in *Shi ji* covers both astronomy and astrology. It begins with describing the constellations and stars in the sky. It divides the whole sky into five gong, or palaces, namely the center, the east, the south, the west, and the north, describing important constellations and stars of each gong, their relative positions, the brightness and colors of some stars, and gives astrological meanings to most of them. It records 89 xing guan, or constellations, about 500 stars. Though the traditional Chinese constellation and star system were set up by Gan De and Shi Shenfu in the Warring States period (475–221 BCE), their books were lost although some of their contents were collected in later astrological books. *Tian guan shu* is the earliest extant work describing the stars of the whole sky. The stars in *tian guan shu* were not simply compiled from that of Gan De and Shi Shenfu but had many differences.

After the constellations and the stars, *tian guan shu* describes the five planets by the sequence of Jupiter, Mars, Saturn, Venus, and Mercury. Sima Qian not only divided the synodic periods of each planet into several phases and described the motions of each phase but also gave astrological meanings for each planet. His description of the five planets was affected by the five phase theory, one of the most important theories in the Han, which connected Jupiter to east, wood and spring; Mars to south, fire and summer; Saturn to center, earth and the third month of summer; Venus to west, metal and autumn; and Mercury to north, water and winter. Besides the connection among natural phenomena, it also included the five virtues of people, and so on. Because the five planets display very complicated motions and they were very important in Chinese astrology, Sima Qian devoted a long paragraph on the five planets.

Following the five planets comes the theory of fen ye, or field allocation, which describes the correspondences between constellations, planets, and so on, and different areas on the Earth. And then follows a brief discussion of the astrology of the sun and the moon. Then it gives several strange names of celestial phenomena, some of them might be comets followed by astrology of the clouds and winds. Then Sima Qian gave a brief history of astronomy, listing a series of names of ancient astronomers and the astrological connections of astronomical anomalies with subsequent political events.

Li shu, or the *Chapter on Calendar*, is mainly composed of two parts: the first describes the history of the calendar, the second gives the calculation process of a calendar. In describing the history of the calendar, Sima Qian emphasized that the appearance of the calendar separated human from spirits. Then people respected the spirits while the spirits downed good seedlings, thus there were no disasters and people enjoyed good harvests. After that there was chaos followed by people striving to make better calendars to delineate the regulation of the universe.

Strangely the calendar for which Sima Qian gave the calculating process was not the Tai chu calendar, the result of the Tai chu calendar reform promulgated in 104 BCE. The Tai chu calendar reform was a famous astronomical event in the Han Dynasty, and Sima Qian was one of its earliest participants. The calendar recorded by Sima Qian is a kind of si fen calendar, or quarter calendar, which got its name because it adopted 365 and 1/4 days as the length of a tropical year. *Li shu* set the precedent of recording the calculating process of the main calendars in the official histories.

As historian, astronomer, and astrologer, Sima Qian set many precedents for subsequent Chinese writers and astronomers.

Xu Fengxian

See also: Chinese Astrology; Court Astrologers; Mundane Astrology

Further Reading

Cullen, Christopher. 2011. "Understanding the Planets in Ancient China: Prediction and Divination in the Wu xing zhan." *Early Science and Medicine* 16: 218–251.
Nakayama, Shigeru. 1966. "Characteristics of Chinese Astrology." *ISIS* 57, no. 4: 442–454.
Pankenier, David W. 2013. *Astrology and Cosmology in Early China*. Cambridge: Cambridge University Press.

STOICISM

Stoicism is a Greek philosophical system associated with Zeno of Citium (334–262 BCE), who founded a Stoic school in Athens ca. 300 BCE. According to the Stoics, the world is an ideally good organism governed by its own rational soul, the *Pneuma* (the active principle, which pervades and animates the universe), and we live in a deterministic universe of cause and effect. Stoic speculation was divided into three parts: logic, physics, and ethics. The Stoics were materialists who found no distinction between matter and spirit. In their view, the universe was comprised of five elements: earth, air, fire, water, and ether (the upper regions beyond the clouds). Upon death the human soul became part of the ethereal regions of the heavens. According to the Stoics everything in the universe is governed by identical laws of Fate, composing a "cosmic symphony." The Stoics were the first to assume that the same physical laws applied to heavenly bodies as to earthly ones. In Stoic thought, moral goodness consisted of discovering our assigned role in the cosmic scheme of things.

Hellenistic astrologers based their speculation on a combination of Babylonian/Chaldean astrological traditions and philosophical thought. The Babylonian cosmological theory of the "eternal recurrence" (the idea that the universe will recur across time and space) influenced the early Stoics. In the Stoic version of eternal recurrence a great conflagration takes place in the cosmos and continues until the planets return to their original location or zodiac sign within the universe. The early Stoic Cleanthes (331–232 BCE) assumed that the gods have divine foreknowledge of the fate of the cosmos and a corresponding concern for human beings. He also assumed that if there are gods there must also be divination. For the Stoics, divination and astrology foretold events that occurred by chance (those things that occur without any clear cause). Stoicism was thus naturally inclined toward astrology because it assumes that austral phenomena follow an observable pattern. Its adherents viewed the position of heavenly bodies as signs of future events. They accepted the connection between the heavens and the fates of individuals but cautioned that the interpretation of this connection was descriptive rather than prescriptive.

Very little formal writing of the Stoics has survived intact. Much of what we know about the views of specific Stoics' regarding astrology comes from the Roman statesman and orator Cicero's (106–43 BCE) *de Divinatione* (a fictionalized dialogue between Cicero himself and his brother Quintus). Cicero claimed that all people, whether learned or ignorant, seeks signs of future events. According to Cicero, the Stoics, and particularly Zeno, defended nearly every sort of divination, including astrology, and looked to the heavens for signs of future events. Cicero singled out Chrysippus (280–206 BCE) and Posidonius for discussion. Chrysippus was perhaps the greatest head of the Stoic school in Athens and his thought is considered identical with Stoicism. He accepted the general validity of astrology and famously said those who are born at the rising of the Dog-star (Sirius) will not die at sea (Cicero). Posidonius (ca. 135–50 BCE) is considered the most scientific of the Stoics. He investigated a wide range of physical phenomena, including astronomy. His explanations of the sun and its distance from Earth, as well as other celestial phenomena such as lunar and solar eclipses, and comets, were renowned in later antiquity. He regarded these phenomena as interconnected in some way by a cosmic symphony. In Posidonius's thought, the Stoic conception of the logos joins with the cosmic symphony to provide the philosophical basis for divination. According to Cicero, the only notable Stoic who rejected astrology was Panaetius (185–110 BCE).

Marcus Manilius, another Roman Stoic, is credited with writing *Astronomica*, perhaps the most advanced ancient Latin treatise on astronomy/astrology. The best-known Roman-Stoic adherent of astrology was Seneca (4 BCE–65 CE), who claimed that the five planets (Mercury, Venus, Mars, Jupiter, and Saturn) plus the sun, moon, and stars exercise sway over human life. These celestial objects pursue different paths and on their slightest motion "hang the fortunes of nations, and the greatest and smallest happenings are shaped to accord with the progress of a beneficent or maleficent star" (Seneca 1963–1965, 59–61).

Wendell G. Johnson

See also: Fate; Hellenistic Astrology; Manilius, Marcus; Roman Astrology

Further Reading

Hankinson, R. J. 1988. "Stoicism, Science and Divination." *Apeiron: A Journal for Ancient Philosophy and Science* 21, no. 2, 123–160.

Hegedus, Tim. 2007. *Early Christianity and Ancient Astrology*. New York: Peter Lang.

Meijer, P. A. 2007. *Stoic Theology. Proofs for the Existence of the Cosmic God and of the Traditional Gods*. Delft: Eburon.

Seneca, Lucius Annaeus. 1963–1965. *Moral Essays*, trans. John W. Basore. Cambridge, MA: Harvard University Press.

Tester, S. J. 1987. *A History of Western Astrology*. Wolfbridge, UK: Boydell.

Wardle, David, ed. 2006. *Cicero on Divination, 1*. Oxford: Oxford University Press.

SUN SIGNS

The sun sign, sometimes known as the birth sign or star sign, is the zodiac sign in which the sun is located at birth or other significant moments. The term is used in two contexts. First there are the sun signs as personality or character descriptions, and second are the sun sign forecasts, the 12-paragraph columns carried in most popular newspapers and women's magazines and now on many popular websites, carrying a reading for each sun sign. Generally known as horoscopes, there is an inevitable confusion between such columns and the horoscope used by most astrologers—the schematic diagram containing astronomical information for a precise time and place. Sun sign horoscopes are composed either daily, weekly, or monthly, depending in the publishing schedule of the host journal, although such restrictions no longer apply on the web. They typically contain between 50 and 150 words of generalized advice and prediction. Both sun sign personality descriptions and horoscopes are simplifications of astrology, allowing them to relate to large groups of people, individuals being able to easily identify their astrological type from their date of birth. The wide dissemination of these columns has led to a popular identification of astrology as a whole with the sun sign.

Even though the zodiac signs' character descriptions were known in classical astrology, the modern concept of the birth sign as a universal signifier of personality and destiny appears to be very recent, developing between the 1900s and 1930s.

Sun Sign Character Descriptions

The attribution of character descriptions to the zodiac signs dates back to the development of natal astrology between the fifth century BCE and first century CE, by which time each sign provided a complete account of individual life including such features as character, profession, and physiological type. The system was sufficiently well known by the late first century CE to be satirized by Petronius in the *Satyricon*.

However, until the 20th century, personality and psychological types were far less important in popular astrology than knowing what days were favorable for particular tasks. Calendars based on the zodiac sign containing the moon offering guidance for appropriate actions for different days were more important than knowing one's psychological attributes. The rise of the sun sign in the 20th century parallels the development of modern psychological astrology.

The broad relationship between the sun's passage through the zodiac signs and communal life was preserved through what became known as Shepherd's Calendars (such as Spenser's *Shepheardes Calender* of 1579) and Books of Hours (of which the most famous example is the *Très Riches Heures du Duc de Berry* of 1412–1416). These related weather and seasonal activities, such as the harvest, to months and zodiac signs.

In the 19th century the description of zodiac signs was usually physical and contained only a minimum of psychological content. The modern personality–psychologically based system is largely based in the reform of astrology undertaken by the theosophist Alan Leo. Leo argued that the sun is the most important astrological planet on the grounds that it represents the solar logos, which transmits divine wisdom into the human universe. He also discarded almost the entire list of external zodiacal attributes, such as profession and physiology, which had been accumulated from the first to the 17th centuries. In his opinion, these were of no use at all if people were to prepare for the coming spiritual New Age, so he set out to create a zodiacal astrology that would fulfill this purpose by encouraging people to reflect on their inner character. His descriptions increasingly set the tone for accounts of the zodiac signs, including the best-selling and influential *Linda Goodman's Sun Signs* (1970). Goodman established the potential profitability of the sun sign books, which have dominated popular astrology publishing since the 1970s. The development of the language of the sun sign as the most prevalent form of popular psychology is evident in the space allocated for the zodiac signs' psychological descriptions; whereas it had been sufficient for Alan Leo to devote a half page to Aries, the sign warranted approximately 24 pages in Bernard Fitzwalter's 1989 *Sun Sign Secrets*.

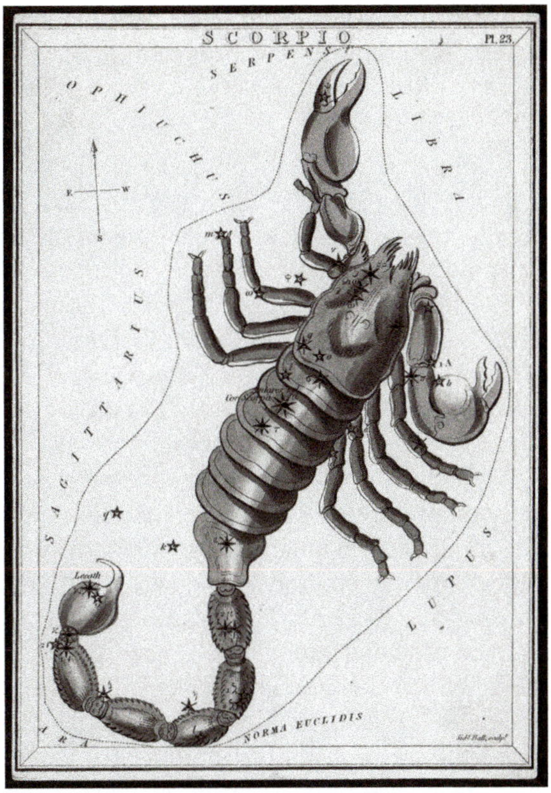

This early-19th-century "constellation card" was designed to be held against the sky to identify the zodiacal sign Scorpio. (Library of Congress)

As summarized in modern astrology the general personality characteristics of each sign are:

Aries: assertive, energetic, self-willed
Taurus: obstinate, stubborn, sensual
Gemini: intellectual, communicate, changeable
Cancer: emotional, nurturing, assertive
Leo: creative, energetic, dramatic
Virgo: careful, precise, practical
Libra: balanced, harmonious, communicative
Scorpio: emotional, secretive, passionate
Sagittarius: adventurous, energetic, optimistic
Capricorn: practical, conservative, ambitious

Aquarius: idealistic, stubborn, revolutionary
Pisces: emotional, sensitive, changeable

The Sun Sign Column

The horoscope column, consisting of 12 paragraphs, one for each of the approximately 30-day periods when the sun occupies each of the signs of the zodiac, became the main vehicle for the transmission of popular astrology from the 1930s onward.

The existence of sun sign columns, though, is a matter of some argument among astrologers, many of whom claim that they are not proper astrology and are responsible for astrology's poor public reputation. The counterargument is that sun sign columns are as legitimate a form of astrology as any other and that they are responsible for astrology's general popularity.

Almanacs prior to the 20th century included forecasts for the year ahead for individuals born on each day of the year, but not grouped together by zodiac sign. The model was maintained by what is usually regarded as the first regular newspaper astrology column, published in the United Kingdom in *The Sunday Express* on August 24, 1930. This included an analysis of the horoscope of the infant Princess Margaret, along with general political predictions and about 50 words per day of birthday predictions for each day of the coming week in line with common practice. The column proved so popular that it became a weekly feature. Current evidence suggests that the first regular 12-paragraph zodiac sign horoscopes columns appeared in *American Astrology* magazine from the first issue onward in March 1933. However, it took a few years for the use of zodiac signs to be generally established. The U.K. *People* newspaper used the names of the zodiac signs in 1935 and a complete 12-paragraph feature was launched in *Prediction* magazine in 1936.

Public familiarity with the sun signs appears to have been widespread in the United Kingdom and United States by the 1950s. They were incorporated into countercultural psychology in the 1960s on the grounds that they provided a means of self-knowledge that connected the individual to the cosmos. The dissemination of such columns was partly driven by technology. By the late 1970s computers were programmed to produce individual birth chart readings and sun sign columns became important as the medium for marketing these. The advent of morning television in the United Kingdom in 1983 created a demand for more content, and the astrologer Russell Grant attracted a huge following in BBC's *Breakfast Time* show. From 1987, the development of prerecorded horoscopes that could be accessed by telephone generated huge profits. Newspapers responded to the new technology by expanding the size of their columns to up to a page (in the case of *Today*) and running regular extra features, such as 12-day specials over Christmas and New Year. Gross income could be at least a £1,000,000 per annum, although there was a rapid decline in the early 1990s as the novelty wore off and companies introduced call-barring technology in order to prevent their employees calling from work. By the late 1990s and early 2000s the web then offered new commercial opportunities as astrologers were able to access a global market and use freely accessible columns as a means offering regular, paid updates to regular readers. By the 2010s YouTube had become another vital medium for marketing and dissemination.

Some columns are written by journalists, as was *The Daily Express* column, "Lord Luck," in the 1960s. Those written by astrologers are usually based technically on a system of so-called solar houses in which the first house is identical with the birth sign, the second house with the following sign, and so on. For example, for somebody born with the sun in Gemini, any planet in Cancer is in the second house and any planet in Leo is in the third house. If the moon is then in Cancer, for an individual born with the sun in Gemini, it is in the second solar house emphasizing money (ruled by the second house). If the moon is in Leo communication (ruled by the third house) is highlighted. To take another example, for an individual born with the sun in Cancer, a transit of Mars (ruling anger) through Leo will be in the second solar house and will signify the possibility of arguments over money. All the planets may be taken into account but as the moon is the fastest moving (spending around two and a half days in each sign) it inevitably plays the most part in daily and weekly columns. Monthly columns tend to emphasize the new and full moons and associated planetary patterns.

Research in the 2000s suggested that 99 percent of British adults know their sun sign and around 75 percent agree that their sign's characteristics were accurate. Evidence suggests that these figures are repeated globally and that sun signs provide a unique means by which individuals endow the minutiae of their individual lives with cosmic significance.

Nicholas Campion

See also: Feminist Astrology; Goodman, Linda; Leo, Alan; Natal Astrology; Newspapers; Omarr, Sydney; Righter, Carroll; Sex and Love

Further Reading

Campion, Nicholas. 2009. *A History of Western Astrology, Vol. 2, The Medieval and Modern Worlds*. London: Bloomsbury.
Farnell, Kim. 2007. *Flirting with the Zodiac*. Bournemouth: Wessex Astrologer.
Fitzwalter, Bernard. 1989. *Sun Sign Secrets*. n.p.: Aquarian Press.

T

TĀJIKA ASTROLOGY

Tājika, literally "Persian" (although derived from Middle Persian *tāzīg* meaning "Arab"), is the designation of the Sanskritized Perso-Arabic astrology that arose as a separate school following the second wave of astrological transmission into India in the early centuries of the second millennium CE. It is thus the form of Indian astrology most closely resembling Western medieval and Renaissance astrology, which similarly rests on Arabic foundations. Although ultimately derived from the same Greek origins as classical Indian astrology, Tājika comprises many technical elements not included in the first wave of transmission about a millennium earlier.

Sources and Early Reception

Perso-Arabic astrology appears to have entered India through the Saurāṣṭra peninsula in present-day Gujarat, which had long been a center for maritime trade, no earlier than the 10th century, as most or all Arabic works that can be identified as Tājika source texts were composed during the ninth century. Although Tājika works emphatically credit a certain "Khindi"—most likely Ya'qūb Ibn Isḥāq al-Kindī, the "philosopher of the Arabs"—with the teachings they present, their most important source seems to have been Sahl Ibn Bishr, a Persian Jew writing in Arabic, who is never mentioned by name. Other uncredited Arabic sources include works by Abū Bakr and 'Umar aṭ-ṭabarī; from the former stems a reference to "Durvītthasa," that is, the first-century author Dorotheus of Sidon, whose writings formed a mainstay of Perso-Arabic astrology. It is possible that the original source text of Tājika astrology was a compendium of excerpts from Arabic authors, mistakenly presented as the sole work of al-Kindī.

More spurious Tājika references to ancient authorities include Maṇittha (pseudo-Manetho), Romaka ("the Roman"), and—often mentioned together—Hillāja and Khattakhutta. The latter pair actually represents a misunderstanding of two interrelated technical terms in Persian, *hīlāg* (Arabicized form *hīlāj*) and *kadkhudāh*, known in the West under the Latinized forms hyleg and alcochoden (with variants), both related to life span calculations. Although the words *hillāja* and *khattakhutta* appear in their proper sense in early Tājika works, later generations of authors mistook them for personal names, suggesting a lack of familiarity with Persian as opposed to Arabic.

There is some evidence to suggest that the earliest known Tājika works in Sanskrit were composed in the latter half of the 13th century by authors who were either Jains or members of the non-Brahman Prāgvāṭa (Porwad) community encompassing both Jains and Hindus. The most influential of these authors, Samarasiṃha, was reinvented as a Brahman by later Tājika tradition. Not all Brahmans were accepting of the foreign science, however, and several Tājika works include apologetic passages defending its use by arguments that range from the mythological (Tājika originated with the Hindu sun god Sūrya, cursed to be born on Earth as a Western barbarian) to the pragmatic (Tājika is worthy of study because its predictions come true), while admitting its dependence on "Brahman-hating Turks."

Technical Content and Creative Misunderstandings

Like classical Indian astrology, Tājika employs a sidereal zodiac and a sidereal definition of the true solar year. Similar sidereal values utilized by the Persians are found in some medieval Arabic works preserved in the West, such as the so-called *Liber Aristotilis* attributed to Māshā'allāh Ibn Atharī. Although the only surviving (but possibly still incomplete) work by Samarasiṃha, originally known as the *Karmaprakāśa* but later also as the *Manuṣyajātaka, Tājikatantrasāra*, or *Gaṇakabhūṣaṇa*, deals with genethlialogy or natal astrology in a broad sense, Tājika astrology has for many centuries been chiefly associated with two other branches of the art: on the one hand, *varṣaphala* or annual revolutions (known today as solar returns), a subset of genethlialogy focusing on predictions for each separate year of life; and on the other, *praśna* or interrogations (also known as horary astrology). The latter branch of astrology also exists within the classical Indian tradition, albeit in a technically different form; the former is unique to the Perso-Arabic school. Tājika texts on both topics again chiefly depend on works by Samarasiṃha, only fragments of which survive today.

Among the doctrines distinguishing Tājika from pre-Islamic Indian astrology, the most conspicuous is that of the aspects, closely resembling those of the Greek, Perso-Arabic, and later European traditions: within its individual orb of light, each planet casts two sextiles, two squares, two trines, and an opposition, in addition to the conjunction. These aspects also form the basis of most of the so-called 16 *yogas*, adapted (with some misunderstandings) from a list given by Sahl and including the configurations known in Western literature as application and separation, translation and collection of light, prohibition and return of light, reception and nonreception, being void of course, and committing strength and disposition—all prominently used in horary astrology.

The zodiacal dignities of the planets constitute a particularly complex area. The Perso-Arabic notion of five dignities (domicile, exaltation, terms, triplicity, and face or decan) was preserved by the Tājikas but with some confusion regarding the identity of the last two, which are often conflated to make room for the classical Indian concept of ninth-parts (*navāṃśa*). The latter is identified by some authors with the *musallaha* (from the Arabic *muthallatha*, actually "triplicity"), while the Sanskrit translation of the same word (*trairāśika*) is understood to refer to the decans. Later generations of Tājika authors added more zodiacal subdivisions, resulting in a separate list of 12 dignities.

Other elements of Greek astrology introduced to India for the first time by the Tājika school include the joys of the planets—some of which depend on the division of planets into a diurnal and a noctural sect, although this principle was imperfectly understood—and the mathematically derived points known as lots (*sahama*, from the Arabic *sahm*; often known in the modern West as "Arabic parts"). The number of lots gradually increased from 32 in the earliest Tājika sources to 50 and later 75 during the Mughal period, indicating unacknowledged influences from additional Arabic sources with the passing of time.

Fragmentary and poorly understood examples of the prognostic technique known in the West as primary directions are scattered throughout Tājika literature, beginning with the *Karmaprakāśa*; the technical term *kisimā* (from the Arabic *qisma*, "division," referring to time) is sometimes met with. The chief prognostic method of the Tājikas, however, is the annual horoscope itself, in conjunction with the annual profection of the ascendant (known as *munthā* or *inthā*, with variants, from the Arabic *muntahā* and *intihā*ʾ, respectively). Particular importance is attached to identifying the planet ruling the year, a more complex procedure than that found in standard Arabic authors, but still unmistakably Perso-Arabic in character. A continuous annual profection of just over 12 days per degree is known but not typically connected with the *munthā*. Other methods for dividing the year into smaller units for the purpose of detailed prediction include a number of *daśā* or chronocrator systems in the Indian style. Some of these (such as *pātyāyinī*, *haddā-* or *tāsīra-daśā*) are based on more or less imperfectly understood Perso-Arabic concepts—the last two names being derived from Arabic *ḥadd* (terms) and *tasyīr* (direction), respectively—while others (such as *muddā-viṃśottarī*) are miniature versions of classical Indian *daśā* systems. Some Tājika texts also outline monthly and even daily revolutions for the same purpose.

Continued Transmission and Modernity

The dissemination of Tājika appears to have been slow at first, and chiefly confined to the Gujarat area at least up to the end of the 14th century. Some evidence suggests a break in transmission in the generations immediately following Samarasiṃha, which may account for the lack of a continued tradition of Tājika genethlialogy in a broader sense. Major Tājika works of this early period include Tejaḥsiṃha's *Daivajñālaṃkṛti* (1337), Haribhaṭṭa's *Tājikasāra* (1388), and Keśava's *Varṣaphalapaddhati* (late 15th century). During the Mughal era, the eastward and southward spread of Tājika gained momentum, and Tājika works proliferated in the 16th and 17th centuries. Without question the most important of these was the *Tājikanīlakaṇṭhī* (1587) by Nīlakaṇṭha Daivajña of Benares, astrologer royal to the emperor Akbar (r. 1556–1605). According to the Tājika encyclopedist Balabhadra—himself a student of Nīlakaṇṭha's younger brother Rāma Daivajña—Nīlakaṇṭha belonged to "the modern Tājika school," contrasted with "the ancient Tājikas." These modernists were chiefly Brahmans, criticized by some of their contemporaries for "not understanding the tradition of the Yavanas [Muslims]," but their version of Tājika still won the day: the *Tājikanīlakaṇṭhī*, having eclipsed the work of Samarasiṃha, remains the most widely studied Tājika textbook today.

In Mughal times, classical Indian astrology and Tājika were typically practiced separately, by members of hereditary communities who preserved astrology, like other traditional knowledge systems, as their intellectual property. Since the late 19th century, when Hindu astrology began—under Western influence—to be popularized and, to some extent, reformed, it has become more usual for practitioners (typically of the professional middle class, practicing astrology as an avocation) to combine the two, implementing elements from each according to their own understanding and predilections. Today, Tājika is thus subsumed under the modern paradigm of "Vedic astrology," its extra-Indian origins largely forgotten, ignored, or even denied.

Martin Gansten

See also: Decans; Indian Astrology; Islamic Astrology; Lots; Primary Directions

Further Reading

Gansten, Martin. 2012. "Some Early Authorities Cited by Tājika Authors." *Indo-Iranian Journal* 55, no. 4: 307–319.

Gansten, Martin. 2014. "The Sanskrit and Arabic Sources of the *Praśnatantra* Attributed to Nīlakaṇṭha." *History of Science in South Asia* 2: 101–126.

Gansten, Martin, and Ola Wikander. 2011. "Sahl and the Tājika Yogas: Indian Transformations of Arabic Astrology." *Annals of Science* 68, no. 4: 531–546.

Pingree, David. 1997. *From Astral Omens to Astrology: From Babylon to Bīkāner*. Serie orientale Roma 78. Roma: Istituto italiano per l'Africa e l'oriente.

THAI ASTROLOGY

Finding the exact origins of astrology in Thailand is impossible. Astrology in its classic forms was brought to Thailand during the long period of Indianization that had its greatest impact in Southeast Asia from roughly the first century CE until around the end of the first millennium CE. Brahman-Hindu law, political institutions, and architecture as well as the Hindu and Buddhist religions all flowed into Southeast Asia over these centuries. By the end of the 14th century, Thailand (and nearly all of mainland Southeast Asia) had adopted a Theravada Buddhism permeated with local animist belief and practice. The most common link between Buddhism and astrology is that Thai astrology claims to read the present and future karmic results of a person.

Among the many Sanskrit texts brought into Thailand covering law, governance, and epic literature were astronomical-astrological texts of *Jyotir*, more commonly known as Indian astrology. Indian astrology was shaped and reshaped by Thai culture creating distinctive astrological beliefs and practices and is known as *Horasaat* (Sanskrit: *horashastra*). The fundamentals of this Indo-Thai astrology concerning the zodiac signs and heavenly bodies correspond to Western astrology with the important additions of lunar mansions and the north and south lunar nodes as the gods Rahu and Ketu. Traditional Thai astrology still does not use Neptune and Pluto in making a chart, though Uranus has been included and there are some schools of Thai astrology and individual astrologers who do include all three of these planets. As in classical Indian Astrology, Thai astrology and Thais in general to this day believe astrological heavily bodies are gods (deva, Thai: *tep*) as well as material astronomical objects. Presently in Central Thailand the worship of Rahu as the god of luck and fortune has become quite popular.

In addition to Indo-Thai astrology, Thais have practiced a variety of fortune-telling systems including palm reading and spirit possession. A very popular system is the "Prediction by Year of Birth" (more technically *bee nakasaat*) using a 12-year cycle with each year represented by an animal (similar to what is known in English as Chinese Astrology, although how the system arrived in Thailand is obscure). In the Thai context this system ignores a connection to the heavens as the title suggests. It is more a calendrical fortune-telling system where Thais, including the practitioners, connect a year with an animal (and all its meaning) and it ends there; no further theory or thought as to constellations and the heavens follows.

By contrast, the popular system *Mahataksa* (Sanskrit: *mahataksha*), the other true astrological system and also Indian derived, is based on the day of birth and maintains a direct connection between the day and the heavenly body that influences that day (Sunday through Saturday: sun, moon, Mars, Mercury Wednesday daytime, Rahu Wednesday nighttime, Jupiter, Venus, and Saturn, respectively). The days and these heavenly bodies are plotted in a square divided into eight-squares surrounding a ninth central square. Most Thais do not think much beyond the day itself; however, texts, charts, and practitioners who use *Mahataksa* all refer to the heavenly bodies—gods—involved. While the simplicity of using the day of birth suggests a simple system, the variety of influences assigned to each day/god combine with placement and movement of personal "houses" (*taksa*) during one's lifetime render it a more complex system. Practicing astrologers consistently use Indo-Thai astrology and *Mahataksa* in tandem cross-checking between the two to add depth to a prediction. *Mahataksa* has been popular in part because it does not require the astronomical skill or information necessary for Indo-Thai astrology.

Indo-Thai Astrology was the monopoly of the premodern Siamese royal court and other lesser royal courts, given that it required some skill at astronomy, availability and knowledge of specialized texts, and money to support its specialized practice. It was also the occupation of Brahmans who, despite the Hindu title "Brahmans" (*prahm*), are in effect Thai animist-polytheist priests; Brahmans are still attached to the palace. A primary function of court astrologers was to find the auspicious moment to begin or perform important activities. For the general population, Indo-Thai astrology was more or less unknown.

Apart from scheduling royal life and events, a main use of court astrology was to make predictions for war: finding auspicious times for declaring war, marching an army and choosing a day of battle, as well as predictions on success or failure in battles and of the war itself. Astrology still plays a key role in the Thai military which uses it for purposes ranging from assigning new soldiers their specialization to finding the auspicious time to stage a coup d'état. Thailand, or rather Bangkok, has its own birth chart (*duang meung*) placed under the city pillar at its installation probably in 1782 by the first king of the still ruling Chakri dynasty. Since its production this chart has been read again and again by astrologers who generate a plethora of predictions about the future of the country.

Outside the palace, fortune-tellers are overwhelmingly Theravada monks, despite the textual admonishments against practicing or "earning a living" by fortune-telling (included in a list along with many other worldly activities). Thais go to Buddhist temples to consult monks learned in astrology and fortune-telling to ask for auspicious times for events such as weddings and consecrating a new home and for naming a new born baby.

The 20th century saw a democratization of astrology. The mass printing of calendars and charts listing the positions of the heavenly bodies allowed everyone easy access to the basic information needed for making a birth chart. There was also attempts to purify the Buddhist sangha which included suppressing fortune-telling and other magical practices. This helped push fortune-telling outside the temple walls and provided new opportunities for existing lay fortune-tellers as well as producing new ones. Lay astrologers still frequently work just outside the temple grounds; sometimes even within the temple grounds. But this monastic reform never had any lasting effect on the Thai monastic order and today Theravada monks still dominate in magic, though lay Indo-Thai astrologers have become more numerous. During this democratization, women began practicing astrology, moving beyond traditional roles of fortune-telling as spirit mediums. Presently there are many women Indo-Thai astrologers. However, Buddhist monks retain the advantage of religious charisma which lends weight to their predictions.

Thai astrological terms remain close to the Sanskrit originals as fundamental terms were transliterated into Thai script, rather than being translated into Thai or creating a Thai equivalent. Although the Thai language has a host of Sanskrit loan words, the average modern Thai is familiar only with the most common terms of astrology—auspicious time (*reuk*), zodiac (*rasi*), and so on—because astronomical terminology is specialized. In fact, the Thai word for astrology, *horasaat* (Sk. *horoshastra*) the "hour science," for most Thais does not carry the specific meaning of "astrology" but rather has a general meaning of "fortune-telling" or "divination." When this author tells Thais that he researches *horasaat* they invariably hold out their hand for their palm to be read. When Indo-Thai astrology is then summarily explained, Thais frequently do not know what a birth chart based on the heavenly bodies is, but they are nevertheless happy to get a prediction based on it. For most Thais the prediction is important, not the system that generates it.

In contemporary Thailand, bookstores have sections on astrology and "prediction" (*horasaat* and/or *kanpayakorn*) which are filled with mostly annual premade prediction books and teach yourself manuals. The influx of other traditions including Western astrology and Uranian astrology is displayed on these book shelves and in the popularization of Western astrological symbols in books on traditional Thai astrology. This importation of Western astrology is part of a general trend of importing a variety of fortune-telling techniques ranging from Chinese facial reading to Tarot Cards ("Gypsy Cards" for Thais).

There are several Thai astrological associations that offer courses, consultations and venues for astrologers to meet. Bangkok has one prominent book store that specializes in selling and printing books on fortune-telling as well as selling the basic few items used by a traditional Thai astrologer. Most important are the calendars listing all the positions of the heavenly bodies over the years and various styles of wheels for plotting the ascendant; these also note information for quick reference. There are small cards for recording a birth chart and key astrological information, as well as ink stamps of a circle divided into 12 sections to stamp on paper for making a handwritten chart.

Day of birth and sun sign predictions are ubiquitous in newspapers and magazines, despite the fact that sun sign prediction is not used at all in traditional Thai astrology. Currently there are several cable TV shows where an astrologer takes calls and then makes the caller's birth chart followed by predictions; usually the astrologer relies on computer software to plot the chart and produce a basic reading. A very popular astrology TV show, *Seuk 12 Rasi* (*Fight [between the] 12 Zodiacs*) airs Sundays at 12:15 running until 13:00. The show is a clever combination of celebrity guests and celebrity gossip combined with a few serious sun sign readings all taking place in a game show–style atmosphere.

Astrology is a part of life for most Thais. They may not know how a system works but they are always eager to hear a prediction. Of course astrologers are not on every street corner, but it is quite easy to find one by looking around, asking friends and acquaintances, visiting a temple, and now on the Internet. Or one can always buy a book. Many Thais qualify their interest in astrology by saying that they know it may not be correct and one should not blindly believe or follow a prediction; however, this statement appears less a statement of true feeling and more an attempt not to look too credulous. As with karma and nirvana, spirits and ghosts, Thais believe in astrology.

Matthew Kosuta

See also: Astrotheology; Buddhism; Court Astrologers; Indian Astrology

Further Reading

Cook, Nerida M. 1989. *Astrology in Thailand: The Future and the Recollection of the Past*. PhD diss. Australian National University.

Kosuta, Matthew. 2016. "A Thai Woman, Her Practice of Thai Astrology, and Related Gender Issues." *Journal of Traditions and Beliefs* 3, no. 9.

Wales, H. G. Quariitch. 1983. *Divination in Thailand: The Hopes and Fears of a Southeast Asian People*. London: Curzon Press.

THEOSOPHY

Theosophy, from the Greek *wisdom of God*, is a part of Western esotericism that deals with philosophical and mystical knowledge of nature and life. Since the establishment of theosophy, astrology has been an integral part of theosophical studies, providing theosophers with methodological and intellectual tools to speculate about the structure and purpose of the universe and its relationship to mankind. In turn theosophy introduced new ideas to astrology and influenced the popularity of astrological practices.

Historians of science and religion distinguish two "golden" periods in the history of theosophy: the end of the 16th through the 17th century, during which the major corpus of theosophic knowledge was produced; and the second part of the 19th century characterized by the revival of theosophy and its advancement into what theosophers consider the spiritual heritage of mankind by incorporating non-Western traditions.

The first golden period of theosophy is characterized by the formation of its intellectual foundations. Scholars often associate the emergence of theosophy with the period of intellectual revival in Europe during the 14th–15th century, and the need to incorporate diverse currents of studies from humanities and sciences into a coherent corpus of knowledge. The main scholarly traditions that influenced the formation of theosophy were Neoplatonism, neo-Pythagoreanism, Alexandrian Hermeticism, and Kabbalah. Astrology along with alchemy gained prominence as the common components to all currents of theological thought. What distinguished astrological studies was that they relied on a perspective of nature associated with *magia*, or a mode of thinking about the world as alive, and combined mysticism with chemistry and physics.

This period is associated with Paracelsus. Paracelsus introduced to Western esotericism its foundational worldview, arguing that the universe was interconnected by the complex networks of correspondences on all levels of reality. His follower Heinrich Khunrath (1560–1605), also a German medical man, developed this view further. Khunrath not only believed that all things in the universe are connected, but also argued that outward appearances of bodies and particularly symmetries of things disclose their inner characteristics. Khunrath is also credited with coining the term *theosophy* in its present meaning.

Paracelsus was primarily interested in astrology associated with magical knowledge of the relationship between men and stars. He stressed that medical theory and practice must rest upon Christian piety and the physician's knowledge of the celestial and chemical fundamentals of nature. Like Paracelsus, Khunrath aimed to connect the science of healing with the word of God. He believed that because the body was the place where the soul dwelled, medical practitioners must allow God to teach them through hypnotic visions and dreams on how to unite with supernatural entities, such as spirits, to learn the secrets of the universe (Forshaw 2008, 67–68).

Like Paracelsus, Khunrath accepted mystical studies of the nature for the purposes of healing. He applied astrology, alchemy, magic, and also geomancy, a form of divination using abstract symbols to represent a cosmic model to establish the relationship between macro- and microcosmos. Khunrath developed Paracelsus's speculations about interconnections of reality by taking these ideas outside of medical practices and connecting them with esoteric knowledge, which is why scholars credit him as one of the three founding fathers of theosophy, along with

German Lutheran mystic Johann Arndt (1555–1621) and theologian and alchemist Valentin Weigel (1533–1588).

During the 18th-century Enlightenment theosophy and astrological studies lost popularity. Only in historical fields did some interest as to the origins and main doctrines of theosophy remain. One of the scholars who examined the history of theosophy was Johann Jakob Brucker (1696–1770). His critique of different theosophical currents helped establish common characteristics shared by theosophers. For Brucker, theosophers penetrated mysteries of nature by magical means. They acted upon nature by commanding the spirits that resided in all things, and by using the signatures that were the images of divine substances also found in all things. Brucker identified magical astronomy and alchemy as the main tools of theosophical studies.

The second "golden" period in the history of theosophy fell within the second part of the 19th century and lasted until the beginning of the 20th century. This period is associated with the influences of the Russo-German aristocrat Helena Blavatsky (1831–1891) known for her book *The Secret Doctrine* (1888), and for her establishment of the first Theosophical Society in New York City in 1875. Blavatsky traveled to Tibet and India and enriched the traditional corpus of theosophical knowledge by introducing teachings from Hindu and Buddhist traditions.

This portrait of Helena Petrovna Blavatsky, the founder of Theosophy, captures some of her intensity. (Blavatsky, Helena Petrovna. *Isis Unveiled: A Master-Key to the Mysteries of Ancient and Modern Science and Theology*, 1891)

The revival of theosophy during the second part of the 19th century is characterized by the renewed interest in occult knowledge in Europe. In part, this happened as a response to the development of science, as some discoveries seemed particularly hostile to social values given that mystical knowledge of nature remained popular. Astrology became particularly popular because it offered a compromise between science and mysticism. Astrologers used astronomical facts of the positions of the planets, the sun, and the moon, in relation to the zodiac to predict events in nature and people's lives, something that science with its objective methods was unable to do.

At the same time, and as a part of evolved theological teachings, astrology, unlike other aspects of traditional Western theosophy,

Madame Blavatsky on the Origin of Astrology

The founder of Theosophy, Helena Petrovna Blavatsky, believed that astrology originated among the priests of ancient Egypt, a theory for which there is little evidence. However, Theosophists, like other believers in ancient wisdom, tended to look to Egypt as its ultimate source:

> The Egyptians and the Chaldees were among the most ancient votaries of astrology, though their modes of reading the stars and the modern practices differ considerably. The former claimed that Belus, the Bel or Elu of the Chaldees, a scion of the divine Dynasty, or the Dynasty of the king-gods, had belonged to the land of Chemi, and had left it, to found a colony from Egypt on the banks of the Euphrates, where a temple ministered by priests in the service of the "lords of the stars" was built, the said priests adopting the name of Chaldees. Two things are known: (a) that Thebes (in Egypt) claimed the honour of the invention of Astrology; and (b) that it was the Chaldees who taught that science to the other nations. Now Thebes antedated considerably not only "Ur of the Chaldees," but also Nipur, where Bel was first worshipped—Sin, his son (the moon), being the presiding deity of Ur, the land of the nativity of Terah, the Sabean and Astrolatrer, and of Abram, his son, the great Astrologer of biblical tradition. All tends, therefore, to corroborate the Egyptian claim.

Source: Blavatsky, Helena Petrovna. 1892. *The Theosophical Glossary*, 39. London: Theosophical Publishing Society.

retained its central position. Alchemy became marginal, and Christianity lost its hold on theosophy and esotericism in general. The revival and evolution of theosophy introduced notions of karma, reincarnation, and psychology of the soul to astrology, and also influenced the popularity of astrological practices. Thus, astrology united occult and scientific practitioners and was also enriched by the new theosophical teachings. One of the key people who introduced these new concepts to astrology was William Allen, known as Alan Leo. A lifelong Theosophist, as members of the Theosophical Society are referred to, in 1914 Leo helped found the Astrological Lodge, a London-based organization of Theosophists devoted specifically to astrology, serving as its first president. The Astrological Lodge is still in existence as a leading body in British astrology. Theosophists have been active in the founding of many other astrological organizations. However, the Theosophical approach to astrology was controversial, and many astrologers found Theosophists to be insufficiently rigorous and mathematical in their astrology, and too focused on character analysis rather than prediction.

Theosophy also contributed to a revival of interest in astrology in Germany, one that found artistic expression in the composer Gustav Holst's astrologically influenced suite, "The Planets." Hugo Vollrath's Leipzig-based Theosophical publishing house founded in 1906 brought out a popular "Astrological Library" which continued into the 1920s. Along with another Theosophist, Karl Brandler-Pracht (b. 1864), Vollrath also launched an astrological periodical. (Vollrath would later join the Nazi Party and attempt to blend Theosophy and National Socialism.)

Theosophy's influence on astrology was not limited to England, Europe, or North America or the Western tradition, but extended to India, an area where Theosophy was very active. The revival of the Indian tradition in astrology, which later became known as "Vedic Astrology," was largely the work of Indians connected with the Theosophical movement. The area near the Society's first Indian headquarters, Chennai in South India, became a hub of printing of astrological texts, although the Indian astrologers influenced by theosophy were more interested in traditional predictive astrology than were the Western theosophic astrologers. An English translation of Varahamihira's *Briajjātaka* by an Indian Theosophist, N. Chidambaram Aiyar, was published by the Theosophical Society in 1885. The dominance of South Indians in modern Indian astrology is in part a legacy of the decision of the Theosophical Society to locate there. Theosophy also opened the door to exchanges of ideas between Indian and Western astrologers.

The astrological practices that emerged among theosophers during the 20th century were only seemingly analogous to those of the early modern period. While some practitioners similarly to their medieval predecessors devoted time to divination, or reading of the charts associated with the health of a particular person, those who gained prominence utilized an emerging field of psychology, especially associated with the work of Carl Jung. Among the most influential practitioners of Jungian astrology was Dane Rudhyar, a member of the Theosophical Society, who influenced a shift in astrology from predictions to psychological chart readings. Other notable astrologers influenced by Theosophy include Walter Gorn Old (1864–1929), known by his pseudonym of "Sepharial"; Marc Edmund Jones (1888–1980), the American inventor of the "Sabian symbols"; and Charles Carter (1887–1968), the second president of the Astrological Lodge and the leading English astrological writer of the mid-20th century.

Theosophy and astrology are difficult to separate, given their common worldview and shared ideas and practices. They both continue to evolve, responding to changes in the social and scientific climate, despite their marginal intellectual position.

Louis Gosart and Ulia Popova

See also: Astral Magic; Astrological Associations; Leo, Alan; Paracelsus; Pythagoras of Samos; Rudhyar, Dane; Transpersonal Astrology; Yeats, William Butler

Further Reading

Faivre, Antoine. 1994. *Access to Western Esotericism*. Albany, NY: SUNY Press.

Faivre, Antoine. 2000. *Theosophy, Imagination, Tradition: Studies in Western Esotericism*. Albany, NY: SUNY Press.

Forshaw, Peter J. 2008. "'Paradoxes, Absurdities, and Madness': Conflict over Alchemy, Magic and Medicine in the Works of Andreas Libavius and Heinrich Khunrath." *Early Science and Medicine* 13, no. 1: 53–81.

Hammer, Olav. 2003. *Claiming Knowledge: Strategies of Epistemology from Theosophy to the New Age*. Leiden: Brill.

Kurlander, Eric. 2017. *Hitler's Monsters: A Supernatural History of the Third Reich*. New Haven, CT: Yale University Press.

TRANSPERSONAL ASTROLOGY

Transpersonal astrology was a term first used by Dane Rudhyar in 1930 and developed in his later works. It referred to a form of astrology that went beyond psychological description and analysis, and instead recognized astrology as a spiritual path that opened the individual up to spiritual forces that could transform consciousness. The term also refers to astrologies inspired by the work of the transpersonal psychologists such as Roberto Assagioli (1888–1974) and Stanislav Grof (b. 1931). Such psychologists came from the humanistic tradition in psychology, established by those such as Abraham Maslow (1908–1970), but ultimately stemming from thinkers such as Carl Gustav Jung and William James (1842–1910). The common theme of transpersonal psychology is the linking of personal and spiritual factors in the individual, with human beings seen as spiritual beings capable of self-realization. Additionally, transpersonal psychologists are often concerned with higher states of consciousness and peak (mystical) experiences.

Transpersonal astrology took on an overtly spiritual tone, and can be likened to a path of initiation. The individual walking this transpersonal path opens themselves up to spiritual forces from a realm beyond personal consciousness. Such forces descend to transform the consciousness of the individual, preparing them for a new age of human civilization. In practical terms this form of astrology was similar to Rudhyar's earlier psychological versions, with the aim being to become an individualized, autonomous person. The crucial difference, however, was the recognition that in using astrology to do this, one opened to spiritual forces and thereby became a meeting place for the descent of spirit and the ascent of matter—these two finding their common ground within the human psyche (Rudhyar 1980, 99–100). Individual development and transformation were also important to the wider collective, paving the way for a more enlightened age with the individual's growth in this life connected with the working out of karma within a greater scheme. Rudhyar suggested that development might particularly occur when the outer planets, Uranus, Neptune, and Pluto, are making major aspects to the birth chart.

The transpersonal psychology of Assagioli found particular resonance with some astrologers. Assagioli developed a form of psychology which he called psychosynthesis, the aim of which is to find the unifying center of the Self around which a new personality may be built. This rests on a model of the psyche which has different layers of consciousness, Lower, Middle, and Higher or Superconscious, and which recognizes Jung's Collective Unconscious (humanity's shared layer of psyche). The Superconscious realm is the one associated with higher intuitions such as altruistic love, genius, and illumination, and in this realm we find higher psychic functions and spiritual energies (Assagioli 1965, 17–29). Assagioli also developed a theory of sub-personalities, the idea that each individual plays a variety of roles in life with different sets of personality traits dominant in each setting. In extreme cases, these different personalities become excessively distinct, which leads to multiple personality disorder (Assagioli 1965, 74–77).

Examples of Assagioli's ideas in astrology may be found in the work of Howard Sasportas (1948–1992). Sasportas suggested subpersonalities could build up around archetypal drives and principles represented by planets and signs in the birth chart. For example, Mars conjunct Jupiter in Aries on an angle of the chart could suggest a subpersonality akin to a warrior god or a knight determined to fight for a cause while the sun in Capricorn trine Saturn in Virgo might suggest a subpersonality who is very orderly, efficient, and strict (Sasportas 1987, 170–172). Elsewhere Sasportas discusses the superconscious, linking this realm of beauty, light, and love with the planet Jupiter and, like Rudhyar, with the outer planets Uranus, Neptune, and Pluto. He additionally associates the 9th and 12th houses of the birth chart with the experiencing of superconscious or transpersonal energy (Sasportas 1988, 169–253). Assagioli's work also played a major role in the development of Huber Astrology, developed by Bruno and Louise Huber. The "Huber Method" aims to use astrology for psychological and spiritual growth. Originally developed in the German language, this type of astrology has been available in English since the 1980s.

In 1982, Sasportas and Liz Greene (b. 1946) opened the Centre for Transpersonal Astrology in London, U.K. The name was changed, however, just one year later to the Centre for Psychological Astrology (CPA) in recognition of the fact that psychological astrology, which the CPA came to epitomize, rested on a variety of approaches wider than those of the transpersonal psychologists. It may therefore be argued that while transpersonal psychologies were incorporated into wider psychological approaches to astrology, "transpersonal astrology" itself moved to greater emphasis on the psychological over the spiritual and was subsumed under the wider umbrella of "psychological astrology."

Also worthy of note are the astrological investigations of transpersonal psychologist Stanislav Grof. Initially dismissing astrology as a pseudoscience, Grof's extensive study of non-ordinary states of consciousness in conjunction with astrologer and philosopher Richard Tarnas (b. 1950), led him to assert that astrology, particularly through planetary transits, is able to predict and illuminate the archetypal content of nonordinary states of consciousness (Grof 2011, 66). For example, during a transit of Saturn and Pluto an individual in an altered state of consciousness is more likely to experience oppression and constriction, or terror and dread, qualities associated with the combination of Saturn and Pluto (Grof 2011, 77). Grof argues that the existence of transpersonal experiences indicates an ensouled cosmos imbued with consciousness and intelligence and moreover that such experiences are correlated with the inner nature of the universe. This work has led Tarnas to develop a form of astrology known as archetypal astrology, which argues that archetypal forms permeate both the human psyche and the cosmos and can be understood through the movements of the planets in relation to each other and their positions in the birth chart of each individual.

Laura Andrikopoulos

See also: Age of Aquarius; Feminist Astrology; Jung, Carl G.; New Age; Rudhyar, Dane

Further Reading

Assagioli, Roberto. 1965. *Psychosynthesis.* London: Penguin.

Grof, Stanislav. 2011. "Holotropic Research and Archetypal Astrology." *Archai: The Journal of Archetypal Cosmology* 1: 65–88.

Rudhyar, Dane. 1980. *The Astrology of Transformation.* Wheaton, IL: The Theosophical Publishing House.

Sasportas, Howard. 1987. "Subpersonalities and Psychological Conflicts." In *The Development of the Personality*, ed. Liz Greene and Howard Sasportas, 163–221. York Beach, ME: Samuel Weiser.

Sasportas, Howard. 1988. "The Quest for the Sublime." In *Dynamics of the Unconscious*, ed. Liz Greene and Howard Sasportas, 167–253. York Beach, ME: Samuel Weiser.

Tarnas, Richard. 2006. *Cosmos and Psyche: Intimations of a New World View.* New York: Viking.

V

VALENS, VETTIUS (SECOND CENTURY CE)

Vettius Valens (probably b. February 8, 120 CE) (Valens 1986, v) was a practicing astrologer from Antioch, Syria, now Antakya, Turkey. He is known for his nine-book treatise on astrology, the *Anthologies (Anth.)*, written in Greek probably between 150 and 170 CE (Riley 1996, 5–6). This text is one of the most important extant documents on the doctrines and techniques of Hellenistic astrology, that is, the astrology practiced in the Mediterranean region between roughly the second century BCE and the seventh century CE. In addition, Valens's work is a source for otherwise unattested Greek vocabulary of the Greco-Roman period, and for quotations of ancient authors. Thus his work has value beyond astrology's parameters.

Valens addresses the *Anthologies* to his student, Marcus (a practice similar to Ptolemy's, who addressed his astronomical and astrological treatises, the *Almagest* and the *Tetrabiblos*, to someone called "Syrus"). We know little about his personal life except for brief information provided within discussion of the topics of his astrological treatise. He uses what is likely his own birth chart (February 8, 120 CE) in a number of examples, and even includes the date of his conception (May 13, 119 CE) (*Anth.* I, 21.17–26; III, 10.4) (Frommhold 2004, 110–118; Hübner 2008, 111; Heilen 2015, I, 254).

To further his knowledge of astrology, Valens claimed to have made a journey to Egypt, where he found a teacher, he says (*Anth.* IV, 7.11), through the guidance of his personal daimon (a kind of guiding and protecting spirit popularized by Plato). With other passengers, five of whose birth charts he details in addition to his own, he was on board a ship nearly wrecked sometime in 154 CE (*Anth.* VII, 6.127–60). (The exact date is uncertain because Valens does not state it directly, but only refers to the ages of the participants and their astrological circumstances at the time.) He uses this near catastrophe to illustrate astrological doctrines of the ascensional times of zodiac signs and planets ruling different periods of life, as well as an example of how fate works astrologically (in this case, it was benefic circumstances in each of their nativities that allowed them to survive). From time to time he makes brief philosophical digressions. From these we can determine, at least, that he was familiar with some of the popular philosophies of his day, including Platonism, Stoicism, and Hermeticism. However, his philosophical outlook may best be described as eclectic.

There are two critical editions of Valens (W. Kroll 1908 and D. Pingree 1986). Five partial or full translations have been made of the *Anthologies*, one in French, one in German, and three in English. Riley's English translation can be recommended for ease of access and accuracy.

Extant versions of the text are somewhat problematic in content, organization, and condition (Riley 1996, 21–22). The foundation text on which the manuscripts depend is said to date to the fifth century CE, based on dates of ancient additions to the text (Valens 1986, xii; Riley 1996, 21). The three most important manuscripts are *Marcianus graecus* 314, ff. 256–286; *Vaticanus graecus* 191, and *Oxonienses Seldeniani* 22 and 20, now, respectively, in the Marcianus Library in Rome, the Vatican, and the Bodleian Library, Oxford (Valens 1986, vii–xi).

The earliest version of a doctrine appearing in later manuscripts of Valens is a parchment fragment of the sixth century CE (known as *PGM* L: Betz 1992, 283) now in the Nationalbibliothek, Vienna, inv. no. 8033), which contains on its *verso* a close paraphrase of a section of Valens (*Anth.* II, 20.5). However, there is no way of knowing whether this is an actual quotation from Valens, or whether the writer of the parchment and Valens were drawing on the same original source (Greenbaum and Naether 2011).

The *Anthologies*' nine books appear roughly in chronological order in the present editions, but are not particularly systematic in their organization: the same topic may appear in different books. In addition to the common information often found in astrological texts—sections on the zodiac signs, planets and their meanings (Book I), as well as descriptions of the 12 places in the astrological chart (Book II)—*Anthologies* outlines forecasting techniques used by Hellenistic astrologers. Valens attaches great importance to length and quality of life predictions (beginning in Book III), and provides a number of techniques for ascertaining these. Some techniques emphasize the Lots of Fortune, Daimon, Eros and Necessity (see Greenbaum 2016). Some appear only in Valens. One is his use of "time-lords" (*chronokratores*, planets ruling a specific period of time) in the doctrine he calls "Aphesis" (release) from the Lots of Fortune and Daimon, in which the planet ruling the sign of the Lot of Fortune or Daimon begins the list of planets ruling periods of life (*Anth.* IV, 4–10). He also outlines different ways to ascertain crisis periods, the predictive systems known as profections (*Anth.* IV, 11–25), and decennials (*Anth.* VI, 6; also in Firmicus Maternus and Hephaestio of Thebes).

As a practicing astrologer, Valens demonstrates the tasks performed by an astrologer for his clients. His case studies, using many charts (123 examples, the most in any extant ancient text), give a unique view of astrology's actual practice in the Greco-Roman world of the second century CE. Though his views of fate are contradictory at times, they reveal his struggle to understand how destiny, choice and providence combine in the events of a life.

The importance of Valens's text moreover, lies beyond his service to astrology. He supplies quotations from around two dozen authors, including the astrologers Critodemus, Nechepso and Petosiris; mathematicians and astronomers Meton, Soudines, and Kidenas; and the legendary "Orpheus." His work transmits vocabulary unmentioned in any other Greek text (*hapax legomena*); his mention of various occupations gives a window into labor practices in his era (Cumont 1937).

The afterlife of Valens continued in the Medieval and Renaissance periods. Valens was known to astrological writers in Arabic, who called him Walis (from the Greek Οὐάλης), including Māshāllāh and Abū Ma'shar; the historian al-Nadīm's *Fihrist* also notes nine books of "Walis" (Riley 1996, 21).

Dorian Gieseler Greenbaum

See also: Abū Ma'shar al-Balkhī; Fate; Firmicus Maternus, Julius; Hellenistic Astrology; Māshāllāh; Ptolemy; Roman Astrology

Further Reading

Betz, Hans Dieter, ed. (1992) 1996, repr. *The Greek Magical Papyri in Translation, including the Demotic Spells*, 2nd ed., vol. 1, *Texts*. Chicago: University of Chicago Press. Available at https://www.academia.edu/3158348/The_Greek_Magical_Papyri_in_Translation_including_the_Demotic_Spells

Cumont, Franz. 1937. *L'Égypte des astrologues*. Brussels: La Fondation Égyptologique Reine Élisabeth.

Frommhold, Katrin. 2004. *Die Bedeutung und Berechnung der Empfängnis in der Astrologie der Antike*, vol. 38, Orbis antiquus. Münster: Aschendorff.

Greenbaum, Dorian Gieseler. 2016. *The Daimon in Hellenistic Astrology: Origins and Influence*. Leiden, Boston: Brill.

Greenbaum, Dorian Gieseler, and Franziska Naether. 2011. "Astrological Implications in the 'Lot Oracle' *PGM* 50." *MHNH* 11: 484–505.

Heilen, Stephan. 2015. *Hadriani genitura. Die astrologischen Fragmente des Antigonos von Nikaia. Edition, Übersetzung und Kommentar*, vol. 43, Texte und Kommentare. 2 vols. Berlin: De Gruyter.

Hübner, Wolfgang. 2008. "Vettius Valens." In *Complete Dictionary of Scientific Biography*, vol. 25, 111–113. Detroit, MI: Charles Scribner's Sons.

Komorowska, Joanna. 2004. *Vettius Valens of Antioch: An Intellectual Monography*. Kraków: Ksiegarnia Akademicka.

Riley, Mark. 1996. "A Survey of Vettius Valens." http://www.csus.edu/indiv/r/rileymt/PDF_folder/VettiusValens.PDF

Riley, Mark. n.d. "Draft translation of Vettius Valens, *Anthologiai*, Books I–IX." Unpublished work at http://www.csus.edu/indiv/r/rileymt/Vettius%20Valens%20entire.pdf

Valens, Vettius. 1986. *Anthologarium Libri Novem*, ed. David Pingree. Leipzig: B.G. Teubner.

VARĀHAMIHIRA (505?–587 CE)

Varāhamihira was an Indian scholar whose work encompassed the fields of mathematical astronomy, natural astrology, and horoscopy. His most significant works include *Pañca-siddhāntikā*, *Brhadyātr*, and *Bṛhajjātaka*, and *Brihat-samhita*.

Like many Sanskrit scientists, much information on Varāhamihira is obscure. In his work the *Bṛhajjātaka*, Varāhamihira mentions that he is a son of Adityadasa, who lived in the city of Avanti and was also a scientist native to the city of Kāpittaka. Scholars tend to believe that Kāpittaka (now Kayatha, in central India) is the birthplace of Varāhamihira (Puttaswamy 2012, 141). Varāhamihira was also a devotee of the Sun God: not only did he address the sun in the beginning of many of his works, but also the second part of his name, "mihira" derives from Mithra, the Iranian Sun God (Shastri 1969, 20). Utpala, a 10th century scholar and known commentator of Brihatsamhita, saw Varāhamihira as the incarnation of the sun, who came down to the world of humans to save the *Jyotiḥśāstra* teachings from destruction (Shastri 1969, 1).

Varāhamihira was an heir to a great Indian tradition in astrology that emerged from combination of the ancient Vedic texts (the oldest scriptures of Hinduism), strong knowledge of mathematics, and the observation of the heavens. Within the Vedic tradition astronomy, or *Jyotiḥśā*, was one of the six sciences of Indian scholarship. Teachings composing *Jyotiḥśā* were termed the *Jyotiḥśāstra* (from Sanskrit *śāstra*, teaching; *jyotih*, light, star). They consisted of three kinds: *tantra* or *ganita*, mathematical astronomy; *samhitā*, study of divinations and omens and their practical application (i.e., to forecast weather and natural disasters and historical and political events); and *horā*, astrology and, specifically, horoscopes. As a rule, the texts composing *Jyotiḥśāstra* teachings have been written in verse (as other forms of teachings). The demands for poetic meter in expressing knowledge of the heavens created a number of difficulties for contemporary scholars. While a significant number of these texts were created, and, as one scholar suggests, still exist, this form of knowledge is decaying given how few scholars are trained to work with these teachings (Pingree 2003, 46).

Varāhamihira mastered all the three branches of *Jyotiḥśāstra,* becoming a *jyotiṣi* of outstanding talents, and thus was both an astronomer and an astrologer. He worked not only with works from the Vedic tradition, such as for example those composed by Aryabhatta (476–550 CE), but also with the works of astronomers from Babylon, Greece, and Rome. Greek astronomy was particularly influential in India, in part because Greek astronomical texts were translated into Sanskrit, Pahlavī, and Syriac (Pingree 1976, 109).

One of Varāhamihira's most influential works is the *Pañca-siddhāntikā* (also *Pañcasiddhāntikā*), or *The Five Astronomical Canons*, a treatise on *tantra* (mathematical astrology), dated around 575 CE. In this work, Varāhamihira discusses five astronomical doctrines, or *siddhantas*: "Paulisa," "Romaka," "Vasistha," "Sūrya," and "Pitamaha." The first two—"Paulisa" and "Romaka"—are attributed to have origins in Babylonian and Greek astronomy. Scholars consider this work of great scientific and historical value, given that it is, arguably, "the only" (as one scholar puts it) text that contains all five astronomical doctrines and also the views of early astronomers whose works have been lost (Shastri 1969, 26).

Varāhamihira's other two well-known works, the *Bṛhajjātaka* and *Brhadyātrā*, deal with the two other *Jyotiḥśāstra* teachings, *samhitā* and *horā*. These works enjoy great popularity and have many commentaries in Sanskrit and in modern Indian languages. Finally, *Brihatsamhita* (also *Bṛhat Saṁhitā*) deals with horoscopy (the signs of the zodiac; connections between planets of the signs; planets, and their periods), or *daśās* (Sanskrit "planetary periods"). The study of *daśās* was significant in predicting the movements of a person's life (i.e., misfortunes, periods of prosperity) by examining the connections between the movement of planets and lives of people. For example, Sanskrit astrology projects that a person's life ideally lasts 120 years. It is divided into nine *mahādaśā* (great planetary periods). These *mahādaśā* last from six to 20 years, and are further divided into nine *antardaśā* (planetary sub-periods). Depending on the kind of the planet that governs a certain period and sub-period of a person's life as well as the position of the planet(s) in the person's horoscope, the *daśās* are classified into three kinds of periods: "abundant" (*sampūrṇa*), "empty" (*riktā*), and "malefic" (*aniṣṭaphalā*). The fluctuation of a person's fortune (that is given to a person at the moment of birth) also fluctuates depending on the period his life enters (Guenzi 2012, 50). *Brihatsamhita* covers a range of topics concerning the interests of ordinary humans, astrology, and the movements of planets.

Varāhamihira's teachings also offer a glimpse into the everyday life in the Gupta Empire. Although his books were about mathematics, astronomy, and astrology, they also included information about religion, clothing, jewelry, business, food, and literature that were integral parts of the life and practice of the scientists of the time.

Thomas Gosart and Madhumita Kaushik

See also: Indian Astrology; Theosophy

Further Reading

Guenzi, Caterina. 2012. "The Allotted Share: Managing Fortune in Astrological Counseling in Contemporary India." *Social Analysis* 56, no. 2: 39–55.

Pingree, David. 1976. "The Recovery of Early Greek Astronomy from India." *Journal for the History of Astronomy* 7, no. 2: 109–123.

Pingree, David. 2003. "The Logic of non-Western Science: Mathematical Discoveries in Medieval India." *Daedalus* 132, no. 4: 45–53.

Puttaswamy, T. K. 2012. *Mathematical Achievements of Pre-Modern Indian Mathematicians.* London: Elsevier.

Shastri, Ajay Mitra. 1969. *India as Seen in the Brhatsamhita of Varahamihira.* Delhi: Motilal Banarsidass.

VILLENA, ENRIQUE DE (1384–1438)

The Spanish humanist scholar Enrique de Villena translated classical works into Castilian and wrote treatises on topics such as the plague (1422), consolation (1424), and the evil eye (ca. 1425). His interest in astrology started at a very young age during his education in the Catalan courts of Pedro IV *el Ceremonioso* (1336–1387) and Juan I *el cazador* (1387–1396) where astrologers, including Jews and Muslims, flourished under royal protection. Notorious as an astrologer during his life, his books were burnt at the stake after his death by the bishop of Cuenca, Lope de Barrientos. Villena became legendary as a *magus* seduced by the devil, which, fostered by Spanish theater and literature, led several works of astrology to be attributed to him during the modern period.

The Castilian *Tratado de Astrología* was found, severely burnt, at the end of the 19th century by Manuel Serrano y Sanz, friend of the great scholar Marcelino Menéndez y Pelayo, and is now located in the National Library of Spain (Res/2, I, 49 h). The fire damage led to doubt whether if it was a true manuscript that survived Barrientos' stake or another apocryphal work. Although authorship has been strongly debated by modern scholars, the manuscript was produced right after Villena's death by a certain Andrés Segovia, who claimed to be copying Villena's original.

The *Tratado* is divided into two parts following Aristotle's *Physics*. The first analyzes the four elements and the second the influence of the celestial spheres over the terrestrial realm. As in his *Exposition of the Psalm Quoniam videbo*, Villena questions the alchemists' attempt to achieve the *quintaesentia* out of wine, defending astrology over alchemy in line with many other medieval astrologers. In his chapter "On the debate that the wise hold about astrology" [*De la disputaçión que fazen los sabios açerca de la astrología*] he builds his Christian apology for judicial astrology and its compatibility with free will.

Villena appropriated biblical discourse citing several passages of Peter Comestor's paraphrased bible *Historia Scholastica* which acquiesce in astrology and magic. He defends magical and astrological representations of Jewish cult objects like the Tabernacle and the Temple, represents Moses as an astrologer and practitioner of talismanic magic, and builds an original *Prisca Theologia* which identifies Zoroaster as the founder of magic.

Villena, as can be seen in his *Tratado de la Fascinación*, was in contact with Juan I's Jewish astrologer, Hasdai Crescas, and his disciple Zaraya Halevi, both of whom thought that the Temple's utensils and the Tabernacle received celestial influences which the magician could operate. These elements, among others, clearly allow attribution of the *Tratado de Astrología* to Villena.

Mariano Villalba

See also: Astral Magic; Christianity; Legal Regulation of Astrology; Medieval European Astrology; Renaissance and Reformation Astrology

Further Reading

Cátedra, Pedro, and Julio Samsó. 1983. *Tratado de Astrología atribuido a Enrique de Villena*, Barcelona: Editorial Humanitas.

Villalba, Mariano. 2015. "El Tratado de Astrología atribuido a Enrique de Villena. Esoterismo en la corte de Juan II de Castilla." *Magallánica: revista de historia moderna*, no. 3, 186–216.

Villalba, Mariano. 2016. "Esoterismo y poder en Castilla y Aragón. Enrique de Villena y su *Tratado de la Fascinación* (1425) y *Tratado de Astrología* (1438)." Tesis de Maestría en Sociología de la Cultura y Análisis Cultural, Universidad Nacional General San Martín.

Y

YEATS, WILLIAM BUTLER (1865–1939)

William Butler Yeats was the foremost Irish poet of his day. Through his poetry, his political activity, his revitalization of the Irish theatre, and his devotion to Celtic mythology, he exercised a powerful influence on Irish culture that still reverberates today. But behind the public image of authority Yeats cultivated lay a private self profoundly motivated by astrology and mysticism, studies in which he was closely involved throughout his adult life and without which much of his poetry cannot be fully understood.

Yeats's fascination with astrology was one aspect of the interest in mysticism he exhibited from an early age. He was close friends with his maternal uncle George Pollexfen (1839–1910), an enthusiastic astrologer who cast the young Yeats's horoscope. By the age of 20, Yeats was presiding over the Dublin Hermetic Society, and within another five years he had joined the Hermetic Order of the Golden Dawn in London, where he learned a variety of esoteric techniques among which astrology was a vital component. Yeats was to remain a member of this Order for about 30 years, and by 1900 he was in charge of the Isis/Urania temple in London. As late as 1923 he was still a member of the Irish Astrological Society. Toward the end of his life he declared, "The mystical life is the centre of all that I do and all that I think and all that I write" (Graf 2000, 13).

Yeats's earliest surviving astrological manuscripts date from 1889 and from 1908 he compiled a series of astrological notebooks. Six survive, containing horoscopes of family, friends, and literary and political figures. He also corresponded with professional astrologers. His notebooks and letters reveal that he used astrology for every aspect of his life, including running the Abbey Theatre in Dublin. Virginia Woolf commented in her diary in 1934 that Yeats would "never do business with anyone without having their horoscopes" (Campion 2009, 245). Letters to Pollexfen include details of people for whom Yeats wished a horoscope to be interpreted, and he himself offered astrological advice to some of his friends and lovers. Yeats described his own poetry in astrological terms, noting that around 1914 his style changed from lunar to a solar influence. He also kept a close eye on his horoscope, commenting in his journals on natal aspects and their effects upon his character, as well as noting transits and progressions.

Through consulting his horoscope, Yeats decided that he should marry in October 1917. He proposed to Iseult Gonne, who when she was 15 had jokingly suggested to Yeats that they marry; he had refused, citing an excess of Mars in her horoscope. When he proposed this time, she rejected him.

He then promptly courted and married Georgie Hyde Lees (1892–1968), a longtime acquaintance who was herself a highly skilled astrologer and whom he already knew well enough to have sponsored her initiation into the Golden Dawn. The couple were well aware that their shared interest in magic and astrology would be a strong bond between them; they could hardly have known, however, the profound effect of marriage on Yeats's work. He would be creatively revitalized and find a powerful new voice in which to write some of the finest verse of the 20th century.

During the Yeatses' honeymoon Georgie, distressed by Yeats's continuing obsession with Iseult, distracted him by trying automatic writing. So excited was Yeats by the results of this experiment that he and Georgie devoted a few hours each day to her trance work. The "communicators" were specific about their purpose; they announced, "We have come to give you metaphors for poetry" (Yeats 1966, 8). Yeats himself stated that as a result "my poetry has gained in self-possession and power" (Yeats 1966, 8).

Yeats recorded the results of five years of this trance writing in *A Vision*, an astrologically based prose text that he considered his finest and by far his most important work. So seriously did Yeats regard this book that he rewrote it at least seven times. After publishing the text privately in 1926 he continued to work on it, publishing the final version in 1937.

Yeats gradually built up from the trance communications a coherent body of esoteric knowledge, setting out a theory of historical cycles and a system for describing all possible types of human psychology. All is explained through astrological symbolism, the entire system being based on various applications of the idea of a regularly recurring cycle such as those made by the sun, moon, and planets around the zodiac. The longest cycle of which Yeats writes is the Platonic concept of the Great Year, the period taken for each planet to return to its original zodiacal position. The shortest is the Arabic system known as the Mansions of the Moon, marking 28 monthly lunar phases that Yeats used to create a theory of human psychological types and which he described in his poem *The Phases of the Moon*. Yeats and Georgie seem to have had a great deal of private fun out of their system, and were sometimes overheard discussing which phase of the moon described a new acquaintance.

Readers of Yeats's poetry who are baffled by his frequent mention of "gyres" will find the meaning in *A Vision*. Yeats saw historical eras as progressing in a predictable rhythm, one civilization rising as another falls. He symbolized this by the complex motions of two interpenetrating cones spinning in opposite directions: these are the gyres. In his apocalyptic poem *The Second Coming*, Yeats describes the 20th century according to his theory; the birth of Christ two thousand years ago called forth an opposing force whose time has now come:

> what rough beast, its hour come round at last,
> Slouches towards Bethlehem to be born? (Yeats 1994, 159)

The systems described in A *Vision* gave Yeats a coherent philosophy upon which much of his poetry from *The Wild Swans at Coole* (1919) onward is based. Indeed, without his knowledge of astrology, some of his greatest poetry would never have been written.

Ruth Clydesdale

See also: Astral Magic; Astrological Associations; Theosophy

Further Reading

Campion, Nicholas. 2009. *A History of Western Astrology*, vol. II. London: Bloomsbury Continuum.

Graf, S. J. 2000. *WB Yeats: Twentieth Century Magus*. York, ME: Samuel Weiser.

Harper, George Mills, ed. 1975. *Yeats and the Occult*. Toronto: Macmillan.

Jeffares, A. Norman. 1988. *W.B. Yeats; A New Biography*. London: Hutchinson.

Maddox, Brenda. 2000. *George's Ghosts: A New Life of W. B. Yeats*. London: Macmillan Picadorn.

Saddlemyer, Ann. 2002. *Becoming George: The Life of Mrs W. B. Yeats*. Oxford: Oxford University Press.

Yeats, W. B. 1966. *A Vision*. New York: Macmillan.

Yeats, W. B. 1994. *Collected Poetry*. Ware: Wordsworth.

Z

ZADKIEL

Zadkiel was the name under which one of the longest running British astrological almanacs was published. (In Kabbalistic astrology, Zadkiel is the Angel of Mercy and associated with the planet Jupiter.) The original Zadkiel was Richard James Morrison (1795–1874), a retired Royal Navy officer. The first issue appeared in 1831, under the title *The Herald of Astrology* with "Zadkiel Tao Tse" as the author. It was modeled on *The Prophetic Messenger*, an almanac produced by the pseudonymous "Raphael" which had first appeared in 1826. (Raphael was Robert Cross Smith [1795–1832].) The name was changed to *Zadkiel's Almanac* in 1836. It was a success, outstripping *The Prophetic Messenger* and selling around 44,000 copies by 1861.

Morrison published other astrological works, including a revised edition of William Lilly's *Christian Astrology* titled *An Introduction to Astrology* (1835). His approach to astrology was spiritual and mystical, ascribing the influence of the planets to their governing angels rather than their physical properties. Morrison was also a leader in switching from the traditional square outline of the horoscope to the modern circular one. He most prominently appeared in the public eye in the course of a lawsuit. The 1861 *Zadkiel's Almanac* had predicted danger to the Prince Consort Albert, who died on December 14 of that year. The accurate prediction attracted some attention, as skeptics put it down to blind chance and attacked Zadkiel as a charlatan. Zadkiel's identity as Morrison was revealed by another Naval veteran, Sir Edward Belcher (1799–1877), who accused Morrison of working con games by claiming to reveal spirits by means of a crystal globe. Morrison had indeed used a crystal for scrying, but sued Belcher for libel for claiming that the visions were fraudulent. The subsequent trial focused more on scrying than on astrology, although Zadkiel's astrology was mocked during the proceedings and in the press coverage of the trial. The court found for Morrison, but awarded the derisory sum of 20 shillings.

Zadkiel's Almanac continued to sell reaching a circulation of about 80,000 by 1870. Morrison died in 1874 and the almanac was passed on to R. V. Sparkes, who died in 1875. The third Zadkiel was Alfred James Pearce (1840–1923), who brought out the almanac until his death. Pearce used his position to fight both the skeptics without and his enemies within the field of astrology as well. Pearce particularly loathed the new theosophical astrology as practiced by Alan Leo and others, which he regarded as unscientific and insufficiently rigorous. His own astrology was far less spiritual than Morrison's, demanding a high level of mathematical skill, and Pearce was devastating in his criticisms of astrologers he considered mathematically unqualified. *Zadkiel's Almanac* continued to prosper in his hands, reaching a circulation of over one hundred thousand. It closed in 1931, eight years after Pearce's death. Its old rival *The Prophetic Messenger*, now *Raphael's Astronomical Ephemeris*, continues to the present day.

William E. Burns

See also: Almanacs; Astral Magic; Theosophy

Further Reading

Curry, Patrick. 1992. *A Confusion of Prophets: Victorian and Edwardian Astrology.* London: Collins and Brown.

ZODIACS

The zodiac is the group of 12 constellations along the ecliptic that define the path of the planets across the sky. Zodiacs have been used globally since antiquity and have influenced cultural developments outside astrology in areas including art and architecture, religion, and popular culture. Visual representations of the zodiac, typically in a circular format, are also referred to as zodiacs.

The earliest known zodiac appeared in the eighth century BCE in Mesopotamia. This early zodiac was formed on the basis of 36 stars that correlated with the 12 months of the Mesopotamian calendar with accompanying phases of the moon. The purpose of the Mesopotamian zodiac was to anticipate astronomical information and to keep time. The idea that zodiac signs number 12 was first developed by the Babylonians, and has enabled zodiac signs to be correlated with other groups of 12, such as the tribes of Israel, the Apostles of Jesus, and the Olympian gods of ancient Greece. The Babylonians also introduced the tropical zodiac commonly used by Western astrologers which followed the 12-sign zodiac structure and was based on seasons, so the first zodiac sign of Aries started at the start of spring, Cancer in the summer, Libra in the fall, and Capricorn at the time of the winter solstice. This order influenced the astrological meanings of the zodiac signs, for instance all of these signs are cardinal signs associated with birth and the start of new things.

Along with other elements of Mesopotamian astrology, the zodiac was further developed by Hellenistic Greeks. Zodiacs appeared in the second century BCE in Hellenistic Egypt. The organization of the zodiacs according to stars was a Hellenistic Greek development as opposed to an Egyptian one, however. A particularly novel aspect of ancient Greek zodiacs is that the signs of the zodiac were each assigned to a particular part of the body. Because the signs of the zodiac were correlated to particular stars within constellations, the stars became associated with the body parts. This construct of the unity of celestial bodies with the human body fits in an ancient Greek cosmology in which the universe and its accompanying parts are whole, a Stoic principle. The familiar association in the Western astrological

The Dendera Zodiac dates from the first century BCE. It is a product of the Hellenistic Ptolemaic dynasty of Egypt. (Wellcome Collection)

tradition between zodiacal signs and animate life—plants and animals—is seen in the start of the classification of zodiacal signs with animals through Egyptian medical practice which assigned animals to different parts of the body. Because zodiacal signs had been relegated to certain parts of the body, astrological medicine was impacted by this categorization. In Hellenistic Egyptian astrological medicine, the zodiacal signs were said to be responsible for ailments of a particular body part. The pathology of illness was believed to emanate from astrological location and placements at a person's birth. The tradition of associating each sign of the zodiac with a body part and its afflictions has continued to the present day. Zodiacs had many other purposes in Hellenistic society, including their use in "architecture, painting, maps, and coins" (Bobrick 2005, 20). Additionally, they were used for electional astrology, "the coronation of Antiochus I (a ruler of the Hellenistic Seleucid dynasty) correlated with planets being in Leo" (Bobrick 2005, 23).

While Hellenistic Greeks were responsible for much astrological growth, societies to the east developed the zodiac in different ways. Sidereal zodiacs were developed by astrologers in India and were not oriented to the seasons, but to the fixed stars. Indian astrologers' zodiacs were more astronomically advanced than those of the Babylonians. Tibetan astrologers also sought further development beyond the Western astrological model. Differences in the approaches can be seen in how Tibetan astrologers referred to the signs as houses, instead, or how "the zodiac was divided into twelve sections of 30 degrees each, or 360 degrees, with each degree having sixty minutes" (Berzin 1987, 19). Tibetan astrologers had developed a system for telling time that was beyond the celestial one that Western astrologers prized. Tibetan astrologers developed the idea that there are "three types of days: zodiac, solar, and lunar" and that a "zodiac day is the time it takes for the sun to progress one out of 360 degrees of the zodiac." Tibetan astrologers created a system of telling time that allowed the public to access the day and time more accurately than merely understanding the time of day by way of visible astronomical evidence.

The rise of Christianity in the Roman Empire led to tension with astrology. Western astrology, as scientifically focused as it was, did embrace a connection between "religion and the calendar" in terms of issues like the date of Easter. During the Middle Ages zodiac signs were still not primarily associated with personality as they are today. Zodiacs still recorded astronomical knowledge but embraced religion as well. In the Middle Ages, "Zodiacs on coins and gems are associated with the sun, with the sun and moon, with the planets and their gods—especially with Zeus (Jupiter) chronocrator—and all seem to be connected with religion and the calendar" (Tester 1987, 104). The religious element was very new but the need to tell time by using zodiacs was traditional. It is critical that contemporary onlookers to medieval zodiacs are mindful that "the time and the date meant something very far from what they mean to us" and that so-called zodiacs did not include information about each zodiacal sign but information about solar and lunar placement in the zodiac. To medieval men and women, telling time involved directly seeing "the positions of the sun and of the moon." Zodiacs were consulted so frequently that Geoffrey Chaucer referred to zodiac sundials, devices dating to Hellenistic Egypt, in the Prologue to the Canterbury Tales because zodiacs were the primary means of telling calendrical time.

Another testament to the immense importance of zodiacs in the Middle Ages is in their use in Books of Hours which were texts that contained the dates of feasting days and other religious observances. The Books of Hours also put forth zodiacal information that astrologers had approved. The Books of Hours were one of the most widely read documents in the Middle Ages, second to the Bible and almanacs. Zodiacs were embraced by some religious authorities and therefore had a popular purpose in the Middle Ages. Zodiac frescoes and coins appeared in Islamic societies as well. The continued production of zodiac frescoes and other use of zodiacs by clergy members demonstrates the endurance of astrological thought into the Renaissance, with the commencement of some skepticism toward astrological thinking which exacerbated in the Enlightenment.

Sabian Symbols

The Sabian symbols, a set of 360 symbols, one for each degree of the zodiac, were the joint creation of American astrologer Marc Edmund Jones (1888–1980) and the psychic Elsie Wheeler in 1925. Jones's *The Sabian Symbols in Astrology* (1953) is considered the classic statement. The symbols are not pictures but short descriptive statements. Most involve people, such as the 11th degree of Aquarius, "During a Silent Hour, a Man Receives a New Inspiration which May Change His Life." A few are more abstract, such as the sixth degree of Aries, "A Square, with One of Its Sides Brightly Illumined." Some are clearly Christian in origin (Jones became a Presbyterian minister) and several reflect a culture influenced by mysticism and Theosophy. One example is the 29th degree of Virgo, "A Seeker after Occult Knowledge Is Reading an Ancient Scroll which Illumines His Mind" or the second degree of Libra, "The Transmutation of the Fruits of Past Experiences into the Seed-Realizations of the Forever Creative Spirit."

The term *Sabian* is derived from the "star-worshippers" of the Mesopotamian city of Harran during the Islamic period, and Jones used it for several of his projects, including an occultist group called the Sabian Assembly, which is still in existence. Among the astrologers outside Jones's immediate circle intrigued by the symbols was Dane Rudhyar. They continue to be used by some astrologers in the Western tradition.

The Neoplatonism and magical thinking characteristic of Renaissance astrology led some to see the Zodiac as fundamental to the nature of the universe. Marsilio Ficino, drawing from the ancient astrologer Manilius, believed that each sign of the Zodiac possessed a soul (identified as the soul of the principal star of the constellation), which could be identified with an Olympian God. He suggested that the ideal city be divided into 12 parts so that it could be governed in the same way as the heavens, divided into 12 zodiacal signs.

After the Enlightenment, zodiacs were used frequently in the 20th century. Zodiacs were used in the construction of the Library of Congress: "There is a zodiac band on the bronze door on the entrance to the Library, a zodiac clock in its main rotunda, zodiacs in the southeast pavilion, and in the marble floor of the Great Hall" (Bobrick 2005, 254). Zodiacs were also used while building the National Academy of Sciences, "a bronze statue of Einstein outside the National Academy of Sciences shows him contemplating a star-spangled marble horoscope for April 22, 1979, his right foot resting on two stars—Bootes and Hercules" (Bobrick 2005, 254). Margaret Mitchell based some of her characters in her best-selling novel *Gone with the Wind*, the inspiration of the film of the same name, in part on the zodiac signs. Thus Aries, ruled by Mars, "the red planet, inspired Scarlett O'Hara, hence her name" (Bobrick 2005, 278). The sun sign astrology column, the most popular form of astrology through most of the 20th century, remains organized by astrological sign in the traditional zodiacal order from Aries to Pisces. The signs of the Zodiac have become a kind of linguistic shorthand people use to describe and analyze their own personalities and those of others.

Isabel Lasch-Quinn

See also: Decans; Electional Astrology; Fixed Stars; Hellenistic Astrology; Horary Astrology; Horoscopes; Islamic Astrology; Natal Astrology; Sun Signs

Further Reading

Battistini, Matilde. 2007. *Astrology, Magic, and Alchemy in Art*. Los Angeles: Getty Publications.

Berzin, Alexander. 1987. "An Introduction to Tibetan Astronomy and Astrology." *The Tibet Journal* 12, no. 1: 17–28.

Bobrick, Benson. 2005. *The Fated Sky: Astrology in History*. New York: Simon and Schuster.

Kaske, Carol V. 1982. "Marsilio Ficino and the Twelve Gods of the Zodiac." *Journal of the Warburg and Courtauld Institutes* 45: 195–202.

Saliba, George. 2004. "The Role of the Astrologer in Medieval Islamic Society." In *Magic and Divination in Early Islam*, ed. Emilie Savage-Smith, 341–370. Aldershot, UK: Ashgate Variorum.

Tester, S. J. 1987. *A History of Western Astrology*. Wolfbridge, UK: Boydell.

Glossary

Almuten: An Arabic term for the chief planet in a horoscope. There were complicated formulas for determining an almuten.

Ascendant: Point where the ecliptic cuts the Eastern horizon. The sign occupying that point might also be referred to as the ascendant or ascending, as might planets occupying that sign. Cusp of the first house.

Aspect: The angle between two planets at different points on the ecliptic. Astrologers vary on which aspects are significant. Basic aspects include conjunction, opposition (180 degrees), trine (120 degrees), and square or quartile (90 degrees). The overall development of astrology has been toward using more and more aspects, including those produced by dividing the original aspects such as sextile (60 degrees), semisextile (30 degrees), and semisquare (45 degrees). Some contemporary astrologers also use aspects based on dividing the ecliptic into fifths or sevenths. At a given moment, an aspect can be applying (moving into position) or separating (moving out of position).

Conjunction: An aspect; the appearance of two or more planets together at the same place in the sky. Astrologers vary on how close together the planets have to be to count as a conjunction.

Cusp: The dividing line or border area between houses or signs.

Descendant: The opposite of the ascendant, the point where the ecliptic cuts the Western horizon. Cusp of the seventh house.

Ecliptic: Apparent path of the sun around the Earth.

Ephemeris: A chart or table enabling an astrologer to determine the position of a celestial body at a given day or time. In contemporary astrology, the work of an ephemeris is usually done by software. The plural of ephemeris is ephemerides.

Exaltation: A relation between a planet and a sign weaker than rulership.

Great Conjunction: The term refers to conjunctions of Saturn and Jupiter, the rarest conjunctions, taking place around every 20 years. The conjunctions rotate between triplicities of zodiac signs about every 200 years. Some reserve the term for the first conjunction in a new triplicity. Great conjunctions are particularly important in mundane astrology.

Horoscope: (1) A diagram of the heavens, showing the relative position of planets, the signs of the zodiac, and other celestial phenomena at a particular moment in time, for use in foretelling events in the life of a person or institution, answering questions, etc. (2) In sun sign astrology, a prediction or set of predictions for a particular sun sign.

House: A division of the sky into 12 zones, usually beginning from the ascendant. There are many ways of calculating houses.

Hyleg: In a natal horoscope, a planet situated so as to influence the life span of the subject. There are different procedures for identifying the Hyleg. However, as many modern astrologers view life span predictions as unethical, it is not used much today.

Imum Coeli: The point opposite the midheaven. Cusp of the fourth house.

Islamicate: Of Islamic civilization but not necessarily Muslim; for example, a Jewish astrologer such as Mashāllāh working in a Muslim-dominated society would be Islamicate.

Joy: A relationship between a planet and a sign weaker than lordship or exaltation. There are various ways of calculating joy, but it is not used much by modern astrologers.

Katarchic Astrology: Astrology of a particular moment in time other than the birth moment. Usually divided into electional and horary astrology.

Lunar Mansions: A division of the ecliptic into 28 parts, based on the 28-day cycle of the moon. Particularly important in Indian astrology, where they are known as *nakṣatras*. Also referred to as the "Mansions of the Moon."

Lunar Nodes. The two points where the orbit of the moon crosses the ecliptic. These points move through the zodiac in a cycle lasting approximately 18 years. The ascending node is where it crosses south to north, the descending it where it crosses south to north. In Western astrology they are known as the Dragon's Head and Dragon's Tail, respectively; in Indian astrology (where they are treated as planets) as Rahu and Ketu.

Midheaven: The point where the ecliptic crosses the prime meridian. Cusp of the tenth house.

Planets: The seven original astrological planets are the sun, the moon, Mercury, Venus, Mars, Jupiter, and Saturn. In astrology, the sun and moon are considered planets although they are also put in a special category as "luminaries." Since the 18th century, the newly discovered planets of Uranus, Neptune, and Pluto have been incorporated into astrology. Some systems of astrology, such as the Hamburg School, use additional "planets" for which there is no scientific evidence.

Retrograde Motion: The motion of a planet, as viewed from Earth, when the planet appears to be going backward through the zodiac.

Rulership: A relation between a planet and a sign, by which the influence of the planet is increased when in that sign and by which the planet exerts an influence over the sign even when not present. Rulership is the strongest of these relationships, which are collectively referred to as dignities. Also referred to as lordship.

Solar Revolution: In reference to a natal or mundane horoscope, the moment when the sun reaches the exact same point in the sky it occupied during the original horoscope. A new horoscope drawn at this moment can be applied to the subject of the original horoscope, often to give predictions for the coming year.

Transit: Period when a planet moves through a particular sign or region of the sky.

Trigon or Triplicity: A division of the zodiac into four groups of three signs, each associated with a traditional element: earth, air, water, and fire: Fire—Aries, Leo, Sagittarius; Water—Cancer, Scorpio, Pisces; Air—Gemini, Libra, Aquarius; Earth—Taurus, Virgo, Capricorn.

Void of Course: A planet is said to be void of course when it will not form any more aspects with other planets until it passes into another sign. This is usually applied to the moon.

Selected Bibliography

Books

Adorno, Theodor W. 1994. *Adorno: The Stars Down to Earth and Other Essays on the Irrational in Culture*, ed. by Stephen Crook, with an Introduction. London: Routledge.

Allen, Don Cameron. 1941. *The Star-Crossed Renaissance: The Quarrel about Astrology and Its Influence in England.* Durham, NC: Duke University Press.

Azzolini, Monica. 2013. *The Duke and the Stars: Astrology and Politics in Renaissance Milan.* Cambridge, MA: Harvard University Press.

Barnes, Robin. 2015. *Astrology and Reformation.* New York: Oxford University Press.

Barton, Tamsyn. 1994. *Ancient Astrology.* London: Routledge.

Barton, Tamsyn. 1994. *Power and Knowledge: Astrology, Physiognomics and Medicine under the Roman Empire.* Ann Arbor: University of Michigan Press.

Battistini, Matilde. 2007. *Astrology, Magic, and Alchemy in Art.* Los Angeles: Getty Publications.

Beck, Roger. 2007. *A Brief History of Ancient Astrology.* Malden: Blackwell.

Bobrick, Benson. 2005. *The Fated Sky: Astrology in History.* New York: Simon and Schuster.

Campion, Nicholas. 2012. *Astrology and Cosmology in the World's Religions.* New York: New York University Press.

Campion, Nicholas. 1994. *The Great Year: Astrology, Millenarianism and History in the Western Tradition.* London: Penguin.

Campion, Nicholas. 2008. *A History of Western Astrology, Vol. I: The Ancient World.* London: Bloomsbury.

Campion, Nicholas. 2009. *A History of Western Astrology, Vol. II: The Medieval and Modern Worlds.* London: Continuum.

Capp, Bernard. 1979. *English Almanacs, 1500–1800: Astrology and the Popular Press.* Ithaca, NY: Cornell University Press.

Carey, Hilary M. 1992. *Courting Disaster: Astrology at the English Court and University in the Later Middle Ages.* New York: St. Martins.

Chevalier, Jacques M. 1997. *A Postmodern Revelation: Signs of Astrology and the Apocalypse.* Toronto: University of Toronto Press.

Curry, Patrick. 1992. *A Confusion of Prophets: Victorian and Edwardian Astrology.* London: Collins and Brown.

Curry, Patrick. 1999. *Prophecy and Power: Astrology in Early Modern England.* Princeton: Princeton University Press.

Curry, Patrick, ed. 1987. *Astrology, Science and Society: Historical Essays.* Woodbridge, UK: Boydell.

Curry, Patrick, and Angela Voss, eds. 2007. *Seeing with Different Eyes: Essays in Astrology and Divination.* Cambridge: Cambridge Scholars Publishing.

Curry, Patrick, with Roy Willis. 2004. *Astrology, Science and Culture: Pulling Down the Moon.* Oxford: Berg.

Curth, Louise Hill. 2007. *English Almanacs, Astrology and Popular Medicine.* Manchester: Manchester University Press.

Dooley, Brendan. 2002. *Morandi's Last Prophecy and the End of Renaissance Politics.* Princeton: Princeton University Press.

Dooley, Brendan, ed. 2014. *A Companion to Astrology in the Renaissance.* Leiden: Brill.

Garin, Eugenio. 1983. *Astrology in the Renaissance: The Zodiac of Life*, trans. Carolyn Jackson and June Allen. London: Routledge and Kegan Paul.

Geneva, Ann. 1995. *Astrology and the Seventeenth Century Mind: William Lilly and the Language of the Stars.* Manchester: Manchester University Press.

Genuth, Sara Schecner. 1997. *Comets, Popular Culture and the Birth of Modern Cosmology.* Princeton: Princeton University Press.

Gerson, Stephane. 2012. *Nostradamus: How an Obscure Renaissance Astrologer became the Modern Prophet of Doom.* New York: St. Martin's Press.

Grafton, Anthony. 1999. *Cardano's Cosmos: The Worlds and Works of a Renaissance Astrologer.* Cambridge, MA: Harvard University Press.

Green, S. J. 2014. *Disclosure and Discretion in Roman Astrology: Manilius and His Augustan Contemporaries.* Oxford: Oxford University Press.

Hayton, Darin. 2015. *The Crown and the Cosmos: Astrology and the Politics of Maximilian I.* Pittsburgh: University of Pittsburgh Press.

Holden, James H. 2006. *A History of Horoscopic Astrology.* Tempe, AZ: American Federation of Astrologers.

Howe, Ellic. 1967. *Astrology: A Recent History including the Untold Story of Its Role in World War II.* New York: Walker.

Jerome, Lawrence E. 1997. *Astrology Disproved.* Buffalo, NY: Prometheus.

Kjellgren, Martin. 2011. *Taming the Prophets: Astrology, Orthodoxy and the Word of God in Early Modern Sweden.* Lund: Sekel Bokforlag.

MacNeice, Louis. 1964. *Astrology.* Garden City, NY: Doubleday.

Maxwell-Stuart, P. G. 2012. *Astrology: From Ancient Babylon to the Present Day.* Stroud, UK: Amberley.

Monod, Paul Kleber. 2013. *Solomon's Secret Arts: The Occult in an Age of Enlightenment.* New Haven, CT: Yale University Press.

Newman, William R., and Anthony Grafton, eds. 2011. *Secrets of Nature: Astrology and Alchemy in Early Modern Europe.* Cambridge, MA: MIT Press.

Parel, Anthony. 1992. *The Machiavellian Cosmos.* New Haven, CT: Yale University Press.

Perinbanayagam, R. S. 1982. *The Karmic Theater: Self, Society and Astrology in Jaffna.* Amherst: University of Massachusetts Press.

Phillipson, Gary. 2000. *Astrology in the Year Zero.* London: Flare Publications.

Ryan, Michael. 2011. *A Kingdom of Stargazers: Astrology and Authority in the Late Medieval Crown of Aragon.* Ithaca, NY: Cornell University Press.

Smoller, Laura Ackerman. 1994. *History, Prophecy and the Stars: The Christian Astrology of Pierre d'Ailly, 1350–1420.* Princeton: Princeton University Press.

Sommers, Susan Mitchell. 2018. *The Siblys of London: A Family on the Esoteric Fringes of Georgian England.* Oxford: Oxford University Press.

Tester, Jim. 1987. *A History of Western Astrology.* New York: Ballantine.

Traister, Barbara Howard. 2001. *The Notorious Astrological Physician of London: Works and Days of Simon Forman.* Chicago: University of Chicago Press.

Wedel, Theodore Otto. 2005. *Astrology in the Middle Ages.* Mineola, NY: Dover.

Whitfield, Peter. 2001. *Astrology: A History.* New York: Abrams.

Zambelli, Paola, ed. 1986. "*Astrologi Hallucinati*": *Stars and the End of the World in Luther's Time*. Berlin: Walter de Gruyter.

Websites

American Federation of Astrologers. https://www.astrologers.com
Guinard, Patrice. Digital International Astrology Library. http://cura.free.fr/DIAL.html
Houlding, Deborah. Skyscript. http://www.skyscript.co.uk
Phillipson, Gary. Astrology in the Year Zero. http://www.astrozero.co.uk
Research Grants for the Critical Study of Astrology. http://www.astrology-research.net
Smit, Rudolf H. Astrology and Science. http://www.astrology-and-science.com /

About the Editor and Contributors

Laura Andrikopoulos is a postgraduate tutor for the MA in Cultural Astronomy and Astrology at the University of Wales–Trinity Saint David. Her research interests center on the history of modern astrology, particularly psychological astrology, and the philosophy of astrological practice in the modern world. Laura is a former president of the Faculty of Astrological Studies, U.K.

Bernadette Brady holds a PhD in Anthropology (2012) and an MA in Cultural Astronomy and Astrology (2005). She is currently a tutor in the Sophia Centre for the Study of Cosmology in Culture at the University of Wales–Trinity Saint David, U.K. Her research interests are the role of fate in contemporary astrology, the religious and cultural significance of stars and star phases, and the union of mythology with landscape in its potential to capture earlier astronomies. Recent publications include work in Egyptian astronomy (2012), the orientation of the Solstical Churches of North Wales (2017), and the solar discourse in Cistercian Welsh abbeys (2016). Apart from journal papers she has also authored *Cosmos, Chaosmos and Astrology* (2014).

William E. Burns is a historian who lives in the Washington, D.C., area. His books include: *An Age of Wonders: Prodigies, Providence and Politics in England 1657–1727* (2002), *Science and Technology in Colonial America* (2005), *Knowledge and Power: Science in World History* (2010), and *The Scientific Revolution in Global Perspective* (2015).

Josianne Leah Campbell has an MA from the University of North Carolina–Charlotte and is instructor of English at York Technical College. She has enjoyed a long career as a professional educator, and her research and teaching expertise lies in the field of literature, folklore, and popular culture.

Nicholas Campion is Associate Professor of Cosmology in Culture and program director of the MA in Cultural Astronomy and Astrology at the University of Wales–Trinity Saint David. His books include the two-volume *History of Western Astrology* (2008–2009), *Astrology and Popular Religion in the Modern West* (2012), and *Astrology and Cosmology in the World's Religions* (2012).

Ruth Clydesdale, MA, DFAstrolS, is an independent researcher, writer, and lecturer who specializes in the study of astrological and esoteric aspects of art and literature. Her publications include contributions to conference proceedings and articles published throughout the United States, the United Kingdom, and Europe. She has taught History of Renaissance Art at City University, London.

Brendan Dooley has a PhD from the University of Chicago (1986) and is currently Professor of Renaissance Studies at University College Cork, Ireland, where he came after previous assignments at Harvard, Jacobs University Bremen, and the Medici Archive Project. Some recent books include *Angelica's Book and the World of Reading in Late Renaissance Italy* (2016); ed., *Brill's Companion to Renaissance Astrology* (2014); *A Mattress Maker's Daughter: The Renaissance Romance of Don Giovanni de' Medici and Livia Vernazza* (2014); and *Morandi's Last Prophecy and the End of Renaissance Politics* (2002).

Barbara Dunn was formerly an undergraduate/postgraduate at the London School of Economics and Political Science, in receipt of a scholarship from the Social Science Research Council. She subsequently conducted independent research into astrological knowledge/practice, while pursuing a career as a freelance astrological consultant/columnist for U.K. and European publications. Having authored four books published between 1994 and 2009, she continued her studies at the University of Exeter, graduating with an MA in History. She is currently a PhD candidate, in receipt of a doctoral studentship from the Wellcome Trust, researching the application of astrology to medical matters in early modern England.

Benjamin N. Dykes is a leading translator of Latin and Arabic who taught philosophy at the universities in Illinois and Minnesota. In 2007 he published Guido Bonatti's complete *Book of Astronomy* and since then has translated and published numerous traditional works in all areas, including the introductory *Traditional Astrology for Today* (2011). He is currently translating works from Arabic. He offers the *Logos & Light* philosophy lectures on MP3 and speaks to astrological audiences worldwide. See www.bendykes.com.

Kyle Falcon is a PhD candidate at Wilfrid Laurier University in Waterloo, Ontario, Canada. His dissertation, funded by the Social Sciences and Humanities Research Council of Canada (SSHRC) focuses on the ways in which spiritualism and psychical research was part of the Great War's battlefield and home front experiences, as well as the war's cultural memory in Britain. His broader research interests include 19th- and 20th-century European history, war and society, the history of science, and religion and society.

Vittoria Feola is a Lecturer in Early Modern History at the University of Padova, Italy, and the president of Scientiae Inc., www.scientiae.co.uk. She earned her PhD in History from Cambridge University (2005) and has held subsequent fellowships in Brussels, Paris, London, Vienna, and Oxford. Feola has published widely on the relationship between antiquarianism to science, the modes of early modern intellectual communication, and the history of collections.

Benjamin Franz serves as the coordinator of Cataloging and Metadata at Medgar Evers College CUNY. A student of the intersection of science, religion, and culture, he has published on topics concerning eschatology, Tintin comics, *The Simpsons*, rock and roll, and reference librarianship. He resides in East Orange, New Jersey.

Martin Gansten is a Sanskritist and historian of religion specializing in Indic religions as well as in astrological and divinatory traditions across cultures. Although the main focus of his research has been on South Asia, he has written on aspects of astrological history from

Hellenistic Egypt to 19th-century Britain. He received his doctorate from Lund University, Sweden, where he has taught since 1998 and is now docent.

Demetra George, MA, looks to classical antiquity for inspiration in her pioneering work in mythic archetypal astrology, ancient astrological techniques, and translations from Greek. She is the author of *Astrology for Yourself* (1987), *Asteroid Goddesses* (1986), *Mysteries of the Dark Moon* (1992), *Finding Our Way through the Dark* (2008), *Astrology and the Authentic Self* (2008), and *Ancient Astrology: A Practitioner's Guide* (2018). She lives in Oregon, has an active consulting and teaching practice, lectures internationally, and leads pilgrimages to sacred sites in the Mediterranean. www.demetrageorge.com

Louis Gosart is a graduate of Stanford Online High School. Among his favorite subjects are history of science and astronomy. He also is an aspiring journalist and writer, and an excellent cook.

Thomas Gosart is a student at the Honors College at Rutgers University studying physics and classics. His current research is on particle and nuclear physics, with a particular focus on heavy ion collisions. He enjoys journalism and will pursue a graduate degree once he graduates.

Dorian Gieseler Greenbaum received her PhD from the Warburg Institute in 2009. Her book based on her doctoral research, *The Daimon in Hellenistic Astrology: Origins and Influence*, was published by Brill in 2016. She is a tutor at the University of Wales.

Darrelyn Gunzburg teaches in the Sophia Centre for the Study of Cosmology in Culture at the University of Wales–Trinity Saint David. She received her PhD from the University of Bristol (2014) with a thesis entitled "Giotto's Salone: An Astrological Investigation into the Fresco Paintings of the First Floor Salone of the Palazzo della Ragione, Padua, Italy." Her research interests lie in the art historical and visual astronomical exploration of frescoes in medieval Italy, as well as the orientation of Cistercian abbey churches in Wales, the United Kingdom, and Europe. She is the editor of *The Imagined Sky: Cultural Perspectives* (2016) and has written extensively for *The Art Book* and *Cassone: The International Online Magazine of Art and Art Books.*

Justo Hernández got an MD in 1983 (Universidad de Sevilla), an MA in 1987 (Universidad de Navarra), and a PhD in 1997 (Universidad de Valencia). He is a scholar in Renaissance medicine and a member of the AAHM (USA), the DGGMNT (Germany), the RSA (USA), the SEHM (Spain), and a fellow of the RSM (Great Britain). He is an assistant professor of the History of Medicine in the Universidad de La Laguna (Tenerife, Canary Islands, Spain) from 1992.

Wendell G. Johnson is Head of Reference and Research, University Libraries, Northern Illinois University. He has contributed to numerous ABC-CLIO publications and most recently edited *End of Days: An Encyclopedia of the Apocalypse in World Religions* (2017). He is the general editor of the *Journal of Religious and Theological Information.*

Madhumita Kaushik is a writer and linguist studying at the Honors College at Rutgers University. She is interested in creative writing and Portuguese and aspires to be a professor of Spanish and English literature.

Matthew Kosuta is a lecturer at the College of Religious Studies, Mahidol University, Thailand, since 2006. He specializes in Theravada Buddhism, Thai religion, astrology, and divination in Theravada Southeast Asia, and works extensively on religion and war. He is currently the director of the International PhD Program and a vice dean.

Jeffrey Kotyk received his MA in Buddhist Studies from Komazawa University in Tokyo (2011). He later moved to Leiden University, where he earned his PhD in Asian Studies (2017) with a dissertation related to Buddhist astrology in East Asia. He is presently researching medieval Chinese and Japanese traditions of horoscopy.

Isabel Lasch-Quinn's hobbies include running, learning Italian, and reading nonfiction, especially in the social sciences. Her undergraduate studies included an interdisciplinary but primarily historical thesis on the cultural diffusion between the East and the West that resulted from the written legacy of Ibn Al-'Arabi, a prolific 12th century Andalusian Sufi scholar.

Martin J. Manning is the museum librarian with the U.S. Diplomacy Center, U.S. Department of State, and curator of the Public Diplomacy Historical Collection. He was also a researcher at the National Portrait Gallery, Smithsonian Institution, Washington, D.C., where he worked with the senior historian on exhibitions. His areas of research and expertise include U.S. diplomacy, popular culture, world's fairs, propaganda, and library history. He has a BS from Boston College and an MSLS from Catholic University of America. His publications include *American Revolution: The Definitive Encyclopedia and Document Collection*; and *Media and Propaganda in Wartime America*, coedited with Clarence Wyatt (both for ABC-CLIO).

Justin Niermeier-Dohoney is a PhD candidate at the University of Chicago, an associate of the Morris Fishbein Center for the History of Science and Medicine, and an adjunct lecturer at Indiana University Southeast. He specializes in the history of early modern science, natural and environmental history in England and the Atlantic world, the relationship between alchemy and the life sciences, and astrology, especially in the context of early modern climate theory. He is currently completing his dissertation, which explores the influence of vitalistic alchemy on agricultural improvement projects in England and colonial North America in the 17th century.

Annamarie O'Brien is an American Studies doctoral candidate at Pennsylvania State University Harrisburg, specializing in contemporary folk and popular culture. Her research interests include expressive practices online, vernacular visual culture, gender, race, and embodiment. O'Brien has published work on Black fitness imagery (*Race and Ethnicity in Digital Culture: Our Changing Traditions, Impressions, and Expressions in a Mediated World*, 2017), online performances of Japanese femininity (*Popular Culture in the 21st Century*, 2013), and depictions of motherhood in comics (*ImageText*, 2014). In 2016, O'Brien received the Bill Ellis prize from the American Folklore Society for her work examining contemporary astrology practices online.

Ulia Popova is a legal and policy historian with a focus on advocacy research. She has an interest in history of science. She enjoys working with her students on research and publication projects.

Arno Rombouts studied History, Political Science, and Economics at Ghent University, Belgium. He wrote a Master's thesis "Enlightened by the Stars" on the presence of celestial influences in 18th-century European medical works. His research interests related to history cover—among others—Enlightenment scientific and political thinking, as well as the use of "Enlightenment" in modern political discourse.

Micah T. Ross has been a postdoctoral researcher under Kuang-tai Hsu at the National Tsing Hua University in Hsin Chu, Taiwan. He has studied Sanskrit astronomy and astrology at Kyōto Sangyō University and served as a researcher at the Institute d-Etudes Avancées and within the REHSEIS workgroup of Université Paris 7, both in Paris. He graduated from the Department of the History of Mathematics at Brown University in Providence.

Liana Saif is currently a British Academy postdoctoral fellow at the University of Oxford's Institute of Oriental Studies. Her scholarship focuses on Islamicate civilization's esoteric thought and occult traditions in the early medieval period (8th–13th centuries). She is also interested in the intercultural exchange of esoteric and occult ideas between the Islamicate world and Europe in the Middle Ages and the Renaissance. Her book, *The Arabic Influences on Early Modern Occult Philosophy*, was published in 2015.

Keith Snedegar earned a DPhil in modern history at the University of Oxford and was a postdoctoral fellow at the University of Cape Town. He is now a professor of History at Utah Valley University. His interests include medieval European science and African indigenous knowledge systems.

Susan Mitchell Sommers has a PhD and an FRHistS and is professor of History at Saint Vincent College in Pennsylvania, where she teaches Early Modern European history. Trained as a political historian, much of her recent work deals with freemasonry in the 18th century. Her forthcoming book, *The Siblys of London: A Family on the Esoteric Fringes of Georgian England*, will be part of the Oxford series on Western Esotericism.

Lakshmi Srinivas is associate professor of Sociology at the University of Massachusetts, Boston. She is author of *House Full. Indian Cinema and the Active Audience* (2016) and numerous articles on Indian cinema and its audiences.

Mariano Villalba was born in Buenos Aires in 1986. He holds a BA in History at University of Buenos Aires and an MA in Sociology of Culture. He is currently a PhD candidate in Sciences of Religions at University of Lausanne with a Swiss Government Excellence Scholarship.

Arthur Williamson is a professor of History (Emeritus) at California State University, Sacramento, where he also served as Dean of Graduate Studies. He specializes in intellectual history, the history of political thought, and British history during the early modern period. His most recent book has the title, *Apocalypse Then: Prophecy and the Making of the Modern World.* His "Roman Past, Jewish Future: Prophecy, Poetry, and the End of Empire" will appear shortly in *Roman History in Sixteenth-Century English Cultural History*. He is currently working on a volume under the title, *"The Nation Epidemicall": Scotland and the Rise of Political Economy*. He has taught at the University of Chicago, NYU, and Washington University, St. Louis, as well as the California State University.

Xu Fengxian, PhD, is a professor at the Institute for the History of Natural Science, Chinese Academy of Sciences, with a main research field of the history of Chinese astronomy, archaeoastronomy, and the comparative study of astronomy in different early civilizations.

Jennifer Zahrt, PhD, is an author, publisher, and historian of astrology specializing in the German cultural sphere. She has taught and lectured in the United Kingdom, the United States, Canada, and Germany. Zahrt founded and runs Revelore Press, and coruns the Sophia Centre Press with Dr. Nicholas Campion. She hails from Seattle, WA. www.jennzahrt.com

Index

Page references to main articles are indicated by **bold type.**